THE POSTWAR UNIVERSITY

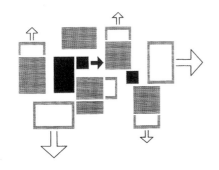

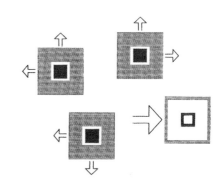

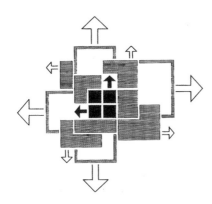

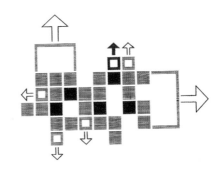

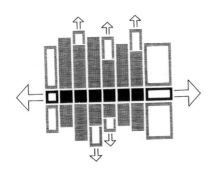

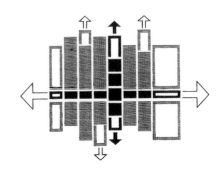

THE POSTWAR UNIVERSITY
Utopianist Campus and College

Stefan Muthesius

Published for the
Paul Mellon Centre for Studies
in British Art by
Yale University Press
New Haven and London

For K.M.-M.

Frontispiece: Plan types for universities in the late 1960s. The most frequent type of layout in which the campus is divided according to the main functions of the buildings. From top left: 'Bereichstyp' or 'zoning' principle; molecular type (San Diego and York); central type (as at Johannesburg and Konstanz); grid type (Loughborough and Berlin, Freie Universität); linear type (Bath and Ulm); cross type (Bochum and Regensburg). By that time planning thinking had assumed a considerable complexity. Three major planning issues are abstracted here: the concentration of campus life (in red: the major communal structures), movement on campus, and extendibility. The aim of such drawings was to show, not a static distribution of buildings, but the dynamic performance and aspirations of an institution. By Peter Jokusch, of the Stuttgart University Institute of University Planning. (Linde (1970) vol. 4, pp. 167–82; cf. *AD* 11-1974 p. 709).

Designed by Mary Carruthers
Set in Bembo by Best-set Typesetter Ltd., Hong Kong
Printed in China through World Print Ltd

Library of Congress Cataloging-in-Publication Data
Muthesius, Stefan.
    The postwar university : utopianist campus and college / Stefan Muthesius.
       p. cm.
    Includes bibliographical references and index.
    ISBN 0-300-08717-9 (cloth : alk. paper)
    1. College facilities – Planning – Cross-cultural studies.   2. College buildings – Planning – Cross-cultural studies.   3. Campus planning – Cross-cultural studies. 4. Universities and colleges – History – 20th century.
LB3223.M83 2001
378.1'96 – dc21

00-043768

CONTENTS

ACKNOWLEDGEMENTS

The author wishes to thank, first of all, those who were prepared to be interviewed: Hans-Joachim Aminde, Lord Annan, Lord Briggs, Sir Andrew Derbyshire, Gabriel Epstein, Sir Leslie Martin, Guy Oddie, Sir Denys Lasdun, Horst Linde, John Richards, Frank Thistlethwaite.

Among those who helped most were: Michael Brandon-Jones (photographs), Mary Carruthers (text), the RIBA Library London, the Cambridge University Art and Architecture Faculty Library, the Library of the Institute of Education of London University, the Institut für öffentliche Bauten der Universität Stuttgart (Hans-Dieter Laubinger), Peter Dormer, Fred Beuttler (UIC Chicago) and Geoffrey P. Williams (Archivist SUNY at Albany), Maria Schorpp (Universität Konstanz) and Hannah Brown and Marjorie Rhodes (World Art Studies UEA).

Among the many others were Rachel Arnold (Churchill College Cambridge), Kathleen Bain (Trent University), Karen Baxter, Michael Behal (Tübingen), Gemma Bentley (Downing College Cambridge), Douglas A. Bicknese (UIC Chicago), Diana Brooks (London), Nicholas Bullock (Cambridge), D. Caleb (Surrey), Louise Campbell (Warwick), Nathaniel Coleman (Boston), Julie Dyson (Leeds), Laurence Eble (CNOUS Paris), Robert Elwall (RIBA), Frances Fournier (Simon Fraser), Jan Gehlsen (Hannover), Miles Glendinning (Edinburgh), Andrew Gilmore (Edinburgh), Thomas Hall (Stockholm), Astrid Hansen (Frankfurt am Main), Tanya Harrod, M. Boone Hellmann (UCSD), Ulrich Hunger (Göttingen), Norbert Huse (Technische Universität München), Neil Jackson (Nottingham University), Pat Jacoby (UCSD), Ludmilla Jornanova (World Art Studies UEA), James D. Kornwolf (William and Mary College Williamsburg), Jean-Michel Leniaud (Ecole Pratique des Hautes Etudes Paris), Jörg Lorenz (Ruhr Universität Bochum), Thomas McCormick (Wheaton College), Horst H. Moller (Göttingen), Joanna Motion (Kent), Katarzyna Murawska, Michał Murawski (Norwich), Michael Murray (London), Bianca Muthesius, Patricia F. Owen (Sarah Lawrence College), Adrian Parry (Higher Education Funding Council Bristol, successor to the UGC), Michael Paulson-Ellis (UEA), Monica Pidgeon (London), Marco Polo (Canadian Architect), Mme Ponsart (CNOUS Paris), Eckehard Pook (Konstanz), Nicholas Ray (Cambridge), Irene Reti (UCSC), R. Shackle (Colchester Public Library), Deirdre Sharp (Library Archive UEA), Peter Smithson (London), Dr A. Spiller (Freie Universität Berlin), A. Tarrant (Surrey), Paul Thompson (Essex), Jennifer A. Thelander (UCSC), Rex Thorpe (Churchill College Cambridge), Pamela T. Wilson (Time Inc. New York), Miss S. Wilson (Lancaster Public Library), Cathey Webb (Higher Education Funding Council).

INTRODUCTION

This book goes back to a time after World War II, when educational reformism united with a new social and architectural impetus. With the universities this movement reached its high point during the 1960s. However, the book concentrates on two 'traditional' institutional models of higher education; the chief claim is that by studying the mutations and combinations of campus and college we gain a more comprehensive understanding of the utopianist mood which shaped the institutions and their architecture.

The institutions which research and teach *Wisssenschaft* – the academic pursuit of the human and natural sciences – have, for a long time, been geographically specific. Hence this book is, first of all, divided by countries. Moreover, from at least the nineteenth century onwards, 'campus' and 'college' developed as largely Anglo-American phenomena. The college in particular as an institution of higher education was hardly cultivated in other countries, at least not at university level. That said, the USA and England also diverged from each other. The USA produced a vast variety of institutional solutions and in particular created the model of the out-of-town campus, while in England the venerable model of Oxbridge – which both countries treated as a 'common heritage' – dominated thinking and let the institutional practices of the newer universities in the provinces appear less important. In the 1960s, however, England created new kinds of institutions in which elements of the American campus and elements of the English, as well as the American, college are fused, a movement, which, in turn, spilled over into the whole of the English-speaking world, including the USA. West Germany is also dealt with at length, because of the strong English and American influences after the war and because originally the definition of 'university' in English-speaking countries owed something to the older German model. Near the end of the book comes a brief survey which looks in a more straightforward way at the utopianist campus design as the globalised architectural and planning movement it had become by the mid-1960s, with France heading the newest trend, the reintegration of the campus into the town.

Today, the most sensitive issue for universities is academic ranking. It must be stressed that this book wants to avoid giving any impression of devising an academic pecking order. It does not deal with aspects of 'pure' research, nor, with the actual content of academic teaching. However, generically, the evaluation 'academic', or 'of a high academic rank' is constitutive of any institution individually, of groups of them (e.g. 'Oxbridge') and of the institution 'university' as a whole. This book deals only with institutions within a relatively unified sector of 'university rank'. Thus it excludes what in Britain is called 'further' education, or the 'Fachhochschule' sector in Germany. In the USA the lower borderline of 'higher education' is rather less sharply drawn.

Another ranking which might have been expected from this book is that of the buildings as architecture. This, likewise, can hardly be undertaken here. There can be, in this context, no selection of ensembles or individual buildings according to the reputations of the designers, as they have been established in the critical press or in subsequent architectural histories and monographs. However, as with academic ranking, architectural quality is also a constitutive of our types of building and for the institution as a whole. An institution of rank must choose an architect of rank. Hence this book only deals with a 'high' level of architecture. And yet, architectural rank is hardly ever in the same way constitutive, as academic rank, of the general reputation of a university. Few students or scholars would choose a university purely because of its architectural standing. Does that relegate the study of university architecture to the sidelines? The way in which 'architecture' does matter to most users of a university is the way it is wedded to its institutionality. We are usually impressed by the beauty of the college chapel or the size and decor of the main administration or social building and we expect at least some such elements to be present on any reputable campus. A minimal expectation on an older campus would be a suitable architectural frame for the celebratory rituals of academe. The architectural expectations for a post World War II campus or college is more diffuse. We would certainly count upon an institutional presence, brought about by a lively and dense assembly of people. To find the right architectural image for a lively institutional presence was one of the chief aims of 1960s late Modernism. Broadly speaking, two styles of university ensembles matter in this context. Firstly, old Oxbridge: clearly many choose these institutions, or venerate them, at least partly because of the architectural image and the apparent seamless unity between architectural image and institutional life. Secondly, New University Modernism: to impress through an institutional/architectural image was precisely what they, too, were aiming for.

INSTITUTION, SOCIAL-EDUCATIONAL ETHOS, COMMUNITY, UTOPIANISM

While the nature of 'college' and 'campus', as well as campus and college architecture will evolve in the narratives that follow, the key characterisation in the title needs some preliminary consideration. The term utopianist is far from straightforward, in fact it encapsulates most of the problems which one might want to read into this book, social, political, architectural, as well as epistemological.

To begin with, however, one may ask, are there perhaps less problematic adjectives? 'New' was the word appended to the foundations of the 1960s in England and it made a considerable impact in a country where the notion 'university' was so much wedded to the old age of Oxbridge. In the USA, where higher education had been subject to continual change for a long time, the term 'new', as such, would have made little impression in the 1960s. 'Reformuniversität' was the prevalent West-German term, in the context of that country's general search for a 'Universitätsreform', yet, such a word found little use in the USA, and even less in England. 'Experimental' (and more or less the same would apply to 'radical') was a quasi-official term used in the case of a few small American colleges, as well as being used unofficially among some English protagonists, and yet, it could hardly have served to create broad public confidence in large new institutions. Similar dilemmas applied to 'progressive'. 'Modern' would have served a similar purpose as new, but is, in fact, a more problematic term. It, too, found surprisingly little use in our context. Institutionally and educationally many new foundations contained too much that was purposely 'traditional'. Architecturally, 'modern' appeared to serve well for many of the efforts of the 1950s and early 1960s, yet, classic Modernist 'functionalism' already appeared outdated to many architects in England and the USA by the mid-1960s. Finally, 'model university', or 'ideal university', in analogy to the fairly common terms 'model town' or 'ideal city', would sound incongruous, or at least unusual; nor can 'idealist' be used in either its philosophical or in its common-parlance meaning.

Yet, before we turn to the adjective utopianist we must investigate the substance to which it is attached, and that under three headings – institution, education and community. The sociological term 'institution' denotes what this investigation is primarily about – using its commonplace definition rather than a more recent, all-comprehensive socio-anthropological understanding: a corporate body, an organisation of a fairly large size and usually all in one place. Rather than concerning itself with the actual practical functioning of this institution, its organisation and administration or the mundane performance of its buildings, this book shall deal more specifically with its professed principal and 'deeper' aim: 'university education'. To begin with, there are grave ambiguities with regard to 'higher education'. If the aim of teaching in university is that students acquire the academic content, then, again, this falls outside the remit of this book. There were, and are, plenty of university theorists who saw no necessity for anything beyond that straightforward process of acquiring. The crucial question was whether the normal university student, aged 18–21, or even 17–20, was, or was not to be considered an adult. 'Higher educationalists' from the late 1950s to the mid-1960s mostly avoided a clear answer. In any case, we never meet with much emphasis on actual pedagogy. It is actually hard to find a definition of the frequently used term 'university education' and this book does not attempt to provide one either. Rather, the accounts which follow take on the beliefs of its protagonists, namely that the institutional functioning and educational effort of a university were broader concerns which are best summarised with the term 'social' and whose specific institutional manifestation was characterised as 'community'.

None of the three terms, institution, education or community, can, by itself, convey the enthusiasm, the intensity, the sense of unity, or the new kind of totality in which the New Universities were seen. The aim was to maximise and optimise the performance of the institution. To begin with, the state vastly increased expenditure. To most, stating the actual figures did not mean very much, but accounts would begin by citing that student numbers 'had doubled within . . .'. The reasons given were all-comprehensive: there was a 'national need' for each country to broaden and deepen education; there was a desire to at least supplement the old elitism that higher education traditionally entailed. In Britain, in particular, Welfare State policies meant a new unity of society's aspirations, a sense of 'for all', which aimed to phase out both elitism and charity. The creating and reforming of institutions was a primary activity of the Welfare State and it seemed to require the utmost zeal. The demand to expand numbers was, of course, met by the caution, even the worry, that 'quality' might suffer. This was particularly prevalent in all the German pronouncements. In the USA the solution was pragmatic: expansion at the top end, in postgraduate studies, as well as at the bottom end. In Britain it was the particular intensity of the new Welfare State ethos which seemed to guarantee the combination of quality and quantity in new kinds of institutions.

Whatever else was meant by 'education', we are probably at the height of the belief that education is best achieved within the framework of a fairly large, or at least a complex institution. Acquiring the cultural and political values of society is actually called 'socialisation' and a school can be seen as the 'microcosm of society'. Knowledge and values are acquired not only by taking on board what the teacher says and demonstrates but by fitting in with other members, with all other members of the institution. A new kind of continuity also began to prevail. Up till now, time spent at university was divided into periods of heavy instruction or examination, interspersed by the high seriousness spent in the rituals of chapel and congregation, but also alternating with periods of relaxation or undefined personal and social activities. Now the concept was that every moment spent at college was equally important for the development of the students' personality. The newly popular terms 'experience' and 'environment' signify this continuous process.

As such, 'community' may seem an impossibly broad term to use. But it is, of course, precisely its breadth that makes it so popular and which at the same time helps to give it conviction, as regards its practical usefulness, but also, and above all, for its moral values – the ethos of the individual's engagement for the wider group within which he/she finds herself. Ferdinand Toennies's definition of *Gemeinschaft* dates from the late nineteenth century. But the term community began to be taken on board only very gradually, during the interwar period, and very much more strongly in the years after World War II (after the World War II 'communal effort'), by most town planners and educationalists. Sociologists kept referring back to Toennies, although his concept had been extended almost beyond recognition. To Toennies, community meant the unreflected togetherness of small, mostly ancient groups, tied by 'natural' links, such as family or work, which guaranteed contentment, precisely because it was unplanned. 'Community' now included groups formed intentionally, even rationally; hence virtually all communities dealt with in town planning and education are now called 'intentional communities'. By the 1960s, 'community' values could be applied to a vast range of social setups, from the small village to the large modern city. During the 1960s and 1970s, the key manifestation, the most exciting and desirable form of community seemed to be the 'urban' one. What was crucial in Toennies's concept of *Gemeinschaft*, of course, was its juxtaposition to *Gesellschaft*, society, but what was crucial in the postwar decades was the way in which 'community' still carried these seemingly deep, even primeval values, even though it had taken on board so many factors, such as rational planning, which Toennies had classified under society.

Educational institutions were prime candidates to inculcate the new intensified postwar sense of community in the citizens. In order to achieve this, it appeared plausible that the educational institution itself should be an ideal community. One is sometimes tempted to apply the characterisation of 'total institution', though not, of course, of the kind found in the prison or asylum. What certainly many of the new universities did show was an acute concern, or 'care', for the whole of the student's life, including the time when he or she was not actually studying. Thus the 'college', in its most comprehensive sense, including the students' 'living' quarters, is the central institution discussed in this book. One of the crucial issues was the question of the optimal size of such an educational community; there was a dichotomy between smallness – the small group clearly being the educationalist's preference – and the new socio-political demand for quantity – referring us back again to the challenge of squaring the circle of quality and quantity.

To the educationalists of the later twentieth century the 'intentional community' should thus be a voluntary, not an instinctive or an enforced one. It is probable that the 1950s and early 1960s marked the high point of this concept of 'liberal' education. The institution still carried much of the older notion of authority and was still held together by the teachers' and the recipients' conviction of the necessity of that authority. Reading the literature on student residences in England in the 1940s we note a two-part discourse: firstly, about the moral and social values to be imparted, which are taken as read, and secondly about all matters practical. By the time of the Niblett Report on halls of residence in 1957 practicalities hardly mattered but there is a much heightened socio-psychological concern about the way members of the halls of residence should and would participate and internalise the moral and social values on offer. But a period defined as a 'high point' also means a period of transition. By the early 1960s the strength of the institutionalist concept of education was already being sapped away. A shift occurred from the functionalist/behaviourist slant and the strong social policy-orientation which had laid the chief emphasis on socialisation, towards a new interest in the cognitive factors and in the cultural make-up of the individual. The closed institution 'school' is broken up by the new attention given to the diverse backgrounds of the pupils – an inevitable consequence of the politically-demanded widening of education. Generally speaking, we move from a climate of consensus-seeking to a climate of argumentativeness, a new stress on 'change' and 'flexibility'. Applied sociology moved from serving certain social policy aims to the analysis of the social state of affairs as it existed. One of the key terms of the mid-1960s was 'spontaneity', a word that stood at the transition between the two phases: on the one hand it is something that stems directly from the individual, something that by definition cannot be planned; on the other hand the planners were hell-bent on devising an environment that would encourage spontaneous social contacts. What complicates the historical position of some of the 'model' universities of the 1960s was the way they straddled both phases of educational institutional thought. By the 1970s, however, the impetus for comprehensive institutional planning had gone – and the money had run out, too.

Returning to the main, the decisive term in the title of the book, no evaluative adjectives can be formed directly from the words institution, education or community – although 'educationally purposeful universities', or 'institutionally strongly worked-out universities', or 'community-value universities' would come closest to the meaning of the book. ('Communitarian' cannot be used as it has lately been 'booked' by a quite specific socio-political movement). There is, however, and has been for a long time, a term which unites most of the values enunciated here – newness, experiment, the striving for the ideal, community feeling and a firm, newly created, totalised institutionality. 'Utopian', although not principally or overtly concerned with the education of the young, does usually demand strong coercive or voluntary reshaping of the users' behaviour. There is only one small problem: utopia is basically defined as non-existing. This, however, has not held back the use of the adjective on many occasions and for new institutions of all kinds. It is hoped, here, that 'utopian*ist*' may sound more down-to-earth than 'utopian universities'. There is, lastly, and most importantly, the issue of building layout and architecture: many of the most noted examples of utopian conceptions entailed built utopias. It is not possible here to even attempt a short summary of utopian planning. Suffice it to point out that what principally makes the plan of such a utopian settlement, or ideal city, look community-orientated is the way it stresses the meeting of people, usually in a central place. 'Rubbing shoulders all the time' was the university founders' and their designers' ideal.

Utopian, furthermore, puts an emphasis on the planning phase of an institution. Utopianist is meant to stress in the context of this book the fact that it is not just about grandiose plans, but about their realisations, however partial and however much hit by Welfare State shoe-string conditions. 'The utopian versus the realistic. Many associated with the new university have utopian, or at least highly idealistic goals but they soon find their aspirations impeded by reality,' wrote the Canadian university founder Murray G. Ross. This may have been, Ross continues, 'devastating for some', but it was also 'tension producing' for others. As with 'institution' and 'community', there have been recent attempts to break up the notions and values of utopia as rigid, finite structures and to include something of the 'tension-producing' element into its very definition. It is this spirit of a 'critical utopia', even of a 'process' of utopia which can serve the analysis, especially when faced with a diversity of utopian solutions. There is a further recent trend, namely to consider utopias more from a users' point of view. A total utopia never was, and never will be realised simply because there never will be the universal agreement needed for such a step. But there always were, and probably there always will be 'consensual' utopias, where some users more or less voluntarily conform to the new ideals of an institution, and often only for a limited time. Universities are, of course, examples of the latter mode: while to the teachers and to the designers the state of being at the institution is a quasi permanent one, the university's main users, the students, enter the educational contract for a strictly limited, and actually a rather short period of time – at Oxbridge this usually amounts to nine times eight weeks, with major breaks in between.

It does not, however, suffice here to define utopia by itself. It must be placed into the context of a much more complex web of socio-political terms. The break in the conception of an educational university community already referred to, the new 'liberalisation' of the mid-1960s, soon led to the advocacy of new and unprecedented amounts of freedom and resulted in calls for the outright rejection of all 'authority' and, in turn, to attempts to form much more informal kinds of student communities. Virtually all commentators, among them recent historians of utopia, agree that this constituted a strong utopian movement. Now from this viewpoint the main institutions in this book should precisely not be called utopian, but its 'opposite', namely 'ideological', meaning that, far from creating new values, they were upholding, overtly or covertly, old values, in order to support an existing social and political system. As Paul Ricoeur wrote in the early 1970s, 'ideology has always the function of preserving an identity, whether of a group or individual; utopia has the opposite function, it shatters reality'. Following a plethora of political and sociological-philosophical analyses of ideology from the 1840s to the 1980s we could extend the term ideology and use 'authority', 'hegemony', 'legitimising power', or just 'power', as well as 'mythification', 'discursive formations', or 'representational strategies' to analyse our institutions and the intentions behind them. But this would still not mark the end of the debate: utopia and ideology are seen not only as opposites, but in many ways as closely related to each other. However, while for Mannheim and Ricoeur they are both necessary ways of thinking, for Marx and Engels they are detrimental; what is needed is only critique, the demasking of ideology and utopia.

To adopt a methodological radicalism by foregrounding any of the terms above, especially ideology, would not appear useful or plausible for this book. 'Utopianist' must remain as a generalised characterisation, principally connoting a united effort and a strong claim for 'change'. It would not seem fair to let the whole effort of the reformers of the years to 1965 be governed by the considerations of 1968 and the accompanying very specific socio-political discourses (even if these had a long pedigree). The book does devote some pages to the perceived institutional-political problems within the episode of 1968 in England and elsewhere, as well as to the way in which, internationally, some planners and designers disclaimed their earlier utopian or utopianist efforts. The movement of 1968 certainly brought major changes as regards the functioning of the institution, especially by claiming a greater openness towards the surrounding community. However, it was also in many ways directed against planning and against architectural 'solutions'. A heuristic decision has thus been made here, namely to descend from the plane of 'pure' sociological and political debate to a narrower definition of the institutional as the concretely, the individually planned and built institution. The primary concern in this book on utopianist universities cannot lie with the 1968 'utopian moment' of the student revolt which showed a disregard for built institutions (while still using them for their own congregations) but in the solidly built new utopianist institutions which preceded it.

The term 'utopianist', finally, gains justification through reflecting on one of the common denominators of the years 1960 and 1968, even if that was only a negative one. The desire to act against instrumentalism, or reductive instrumental rationality, united American liberal educationalists with 'traditionalist' English ones and German Humboldtians, as well as with most postwar Western Marxists. They all regretted and fought an institutionality which was expressly devoted to the 'mere' fulfilling of 'practical' aims, which, in university terms, meant the 'simple' 'production' of vocational degrees. Many, in fact, shared an aversion to all technocratic elements in education which was seen as limiting the 'human potential'. The 'battle' against, or the concrete attempts to limit, instrumentality in the institution is one of the constant sub-themes of this book. In fact, the real, effective opposition to what is dealt with here came somewhat later, during the 1970s, with new, or renewed convictions among monetarist liberals and technologists aligning themselves with the idea that Modern, scientifically-steered societies have no need for either utopias or ideologies, ironically a belief mainline socialism or communism had also held for a long time. Now both movements, that of the early 1960s universities, and that of 1968, appeared out of date.

As far as the architects' own discourses were concerned this book assumes a relative simplicity, at least for the years up to the later 1960s. Architects, we take it, mostly operated with a clear and simple theory which largely kept them free from any substantial fear of a conflict or clash between ideals/ideologies and instrumentality. To put it bluntly, the busy generation of postwar architects had little time for theory. A utopian frame of mind was, in any case, something almost normal. On the whole, architecture was still comprehended under Vitruvius's three headings, *utilitas*, *soliditas* and *venustas*; meaning that, firstly and secondly, a building serves all material-practical purposes economically, and that there need not be any argument about this. Campus and college buildings are there to 'serve' the client, the institution. But at the same time – the third Vitruvian heading – a building must aspire to something 'more'. That higher value, or art value, may exist in an autonomous sphere, even in isolation of social, moral and political values. But architects, especially utopianist-Modernist ones, also believed that it was precisely this 'higher' architectural value which might serve, or better still, might be combined with, or might at least help to lend credence to, the social, political and moral values of an important public undertaking, such as a university. In fact, studying the career of many Modernist designers one notes that the sense of heightened artistic power, or demeanour, goes hand in hand with heightened claims to 'social' power and the strongest possible influence over social policy.

The difficulty comes with the question as to what exactly this 'higher' element of architecture consists of, and how it is to be installed. Here nineteenth- and twentieth-century trends brought new formulations and new values. Traditionally, one simply added ornament to what was perceived as the utilitarian body of a building. This ornament could, in addition to its function as 'art', carry symbolic meaning, symbolic, say, of the religiosity of the church or the authority of a government or an educational institution. In the twentieth century architects and their critics developed new concepts of 'form' and of 'space' and set these apart from the older methods of adding ornament. Part of the trends which shaped the architecture of higher education and the 'reform' movements dealt with here stem from the Pugin/Gropius conviction that the useful must be identical with the aesthetically valuable. This strand of Modernism was desperately trying to get away from the duality use/ornament, once and for all. To put the Modernists' credo in its most banal formulation, 'architecture' should not entail additional cost. There should no longer be a difference, 'architecturally', between a mass and an élite institution. And yet, the old duality persisted, especially in the USA, where practicality cum economy and 'aesthetics' were usually mentioned separately, and were to some extent still juxtaposed. The crux of the matter is that the relationship between the various elements of the 'architectural' and the 'utilitarian', between ideal and instrumentality, is always formulated and 'solved' individually, and differently, in each building undertaking – whatever the style.

Short-circuiting the detailed issues just outlined, the methodology of this book can be sketched out more simply. First of all, it presents chronicles of each institution, mainly as regards their underlying ideals, and their plans and built forms. It is characteristic of this approach that even most of those elements of a plan that one might call practical, for example, the introduction of small kitchens in student residences, are taken to be derived at least partly from idealist (social/moral) considerations. The chief agents in the story are the patrons, the clients of the institutions, as well as the planners and designers. The study of patronage necessitates a division of the book into countries, according to the ways in which the organisations of higher education are/were shaped nationally. As regards the actual narratives, we mostly proceed in a time-honoured way: an idea, an aim, is cited and then a number of buildings are examined as to whether they fulfil this aim. The early 'social history or architecture' of the 1950s to 1970s thus kept to the tradition of the basic history of ideas approach. That approach then turns into more complex ways of investigating the development of the ideas, their dialectics and the way they never appeared settled for long, thereby uncovering matters which had remained unspoken. This means, furthermore, that we can bypass some of the essentialisms which the older kind of history of ideas usually leaves intact. Such an approach is crucial when dealing with Modernism. Today, the terms 'Modern', or 'Modernity', as such, no longer make much sense. The issue of what is, or would be modern today, in the simple sense of 'up to date', cannot be broached here. Instead, the topic is Modernism; its axioms appeared sacrosanct at the time, yet, today, it must be seen as a movement that came and went. In a further methodological turn we adopt a more sociological or socio-historical kind of investigation (as distinct from just citing 'social' ideals or social policies) and relate the ideals/aims more closely to the social and professional structures and processes within which the diverse agents operated, whether patrons, critics or designers. This can help to break the intentionalist circularity, the self-fulfilling-prophesy effect that the history of ideas approach usually entails. (Getting to know the sources, the historian usually finds the exact quote to fit his or her trajectory.) We finally reflect on the rhetoric, as such, concentrating not on the contents of the messages, but on the style of their formulations.

So far it might appear that the subject of investigation is the groups who initiated the processes and buildings. What about the recipients? This book does not consider the users of the new universities, that is, the students (or the lecturers, the administrative and support staff as well as the parents and the general public) as separate 'agents'. In the context of this book the recipients, generically, are treated as nothing other than what the 'initiators' intended them to be. The particular historical situation which applies to the 1960s was, however, that the recipients, certainly the main group of them, the students, began to change their minds and instituted what they saw as a new kind of student, a student body which emphasised its own mode of existence, and often in opposition to the teachers and ideologues/reformers. This book deals with the beginning of this phase, and chiefly with the way the new movement influenced the assessment of the recent plans and buildings. It ran parallel with a new general user discourse, formulated mainly by planners and architects. This is not to deny that a useful material culture study could, and should be written, on the lives and lifestyles on campus and college. It would entail a more general sociological, as well as psychological, analysis of the 'ordinary' daily use of university buildings. Care should be taken that these investigations are conducted historically. It would be naive to construct a scenario in which the intentions behind, and the realisation of a building, are treated as history while the question of the 'results' of those intentions and the subsequent uses of the buildings are seen as somehow belonging to a static present. In any case, this account stops in the early 1970s, when the period of enthusiasm for university architecture was followed by a period of disappointment and retrenchment, which, in turn, was followed by a period of consolidation into the 1980s, ending with an upsurge in building only from the late 1980s. What characterised the attitude of all those years towards the efforts of the 1960s was simply silence.

In the end, we must return to the most general meaning of utopia as simply a set of values which are considered 'higher' than usual. This leads to the historian's chief epistemological issue: what values does a book contain and to what extent are they upheld? At that point an interest has to be declared: the author speaks as an insider, as somebody who has taught for a long time in one of the institutions dealt with in this book. A fairly recent American conclusion in a somewhat similar book makes the issue of the values contained in institutional architecture sound very straightforward: '[Campus and college] architecture . . . [are] the vehicle[s] for expressing utopian social visions . . .'. While such an essentialist definition no doubt catches some of the spirit of the 1960s, it appears too simplistic today. It only allows for a fixed signifier-signified relationship, it does not deal with the possibility of Modernist designers' independent architectural-formal aspirations which might not want to symbolise anything; it leaves no room for the dichotomies practical/ornamental, and there appears no way in which the visions as such may be questioned. Today, a fairer way of dealing with values is by apportioning priority among various sub-values and by sifting between those which are questioned here and those which are taken for granted. To begin with, the most basic term of all, 'social' – whether valorised or not – is not questioned, nor even defined. There is no argument here with the ostensible, basic aim of the new universities which was to expand higher education. The question whether this could have been done more cheaply and more effectively through the expansion of older universities is considered, naturally, as less important in this context. The socio-political framework, the postwar Welfare States of various kinds which chiefly generated this expansion, is not questioned either. Neither can an elaborate definition of university education be offered. Institution is clearly a key term, if not the key term, in this book. The desirability of a degree of institutionalisation, of institutional coherence, is taken for granted, and yet a determination of the maximal or optimal degree of institutionalisation cannot be attempted here.

Ultimately this book is about the built, or the intended permanent frame of the institution. In the end it is the designer's point of view that counts most. It was architects who most wanted a unified campus architecture. This book does not set out to classify the designers' work according to the characteristics of Modernism or any other style, but according to the ways in which the designer tries his or her utmost to enhance the working of the academic-educational institution – not as a manifestation of a single utopian vision, but as a response to utopianist particulars, to notions about the detailed functioning of the institution. The highest aim of the designer and the client was the unity of all the complex factors, a totality, culminating in the combination of campus and college. Optimum unity of effort and design is, of course, the basic aim of any utopian project. Thus the heroes of this book are specifically those institutions in which the strong architectural and the institutional-social factors are most neatly combined; and yet, they are not taken as approximations to the definitive utopia but each in their utopianist individuality.

USA: CAMPUS VS. COLLEGE

Although knowledge has no visible bulk, it requires space as surely as students do.
(Clark Kerr)

THE POST WORLD WAR II MULTIVERSITY

When considering utopianist university design there is a lot to be said for taking the USA as a starting point. Two simple facts should be considered: during the whole of the last two centuries no other country founded such a vast number of institutions and conducted such a thorough and diversified discussion on all aspects of higher education. After World War II, the USA took the world lead in academe. At the risk of adding to the mountains of writing that already exist, the basic rationale here is twofold: to take a look from outside and to help prepare for the rest of the book, by providing initial definitions of campus and college.

In 1973 Clark Kerr, president of America's largest educational institution, the University of California, closed a new edition of his tract, *The Uses of the University*, by reminding his readers not to forget the 'relation of the university to the eternal search for Utopia'. More recently, in his comprehensive and balanced work on American university architecture, Paul Venable Turner concludes that these buildings have been 'shaped by the desire to create an ideal community, and have often been a vehicle for expressing the utopian social visions of the American imagination'. Utopian, in turn, can be synonymous with 'American' and many other such key terms, as justice, compassion, truth, nation. The values of the major American institutions are claimed to be those of the country as a whole. The institution closest to the university would be the American school whose ethos and architectural splendour is often not a long way behind. Even for an analyst of universities who normally stayed clear of strong rhetoric, the sociologist David Riesman, higher education was 'everyone's right'. By the early 1970s this idea culminated in more down-to-earth statements: 'no student who wants to attend college should be prevented from doing so' (President Nixon before congress in 1971). Equally important was the idea that having entered the system even at the lowest levels, the chances for advancement were strong (Ben-David).

The normal trajectory would thus be to state the utopian aims and then to measure the reality against it. The chosen procedure here will be mostly the opposite one. Utopianism, as opposed to utopia, is always a matter of degree, it exists in constant argument, not only with anti-utopianism – which will concern us much further on in this book – but also with non-utopia, with simple pragmatism, or calculated instrumentality, and that within each of the sub-discourses, within each of the professions dealing with the universities. When we come to the story of the English New

Universities of the 1960s, we will meet a more united stress on utopia within a single episode, whereas in order to properly evaluate some of the peaks of postwar American university design, we have to begin with diverse elements in diffuse debates, going backwards and forwards between imagination and reality, between idealism and instrumentalisation, between high and low. For Turner, the twentieth-century manifestations of utopia are identical with the peaks of architectural quality. In our context, the definition of utopianism concerns wider, non-architectural aspects of the institution and a greater number of agents than just the architect and his or her immediate clients or university founders, as they happened to be on the architect's side; we also need to take note of the aspirations of the educationalists, as well as of the college psychologists and the campus planners, all of whom emerge as strong subgroups in our period. The architects, too, are jostling for position in the aim to create the ideal institution; at the same time each profession wants to stress its own expertise and importance. These considerations form the major subtext of this chapter.

For American historians and analysts of the university only three countries matter: England, Germany and the USA. 'To the English concept of the educated gentleman and the German concept of scholarly research for its own sake, the American university added another dimension, namely, that higher education to justify its own existence should seek to serve actively the basic needs of American life'. Sharper opinions may be found earlier, calling 'Oxbridge an expression of English aristocracy . . . Berlin and Leipzig representatives of German imperialism . . . and the small colleges in [America] the expression of the democratic spirit which is the true American spirit'.

On the whole, though, can American higher education, with its 3,000 or so institutions (in 1993), be called a 'system' or an organisational or constitutional unity? True, there has been, for some decades now, much state and central government finance, and many institutions are linked by a system of accreditation in order to ensure the comparability of degrees. But American colleges and universities are not 'of the state' as those in most other countries. Neither would, today, the term 'private' fully express their status; what matters here is that virtually every institution, 'private' or 'state', forms an independent organisation, for which 'non-profit-making' is probably the best characterisation. To cite again an American notion of the situation in Europe: the old English universities are run by faculty, most Continental European ones by the state, while American colleges and universities are normally run, not unlike large businesses, by their Boards of Trustees, with a strong president at the helm. Each institution is furnished with its own large administration, free to shape itself as it sees fit. The primary task is to attract donations as well as good students, through maintaining an image of quality, or a particular historical or religious identity. Institutions range from those with the emphasis on pure research and an international reputation to the localised junior college – to the level of English 'further education' or even of the German higher schools – with innumerable shades in between; size varies from a few hundred to tens of thousands of students.

In the context of our investigation of the shapes of institutions, however, these differences or rankings do not carry much significance. Any institution may call itself 'university'; or may bear the name 'college', from Harvard College to the remotest community college. The ranking scale is simply seen as a reflection of the uneven distribution of wealth and established reputation in society generally, which is taken for granted and thus does not interfere with the utopian project as a whole. It largely concerns purely academic standing and not necessarily the socio-educational aspects of the institution which are the main parts of the American utopian mission. It was the utopian trajectory which gave unity to the project of the generic American college, while the notion of freedom accounts for its diversity. There is thus no single model of a university and there was also, in the years post World War II, no movement strictly comparable to the European ones of creating entirely new, 'reform' universities. Only a small number of states devised such policies 'from above', for their own public universities. In principle and in practice, each American institution was in charge of its own image and its own constant reform.

The high rhetoric, such as Clark Kerr's, more often than not contained a historical dimension which the utopian spirit could turn into statements such as 'the true American University lies in the future', but which, characteristically, always included both a measure of dissatisfaction with, as well as a measure of pride in the American past; as Alan Touraine, the French sociologist of the 1970s, noted, compared with France, most American universities are quite old. Any history of American higher education would stress: 'the foundations . . . laid in colonial time . . . still standing in the twentieth century'. However, this did not mean a straightforward line of tradition. Characteristic, in fact, were continuous intense discussions and searches for new models, at least from the post bellum period onwards. America then began to import from Germany what was characterised as 'learning for its own sake', synonymous with research, or postgraduate studies, and played down the older English social character of the institution. It was at this point that the term university was firmly introduced. Johns Hopkins at Baltimore, for instance, no longer wanted to call itself a college. It was also the time of the large new, state-founded 'Land Grant' campuses. With it came the response to the vast need for technical education which, contrary to many of the European developments, remained within the realm of higher education. However, as elsewhere, a strong duality developed: technical and practical subjects vs. humanities, corresponding to the English polarity vocational / educational or the German opposites *Fachwissen* and *Bildung*. As the strong social stratification of the country kept its hold, the first was normally located at the lower end, the second at the higher end, not only in social but in academic terms as well. This, in turn, became firmly linked, during the early twentieth century, with the polarity of large state vs. small private institutions.

However much stress there is on historical unity, the new developments in the three decades after World War II did form a distinctive period in the history of American higher education. As regards general expansion, the USA started a dozen or so years before the Europeans. The first major impetus came with the Veterans' return in 1945, which must also have had something to do with the 'war babies' wave in the 1960s. In 1947–8 a Presidential Commission published *The Higher Education Report for American Democracy*, the 'first comprehensive rationale for mass higher education'. In 1957 a most momentous and unexpected incentive occurred in the form of the 'Sputnik shock' which drove efforts to raise both quantity and quality. Federal financial contributions had already risen rapidly since the Depression in the 1930s. By 1970 federal and state aid to education amounted to 71 per cent (in Britain, in 1966–7, the figure of state finance was 87 per cent) and money from other sources also increased and enabled the old and privileged private institutions to flourish, too. The actual overall

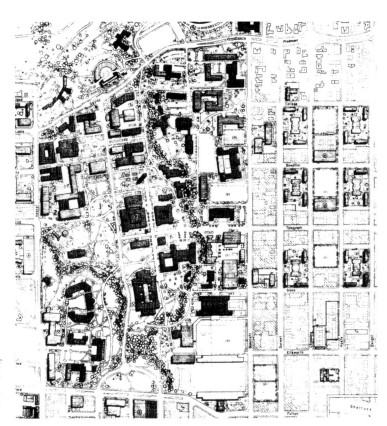

1.1 The multiversity: University of California Berkeley 1959. To the designers of the 1960s it appeared a typically planless campus. (*ARec* 9-1959, p. 162)

cost of 'producing' a graduate kept rising, until about 1970, by 5 per cent per annum. Uncountable numbers of new institutions were founded each year, usually by the state, the vast majority as junior or community colleges. Between 1963 and 1975 the total number of universities and colleges doubled. Total student numbers rose from 2.7 m in 1955 to over 7 m by the end of the 1960s. A further measure of equality was the rise of the proportion of women, from 38 in 1960 to 51 per cent in the late 1970s, and of blacks, from 6.6 in 1960 to 13 per cent in the late 1970s. The proportion of American youth in higher education, about one half, was very significantly higher than the equivalent measure in British higher and further education (even after taking account of the high American drop-out rate, 40–50 per cent). Equally important was the increase at the upper end so to speak. Between 1955 and 1968 graduate enrolment trebled, from $\frac{1}{4}$ million to $\frac{3}{4}$ million. The chief perception was simply that of expansion in all directions.

There was widespread agreement that 'Americans today have higher expectations of the university than they do of practically any other social institution'. 'Higher education, including the research complex, has become the most critical single feature of . . . modern society' (Talcot Parsons). Moreover, the old conundrum of unity and diversity had taken a new turn. The traditional triad of education, scientific research and, at a lower level, technical instruction, were now moulded into a heightened perception of their equal usefulness to society. A new kind of institution had arisen which to some extent levelled the differences between the old diversity of institutions: the multiversity. It could mean a single large campus, or a confederation of sites.

14

1.2 Clark Kerr, President of the University of California 1958–7 and initiator of the campuses at Irvine, San Diego and Santa Cruz. (C.M. Otten, *University Authority and the Student. The Berkeley Experience*, Berkeley, 1970)

The main issue of the 1960s became, in fact, the multiversity itself and what was considered wrong with it. 'The multiversity is a confusing place for the student', wrote Kerr, 'he has problems of establishing his identity and sense of security within it'. The multiversity could, in fact, be seen as no more than an unplanned conglomerate of a variety of institutions. Until the later 1950s it usually suffered from lack of funds, inadequate facilities, unsophisticated administration and uncontrolled proliferation of disciplines. The new stress on scientific research, the newly perceived national need for it, had led to a neglect of the masses of undergraduates. The multiversity seemed, in fact, to have strayed away from the central concept of American higher education. It no longer seemed a part of utopia; utopia could not consist simply of increased numbers (figs 1.1 and 1.2).

How could the multiversity's problems be solved? The answer was seen to lie in institutional diversity. Campus and college were understood as contrasting institutions. Campus entailed comprehensiveness and spread, while college stood for concentration and strictly limited size. As time went on, college and campus were also seen to complement each other, and finally there were the attempts to combine them. We may thus speak of a dialectic of campus and college. The multiversity, would clearly be classified under campus. But if this meant that a 'campus' was increasingly associated with just accommodating numbers, one could expect a new attention to be given to the college by all those who professed to pursue quality. At the same time, the ethos of the general expansion of higher education would never be lost sight of.

LIBERAL COLLEGE TO STUDENT PERSONNEL SERVICE

So far we have characterised the nature of the utopianist system of education as one that is open to the country as a whole. The individual utopianist institution, however,

1.3 College students (possibly in a 'Living and Learning Centre') *c.* 1960. (C. Rieker and F.G. Lopez, *College Students Live Here*, New York, 1961, p. 7)

functions rather by shutting itself off from its environment. This double-facing is reflected in the use of the cherished term community: it signifies both the wider locality outside the institution, and the institution itself, or more precisely, the shared aims, the unity of, and within, that institution. And yet, the remit of the college is broader than that of the university – or so it seemed from the standpoint of the defenders of virtues of the small college. Their fear is, as was alluded to in the Preface, the instrumentalisaton of academic training; to the ideologist of the small college, the danger of the multiversity is not just that of containing anonymous masses, but an excessively narrow vocational view of the acquisition of academic knowledge. Within the college the main task is often formulated as the inculcation of 'education', as well as, or rather than, the imparting of academic knowledge. Returning, however, to the larger issue of widening university provision as a whole, one of the problems which the following will be battling with is whether any new developments in college education should be instrumentalised again, and put into the service of the acquisition of academic knowledge in a larger institution, or whether college education should always be understood strictly as something that exists by and for itself. Put more simply, once again, the alternatives seemed 'training' the masses and 'educating' the elite (fig. 1.3).

The favourite term 'liberal arts college' is derived from Antiquity and the Middle Ages and perpetuates an expression most confusingly used in the English language. Only fairly recently the principal meaning of 'the arts' was changed to 'the humanities' and there are still arguments as to how much of the social sciences and even of the natural sciences should be included. The word that matters most in our context is 'liberal'. 'Liberal education' characterises the non-vocational branch of academe. Crucially, from the later nineteenth century onwards, this also entailed the notion of 'Lernfreiheit' (Clark Kerr), or electivity: the student could choose what to learn and was given part of the responsibility to structure his or her course. This, in turn, was

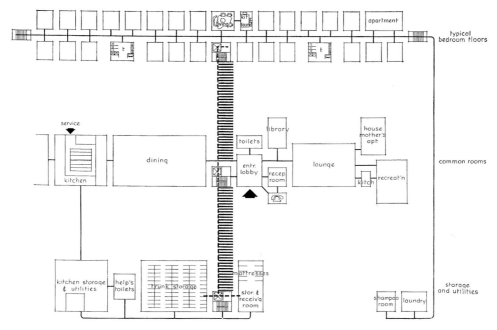

1.4   Schematic plan of an American residential hall 1947. (*ARec* 12-1947, p. 82)

linked to an ever greater emphasis on subjectivity, on the personality of each student, and on the individualised and intensive interchange between teacher and taught. By no means did this weaken the idea of a close community; on the contrary, a community would be strengthened through each individual's commitment to it. But it had to be small. A new, immense value was placed on the small institution – provided this was coupled with a perception of quality. From the later nineteenth century onwards a number of colleges, especially on the East Coast, such as Swarthmore or Bryn Mawr, managed to keep, or even increase their social and academic standing, while, or even because of, remaining small and intimate. They always adhered to the label 'college'. 'Liberal studies find their greatest charm amid the old associations and their natural home in the peace of rural life'. This was *a fortiori* true for womens' colleges which 'courageously claimed a male preserve . . . that of the liberal arts college' and which 'shaped their communal life . . . and transformed their college landscapes into the settings of their own dramas of college life', to cite Helen Horowitz's *Alma Mater*, a richly detailed account of precisely those lives and landscapes in the East Coast women's institutions.

A two-fold development must now be noted with regard to the 'college'; on the one hand, small institutions found it harder to exist, and, especially in the period of the multiversity their numbers diminished. For instance, of the 300 womens' colleges in 1960, only 146 had kept their independence by 1973. On the other hand, major older universities of the highest academic reputation had begun to build sub-units from around 1900 onwards after the small college model, notably, Princeton, Yale and Harvard. At a time when these institutions as a whole could no longer be called a 'college', their 'residential colleges', or residence halls, provided some academic, and much moral tuition; their architecture, and the way it was meant to recall Oxbridge will concern us below.

Discussions about all aspects of higher education were gaining momentum and included the voices of major intellectuals, such as John Dewey, which, in particular, led to countless reformulations of the 'liberal' ideal and which carried on, virtually unchallenged, into the 1950s and beyond. They often began with a reference to the nineteenth-century English champion of a reformed Oxbridge, Henry Newman. The principal target was the instrumentality of the vocational: 'support [must be given] from a disinterested respect for the value of education . . . the ultimate criterion of the place of higher learning in America will be the extent to which it is esteemed not as a necessary instrument of external ends, but as an end in itself'. A major change, however, occurred within this movement around 1930. The retrospective trend began to be replaced by one which stressed the new. Now the term reform came into its own. Small, or very small 'Reform Colleges' not only took the lead in innovation but became desirable, even fashionable places to study. They were usually newly founded, or had been taken over by educational gurus, such as Alexander Meiklejohn (*The Experimental College*, 1932). Most of the movements did, however, perpetuate a hostility towards the new technical world, such as the group which advocated concentrating on the reading of the 'Great Books'. Others took a more 'modern' line, such as Bennington and Sarah Lawrence and preached an intensification of democracy and equality. Another important element was the search for more elaborate procedures in practising the life of a small community, in the 'communal expressive' group. A smaller group of 'aesthetic-expressive' colleges, to use another one of David Riesman's labels, such as Black Mountain College, of the 1930s, believed in the general educational value of personal expression through the fine arts and artistic crafts. Later on we shall come to find links, in some cases of the 1930s and 1940s, between educational reform and architectural reform. After World War II, the reformist message continued but was increasingly overshadowed by a dichotomy of the egalitarian aspirations and the elitist reality of the small college. The task, as seen by many, especially in California, was to incorporate some reform elements into the multiversity, especially the close teacher student contact, or the 'liberal education' kinds of subjects, for instance in 'General Studies' courses.

We have, however, not yet provided the essential characterisation of what happens in the college itself. In the USA, as in England, 'university' stresses the academic learning and research processes, while 'college' makes the point that all other aspects of a student's life are also catered or cared for. It is this care which grew into an enormous complex of preoccupations, shared by a number of agents, educational philosophers, administrators, psychologists, architects and others. Embracing it all was the continued concern for liberal educational values with the overriding goal of connecting all the elements into one great whole. To provide only one example of the innumerable highly charged social-moral formulations, taken from the bible on the subject, Nevitt Sanford's *The American College* of 1962:

> The academic community must be an assembly of men and women humble enough yet secure enough to exhibit to one another their doubts, the weaknesses, and at times their wretchedness. This is the price of knowledge and truth . . . foster the understanding and the free but organised search for new forms of thinking and living, and you will be educating people.

It was the reform movements of the early decades and some of its leaders, such as

Theodore M. Newcomb, who helped to formulate the new methodologies of the post World War II concern for, and ensuing science of, college life. Basically, the concern for the student goes back to the kind of responsibility upheld by every traditional institution, the disciplinary one, to ensure the orderly behaviour of its inmates. One has to remember that, traditionally, the age of American students ranges between 17 and 21 years – 'most college students are adolescents' (Dugald S. Arbuckle 1953). A principal concern was for the student's 'mental hygiene' (used in 1953 without quotation marks), though this authoritarian attitude would rapidly diminish in the 1960s. But we must look for yet another major source for this development. It lay with the way post World War II academics generally insisted that nothing but rigorous scientific methods will do. The 'Student Personnel Services', as they developed from the 1940s to the 1960s, had to move into the scientific sphere, too. A language arose, sounding entirely professional and different from that of the earlier philosopher-educationalists and different from the generalised rhetoric used by the college presidents. It was the discourse of the psychologist, in particular the behavioural scientist. Psychologists had moved away from moralising analyses of an individual's character traits and concentrated, instead, on his or her 'environment', or, to cite the college jargon, the 'press', meaning less the actual physical environment, but 'peer group influence' and the general mental atmosphere of the place. A new group of academic researchers then took these 'independent, situational variables' and treated them with much arithmetic and tabulations. A whole culture of student care arose, practised by professionals within the institutions, numbering thousands in all, and with their back-up of a great number of researchers resulting in a vast body of publications.

It is important to note again that the student personnel services were strictly not concerned with the contents of teaching. However much their origin lay with the liberal educational ethos, they now sidelined an important tradition of that movement, namely the advocacy of the humanities for educational purposes, as well as the non-vocational stance of liberal education. On the other hand, this meant that the new 'services' operated for all students, they served all 'college men'. According to the faction of college psychologists, all students at one time or another needed their help. Thus one might even conclude that the student personnel service functioned as a genuinely new unifying element, it included everybody in the multiversity, and that therefore it did take the idea of the college, as togetherness, into the larger university, and therefore did help to reduce the gap between 'mass' and elite.

Against that, however, speaks the continuing proliferation and diversification of the groups serving the well-functioning of the college. 'The college psychologist helps the individual, the college administrators strive for order in the community.' Most evaluations of the student services reveal their straightforward instrumentality. Their chief purpose was, simply: 'the correlation between college press and productivity', that is, academic success and the prevention of 'attrition', or dropping out. While the investigations bristled with graphs and mathematics, the main conclusions were mostly of a devastating simplicity. For instance, 'freshmen-to-senior changes in several characteristics have been occurring in considerable uniformity in most American colleges and universities in recent decades'. The recipes, too, in the end, had to remain vague. A key term was 'fit': the correspondence between the college environment and the mentality of the student. Agreement could not be reached as to the degree of 'fit' which was desirable. The earlier radical reform college could aim for a strong lack of fit, at least initially, so that the student's character and outlook could be changed and moulded into the desired direction. The psychologists of 1970, however, oscillated between concluding that too strange an environment would elicit resistance on the part of the student, with effects that were educationally counterproductive, and, on the other hand, that too close an initial fit would mean a lack of challenge and would elicit no change in the student's character at all. Indeed, it was said that 'the typical college graduate is a cultural rubber-stamp for the social heritage as it stands, rather than the instigator of new patterns of thought and new standards of conduct'. In other words, somehow, the reformist impulse appeared to have evaporated during the 1960s and the aims and the ethos of the institution college were less clear than ever before.

The college's concern for the lives of students was normally most wide-ranging. 'We house and feed them and find ways to teach them' thus President Esther Raushenbush of Sarah Lawrence, one of the most prestigious small womens' colleges. One should note the order of the tasks as outlined here. To take the second, virtually all institutions of higher education, anywhere, take the feeding of the students for granted. The vast majority also built facilities in the centre of the campus for further aspects of the social and recreational life of the students. In Anglo-Saxon countries these are usually called 'students unions', built and financed by the university, but often administered by semi-autonomous student organisations. There was never any argument as to their basic use and the need for them. However, their complexity increased during the postwar years; a great variety of 'campus centres' were created which catered for further cultural purposes; there was often a lavish 'arts centre', which of course, could be seen as the substitute of the old college chapel.

The major area of the college not devoted to teaching was the student's 'residence'. It has come to be recognised as the overriding characteristic of the Anglo-American college and university education as a whole. Until the mid to later nineteenth century this English tradition continued in America, but with the new wave of the publicly financed campuses of largely local or regional intake, as well as the influence of German university culture where the student residence was virtually an unknown entity, many American universities – as well as most of the English 'Civics' and 'Redbricks' – expected students to find their own accommodation. But from the mid-twentieth century a vast number of student residences were again built, the College Housing Loan programme from the early 1950s made obtaining finance easier, and the Higher Education Facilities Act of 1963 further encouraged the construction of 'cheap shelter'. Total provision could, of course, only be dreamt of. Until the early 1970s precise figures seem hard to come by, but it appears that about half the American student population commuted to the university, while a further one-third, or more, lived in purpose-built accommodation, which was somewhat like the situation to Britain, although there the proportion of students living at home was much smaller (figs 1.4 and 1.5).

The very first American colleges included student residences just as their English models in an all-purpose building. Later on, during the eighteenth century, and departing from English customs, residences were usually accommodated in separate buildings. In his celebrated early nineteenth-century model university at Charlottesville, Virginia, Thomas Jefferson carefully coordinated them with all the other functions. On the average campus, however, residences occupied rather undistinguished, barrack-like buildings. The traditional American residence thus moved some way away from its Oxbridge origins. Most accommodation consisted of dormitories – a term unknown in the university context in England – meaning long corridors, often twenty rooms on either side, with sparse sanitary facilities, each room sleeping two or more – single rooms remained the exception in the USA for a long time. There was usually no space anywhere in the dorms where the student could do his or her actual studying.

There was a further element in the diversification of life in the college. From the affluent later nineteenth century onwards, students took their lives, so to speak, into their own hands, or rather, were helped by their parents and the alumni, who built for them great numbers of club-homes, called fraternities and sororities, which included dormitories and a great number of social facilities. A society within a society arose, entertainments of all kinds, initiation ceremonies, drinking, dating, useful contacts within the social elite. England had nothing to offer in comparison – although some aspects of student life at Oxbridge have been looked at and judged in somewhat similar terms – whereas the German *Studenten-Verbindungen* offer strong comparisons during much the same period (see page 208). If we include the vastly expanding facilities for athletics, which seemed to dominate life on the old campuses during the early twentieth century, we arrive at a description of life in the American college town in which student socialisation had become an independent entity.

But this is, of course, a later twentieth-century view. Earlier, the strong old moral-educational beliefs, combined with the stability of the hierarchical social structure would take this performance of the adolescent elite for granted. To the new educational-sociological and reformist kind of thinking the separateness of the old dormitories and the fraternities provided a challenge to devise a 'reintegration of curriculum and extracurriculum' (Brubacher and Rudy). The provision of the students' unions and campus centres mentioned above – a 'movement' which began around 1900 – were part of the attempt to re-include social and recreational elements into the centre of the university.

Around 1900 we also witness attempts to 'return' to the full scale Oxbridge College – in actual fact it amounted to a parallel with the new English concept of the student 'hall of residence', or, as the Americans say, 'residence hall', with just some academic teaching, as well as some 'moral' instruction. It began chiefly at Princeton, then took off at Yale after World War I and reached Harvard shortly after. Particularly striking and in many ways novel was the way in which architectural design was put into the service of the educational aims. As the architect, Ralph Adams Cram, remarked about his Princeton College in 1910: 'half college and half monastery', it 'sways men's minds and exalts their spiritual consciousness by means of the subtle influence of solemn architecture'. The attraction of old Oxford seemed overwhelming and the allegiance could not have been more outspoken at times: 'we seem to have added to Princeton the age of Oxford and Cambridge' (University President Woodrow Wilson). Harvard chose the term 'Houses' for its version of the college/residence hall, also arranging them on an open courtyard principle, though this time the style is not Gothic but an early Georgian manner which approximates the early buildings on the USA's oldest campus. Each of the seven Houses accommodates 400 students, with copious social-recreational facilities, as well as those for teaching, directed by a House Master, an academic of some standing. The teaching is, of course, only supplemental to that in the main parts of the university. There was one major Oxbridge planning element adopted at Princeton and Harvard, the 'staircase principle', giving access to a smaller number of rooms – at variance with the traditional American dormitory access via corridors. Harvard's Houses remained models for the internal organisation of student residences for a long time while 'Collegiate Gothic' conveyed the image of a complete and integrated institution and was at times applied to a large campus, such as Chicago or Duke. Finally, it must be stressed that nothing of that scale and intensity was ever built in England itself (cf. fig. 1.7).

To obtain strong institutionality by means of strong architectural images was an important innovation, but one could not expect it to find widespread adoption, for reasons of simple finance, as well as for unspoken reasons of status. A more specifically architectural idea of the college will be taken up again with the Modernist style. We must here return to the kind of discussion about institutions to which the 'college' has been subjected so far. Research of the kind arising from, and used for, the student personnel type services was, of course, also conducted for student residences, though not much of it appeared before about 1970. Investigations concentrated on the internal world, the peer group issues, or questions as to the allocation of applicants to specific residences or problems of coeducation. From an English point of view there seems to have been comparatively little research on socialisation for its own sake. The crucial question for our context, was, however, the relevance of student residences for the campus as a whole. And here we begin, again, to encounter hesitation. The major comparison was between students in residence and those commuting, and whether this was making a difference in academic attainment. It was estimated in 1977 that 'residence adds about 12 per cent to a student's chance of persisting in college and graduating'. In a summary of the research of two or three decades we read vaguely that students in residence are more likely to change their attitude, beliefs and values than those staying at home, but students 'do not perform better academically'.

There was always a very general agreement that more residences were needed and through the whole of university and college expansion the proportion of residences kept pace. But there were also many kinds of dissatisfactions and disagreements. The English ideal was venerated, but ultimately considered as too expensive for the USA. Occasionally, the English mode was felt to offer too little: 'For education to take place, faculty and students on campus must be involved in activities important and rewarding to both. Coffee and doughnuts will not do; and no improvement is to be gained from switching to tea and petit fours.' In 1963, the campus planning expert Richard Dober, tells us that the importance of residences in general is 'still debated'. Some objected outright to student residences, namely those who felt comfortable and independent in the fraternities and sororities. Brubacher and Rudy, in their comprehensive history and analysis concluded that educationalists still needed to find 'a way to integrate more closely [the American residences] with the educational objectives of higher learning'. The tail end of an old phenomenon coincided with the beginning of a new phenomenon, the new 'student culture' view of independence. It must be noted, though, that the strength of the residential tradition in America prevented the radical rejection of university-organised student residence as we shall witness it in 1960s West Germany. Some tried a pluralistic solution – students could stay in the dormitories according to the rules set by the institution, others may live where they can do as they please. Special groups included graduates and married students (beginning around 1960); the issue of the coed dormitories was first noted around 1960; there were the ethnic minorities in 'bi-ethnic dorms'and there were 'Theme Houses', i.e. halls for international groups of students. Residences now had to suit particular groups. At the same time new variations of academic supervision in hall kept springing up. According to Riesman, Michigan State 'pioneered' the 'living and learning unit' in the early 1960s.

Another version of the institution was the community college, a new name for, and an expansion of, the junior college, catering throughout for a lower class of degree and for a strictly localised area. Politically, there was unilateral support for this extension of higher education 'downwards'. The number of community colleges grew substantially, particularly from the late 1960s. Between 1973 and 1980 alone student numbers doubled. It was seen, however, as a borderline type of college: 'more than a high school, less than a university'. A community college was not a college, strictly speaking, as it did not normally include student residences. On the other hand, 'because much of the social life of the living-in college is missing', there had to be a special emphasis on the communal student facilities of the 'union' kind mentioned above, located in the centre of the complex. On the whole, because of a lack of complexity, this type of institution did not take part, so to speak, in some of the debates conducted here. And yet, the new proliferation of the term college revitalised this venerable institution and supplemented its old elitist image. 'Community', too, was invigorated, in two senses of the word, as a self-contained institution and as a service for the locality around it.

What emerges from this section so far is that the definition of the American 'college' had become increasingly blurred. Its older chief aim, 'education', became ever more difficult to define. Its 'true' American version was that of a completely self-contained institution which is both a small university in the fullest academic sense of the word and a fully self-contained living unit, at least as far as the students are concerned. At the other end of the spectrum is the plain block of student dormitories with some 'built-in' supervision facilities. However, following the sketch of the college we must return to the chief issue of this book, the university as a whole. In the old days, the American college was identical with the American university. At least from the beginnings of the multiversity onwards this was no longer the case. Moreover, during that period, as already mentioned, many small colleges folded or were amalgamated with larger neighbouring institutions. On the other hand, there was a mushrooming of diverse sub-units on the larger campuses which contained at least some elements of the old college type. There was one attempt, the last, one is tempted to say, at a rational combination of college and university: the Cluster College, or Satellite College, where a number of residence hall units are grouped around a larger 'university center', serving major communal functions, postgraduate students etc. A start was made in the 1920s in Claremont, California. The most sophisticated effort of this kind, the University of California Santa Cruz group of colleges, will concern us below.

Unity and a strong institutionality are what we have been looking for. 'Multiversity' denotes diffuseness, but 'college' by this stage, during the 1960s, becomes very imprecise, too. What was it that chiefly created the unity of the whole institution? According to Brubacher and Rudy, 'the characteristic expression of [the] new concern for the "whole student" and for the establishing of a new unity in the American college [which here includes, of course, the 'university'] in the twentieth century came to be the student personnel movement'. But they conclude their account on this topic with a sceptical note: 'There is no question that the American college student has become . . . the most thoroughly guided and counseled student in the world'. Doubts had, in fact, set in as to whether 'student moral educational and psychological guidance' was the institution's most useful aspect or function. The old educational morality which held the institution together, was no longer strong. The characterisation of the student personnel services above as 'instrumentalist', i.e. as aiming chiefly at maximising degree performance, left us in doubt as to whether they were really that much concerned with the institution as a whole. It was found, in fact, that the unifying ideal of the liberal arts college or university had been divided into the concerns of a number of separate professions. Was there still a desire for unity? If so, who could help to bring it about? We shall now turn mainly to plan and architecture. Did those professions compete with, or against, the educators and psychologists in the search for unity or did they all work together? How much advice could a designer gain from the study of the pronouncements outlined so far? A statement by David Riesman, when summing up the Harvard Houses under the heading: 'Some Utopian Conclusions', may make us doubtful: 'Unfortunately we know no formula for determining optimal community size', perhaps not a profound remark, but certainly a perceptive one.

CAMPUS PLANNING

The protracted search for the unity of the institution of college or university can be brought to a conclusion through the use of a single term: campus. First met with at Princeton University in the late eighteenth century, the Latin word campus, meaning 'field', became common as an expression for an ensemble of buildings (usually) for higher education. Thus campus indicates primarily a location. The term underlines the self-containedness of the institution and thus its separateness. Often a campus is situated on the edge of, or outside, the town. Obviously, a campus could not exist without the institution, be it 'college' or 'university', yet the independence of the term 'campus' often appears strong. Through time, 'campus' assumed something of the meaning of an institution itself.

For Turner, campus planning is a thoroughly 'American tradition'. The initial layout of a set of buildings of any kind in an American town differs substantially from that of most European ones through the well-known facts of spaciousness and rectiliniarity. Early American colleges and campuses invariably consisted of a number of blocks, at right angles to each other; the nearest European equivalent was perhaps a group of barracks, placed on the edge of a town. 'Architectural' treatment consisted of the time-honoured Western fashion of marking out the central block with some ornamental features. During the nineteenth century the single, but complex palace became the preferred model for a new college. It was around 1900 when more conscious attempts were made at a visual planning of the many new large universities. As for exhibition design and town planning (the 'City Beautiful'), the American version of French 'Beaux Arts' planning became the model for higher education and, coupled

1.5   University of South Florida, Tampa, begun 1957, view of c. 1964. (Ross)

with the help of the new and much more impressive ways of the pictorial representation of the projects, stupendous campuses were devised. A multiaxial layout and the
careful scaling of the height of buildings, together with central public spaces and sensitive landscaping provided a hitherto unknown sense of visual unity.

Between the wars there followed a hiatus in grand campus design, while architectural and planning interest was centred more on smaller-scale collegiate buildings. The
first beginnings of International Modernism were, as we shall see, smallish, but during
the 1950s, as Turner demonstrates, a bolder Modernism in East Coast universities, particularly at Yale or Brandeis, was coupled with the conviction that a good campus
can consist of a number of diverse architectural masterworks and with a distrust of
'grand' planning and Beaux Arts uniformity. Wherever the situation allowed it, an
overall low density was preferred, with plenty of greenery, corresponding to new international trends in town planning. Modernist designs in cheaper institutions generally
seemed to go for a plain rectangular slab block, often multistorey, that fitted most
purposes; on the other hand, new kinds of special purpose buildings, especially for
the sciences, had to be devised. Meanwhile, the multiversities grew more rapidly and
coherent plans became harder to uphold. There was an increased need to plan for
extendibility. In some cases, such as at the University of South Florida, this led to a
way of leaving vast spaces around the initial buildings, to be filled gradually in years
to come. One of the major new problems was automobile access. Less visible manifestations of new technology were the new 'teaching machines', i.e. audio-visual aids,
as well as computerised central timetabling (fig. 1.5).

University planning became more than ever before an organisational, technical
process. Modern town planning thinking, as developed around 1900 in Germany and
the USA, especially the idea of the careful division of functions ('zoning'), had entered

the university world for some decades and many institutions had devised 'master plans' for future expansion. But by now the old days appeared to be characterised by 'hit and run techniques', 'educated guesses by the president or the board of trustees', or by academics who thought that a Nobel prize in chemistry enabled them to act as architects. Older universities, like Harvard, could now be dubbed 'a loose confederation of departments held together by the allegiance to the central heating plant'. From the late 1940s, increasingly, a full-time member of the administration became responsible for campus planning, an agency that could later be subdivided into 'programme analysts' and 'space experts'. We thus meet another group of specialists in the field of creating universities. They, too, created their professional bodies and research groups, such as the Society for College and University Planning, a subgroup of the American Institute of Architects (AIA) or the New York based Educational Facilities Laboratories Inc., supported by the Ford Foundation, as well as consultant firms, such as Dober, Walquist and Harris Inc., of Boston. In 1963 its Richard P. Dober laid down the new science in his comprehensive work *Campus Planning*.

Utmost rationality pervades all their considerations. 'Campuses grow by logical building increments'. The main steps in planning entail a translation of quality and quantity of need (strictly divided into diverse functions) into space requirements, or 'planning modules'. Each major teaching unit, as well as communal and administrative functions, will be accommodated in its own distinct building and on a distinct part of the campus. Then there is the given, the site, a minimum of 400 acres (161 hectares). 'Relatively flat' sites are best; Dober assumes that normally several sites 'will present themselves for comparison and selection'. Roads are divided into major and minor ones and the campus as a whole is circumscribed by a ring road. There has to be a certain proportion of open parkland and a staggering amount of parking space; 'UCLA is a four-year university – or five years if you park in Lot 32' (Bob Hope). The key international Modernist term 'space' plays as yet a subordinate role: the buildings, the 'physical elements' of the campus are primary, 'the circulation systems are subsidiary considerations' – although there is an emphasis on the pedestrianised central area, or 'pedestrian precinct' for its own sake and Dober shows his sensitivity in the way he pleads for a 'gradual pedestrian-scale transition from parking lots to campus buildings'. Above all Dober insists on greenery. Members of the university 'need physical and psychical relief from the demanding and occasionally restricting communal life'. Residences are invariably located at the periphery. Dober reaffirms his allegiance to zoning: 'rarely do people eat, sleep and work in a single environment' and even as regards the diversified student residences, for singles, married couples etc., he advocates separate locations, as the 'social and living patterns of each group might be in conflict' (fig. 1.6).

Once all this is established, we can look at 'the planning module as a chess piece and the campus as a chessboard. Each move has consequences for all other pieces.' Yet, this metaphor is not pursued, for obvious reasons, because unlike chess, nothing ever drops off the plan of a campus. The ultimate aim is, in fact, 'to bring all things forward into balance'. This balance consists mostly of a straightforward concentric scheme, from the 'academic centre' to car parks at the periphery. Once it is all put together, then the campus, for Dober, is complete, 'final'. Dober's vigorous drawings, half life-like, half schematic, carry a considerable conviction of visual unity and are to an extent reminiscent of the Beaux Arts approach; of course, Dober has abandoned

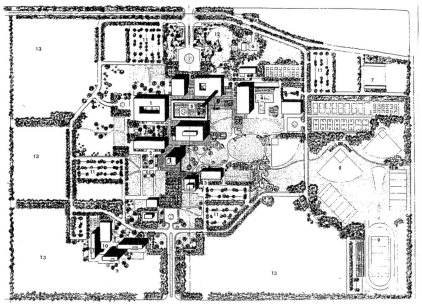

1. ACADEMIC CENTER   5. CAMPUS CENTER   9. STADIUM

2. SCIENCE CENTER   6. CAMPUS RESIDENCE   10. STUDENT HOUSING

3. ARTS CENTER   7. CORPORATION YARD   11. PARKING

4. PHYSICAL EDUCATION CENTER   8. ATHLETIC FIELDS   12. LAKE

13. FUTURE USE

PHASE I. CAMPUS MASTER PLAN

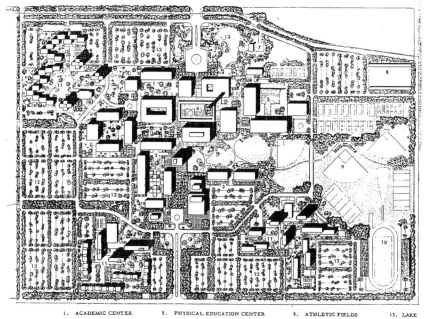

1. ACADEMIC CENTER   5. PHYSICAL EDUCATION CENTER   9. ATHLETIC FIELDS   13. LAKE

2. SCIENCE CENTER   6. CAMPUS CENTER   10. STADIUM

3. ARTS CENTER   7. CAMPUS RESIDENCE   11. STUDENT HOUSING

4. UNASSIGNED CENTER   8. CORPORATION YARD   12. PARKING

ULTIMATE CAMPUS MASTER PLAN

1.6   R. Dober, from *Campus Planning*, New York, 1963 (showing, bottom, Sonoma State College California, Master Plan, by J.C. Warnecke and Associates).

Beaux Arts historical styles. 'It is not usually necessary to establish . . . illustrative three-dimensional designs for typical long-range plans'. 'The planning module *may* imply preliminary architectural design' (my italics). In the case of residences, it is enough to 'express' them in 'density, acreage, floor area ratios and building heights. These controls are sufficient to establish a design structure. . .'. The word 'aesthetics' crops up furtively in some places. Dober feels that he does have to provide a quasi architectural theory because his clients invariably entertain images of historic campus architecture. He therefore distinguishes between 'campus form', which comes about through planning, and 'style'. The latter has to be understood 'as a family resemblance among a group of buildings'. Dober mentions many styles, and only very hesitantly recommends Modern. Modestly, yet explicitly, Dober concludes that campus planning must be seen as a distinct stage in the process of building a university: 'The recognition of what has to be done to solve the planning problem is no less a professional skill than solving the problem itself [i.e. finding the detailed design solution]'.

We are therefore hardly surprised that Dober's work was not, seemingly, taken up much by the architects with whom we are going to deal, nor does Dober link up in any way with the other discourses cited so far; the term education is hardly given prominence in his book. His concern is for the practical functioning of the institution. For him there is little that links 'social phenomena', educational programmes, or the curriculum, and planning. 'I write as a general practitioner in the art of planning. I am not . . . an educator, nor a scholar. I am giving a . . . view of how campuses are being developed and how present techniques might be sharpened for better results.' 'Results' are, we presume, defined, again, as relating to the good academic performance and the 'processing' of students. We meet, once more, a strictly instrumentalised approach; 'campus planning' does not really profess to be concerned with an notion of the institution as a whole.

ASSIGNING ARCHITECTURE'S ROLE

The remainder of this chapter should deal with the question of whether, and, if so, to what extent, architects helped to devise integrated institutions in the post World War II period. So far, we have stressed a growing separateness of the professions in our field. On first impressions, architecture was no exception. As we saw, Dober even kept planning and architecture apart. The other professions showed little regard for what a campus looked like. 'The architecture of buildings' is a brief entry, incongruously formulated – at least to Modernist ears – in the index of the foremost sociological study of the American reform college by David Riesman. In the behaviourist-psychological literature references to architecture virtually never occur. As we saw, the term 'environment', and even 'plan' or 'design', usually referred to people rather than buildings or spaces. By 'aesthetic experience' writers normally meant the teaching in the visual arts. There was the odd comment that architecture is 'expensive'. We may even read a council that 'energy should be directed not to plant, development, buildings and facilities, but to relations between teachers and students and to the expectations and the conceptual framework which influence the way they work together'.

In those cases where architecture was mentioned by non-architects, and its importance admitted, its purpose appeared strictly limited. Clearly, everybody had to recognise the effects which college architecture was capable of. Historicist architecture from the later nineteenth century onwards showed 'aesthetic and social purpose . . . [and left] an impression of a society apart, transmitting a sense of consecration by "the mysterious guidance" of the associations of the place'. 'My . . . imagination had conceived a college as an assemblage of Parthenons and cathedrals', ran the traditional comment of an alumnus. It may well have been that by 1960 or 1970 many of the modern psychologists and sociologists thought that typical rich American college architecture was 'tasteless and imitative' (David Riesman, 1962). But old attitudes prevailed: 'Alumni are concerned about architectural style, symmetry of building placement, attractive appearance, well kept lawns and preservation of monuments' (J.D. Millett, 1962). Decades later we may still find slight sarcasms, such as calling architectural efforts 'monuments' for university presidents, donors and alumni and 'architecture' still appears as just one among many rubrics concerning university buildings, together with 'flood plan' or 'parking'. Seemingly, matters of aesthetics can be strictly controlled. In the case of publicly funded universities we find that 'the state's art and architectural board reviews [the plans] . . . for the governor's office . . . This independent board . . . typically consists of five members, an architect, an art historian, an artist, a representative of the state's museum of fine arts . . . it is primarily concerned with aesthetics, that is, the exterior of buildings . . . Since all members are well-trained professionals and experts in art and architecture, there is usually a consensus among the board.' Another typical formulation, indicating the separateness of the architectural, it was pronounced in a programme for Chicago Circle in the early 1960s: '. . . full attention [would be] given to aesthetics and economy'.

The contrasts of these quotes with the Modernist and later discourses used by the architects themselves and their critics could not be more striking. However, it must not be assumed that directions are entirely clear among the latter, either. Architectural discourse with regard to university buildings was in itself quite varied. Some of the Modernist campus buildings by the country's most avant-garde and most prestigious practitioners, such as Eero Saarinen's, Gordon Bunshaft's, and Paul Rudolph's at Yale, ultimately belong to the category of the single, impressive building, they were the new towers and porticoes. A rousing short admonition in the *Architectural Record* by John Knox Shear fits in with this line: 'Students . . . [are] impressionable because they are socially unsure, intellectually curious, and generally eager to accept whatever has the approval of an authority presumed to be sophisticated.' He thus felt confident to demand 'experiments in planning and design'. A crucial element in strengthening the authority of the designer is the fact that in a university 'the acreage is large and the authority over its use is almost uniquely single'. Shear mistrusts the trustees', i.e. the clients and their 'righteous double talk of economy and tradition'. There is a special reason for trying to influence the students, for 'today's student is tomorrow's trustee'. Only at the end Shear refers to the actual purpose of the institution: 'universities should build in the spirit they teach'. We shall describe below the way in which a similar but much more comprehensively orchestrated campaign in the *Architectural Review* and the *Architects' Journal* launched the architects' platform in English new university building. A few years later, the American Institute of Architects (AIA) again took concerted action to drive home the importance of their profession in university planning and design. Now the approach is virtually the opposite to Shear's in

1957: utility and economy were the watchwords. Answers to a questionnaire sent out by the AIA to university presidents revealed that 'beauty' came way down in the order of preference. Planning by architects leads to 'rational, justifiable and secure decisions'. By 1970, we may read the opposite again with the call to abandon the 'exclusively . . . utilitarian standpoint . . . Campus aesthetics has become a top priority'.

A more circumspect formulation of the relationship architect-client was prepared by a new executive body, set up for the rapid extension of universities in the State of New York (the 'SUNY' system). First it created, in 1962, a new 'autonomous' organisation, the State University Construction Fund, headed by one of the most powerful figures in American politics, Governor Nelson Rockefeller. The Fund was meant to bundle together all activities, from raising the money, to planning and building. The uppermost of the stated aims was efficiency. After speed, architectural quality was the most frequently underlined objective, and a certain reliance on the designers, that is, the 'total professional and building services' was advocated. To achieve it, 'a system . . . was set up to promote full utilisation of the capabilities of the design professions . . .'; clients should formulate their demands 'flexibly', so as to 'permit creative freedom'. There should be no divisions between planners and architects. On the other hand, there is a continuous stress on 'the rational procedure' which 'avoids incidents of trial and error'; 'decisions [were] to be made concurrently, rather than in time-consuming sequence'. The Fund itself chose a 'different design vocabulary' for each campus, 'for the guidance of the designers'. The process of choosing the architects, not very clearly explained by the professional journal, was to involve those 'of demonstrated ability', those 'who produce high quality'. Following Samuel E. Bleeker's account, it was, indeed, the governor himself who 'fought' for architecture. In his thoroughly traditional understanding of art patronage (whereby 'art' included Modernist art) Rockefeller held that 'architecture' costs extra money and this also entailed the conviction that 'fancy' was not normally needed for Welfare projects, such as public housing, but that universities did need it. Rockefeller was convinced that to 'bridge and highway builders sensitive design was foreign', while the private architect 'needs autonomy over his or her design', and that this 'kept the best architects from state projects'. In early 1963, in an extraordinary attempt at, so to speak, the private initiation of state patronage, Rockefeller invited sixty of 'the nation's top architects' to his mansion to show off his own interest in modern art and to 'work his magic' to convince them to design for his state campuses. Indeed, gradually the elite of the East Coast designers did join, though mostly just for individual buildings (see below page 42). Was one of the underlying motives the unspoken competition between SUNY, the New York State organisation and the massed and powerful private institutions of the East Coast (figs 1.19 and 1.22)?

It thus appears that the architectural discourse differed strongly from the others in higher education. It was more strictly evaluative and usually proceeded by a high degree of selectivity. In architecture, the chief traditional principle was now to select according to notions of 'artistic', or 'aesthetic quality'. In order to arrive at a broader and fairer assessment of layout and design, literally each campus ought to be examined by itself, especially in respect of the chief issue here, the relationship between the design and the utopianist-institutional concept. The complete freedom with which institutions can be founded, which we postulated at the outset as one of the characteristics of the American 'system' makes it likely that even an academically obscure institution could come up with unusual planning solutions. In practice, we have to adhere to a selection that was made at the time by a self-appointed, nationwide, even international architectural establishment. The choice of the post World War II buildings in Turner follows virtually entirely from two of the four major American architectural periodicals, *Architectural Forum* and *Architectural Record*. Ostensibly they address the profession but in the way in which they concentrate on short texts, splendid drawings and striking photographs their chief aim was more likely to help with convincing the prospective client. The architects, in turn, would maintain that the clients do not have much intrinsic understanding of architecture and that what the administrators and the money-givers were primarily after was attractive drawings, 'the desire to make a modern building resemble an illustration from a history book' and to 'design a pleasing facade and devise the interior into suitable cubicles'. When President Johnson addressed the American Architects' congress of 1965 he pleaded 'may your success be so great that ours will be remembered as the Age of Beauty'. We are witnessing here a way in which the understanding of architecture in the USA differs from that in contemporary Welfare State Britain, in Germany and even in Canada, at least as far as our field of higher education is concerned. Individual, instrumentalised professional interests vs. utopianist 'wholeness' continued to be an issue.

INTERNATIONAL MODERNIST COLLEGIATE

This brings us, of course, to the heart of what Modernist architecture was supposedly about. In our earlier deliberations about the nature of the American college, specifically architectural issues, as well as designers, seemed to play only a subsidiary role. It is characteristic that in the discussions about many Modernist buildings it is the architecture and the designer who seem to play the key role while all other issues and agents seem subsidiary. This is due to the way in which most Modernist architects claim that it is they who cater expertly for all conceivable aspects and that their style and their procedure is what creates the unity of all the efforts within the institution. The history of Modernism in architecture is treated by American architectural historians as diversely as elsewhere, from hailing its identity with the postwar effort and positive American values to associating it with American imperialism, to, lately, a virtual silence (Dell Upton), as well as restatements of Modernism's utopianist wholeness (Harries). In an older history we read that, by 1960, Modern architecture's 'aesthetic . . . victory was complete . . . there were hardly any enclaves of the old eclecticism' – somewhat late, one may say, although we shall see that English university architecture was even less 'advanced'. Turner is much more cautious, claiming that there are several diverse strands in that movement. Moreover, he is often at pains to link its concepts of planning back to the 'American tradition'. Briefly, one may distinguish four major divisions in Modernist university architecture: the expensive single-purpose structures by the internationally recognised masters, usually in the top-rank institutions; the more utilitarian solutions up and down the country; the very large unified campus buildings and the small and more informal groups of chiefly residential units. The centre of this last development lay, from the late 1930s, with Walter Gropius, who had been called to teach at Harvard in 1937.

'The Bauhaus, undone by Hitler, lives a flourishing life in America' (David Riesman). Some have interpreted this episode as a purely European import; others stressed the way Americans were quickly assimilating foreign trends. There is, in fact, a complex relationship between Modernism and previous modes of Anglo-American college architecture. In what must have been a rather courageous line to take in 1952, at the height of the first flourish of Modernism in New England, MIT architectural historian Albert Bush-Brown drew close parallels between two seeming adversaries, the Neo-Gothicist Cram whose college buildings at Princeton have been mentioned above, and Walter Gropius. 'Both Cram and Gropius believe that their architectural missions are profoundly cultural . . . Both [are] the best exponents of the interrelation between educational and social philosophy and architecture.' Moreover, Gropius – in spite of his frequent chiding of nineteenth-century eclecticism – actually shared a certain kind of Medievalism with Cram: 'Their mission' Bush-Brown continues [is] to create that unity which was characteristic of the medieval craft community'. Both Cram's and Gropius's enthusiasm ultimately went back to the Romantic movement, from which two lines can be drawn, an English line, to Cram via Welby Pugin, who first dreamt of a socio-architecural revival of a medieval college or almshouse in the 1840s, and a German line extolling the togetherness of designers and craftsmen building the cathedral, its last showing was in the 'cathedral' of Gropius's Bauhaus Manifesto in 1919 (figs 1.7 and 1.8).

What was striking was the link-up between American reformist colleges and the new European Modernism. We cannot explore fully the complex twists of the 'progressive' vs. the retrogressive/anti-technological. Gropius heavily contributed to these twists in the way he chided the American Neo-Gothic colleges for their past-mongering. To the Americans this seemed to go along with the way they traditionally perceived the German university ideal as instrumentalist-technological; while their's was the American-English 'liberal', 'humanist' ideal. The 1930s American college reformers were mostly adhering to the latter. But Modern vs. traditional higher education was not the principal issue. The fact was that the 'German' educational thinking that came with Gropius's Modernist architectural-social ideals had virtually nothing to do with the German university, past or present. The origins of the educational philosophy and the practical experiments which emphasised learning by doing, by experiencing, rather than by training the memory, go back to the early nineteenth century, to Pestalozzi and Froebel; as Bush-Brown emphasises, 'Americans [had] visited the same Swiss schools . . . from which the German educators . . . and ultimately Gropius got their ideas'. German-American exchanges continued after World War I, between, for instance, the educational philosophers Georg Kerschen-steiner and John Dewey. A new early twentieth-century kind of institution, the *Land-schulheim* (or *Schullandheim*), i.e. high school courses conducted in country isolation, might well be likened to the liberal college ideal, especially in the way in which great emphasis was laid on mutuality among pupils. By 1948, Harvard President James B. Conant, who had been instrumental in getting Gropius across (his own study of German higher education going back to 1927) attempted to give the relationship between liberal education and the 'modern world' a positive turn: '. . . by relating their educational undertaking to ethics, the welfare and body politic, and the emotional stability of the individual, humanists [i.e. supporters of liberal education] can make an overwhelming case for the importance of their mission'. It is thus possible, in a complex way, to stress elements of continuity between the liberal / historicist collegiate and a new Modernist collegiate.

Meanwhile, crucial changes had occurred with the layout of educational buildings. Modernists replaced the great theme of the 'monastic' mode, the courtyard, with the plain rectangular block. This was the result of scientific and practical considerations, largely those of creating maximum light and fresh air for all occupants. For student residences it appeared a straightforward solution – not all that different from the traditional American dormitory block, in fact. For some designers of the interwar period this slab block, however, also provided a starting point for a complex coordination and linking of the blocks by low passages. We can begin with Gropius's first educational projects in the mid-1920s, such as the Philosophische Akademie at Erlangen, a short-lived reformist institution where the clients' and the designer's task was to 'create the architectural conditions for a community in which work and life come into close connection'. The Bauhaus building in Dessau brought a more complex, as well as compact, version of this proposition. In the mid-1930s Gropius practised it again in England, at Impington Village College near Cambridge (in actual fact a special kind of secondary school) for the educational reformer Henry Morris. There is a 'sense of congruity between form and social intention: the relaxed grouping of class room, community space and shared hall' (Andrew Saint), the latter, the wedge-shaped auditorium, had by now become a trade mark of International Modern. The inclusion of informal curved elements perhaps followed Le Corbusier's 1930 Pavillion Suisse hall of residence in Paris (fig. 1.8).

A number of small, more or less reformist East Coast colleges took up the new style, or were at least planning to do so, in the late 1930s. During 1937–8 Gropius was invited, with Marcel Breuer, to submit designs for arts centres at Wheaton College, Norton, Massachusetts and for William and Mary College at Williamsburg, Virginia. Modified versions of the Impington plan were supplied. By those years, a number of American designers also supplied similar Modernist designs. Another competition of 1938, for Goucher College, Baltimore, Maryland, demanded a design which 'should reflect progressive principles in education'. Built after World War II (by John C. B. Moore and Robert S. Hutchins), its Modernism consists in the relatively unaxial grouping of buildings and the lack of historical style references. In 1939 Gropius planned a more complex version of Impington for Black Mountain College, Lake Eden, North Carolina, the most artistically-minded of all the American colleges, and a Bauhaus exile stronghold.

Gropius's major work in this series (with his firm, The Architects' Collaborative, or TAC) is the Harvard Graduate Center residence hall of 1950. Considering its average size, bedrooms for 575 students and associated canteen and club rooms, and the way it was built exceptionally cheaply (at a quarter of Harvard's normal costs), the Graduate Center attracted an extraordinary amount of interest. It consists of the usual assembly of low slab blocks, but they are now more carefully linked by way of bridges and covered pathways. The main communal block is slightly emphasised by a curved plan and different window formations. The overall layout now marks out more carefully the circulation patterns and the photos of the period stress the complexity of views through the whole group. 'Space' becomes a major term in the discussion; 'flowing space', the 'merging of spaces', the attempt to enhance the outside areas of the building, to emphasise the communal areas, the 'outdoor living rooms', which keep to 'a reasonable human scale'. Gropius, as usual, was ready with a full-worded statement about the links between architectural and socio-educational factors: he

1.7 Wellesley College by Day and Klauder, mainly 1930s. (Courtesy Wellesley College Archives)

talked of '. . . the philosophical concept of communal living, of co-operative activity and of interchange of ideas' and declared that 'living in this kind of a group of buildings, a young man may unconsciously absorb ideas and principles that would seem abstract and remote in the classroom, but which, translated into concrete, glass, light and air assume a convincing reality'. Gropius still felt he had to defend his Modernist style against the imitators of the past; on the other hand he prided himself on taking up some of the visual qualities of Harvard's traditional 'yards': 'As orderly as the original Harvard Yard, and yet as free and easy-going as a modern community centre' (fig. 1.9).

Gropius and his TAC henceforth designed a number of intricate schools and university buildings worldwide, but none of them were as ambitious as the University of Baghdad, planned from 1957 but not completed until the 1980s. There was very little indication from the client as to what was required and thus TAC felt they had to start from scratch. On a sizable campus, 2 by 1.5 kilometres (1.5 by 1 mile) and 8 kilometres (5 miles) from the city, the target was 12,000 students. There is a new element of flexibility: the major teaching facilities were to be housed interchangeably, in an attempt to facilitate contacts between disciplines. The first project of 1958 contained a novel solution of the parking problem – the elevated central piazza. The great hall, the administration tower and the purely ornamental gateway arch appear fixed and grand. But the overall plan shows neither the axial order of the Beaux Arts and early Modernist manners, nor the freer, but still rectangular grouping preferred by Dober. Instead, we note a loosening of the right angle, almost, one might say, a random grouping, if it had not been for the dense togetherness of the individual complexes of teaching or residential blocks. The term cluster comes to mind, proposed by Peter and Alison Smithson in England as early as 1957, to which we shall come much further on in this book. There is, however, a special reason for the high density: the close proximity of all the buildings was to help with keeping out the burning sun. These climatic

34

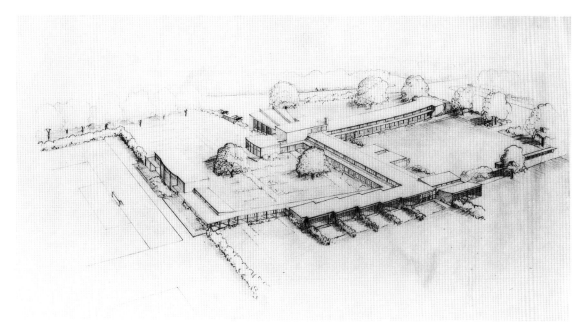

1.8   Impington Village College (Cambridgeshire) by Walter Gropius and Maxwell Fry 1938–40. When Gropius moved to England he developed a version of the International Modern style which does not squeeze individual functions into pre-conceived blocks (cf. 1.19) but accentuates them individually by spreading them out. The layout then stresses the links between them, much in the manner of the nineteenth / early twentieth-century collegiate plan. (British Architectural Library London)

concessions and the onion shape of the mosque appear to be virtually the only 'Arabic' elements in the design. For Gropius the strong contrasts of light and shadow cause 'significant rhythms', which 'tend to express the meaning of universitas, which is "wholeness", offering a creative setting for a fully, well integrated life for the students'. Later on Gropius's explanation is even more simple: 'As a whole the university is the

1.9   Harvard University Graduate Center, student residences and common rooms by Walter Gropius/The Architects' Collaborative, 1949. (Courtesy Harvard University)

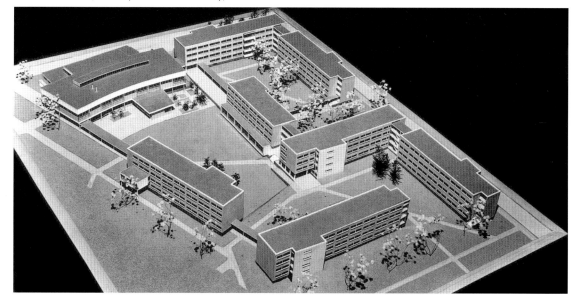

35

chief problem of modern society, which, quite simply, consists of education'. Widely published at the time, with distinctive, perspective views, Gropius's design for Baghdad was perhaps the most important project of its date and had possibly more influence overseas than in the USA itself (figs 1.10 and 1.11).

From about 1960 we find a large number of groups of student housing by most of the eminent designers, especially in the prestigious universities. Gradually, the straight economic slab block of the 1940s to 1950s went out of fashion. As in contemporary Oxbridge, a group of residences seemed a good use for an alumni donation and could be added easily to the already diverse campus buildings. There is always an emphasis on communal spaces. But the way this is done varied tremendously (fig. 1.12). One of the most serious-minded solutions were the Erdman Hall Dormitories of Bryn Mawr College, Pennsylvania of 1960–5 by Louis Kahn. This is a strict geometric expression of centrality on a plan which made it possible to provide almost wholly self-enclosed and ample interior lightwells as communal spaces. In some ways another extremely well-known group, the versatile Eero Saarinen's Morse and Stiles Colleges for Yale of 1960–2 is the opposite, a wildly irregular layout, creating a number of leafy semi-courts, with communal facilities at the 'hinges'. Here there are twelve individually shaped rooms per staircase on the Oxford model (which, of course, was, by then, also the Princeton, Yale and Harvard model); like Kahn, Saarinen no longer goes for Modernist complete glazing, but for solid, heavy walls. Nevertheless, 'the courtyards make a convincing statement for the collegiality and interaction of groups gathering together' (Robert A. M. Stern). Saarinen apparently went to Oxford as well as to the San Gimignano in Tuscany, the English Townscapists' (see below p. 91) favourite Italian Hill Town (fig. 1.13).

What matters most in our context is that these residence halls and colleges were architect-initiated, in the sense that their institutional characteristics were to a large extent the result of the designer's convictions of the link between architecture and individual or social behaviour. Within a total picture of the academic and social policies of higher education, however, their contribution must not be overrated. These halls or 'colleges' can be seen in the context of a tradition of experimentation in the top East Coast institutions, as well as in the tradition of purely architectural innovation and individuality. We must bear in mind some of the chief perceptions of the period, the contrast between the rich college and the mass higher education campus. However, we should note that the same experiments were taking place at least in some of the latter universities. As they were likely to lack architectural kudos they have not received the attention they deserve, at least from an architectural-institutional point of view. Robert M. Crane, Dean of Students of the University of Illinois, in 1963, presented the usual arguments in favour of student residences and gave a detailed analysis of various kinds of halls in a number of universities, using a certain amount of new architects' language, such as 'design for living'. Most eye-catching in its plan is the Alfred and Matilda Wilson Hall at Michigan State University by Ralph R. Calder and Associates, reminiscent of the archetypal architectural-institutional model of the eighteenth to nineteenth centuries, the panopticon: individuals surrounding a communal core. The relative lavishness of that core is all the more astonishing as it was built at a time when a 'housing shortage necessitated housing three students in rooms designed for two'. Crane is, however, not clear at the end as to whether the 'college' should be the norm. He talked of the return to the "collegiate" experience on the large campus', but he also says: 'These designs for living

1.10   Baghdad University, engineering library and part of central plaza. (W. Gropius and others, *The Architects' Collaborative*, London, 1966)

1.11   Baghdad University, planned from 1959 by Walter Gropius/The Architects' Collaborative. In the centre: auditorium, administration building, office tower, student center, art gallery and museum; around it are grouped the academic buildings. Adjacent to the centre are the student residences and along the river faculty housing. (W. Gropius and others, *The Architects' Collaborative*, London, 1966)

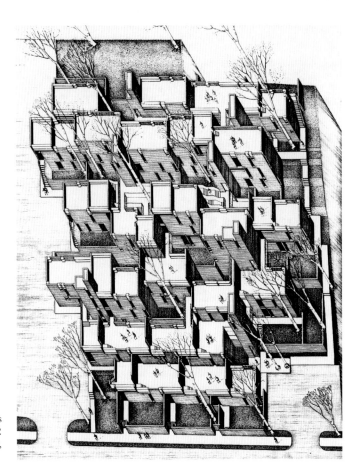

1.12 Yale University, married students housing, by Paul Rudolph 1960. (P. Rudolph, *Dessins d'Architecture*, Fribourg, 1979)

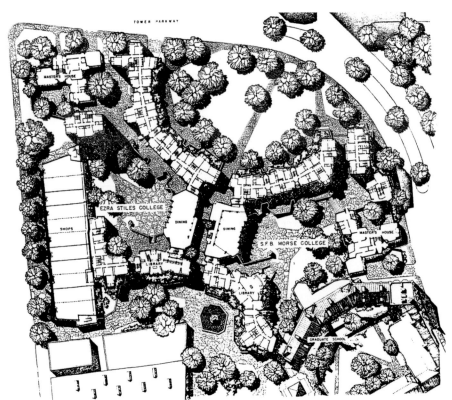

1.13 Yale University, Morse and Styles Colleges, by Eero Saarinen 1960–2. (A.B. Saarinen (ed.), *Eero Saarinen*, New Haven and London, 1968)

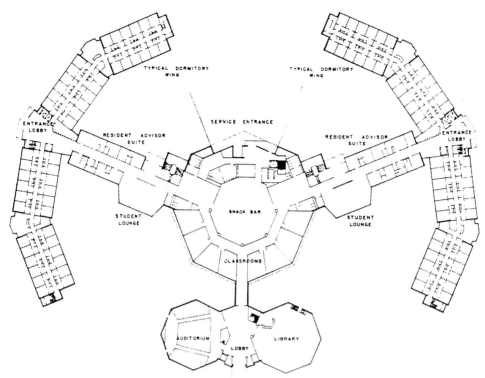

1.14　Alfred and Matilda Wilson Hall, Michigan State University, by R.R. Calder and Associates, *c.* 1960. A block for 564 women and another one for 560 men with communal facilities in the centre. (*American Association of Architects Journal* 9-1963, p. 81)

should not necessarily dominate a campus scene, for there are many other kinds of living experiences to be considered' (figs 1.14 and 1.15).

Searching for a fully unified institution, one may turn at this point to the community colleges. They were usually strictly limited in size, thus the major problems of multiversity diversity would not arise. A typical college comprised 3,000 students on 150 acres (61 hectares) and could cost about $10m to build. As has already been

1.15　Alfred and Matilda Wilson Hall, Michigan State University. (*American Association of Architects Journal* 9-1963, p. 81)

emphasised, this institution normally lacked one major ingredient of the 'college', the residential section, and for that reason it is marginal in any story of the traditional college. Comparisons with the campuses of important universities are also normally limited because of the lack of a major library or other kinds of prominent central university buildings. In most cases, economy was perceived of as an additional virtue and could further the aim of unity in concept and in appearance. The American Institute of Architects recommended a 'more active and continuous exchange of ideas between architect and client, compared 'with the traditional practice'. By the 1970s the community colleges were receiving much attention, even from the top echelons of the architectural world. 'Many . . . campuses are handsome places which generate pride in the students and faculty who use them, and in the community whose votes paid for building and operating them.'

An eminent practitioner who preached the social and educational virtues of the community college and earned very high architectural recognition for his own examples was Ernest J. Kump. Rooted in California, Kump's national recognition was based on his work there, in particular on his innumerable designs of schools and his systematisation of their planning and construction. Approaching design for higher education from the 'lower end' was not degrading; as we saw, it was highly relevant in Gropius's case. As with Gropius, no comment, no analogy was too strong to drive home Kump's convictions about the socio-educational effects of school architecture: 'A school campus encompasses practically every space or building function necessary in man's social complex'. Hence he speaks of 'the total objectives in campus planning'. But his own article on the community college lacks specificity. What he chiefly means by 'total' turns out to be a broadside against 'mere technical efficiency', and a lack of care for 'total architectural objectives, including expression'. His major recipe for any good campus is to limit its size. Kump's Foothill College, Los Altos Hills, built between 1959 and 1962 for 3,500 students received widespread praise. Kump does not adhere to the prevailing assembly of long rectangles but uses chiefly a square component, or combinations of it – which he had just developed, as a 'module', for schools, but which was also not unlike Gropius's plan for Baghdad. Descriptions concentrate not so much on the buildings but on 'the impressive unity, achieved by a searching use of basic structure to create harmonious volumes of space', or 'of series of 'outdoor "rooms"'. Their intended function was carefully differentiated, from the many small, intimate patios to a large formal area for outdoor assembly. Finally, Kump strongly unified the campus through the consistent use of local redwood and the prominence of the roofscape over the mostly one-storied buildings. This 'Bay Region Style' was interpreted as suiting the local community. '. . . an entire community instantly felt at home . . . Above all there is genuine warmth' (figs 1.16 and 1.17).

CAMPUS: 'MODERN' AND BIG. ALBANY

American Modernist architecture was, by the early 1960s, divided into two major factions. We must briefly look at the one opposed to what has been discussed so far, that is those designers who opted for strict rectilinearity, preferably combined with large size and often with symmetry and achsiality. In higher education the two trends may be related back to the old factions of Gothic and Classical and thus to the smaller

1.16 Foothill Community College Los Altos, 'Typical informal court'. (*AFor* 11-1959, pp. 138–9)

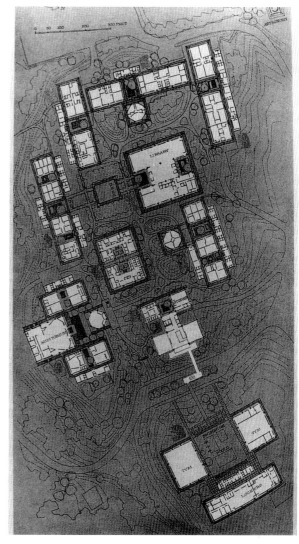

1.17 Foothill Community College Los Altos, 1959 onwards, by Ernest J. Kump. (*AFor* 11-1959, p. 134)

kind of college building and to the grand Beaux Arts campus, respectively. A design that shows the transition from Beaux Arts to Modernism is Church College, Hawaii, begun in 1955 by Harold Burton. This sports a geometric Classical portico in the centre of a very rigid main frontal block. Behind are two symmetrically placed residential blocks. All buildings are of the same height and are flat-roofed. By that time, Mies van der Rohe's Illinois Institute of Technology (IIT) Chicago campus, begun in 1938–9, had already been heavily publicised. In his final design Mies provides a good number of separate rectangular blocks, laid out in strict rectangular fashion with rather undefined spaces between and without any of the linking passages beloved to the Gropius school. In what may be a singular case, Mies seems to have refrained from claiming particular qualities of educational or social impact for his buildings; this, and Mies' well-known reluctance to let the individual function of a building speak and give buildings diversity, distances this campus from the American tradition perhaps more than any other university building. The USA's busiest architectural firm SOM (Skidmore Owings and Merill, in this case Walter Netsch, cf. p. 196) then applied some of Mies's severity of repetition in their United States Air Force Academy at Colorado Springs, but adapted it in a rather un-Miesian metaphor of military drill.

Altogether, this Modern-and-straight faction is far more difficult to trace and to assess than the collegiate one. Its most important university campus, Edward Durell Stone's State University of New York at Albany, was a *bête-noire* for critics and subsequently even for historians. It is crucial to keep Albany's assessement by the critical elite apart from the way in which the complex actually fits in with the major issues of campus design of the 1950s and 60s. We have already mentioned the large organisation which the 'Empire State' under Governor Nelson Rockefeller started from 1960. The institution itself was very young, or rather, it had only just 'graduated' to full university status from a minor college, housed mostly in ramshackle buildings inside the town. Rockefeller took the initiative and he virtually forced the Golf Club to leave the required site. Speed was of the essence, Stone was appointed in late 1961, the model presented in the summer of 1962, the first buildings opened in the autumn of 1964 and the whole was essentially completed by 1969, for 10,000 students at a cost of just over $100m. The architect's model looked grandiose and its realisation came very close to it.

Stone was chosen as 'a Pioneer Modernist'. We noted how the New York state authorities prided themselves on being efficient both economically and architecturally. Stone, however, on occasions, stressed that he was 'free from all limitations'. He had two very clearly defined ideals: 'a great formal composition in a pastoral setting', and Venice: banish the automobile. It followed, for him, that the standard kind of American campus with its spread-out diverse buildings (as had, in fact, been proposed the year before at Albany by Rockefeller's architect friend, Wallace K. Harrison) could not have led to a grand form, but certainly to many roads. Stone united all the major teaching and social functions into one large, over 1,500 feet (500 metres) long rectangle. All vehicular service access is from underneath the podium on which the whole is built. Other users' cars are parked a long way away, mostly on the perimeter, and there is a complex network of pedestrian ways. The functions of individual buildings, such as the library and the theatre are not easily distinguishable from the outside. What is evident is rather the communication network, the covered passages outside and inside the complex which take a considerable amount of space. At this point

1.18   State University of New York at Albany, air view, by Edward Durell Stone. The 'Academic Podium' with the Water Tower, next to it, projecting, the campus centre; to the left of the Water Tower the central library, to its right the performing arts centre, the faculties take up the periphery; the smaller quadrangles are residential halls and residential towers. (University Archives, University at Albany SUNY)

1.19   Albany State University of New York presentation of model with Albany Mayor Erastus Corning and Governor Nelson Rockefeller in 1962 (Stone was absent). (University Archives, University at Albany SUNY)

1.20   Albany State University of New York Colonnades. (University Archives, University at Albany SUNY)

Stone harks back to the old college idea, to Harvard, and also further afield, to Islamic and Pompeian courts, intending the inner courtyards at Albany to offer the 'cloistered calm . . . of a college campus'. Where it comes to the structural detail, Stone stresses economy as well as beauty: everything is built up on a 16 inch (41 cms) module of 'white concrete' cast in situ. With that much laid down by the 'free' architect, it appears that Stone left the inside of his structures, in a rather Miesian way, relatively free, to be planned by the users. As regards expandability, it played some role in the discussions, and was to be achieved simply by erecting further square courts. The student residences Stone wanted as separate units but not dispersed, as Dober still advocated. Their court shape repeats the centre but also contains a tower block. With their twenty-three-storey verticality, *reciprocal* to the (three-storey) horizontality of the rest, the student residences could not have been more clearly related to the whole (figs 1.18–1.20).

The way Stone and his patron openly preferred an independent parkland campus, outside the town, continued the old campus tradition. Dober recommended a flat area: Stone began by levelling his site. But the way in which Stone combined an institutional building of an unprecedented size with a radical degree of visual unity decisively breaks away from the 1950s mode of dispersion to which Dober in 1963 was still fully adhering. In that sense, Albany may be grouped with the North American buildings of a later chapter – the 'one building campus'. Stone's strict pedestrianisation was also in step with the latest planning thinking. Above all, Stone's Albany was 'his'; it was one of the major 'architect's universities' of the period and in this particular sense it also has much in common with the highlights of our next chapters. Like all new campuses, especially 'architects'' ones, Albany received some user criticism, but this was minimal compared with Chicago Circle or some of the English new universities. Stone, however, was, by then, manoevering himself into an unfashionable corner, that is, as far as the critical establishment was concerned. Two elements accounted for this: his insistence on symmetry and his repetitious detailing which was held to be 'decorative' (the 'decorated box' – Robert Stern). In the case of Albany, this led to the reproach of 'no variety, [no] choice', or 'hypocritical authoritarianism'. But there were other factors at work; Rockefeller's grandiose undertaking was considered plebeian among the East Coast academic and architectural elite. This would, of course, not be voiced directly, but it was revealed in statements such as: 'Needless to say, some of the students are thrilled. Boys and girls from upstate farms and small towns find the environment exhilaratingly urban', so Ervin Galantay, professor of architecture at Columbia University. Stone insisted on what appeared to be an older kind of aesthetic of the 'formal'; he made clear that he did not care for the critics and was happy with appreciations from non-professionals. To some critics, his buildings could thus appear as cheaply commercial: Albany seemed like a 'Cecil de Mille spectacular' (Galantay). A much smaller campus designed for the authority which New York saw as their great rival, California, namely John Carl Warnecke's College Heights, San Matteo of 1964, took its cue from Stone, with its strict repetition of the same decorative-constructional motif of the arcade, and was also criticised as 'glib' and 'vacuous'. Later, the layout of the new New York State University Campus at Purchase softened the formality and at the same time provided a maximum of individualist architectural opportunity by having single buildings designed by several members of the avant-garde (fig. 1.21).

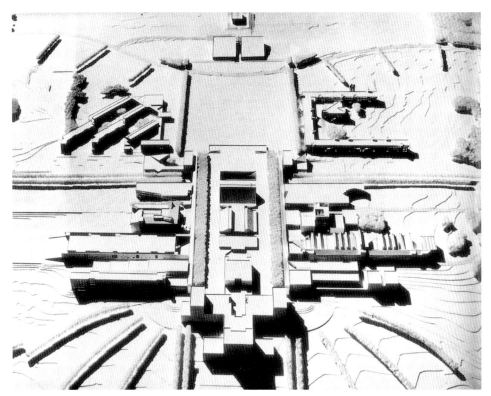

1.21   Purchase, State University of New York College at Purchase. Layout by Edward Larrabee Barnes Associates, designed from 1967. (*AFor* 11-1970, p. 34)

Within the context of university design, the criticisms of Modern and big seem, once more, to demonstrate the strength of the Gropius-derived kind of Modernism. By the later 1960s the majority of designers almost everywhere had turned against the grand single form, even Mies's star was sinking. As regards higher education one is tempted to express this, again, in terms of the preference, ultimately, of the Gothic Revival college tradition, with its infinitely variable conglomerates, where each major part of the institution can be clearly identified and which, above all, appeared to cater better for the socio-psychological well-being of their inmates. The critic who complained of 'uniformity' at Albany duly referred to 'the English collegiate towns . . . the colleges . . . each with its marked identity'. Conversely, though, one might stress that it is Albany which stands out from the ubiquitous collegiate mode, as well as from the multiversity jumble.

A NEW COMPREHENSIVENESS IN CALIFORNIA

The last word in how to extend and unify the multiversity campus *and* to make it more intimate, had not yet been spoken. The problems of the relationship between large and small and, remembering Riesman, the difficulty of determining the 'ideal size of the community', continued to irk. 'To make the university seem smaller, even as it grows larger' was the chief axiom for the new developments in California.

True to the state's image of rapid and enlightened advancement during the 1960s, California took the lead in establishing institutions with a pronounced new character, or, in any case, with a stronger rhetoric of the new than elsewhere. In no small measure this was due to Clark Kerr, America's most powerful university president. Internationally educated, at Swarthmmore, Stanford and London (LSE), he had been chancellor of Berkeley until 1958 and then president of all the universities of the state until 1967 (when he was purged, after the student revolt, by the new governor, Ronald Reagan), as well as being chairman of one of the busiest research institutes, the Carnegie Commission on Higher Education. California's master plan for 1960–75 was without precedent. Kerr created an international platform for its launch with his lectures at Harvard in 1962, entitled *The Uses of the University*. He appears as both a shrewd administrator and a cautious visionary. Of Quaker background, an economist by calling, with a speciality in labour relations, Kerr had demonstrated his left wing/coop movement leanings in the years of the New Deal. His tract on the university in general takes up a venerable tradition, going back at least as far as Cardinal Newman. Fluent in the history of medieval to nineteenth-century Paris, Oxbridge, and German Universities, his historical references lend an element of dignity thoughout, culminating in statements like 'the great universities have developed in the great periods of the great political entities of history'. There is only one major detailed theme in the book, and that concerns the underpinning of the project in the State of California (somewhat reminiscent of the arguments of the New York State Fund) and the desirability, the necessity, of the Federal Grant University system – all based on the assurance that this system can 'maintain and even increase the marking of excellence', or, put at its briefest: that one can combine quantity with quality. Here, Kerr speaks for the founders of most of the new universities dealt with in this book. At one point he refers to what he considered the admirable system of state organisation and finance of higher education in Britain, the University Grants Committee but his new Californian system goes very much further in its power and directives.

The rest of his book is an elegant flourish about the multiversity. Using the oldest tricks of rhetoric, such as the dialectic of modesty, he writes, for instance of the role of the university president: 'The president of a multiversity is leader, educator, creator, initiator, wielder of power . . . But he is mostly a mediator.' Yet neither the chapter 'The Idea of a Multiversity', nor the analysis of one of the premier examples of them, the University of California at Berkeley, nor the chapter on the 'Future of the City of Intellect' give us any concrete clues as to how students were to live or to be taught, nor what the college or campus should look like; the main purpose of the book is simply to assure us of the plausibility and greatness of the undertaking. It abounds in metaphors, such as 'a multiversity is inherently a conservative institution but with radical functions', and likens a university to a 'mechanism' as well as an 'organism'.

However, the facts resulting from the master plan of 1960 were soon there for all to see. A gigantic building programme was under way. California's higher education at all levels comprised, in total – including the private sector – 220,000 students in 1957, 350,000 in 1965, and by 1975 650,000 were envisaged. In 1962 alone $100m were spent on construction, derived from loans as well as state 'appropriations'. One solution for the problem of the multiversity was the strict coordination of all institutions within the 'public system of higher education' (which in California amounted

46

to two thirds, a much larger proportion than in New York State), into three levels: junior or community colleges, state colleges, and universities, the latter with highly selective admission procedures ('the top 12.5 per cent'). A crucial factor was a clear statement about the size of each institution. With Charles Luckman, President of the Board of Trustees of California State Colleges, himself an architect, we meet at last somebody who addresses all the major issues in a coordinated way. The long title of his very brief outline is:

Architectural Synthesis of Educational, Financial and Physical Requirements – Guiding Consideration, Human Scale and Human Factor . . . The determination to achieve academic excellence of all our colleges . . . we must have the closest kind of coordination between three of our major trustee committees. These are Committees on Educational Policy, Finance, and Campus Planning. The reason is so simple, it is sometimes overlooked. To achieve academic excellence, we must first have the right educational curricula, both in context and faculty, then be able to finance [them] . . . our campus planning must result in a physical environment that is conducive to the achievement of academic excellence. All educators [are against] memorising and [for] learning to think. This places a high priority on the importance of the surroundings for the teachers . . . and for the students.

In turn, this should lead to a '"humanation" of architecture – the proper consideration of space, light and air; the development of semi-enclosed patio areas, benches, landscaping; and, now and then, even the use of a bit of water. In short, the human scale and the human factor is a guiding consideration'.

Behind this newly foregrounded social-architectural ethos was another eminence, William Wilson Wurster, Dean of Environmental Design at Berkeley, who, with Kerr as chancellor, had devised the 1955 Long Range Development Plan for the Berkeley Campus. Wurster was a Californian with a belief in the rightness of the local 'Bay Region Style', a Californian vernacular (cf. figs 1.16 and 1.17), and a consequent scepticism for International Modern. However, Wurster had also imbued much of the Gropius kind of Modernism when at Harvard and MIT during the 1940s and was married to the refugee European housing reformer Catherine Bauer-Wurster. Wurster's own buildings are little known outside the USA, and his pursuit of an architectural career can be seen as the opposite of somebody like Stone's. He, and Kerr were also helped by among others, R. Nevitt Sandford of *American College* fame. In addition they followed the model of Harvard Houses and the Oxbridge ideal generally. Berkeley first of all tried to put planning and design into a close relationship and insisted that, on the one hand, only 25 per cent of the land should be covered with buildings, but, on the other hand, that buildings should be 'pulled together into close groups, reflecting functional relationships . . . on tight clusters'. Wurster, as early as 1959, was sceptical about Modernist 'commercial' slab blocks. As regards residences, they should both be fitted with recreational spaces (Kerr: 'youth is vehement and boils over if easy outlets are omitted'), but also placed as closely as possible to the teaching blocks. 'Kerr . . . worked hard to make the campus the center of student interest'. The allegiance to the State of California and the Californian environment meant, finally, that Wurster preferred Californian architects for their programme, and Californian forms, on the model of Kump's Foothill Community College already shown.

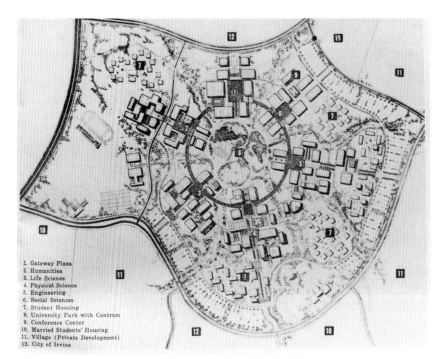

1. Gateway Plaza
2. Humanities
3. Life Science
4. Physical Science
5. Engineering
6. Social Sciences
7. Student Housing
8. University Park with Centrum
9. Conference Center
10. Married Students' Housing
11. Village (Private Development)
12. City of Irvine

1.22   University of California at Irvine, by William L. Pereira and Associates, layout 1964. (*ARec* 11-1964, p. 187)

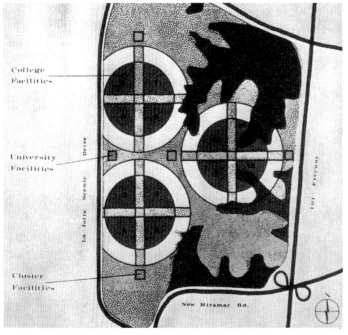

1.23   University of California at San Diego, Robert E. Alexander and Associates, schematic layout 1964. (*ARec* 11-1964, p. 193)

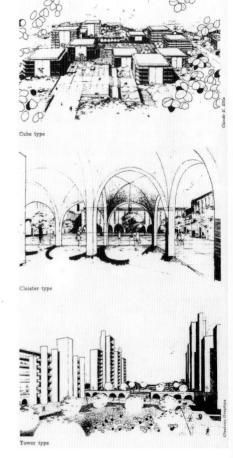

Cube type

Cloister type

Tower type

1.24   University of California at San Diego, proposed college types, 1964. (*ARec* 11-1964, p. 197)

It was for the three new university campuses that Kerr reserved the term 'experiment' – at Irvine, San Diego and Santa Cruz. A major innovatory teaching element was introduced at each: at Irvine the way each student could choose his or her own programme; at San Diego the attempts to bridge C. P. Snow's 'two worlds' (cf. below page 101) of science and humanities, and at Santa Cruz the pass/fail system. Kerr was adamant that all of them should grow to multiversity size, that is to about 27,000 students, the figure, in fact, which their 'mother' university, Berkeley, had reached by then. This size was needed, Kerr argued, to provide excellence as regards libraries, laboratories and cultural facilities. These expectations, however, had to be very much scaled down in the 1970s.

We come finally to Kerr's solution of the problem of the multiversity:

> The big campus lacks the inestimable virtue which the small liberal arts college counted as its hallmarks: the emphasis on the individual which small classes, a residential environment and a strong sense of relationship to others and the campus can and do give. Each of the university's new campuses is an experiment in combining the advantages of the large and the small. Each will offer a different answer to the problems of preserving a sense of individual worth in a world of increasing numbers and of maintaining quality in the face of such numbers.

Irvine was apparently sketched out by Kerr himself and then worked out by William L. Pereira. It opened in 1965. Its outline plans are reminiscent of earlier concepts of ideal towns, notably Ebenzer Howard's Garden City. The centre is formed by a park, with a slender 300 feet (92 metres) 'Centrum' tower. This is surrounded by a 'circle' on which border the complete array of faculties, plus a 'core', containing the central library etc. which also serves as the 'Gateway plaza'. The faculties reach outwards from the circle, like the 'spokes of a wheel' and in between the spokes Pereira planned subsidiary functions, like schools, and houses, in order to help draw in the outside community. All this is placed within a 10 minutes walking distance. The calculation of the walking distance and the claim of its brevity was now becoming a must in all campus planning. Residences are placed a little further outwards and it is stressed that they are 'not directly connected' with academic activities (fig. 1.22). San Diego was envisaged by the architect Robert E. Alexander as a high density complex of three clusters of four colleges (somewhat in the manner of Claremont, see above page 23) with 2,300 students each (and thus, in all, to make the total of 27,000 students, there were to be twelve colleges); each college cluster, in turn, contains major academic facilities. The college, as such, is divided into residential blocks, containing fifty to seventy students, ten on one floor, sharing bathrooms etc. There is in addition, a major centre for all, a 'true center of the communicating arts', and some of the more specialised teaching facilities are accommodated in separate units. In other ways, the residences differ considerably from each other: the 'cube', i.e. Modernist; the '"cloister type", suggested by Christchurch Oxford' and the '"tower"' type, that is, high rise blocks ('San Gimignano'). Each college was to 'have its own distinct character architecturally', evoking stylistic considerations from the earlier part of the century. Little of this was built, however, and the whole plan was drastically revised in 1966, scaled down and the density much reduced (figs 1.23 and 1.24).

Undoubtedly the most complex model of the concept 'small within large' was the

University of Santa Cruz. More literally, this campus now consists of just of a number of colleges and is seen by many Americans as being akin to the 'traditional' English college rather than the American university. Serious planning had begun in 1961, the Long Range Development Plan was issued in 1963 and the first students were admitted in 1965. About nine tenths of the cost, $9m by 1968, was state provided or state-loaned. The founding chancellor was Dean E. McHenry, a political scientist from UCLA and in terms of socio-political outlook a fellow traveller of Kerr's. Thirty-four colleges were planned. This was revised to twenty and by 1978 only eight had been built. There are, at Santa Cruz, some central facilities, a library, a theatre, some buildings for the natural sciences, a sports pavilion ('Field House'), service buildings and some lesser structures, some of which are grouped together approximately in the campus centre but they are far less marked out than usual. Social buildings, in the main, form part of the colleges themselves. What is, first of all, extraordinary at Santa Cruz is not its buildings, but the terrain itself: a heavily wooded, mountainous, even rocky site of 2,000 acres, that is 800 hectares, about 5 kilometres long and 2 kilometres wide (3 by 1.5 miles). This terrain itself does not allow for any kind of centralisation of views, let alone axial arrangements. The master plan was provided by John Carl Warnecke, California's best-known practitior and designer of several state colleges. The landscape architect was Thomas D. Church, from Berkeley and some buildings were by Kump, whose calculated informality we have already met at his Foothill Community College (fig. 1.25).

Each college is designed to cater for about 600 students, 50 per cent of which were residential, a very high proportion for a large university anywhere. The college comes under the leadership of a provost under whom the faculty develops a collegiate curriculum plan, providing a different focus for each college. University-wide, each field of study came also under a board of studies. Students usually received all the first and second year teaching in their college, but only some in their third year. Santa Cruz's aims were restated many times: there was to be a 'climate of curricular innovation', a 'distinctive collegiate environment', 'renewed emphasis on teaching', 'work towards an enriched student-faculty interaction'. A great diversity of teachers were attracted, including some from Oxbridge. There was indeed a perception that Santa Cruz was 'explicitly derived from the medieval colleges of Britain', a perception which, however, betrayed a degree of ignorance of the new situation in England. Closer parallels to Santa Cruz are, in fact, the contemporary 'collegiate universities', such as Kent or York.

It is seldom possible on the campus to see more than one group of buildings. Colleges are usually at a distance of 300–600 metres (1,000–2,000 feet), though some are twinned for economic reasons. The colleges themselves follow neither the traditional European/American courtyard principle, nor do they adhere much to the Gropius kind of flat-roofed parallel ranges, nor again to the spidery kind of plan of York, but consist of a scatter of two- to three-storey blocks which are placed in rather close proximity, next to a complex of communal facilities, with additional small blocks containing teachers' dwellings on the periphery. The first, Cowell College, of 1966, by Wurster, presents large, low-roofed communal facilities and a series of three-storey residential blocks, loosely grouped around green courts. Next door, Stevenson College of 1966, by John Esherick, is denser. With their lively roofscapes all the buildings are bound closer together and the spaces in between take on more the character of a

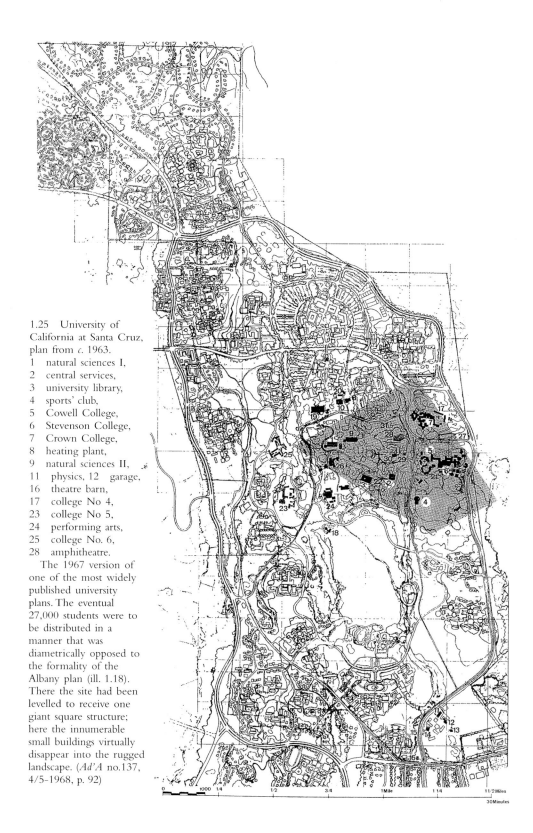

1.25 University of California at Santa Cruz, plan from *c.* 1963.

1 natural sciences I,
2 central services,
3 university library,
4 sports' club,
5 Cowell College,
6 Stevenson College,
7 Crown College,
8 heating plant,
9 natural sciences II,
11 physics, 12 garage,
16 theatre barn,
17 college No 4,
23 college No 5,
24 performing arts,
25 college No. 6,
28 amphitheatre.

The 1967 version of one of the most widely published university plans. The eventual 27,000 students were to be distributed in a manner that was diametrically opposed to the formality of the Albany plan (ill. 1.18). There the site had been levelled to receive one giant square structure; here the innumerable small buildings virtually disappear into the rugged landscape. (*Ad'A* no.137, 4/5-1968, p. 92)

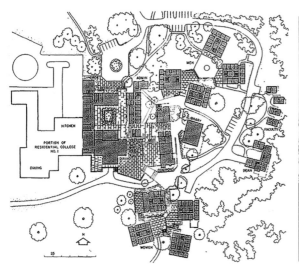

1.26 University of California at Santa Cruz, plan of Stevenson College, by Joseph Esherick and Associates 1966. (*ARec* 11-1964, p. 184)

1.27 University of California at Santa Cruz, Crown College by Ernest J. Kump Associates 1967/8. (M.F. Schmertz, *Campus Planning and Design*, New York, 1972)

small town (fig. 1.26). Crown College 1967 by Kump is denser still but its smaller shapes suggest rather a village kind of atmosphere (fig. 1.27), while Merill College of 1968/9 by Campbell and Wong appears more dramatically integrated with the hills and treescapes. The characterisations 'small town' and 'village' have, of course, little to do with traditional American conceptions; some parallels can perhaps be found in Townscape-influenced housing in some English New Towns from the later 1950s (on the Berkeley English links cf. page 202 below).

While the early overall plan of Santa Cruz was shown in virtually all architectural journal articles and books throughout the world, the actual buildings of the university and its colleges figured more rarely in architectural eulogies. The great exception was Kresge College. Here we reach a peak of American university design of those decades; in its pedagogy and in its architecture, Kresge was the most noted institution of all. The name was derived from its benefactor who otherwise remained unknown. Founding provost was the microbiologist Robert Edgar who was greatly assisted as regards the teaching philosophy by the East Coast-trained reformist and Carl Rogers-influenced psychologist, Michael Kahn. Much of the 'humanistic psychology' sounds like that of the experimental colleges of the previous thirty years: 'a living-learning community which concerns itself with human as well as intellectual needs . . .'. But Freudian and Jungian psychology was now taken further in the very small formal-informal groups ('family' or 'kin groups'), engaging in new 'encounter and sensitivity training techniques'. Thus, in a way, Kresge adopts elements from the psychology of the student personnel services, yet it does not use them in the same plain instrumentalist way – after all, there were no grades at Santa Cruz, only pass and fail. There was, finally, a straightforward hedonistic element, a new spontaneity in order to 'encourage students to let go, to explore, to enjoy.' The central ethos was perhaps best expressed by stressing 'participation rather than efficiency' (David Riesman).

It is a common perception that the extraordinarily intense social-educational concept of Kresge College found its match in the architecture. It was provided, from

1970, by Charles W. Moore, a somewhat anti-establishment-minded designer, at home both on the East and the West Coasts, who believed in complexity, strong colour and a Post-Modern relaxed attitude towards architectural theory and history. Kresge's basic type adheres to the common – and economic – formula of the rectangular two- to three-storey blocks, in this case containing mostly eight four-bed-apartments as well as accommodation in 'dormitory form'. There are a number of faculty residences, the provost's house and diverse communal buildings, the latter, however, appear much less separate than, say, in the first college, Cowell. Furthermore, the architect tries to go beyond the scatter method of arranging all these buildings; by lining them along both sides of a consolidated public street, 1,000 feet, or 300 metres long. Of course, it is a pedestrian precinct, yet not in the common, formal manner, but in the old 'village' way. It is the kind of space that one finds in newer models of dense 'Mediterranean' holiday villages, ultimately going back beyond English Townscape to a Sittean and Unwinian understanding of the traditional English, German, or Italian small town. Moore's own special style of design is the constant screening off and opening of spaces. However, it is not enough to talk – as with the other colleges at Santa Cruz – about the 'blocks' themselves but there are innumerable features, such as covered porches, balconies, external staircases, gateways, pergolas etc. which define and rede- fine the public-private borderline. Many of these features are given closely defined public functions, or rather, each 'public' function is made a special formal feature of, say, the post office, the laundry, the garbage compartment, the rostrum, the 'amphi- theatre' etc. – in an almost playful way, heightened by the intense colours, and always strongly contrasted with white (figs 1.28–1.30).

In what particular ways did this architecture fit in with the college philosophy? Within the college there is one block with a special experimental arrangement, experi- mental in an educational-psychological, as well as architectural sense. It contains the 'Octet Units', each 'octet' presenting an open living space, rising through three storeys; here the inhabitants are left to their own ways of arranging living, study and utility spaces. Another feature helping to create the desired sense of communal openness is the way in which many rooms or apartments look on, and feel very close to the village street – by comparison the other college plans resulted in a much greater degree of separateness. Kresge is probably the peak of the development of both the traditionalist and the Modernist devising of spaces, private, semi-private and public. Above all, according to Klotz, there is a complete lack of hierarchy and an avoidance of a sense of monumentality – still present in most of the other designs of the Uni- versity of California. Indeed, Kresge adopted a mode tried in some of the English new universities, Lancaster in particular, where there is virtually no differentiation according to institutions, meaning that it is hard to pick out the library or adminis- trative building from the residences. The process of merging into a whole is com- plete. For Moore, finally, it was the 'joyous academic celebration' as well as a certain 'insouciance' which mattered most.

AN INTEGRAL APPROACH?

If utopianism means anything, then it must entail acting in unison when creating an institution. One can easily cite elements which were shared without reservations:

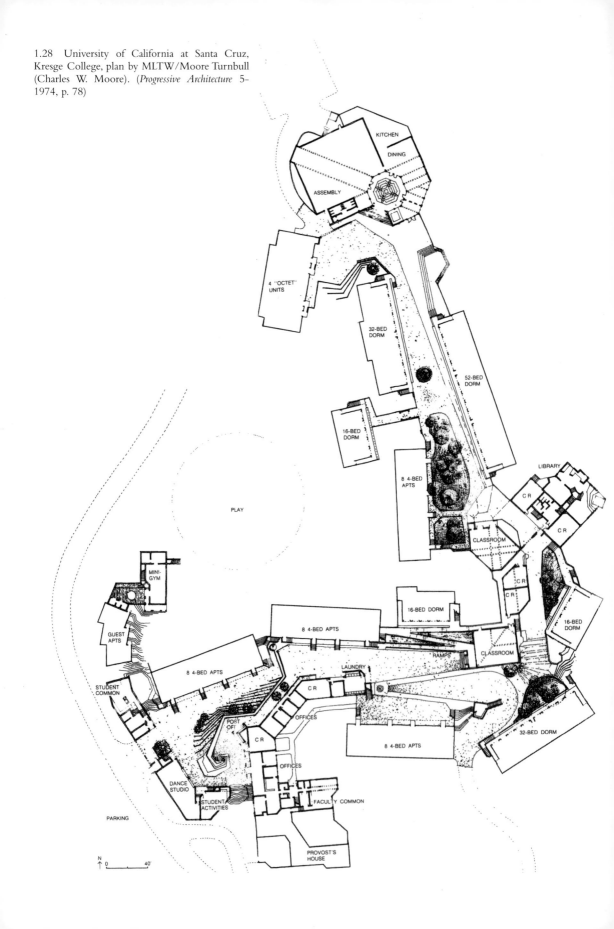

1.28 University of California at Santa Cruz, Kresge College, plan by MLTW/Moore Turnbull (Charles W. Moore). (*Progressive Architecture* 5-1974, p. 78)

1.29   University of California at Santa Cruz, Kresge College 1970–4. (Courtesy Don Kenny UCSC)

1.30   University of California at Santa Cruz, Kresge College. Fountain Court of the Assembly Building. (*Progressive Architecture* 5-1974, p. 83)

terms like 'community'; the way a small college was believed to provide a highly desirable kind of atmosphere, or the way in which a large campus had to be laid out efficiently in order to assure its optimal functioning. These elements had, however, been around for several generations and they were part of the generalised American utopia of education with which we started.

The fact now was that the sub-discourses which had developed from the 1930s and 1940s lacked coherence and inter communication. The general rhetoric, used by university administrators and those involved in the founding and financing of institutions remained a strong ornament. But, by definition, this rhetoric could not deal with any detailed professional concerns. We then examined the discourses of those who felt in charge of the whole of the student's extracurricular affairs, the student personnel services, which were of interest here because they presupposed a certain kind of unity of the institution. They grew enormously during the 1950s and 60s and began to replace another, older kind of university discourse, the educational-moral one. Ostensibly the strongest discourse to concern itself with the whole was 'planning'. However, it too, became a seemingly separate operation, it hardly touched on architecture, while Modernist architects usually took planning for granted and did not see why it should be made a separate issue. The conglomerate of all these factors, meaning at the same time, the non-collaboration of all these discourses, was, in fact, the 'multiversity'. As Kerr remarked: 'the idea of a multiversity has no bard to sing its praises, no prophet to proclaim its vision'. It was the issue of the reform of the multiversity which this chapter set out to investigate. Was it reformed? If so, how much did architects have to do with that reform?

The architects' discourse, too, appeared a relatively closed one. We have already stressed that the architectural historians' set of buildings was largely chosen, initially, by the 'architectural world' itself, that is, by the specialist architectural periodicals – although some attempt has been made in this chapter to broaden the spectrum. On the whole, the interest in university architecture has been limited to the extent it figures within the work of those who are, or were, considered masters. Seemingly inevitable was the selection of relatively expensive buildings (though there were very notable exceptions in that respect, for instance Gropius' Harvard Graduate Center) amongst the most prestigious institutions. In any case, these masterworks on campus were mostly relatively small individual buildings or complexes. In the critical analyses of some of the famed buildings, especially those by Louis Kahn, sometimes a gap opened between the severe criticism of their practical usefulness and the praise of their formal qualities, which further pushed these buildings into their own sphere of architects' architecture. While it was usually not difficult to find some professional voice to confirm an overall educational intention, American designers, although often quoted at length in the most general terms for their artistic and socio-political outlook, appear uninterested in the detailed, committed analysis of the plans and buildings for universities, quite in contrast to many of their English and European confreres. Turner's book, again, appears as a concluding example of this state of affairs; while sounding, at the end, reassuring about the links between architecture and institution, it does not go much into detail about the actual links, at least in the period in question. We shall see that there is a fundamental contrast between the USA and England, certainly in the 1960s, in that English socio-academic innovation seemed to go together neatly with architectural innovation, propagated by a much more united architectural and planning profession and their spokespersons. In a very limited way the obscure – in terms of high architecture – periodical *College and University Business* made a courageous attempt in 1970 to cover the whole architectural effort of the country by asking 2,309 chief financial officers and 1,423 architects to nominate their latest best designs. In its selection the journal most carefully mixed practical financial detail with up-to-date architectural jargon, and selected known as well as unknown institutions.

The neglect was mutual. It may be understandable in the case of the student personnel services which did not want to stray from their professional position in the conception of a good university. But even a broad-minded, yet critical analyst/chronicler, moreover one who probably had studied more campuses in greater detail than anybody else, David Riesman, manages to present a close analysis of life and teaching at Kresge College without any detailed or principled reference to the architect and his design, save for a brief mention of the 'Octets' – and this for a group of buildings where intense pedagogic and intense architectural aspirations were supposedly closely combined. A little later Riesman puts in some praise of the architecture of Santa Cruz, and yet, also refers to 'the still poorly understood relations between architecture and learning, inevitably plagued by changing user's values and tastes'.

It is probable that the lack of mutual understanding can be explained through the narrow instrumentality which each of the professions were locked into, and which, in turn, may be explained through the way most of the discourses developed so rapidly in academic terms. As it was said about the planning and building professions in 1970: 'Essentially the major groups work alone, in the sense that experience and "know how" tend to separate them functionally. A total effort of coordination is not considered essential.' But there is a deeper issue here. At the beginning of this chapter it was stated that the vast scale of academic ranking did not constitute a problem for our investigation. Indeed, the quantitative expansion was each profession's first aim. But to raise quality, to insist on a high position within the system, was, of course, equally important. The fact was that new hierarchies had arisen within the various branches of overall reform. It appears strongest in the field of psychology. There is the 'lowest' strata of those who deal with the practical day-to day psychological or sociological advice. There is the next strata – a nationwide academic network of those who empirically research into college psychology or sociology. There is, or at least was during the 1960s and 70s, a higher strata of sociological research into reforms within the old academic top range (e.g. Riesman's work), where the discourses of the first two levels are rarely mentioned.

It must not be omitted to say, of course, that all these discourses, in themselves, constitute a remarkable achievement. But in our context of the utopianist university, the lack of mutuality, of unity, brings us back to the multiversity once more, to confirm, once again, that the multiversity could, by definition, not be a utopianist university. For our account, we 'found' a small number of clearly utopianist universities in the USA; how many there really were, is impossible to say here. In spite of the Anglo-American similarities, age-old and new, it must be noted that we will face a rather different situation in England, as well as in Germany, as regards utopianism and its discourses: particularly in Germany where all those involved made sure that their contributions were well heard. There were, in fact very few New Universities in the USA, in the sense of a fully comprehensive institution of high academic rank. Certainly one cannot speak of a homogeneous group of new universities; which, ultimately relates to the fact that institutions in that country are traditionally more individualised. They simply could not all be expected to follow a single new direction.

Lastly, there is a problem here of chronology, of the rapid change of theories and fashions in architecture and planning itself. Riesman's remark about the fickleness of the users was not at all out of place during the later 1970s. By that time, a different climate applied to critical architectural opinion, as regards the power and predictability of design, which differed fundamentally from the beliefs held up to the early or mid-1960s. Surprisingly early, in 1966, the leader of Santa Cruz, Dean McHenry, pronounced – perhaps he wanted to sound informal at a conference – the following low-key analysis: 'The fact is that physical planning cannot ensure educational soundness – it can only help it along. The fact is that small numbers cannot guarantee educational soundness – they can only make it more easily attainable. Put quite simply, we believe that the thing that will make the college work – given the assistance of a sympathetic physical and educational plan – is the fact that it will be to the peoples' advantage to make it work'. So much for all the efforts to bypass instrumentalisation and to assert the institution's primary educational-social effect on the individual!

In the end, however, one may take a simpler view. Instrumentalisation or not, who would put into question the academic superiority of American universities post World War II? Can anybody really provide clear proof that the multiversity has been detrimental to the educational effort, however defined? If everybody insists on keeping to the utopia of the small college, the utopia of higher education for all can never be achieved. In contrast to what was considered the shapeless German Massenuniversität, the American multi-university might still be considered at least a conglomerate of institutions. In terms of architectural patronage, it may be noted that all the important new campuses discussed here – and we may also include Chicago Circle, to be dealt with in Chapter III – are state universities and together they do present some counterpoint to the private university architectural establishment. As regards utopia, more narrowly speaking, there was an increasing faction who maintained that where there is no utopia, there will not be dystopia. Some of the much-vaunted integrated campuses of the New English University movement, brought, arguably, just that. However, this means jumping too far ahead. The next two chapters present the utopianist university argument in full, in England and in North America, and will include new battlecries for both college and campus, as well as a newly defined 'urban' ideal. After that we shall see how new ideas of student life began openly to denigrate the older and newer kinds of liberal institutionality and helped to 'bring down' both college and campus.

You do what you like with what you have got and I will do what I like with mine. We have tried in this place to say of every building: 'This does not belong exclusively to anybody'.

(Lord Fulton on The University of Sussex).

COLLEGE AND CAMPUS

Compared with other major countries, the world of the English university was small. 'Conservative' and 'elitist' were terms often used. While the situation in the USA was characterised as a vast and complex hierarchy, the English setup was much simpler: there were the two old foundations and 'the rest'. Institutions below 'the rest', i.e. the lower ranges of 'higher and further education' do not concern us here. Moreover, little change occurred until the early 1960s. Student numbers even shrank in the early 1950s and real growth only started in the late 1950s. A wide-ranging institutional analysis, as in the previous chapter, does not appear necessary at this point. We can concentrate more straightforwardly on new institutional planning and architecture. In a subsequent section we shall discuss the agencies, especially the University Grants Committee, the central authority in Britain, which initiated much of what was new. Trying to sum up what accounted for the high renown of English higher education, the key would surely be the institution, in the simple sense of a place, an environment in which large or small groups interact. The college quad, whether Gothic or collegiate modern, was seen as a guarantee of the kind of socialisation needed to foster academic and educational progress. And yet, by no means all university buildings in England were colleges. The university as a larger unit, as a 'campus', was becoming a planning issue here, too. In turn, this led to much rethinking of the role and shape of the college.

CAMPUS: CIVICS, REDBRICKS AND OVERSEAS

Conveniently, the term campus can be applied to all English universities outside Oxford and Cambridge (though early nineteenth-century Downing College, Cambridge, has been cited as the first ever proper campus layout). It must be remembered that it was the 'Civics' and 'Redbricks' (the nicknames for the provincial foundations of nineteenth and early twentieth century, respectively) which were vigorously expanding during the 1950s, though, of course, from a modest base. While Oxbridge built virtually nothing, the older and newer Civics, as well as London, added many large and imposing buildings to their conglomerates, for instance in Bloomsbury (fig. 2.1). They often showed impressive architectural features, impressive in the sense of the late classical tradition that was deemed appropriate for government and most municipal commissions from the 1930s into the 1950s. After the mid-1950s one issue came to the fore: the adoption of the Modernist architectural style. This late date might appear surprising; had International Modern not been introduced in Britain at least by the late 1930s? Had not most architects working in public offices, for housing and schools, adopted it enthusiastically from at least the end of the war? We must be aware that these architects formed part of a design elite, and that most patrons, including the clients and users of the Civics – and even at Oxbridge (Oxford's 'semi-traditional' Nuffield College, completed in 1960, being a case in point) did not usually belong to this Modernist elite. It was the architectural critics who rather suddenly took up the issue of 'Modern' university architecture in late 1957.

We may, however, consider the architecture of the Civics generically as a tradition which was proudly different from Oxbridge. Apart from campus and college there was a third major type of university building, the single impressive dominating structure, comprising all sections of the university, except residences; Victorian in Glasgow, Edwardian in Birmingham and American 1920s Moderne for London's Senate House. The chief symbol was the tower. The tower of the Parkinson Building of Leeds University mingles well with several other civic structures of the same style. After about 1950, however, designers lost confidence in such kinds of symbols, while town councillors would not want to spend money on them when there seemed so many more pressing needs. Moreover, to squeeze many different functions into one large building appeared increasingly impractical. A stolid sobriety, or one might say, a Neo-Georgian utilitarianism, was the result for most new single-function university buildings – only to be faced with the criticism of dullness by the mid-1950s. Many supporters of Modernism felt that any kind of grandiosity ought to be ridiculed.

In the ensuing complex arguments about university design it was less the overall density of the Civics which was now attacked, but rather the way in which massive buildings were placed next to each other without apparent thought or overall concept. One had to, first of all, come back to basic types. The critic Lionel Brett speaks of two: 'the college theme . . . recovered, and the viable campus development'. The term campus was new for Britain and had come directly from the USA. Its circulation grew slowly, its main use became that of loosely referring to any group of academic buildings belonging to one institution – except, of course, at Oxbridge. The most significant message of the term campus during these early years was that a university had to be based on some overall concept. The UGC was by then asking for master plans, or development plans from all institutions, but they were slow in coming; nevertheless, the *Architects' Journal* in 1958 carefully recorded a great number of partial planning measures. With the idea of the campus, in its Modernist form, went the idea of zoning. A zoning plan means that one begins by dividing up a complex into its major purposes, and then one allocates different localities to those purposes in order to achieve their optimal functioning. However, there was, in Britain, as yet little opportunity for such comprehensive measures to be taken; perhaps the layout plan for Manchester University of 1958 was the best example of a rigid differentiation of functions, into humanities, sciences, medicine, social buildings and student residence.

In America, zoning could often conveniently be combined with the older types of formal town planning. For Britain, however, a rigid 'New Dehli Style of layout' could no longer be a model. Brett defined the 'campus' more narrowly, and somewhat hes-

2.1 University of London, Senate House (in the distance), from 1932, by Charles Holden. 'The University Garden as it is going to be'; a picture of the kind of calm dignity which was precisely what the 1960s wanted to leave behind. Watercolour by Cyril Ludford after the plans of Charles Holden 1943. (S.C. Roberts, *British Universities*, London, 1957)

itantly, as a 'university in a garden'. The most convincing example to that date in England was probably Nottingham University, situated prominently on a hill outside the city, on ample grounds, centred around a typical 'civic' prewar building with a tower. After World War II, a lot of building went on, ambitiously led by Vice Chancellor Bertrand Hallward, with a number of prominent designers. From 1948 they were led by the consultant planner, Sir Percy Thomas, bringing with him a Welsh–American experience in Beaux Arts city layout, and in 1954 one of the country's ·most respected landscape designers, G.A. Jellicoe was engaged to further unify the whole. A number of halls were built around to the edge of the campus, thus achieving a degree of campus self-containedness unusual for Britain's civic universities. In that sense, civic Nottingham was more akin to some of the newer 'Redbricks', like Reading or Exeter, largely of the post World War II period, which could be called campuses and which, from the start, attained a high degree of residency (Reading, after all, was founded from Oxford). However, it was hard to get it right in those days. Redbrick's planning was now considered too informal and too spread out; there appeared to be a lack of coordination and the overall density was considered far too low. There was much agreement, subsequently, that Sussex was the first proper campus university in the country. Sussex, however, was also soon considered lacking in density and the way in which the other New Universities went on record in their rejection of the spread-out type of campus plan meant that the reputation of the campus concept in Britain had already suffered. Its common use does not carry much serious institutional or architectural meaning.

2.2   Birmingham University project, view towards the new residences, by Casson and Conder 1957. (*AJ* 31-10-1957, p. 649)

Nevertheless, a number of overall campus plans caught the limelight in those years. All planners of the 1950s had to cope with existing buildings, but they tried hard to provide a sense of completeness. Casson and Conder took the lion's share; first at Cambridge (see below page 65) and then in the task of the reorganisation of the sprawlingly large and very incomplete-looking campus at Birmingham University in 1957 (fig. 2.2). What is conveyed in their drawings – for Birmingham as well as for Cambridge – is a formal-spatial concern with the old courtyard principle; they wished to adapt them but in so doing to keep the courts partly open, in order to let space flow between the blocks. There is an avoidance of axiality and generally a 'return to picturesque traditions'. Much attention was given to Sheffield University's competition of 1953 for Western Bank; it was in Sheffield where Modernist architecture really entered into British academe (the best known entry, by the Smithsons became relevant much later, see page 91); chiefly in the form of a steel and glass tower block of nineteen stories for the Arts and Architecture section, not completed until 1959. Indeed, many civics began to plan at least one high-rise block. Sir Basil Spence believed that his ten-storey engineering tower at Southampton would 'hold together the hinterland of huts and redbrick blocks' (fig. 2.3). On the whole, however, these plans, revolutionary though they must have seemed to their patrons and their early users and notwithstanding the fact that most of them were designed by major architects, were not to receive much national attention when they were finally built. This was due, firstly, to the way in which Cambridge began to reassert itself, and soon, of course, to the way in which the New Universities insisted that good planning meant planning from scratch.

There was one more area of activity for British university planners and designers, the care for education in the overseas territories. It was strongest in regions where there was least of it, as in middle Africa. Major efforts began after 1945. The adherence to the trusted models at home was strong: 'Camford' standards, Greek and Latin, guaranteeing quality through the London External Degree system. There were ample design opportunities, although the building process was usually slow. The first major project was the University of Ibadan in Nigeria, founded in 1947. Building began in the early 1950s to the designs of Maxwell Fry, at that time England's foremost Modernist social-reformist designer, for whom reformism included 'Third World' activ-

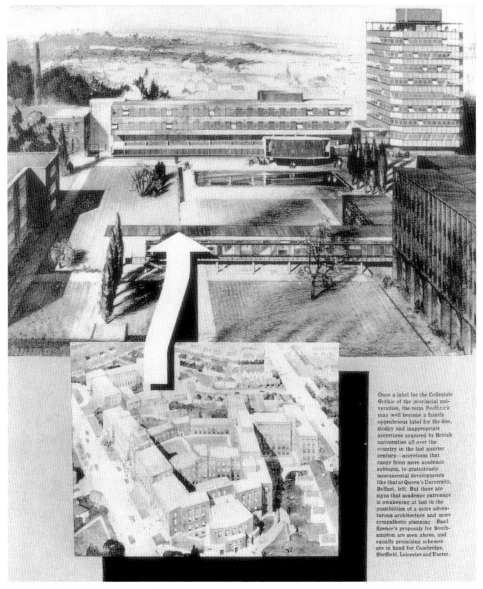

Once a label for the Collegiate Gothic of the provincial universities, the term *Redbrick* may well become a faintly opprobrious label for the dim, stodgy and inappropriate accretions acquired by British universities all over the country in the last quarter century—accretions that range from mere academic subtopia, to gratuitously monumental developments like that at Queen's University, Belfast, left. But there are signs that academic patronage is awakening at last to the possibilities of a more adventurous architecture and more sympathetic planning—Basil Spence's proposals for Southampton are seen above, and equally promising schemes are in hand for Cambridge, Sheffield, Leicester and Exeter.

2.3 The *Architectural Review*, 1957: bad into good: Queens University Belfast and proposals for Southampton University, by Basil Spence. (*AR* 10-1957, p. 234)

ities. One general recommendation for the damp heat of those regions was to spread buildings far apart. Apparently it was due to the principal, Dr Kenneth Mellanby, that a 'much more concentrated scheme [was adopted], reducing the minimum distances to be walked, and stressing the corporate and collegiate character'. African universities were deemed to require almost 100 per cent student residence. At Ibadan each student had a separate study-bedroom (at that time a luxury) in a series of 'colleges', i.e. halls of residences which also had lavish provisions of dining rooms, common rooms and quiet rooms. The most remarkable feature of Ibadan was probably that it neither followed the older axial campus planning nor the newer kind of International Modernist Zeilenbau formation (see Chapter VI) and the associated rational zoning policies, but adhered to a series of semi-open courtyards. The colleges are grouped

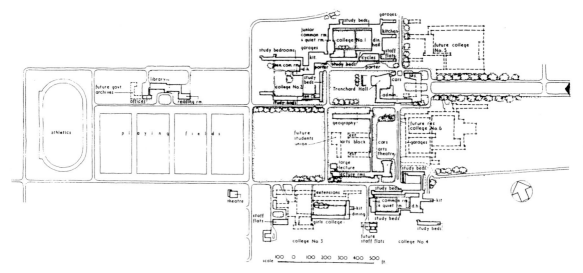

2.4   Ibadan, Nigeria, University College by Maxwell Fry, from 1950; showing the main permanent buildings only. (*AD* 5-1955, p. 154)

close to the central communal and teaching buildings. It is the wedge-shaped halls which give their style away: Ibadan forms part of the International collegiate which Fry had helped to establish with Gropius in the 1930s (Impington, see page 35). Everybody was proud of Ibadan's Modernity, at the time the largest group of Modernist buildings in the whole country (fig. 2.4). Later designs by English architects began to consider the *genius loci* more carefully, e.g. the (unbuilt) ultra low-density design by James Cubitt & Partners for the University of Nigeria at Nsukka with adobe-built student residences (fig. 2.21). Another chapter was South Asia, where normally a more urban character seemed to be required, for instance in the vast 1959 scheme by Raglan Squire Partners for Panjab University at Lahore. Soon there was to be considerable international competition in the field of university design with a plethora of models to follow (see Chapter VI).

Only one plan for a complete new institution in England became known in those years, Arthur Ling's Coventry University College of 1958, a precursor of Warwick University. Here we find a disproportionately large public arena, made up of two squares, with adjacent 'public buildings' (Great Hall, Theatre and Art Gallery) and an American-type 'tower of learning'. The lower square, surrounded by a 'cloister, provides an inward looking setting for the social life of the University'. 'A self-contained community complete in every respect . . . where the pursuit of knowledge and the life of the community would be synonymous'. But such a lavish provision for a tiny number of 670 students could hardly be expected to serve as a model for the new expansionary times of the 1960s. Ling's proposal equated the university with a large Oxbridge college (fig. 2.5).

THE NEW CAMBRIDGE CONTRIBUTION

While hardly anything stirred in Oxford, by the late 1950s Cambridge was rapidly becoming a hotbed of architectural advance. Oxbridge college patrons were considered

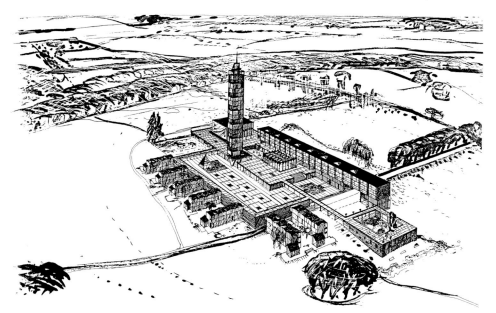

2.5   Coventry, plan for a University College, by Arthur G. Ling and R.S. Johnston 1958. (*Proposed University College Coventry* (Coventry Central Library))

notoriously unable to decide on 'good architecture'. Because of the traditional corporate decisionmaking process any college fellow could block decisions, on any grounds. Cambridge had a bad reputation to live down, namely Christ College's rejection of Walter Gropius's Hobson Street Building in 1937 – whereupon Gropius settled in Cambridge, Massachusetts and copiously influenced American campus architecture. A remarkably comprehensive plan was Casson and Conder's Sidgwick Avenue Art Faculties, first prepared in 1952/3 and built from 1956. It adopted the principle of the courtyard, but in the Modernist vein the buildings are lifted on stilts almost throughout, while the ashlar of all the walls adheres to the tradition of major college and pubic buildings. It was Sir Leslie Martin's appointment as head of the Cambridge School of Architecture in 1956 which had a major effect on the scene. Martin had impeccable Welfare State credentials, having worked in the London County Council's Architects' department, which some, at that time, held to be the most eminent architectural office in the world, its chief output being public housing. Martin built relatively little himself but exercised his influence through his disciples, especially Colin St John Wilson, who was highly influential with his small School of Architecture building, in New Brutalist severe brick and concrete. Martin's influence was soon extended into the sphere of the New Universities as well (see page 139). In Cambridge he acted chiefly as a mediator although there was not much that could be attempted as regards overall campus planning. An earlier plan by Holford (1950) and later those by Robert Matthew Johnson-Marshall and by Chamberlin Powell and Bon had had little effect.

Proper patronage could only come from an individual institution, from a college. Most old colleges expanded with new halls of residence, preferably close to the old buildings. For almost eighty years there had not been a new foundation. But by the late 1950s some argued that existing colleges should not be extended ad infinitum. In early 1958 Senate decided to give way to what was felt to be a national need for training scientists and went ahead with a plan for Churchill College. It was to be large, 600 undergraduates and 60 fellows, on a suburban site, with plenty of space for

2.6　Cambridge Churchill College Competition: Chamberlin, Powell and Bon 1959. 'View from the East with the Chapel in the Centre, and opposite the tower, with porter's lodge at the foot, which marks the entrance.' (*AJ* 14-8-1959 pp. 16–17)

expansion, to be paid for by appeal, which eventually reached over £2.8m. The chief movers were the 'energetic and youthful' new provost of King's, Noël Annan and the Master-elect, Sir John Cockcroft. They duly invited twenty members of the architectural profession to present plans, without fee. The assessors, between them, comprised the major architecture establishment figures, Sir Basil Spence, Sir William Holford and Sir Leslie Martin. Churchill was an important and well publicised competition, because university projects rarely proceeded this way, and also because literally no living architect had ever designed a major college before. Many of them subsequently went on to design the New Universities.

The general stipulations for Churchill College were very much in line with the new thinking for university architecture, formulated by the architectural critics (see page 104): a distinguished design; a 'clearly identifiable group of buildings for a college community; capable of development'. But although the trustees had stipulated rooms around courts accessible by frequent staircases, solutions varied very widely. The four finalists of the first stage were very different from each other and it appears that they were chosen for their striking and unusual features: the jagged contours of the Howell Killick Partridge project, the extravagant kind of civic centre by Chamberlain Powell and Bon – we shall meet these intense designers again shortly in Cambridge, as well as with the town centre university in Leeds – and Stirling and Gowan's combination

2.9 (*far right below*)　Cambridge Churchill College Competition: Stirling and Gowan. 'To . . . create an internal environment, private, enclosed and protected'. 'The outer ring of college rooms encloses the great court . . . [establishing] the entity of the college at the first stage of building operations'. Between the two residential blocks on the left is the library, front right the assembly hall and dining room, far right the Master's Lodge. (*AJ* 14-8-1959, p. 27)

Churchill College Cambridge: The significance of the competition for Churchill College Cambridge lay chiefly in the way in which it was a novel task for English architects, as for many decades there had not been a major new design for a college. As a result, the cream, and avant-garde, of the profession supplied an astonishing diversity of designs, a diversity which turned out to be a rehearsal for the diversity of the New University plans by virtually the same group of architects.

2.7 (*left*) 'Boston Manor. The Living Suburb', design for a high-density suburb, by Chamberlin, Powell and Bon 1958. Part of town centre with six-storey housing quadrangles and low-rise housing beyond. For these architects there seemed virtually no difference between a university plan and a city plan. (*Architecture and Building* 10-1958)

2.8 (*below*) Cambridge Churchill College Competition: Howell, Killick and Partridge. (*AJ* 14-8-1959, pp. 21–6)

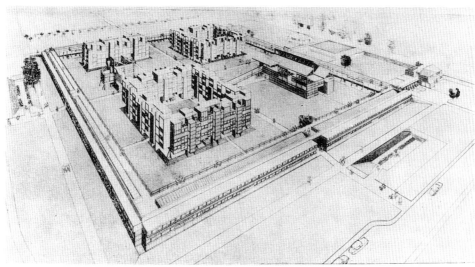

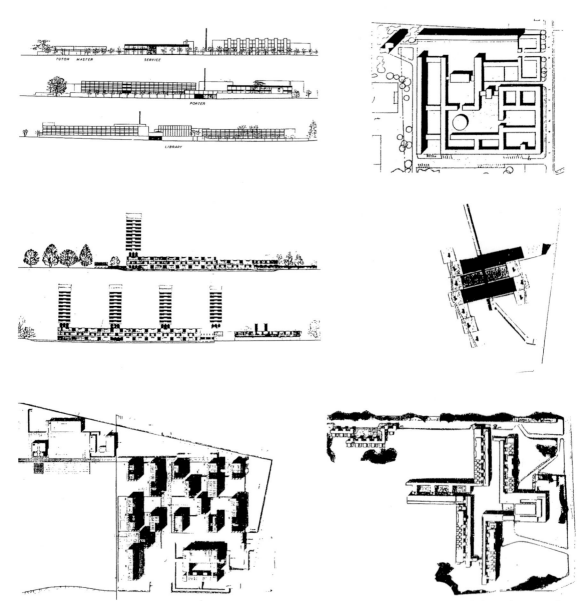

2.10 Cambridge Churchill College Competition, a selection of the remaining entries. Top left: Robert Matthew Johnson-Marshall; top right: Lionel Brett (Lord Esher); centre left: The Architects' Co-Partneship; centre right: Peter and Alison Smithson; bottom left: Yorke, Rosenberg and Mardall; bottom right: Fry, Drew, Drake and Lasdun. (*AJ* 13-9-1959, pp. 124–5, 137, 122–3, 126–7, 133, 122–3)

of urban density, college quads and defiant axiality – the latter anathema to current beliefs. The great majority of the remaining sixteen proposed diverse versions of the quad, though what varied greatly was the height of buildings; at least seven proposed some structures of above four stories. Peter Smithson differed most strongly from the rest by proposing a 'modern hotel' kind of building (figs 2.6–2.10).

The winner was Richard Sheppard, Robson and Partners who proposed the most quiet designs of all, chiefly a series of densely interlocking quads, with staircases each leading to twelve or so rooms. A well separated and elaborate central complex of communal building completes the whole. Buildings are low, consistently two or three stories. It was not Modernist concrete which was to dominate, but dark brick, with

2.11 Cambridge Churchill College Competition winning entry by Richard Sheppard, Robson and Partners 1959, central court area (looking rather different from what was built). (*AJ* 14-8-1959, pp. 6–7)

2.12 Cambridge Churchill College by Sheppard, Robson and Partners, 1960–4, view towards dining hall and view into a court towards the left

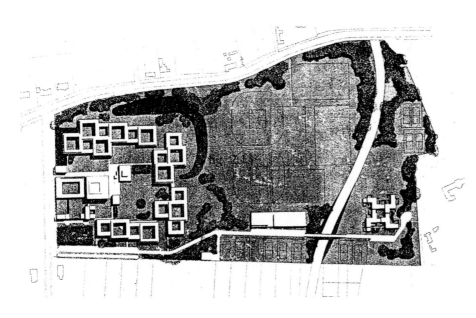

2.13 Cambridge Churchill College Competition entry by Sheppard, Robson and Partners 1959, outline plan (the built layout is much more open towards the main lawn). (*AJ* 14-8-1959, pp. 6–7)

concrete for the horizontal structural parts. Inside, in the hall and in the refectory, the same materials are shown, enriched with a profusion of teak and pine, producing an altogether darkish effect. After its formal opening in 1964 much critical ink was spilt; all appreciations take on the question as to whether or not Churchill may be called a Modern building. There was definitely an institutional traditionality in the insistence on quads, in the lavishness in which the central communal functions were provided for. On the other hand, the lack of achsiality, the frequent turns and corners of the quads and their relative openness were typical of avant-garde housing layout of the early 1960s, as was the way the materials were left raw, 'unfinished', unpolished; thus the design had moved on from established International Style Modernism, and its more delicate forms of Gropius's colleges of around 1950. In any case, Churchill College seemed 'plain blunt and bulldogishly English, like the founder himself' (Michael Webb); for Annan, the original client, the most important factor was the look of 'quality' while one might remain 'indifferent to the design'. Banham summarised Churchill College with a simple 'informal but grand' – although he insists on 'contrives to be grand' because he himself did not believe in a Cambridge 'College tradition'. Nobody, however, had any doubts over the building's comfort: 'everywhere the emphasis is on sociability and multiple use'. As a member of its type, as a college, Churchill appeared a complete success (figs 2.11–2.13).

A few years after the Churchill competition two of its entrants were given commissions for complete colleges of a smaller size. Fitzwilliam (Stages I and II 1961–7) by Denys Lasdun and New Hall (Stages I and II 1962–6) by Chamberlin Powell and Bon serve around 200 students each. Lasdun adhered more closely here to the traditional 'quad' idea than in his Churchill design, although he transformed the plans into a kind of square snail, with the public rooms at the centre. Much of the complex

70

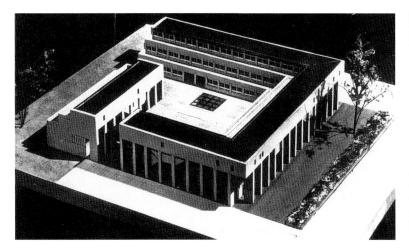

2.14 (*far left*) Cambridge New Hall by Chamberlin, Powell and Bon 1962–6. (*Ad'A* 137 4/5-1968, p. xxxi)

2.15 Cambridge Harvey Court (Gonville and Caius College) Sir Leslie Martin and Colin St J. Wilson with Patrick Hodgkinson 1960–2. (*Casabella* 6-1961, p. 15)

had to be built to stringent UGC standards and is treated rather repetitively inside and out. New Hall was a Women's College, likewise with bedrooms to UGC standards. Here the choice was for the Victorian 'female' college type of basic corridor access rather than the traditional 'male' version of the frequent staircase access. The strongly emphasised centrally-placed multi-towered dining room occasioned some puzzled comments as to the possibly male interpretation of forms combined with the female whiteness of the concrete (fig. 2.14).

Lastly, there is Harvey Court, designed during the late 1950s and built 1960–2 by Leslie Martin and his associates. Although it is not a proper college, but only a medium-sized hall of residence for Gonville and Caius College, unlike most extensions of colleges it is not treated as a more or less straightforward block, or series of blocks of rooms, but as a quad. But Harvey Court transforms this old formula into a late Modernist multilevel structure, with car parking spaces and communal facilities at the bottom and rooms above; moreover, the rooms are set back so as to allow more light and more privacy, as well as creating a very strong front and back contrast. This, in turn, is combined with another re-interpretation of the old quad idea: the outside face is closed and even appears forbidding, doubly emphasised by the all-brick facing, whereas the inside of the quad is light and open. Martin brought in two related arguments for his college revival. Firstly, he maintained that among university buildings those for teaching will be subject to changing purposes while student residences are likely to remain the same. He then reiterated that 'in the case of student life' the 'residence itself should be the primary medium of higher education'. On the whole, the 'architectural conception of the court is more lasting than superficial changes of style' – a crucial hint for so much 1960s university planning. The way in which the design resembles what in public housing began to be called 'low-rise high-density', leads further to statements regarding the 'intrinsic desirability' of 'the "urbanity" of city life' (fig. 2.15). However, in 1970 Nicholas Taylor notes the limitations of these concepts when applied to 'Cambridge's most important postwar building': 'A single "urban" building, however, does not make a city . . . caught in a nexus of college property ownership which dictates separate plots, separate buildings and separate architects . . . each of them building its own disconnected fragment in suburbia.' We shall see that it is precisely these kinds of arguments that pervade the planning of some of the New

2.16 Oxford St Catherine's College by Arne Jacobsen 1960–4. The main entrance is at the top (adjacent to the Master's Lodge), the service entrance to the right; the long ranges contain the bedrooms; to the left of the central circular lawn are the library and the lecture hall, to the right the hall with kitchen and service rooms. (*AR* 10-1963, p. 279)

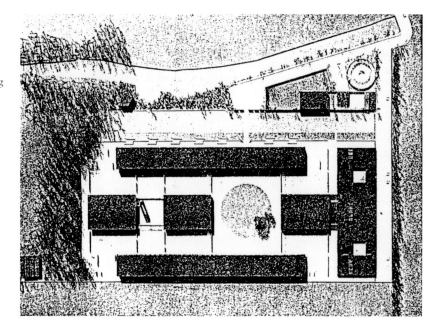

2.17 Oxford St Catherine's College.

Universities and their efforts to be 'urban', and we shall examine, in turn, whether their attempts were judged to be successful. It only remains to be mentioned that when the next major college was designed, Robinson, in 1974, ideas about college planning had changed considerably: a college was now seen as a complete small town.

Oxford's contribution in this context is very much smaller. There was no school of architecture, let alone one that stressed planning and public service, or 'urban' issues, as at Cambridge under Martin. Oxford's interweaving of town and college presented the ideal in any case and there seemed no need for any new thinking. Leslie Martin

himself made a contribution to the issue of the proper combination of communal and secluded spaces in his Three Libraries complex (Oxford University Library Group). Oxford's one spectacular contribution was a quasi newly founded College, St Catherine's, a fairly large undertaking, though with 400 students smaller than Churchill, to which its history ran parallel. In single-minded fashion the Master, historian Alan Bullock, pursued the idea that the 'best' and most Modern architecture was not likely to be expected from Britain and chose the Dane Arne Jacobsen (in early 1959). The architect then went away and produced a design. Bullock tells us about the moment of revelation: he waited for Jacobsen and the model at London Airport: 'we nearly unpacked it in the customs and I saw at once that was "it"'. From then on 'I fought hard to give him a free hand' – a kind of client-architect relationship which we will find again with the vice chancellors of the New Universities, such as Norwich or Lancaster. St Catherine's uses two elements which made it more strictly Modern (and yet we are told that it was not meant to look like 'an ordinary standard modern building'), namely, absolute rectilinearity and much use of glass. Its layout is 'simple', with clearly distinguishable units, mostly well separated from each other. In the end, Bullock, like almost all teachers of his generation, wanted the whole to be 'the visible expression in architectural form of the university as a community living together'. Indeed, one of the 'open community' elements was taken to be the way in which the students rooms are utterly exposed through the all-glass external walls. Arguably, at St Catherine's, 'community' went to a degree of denying privacy greater than anywhere at Cambridge; at the same time there is also a high degree of 'suburban' secludedness here (figs 2.16 and 2.17).

COLLEGE, HALL OF RESIDENCE, STUDY BEDROOM BLOCK

Unlike the heavily protected term university, 'college' can be used for all kinds of higher grade schools, all kinds of institutions of 'further education', or for a whole university, as with the individual 'colleges' of London University. To begin with, our concern is strictly with the Oxbridge type of college. The overriding characteristic of Oxbridge's approach to university education is to include concern for those periods when the student is not actually studying. The story of post World War II British university education is that this concern is not restricted to Oxford and Cambridge but that the majority of universities now aspired to this 'residential ideal'. A magic statistic was the proportion of students in university-built 'residences'. In Oxbridge it was around 50–60 per cent; only very few universities reported more, with Durham at 68 per cent and Keele at 100 per cent; there were also some as yet small Redbrick universities, Reading, Southampton, Exeter as well as Nottingham who strove for a very large proportion of students in residence. The lowest figures came from the large conurbations, especially London, or Manchester with 20 per cent. The critical corollary figure was that for students studying away from home; on the whole, studying and living at home was not considered advantageous. Averages were going down: in 1938/9 58 per cent left their home, in 1961/2 it was 80 per cent. One of the most remarkable developments in the expansion of British higher education after the war and especially during the 1960s was that both the number of students overall and the proportion in university residences greatly expanded. In 1961/2 that proportion

was 28 per cent, in 1974/5 45 per cent. It meant that approximately 70,000 extra beds were being provided during these years alone.

The rest would use lodgings, sometimes controlled, or 'approved', by the universities. While there was the occasional voice which listed advantages of 'lodgings' or 'digs', the disadvantages seemed only too obvious. To 'take in lodgers' was a world that is largely forgotten now: families or single persons would have a room to spare and needed additional income, usually in the older kinds of cramped houses, where quiet study was often not possible. Moreover, during the 1950s, with rapidly rising standards of living and more and more old houses being cleared away, fewer and fewer places were available. Thus university residences were becoming simply a condition of the expansion of student numbers. But, as has been made clear previously, such a quantitative argument would not suffice in this discourse. UGC Chairman Keith Murray was always adamant: 'We consider that university residence is desirable on educational grounds'. The Robbins Report of 1963 demanded more residences, too – without giving much detail as to how to achieve the aim. There were demands that every university should make at least one year of university residence compulsory.

Thus, why not just extend all universities by building Oxbridge-type colleges? There was the occasional demand simply to revert to this solution. But there would not have been agreement as to the teaching function of the college. In the older civics, in particular, it would simply not have seemed appropriate to lose even some of the central teaching functions to individual sub-institutions. What seemed, in the postwar period, particularly unsuitable about the Oxbridge colleges was their virtual administrative and academic independence from the 'university'. Within the increasingly complex institutional thinking which this chapter sets out to explore, the old autonomy of the Oxbridge college made less and less sense. However, we do not need to analyse the administrative and institutional peculiarities of the Oxbridge setup; for anybody outside, college life and college customs, as such, appeared something too rarefied to be adopted anywhere else, notwithstanding the fact that during the 1960s Oxbridge college life itself changed greatly and much of the formality was abolished; symptomatic was the abandonment of the idea of a college chapel at St Catherine's and (after considerable argument) at Churchill College. Lastly, there would have been

2.18 (*far left*) Leicester University, Beaumont House student residences (originally a private villa, 1904), now part of Beaumont Hall complex, Stoughton Drive South. (J. Simmons, *New University*, Leicester 1958)

2.19 Liverpool University men's hostel Greenbank Drive 1947–8. 'Library'; clearly this term has little to do with books, but much with relaxation. (*B* 21-5-1948, p. 616)

no hope of adopting the full college system in the state-financed Redbricks or Civics for one plain reason: cost. A more appropriate model at that point were the colleges of Durham, which were much more dependent on the university, yet these were rarely mentioned. Britain's numerous small Teacher Training Colleges usually excelled with a high proportion of residence. Moreover, their origins in the church colleges of the nineteenth century were close to the philosophy of Newman or Arnold which also informed much of the ideology of Oxbridge. However, because of their lower academic status they could hardly serve as direct models.

That said, elements of Oxbridge college life remained the ideal and ideologists and designers continuously tried to adapt the old elements into novel institutional and architectural solutions. All seven of the New Universities took up Oxbridge institutional elements. It was the provincial wanting-to-be-a-college, the Hall of Residence, as it was grandly called (hall, itself, being an old Oxbridge synonym for college), which forms the single most important institution in our whole investigation. It is, however, in many respects important to keep hall and college apart. Early halls could sometimes be more self-contained than even an old college. They were usually set up by private funding and often did not come under the university's authority. An early and orthodox view is that of John Murray, principal of what was to become Exeter University, in 1948. We read, generally, of 'authority', 'spirit', 'moral and social influence'; of the need for a warden 'with pastoral gifts', that the 'matron should be a person of good social class', of 'disciplinary values', of 'accepted hierarchy . . . domestic and garden staff': the 'real unity rests on the admission of these differences'. More striking even are the physical conditions: within an analogy to the home, rather than a large institution, it is best to use 'fine old homes' which should have their own grounds, 10–15 acres, 'of rural and sylvan aspect', 'two or three tennis courts'; 'an urbanised hall is a sin against youth'. Clearly, the ideal of the university hall overlaps with that of the old-style boarding school, mixed with elements of the gentlemen's club (figs 2.18 and 2.19).

A much more practical line is taken in Keith Murray's Report of the same year, 1948, by the later Sir Keith, indeed, the future UGC chairman. His approach is more strictly instrumentalist: a hall must create conditions of privacy, silence, warmth, light, good meals, reference books etc., which 'make for quicker and better results'. Murray lays down the exact facilities required to fulfil such aims. 'Rest' in particular is mentioned again and again: the purpose of the common room is 'to relax in attractive, comfortable and restful surroundings . . .'; the students should be 'living in an atmosphere of academic calm'. There is much detail about the service aspect. Very high standards are taken for granted by Keith Murray, too: one member of staff for five students. There is some dispute over the ideal size of the hall, for John Murray sixty to seventy is the maximum; for Keith Murray it is 100–150; the latter figure was considered good for economy – a rare consideration in those early days. Students should, and were, selected as to their suitability for the life of those communities. Finally, halls for women would differ somewhat from those for men (women 'needing laundry and sewing rooms and hairdressing cubicles, men need a boot room'). The cost: normally a cool £1,500 to £2,000 per student place; it was reckoned that the communal facilities accounted for 50 per cent of it. Keith Murray reports suggestions to achieve economies through combining the kitchens of two halls; not for him, as this would 'abolish a healthy competition between halls to build up a reputation for their cuisine'.

Nine years after the Murray Report another detailed investigation appeared; again under the auspices of Sir Keith Murray, now the UGC chairman. It seems largely coloured by the outlook of sub-committee chairman, William Roy Niblett, professor of education at London University; we have already briefly cited the educational convictions of another member of the sub-committee, Alan Bullock, and we shall have the opportunity to discuss Eric James's educational university philosophy at York. Niblett does not see any reason to discuss or amend the practical stipulations in the Keith Murray Report. His aim is to restate what Murray only occasionally refers to, the hall's socio-educational ideology and to give advice about the academic-educational running of the hall. The Niblett tract is drenched in moral-educational language. The same basic theme is repeated innumerable times; exaggerations abound: the new kind of hall 'requires a revolution of mind and attitude', or near tautologies: 'much of the liberalising and civilising power of an education is exercised imperceptibly by the values powerfully embodied in it'. Living at home or in lodgings cannot possibly do the student any good, according to Niblett. The hall 'avoids the real difficulties of living daily in two atmospheres'. As regards the running, Niblett again abounds in general exhortations: 'a blend of dignity and informality in the conduct of its affairs', 'one should pass easily from the ceremonious to the simple mode' of behaviour. Niblett underlines the importance of the formal dinner, with students being waited upon 'every evening'. There is one major presupposition in the way Niblett stresses the necessity of the hall: the increasingly frequent low social background of students: 'they arrive in hall shy and awkward, leave as a pleasant and balanced personality'; 'life in hall turns schoolboys into adults, prepared to take their part in the community'.

The Niblett Report was soon chided for being not a sociological investigation but simply a statement of opinion. But there is no doubt that it helped to keep up the momentum in the debate on the provision of student residences. Although there is little discussion about the layout of a hall, Niblett did, however, opt for small groups of rooms on the 'staircase plan', or in '"parlour groups"', where a number of study bedrooms cluster around a small common room', which became the most influential factual remark in the whole report. Niblett's architectural ideas appeared straighfor-ward, they had remained those of the pre-Modernist days: it was enough to provide buildings of quality and 'dignity'.

However, by 1960, the Hall of Residence was suddenly beginning to appear out-dated. It was the very demand for it that brought about its demise. What had rarely occurred to the providers earlier on now struck home. Halls were too expensive. This fact now also led them to appear impractical. Halls were usually located at some con-siderable distance from the teaching buildings, especially in London. 'University life tends to be reduced to a long bus ride'. This meant that the elaborate facilities were completely empty for most of the day. If halls were to be kept to the Niblett size of 120 or 150 students, how could one find, or afford five or ten new sites, let alone build on them. For the provincial student, to live 'in hall' was, in fact, a privilege. The great majority of halls were the result of private benefactions, hence they were often based on suburban mansions. By the late 1950s the UGC made clear that it would not, in principle pay for the building of student residences; it only gave funds towards the cost of the design and towards the fittings. In order to obtain this help, the uni-versity had to stick to the UGC's cost limits. In 1958 the UGC wanted to bring down the figure for one student's accommodation from £1,500 to £840, calculating it simply for a room of 225 square feet (21 square metres). By 1960 the figure was £945. Robbins later suggested that rooms could be had for £600 in converted old houses; by the late 1960s, as we shall see, Lancaster and East Anglia began to build rooms for about £700 plus.

What few people appear to have foreseen was the considerable change in students' habits, especially a turn away from formal dining, and a new preference for cheap cafeteria self-service and towards their own cooking. During the 1960s many Oxbridge colleges abolished, or reduced formal dinners, and the general bar became a new focus of college life, for seniors and juniors alike. Universities were beginning to give up their rules regarding presence in college, for instance the 'exeats' for going away, or late visiting. Brett already in 1957 remarked about the 'superfluity' of all the common rooms in the halls; the main requirement was the private room for each student. Another factor which ran alongside was the growing distrust in the educa-tional paternalistic ideals. Suddenly, after so many assertions about the forming influ-ence of halls, it was remarked that 'we do not know' about major aspects of student residence. We now witness the onset of empirical sociological research. More left-wing orientated sociologists, like Peter Marris, stated in 1963 that the 'residence in the halls does not influence the pattern of social life very profoundly', it might even 'impose arbitrary segregations' or 'retard the process of reaching maturity'. In any case, students increasingly preferred to live entirely unsupervised.

A look towards Scandinavian and other Continental countries in the early 1960s gave the final push. There, many students lived in rooms grouped together as flats, often twelve or more rooms plus a 'farmhouse kitchen', bathroom and toilets – though students in Scandinavia tended to be somewhat older. We now witness the beginning of a new and definitive type of student residence, the 'study bedroom'. In some cases minimal academic and moral supervision remained, by placing tutors' flats adjacent to the students' rooms, and some extra communal rooms were often still provided. But the chief spheres of socialising were now the small kitchen/common rooms and the students' own rooms. Niblett's objections to sleeping-only accommodation were not heeded. But the emphasis was not merely on socialisation, of whatever kind. 'Study' also meant a new emphasis on the student's private sphere, and the cramped, and often shared bedrooms of the older kind were usually not conducive to that. In retrospect it appeared that in the old type of hall the student's own solitary study had not been of a high priority – it was subordinated to the organised togetherness of the dinning rooms, common rooms, and even the hall's library.

Lastly, the issue of mixed student residences came to the fore. Although the question of coeducation had been raised occasionally, the thought of a mixed hall could hardly be entertained during the 1950s. Jellicoe's grand campus plan for Nottingham of 1955 separates the splendid arrays of men and women's halls into two distinct groups. Increasingly though, by the early 1960s, colleges (of all kinds) were beginning to go coed. By 1965, Kent, Lancaster and Essex residences claimed to be the first in doing the same, the latter accommodating men and women on alternate floors, while York placed them in different wings. From the late 1960s changes in social habits quickly left all institutional measures behind and by the mid-1970s we read that 'living together is openly accepted'. Arguably, nothing changed the character of university life so much as the growing proportion of women, and the growing mix of the sexes. And yet, there is little comment about this, at least during the 1960s. The actual proportion of women grew rather slowly, from 25 per cent in 1962 to 34 in 1973. But there were strong divergences: in Oxbridge it was traditionally low (12 per cent in 1962), and the change to the coed college hardly started before the 1970s, while the New Universities contained male and female students in about equal numbers from the start (Sussex began with 67 per cent women).

Finally, one has to be reminded that all the criticism and changes took place while, in the context of general university expansion, a vast number of student residences were actually being built. In practice, the character of a hall, the degree of paternalism or student independence was due to a host of factors. The terms 'residence' or 'hall' kept on being used. It was often simply the sheer size of many of the new developments which left the old atmosphere of villa-cum-club-cum-boarding-school behind (figs 2.20 and 2.21).

Needless to emphasise, the actual layouts varied greatly. Many major architects now concerned themselves with the type, lavishly at Oxbridge (see page 64) and more economically in most other universities. One of the largest of the complexes was Richard Sheppard's Weeks Hall of Residence ('Hostel'), Princes Gardens, South Kensington for Imperial College, London, planned from 1957. There were to be more than ten floors with over 1,000 rooms in several blocks surrounding a large court. The way in which, on each floor, eight rooms are grouped around a staircase, accessible from the ground and fourth floors respectively, provides a combination of a modern mass institution with the Oxbridge model and was dubbed 'community life in modern buildings'. Above all, the block is only a few steps away from the teaching buildings (fig. 2.22). Some of the most noted experiments of the early 1960s were conducted in Leeds. A very large looking complex, Bodington Hall, was built for 600 students from 1959, $9\frac{1}{2}$ miles (15 kilometres) away. Chamberlin's Plan of 1960 (fig 2.31) then envisaged as many as 3,000 students living on campus. As an 'experiment', Leeds built two kinds of accommodation side by side: a hall of residence, the Charles Morris Hall, and a study bedroom block, the Henry Price Building, originally planned, each, for about 200 students. The differences between the two types are,

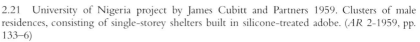

2.20 (*left*) Nottingham College of Arts and Crafts, student residences ('vertical college'), project by D.I. Brindle *c.* 1959 – a kind of experiment that was very rare. The drawing was not published in an English architectural journal. (*BW* 51/52, 21-12-1959, p. 1489)

2.21 University of Nigeria project by James Cubitt and Partners 1959. Clusters of male residences, consisting of single-storey shelters built in silicone-treated adobe. (*AR* 2-1959, pp. 133–6)

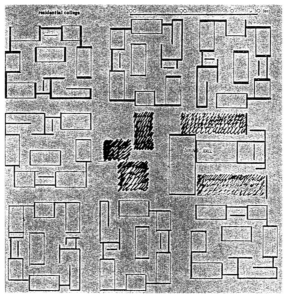

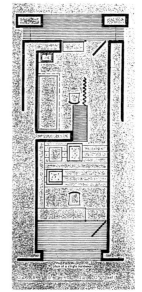

however, not immediately clear and appear to consist chiefly in the greater and lesser amount of communal facilities, respectively. The UGC architects' department itself built an 'experimental hall', Whiteknights, for Reading University, a rather low and spreadout building, in keeping with the park-like quality of the campus (fig. 2.25). The chief designer, Guy Oddie, purposely created an unspectacular look, 'a quiet air of dignity without stuffiness'. Manchester University was building a very large complex, out in the suburbs, at Fallowfield, and devised a composite name to please all preconceptions, Owen's Park Student Village, for 1,500 inhabitants, with blocks of variously sized bedrooms and numerous eating facilities interspersed (fig. 2.24). Six to twelve students share a 'pantry'. There is also a nineteen-storey tower block – the idea that a tower was an economic way of providing large numbers of rooms around

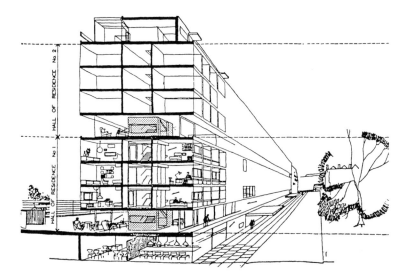

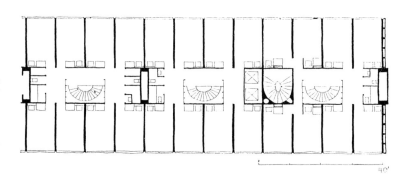

2.22   London Imperial College of Science and Technology, Weeks Hall, Princes Gardens, Sheppard, Robson and Partners 1964–8. 'Stacked Colleges': The 'Halls of Residence nos 1 and 2' comprise four floors each, of which three floors are for bedrooms, accessed by subsidiary internal ('Oxbridge-type') staircases (see fig. 2.23), and one floor for common rooms. The main staircases (and the lift) are indicated by the way they do not open into the intermediate residential floors. (R. Dober (1965), p. 13; *AR* 10-1963, p. 294)

small social centre had been voiced as early as 1957. The Carnatic Scheme for the University of Liverpool at Mossley Hill included three tower blocks within a quasi-town in a park, while a more leisurely, yet unified, but also most unusually shaped layout was provided by Gillespie, Kidd and Coia at the 'The Lawns', Cottingham, for the University of Hull. Its striking forms were given the best critical treatment, not, as with the others, in the *Architects' Journal*, but in the *Architectural Review*.

In spite of their architectural novelty one may see those complexes as end-points of a development, late descendants of the hall of residence idea. It was still the university who felt it had to cater for all aspects of student life. By the later 1960s and the early 1970s thinking about student residences was moving on again. One of the characteristics of the situation was the further broadening of research. The field of student support services differed considerably from that in the USA. The student mental and physical health services in England were catching up slowly; their aims were entirely practical; academic research was, however, devoted far more to socio-logical and socio-psychological issues and was kept, in contrast to its American counterpart, at a distance from simple instrumentality. We have already cited the apparently sudden realisation in around 1960 of their ignorance of the way residences 'work'. In 1965 Niblett organised the 'Centre for the Study of Educational Policies' in his

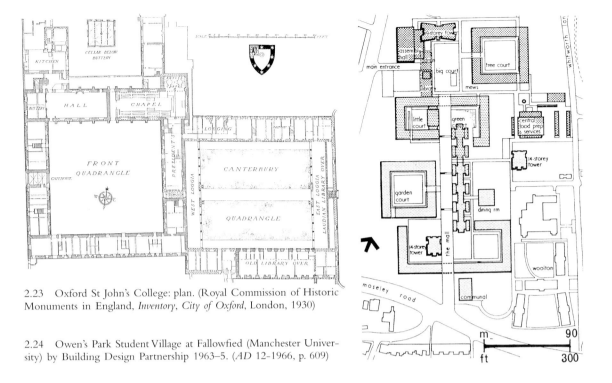

2.23 Oxford St John's College: plan. (Royal Commission of Historic Monuments in England, *Inventory, City of Oxford*, London, 1930)

2.24 Owen's Park Student Village at Fallowfied (Manchester University) by Building Design Partnership 1963–5. (*AD* 12-1966, p. 609)

2.25 Reading University Whiteknights Hall by the Architects' Group of the University Grants Committee (Guy Oddie, Roger Clynes) 1963–5. (*AJ* 3-3-1965, pp. 527–9)

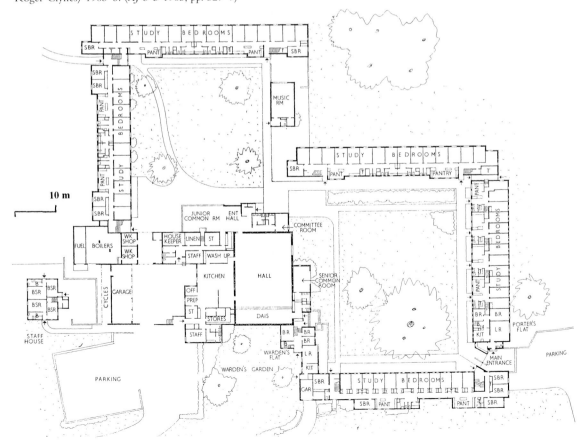

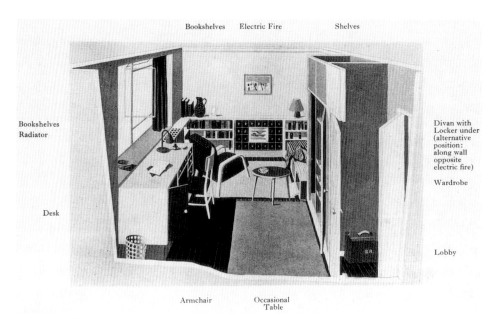

Bookshelves   Electric Fire   Shelves

Bookshelves
Radiator

Desk

Divan with
Locker under
(alternative
position:
along wall
opposite
electric fire)

Wardrobe

Lobby

Armchair   Occasional
Table

2.26   Study bedroom, model drawing, 1948. ([K.A.H.] Murray Report (*The Planning of University Halls of Residence, . . . Report of a Commission appointed by the Committee of Vice-Chancellors and Principals of GB and Ireland*, Oxford, 1948)

2.27   Study bedrooms compared. (*AD* 12-1966, pp. 613–14)

University of Essex tower blocks

Finance: UGC
Gross area of RCU: 125·5ft³
Cost per RCU: within £945
Cost of furnishing RCU: £140
Services: central heating and lighting
Communal facilities: kitchen/dining room, laundry trunk store and telephone
Grouping: 13 or 14 rooms arranged as a flat, including a kitchen/dining room containing two cookers, two sinks and four refrigerators.
Occupancy of s/b: single

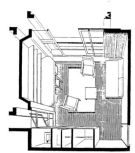

Graduate building, Corpus Christi, Cambridge

Finance: private
Gross area of RCU: from 160 to 210ft³
Cost per RCU: £2700
Cost of furnishing RCU: £180
Services: half the rooms have a washbasin; background heat by grille tube with a fan booster controlled and paid for by the student; one fixed light and two socket outlets (electricity paid for by the student)
Communal facilities: a washroom, two w.c.s, a bathroom and kitchen on each floor; a laundry and common room shared by all students
Grouping: 12 rooms per stair
Occupancy of s/b: single
Remarks: standards are intended to be higher than in a normal undergraduate hostel

Owen's Park tower block, University of Manchester

Finance: UGC
Room area: 100ft³
Cost per RCU: £1450
Cost of furnishing RCU: within £150
Services: low pressure hot water heating, lighting points with circuit breaker for each room
Communal facilities: washrooms, small kitchen for light meals, laundry, and storage
Grouping: four groups of twelve rooms on two floors sharing meeting/common room. Also within the building are two music rooms, TV room and dark room
Occupancy of s/b: single

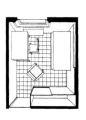

University of Lancaster

Finance: UGC for first college, private for second and third
Gross area of RCU: 145ft³
Cost per RCU: £900
Cost of furnishing RCU: £150
Services: heating and lighting
Communal facilities: washroom, cleaner's room, utility room and kitchen/lounge
Grouping: 10 rooms arranged as a domestic flat with communal facilities
Occupancy of s/b: mainly single, 20–30 per cent double
Remarks: rooms are arranged in three-storey buildings around courts, with penthouses for administrative staff and teachers

2.28   Study bedroom, Warwick University. (*AR* 4-1970, p. 296)

In 1965 Niblett organised the 'Centre for the Study of Educational Policies' in his Institute of Education at London University and the influential Society for Research into Higher Education began its activities in 1967 from the same base. For these researchers, all previous investigations were lacking in precision and plausibility. They now set off on a vast scheme of fact and opinion gathering and close analysis. The result, after some six years, was, however, inconclusive. It abounds in statements such as 'there is no evidence that' and its final conclusion is: 'We cannot say that residence makes an essential contribution to liberal education'.

Students at the age of 18 were now undeniably considered to be adults. As early as 1966 it was asked why the university should be dealing with student residences at all; students were no different from ordinary citizens. A little later the National Union of Students complained that the state, which was normally very concerned with housing for special groups such as the elderly, did not provide for the student part of the population; it even hinted, paradoxically, at the privileges of older halls: why should students be provided with such 'luxurious accommodation'? Most student residences still cost more to build than the equivalent unit of accommodation in council housing. In the 1970s, the architectural critic John McKean held categorically that there is no such thing as student housing, only housing. Even rooms in older houses could work satisfactorily. The custom of students getting together to rent a house was apparently just beginning at this time. Finally, we must remember that 'community' was still a live issue with some radical students and though it slightly changed its name – to 'commune' – it could generate internal rules every bit as strict as those of a Niblett Hall. However, the question in the end may again simply be about numbers; notwithstanding all the arguments – would the university expansion of those decades have been possible without university-built student accommodation (figs 2.26–2.28)?

From the student's residence as a quasi separate unit of the university we must turn back to the institution as a whole. On the traditional campus the stately and highly decorated central buildings signified the hub of the social, educational and academic authority of the institution. This authority was especially manifest on particular occasions, such as 'congregation', the day of degree-giving, when the message of the buildings was reinforced by an elaborate ritual. The 1960s did not intend to break with this tradition but the analysis of university life shifted considerably, away from definitions of hierarchical and fixed institutionality towards a more diffuse picture of socialisation – and here the American word comes back in again – the campus. Moving away from the concept of the hall of residence towards the new type of study bedroom block had also meant moving away from a point of firm, self-contained institutionalisation; instead of a medium-sized unit, a hall of, say, 100 students, with central common rooms we now meet an array of much smaller and informal units for eight or fifteen students. One of the most convincing arguments in the Niblett Report had been that a large university is too large for the student to give it their 'loyalty' and that smaller sub-units are needed. However, as was explicitly stated in the USA (see page 24), the issue of size – that is, the optimal size of the larger institution – was one on which educationalists and planners could never settle – although the New Universities' notional 3,000 sounded plausible during the mid-1960s.

One of the customary foci of student life, and one that came prominently into use after the war, is the students union, a kind of club of which all students are members. A familiar example to many is 'the Union' of London University in Mallet Street, large, multifunctional, spacious and comfortable. There is no academic supervision of any kind. Some argued that more of the unions' facilities should be taken over by the halls; others said that with the enlargement of the university one central union could become too big for its members to identify with the institution. Niblett explicitly resisted the enlargement of the students union and claimed that 'some students would prefer new halls . . . to additional student buildings'. The issue of the students union building became a major one in the planning of the New Universities. As we shall see, some of them fiercely insisted that there was no need for it because the way the whole campus had been planned as a complex social unit, as at York, Kent, Essex and Lancaster. The students themselves invariably clamoured for such a building, especially during the period of the troubles around 1970. A closely related major campaign was the advocation of 'membership' of the hall and the provision of special rooms for study for those students who did not sleep there. Nothing new in this, of course, because membership for the whole student body had always been a facet of Oxbridge college life. There could be variations on the theme, such as the St Cuthbert's Society, part of Durham University, which comprised groups of students in lodgings. The corollary of the student's club was the faculty club or senior common room; it too, went through a torturous process of being called into question (though there was very little open discussion on this). Some of the New Universities, Essex in particular, insisted on not providing special facilities for staff at all.

Virtually all parts of the campus were now investigated as regards their social function. It was maintained that the department was the chief 'social unit' of the university; it was even claimed that it provided the only natural opportunity for staff and students to meet informally. So far, in this chapter, we have dealt with the student's 'own' sphere in the university. What has been neglected is the way discussions about universities oscillated between the stress on the sphere of the students' education and the more purely academic and research activities. We noted the entrenched debate on graduate research vs. undergraduate education across in the USA. Like some of the older Civics, the New Universities stressed high-profile research from the start. Within this emphasis there was a new slant towards cooperation among researchers. The choice of the term 'school' for the larger academic unit in some of the Seven was meant to further this aim. A common statement was that the cutting edge of research was found at the borderlines between disciplines. A further idea was that teaching, even that for undergraduate beginners, should be closely integrated with all the research activities of a 'school'. One is reminded of the famous German university maxim: the unity of research and teaching (see page 203). But English university discourse would not normally refer to matters American, nor German, in this context. Indeed, nobody would go so far as the Germans, where there was traditionally no concern at all on the part of the university for the student's life outside the teaching rooms. There was, however, an older notion about a certain contrast between Oxbridge and 'the rest': at least some of the provincial universities would put special stress on research, while Oxford was still perceived to be concerned chiefly with the education of gentlemen. But during the years under discussion, the 1960s, nobody would want to repeat such a statement; after all, the tutorial, or supervision system at Oxbridge did seem the best way to guarantee high-level teaching. There was, however, a special new emphasis on openness and even informality in the teaching process in the New Universities, and there was the occasional remark about 'the rest' (and that could include Oxbridge) being 'stuffy'. In the intricate planning of the main complexes of the New Universities, first at Sussex, and then especially at Lancaster and Bath, there was intensive thinking about the relationship between teaching and recreation spaces.

Another way of discussing the issue was simply to stress the importance of the centre of the university. A lone early proposal came from Eric Ashby in the 1950s, a major Cambridge figure, and one who knew universities worldwide. He advocated longer opening hours for refectories and libraries, in order to attract students and, again, to prevent them spending their time in unsuitable lodgings. One of his statements was to reverberate through university planning in the 1960s – the need to avoid, at all costs, the '9 to 5 university'. In the end, Niblett, too, conceded that students should 'spend as much as possible of their day within the university precincts and that facilities for work, meals and leisure activities therefore need to be provided'. His report went on: 'We therefore suggest that student houses . . . might be established near the main buildings of the university to serve as non-residential halls.' This sounds like a committee's compromise. It must have been Niblett who insisted that such a 'student house' had to be 'under the leadership of its own warden'. No built examples of this mongrel institution are known. Planning, in fact, went the other way, so to speak and it is the more mundane institutions which it was felt necessary to include in the heart of the campus, namely shops, banks, a post office. When Norwich planned its campus, the architects obtained a planning consent very early on from the city which forbade shops on the edge of the university.

We are, in fact, in for a paradigm change in the development of the thinking about institutions and socialisation. To state it in terms of the practical solutions on campus: apart from the meeting rooms within the departments, the best places to meet in the university were the cafes and restaurants. What this meant in practice was not just another kind of sub-institution, but an onslaught on the very kind of institutionalism advocated so far. In the cafes and restaurants, according to the sociologist Peter Marris, relationships would be 'non-artificial'. Exactly the same qualities had been ascribed to the new way of grouping study bedrooms around a small breakfast/meeting room where students could 'meet casually in the small kitchens'; students in university residences no longer congregated according to institutional patterns. The student health expert Nicholas B. Malleson claimed that 'the chance and contiguity element is dominant' – '. . . the fluke . . . of being on the same workbench in the lab'. 'Do not try and impose community structure through supervision and the deliberate mixture of staff and students', but encourage 'unforced associations . . . in smaller groups, through a variety of activities'. Major benefits were expected from new teaching methods 'like the free group discussion'. It was even claimed that the Oxbridge colleges of the Middle Ages had begun as 'unplanned and spontaneous institutions'. Very occasionally we hear a late authoritarian voice: 'We need wardens to encourage contacts among the mass of students . . . [it is] quite unrealistic to expect contacts on a wide enough scale to develop from casual encounters at local bars'.

'Spontaneity' stood for a set of phenomena that to most observers appeared entirely new. It first of all represented a paradigmatic change in that 'youth' was no longer considered a group within society which primarily needed to be directed by other agents of society, but one which had, and was somehow entitled to have, its own mode of existence. As far as general architectural discussions were concerned, this coincided with the perceived 'emancipation' of the users vis-à-vis the design authorities (see page 287). It also meant a further strengthening of the sociologists' position vis-à-vis the pedagogue: the latter now had to learn about, and to respect, a new phenomenon, 'youth culture'. Its particulars, such as the meteoric rise of the Beatles, do not concern us here; what was crucial, however, was the overall positive picture of the movement that pertained during the early to mid-1960s: 'idealism, spontaneity, intuitiveness, honesty, volatility'. Its protest potential as well as the trend towards permissiveness still appeared mild.

Within the university this profound change in educational policy and institutional thinking needs to be reviewed once more from a wider angle. Clearly, much of the new thinking was spurred by economy: the old paternalist institutionalism was simply too expensive. Traditionally, 'university' signified an exceptional environment which was provided for a small number who should be nothing but grateful for it. No arguments were conducted as to whether or not these kinds of institutions 'worked'; they would unfailingly impress the lower-class kid. Hence the simple instrumentalism still found in the Murray Report on Halls in 1948. Niblett's institutions were still paternalist, but his message was more general and less instrumentalist. In 1957, when cries to turn Britain into a efficient technological society were at a high pitch, he wanted 'community' to be something more intentional, to be more deeply felt, as a commitment by all the inhabitants of a hall, in the 'liberal arts' sense. It was only around 1960, when the modern Welfare State axiom, state services for all, entered the universities. It meant that anything that smacked of privilege had to be phased out. Paternalism became severely discredited. In education, as in all other spheres of life, everybody was to be 'equal'. This greatly weakened the notion of imposed special institutional structures. Students had their own forms of community life. The earlier definition of an institution was to organise everybody according to pre-set patterns. A new definition of the institution university, apart from anything narrowly connected with learning or research, was that it provided occasions and places for members to practice any social habit they might bring with them or might care to acquire; a multilayered institution, much left to the accidental; certainly not monolithic or hierarchical. The most important quality of association was spontaneity. A great diversity of meeting points were needed.

This new movement, however, did not, as yet, point towards the complete dissolution of the institution. It was only around 1970 when some ideologists postulated the university as an atomised institution. We have already quoted McKean saying there was no student housing, but only housing – a university dissolved into small ad-hoc groups of whoever happened to want to teach or learn, wherever and whenever. It was a time when many academic town planners preached total indeterminacy and interchangeability which will be dealt with below in the chapter of late 1960s planning notions and new concepts of the 'user'. Until the later 1960s 'the sense of identity with the whole university' was usually still a strong one. When the American university planning theorist Richard Dober came to England in 1964 he was completely taken in by the English thinking of that moment, the search for a unitary interpretation of campus life. In what he calls 'the continuous teaching environment', Dober notes the avoidance of 'rigid distinctions between instructional, communal and residential buildings [which] reduce the opportunity for casual and undirected attachment'. What is needed, instead, according to Dober is a 'physical design that spreads activity points – meeting places, so to speak – throughout the campus . . .' (see page 195). Indeed, the dovetailing of college and campus was to be the intense concern for the planners of most of the New Universities, overtly at York and Lancaster, implicitly at Essex and East Anglia and explictly rejected only by Warwick.

In an attempt to sum up these complex issues of university community and university residence community, of college and campus, or college vs. campus, we can cite three factions. One is tempted to begin with an educational Left and Right. On the one hand, the new Welfare State, as voiced, for instance, in the Robbins Report where all students are adults, student residence is a practical issue; and on the other, the old guard with its wardens 'in loco parentis', where the university is seen as a substitute for the (smart) home. As we shall see, the New Universities put themselves right into the 'Centre': the university would care for every aspect of the student's life by providing special institutions, or sub-institutions; and these institutions, residences, central social and academic facilities must be related to each other as closely as possible – while in 1958 Niblett had still maintained that good academic supervision in halls is more important a factor than geographical nearness to the campus. Facilities should also no longer be rigidly 'zoned' as in the older Civic or Redbrick setup, or on the older Modernist type of campus. But there was now no agreement as to how all these relationships should be planned in detail. Some still verged towards paternalism (Kent), others took the greatest pains to stress a 'freer' kind of association (Essex). The sociologist R.H. Halsey's convenient summing-up of 1961 held true until about 1965: 'The evidence, on balance, suggests that student opinion continues

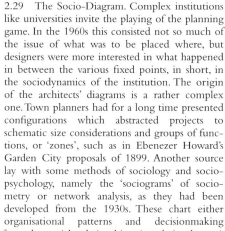

INDIVIDUAL · · · · GROUP · · · DEPARTMENT

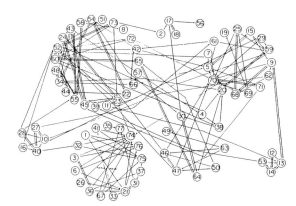

2.29 The Socio-Diagram. Complex institutions like universities invite the playing of the planning game. In the 1960s this consisted not so much of the issue of what was to be placed where, but designers were more interested in what happened in between the various fixed points, in short, in the sociodynamics of the institution. The origin of the architects' diagrams is a rather complex one. Town planners had for a long time presented configurations which abstracted projects to schematic size considerations and groups of functions, or 'zones', such as in Ebenezer Howard's Garden City proposals of 1899. Another source lay with some methods of sociology and socio-psychology, namely the 'sociograms' of sociometry or network analysis, as they had been developed from the 1930s. These chart either organisational patterns and decisionmaking processes, or sets of psycho-social relationships (or their absence) between individuals or groups. In many cases these socio-diagrams serve not only as a mere schematisations, but also as exhortation or evocation. It appears that the 1960s presented a particularly strong overlap between all the disciplines: the sociologists put increased emphasis on real location (rather than presenting purely numerical values), while the planners and architects abstracted and generalised to a considerable degree from locational-spatial reality. As Jacob L. Moreno, the founder of sociometry once remarked: arranging neighbourhoods is commonly done 'by accident or according to architectural or industrial planning . . . the architect of the future will be a student of sociometry'.

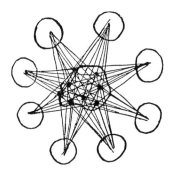

From the 1950s we note further metaphorising and analogising, especially with molecular and cell-biology. It was the apparent great simplicity which made these drawings so convincing, for instance in Le Corbusier's innumerable sketches. Sketchiness and immediacy could be seen as directly related to the 'organic', but, of course, they also fed on the notion of the designer as original artist and guru. Among the acknowledged sources of Alison and Peter Smithson's socio-diagrams from the mid-1950s were the paintings of Jackson Pollock and Jean Dubuffet. In Kevin Lynch's *The Image of the City*, a 'book about the look of cities', we frequently meet versions of the biologistic sociogram which are meant to help directly with a city's or a district's 'imageability'. In a wider sense the architects' socio-diagrams presented a conundrum central to Modernism: artistic freedom and variety coupled with social policy convictions. Each one of the diverse solutions was considered optimal, socially and architecturally. By the later 1960s we observe a new kind of diagram in which lines are straightened and a grid pattern is regarded as a 'neutral' communication 'matrix' (cf. ills. 5.1 below etc.). From top to bottom: C. Perrow, *Complex Organizations*, Dallas Tex. 1979 (1972), pp. 217–18. J.L.

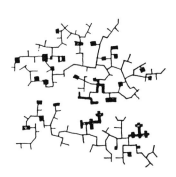

Moreno, *Sociometry Reader*, Glencoe IL 1960, p. 79 (Relationships between the inhabitants of Atiro and Pueblo Nuevo, 1949); Le Corbusier and F. de Pierrefeu, *The Home of Man* (*La Maison des hommes*), London, 1948: Paris and satellite towns; A. and P. Smithson, 'Appreciated unit', *Team X Primer*, London, 1968; K. Lynch, *The Image of the City*, Cambridge MA, 1960, pp. 5, 40.

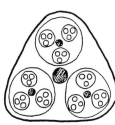

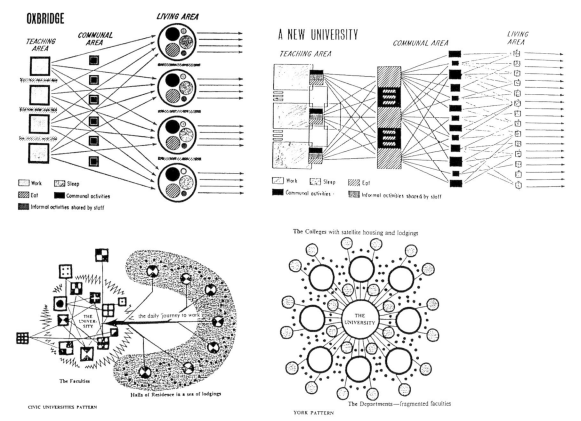

2.30 A diagrammatic representation of the functioning of various types of universities. Above: Peter Marris, 'Halls or Digs for Students?' (*New Society* 16-5-1963, pp. 8–10). Below: York Development Plan, 1962.

Beyond the chief message, that of the integration of university and student life, there is much that is divergent and even contradictory in these drawings. Marris essentially pleads for the place of interdisciplinary teaching to be considered the main focus of 'university communal life'. The York drawings introduce yet another element to diagrammatic presentation, a representational factor which goes beyond the purely schematic and locational, namely caricature, in the way elements of the 'civic pattern' appear diversified and scattered. The ideal plan for York, finally, is highly problematic. Whereas the 'fragmented faculties', the grey dots, do indicate the way subjects are dispersed, the large centre 'university' presents precisely the kind of concentration which York wanted to avoid, namely by means of the dispersal of central social facilities into the colleges. Overall, the diagram of York presents a geometrical ideal which takes on a life of its own.

to be inspired by the collegiate ideal. The task of university planning is to interpret this ideal realistically for expanded numbers of varied social origin.' Cambridge man Frank Thistlethwaite, vice chancellor of East Anglia, did not hesitate to call the plan for his enormous-looking new campus 'a college writ large' (figs 2.29 and 2.30).

TOWN PLANNING AND PUBLIC HOUSING PARADIGMS:
PRECINCT, TOWNSCAPE, URBAN CLUSTER AND THE ELEVATED PEDESTRIAN

Further on in this chapter we will meet the term 'architects' universities'. Such an expression could arise because the architects were staking their claim to be involved in higher education construction in a forceful, even cunning way. But we may also state that we have reached a natural point where the designer of a campus, or a block of residences 'takes over'. So far, all our spokespersons have been academics, administrators and sociologists of education. It appeared, moreover, that from about the mid-1960s onwards their researches were ending either in doubts or even in the complete rejection of educational traditions. For the architects of the years 1962–6, such an outlook did not apply. Naturally, a negative or sceptical attitude would have been detrimental to acquiring a commission. But the architects did believe in models for dealing precisely with the kind of job required, a community of several thousand, much of the time closely involved with each other. The watchword was 'urban'. The architects had developed this concept from the 1940s in conjunction with town planners, housing officials and sociologists. From the late 1950s they saw themselves as the main protagonists of a new urbanist movement. They thus felt comfortable with the planning of, if not large institutions, but certainly of close-knit communities and had no qualms whatsoever in 'taking over' from the educationalists.

Planning a university presented 'no difficulty' to architect-town planner and critic Lionel Brett in 1957:

> Universities don't need industry or marshalling yards, back gardens or allotments, universities don't generate their own motor traffic [sic] or have to accommodate masses of other people's. None of these disintegrators have to be grappled with. Universities have the priceless advantage, for the planner, of pedestrian circulation, self-containment, strictly limited size, and buildings of high quality and varied function and outline.

In short, the university is, or could be an ideal town. As is well known, proposals for urban utopias are as varied as the periods which produced them; furthermore, utopias could be retrospective as well as progressive. Just for the record again, Brett concludes that the only two examples of the ideal city of learning in England are Oxford and Cambridge. As Mark Girouard put it a little later: 'freedom from traffic, interpenetration of buildings and greenery, the Oxford and Cambridge colleges are right in line with the most modern principles of planning'.

The idea of a university as a town goes a long way back. Even within International Modernism, the tradition reaches back to the 1930s. William Curtis, in an important early contribution to the theme, has traced the way in which Le Corbusier 'treated the problem of the university as a pretext for the demonstrations of collectivity and urbanism'. In his book of 1937, *Quand les cathédrales étaient blanches*, Le Corbusier is enchanted by the American college and campus: 'Every college and university is a urbanistic unit in itself, a town, small or large.' Curtis then traces the same spirit – more or less convincingly – through Le Corbusier's hall of residence of 1930, the Pavillion Suisse in the Cité Universitaire in Paris, via Stirling's Florey Building and the Smithsons' addition to St Hilda's College (both in Oxford) and then through to the 'cité lineaire' of the University of East Anglia. Later, Curtis followed a similar theme in one of Le Corbusier's last buildings, the Harvard Centre for the visual Arts in Cambridge Massachusetts, and especially in the way Le Corbusier devised an elevated walkway, taking up a pre-existing communication line, right through the middle of his square building.

It has been stressed that twentieth-century American campus planning corresponded closely to the precept of zoning, allocating each function its separate location. Major efforts of avant-garde English town planning during the years 1953 to 1970 were directed against the rigid separation and spreading-out of functions. By 1957 Brett wanted universities to get away from the 'postwar loose scatter . . . in a parkland'. Four years earlier the *Architectural Review* had launched its heaviest attack on the low density of the celebrated English New Towns, such as Harlow, vilifying them as bland, monotonous, as 'prairie towns'. Michael Brawne and Michael Cassidy tried to draw analogies between the concepts of rigid zoning thinking in towns and universities when they contrasted the 'finite areas', such as the 'neighbourhoods' in the New Towns with a 'fluid group structure' kind of understanding of a town, or a university. There was a new concern for the centre. A key term of the 1950s was 'precinct'. Its chief quality was its liveliness and this was achieved by irregular layout, by spatial surprises, by being bordered with a variety of buildings. A new style of sketchy and lively drawings of towns, or, rather, of glimpses of town life, was developed by Gordon Cullen who worked closely with the *Architectural Review*. His proposal for a 'University Forum' for Imperial College, London in 1955 was a direct application of townscape visualisation. Models for picturesque townscape were the smaller old English towns, but also the 'Italian Hill Towns 'of Tuscany or Umbria. In order to achieve self-containedness, it was best to exclude vehicular traffic from a precinct. Casson and Conder's 1953 plan for the Cambridge Arts Faculties was the first to try and import the feel of a pedestrian precinct into a university. With their extremely sketchy drawings they tried to get across a new sense of the whole of the 'the living stream of university life'.

Architects thought nothing of switching from housing to university planning, and then possibly back to housing. For instance Patrick Hodgkinson used his and Martin's ideas of Harvey Court at Cambridge (fig. 2.15) in his giant public housing blocks at Brunswick Square in Bloomsbury. An ambitious scheme of comprehensive and dense town centre planning, the Barbican in the City of London, was followed by an attempt at a dense kind of suburban planning, 'Boston Manor' of 1958 (fig. 2.7); the designers, Chamberlin, Powell and Bon then tried very similar forms for their Churchill College entry (fig. 2.6), and finally in their plan for Leeds University of 1960. As regards the plethora of its 'urban' elements, high density, pedestrianisation, contact with the city centre and more, as well as with its complex buildings from the mid-1960s onwards, Leeds became the most notable university extension in England of its time (figs 2.31–2.33).

By 1960 the architectural avant-garde had been shifting their concerns again, to two related concepts, 'communication' and 'association'. In the writings of Peter and Alison Smithson, the notion and value of community was subtly bent into an intense concern with urban microspaces, that is, with what happens at the borderline between the private and public sphere, for instance the contacts around the front door of a house or flat. On the other hand, 'community' was re-interpreted as communication, within the smaller sphere of contacts between flats, or in the larger sphere between blocks of flats or between parts of towns. To the Smithsons, human settlements had to be understood as 'clusters' of activities, or as 'nodes' in a network of communications. An essential part of this organic metaphor (strictly organic, in the sense of using biological metaphors), was its non-diagrammatic look, that is, there was no conventional diagrammatic, straight line-rectiliniarity. To the Smithsons right angles or strict separational zoning all came under 'mechanical' and were alien to the nature of human

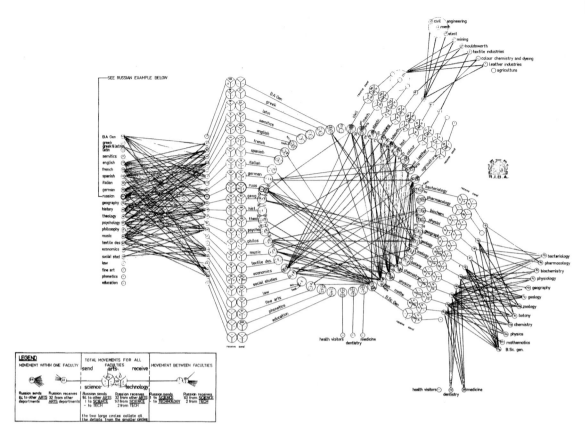

2.31   Leeds University: analysis of the relationship of departments (forecast for 1970). 'The circle of departments shows their relationship within different faculties and the columns outside the circle show the relationship of departments within the same faculties. The circles include the numbers of students which any one department sends to, and receives from, other departments. The number of departments which send to, or receive from, any one department is shown by the lines converging on that department.' (*University of Leeds Development Plan*, Chamberlin, Powell and Bon, publ. Leeds University, 1960)

settlements. Human communication does not proceed along straight lines and right angles but is more likely to take a diagonal or a slight curve. The essence of any human settlement or institution was represented in its communication network – all of which clearly ran parallel also to the 'new spontaneity' movement.

Now the separation of pedestrian and vehicular traffic became an even more intensely pursued issue. English designers once more joined a European Modernist avant-garde tradition which reached back to St Elia and Le Corbusier of the 1920s, where communication lines were singled out into separate elements, such as platforms or bridges, thereby linking all buildings into a single conglomerate. Indeed, after the first approximation in the London housing project for Golden Lane of 1952, the Smithsons' first major manifestation of clusters linked by communication lines was their entry for Sheffield University of 1953, a key image until well into the 1960s (fig. 2.34), and its first application, in turn, was the giant Park Hill Housing estate in Sheffield. In terms of intense complexity of single-building town centre planning, Cumbernauld in Scotland became the admired example in the early 1960s, while in terms of a balanced large new town the Hook New Town project of 1961/2 became a much cited model (fig. 2.95), containing as it did a very large central, elongated

2.32   Leeds University 1960 by Chamberlin, Powell and Bon. One notes the way in which all the buildings are linked. The subsequent revisions considerably increased the density and made very extensive use of the Smithsons' concept of street decks and bridges. (*University of Leeds Development Plan*, Chamberlin, Powell and Bon, publ. Leeds University, 1960)

2.33   Leeds University, part of Chancellor's Court by Chamberlin Powell and Bon from the mid-1960s.

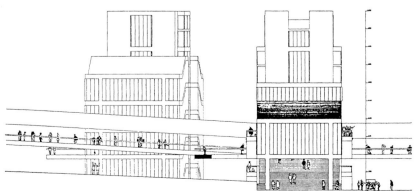

2.34   Alison and Peter Smithson: project for Sheffield University 1953: 'Patterns of pedestrian movement are the key to the architectural organisation of the building'. (A. and P. Smithson, *Urban Structuring*, London, 1967, Courtesy P. Smithson)

and elevated pedestrian precinct with a vehicular zone underneath. In fact, one of its designers, Hugh Morris adopted the abandoned Hook project directly for Bath University. This kind of elongated centre was sometimes called the 'spine'; one could also speak of 'linear planning', but in those years that line was usually bent to a greater or lesser extent. Soon, a further term was applied to this kind of structure, no matter whether a town, a shopping centre, an office complex, a holiday colony or a building for teaching: 'megastructure'. Moreover, this kind of conglomerate, and anti-diagrammatic planning in general, seemed to lend itself to easy extendability, an issue which rapidly gained importance around the mid-1960s. So much so, that the newest avant-gardes of the 1960s, such as London Archigram Group, rejected any 'permanent' structures. But their effect on university planning takes us well beyond the Seven New Universities and will thus be considered towards the end of the book.

THE 1960S NEW UNIVERSITIES

'. . . the alliance of the Franciscan with the aristocrat.'
(A. H. Halsey)

The foregoing may be concluded by formulating a very simple recipe: take the town-scaped precinct, the cluster, or the pedestrian spine, fit the individual purposes of the university into and around it, and declare the whole as an ideal fulfilment of the '*academic* community.' This was not to be a dream, but a reality, not only once, but more than half a dozen times over. The actual 'Seven' were very quickly considered a success all-round, academically, institutionally and architecturally. If one looks more closely, the success story was chiefly that of the group as a whole. Individually, as we shall see, such a positive image could not be upheld by every institution in every respect.

The early success of the New Universities could be seen in various lights. To the general public at home, nothing like it had ever happened before in the realm of higher education. The publicity given to them was unprecedented; they were the 'darlings .of the *Sunday Times*' and the *Daily Express* and *Daily Mail* now engaged special correspondents for higher education. To continental European university reformers its was the decisiveness and seemingly unbureaucratic efficiency that impressed most: 'England, Du hast es besser' exclaimed Gerhard Hess, the founding rector at Konstanz. To many architects abroad, the continuation and modification of the cherished English college tradition was intriguing to observe. In a comparison with the American architectural world one notes in particular the strength of the architect's convictions, coupled with their clients' belief that their architect is in tune with the academic and educational aims of the institution.

THE UNIVERSITY GRANTS COMMITTEE AND THE LOCAL FOUNDERS

The success story of the new Seven is often associated with the Robbins Report of 1963 which recommended a drastic expansion of numbers and a social broadening of the student base. It thus became synonymous with university reform generally.

There is the broad picture of the rapidly growing state dependency of the universities, from 53 per cent in 1946 to 83 per cent in 1966; in actual terms, the rise of state contributions was staggering, from £7m to £157m per annum. A notion of a 'national need' had arisen which gradually replaced the simpler notion of education being provided to the measure it was wanted or could be afforded. Indeed, the number of university students rose from 108,000 in 1960 to 228,000 in 1970 (compared with 85,000 in 1950 and, 299,000 in 1980) as a proportion of the age group it rose from 7 per cent in 1960 to 14 per cent in 1970.

It is, however, crucial in our context to note that the seven New Universities were founded before the Robbins 'wave' of reform. As they grew so slowly during the 1960s, they did not even contribute much to the desired, and real, increase in student places, and, even more significantly, they gave no real impetus for the broadening of the social base. The New Universities of the early 1960s constitute a university reform *sui generis.* Its beginnings lay in a simple calculation. Until 1955 it was believed that the expected increase in student numbers could be accommodated in the existing institutions. Thereafter, demands arose to speed up the increase; at the same time there was a consensus among academics that a figure of 4,500 should not be exceeded for most universities. The result was that several new universities were needed. While the government deliberated, the banging on its doors by local promoters of Brighton helped to speed up the process.

Founding a new university involved a protracted interplay between the state and local pressure groups. We must begin by stating that the New Universities were the first in Britain to be founded entirely by the state, or, to be precise, by the eminently subtle organisation of the UGC, the University Grants Committee. Endless ink was spilt in the attempts to define this body equivocally. Did it 'belong' to the universities or to the government? It was, in fact, a branch of the Treasury, established in 1919, but was incorporated into the Department of Education in 1964. In its day-to-day existence and its chief self-understanding it was a meeting point for senior dons from all British universities at its offices in Belgrave Square. The committee centred around Sir Keith Murray (later Lord Murray of Newhaven), its chairman from 1953–63. Murray was a Scots Presbyterian, Oxford and Cornell educated, who had become rector of Lincoln College Oxford after the war. There was not very much in the way of a predominant academic specialisation, but Murray was held to 'possess the full range of administrative skills with scarcely a whiff of the bureaucratic'. The UGC was only one of his innumerable agendas. The precise moment of decision with regard to the New Universities is somewhat shrouded in darkness (there was no early debate in parliament about the issue), what really mattered was the individual 'Treasury approval'. This process lasted from February 1958, when the University of Sussex was 'government-announced', to November 1961, when the last of the Seven, Lancaster, was approved (see page 305 for a detailed list of the progress of the Seven) (figs 2.35–2.37).

The other agent was the local one. One of the crucial differences between Oxbridge and 'the rest' was the former's complete independence from local or national decision-making, notwithstanding the fact that much of Oxbridge was originally founded by the Crown or the national 'establishment'. All the other English universities had been founded through local initiative. The New Universities carried on precisely where the last Redbricks, such as Exeter, had left off. But for those institutions, relying on local initiative and local funding had inevitably meant slow progress, and

2.35 Sir Keith Murray in 1964 as Honary Fellow of Downing College Cambridge. (Photo Courtesy Michael G. Murray)

2.37 (*far right*) Sir John Fulton and Sussex University. (Courtesy Jane Bown, *The Observer* 14-6-1964, p. 12)

2.36 Sir Eric Jones. (*ST* 17-6-1962 (Magazine) p. 28)

the state (or, rather, the national academic establishment) gave only piecemeal recognition; in practice this had meant a dependence, for decades, on the validation of all their degrees by a more senior university, usually London. Now the new situation gave the whole process a completely different impetus, a much quicker start, and a much closer interaction between national and local agents. Completely new universities were to be had, so to speak; but the local interest groups were made to compete for that national money. The government, for its part, saved itself much trouble, especially in the search for locations (there was merely a stipulation that two of the new foundations should be located in the north) (fig. 2.38).

There were, indeed, at some time in the early 1960s, up to thirty towns who desired a university. A number of them had rapidly gathered together formidable organisations; committees proliferated and practically everybody of any consequence in the town or in the county took part. Usually there was somebody particularly adept at leading this band, such as the Brighton Education Officer, W.G. Stone. These Promotion Committees as they came to be called had to come up with proof of 1) profound and informed local enthusiasm, 2) already existing local institutions of an academic nature, 3) the likelihood of substantial financial donations and recurrent support from the local authorities, 4) a reservoir of rentable rooms for students and 5) and most importantly, a site. After an intensive process lasting up to two years with constant toing and froing to London, the final letter would come from Sir Keith, saying that 'the UGC have now been authorised by the Government', i.e. that the money was now on offer. At that point, local power retreated somewhat as the academic organisation gathered pace, but on the whole the administrative structure of the New Universities was to follow the 'provincial', rather than the Oxbridge custom in maintaining strong 'councils', i.e. a governing body made up chiefly of local 'lay' members.

There was, however, a carefully devised general rationale behind the UGC's choice of locations. Unlike the great majority of the earlier provincial foundations the Seven

were to be located not in the major centres and industrial conurbations, but in medium-sized, even smaller towns, preferably of the non-industrial, county-town type, and preferably those with national historical associations, as at Lancaster. There was a sense in which the picturesqueness of a medium-sized town could be considered a national asset – for that reason, for instance, Colchester, was preferred to Chelmsford – and a large cathedral, as at Norwich, Canterbury and York was seen as a building of national status. That said, the UGC's stipulation to situate the campus outside the town – *c*. $1\frac{1}{2}$ to 4 miles (2–6 kilometres) on a minimum of 200 acres (81 hectares) for 3,000 students – meant that although the New Universities were associated with provincial towns, they were, in fact, not of the towns. The reasons given were mainly practical ones, but there were also those of aesthetics, the parkland campus ideal, and, more importantly, of ideology. All seven locations possessed a country house on, or near the site, or, at the very least a picturesque farmhouse. In nearly all cases these 'historic houses' provided the first seat of administration. Thinking of East Anglia, and to a lesser extent of Essex and Sussex, one should remember that, traditionally, the larger estates in the shires were seen to rank socially and culturally above the nearby towns. When, in 1960, some Norwich architects and their civic supporters argued for a city-centre location, their opponents defended the out-of-town site by pointing to the way in which a university on Ber Street would look 'dismal and unattractive and [would] provide unpleasant views of the railway sidings, the electricity power station and the new gas works'. The UGC hardly even listened to any such debates.

We may thus call the whole foundation process a clever management of perceptions. The local elite of Norwich, or Brighton proudly felt that without their effort

2.38 York petition to the University Grants Committee 1947. (PRO UGC 218 7, Memorandum February 1947)

We beg to lay this statement before you, in the hope that, here, a beginning may be made, in the way which the existing University authorities deem the most valuable and practical. The goodwill of the City is strong and active; we trust that the response may be such as will make a full call upon it.

We have the honour to be,

Your obedient servants,

Fred Gaines
Lord Mayor of the City of York.

Cyril Ebor:
Archbishop of York.

G. W. Wrangham.
Recorder of the City of York.

C. F. Vanderson
Sheriff of the City of York.

Eric Milner-White
Dean of York.

Geoffrey R. H. Smith
High Sheriff of Yorkshire.

Corlett
Member of Parliament for York.

G. J. Harris
Chairman, Rowntree & Co., Ltd.

Noel Terry
Chairman, Joseph Terry & Sons, Ltd.

J. Hayman
Chairman, York Education Committee.

W. Patterson
Chairman, York Trades Council.

J. B. Morrell
Chairman, York Civic Trust.

Madge Butterfield
Chairman, British Federation of University Women (York).

Oliver Sheldon
Governor of the Company of Merchant Adventurers of the City of York.

there would not have been a university near their town (it would have gone somewhere else), while the state (or the government, of either colour) could be satisfied with the fulfilment of the 'national need'. And yet, the Seven could not be said to be 'local' universities – to the extent that this was seen to be the case of the Civics and Redbricks, nor were they ever proper 'state' universities, in the sense of those of the State of New York, or California. Strictly speaking, there was only one major 'agent', the academic, or, to be precise, a self-appointed core group of professors and vice chancellors, exercising 'de facto control of elitist institutions by like-minded members of the elite'(A.H. Halsey) and practising a 'hands-on, highly personal style of operation' (Michael Shattock). Keith Murray remembered it as a '"clubbale", enjoyable, eminently reasonable, objective'. Murray, too, was first and foremost an academic, albeit mostly in the sense of an academic organiser, a mediator of corporate bodies. 'Independence' 'academic freedom', 'academic autonomy', these were the watchwords of Murray and his group, but, of course, other kinds of comments and rumours went around, for instance that the pleasant locations were chosen primarily in order to help with attracting 'good' academic staff (*The Observer*).

Phase one of the local foundation of the university was immediately followed by phase two of the UGC's machinations, the academic organisation. Now the UGC took the reins, the locals were excluded. Murray put together the 'Academic Planning Boards' (APB) for each new institution. It always contained a vice chancellor (of another university) and there was a calculated small overlap between all the boards of the Seven. The groups' main functions were to devise an academic plan and to make sure that the independent institution would keep 'satisfactory academic standards'. Unlike the other provincial universities, who had had to wait for independence for decades, the new ones would receive full degree-granting rights from the start. Finally, the Academic Planning Board had to find the vice chancellor. This done, the university was born at last, and it was 'born free' (Lord Fulton).

THE BALLIOL / 'LIBERAL' ETHOS. KEELE. THE 'SCHOOLS' SETUP

'Independence' was seen as the prerequisite of 'innovation'. Innovation was, one might say, compulsory in this situation. '$\frac{1}{3}$ numbers, $\frac{2}{3}$ new ideas', was Murray's demand. Within a simple hierarchical system it would have been a fight for a place as high up the academic ladder as possible; within the Oxbridge vs. the Rest situation, the stakes were upped much more: none of the New Universities wanted to be classed along with 'the rest'. At times it appeared that the spokespersons of Sussex et al. took issue with the whole of higher education in Britain. Potted histories of English higher education took a patronising attitude: 'a patchwork of history', 'haphazard growth' (Boris Ford). One of the most venerable British institutions could now be chided roundly as 'elitist, hierarchical, intensely competitive, too narrowly specialised'. Splendid but arrogant Oxbridge and eager but dull Redbrick were constantly played off each other. The New Universities' greatest challenge was to meet a vociferous minority, including dons like Kingsley Amis (at Peterhouse, Cambridge), who warned of an impending drop in quality, the familiar 'more means worse argument': 'University graduates are like poems or bottles of hock, and unlike cars or tins of salmon, in that you cannot decide to have more good ones'. Asa Briggs of Sussex, however, untiringly assured his audiences that 'quantitative expansion was coinciding with qualitative reorientation'.

Clearly, there was an educational zeal, a passionate attempt to inculcate certain values. General educational discourse still sounded eminently simple. The Robbins Report talked of 'not mere specialists but rather cultivated men and women'. Nineteenth-century formulations, such as John Stuart Mill's 'men are men before they are lawyers or physicians . . . and if you will make them equable and sensible men, they will make themselves capable and sensible lawyers or physicians', still held sway; John Newman's and Matthew Arnold's writings from the same period were likewise still compulsory reading. From the early English pamphletists we must turn, once again, to the American 'experimental college' of the interwar period (see page 18) and from there to the postwar realisation of the failure of the old German university and its high ideals during the Nazi period. In 1949, Sir Walter Moberly's book, *The Crisis in the University*, deals surprisingly little with university matters as such, and one hardly gets a sense that the university itself was in crisis, definitely not at Oxford. What the book amounted to was a plea for students to be taught the political and moral problems of the world at large, in order to fight the modern threats of specialisation, mechanisation and secularisation. Here, as in the writings of F.R. Leavis, the English ideal came close to the American 'liberal' ideal, although the English tended to use this term much less frequently. For once, it did not sound quite right for the Christian and/or socialist outlook of many reformers, neither would they want to stress the arts at the expense of the sciences, nor did they want to put exclusive emphasis on undergraduate teaching.

An academic uniquely placed into all these contexts was Alexander Dunlow Lindsay, later Lord Lindsay of Birker, with experience in the USA as well as in pre- and postwar Germany (see page 207). His actual 'home' was Balliol College, Oxford, where he had been a philosophy teacher and long-time warden; Balliol, the elite school, which cultivated an image of strong personalities among teachers and taught, as well as that of 'a close-knit . . . community . . . with such intense communal, intellectual curiosity'. On balance, it prided itself with the public-figure alumni, rather than the pure academic. In 1949 Lindsay left Balliol and founded the University College of North Staffordshire, later named Keele University. It can clearly be seen as an 'experimental liberal arts college', remaining small, under 1,000, for a long time. It introduced a four-year degree, with the compulsory combination of arts and sciences in the first year, and it was almost wholly residential. Situated virtually in the country, near Stoke on Trent, around a lavish Victorian country house, Keele differed decisively from the contemporary 'University Colleges', i.e. the younger Redbricks. The fact that it could from the start validate its first degrees links it with the 1960s New University movement. However, by the later 1950s Keele had remained very small and was held not to have done particularly well in most respects. It subsequently developed into a fully-fledged, but somehow normal university. Moreover, English university reformers of the late 1940s, even the socialist-minded ones, including indeed the socially conscious Lindsay, had not yet grasped one major issue: the expansion of student numbers generally. In an astonishing statement in late 1958 Niblett maintained that 'a remarkably high proportion of . . . our young people today go to university' (it was then 4.1 per cent). To Lindsay, Moberly and Niblett the essential task of a university was to train 'leaders', '. . . to turn out a governing class' (Niblett in 1962). The Seven's founding vice chancellors most definitely belonged to that class: six were Oxbridge men, all 'buccaneers, jostling each other for the prizes of a new university age'. Such a role, of course, could hardly be found at Oxbridge itself, but rather in the provincial universities, and even more so among the American colleges.

Other major founders also came from 'the Balliol Society of Scholars', the philosophy don Lord Fulton at Sussex ('Balliol-by-the-Sea'), as did his philosophy professor, J. P. Corbett, who was also in charge of student affairs, or the philosopher and Dean of Students at Norwich, Marcus Dick. Most of the protagonists of the New Universities, at least the first two, Sussex and York, carried on with the Leavis or Lindsay-inherited educational rhetoric. They talked of 'allegiance', and 'identity', and wanted 'the student to feel like an "insider"' (Niblett). By the early 1960s the elitism of small numbers had, of course, begun to be heavily challenged by the demand for expansion. But to some of the postwar educationalists, such as Eric James, York's vice chancellor, this meant simply redoubling efforts within the old educational mould. 'Students are apt in these days to be directionless . . . their families have been afraid to lay down the law . . . their churches . . . ineffective, [they] live in a subculture . . . pulled strongly in the direction of the dark ages. Universities are in some sense the clerisy . . .'.

The most central of the key words seemed to be, again, community – 'the fundamental notion of community' (Briggs). This notion dated, in Britain, chiefly from the time of World War II, being closely related to the war effort and the utopianist reconstruction after the war. Moreover, it did not suffer from the class connotations of many of the other terms cited. It could be used flexibly in many variants: the 'university community' or the 'community of the university', or rather as the 'university within its community', referring to the people outside. If extra comprehensiveness was needed one could speak of 'the total community'. It was a term that linked people with institutions and, as we shall see, institutions with architectural design. A typical late and more complex definition came from the Oxford historian Marjorie Reeves:

> The academic community is a way of organising a set of personal relationships, of contriving an equilibrium of conflicts, so as to promote an imaginative grasp on living knowledge. Within such a community learning is . . . ideally embodied in the tutorial or seminar group . . . it presupposes the free-ranging and responsible play of the intelligence, informed by passion, and moving always towards a critical comment . . .

Under closer scrutiny, it is hard to assess what was actually 'innovative' with the Seven. First of all, one must stress that innovation hardly concerned the administrative and governmental structure of the institution, nor did major early successes in pure research come to light. As regards subjects taught, there was the exclusion of the more vocational areas, such as medicine or heavy engineering, while on the other hand, there were attempts to claim novelty by introducing subjects that were not taught elsewhere. In the wake of C. P. Snow's *Two Cultures* great stress was placed on bringing together the humanities and the sciences; here, too, Oxbridge provided a model, as Snow had remarked, on almost all the college high tables the two sat together. The chief innovations lay, in fact, in the organisation of the learning processes. One has to remember that Oxford and Cambridge at that time were still predominantly teaching undergraduates (in the humanities the Oxbridge proportion of postgraduate students in 1961/2 was 9 per cent, nationally 10 per cent, in the sciences the figures were 26 per cent and 20 per cent, respectively). For East Anglia, Frank Thistlethwaite introduced 'a highly articulated, Oxbridge type system of student support with advisers, etc.'. As we shall see, some took on the Oxbridge college pattern

2.39 Oxbridge tutorial. (*Deutsche Universitätszeitung* [*DUZ*] 12-1960, p. 23)

almost in its entirety. Other elements came from the USA, e.g. the 'Dean of Students', the officer in charge of student welfare; on the whole, though, the psychological care for students in England did not match up to the vast professional concern in the USA. 'Face to face teaching' was the ideal, tutorials, small seminar groups; teaching through lectures was greatly discouraged. Thus it was that the vice chancellors of York and Norwich, during the 1960s, could speak of the new institutions as 'outstanding teaching universities' (fig. 2.39).

'Redrawing the map of learning' was Asa Briggs's most memorable phrase of those years. At Sussex the momentous decision was to create 'Schools of Study'. The New University pioneers saw two enemies who appeared closely related, subject specialisation and departmental segregation. It was reckoned that three-quarters of all undergraduate degrees in the 1960s were single subject degrees. In Oxbridge several subjects were usually studied one after the other without much thought as to what they had in common. Another important model was, of course, the American pattern of 'majors' and 'minors'. Departments or faculties, it was felt, were stifling institutions, where 'everyone was guarding his or her territory and where change is virtually impossible' (Briggs). The 'school' is a much larger administrative unit than a department; an umbrella, say, geographically speaking, such as European Studies, Anglo-American Studies; in the sciences divisions usually remained more conventional. The school is where the student registers and all the services are coordinated. At both the student and the faculty level subjects are meant to communicate: European history, European literature, European languages. This also meant that several major subjects, such as history French or English, could be taught in several schools. This makes for a complex structure overall. In addition, the course structures were elaborated further with general courses, which all students in certain subjects had to take. These elements were specially important in Essex and Warwick where the notion of the 'school' was weaker and the older kind of single subject departments kept more of a hold. It was the complex web of free and compulsory elements in the syllabus which perhaps characterised most the new teaching patterns of all the New Universities (fig. 2.40). (Cf. Degree Combinations of the Seven, page 307.)

There was, in the end, an unambiguous relationship between the New Universities and Oxbridge, and Oxford in particular. In 1963 the Robbins Report hinted at the need to reduce the dominance of Oxbridge. By then, the New Universities had entered the phase of their greatest success, attracting good staff, from Oxbridge, naturally, and Sussex had selected its first fifty-two students in 1961 from over 500 applicants. The question of whether they would 'equal' Oxbridge mattered less, as, in fact, they had managed to create their own identity and to place themselves comfortably into a new category between the Civics / Redbricks and Oxbridge. Although none of the epithets or nicknames actually stuck for long, such as the 'Plateglass Universities' (Michael Beloff) or the more friendly 'Shakesperean Seven' (Lord Boyle), the author of a verse of 1963 (not the bard himself but Pendennis of *The Observer*) deserves to be quoted in full:

How speaks industrious Warwick,
   Shrewd Lancaster, my noble Lord of York?
      Brave Sussex, ill-starred Kent, ambitious Essex.

WELFARE STATE 'SOCIAL FORM'. THE ARCHITECTS DEVISE COST-CUTTING BRIEFS

'What is the Modern equivalent to King's College Chapel?' asked, in 1964, Sir William Holford, one of England's premier planner-architects, and soon to be elevated to Lord Holford. He was at the time engaged in building the new University of Kent. There is no record of any direct answer. But others also voiced their enthusiasm: the 'New University Movement as exciting as the cathedral building movement of the early 12th century'; 'neither the mind nor the face of Britain will ever be the same again'; 'a long pent-up flood of interest and skills in the planning and shaping of total environments', all of which was, one might say, part of the 'British tradition of architects as briefmakers'. What is more significant than this self-praise is the acknowledgment of the architects' power by those outside the profession. 'All these universities are going to be in a genuine sense, architects' universities'. Boris Ford, professor of education at Sussex, spoke of 'the odd way in which the architects have taken over the academic's job'. What we witness is a remarkable patronage situation: a situation in which the client and the planner-architect were convinced of the mutuality of their beliefs.

There were, in fact, some analogies between the two groups, that is the top academics, centred around the UGC and the group of top London practitioners, 'progressive' in the years after the war, 'established' by the late 1950s. Many found their introduction to university architecture through the Churchill College competition – six of the architects of the Seven were either taking part in it, or belonged to the panel of judges. But the New Universities decided to dispense with competitions as too cumbersome and time-consuming. The search for an architect went by word of mouth, or by simply a letter requesting names from the president of the Royal Institute of British Architects. Thus the situation of architecture vis-à-vis the New Universities and their clients can be explained to a large extent through a small and relatively closed network within a centralised state. After all, there was no separate campus planning profession, as in America; on the contrary, the 'advanced', even the 'established' post World War II architect considered himself or herself highly qualified for any planning task. But our architects, at that time, would not themselves have been content with this explanation. It would have sounded far too simplistic and instrumentalist. Helped by that formidable double organ of professional self-expression, the *Architectural Review* and the *Architects' Journal*, the architects launched a powerful and shrewd campaign to support their involvement in university design in 1957/8.

The architects' initial platform was their defense of the Modernist style: they declared that too many facilities were housed in ill-adapted Victorian structures, makeshift, in a bad state, even in 'slums'. The *Architects' Journal* presented a complete catalogue of the practical advantages of Modern design: higher standards in acoustics, sound and heat insulation, day and artificial lighting, more space, good use of the site, structural strength, services and equipment and, most importantly, value for money, and even speed of building. New construction at that time meant metal and glass – critics could not yet foresee the great variety of constructions that was soon to become available under the heading 'Modern'. By 1958 there were very few examples to be shown, but a number of projects were at an advanced stage, all in the provincial universities, and usually by the most eminent designers, such as Sir Leslie Martin at Leicester and Hull, or Sir Basil Spence at Liverpool, Newcastle and Southampton. But Modernism, contrary to the assumptions of its homogeneity and universal validity, had a great number of faces. The projects cited here, when they had been built, by the early 1960s, did not acquire fame; they were then seen to belong to the great number of 'ordinary', 'routine functional' Modernist buildings. 'The primitive functionalism of prewar and postwar reconstruction proved to be illusory by the late 1950s' (Michael Brawne 1967). Cambridge and Oxford had woken up – and some Civics and Redbricks, such as Leicester, tried to keep up with them – but they now aimed for a rather different kind of building: usually highly expensive and individualist, by a not yet quite 'established' group of younger designers, such as Stirling and Gowan.

There were, in fact, a number of carefully orchestrated strands in the critical agenda of 1957/8. There were simply millions of pounds available for construction, 80 per cent of it state-provided, peaking at £46.1m for the year 1965/6. As for Modernity, the *Architects' Journal* made shrewd use of its ethos, predicting that when the 'most important' clients are educated within the modern architecture of the universities, 'they, in their turn, will help to ensure that [it is] quickly spread throughout the nation by knowing what they are entitled to demand from the architect'. And yet, the 'Modern style' no longer represented the highest value to the architectural press as a whole. The *AJ's* sister journal and high cultural mouthpiece, the *Architectural Review* ran a parallel campaign. In it we find a rogues' gallery of recent buildings, reproduced anonymously and utterly condemned – while it is the *AJ* in which details about most of them can be found, the *AJ* being the more mundane publication which had to be more cautious because it addressed itself to the world of job architects, clients and the building industry. The *AR's* piece was by Lionel Brett (Lord Esher), architect commentator and establishment figure in architecture and conservation. Brett carefully avoids any mundane advocacy of the Modern. His chief aim is to help establish 'the more humane and adaptable approaches that promise an integrated concept of a university and its buildings'. To the designers and critics of the later 1950s who had propounded this kind of view for a decade in housing and town planning, the concern for 'the whole' was axiomatic. It is not the individual building that interests them: 'Administrative buildings, offices, faculty buildings, lecture halls, libraries, student unions; these buildings types are familiar ground to the architects. But what makes a set of them into a University (and not a technical institute) is the way they are lived in day and night [and that] depends how they are arranged.' They considered that 'so far universities [had] failed to integrate [a] sense of community both physically and visually'. While the *AJ* postulates practical Modernist design, Brett concludes with an apotheosis to restore to the designer his synoptic vision and thus re-equip him for his old role at the centre of civilization'. Of course, for Brett, too, 'the ball is in the court of patronage'. Three years later Graeme Shankland, a town planner, underlined again − after having quoted Plato's *Republic* on the importance of good design in education − 'the supreme social importance of the quality of architecture . . . of the universities'. There also had to be a *bête-noire*, it was Keele University which was repeatedly mentioned for its lack of vigorous planning, resulting, it was maintained, from the early failure to appoint a Modernist architect of rank.

As a Canadian architectural journal wrote in 1962: 'While we are dazzled by the stylistic gymnastics of artist-architects South of the border, across the Atlantic the British slowly evolve prototypes of social forms'. The argument goes on to state that 'the British have almost eliminated the architect of individualistic talent' and the journal ends with a demand for a synthesis of 'these basically opposing philosophies'. This statement, however, does not take note of the fact that Britain had a tradition of socio-architectural rhetoric in the utopianist writings of Ruskin, William Morris, Unwin and their followers amongst the critics in the architectural press. For many Modernists, certainly those of the Gropius line, it was precisely their overriding concern that a division between a mundane notion of the technical or empirical-sociological and architectural art should not take place. The architects made sure that the major planning concept, the major sociological intentions, or the social ethos of the building, ranked as highly as the 'art'; in fact, they understood the social and planning ethos to be fused with the art of architecture. There is, in fact, a view in which the British architectural establishment formed part and parcel of new British Welfare State policies. The severe physical and psychic experience of the war led to the call for radical change for the 'New', for creative effort on all fronts, serving the poor and the better-off alike, thereby eliminating the old notion of charity. A good client-designer relationship was almost a built-in factor in this Welfare State procedure. In reality, the architects had been in a no-choice situation after the war: private building was very much restricted. But many of the younger architects actually did imbibe the Gropius kind of postulated unity of the social-architectural project. After the New Towns, public housing and elementary schools, state-provided higher education was a relative late comer. For some of the major designers, such as Chamberlain, Powell and Bon, Leslie Martin, Lasdun and Capon this provided a convenient pattern of succession; they saw the New Universities as a major building block in a natural sequence to Welfare State housing designs.

In some Welfare State social architecture, for instance in the prefabricated schools of the 1950s, the reduction of building costs had been made part of a design and building reform campaign. In other fields, such as early high-rise public housing, the designers and their clients did not always choose the cheapest solution. The New Universities, by common consent, were built cheaply – though in detail, as we shall see, that judgment will be somewhat diversified. Comparisons with buildings at Oxbridge – where the figures were made public – showed that the same task could be realised at the rate of a third or even a quarter of their cost. To cite just one example, Leslie Martin and Colin St J. Wilson's eight-storey William Stone Building for Peterhouse, Cambridge, of 1963–4, which provided rooms for just eight fellows and twenty-four undergraduates, all for a cool £100,000. At East Anglia's 'Ziggurats' that sum meant rooms for 100 students plus subsidiary facilities and one or two tutor's flats (and that in a building of an unprecedented architectural complexity – while standards of space and finishing were, of course, rather lower). Abroad, especially in Germany, there was great admiration, at least during the mid-1960s, for English low-cost building. On rough calculations, Bochum University worked out at £7,000 plus per student, while an English New University, costing £7m to build, for 3,000 students (including a good number of residential places, which hardly applied at Bochum), provided the same for a mere £2,300 per student.

Overall cost aside, the process of building required precise and flexible costing mechanisms at all times. The relationship between the architect and his client was in most cases a constructive one. Here, too, the UGC proved its particular kind of 'double-face': towards the government and the taxpayers it appeared trustworthy; towards the universities and their architects it could be flexible. University and architects had to submit plans to the UGC at several stages of the process. The UGC had, by the late 1950s, created its own department of architectural advice and provided rules for a number of specific purposes, such as the minimum space for a faculty office. There were also some standardised costs limits (we have cited the figures for student residences, page 77). Each campus received a total of about £6m over six years and the institutions topped it up with appeal funds to the tune of £500,000 (Kent) to £2.75m (Warwick). The UGC did, however, stress the factor of discussion and it did not prescribe any architectural concepts, neither for the general plan, nor for the detailed design – as this would have contradicted the spirit of 'experimentation'. It did admonish the universities to first choose a development architect, and then think about whom to employ for individual buildings; however, most of the Seven did not follow this advice. Thistlethwaite of East Anglia, when questioned by Murray as to why he had committed himself to Lasdun for both plan and design, said that he had not been aware of the stipulation. There are reports of the visits of one of the UGC's building officials, Parnis, where he regularly spotted some elements of wasted money. However, this climate was soon to change: already by 1966 there appeared to be less money all round and by 1968 much stricter financial controls were applied. There were some architects, especially Robert Matthew Johnson-Marshall, of York and later Bath, and others, who prided themselves in their financial reliability and who in fact wanted to institute a greater overall rationalisation of building construction, e.g., with the help of Clasp which they used at York – but on the whole, architects hardly went along with this kind of thinking, insisting on their individuality as designers.

When Keith Murray was approached by a Treasury official recommending a stronger presence of the UGC in the decisionmaking of each university, Murray replied by defending his looser reign: 'The University Grants committee policy, as distinct from that of the Ministry of Education or of the Ministry of Health, is to pass as much responsibility as possible to the universities . . .'. Murray shrewdly reasoned that a stricter reign 'would undoubtedly lessen the universities' sense of responsibility and at the same time limit the committee's freedom to assess'. To all intents and purposes English universities, traditionally 'independent', were becoming, during the postwar decades, a part of the state. In this regard, seemingly radical changes were advocated in the Robbins Report in late 1963. Henceforth, all institutions of higher education became part of the 'university system', to use an important term of the report. However, a strong element of independence as regards the academic sphere continued. Socially, the universities could also still be seen to present an image of exclusivity. It was the New Universities' good fortune to be founded and designed when there was still a strong sense of autonomy, and it was their next good fortune to be built while the country as a whole was told to appreciate the general social importance of that institution. The New Universities were thus arguably not part of Welfare State architecture when they were planned, but slipped into this category while they were being built. It was exactly at that point when Essex's gigantic architectural scheme to house up to 20,000 students made its impact. It was the vice chancellor, Albert Sloman, who appeared as the guarantor for the numbers and it was his architect, Kenneth Capon, who vouched for the architectural realisation. It was a formidable team, in the sense of traditional patronage, as well as in the sense of a 'Modern' public project.

MONUMENTALISM ON A PARKLAND CAMPUS: SUSSEX

'The case for radical rethinking'; to 'represent for posterity the twentieth century conception of a university'. Such statements by Asa Briggs of Sussex University abounded during the high years of the New University movement. The speed with which Sussex developed was breathtaking. Within the span of three, or even two years, it had risen to the highest level of British academic institutions. There are three elements in the early history of Sussex. The phase of the unexpectedly rapid growth from 1961 had been preceded by the lengthy and intense local effort to found a modest University College of Brighton. The third factor was the architecture. The quality of Sir Basil Spence's first buildings, opened on time, in 1962, in their blend of novelty and establishment eminence, seemed the exact equivalent to the academic ethos of the institution.

There had been efforts to establish some kind of university or college at Brighton even before the World War I, to be revived during the 1930s and then again in 1946. As for the other applicants who went to the UGC, Norwich and York, the climate was not right. Brighton renewed it attempts in 1955/6. This timing was crucial, as it meant that Brighton was to precede the other two and any further new applicants. The untiring organiser and spokesperson was Brighton's Chief Education Officer, William G. Stone. Apart from the obvious reasons, such as the lack of a university in south-east England and the overcrowding of London university, Stone had developed a distinctive higher and further education policy of his own. Brighton was to have a new technical college and Stone considered that this ought to be balanced by a place for liberal education, 'for [the] humane and liberal elements in our cultural heritage'. If Stone did not actually influence UGC thinking in those years, his ideas were certainly close to those of Niblett and James. Stone even tried to fight what he saw as the unnecessarily strong demand for technical education; on the contrary, he suggested, in order to strengthen Britain's role in the world, that 'trade may follow the greatness of her poetry'. By 1957 more concrete reasons were cited: a good site at Falmer, to be given by Brighton Council, and plenty of student accommodation in off-season boarding houses. By that time, the government climate was turning in favour of new universities, although it took nearly two more years until, in February 1958, the Brighton deputation received the desired answer.

There was one very major general problem to be solved: the new institutions were to be fully-fledged universities from the start and give out their own degrees, undergraduate and postgraduate. A new body was created, to deal with this and other problems, the 'Advisory Committee on Academic Planning' for Brighton, a group in which the local promoters had virtually no say. It was put together by the UGC and made up of eminent academics nationwide (its subsequent versions were called Academic Planning Board). Finally, in February 1959, the Proposed University College of Sussex presented itself as a new institution. Now a 'College Council' took over, composed of members of the Academic Planning Committee, the local education officers and 'eight persons of distinction in the county'. The vice chancellor designate and the architect were also present. By the autumn of that year the vice chancellor took up his post. John Scott Fulton, by training a philosopher, a fellow of Balliol and then the principal of the University College of Wales in Swansea, had before that been closely involved with the foundation of Keele. Balliol and Keele, of course implied: 'general education' as well as 'a rational not an authoritarian relationship between teaching staff and students'. At the same time, Fulton led an 'incredibly varied public life' and was classed as a 'publicist', and as highly 'image conscious'. He was made a life peer in 1966 when he left Brighton to become chairman of the British Council.

It was only during 1960 that planning really got under way. The name of the institution was now upgraded, that is, the word 'college' was dropped by the UGC for the New Universities – this was done at the instigation of Norwich. The projected student number was greatly enlarged, 2,000, even 3,000 students were envisaged after a span of a few years only; Stone's proposal had been for a college of 800. It was decided to open two years ahead of schedule and to complete the first buildings one year early.

Brighton now formulated its celebrated academic structure and programme. A departure from the old pattern of departments, as well as a new interdisciplinarity have been mentioned earlier, and also the way in which a spirit of 'freedom' should be used for innovation and experiment. But only by 1960–1 did Sussex feel 'completely free from the status inhibitions of some of our colleagues in other provincial universities. We did not use the term "morale"; we spoke of elan', to quote again Asa Briggs, a fellow of Worcester College and subsequently professor of History at Leeds who played an increasingly important role in Sussex as its first professor and first pro chancellor (and as vice chancellor from 1967). Briggs's chief enemy was specialist vocational education. 'Merely to turn out enormous numbers of specialists with specialist degrees will [not serve] the real needs of the community . . . in a period of great social and economic changes'. The problem had to be attacked from two angles. Firstly, Sussex abolished both the divisions in departments and faculties and replaced them by 'Schools of Studies' (see page 102). Secondly there was the curriculum. Keele

Chart 1

NOTES

1. The *dates* refer to the October of each year and they record the year in which the School was established or in which the Major Subject was introduced into the School.

2. The *percentages* are very approximative indications of the relative weightings on a time basis of Preliminary, Contextual, and Major Subject courses in the Degree course.

3. The *Preliminary* courses listed are not of equal weight.

4. The individual *contextual* courses are not listed. The Subject Groupings shown represent the most common choices in each School.

5. The *supporting* courses differ and are less common within Schools than are the contextual courses in the B.A. degree course. The boxes are very approximate representations of the nature of those courses in each School.

KEY to Schools of Studies

AFRAS — Sch. of African & Asian Studies
EDUC — Sch. of Educational Studies
ATLAN — Sch. of English & American Studies
EURO — Sch. of European Studies
SOC — Sch. of Social Studies
A.S. — Sch. of Applied Sciences
B.S. — Sch. of Biological Sciences
M.P.S. — Sch. of Mathematical and Physical Sciences
M.S — Sch. of Molecular Sciences (this School was created out of the School of Physical Sciences in 1964, which explains why some of its major subjects are dated earlier than the foundation of the School).

COLOUR KEY. For purposes of national classification the UGC allocates subjects to 18 Subject Groupings. The only groupings relevant to the University are:

Education
Engineering
Other Technologies
Biological Sciences
Mathematics
Physical Sciences
Social Studies
Language, Literature and Area Studies
Other Arts

| | B.A. DEGREE COURSE | | | | | B.Sc. DEGREE COURSE | | | | |
COURSES	AFRAS 1964	EDUC 1964	ATLAN 1961	EURO 1961	SOC 1961	A.S. 1965	B.S. 1965	M.P.S. 1962	M.S. 1964	COURSES
Preliminary (15%)										Preliminary (15%)
History										
Language Values										
The School Course										
										Structure & Properties of Matter
										Mathematics
										Optional Course
Contextual (35%)										Supporting Courses (20-25%)
Arts/Science Scheme										Arts/Science Scheme
MAJORS (50%)										MAJORS (60-65%)
American Studies		1961								
Anthropology, social	1964				1965					
Art		1966	1966	1966						
						1966				Automatic Control
							1966		1966	Biochemistry
Biology		1966					1965			Biology
								1962		Chemistry
								1964		Chemistry, theoretical
Economics	1964			1962	1961					
						1965				Electronics
						1965				Eng. Science, Elect.
						1965				Eng. Science, Mech.
						1968				Eng. with Op. Research
						1966				Eng. with Soc. Studies
English	1966	1964	1961	1962						
French	1966			1961						
Geography	1964	1964		1962	1961		1965			Geography
German				1961						
History	1964	1964	1961	1961	1961					
International relations	1964			1963	1963					
Italian				1967						
Law	1966		1966	1966	1966					
						1965			1966	Materials Science
Mathematics				1964		1966		1962		Mathematics
Philosophy		1964	1962	1962	1961					
Philosophy & Religion	1964									
								1962		Phil. & Theory of Sci.
Physics					1965			1962		Physics
								1962		Physics, chemical
								1964		Physics, mathematical
Politics	1964		1966	1962	1961					
Psychology, developmental		1964								
							1965			Psychology, experimental
Psychology, social	1966			1965						
Religious Studies		1964		1964	1964					
Russian				1961						
Russian Studies				1965						
Sociology		1964	1966	1962	1961					
Total	24	11	9	8	16	13	9	4	4	5	19 Total

2.40 The University of Sussex near Brighton: the syllabi of the early First Degree Courses. The purpose of this schematic representation is to demonstrate the degree of interdisciplinarity of, firstly, all the courses (even across the arts/science divide), and, secondly, within each 'school'. (V.G. Onushkin (ed.), *Planning the Development of Universities I* (reproduced by permission of UNESCO) Paris, 1971)

2.41 (*right*) The University of Sussex, 'Students of Sussex University outside the Arts building'. (S. Maclure, 'The "with–it" university', *The Listener* 25-2-1965, p. 291)

2.42 (*far right*) The University of Sussex at Falmer, near Brighton, by Sir Basil Spence; model *c.* 1960. Falmer House in the foreground, to the left the library, at the back the arts building and the sciences to the right. (*AR* 10-1963, p. 266)

and Oxford (Modern Greats) provided some precedents. All students at Sussex 'belong' to one School, where their 'Major' has to be supplemented by one or more 'Minors'. Finally, teaching was to be in small groups, not through lectures, but face to face, in order to create questioning and lively attitudes, a point argued in great detail by the first professor of philosophy, Patrick Corbett, like Fulton a former fellow of Balliol.

By mid-1961 Sussex had not even admitted a single student when Fulton wrote a long report in *The Times*, entitled 'Balliol by the Sea Faces its Future'. It ranges widely over space and time: 'Throughout the world . . . education is a new religion'; Sussex 'must embrace the values by which universities have been guided through seven centuries'. Fulton stressed that Sussex formed part of a movement of the Seven as a whole and then refers to its primacy within it. (A little later it called four residential blocks after its four sister universities.) It felt it had to go for big; smallness may lead to claustrophobia. After all, already by 1962 there were 3,100 applicants for 400 places. By late 1964 fame had reached an early peak. 'Oxford, Cambridge and London now have to compete' says a leader in *The Times* – and we can even read the first cautious criticisms of the 'PR and Colour Supplement aspects' of the operation. By that time some New Universities, notably York, but also Kent, had actually begun to try and put a new stress on eschewing novelty.

'Unlike London, [Sussex] is beautiful in site and architecture.' The fact that there were completed buildings by late 1962 played an important role in Sussex's early fame. The organisation of the physical plan was a matter primarily for the local promoters (as distinct from the academic), and that again meant largely William Stone. Already by 1957 the Borough Surveyor of Brighton, D. J. Howe, had proposed a modest outline for five buildings on the Falmer site. During the following year, Stone, in constant consultation with the UGC and also with the RIBA, went very much bolder and interviewed some of the most eminent names: William Holford, Hugh Casson, Leslie Martin, Richard Sheppard and Basil Spence. With the last, the choice fell upon the most prestigious of all, certainly in terms of public buildings: Coventry Cathedral and later the British Embassy in Rome, but also a number of commissions at Cambridge, such as the Erasmus Building for Queen's, the first notable 'Modern' building in Cambridge which was also trying to fit in with the landscape of the 'Backs'; his

new buildings in Redbrick, on the other hand, were uncompromisingly Modernist steel and glass (cf. page 62). Spence proceeded with reasonable dispatch at Sussex; invited in early 1959, he produced sketch plans by mid-1959, a model and detailed plans by early 1960; building started in late 1960 and Falmer House and the School of Physics were completed by 1962/3, the library, arts, chemistry buildings by 1964 and 1965 (figs 2.41 and 2.42).

'One of the most interesting and absorbing design exercises I have ever undertaken' declared Spence. This was the client's luck. The designer's luck was the determination, already cautiously voiced by Stone and then forcefully by Fulton (who had just built a large students union at Swansea), to start the campus with a purely social and ornamental building. Its early name, College House was derived from the fact that the university, during 1959 was still called 'college', but it also had something to do with the way in which Fulton initially did not want to build residences. It was thus all the more necessary to provide a venue which – to cite an often repeated phrase – 'should be father and mother to the undergraduates'. Moreover, 'it gave an air of completeness in itself' on a campus which faced years of building activity. As Briggs later said, it was 'our alternative conception to a college system'. The social philosophy of the university stresses that 'care was taken to avoid offensive segregation'; it is not a 'student union building', nor a 'senior common room building'; and an early observer noted: 'Staff and students mix without embarrassment in the Refec-

2.43   The University of Sussex, Falmer House

2.44   The University of Sussex, Falmer House. 1960–2 by Sir Basil Spence,
first floor plan. (*AR* 10-1963, p. 268)

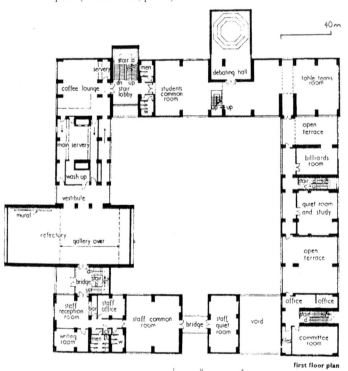

first floor plan

2.45   The University of Sussex, Falmer House
students' common room. (*Ad'A* no. 107 4/5-
1963, p. 17)

tory, Coffee Lounge and Bar'. What is intriguing to note here is that the other six New Universities decided either not to build a general 'students union' or they delayed its building; for most of them this did not turn out to be a happy decision.

Falmer House, as it was soon to be called, is arranged around a quad. It contains several dining facilities and common rooms, including a lavish debating chamber and a two-storeyed refectory which is distinguished outside by a special roof and by projecting slightly into the quad. The building is clearly a version of the Oxbridge College, and one of a most lavish kind. Much of the ground floor is taken up with kitchens and service rooms. But the building also contains as many spaces which are purely ornamental, that is, there is the framework of the building, but it is not filled in, 'like a chest of drawers with some of the drawers left out'. Thus what is most striking about Falmer House is what one must call its purely architectural aspect: a series of massive, irregularly-spaced brick piers, covered by low segmental arches or broad flat concrete bands. Spence admits to two main inspirations: the Colliseum in Rome and the Maisons Jaoul in Paris, Le Corbusier's latest essay in heavy brick and concrete. The unity of the look of the building, a singular feeling that exterior and interior are interchangeable, is further enhanced by the way the same materials are used inside ('to stand up to hard wear by the students'). Falmer House is, on the whole, as lavish as anything at Oxbridge, or as the most ornate of the Classical central buildings of the Civics, yet it seems to stand outside either category (figs 2.43–2.45).

Another function of Falmer House is, or was, to provide a kind of ceremonial entrance; through it runs a central path which leads to the 'Great Court' a large open area which is flanked by the other early buildings, Physics and Chemistry on the right, Arts in the Centre and the Library and the slightly later Gardner Centre for Visual Arts on the left. The detailed treatment is similar in all of them, brick piers and concrete arches or bands, though they all appear to be lower than Falmer House. Most striking is the entrance to the small block of lecture theatres in front of the Arts Building. Spence said: 'the axis of our main entrance archway, this view should, I felt, be terminated by the Arts Lecture Theatres'. At the entrance Spence placed two quasi ornamental concrete pylons, 'a symbol of incompleteness.' This, and the controversial circular chapel (the 'Meeting House', designed like a Sussex or Kent oathouse) completes the first and inner group of Spence's campus.

So much for the buildings, distinguished as they are; but what about the plan? The short answer is that there never really was one. But this answer would not suffice, neither from the point of view of the institution's ethos as a whole, nor in a new general architectural climate in which 'planning problems' were gaining ever more room in the discussions. 'I am against the rigid formal plan' was Spence's simple defence in 1967. Certainly the client never presented what was beginning to be called elsewhere a 'development plan'; how could one have predicted in early 1959 that the modest 'college' of 800 students was to grow into a large institution of 2,000, 3,000 or more? In his numerous, but always sketchy and changeable plans Spence presented one principle of the layout, the court, 'interlocking courtyards fed by service roads', which could simply be added on according to requirements. Unity is, furthermore, provided by the design of the buildings themselves. By 1962/4 Spence simply contended that the first two buildings, Falmer House and Physics had 'determined' the future character of the campus. Recurring features are the concrete 'arch', the use of the same materials, red brick, 'pink Sussex', some knapped flint, copper, and timber painted white. There was, and is, of course, a more important unifying factor, the site. Client and architect (and the eminent landscape architect, Sylvia Crowe) agreed from the outset that the park had to be preserved. It was decided that no building should be higher than the trees. Sussex convincingly demonstrated, from the start, that the out-of-town campus policy of the UGC was working, that, again in Spence's words, a 'peaceful pastoral scene' had been preserved. One further element of planning was to try as hard as possible to hide the cars.

What the critics of the later 1960s missed at Sussex was, as Birks put it the 'careful interrelationship between architectural and academic concepts'. Actual correlations between the individual Humanities Schools and individual buildings were hard to find. Spence's own comments remained on a very general level: he wanted to 'avoid an institutional type of architecture, characteristic of much modern school building'. His architecture 'should help sixth-formers over the fence into manhood and womanhood'. In 1966 he insisted that 'the undergraduate is still an adolescent' who is to receive 'confidence and protection from buildings'. Spence's ideal university architecture is the Oxbridge 'series of interlocking courtyards' and the 'colonnades where friends can walk and talk'. There are a great number of contemporary praises of Sussex, such as '. . . established a university presence'. Spence's ultimate conclusions were even simpler: 'beauty . . . officially "aesthetics" is a dirty word . . . And yet the level of aesthetic appreciation usually marks the standard of achievement of a civilisation'.

Spence's relationship with his clients was the usual Romantic one which also applied to most Modernist commissions: the client hands the designer a brief, the designer goes away and after a while returns to present the drawings. 'Committees do not know the feeling of tension that always exists after a concerted effort to get a series of drawings together', writes Spence. Yet he is polite about his clients; admittedly they did not know themselves much about what they wanted, and for instance they let him design the Physics building before the professor had been appointed. But he praises Fulton saying, 'he gave me a clear idea of the university he wanted to see' and he demanded a 'Sussex esprit'. That seems to have been all, except, for Fulton's ideas about College House. Fulton and Briggs, for their part, said even less. Much later Briggs professed that 'the academics had nothing to do with the choice of Spence as an architect'. In fact, underneath the serenity, there was a somewhat different story to be told. Spence tended to be expensive; he was aware of it, and at times he even liked to give the impression he did not care for UGC costs limits. In 1961 there came a point when the university had to promise the UGC that it would try and be more economic in future. The wider architectural profession, of course, came to know rapidly about the situation and Guy Oddie (of the UGC, one of the more 'hardline' Welfare State cost-conscious practitioners) remembers 'the rascal Spence; if only we could have looked after the Spences, the pounds would have taken care of themselves'. The situation was, however, more complicated than that. The UGC had, in fact, granted some extra money – 'it might be reasonable to allow a somewhat higher expenditure for College House as the centerpiece' – if money could be saved on other buildings. In the end, the cost of Falmer House, £352,000, did not appear all that high and the level of the university's capital spending, £4m by 1966–7, was hardly out of line with its sister foundations.

By the later 1960s some more substantial criticisms of the Sussex 'plan' were voiced. The rapid growth meant that already by 1966 Falmer House was getting too small as a social building and a large refectory centre was created further up the campus. Much of the campus as it had been built by the early 1970s was hardly visible from the central area. The science buildings in particular were spreading up the hill towards the east and were almost completely out of sight. Sussex retorted by reiterating its philosophies of keeping to a certain kind of detailing, and of the principle of unpredictability. Lastly, Sussex did not treat student residences as a priority: the landladies of Brighton in the off-season period provided too good an accommodation, which also seemed to work well socially. However, from 1963, several halls of residence were built further up the valley which do not really form part of Spence's inner campus. Thus, although Sussex's main buildings gave an overwhelmingly good start to New University architecture, as a university plan Sussex was to make hardly any impact at all.

LAST INTERNATIONAL MODERN: WARWICK

The 'best' institutions are normally those whose story is swiftly told, or at least where origins and development can be followed through in a straight line. Of all the Seven this is least the case at Warwick, and yet, this university prides itself of being the largest of the Seven and the most successful one in academic terms. There is not one, but several architectural stories to tell. The main scheme by Yorke, Rosenberg and Mardall (YRM) came last chronologically; in terms of the history of architectural styles, it is the earliest.

Proposals by the civic elites and the church in Coventry went back to 1943 and continued throughout the 1950s; the chief aim was an elite Technological University, such as MIT. The stirrings at Brighton in 1958 spurred Coventry into action, but Arthur Ling's 'Proposed University College' for only 670 students (see page 65 (fig. 2.5)) did not correspond to the UGC's plans for greater expansion. Government assent did come in May 1960, a month later than York and Norwich, and yet, Warwick admitted its first students a year later than the other two. The muscle of the Coventry promoters was considerable, thanks especially to their chief, the car manufacturer Lord Rootes; yet it could not have been the UGC's aim at that time to give a technological slant to any of the Seven because technical education was destined to be strengthened through the new Colleges of Advanced Technology. The image of industry and commerce remained powerful, in the constant stress on an institution that was turning away from the past, towards efficiency and modernity. It took a long time, until late 1962, to appoint the vice chancellor, apparently because of the limited market for such high-powered figures. John Blackstock Butterworth was a lawyer and a fellow, and, by 1962, sub-warden of New College Oxford. His language was among the most dynamic: 'expansionist', 'trendsetters in everything'. He declared that 'No university matters until two fifths of its staff are airborne at any one time'.

It took nearly another year before the chief architects were appointed and planning for the main site could begin, mainly because of the uncertainties over the positions of planners relative to designers. Although the general rule was that the local promoters found the architect, the university kept asking the UGC for advice. Warwick also followed, more faithfully than the other Seven, the UGC directive that at first a planner should be employed for the general layout and that only afterwards the designers for the actual buildings should be chosen. Local supporters were keen on local practitioners, because, as Dr Henry Rees of the local Executive Committee remarked, competitions could be lengthy and architects of national reputation might not act cost-consciously. Waiting in the wings was Arthur Ling, Coventry City architect. Considering the reputation of Coventry and its planning and rebuilding after the World War II destruction, Ling did not seem too parochial a choice. Moreover, he liked to combine his activities as an architect in a public office with the pronouncement of experimental schemes. Butterworth, at least initially, seemed 'unwilling to commit himself' to Ling. By mid-1963 'the architects were anxious to begin sketch plans'. In addition, Sir Donald Gibson, Ling's predecessor as the chief planner of Coventry after the war, recommended the use of Clasp, a prefabricated building method, just at that time famously taken up at York. Ling then became planning consultant and was joined by Arthur Goodman, of the regionally-known firm Grey, Goodman of Derby, for the design of individual buildings and they soon started on the smaller site, the 'East', or 'Gibbet Hill' site. The group lacks the coordination of the small East Anglia 'Village' Campus of the same year but its buildings have served the university well ever since. By late 1963 it turned out that Ling was to leave Coventry. By November, Yorke, Rosenberg and Mardall were appointed as architects for the main site, though Ling continued as overall planner for sometime. Warwick's procedure, clearly, was not a model.

Soon, however, Warwick did get its act together. The university produced a development plan which fell far short of what York had produced in 1962, but it did exceed in detail the purposely vague outlines for East Anglia and Essex. Probably spurred by Essex's adept handling of publicity, Warwick stepped into the limelight on 9 April 1964 at the Institute of Directors in Belgrave Square, London. Such a move was, indeed, needed in order to launch the ambitious appeal for £4m. Warwick obtained the highest sum of all the Seven: £2.75m by 1967. Butterworth's idea was to be clear, simple and big: 10,000, 15,000 even 20,000 students. It was to be 'national' in status, 'first class'. On the other hand, he addressed the local community, speaking of the 'closest possible co-operation . . . to develop the industrial side along up-to-date American lines'. Warwick wanted its image to be that of the 'real world', although, as in the other New Universities, Oxbridge dominated in the first appointments, since nine out of ten professors were educated there. The academic setup was vaguely outlined as a number of 'schools', largely synonymous with faculties, with 'Boards of Studies' to organise curricula across the schools while a notion of the old kind of professorial chair also prevailed. The basic maxim seemed to be freedom of choice for all. It is 'best to let professors in and let them get on with it'; there was to be 'no straightjacket', 'no "complex whole"'.

> It is regarded as essential that the academic organisation should not be influenced by anything other than academic considerations. It is vital to the well-being of the academic disciplines that those working in each of them should be able to work and teach together. The University will not therefore, attempt to interweave teaching with the units of social organisation which are proposed, since that could only be done either by making the social organisation coincide with the academic, or by breaking down the academic groups and dispersing them through the social units.

Thus Warwick was opposed to both the integration of college structures into the whole, as at York or Lancaster, and the domination of 'schools' over subjects, as at Brighton or Norwich.

Ling's 1963/4 University of Warwick Development Plan – hinting at a growth to 20,000 students – was the largest project of its time in Britain. And yet, it excelled in 'townscape' compactness: a '10 minutes' walk' was sufficient to traverse the campus. To achieve this there had to be a complicated scheme for vehicular traffic, a kind of loop road, with assorted pedestrian levels above, and a special feature of Crystal Palace-like multistorey covered streets. On the other hand, the central precinct is still partly open to parkland. It is flanked by lavish communal, or, rather, ceremonial buildings for the arts, including a very large assembly hall, and a gigantic library. The arts teaching blocks border on the residences which shape the outer fringe of the campus and are arranged in courts and semi-courts, plus seventeen-storey towers. The halls are, furthermore, lavishly appointed with dining areas, common rooms etc. Ling thought that each hall should be designed individually and emphasised that he did not possess, as yet, 'the final answer to student living'. A shopping centre, somewhat on the edge, completes the complex; straddling across the motorway, it was to serve the wider neighbourhood.

Ling's proposal looked lively and glossy but it was largely a town planner's and architect's dream and contained little detail. Above all, it was totally unclear how and when the '58 millions' could be found to build it in its entirety (fig. 2.46). Subsequently, during the autumn of 1964, with Ling leaving and YRM taking over, the great plan was quietly abandoned, but no new overall scheme was publicised until later in 1966. When Butterworth asked the UGC's opinions about Yorke, Rosenberg and Mardall (YRM), he was told that they are 'faster . . . a big office' and that they built economically. YRM was a firm with a very strong reputation in public sector work, not so much for schools or housing but for more technically demanding, and often very large complexes, such as Gatwick Airport and St Thomas's Hospital in London. It is very likely that YRM disagreed with much of the Ling plan. In their entry for Churchill College Cambridge they were the only ones who wanted to break decisively with the college image, and designed a version of Zeilenbau blocks (cf. page 68) which amounted to a manifesto against both Oxbridge and Redbrick (and, in effect, Sussex, too): 'Avoid . . . the conscious protective sense of turning in-ness', they said at Cambridge, as well as the 'grand, pompous scale of Renaissance and Neo-Classical Colleges', in fact, avoid any 'subordinance of the needs of college members in order that architectural effects may be obtained' (fig. 2.10).

Beginning at Warwick with the library, the YRM team, led by Eugene Rosenberg himself, chose the most straightforward Modernist type of rectangular structure. All the blocks are essentially the same, though they are not unidirectionally placed in Zeilenbau formation but at right angles. There was a further formula in one of the planning pronouncements of 1963/4 which eminently suited the designers: 'It will not be possible to give physical recognition to individual schools of studies in the plan'. The slab blocks are large, and what makes them look alike is the 20 feet (6 metres) interval framework of in-situ concrete; with their windows set back, the blocks appear boldly patterned and the white cladding gives the whole a clean and very orderly air. Comments by others were mostly very positive during the years 1966–9; 'the University has deliberately chosen to create buildings on the main part of the

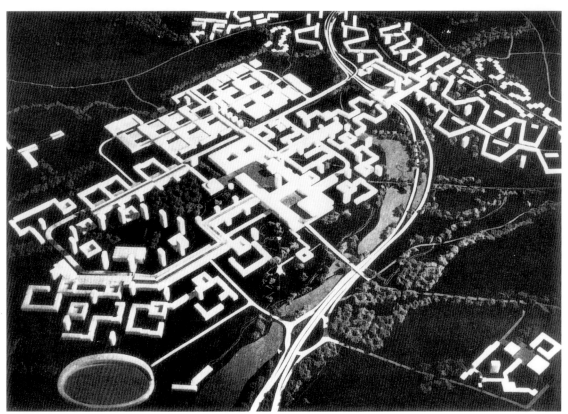

2.46 The University of Warwick at Coventry: Ling Plan 1963/4. (*University of Warwick Development Plan*, by Arthur Ling, publ. University of Warwick, 1964)

2.47 The University of Warwick, by Yorke, Rosenberg and Mardall (YRM) Model 1966. (*AA* 1967, p. 64)

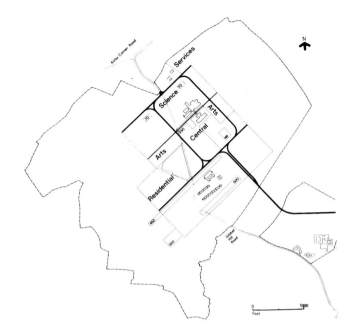

2.48 The University of Warwick, Yorke, Rosenberg and Mardall (YRM). Zoning plan 1966. The plan also shows almost all the buildings of the YRM phase. Bottom right: the Gibbet Hill site. (*AA* 1967, p. 64)

site on a scale with a large university'. The blocks were said to 'look exceedingly solid', 'cool', there is 'strength . . . even nobility'. 'Classic simplicity . . . austerity of outward appearance . . . elegant proportions distinguish them from cheap imitations . . . may be of great value in the general education of a generation of students from aesthetically undistinguished local backgrounds' (figs 2.47–2.49).

While Butterworth rejected the interference of the social with the academic sphere he fully endorsed the earlier UGC line on student accommodation, aiming for a half or even two thirds of the students to be resident on campus. Residences should consist of social groups or units, 'which we call Halls'. Even here, the authorities were cautious: 'Nothing will stop a student living in isolation if he wants to . . .' and further: 'it would be disastrous if the wardens try to build in Oxbridge type traditions rather than let new ones grow out of the way of life in hall'. Warwick chose the full hall of residence concept, but advocated very large units of 1,000 to 1,500 students each. By mid-1965 YRM began with Rootes Hall. The name is a little confusing as it refers to a whole complex of the residences and the separate 'social building'. The four-storey study bedroom blocks contain sections of sixteen rooms, along internal corridors with internal bathrooms, in other words, conforming to the Modern International Style slab block, and even to the Zeilenbau ideal. It must be remembered that they also conform to the UGC stringent cost limits. When Warwick proposed more expensive tower blocks, the UGC said no. The Rootes 'Social Building', on the other hand, is very well appointed and was shaped somewhat after Falmer House at Sussex. It contains all manner of communal facilities, including the proverbial 'airport lounge' (figs 2.50–2.52).

By 1966 YRM were publicising a new development plan. It bore very little relationship to Ling's. The university's demand for the non-interference of social and academic spheres translated into the standard recipe of 1930–50s Modernist architecture

119

2.49 The University of Warwick, entrance to library and science blocks, YRM, 1964–6.

2.50 The University of Warwick, residences (Rootes Hall), YRM 1966. (*AD* 6-1966, p. 302)

2.51 The University of Warwick, plans of residences (Rootes Hall), YRM, 1966. (*AD* 6-1966, p. 302)

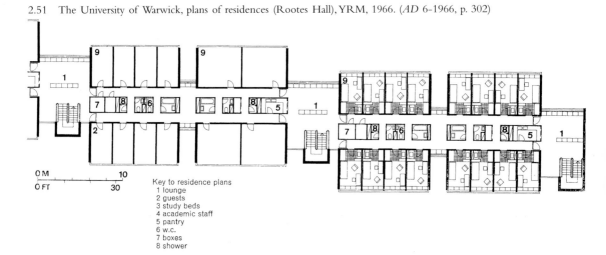

Key to residence plans
1 lounge
2 guests
3 study beds
4 academic staff
5 pantry
6 w.c.
7 boxes
8 shower

2.52   The University of Warwick, 'Airport Lounge' in the Rootes Social Building.

and planning, that is, zoning. YRM envisaged five zones: academic, central facilities, residential (they now avoid the term 'hall'), services and open spaces. What was to hold such a plan together were, of course, the communication arteries, 'a stem of internal roads'. In its final form, the system was to have one-way primary roads, off which secondary roads would lead, giving access to buildings and car parks. Even the 'spine', the central axis of the campus, consisted of a roadway. YRM were not interested in Ling's kind of vertical division of traffic, there is only one small pedestrian bridge leading to the library. Altogether, the plan was seen as severely pragmatic; buildings not immediately necessary, such as lavish 'public buildings near the Library, were 'hoped for', and a pedestrian system could 'be put in hand', if desired. Perhaps the best way of characterising the complex was by Diana Rowntree' in the *Guardian* of 1966 when she described it as a 'town sized machine'. But this town was not so much a postwar Welfare State town, as an office town.

Criticism was bound to arise. The last section of this chapter will deal with the major issues in a new phase of thinking about universities, the 'troubles' and the subsequent soul-searching which affected most institutions of higher education. At Warwick, condemnation came earlier. Already shortly after completion YRM's study bedroom blocks were held to be 'needlessly regimented'. The inconsistencies of the planning process were, of course, known, yet not talked about openly. What hit Warwick was the general condemnation of the classic International style, especially the predominance of right angles and the repetition of forms. It happened earlier in Britain than elsewhere; we shall find an altogether far greater number of slab blocks in France and in Germany. To the majority of British professional opinion Warwick appeared to be 'dehumanised' . . . 'yesterdays' planning philosophy'. So, the university took the consequences and changed planners yet again. By early 1971 YRM had been replaced by Gabriel Epstein (Shepheard and Epstein), of Lancaster fame. Under their aegis, the new wriggly units and small kinds of residential blocks contrasted strongly with YRM. Warwick now also created a number of central social buildings, largely with private money. All in all, Warwick's importance in the context of the unified plans of the Seven New Universities was chiefly one of contrast.

FORTRESS COLLEGE: KENT

The lessons of Warwick could be summed up easily: in an ideal setup there should be a single site, a determined vice chancellor and a single architect who acts as planner and as designer. It needs a fierce commitment and stringent organisation at the start and several years of continuous devotion. The University of Kent fared even worse than Warwick. To the critics it seemed that there never was a proper plan and this criticism began much earlier than with the other Seven, in 1965, when the first buildings had hardly even been completed. Ever since then Kent has been considered the least successful of the group in terms of its architecture. And yet, to leave it at that would be a grave mis-representation. Like Warwick, Kent did proceed according to very specific ideas and produced a set of buildings of major significance. Within our story it brought the high point of the movement of a return to Oxbridge; among the Seven 'paternalistic' Kent was the antidote to 'libertarian' Essex. (It may also be opposed to Warwick, as regards the latter's opposition to mixing learning and living.)

Kent belongs to the second group of the Seven. As with Essex and Warwick, the government announcement and the appointment of the Academic Planning Board came in mid-1961. Its vice chancellor, Geoffrey Templeman, had been registrar at Birmingham University, from where he had been involved with the early planning of Warwick. He was trained as a medieval historian in Birmingham, London and Paris; thus Kent's vice chancellor was the only one of the Seven who had not been to Oxbridge. Was his opting for the Oxbridge model now a way of making up for that? Or was his character (according to later comments), 'personifying the older academic style, diffident and haughty' and disinclined, for instance, to engage himself in public relations exercises to collect donations at the root of it? In any case, for the commentators of the 1960s 'paternalism', 'conservatism', opting 'against egalitarian prejudice' and the Oxbridge option seemed to go together. Templeman, in turn, frequently seemed to find himself on the defensive. Perhaps he suffered from the impact of the rhetoric and success of Sussex and Essex. To him, a university was 'not about running gimmicks'. He did, however, come with strong ideas: breaking down departmental barriers, interdisciplinary curricula etc. What Sussex called schools, Kent called faculties; students took a long Part I in which they combined several subjects, including the natural sciences, and then specialised in Part II. The main teaching method was to be the tutorial. Above all, Tempelman aimed at a 'merging of learning and living' in his colleges.

The local sponsors had made substantial moves to find an architect before Templeman arrived. With the advice of the RIBA's president, William Holford, a long short-list was devised and consulted (of which Lasdun, Leslie Martin, RMJM and

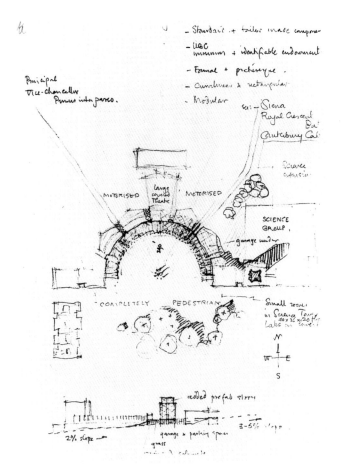

2.53   University of Kent at Canterbury: very early sketch by Sir William Holford, *c*. 1963. (G. Martin, *From Vision to Reality. The Making of the University of Kent at Canterbury*, publ. University of Kent, 1990)

Powell and Moya declined). In the end Holford himself took the job. The men at Kent prided themselves in having chosen a town planner 'among the top few in the world league'. Furthermore, Sir William Holford, RIBA goldmedallist in 1963 and life peer in 1965, also had much experience with university planning at Exeter and Cambridge. Holford presented his first outline plan in May 1963. He had to follow a number of major general formulations by Templeman. The layout should be conceived as a 'single whole from the beginning', a surprising statement in view of all the later criticisms. There should be three kinds of sections – amounting to zones – central buildings, science buildings and residences. Templeman pleaded that they should be quite separate from each other and especially that there should be plenty of room between them initially, so that they could be filled out in time and not get cramped, a formula tried in some American campuses (see page 25). A large terrain, immediately north of the small city, on a hill, offering a magnificent view of the cathedral, was the 'finest site in the country' for any of the new universities. The hill top was clearly the ideal position for the central buildings. The science area could be located on the plateau behind, out of sight, while most of the colleges were to be placed on the road leading up to the hill. Apparently entirely for his own consumption, Holford sketched a giant, concentrated semi-circular building (fig. 2.53), playing, like Spence, with historical architecture – Siena, the Royal Crescent, Bath, Canterbury Cathedral and Birmingham University and, for good measure, an American-type 'Science Tower'. In his actual 'University Development Plan' of 1963–4, a slight document, Holford followed Templeman's recipe of dispersal.

In purely visual terms the early layout of Kent was singular and massively ambitious. There were to be 'at least 10 completely self-contained colleges', all of a similar shape. Spaced widely apart, as isolated units, surrounded by lavish greenery, this ensemble would have made a strong impression. Two of the colleges are close to the central buildings on the top of the hill and form a small core group. This is where we come face to face with the view and Holford tries to make the most of this area in terms of vistas and building impact. In the centre is the large library and the isolated single-storey octagonal Senate Building, designed after Holford's time. For the rest of the teaching and social buildings, on the side of and behind the front range, there appears to be no plan. The criticism in late 1965 in the *Architects' Journal* was devastating – 'buildings spread out in a way reminiscent of the worst attempts at the "grand manner" . . . a bleakness and curiously old-fashioned attempted grandeur and formality'. Moreover, this remained the only major critical account. A little later, Reyner Banham, usually hypercritical of most New University architecture, at least liked the interiors of Kent's colleges.

By late 1963 it became clear that Kent was in a hurry. It wanted to admit a large first intake in 1965. The option of temporary accommodation was rejected. At this point the UGC was particularly favourably inclined. It decided to make an exception from the rule not to pay for student bedrooms, and gave money for most of them in the first two colleges. (In any case, the UGC would pay fully for all other facilities in such a building). Their design was deemed to be within the UGC costs limits, £945 per unit, in conventional construction and the university speeded up building by arranging for a novel form of 'negotiated contract'. By mid-1965 and mid-1966 respectively Eliot and Rutherford College opened. Holford, however, had already had enough. In late 1965 he resigned. A recent Kent chronicle speaks of 'a clash of personalities'. Holford complained that his client did not give him sufficient instructions.

In general terms Templeman echoed the central design policy of the time: 'The thing that really fascinates me is the whole problem of how to design buildings so as to create the sort of community you want'. In 1964 Holford acknowledged his debt to the York Development Plan. But the architecture of the Kent colleges owes very little to the English tradition and differs strongly from what York was building at that time. The only models were the compact square blocks, linked diagonally, at Bryn Mawr College; indeed, Anthony A. G. Wade, the job architect of Eliot and Rutherford, had studied at the University of Philadelphia with Louis Kahn. As Holford states: 'Each college is as compact and as self-contained as it can be made'. A very large number of facilities are fitted into this geometry. The college is made up of four squares, four quads. The basic unit is a group of seven study bedrooms plus one tutor's room and each quad basically consists of four such wings. This is an economic arrangement, because it combines maximum daylight access with minimal corridor length. Many corridors are, however, artificially lit. Contrary to widespread custom, Kent provided no kitchenette or breakfast room with the set of study bedrooms. The insides of the quads contain the other rooms which the self-sufficient college needs: the kitchens and the immensely complex sets of ancillary

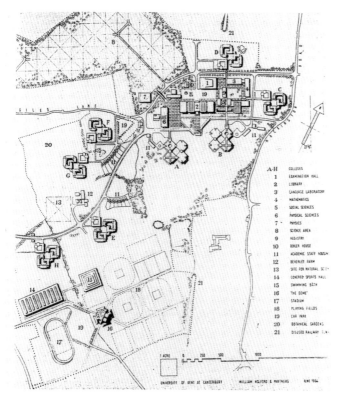

2.54   University of Kent, plan with eight colleges, June 1964, by Sir William Holford. (G. Martin, *From Vision to Reality. The Making of the University of Kent at Canterbury*, publ. University of Kent, 1990)

A-H   COLLEGES
1   EXAMINATION HALL
2   LIBRARY
3   LANGUAGE LABORATORY
4   MATHEMATICS
5   SOCIAL SCIENCES
6   PHYSICAL SCIENCES
7   PHYSICS
8   SCIENCE AREA
9   REGISTRY
10   BOILER HOUSE
11   ACADEMIC STAFF HOUSING
12   BEVERLEY FARM
13   SITE FOR NATURAL SCIEN
14   COVERED SPORTS HALL
15   SWIMMING BATH
16   THE DOME
17   STADIUM
18   PLAYING FIELDS
19   CAR PARK
20   BOTANICAL GARDENS
21   DISUSED RAILWAY TRA

1 ACRE   0   250   500   1000

UNIVERSITY OF KENT AT CANTERBURY   WILLIAM HOLFORD & PARTNERS   JUNE 1964

2.55   University of Kent, air view. (Courtesy University of Kent)

rooms, lecture theatres and seminar rooms (though no college libraries). Most prominent of all are the common rooms and the refectory. The architectural interest inside comes, of course, with the way the four blocks are linked. The way they 'touch' each other at their corners provides for diagonal passages and staircases, which, in turn, lend a special sense of coherence to the inside – once one has acquired a sense of where one is. The external severity has always been associated with the 'contents', though it must also be due to the repetitive and conventional manner of construction (figs 2.54 and 2.55).

During the day, such a complex can hold about 1,000 users. Most non-science teaching takes place in the colleges. About 300 resident students had to be accommodated, with additional facilities for the c. 300 non-resident students, as well as offices and teaching rooms for about seventy tutors (and eight tutors in residence); in addition there were two to three dozen service staff. Only the Master lived in a separate, but adjacent house. The colleges enjoyed, at least initially, a large degree of autonomy, with their own complex administration; however, students would be admitted to the university-wide faculties; thus in this crucial aspect the colleges at Kent differ from Oxbridge; they resemble rather more those at Durham University. The first Master of Eliot, the theologian Professor Alec Whitehouse, had indeed come from Durham. There were, furthermore, the college rules to match the complexity of the plan. All undergraduates were assigned 'moral tutors'. There were strict rules governing visiting hours; the iron gates to the only entrance of the college were firmly locked at night. As at Oxbridge, permission had to be sought for any absences ('exeats'). On the other hand, Eliot claimed to be the first coed university college in the country (though Lancaster claimed this, too). The culmination of college life was the meal time. This was one of Templeman's ideals, the 'community of masters and scholars' eating together, the 'college family united'. In the time-honoured Oxbridge style, undergraduates could not sit down until the Master and the teachers had taken their seats. The surroundings were designed to match. The refectory takes the full internal height of the block, the High Table is, of course, raised, and here we come to the culmination of this vast ritualised space: a huge window opens up the view towards 'Bell Harry', the silhouette of Canterbury Cathedral (figs 2.56–2.58).

Discussions at the time, however, centred around the question as to whether the old college ritual could be upheld. Indeed, many of the rules were soon to be watered down or disregarded. There were other new factors which began to erode the community of the college, as well as its economy, namely the changes in students' dining habits, from the set-hour patterns to highly informal timing. Students at Essex, which, as we shall see, prided itself for having 'no rules', tried to ridicule Kent. The university would counter these reproaches by saying that parents were usually happy with the knowledge that their offspring was well looked after. The later colleges at Kent, indeed, took on a different shape and a less formidable look. The sensitive critics of the mid-1960s, such as Stuart Maclure at the *Listener*, sounded concerned. According to Maclure, Templeman took a 'great gamble' with the college concept, and 'Holford's buildings incorporate these ideas with such uncompromising rigidity that the university authorities have little room for manoeuvre if they want to change their mind'. What was most striking, at Kent, as well as in Maclure's analysis, was the belief in the behaviour-shaping power of the buildings. An even more complex, but also more subtle example of this belief will be found at York.

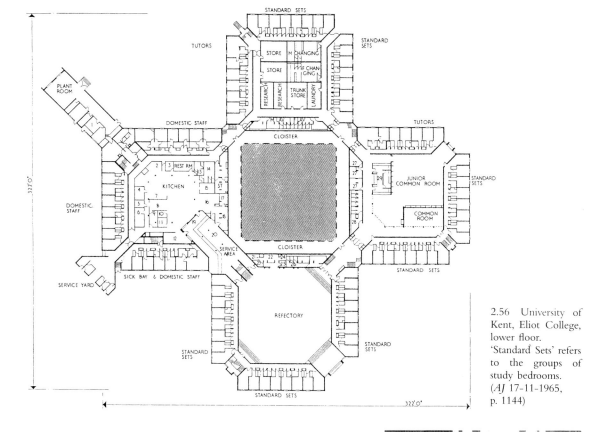

2.56 University of Kent, Eliot College, lower floor. 'Standard Sets' refers to the groups of study bedrooms. (*AJ* 17-11-1965, p. 1144)

2.57 University of Kent, Rutherford College, main entrance

2.58 University of Kent, interior of college dining room towards the High Table from which there is a view of Canterbury Cathedral. (*AR* 4-1970, p. 272)

Although excelling with new academic ideas and striking modern buildings, Warwick and Kent never made it as regards a convincing unity of university design. Sussex had been first on the scene with its highly successful academic concept as well as with an attractive layout and unusual, yet dignified architecture. Most importantly, architecture and academic concepts at Sussex seemed to match immediately. But it was with York and its colleges, chronologically following Sussex, when New University planning and design became an immensely serious issue, in thought and in the practical determination of all concerned.

The University of York has the most distinguished prehistory of all the Seven. Traditions of learning went back to the Middle Ages. As early as the seventeenth century the old 'Capital of the North' had made attempts to found a university and there were several more attempts later. Like other cities, York revived the project in the years after 1945. The notables of the city sent out a memorandum promoting York in glowing terms (fig. 2.38). The UGC rejected the idea, chiefly saying that there were already several universities in the region. But York did not give up. Under the auspices of the local amenity society, the York Civic Trust, the promoters set up a permanent body, the York Academic Trust, to keep up the momentum. Throughout the whole process the financial backing of the Rowntree Trusts and the help of the Rowntree director, civic dignitary and benefactor John Bowes Morell was crucial; it was Rowntree who secured Heslington Hall and the adjacent site. Secondly, numerous small institutions were founded, such as the Institute of Archives or the Institute of Advanced Architectural Studies which tried hard to acquire regional and national importance. They were installed in some of the city's supernumerous medieval buildings, notably King's Manor, which, in turn, helped to fortify what was York's greatest asset, the image of a richly historic city. From there it seemed a plausible step to claim that York, as 'one of the most beautiful towns in the country, possesses much of the ethos of Oxford and Cambridge', or even: 'York's ultimate aim is to establish a university of the status of Oxford or Cambridge'. York's catchment area was conceived not in terms of the region, but of 'the whole English speaking world'.

The government's approval of Norwich and York came in April 1960. Chairman of the York Academic Planning Board was Lord Robbins, who was also about to start the inquiry which two years later resulted in the eponymous report. Its demand for the speedy increase of student places greatly helped the ethos of the New Universities in their early years, although the Robbins Report was not to lay much stress on the residential element in new universities, let alone a strong collegiate bias. Another year elapsed before the vice chancellor and the architects were appointed. From then onwards efficiency reigned. Sir Eric James, who had been promoted to life peer (Lord James of Rusholme) in 1959, was educated at The Queen's College, Oxford, and then became the revered High Master of Manchester Grammar School. Like Lord Robbins, Jones, too, had been much involved with the UGC. The architects, Robert Matthew, Johnson-Marshall and Partners – 'RMJM', or, popularly, 'Rumjum' – were a firm of the most solid achievements, particularly in institutional architecture among which were several university buildings and projects. Their design for Churchill College Cambridge was one of the most radical proposals with a notably industrial look (fig. 2.10). The firm was later to obtain an astonishing three further

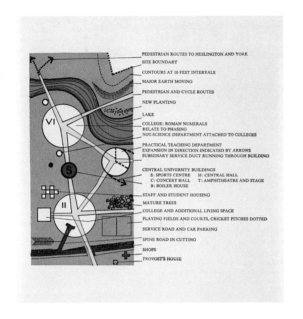

PEDESTRIAN ROUTES TO HESLINGTON AND YORK
SITE BOUNDARY
CONTOURS AT 10 FEET INTERVALS
MAJOR EARTH MOVING
PEDESTRIAN AND CYCLE ROUTES
NEW PLANTING
LAKE
COLLEGE: ROMAN NUMERALS
RELATE TO PHASING
NOT-SCIENCE DEPARTMENT ATTACHED TO COLLEGES
PRACTICAL TEACHING DEPARTMENT
EXPANSION IN DIRECTION INDICATED BY ARROWS
SUBSIDIARY SERVICE DUCT RUNNING THROUGH BUILDING
CENTRAL UNIVERSITY BUILDINGS
  S: SPORTS CENTRE   H: CENTRAL HALL
  C: CONCERT HALL   T: AMPHITHEATRE AND STAGE
  B: BOILER HOUSE
STAFF AND STUDENT HOUSING
MATURE TREES
COLLEGE AND ADDITIONAL LIVING SPACE
PLAYING FIELDS AND COURTS, CRICKET PITCHES DOTTED
SERVICE ROAD AND CAR PARKING
SPINE ROAD IN CUTTING
SHOPS
PROVOST'S HOUSE

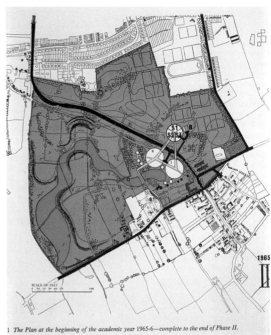

The Plan at the beginning of the academic year 1965-6—complete to the end of Phase II.

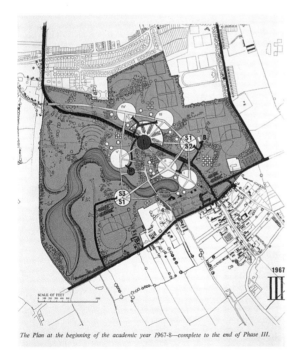

The Plan at the beginning of the academic year 1967-8—complete to the end of Phase III.

The Plan at the beginning of the academic year 1970-1—complete to the end of Phase IVA.

2.59   The University of York Development Plan of 1962 by Robert Matthew, Johnson–Marshall and Partners ('RMJM'; Project Architect: Andrew Derbyshire). A demonstration of the possibilities of extension. (*University of York Development Plan 1992–1972*, publ. University of York, 1962) commissions for new universities (Bath, Stirling and Ulster). The choice had been made by the local Promotions Committee, whose secretary (and future registrar), John West Taylor, had known Stirrat Johnson-Marshall. The actual designer in charge was Andrew Derbyshire who had made his name chiefly in public housing. Bernard Feilden, the noted Norwich architect (we shall meet him again at East Anglia) who was also becoming Britain's premier restorer of cathedrals, York amongst them, took on the lavish refurbishment of Heslington Hall which serves as York's representative headquarters and administration building.

York's relationship with the UGC was cordial, at least under Murray. But 'of all the [early] decisions taken . . . none was more fortunate than the choice of architects' according to the vice chancellor. Reciprocal compliments from the architects can be found in Andrew Saint's account of the university's building history which forms part of his book *Towards a Social Architecture*, on the Hertfordshire schools. Saint stresses the special nature of the way York was planned and constructed, and the spirit of co-operation, of much of 1940s and 1950 British Welfare State architecture. Lord James voiced the conviction of all the great patrons of New University architecture when he stated 'it is very doubtful indeed whether many . . . teachers and administrators realise the way in which the physical form of a university should reflect its academic ideas'. However, the actual relationship between client and architect could vary a lot. At Norwich and Essex, and to some extent at Sussex, there was a like-mindedness as regards the grand ideas of the scheme, while the architect was assured of the client's admiration for his artistic capabilities. The James-Derbyshire relationship was based more on a mutual relentless concern for the nitty-gritty. What was also greatly significant at the early stages of planning was that the number of decisionmakers was small. At York there was initially no committee, not even a building officer; the group nominally consisted of the vice chancellor, the registrar and the two architects, but in practice, the team amounted to James and Derbyshire. Any reproaches for lack of democracy would have been countered by stating that their undertaking was wholly accountable to the public, to the state, and that the planners would make sure that the job would be done with the utmost efficiency and speed; all of which also implied stringent economy, in fact, for architect and client cost limits formed part of the 'challenge'. It must also be stressed that the architect was as consistently devoted to the job as the client, in contrast to most of the other designers, such as Spence, Holford and even Lasdun, who were usually also busy with projects they rated grander than a cost-cutting university in the provinces.

The immediate result of this cooperation was the *University of York Development Plan* which was published in spring 1962. The document is, in fact, one of the most lengthy of its kind; it is less mathematical than its immediate predecessor, the 1960 Leeds university plan, but stronger on the actual details of academic life and the kinds of buildings required. It is, explicitly, a plan, not an architectural design. 'Planning' means in this case, primarily an outline of the practical requirements and their complex inter-relationships. It also means the firm pronouncement of their academic-social-educational philosophy and the schematic portrayal of the spatial relationship of the various elements to serve that philosophy. Hence the book is full of 'sociometric diagrams', two-dimensional statements of relationships (fig. 2.30). Probably most admired by planners was the careful device for York's extendibility, year by year from 1963 to 1970. Yet the principle was straightforward: simply add further colleges (fig. 2.59).

The question of the architect as briefmaker was an issue with every New University. At York the overall plan and the concept of how the institution should work was James's. His motto was 'the identity of architectural and academic purpose'. What, then, was York's principal academic purpose? In the foreword to their plan, James stresses that devising the *Development Plan* was itself a 'deeply educative experience'. Education is indeed the key word in the philosophy of the university. Of the four key 'propositions' the development plan wishes to make, the first two are directly concerned with education, the third with change and extendibility and the fourth with education again, in particular with the effect architectural aesthetics would have on it. Later on James would joke: 'All I wanted to be was schoolmaster' and he seemingly did not mind being called elitist, meritocratic, paternalistic, even reactionary – though it was emphasised that he always had 'a distaste for pomp and circumstance'. In 1965 he concluded a speech about York with mention of its quasi priestly function: 'The academic community, the clerisy, as Coleridge called it, must not merely give society what it needs, but show it what it ought to need'. His desire to keep control seemed a natural corollary. Occasionally he maintained that a university should not grow beyond 3,000 which elicited a remark by one of the officers of the UGC that this would 'indeed [be] his sort of university, where the eye of the VC is on all'.

The usual way to begin a characterisation of a university foundation is to discuss academic content. Most New Universities tried to catch the limelight with proffering new subjects, or at least new combinations of subjects. They all shared the platform of interdisciplinarity. York, however, was least eager to join this trend. There is very little emphasis on any newness of subjects and it was easy on combining subjects. Basically candidates had the choice of whether to go for single or combined studies. As James put it: 'breadth is more likely to be achieved through methods of teaching than by actually laying down courses which aim at broad synthesis'. One may go further and state that at York the academic programme took second place to the educational-social process of conveying it (fig. 2.60).

Colleges had been recommended at York from the very beginning. The Oxford trained York notables advocated them for reasons of tradition and in order to provide a greater opportunity for each student 'to express and develop his personality'; colleges might even 'attract far greater endowments'. In Robbins's York Report of early 1961 we read that colleges 'build up a body of tradition and loyalties'. James, however, wanted to set counterpoints: colleges at York must not 'encourage isolation and a parochial attitude'. Every student and employee of the university was to be a member of a college. But to end the description there would be a grave simplification. What James did take on board was the Sussex line of discouraging subject self-containedness and, like his colleagues, he stressed the way in which subject boundaries are liable to change. But contrary to Sussex and East Anglia, York did not really mind what the units of academic organisation were called. Logically, the division of the university into colleges precluded other prominent sub-units, like 'schools'. In fact, York largely remained with the old structure of single subject 'departments' and added a loose organisation of 'Boards of Studies' in charge of coordinating the combined degrees. What really mattered to James was the dovetailing of the departments with the colleges. It is important to realise that York does not import the Oxbridge model of the autonomous college, which to a large extent determines its own academic make-up. York, of course, puts prime emphasis on the teaching that is done within

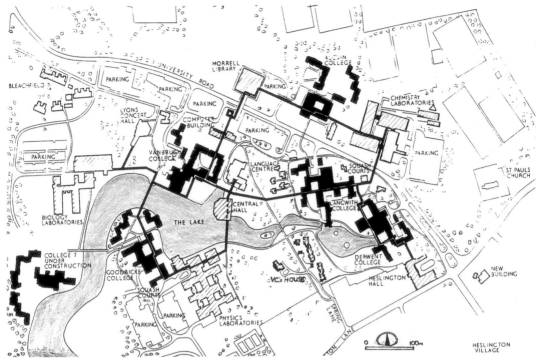

2.60　The University of York, map of colleges by the early 1970s. (*AJ* 23-2-1972, p. 418)

2.61　The University of York, plan of ground floor of Langwith College, 1963–5. The hatched area shows the 'public' walkway leading through the college. (Dober (1965))

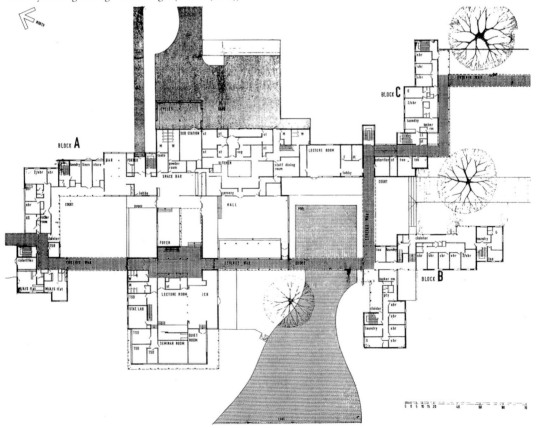

each college, chiefly in tutorials of three to four, but it disperses major subjects over most colleges. Thus the head of the English Department sits in one of the colleges, but most of the other colleges teach that subject, too. Each college was originally intended to have at least three departments.

A striking dialectic arises. On the one hand there is dispersion: no college should be associated with a particular subject, the rigid single subject culture was to be avoided. But, dispersion came to mean the opposite of separation; rather, it would help with 'the mixing of different interests and skills which is one of the chief purposes of university education' and provide 'opportunities for meeting new people and making contacts with fresh ideas which is the raison d'être of the university'. The 1962 plan even maintains that there is much more overlap between arts and sciences than previously held, but reluctantly accepts that, for purely practical and financial reasons, the teaching spaces of the natural sciences have to be kept apart. At times the York principles appear to be raised to a dogma: 'Excessive concentration of any particular function is therefore to be avoided, however convenient it may be either financially or administratively'. One way of optimising room use, or simply, to counter organisational chaos, was to devise the teaching timetable centrally.

There was a corollary in the handling of student applications: they were, first of all, admitted to the subject, to a department; they could then also choose a college; 'otherwise membership is distributed in such a way as to ensure within each college a representative spread of student academic interest'. We are, in a way, at the peak of the integrative philosophy of the New University movement. There should be as little separation as possible between the institution of teaching and the institutions of student life and student residence. In contrast, we have cited already the way in which Warwick was to formulate its opposition to precisely this principle. The York prospectus of 1969 states explicitly 'non-resident members, as well as all resident members of a college spend much of their time in their own or another college'. Linked to the way in which the teaching was dispersed was the insistence on avoiding a separate, or central student union building – in spite of the occasional clamouring for it

2.62 The University of York, interior of Langwith College. Part of entrance lobby, towards the left is the entrance to the large dining hall.

2.63 The University of York, colleges, design 1962/3. (UGC, *University Development 1957–62* (*Parliamentary Paper* Cmnd. 2267 Crown ©, by permission Controller of Her Majesty's Stationery Office), 1964, p. 115ff.)

from the student body. Nothing should substitute, or compete with life in the colleges. Each college had an elaborate structure of self-government, in which student representatives were involved from the start. Each college was urged to work out a limited amount of self-promotion and individuality – sometimes sounding slightly whimsical to outsiders – such as honorary memberships, special college lectures etc. An example of the power and strength of James's educational convictions was the way he argued that the smaller college setup gave wider opportunities for student participation, contrasting it with the way central student unions produce 'comparatively few, almost full-time student politicians'. It meant not only a break with standard modern customs in universities, but with a major Oxford tradition, too.

The size of colleges varied somewhat, but about 300 undergraduates plus 80 graduates and about 45 staff was considered about right. One half of the 300 members would be resident. These figures were based on calculations of very varied kinds. Four hundred was considered about the right economic size for a kitchen as well as the maximum number that could get to know each other within a year or two. This complex institution contains upwards of two dozen different kinds of rooms. Libraries, dining rooms, snack bars, bars, tutors' rooms, lecture rooms of some size, administrative offices, study bedrooms for a whole range of users, and more (figs 2.61–2.63).

All this might seem 'traditional', but the way all these facilities were combined had little precedent. A college at York is planned not concentrically, but centrifugally. It consists of several wings which are flung out in an asymmetrical manner, each surrounded by as much parkland as possible. There is an avoidance of straight corridors. At the outer ends of the wings are the rooms deemed to require most privacy, such as those for married academic staff. Rooms are usually arranged in nuclei of five to ten, sharing bathrooms and a pantry to make snacks. Each staircase has a tutorial room.

Most staircases have their own door to the outside. In the centre are the public rooms and here the communications lines meet. Again, we are told explicitly what should happen there: 'Students, staff, porters, cleaners and visitors, all pass through this space and here one can stop and talk, eat or drink, or walk on', or: 'here students sit and talk' (James). It seems that this sort of statement about their institution mattered more to the authorities than the normal college 'rules'. There were fewer of them than usual at that time. James believed in a low measure of status differentiation. There was no element whatsoever of the Oxbridge 'High Table'; the vice chancellor, it was reported, stood in the same queue for his lunch as the undergraduate. James himself held the college rules to be on the side of 'libertarianism'. Initially he had planned single sex colleges, but then it was decided to mix them, with men and women in different wings.

What the *Development Plan* did not intend to do was to determine the architectural design of the university. Here York, in stark contrast to the perceived old college idea, chose a very new method; Clasp, which stands for Consortium of Local Authorities' Special Programme, a method of building with relatively lightweight steel and precast concrete panels which had been used chiefly for schools by some Midland Towns from the later 1950s onwards. The principal idea of 'systems building' was of course to save cost and design effort by using the same method in as many buildings as possible. Speed of erection and predictability of cost were other virtues. Probably its most important advantage was flexibility of planning, 'ever varying rooms sizes and configurations' as opposed to 'the minimum study bedroom dictated by official limitations'. The system aroused wide interest in avant-garde architectural circles in those years and had reached its high point with a much noted model school erected at the Milan Triennale of 1960. At York Clasp was the chief contribution of the architects RMJM, and reflected part of the 1940s and 1950s ethos of the close collaboration between planners, designers, contractors and the building industry – an ethos that befitted James's idea of the university just as much. RMJM soon continued with it at Bath University. For York, the system was somewhat modified, with greater sound-proofing and additional features like oriel windows (figs 2.64 and 2.65).

York behaved much more like a normal university in building a number of spectacular communal structures, in fact very lavishly catering for large assemblies, theatre and concerts in separate buildings. There are also separate buildings for the sciences. Their placement within the campus as a whole, likewise, does not step out of the usual. Much was made of the park-like grounds of the university, again, nothing unusual for a campus university. At York the parkland was a continuation of the mature garden of Heslington Hall, but much work was also done by the university, and it was cleverly phased before the beginning of building. Virtually all residential rooms have a view of a section of the park. There was much praise of the 'casualness in moving around'. York follows the 1950s and 1960s town planning fashion in strictly separating pedestrian and vehicular traffic. The chief communication lines are the walkways. The way they are all covered by a lightweight roof structure gives them even more attraction. All buildings are linked by this system. Moreover, these passages do not just end at the main door of each college. In fact no college has anything like a front, or a main door – here the contrast with the bastions at Kent is particularly striking. The footpaths seem to linger through the colleges, all in the interests of communication. In this sense, with the system of 'nodes' and linking filaments, this uni-

2.64 The University of York, vice chancellor's house 1963–5.

versity is arguably not an assembly of separate units, but forms a whole, a kind of complete and 'anti-diagrammatic' organism that points forward to the next group of 'urban' university complexes.

York University planning was thus driven by a sense of responsibility to provide for the social and psychological well-being of the student – which was matched by a belief that the right kind of planning would actually generate the desired effects. The overall aim, as the main section of the *Development Plan* of 1962 concluded, was for the institution to achieve the status of a 'community' . . . [rather than] remain merely a mass of individuals'. It declared 'the principles of the plan attempt to lay down a framework on which the right relationships may be established, but they must be carried into the detailed design of the building units if the desired result is to be achieved.' Andrew Saint summarises his account of York University: 'Nowhere else did concentrated thought about what a university ought to be like in a modern democracy come so close to finding physical expression'. With statements like this Saint joins in with the verbal rhetoric of that period of planning and building, an issue to which the book will return later. In contemporary comments and criticisms it would be hard to find that level of praise. Suffice it to say here that as we shall see in a section below, York received less criticism than the other Six, except Lancaster. Consider J. M. Richards's judgment that York had: 'The only master plan that is being stuck to', which was perhaps the greatest possible compliment that could be expected from an architectural critic at that time. But, as in most such situations, there was also much to be sceptical of. First of all, York was not 'cheap'. When the chancellor, Lord Harewood begged his community for money in 1962 he admitted as much: 'the collegiate system . . . relatively expensive'. The cost of a student bedroom exceeded the UGC norms by 10 per cent, although that did not matter too much, as most of the purely residential element, about half of the total of *c.* £500,000, was, for the first colleges, paid out of the university's own funds which, at £1.5m were not among the largest of its date. However successful the landscaping, the UGC also considered it expensive, amounting, as it did, to about 10 per cent of the total building cost. In the later 1960s York's *Development Plan* had lost much of its conviction for the advanced planning community. The UGC held that York's method of expansion, by adding completely new colleges, was more expensive than piecemeal smaller

2.65 The University of York, view over the lake (Langwith College), showing the Clasp building prefabricated system; Heslington Hall is on the far right.

kinds of expansions. Lancaster which had adopted the collegiate system somewhat in the footsteps of York, could score with its more sophisticated recipes for campus expansion.

More tricky is the subject of aesthetics. It is doubtful whether one can uphold Saint's dictum that York was not to be 'a monument to . . . any abstract aesthetics'. The *Development Plan*, in the last four of its 'propositions', states: 'the architect's task is . . . to give the place the kind of order and beauty which will enhance and not detract from, or contradict, the uniqueness of the intellectual and emotional experience'. But James had doubts: 'I want beautiful places for students . . . my architect says beauty is in sticking to the costs limits . . . I am not sure whether this is OK'. The architects continued their brief discussion of aesthetics by mentioning a 'quality of memorableness'. Expressed more simply, Stirrat Johnson-Marshall intended the look of York to be 'in the style of the Cambridge Backs – grass , trees, water, buildings'. The architects thus came close to an image desired by the conservative local founders. In that sense, York belongs to the same tradition as Spence's Sussex. With regard to York's advanced building method, Clasp, there was a continuing worry that it would be lacking in aesthetic qualities. There was thus intensive concern on the part of York's designers to hit the right colour, and to blend it with the landscape, and there was disappointment when cheaper mixes had to be chosen. Yet another critic was reminded of the lower educational origins of the building system and the college layouts: 'York is a disarming place, a glorified secondary school, easy, relaxed, informal'. In the mid-1960s another, seemingly more profound criticism of the York concept arose. Michael Brawne cautiously voiced a disappointment in 1965 when he felt that the 'strongly built form' he anticipated from the plan had not materialised. Others, likewise, found the whole 'scattered', or 'confused'. In the early statements the

137

authorities at York had chided Redbrick as 'amorphous' and demanded York to be 'articulate from the start'. The fact was that between 1963 and 1965 the models for East Anglia and Essex had been thrust upon the public and critics. Perceptions as to what an 'integrative' New University should look like still kept changing. The stakes were upped again: to combine even more intensively the educational concepts with formal distinctiveness. The optimal 'social form' was still to be striven for.

INTEGRATED 'URBAN': EAST ANGLIA, ESSEX, LANCASTER, BATH AND OTHERS

The sequence of the New University campuses here does not entail a chronological, or academic pecking order. It proceeds according to the development of their architects' interpretation of the main academic-institutional task. At East Anglia we arrive at the seemingly closest fusion of academic intention, overall architectural plan and detailed design. There was now an even greater radicalism. East Anglia and Essex professed to reject all previous models of university planning and building: the Civics' and Redbricks' casual assemblage of buildings, of course, the campus of the looser, parkland kind (Sussex), as well as the regular Modernist town planning kind of spacing of blocks (Warwick), and also the college and the hall of residence. The briefest description of East Anglia and Essex is, in fact, that of one continuous building. This amounts not only to a change within a narrowly defined mode of architectural design but also to a departure from the older understanding of institutions. From a static view of a distinct locality, say a centrally placed honorific building, a predetermined, stationary place to meet, design develops towards a dispersal of sub-institutions, fusing them into a whole which is called 'urban', or 'linear', in analogy to a feeling for a town as a certain kind of complex and lively organism. To cite Peter Jokusch, a German architect who had studied all the English New Universities most closely during the 1960s: 'There is not actually an area in the university which is devoted exclusively to social purposes, but there is also no place in the university which cannot be considered a social place.' The cherished institutional-architectural notion of 'community' is subtly bent into 'communication', an encouragement of movement within the one-building complex. This change of thinking to some extent coincided with a profound change in educational-institutional philosophy, entailing an advocacy of the 'spontaneous', rather than the institutional-formal. Certain elements at York did foreshadow this new style, as did Chamberlin, Powell and Bon's 1960 plans for Leeds. Perhaps the best characterisation of what was intended by the new demand for the 'urban' was the fusion of institutional liveliness and architectural image.

As regards the relationship between designer and client/user, the heightened experimentalism could be seen to run counter to the new user 'freedom': the designer's role now seemed to be more high-profile and more dominating than ever before. That this did not always go down well with users and critics was almost a foregone conclusion.

East Anglia

The results, as they appeared by the end of the decade, were awe-inspiring mountains of concrete. Denys Lasdun's University of East Anglia was photo-celebrated by architectural journals all over the world, analysed sceptically by a new group of inde-terminist designer planners and unloved by a great many others. UEA's history is more complex than that of the other Six in the sense that one deals with several phases and agents which bear little relation to each other. In another sense, however, its architecture is more unified. Norwich was third in line after Brighton and York. The first local efforts went back to the 1920s and a new attempt was made in 1947. It was Brighton's and York's progress which galvanised the locals into action again in 1959. The notables comprised a much wider spectrum than at Sussex or York, gentry-cum-businessmen, education officers, county officials, but also academics from Oxford or Cambridge who were eager to help, largely because they loved their Norfolk country homes. The regional net was cast much more widely, comprising Suffolk and even Huntingdonshire – hence the university's somewhat imprecise name. The site was duly set next to a small, but cherished country house, Earlham Hall, long-time home of the Gurney banking family, with precious memories of Elizabeth Fry, the early nineteenth-century social reformer. The government go-ahead came in May 1960, as at York, but it took longer to find a vice chancellor. Dr Frank Thistle-thwaite was a fellow of St John's College Cambridge, a historian of matters Ameri-can, and chosen chiefly because of his clear ideas about UEA's structure. Far less dominant a figure than Fulton or James, Thistlethwaite nevertheless dealt effectively with the formidable group of local founders. He quickly put in place a number of 'schools', each with a firm identity, largely on the Sussex model; he found good heads for them and thus established an early academic reputation. Added to this was a rep-utation for user-friendliness, compounded by UEA's single most important novelty in adopting the American method of 'continuous assessment', rather than relying entirely on final examinations.

UEA opened in a blaze of publicity in October 1963, but this was not the main campus – which was hardly even on the drawing board by then – but the 'Univer-sity Village'. 'A wonderful freshness in outlook – a splendid combination of curiosity and kindness, a self-possession without aggression, of natural egalitarianism without effort' – the journalist from the *Daily Telegraph* must have picked a good day when she came to Norwich in November 1963 and found the well-dressed students of the 'University Village'. It had been built with great rapidity, for 1,200 students (no resi-dences, of course), in prefabricated one- or two-storied huts of wooden panels. More importantly, the layout by the noted local firm Feilden and Mawson and the land-scaping managed to tie it all together pleasantly; users simply felt 'happy'. The vice chancellor and his administration were, of course, residing in Earlham Hall. Thistleth-waite could be quite explicit about his allegiance to 'the county'; with regard to his own residence, a small country house, Wood Hall at Hethersett (fig. 2.66), he stated: 'It seemed desirable . . . for the vice chancellor to be quartered in a house which was known to, and accepted by the County, rather than in some town house in the centre of Norwich'. The power and image of the New Universities' vice chancellors knew seemingly no bounds; at York, James had himself built a house which rivalled Hes-lington Hall, not in size, of course, but in the separateness of its position (fig. 2.65), while Sloman's villa at Essex overlooked the whole campus and was reportedly acces-sible only via a drawbridge.

Yet another world was that of the architect from distant London, Denys Lasdun. As at Sussex, it was the local founders who were determined to engage a national

2.66 The University of
East Anglia at Norwich,
Wood Hall, the vice
chancellor's residence at
Hethersett, Norfolk
(mainly seventeenth
century). (Courtesy
UEA)

2.67 The University of
East Anglia, 'Draft I'
model, April 1963, by
Denys Lasdun and
Partners. Shows the
ziggurat residences and
the 'teaching wall'; while
the other functions are as
yet not clearly distributed
and indicated. (Courtesy
UEA)

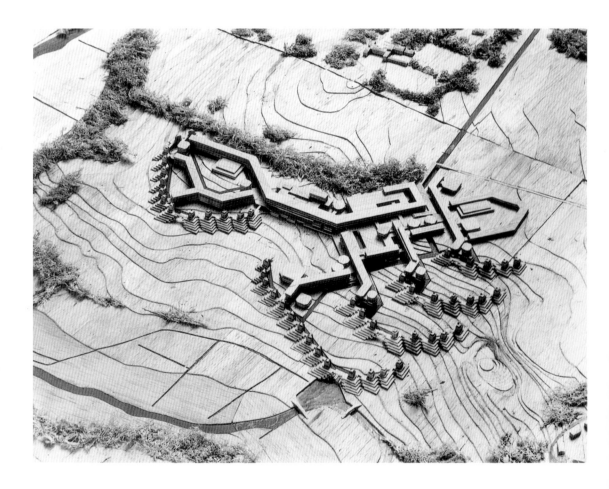

name for their campus. Their unstinting secretary, Gordon Tilsley, replied to unsolicited inquiries by local practitioners that Norwich university was to have an 'international reputation, therefore the architect had to be best that could be procured'. Cautious inquiries produced shortlists of much the same names as before, Spence, Philip Dowson, Chamberlin, Powell and Bon etc. Sir Leslie Martin, a man of immense reputation for both his contributions to Welfare State architecture in the London County Council and for his experimental approaches in his new teaching and design activities at Cambridge University appeared to be the strongest candidate. In July 1961 Martin came to see the Earlham site. He was keen, but when he proposed a procedure which appeared quite normal at that time, namely a division between an overall planner and designer and a number of others working under him, Lord Mackintosh, the chairman of the local founders, replied that 'he would like there to be one mind and one style throughout the university building'. In the end Martin declined, giving his reason that, as a teacher, he should not amass too many jobs at a time. With Mackintosh's dictum in mind it was Thistlethwaite who in October 1961 again began the search for a planner and architect. Memories and sources are hazy as to why Lasdun was approached, but Thistlethwaite was, of course, well aware of what Lasdun was then building in Cambridge (see page 66), and even more so of Lasdun's extensions for Thistlethwaite's own college, St John's (the 'Cripps Building') which in fact remained on paper because they appeared too daring. If one remembers at this point Nicholas Taylor's contention that the new Cambridge university architecture of Martin and others was splendid but that it remained isolated and 'suburban' as regards the environment, then Lasdun's move to a large, integrated university complex appeared a logical step to take.

Not much younger than Spence or Holford, Denys Lasdun nevertheless belonged to a quasi new generation of designers who had only just entered their phase of maturity. They sailed under the label 'The New Brutalists' which was commonly understood to entail masses of raw concrete, but also a new concern for planning in the sense of investigating the spaces of people's movement in towns or housing estates. But this kind of thinking in 'social architecture' was decidedly not that of the RMJM kind of devotion to economic and efficient building. On the other hand, the Smithsons and Lasdun would not want to be concerned with any 'aesthetic' of the kind entertained by Spence or RMJM, of 'added' forms or colour. The real hero of Lasdun and the New Brutalists as a designer and artist was Le Corbusier, or rather, the late Le Corbusier, overpowering yet poetically subtle.

The story of Lasdun at UEA has two opposing sides to it: the outside world, with its national publicity, and the client in Norwich. It took Lasdun well over a year to come up with a model and an overall plan, yet it was only 'an anatomy of ideas', he stressed. His press conference in Norwich on 25 April 1963 made a massive impact, in both the professional and the general press. Lasdun and Thistlethwaite showed what appeared to be a vast model of a most complex conglomerate which was publicised immediately and widely. It was described as 'This beautiful organism . . . this deeply felt and imaginative concept' by Lionel Brett in the *Architectural Review*. The model was, on the other hand, hard to decipher and this probably contributed to the readiness of the media to report Lasdun's rhetoric verbatim, with phrases like '. . . to foster among students a sense of the coherence as well of the diversity of knowledge'. In fact, the architect became the chief publicist of UEA during those years (fig. 2.67).

Behind this public face there was a quagmire of indecision, mistrust and rows going on at Norwich. Everybody was to blame. The university and its numerous groups and committees did not know what they were after, many of the local promoters did not like the architect's style and would have preferred something traditional. When asked about the colour of his concrete, Lasdun's quick reply was 'my concrete will be cathedral-coloured' (it was, of course, nothing of the kind but a creamy colour can, in fact, be found at Essex). Lasdun and his deputies often appeared high-handed and would keep quiet about what they had in mind. There seemed to be no proper control of timing, or finance. The UGC officials threw up their hands in despair and even, at one point, threatened to withdraw their support, which would have meant starting again with the search for an architect and a plan. Through all this, it was the vice chancellor who essentially stood by his architect and the two 'restored order' in late 1963. It then took another year to produce detailed plans and the first buildings only opened in late 1966.

Part of the problem simply lay with the extreme spirit of experiment prevalent on the project. It did not want to admit to any precedent. Lasdun had a habit of professing, when embarking on an important project, that he had never tried 'anything like it before'. In the case of buildings for higher education, with all his work for Cambridge, this was patently untrue. He was flanked by his client who repeatedly declared 'Lasdun had no brief'. More significantly, there was no development plan to speak of either. Lasdun, however, did cleverly provide an image of extendibility in the way the blocks of residences could be added on, but this was essentially a simple architect's image of extendibility. The immense effort that went into devising the plan and nature of York, from the general principles down to the detail, was virtually absent in Norwich. At York it was the decision to adopt a complex integration of college and university that partly necessitated such a procedure. When it came down to what was actually needed in Norwich it did not entail anything out of the ordinary: teaching buildings, library, social buildings, the usual ancillary structures and, from the start, a certain proportion of student residences on campus. Statements like 'living and learning, hand in hand with all the moral and social implications worked out in a total community' had become standard by that time. The conclusion of all this is that UEA, in its original parts on 'University Plain', is the work of the designer and the designer only. In fact, there was a process of evolution within the architect's work: Lasdun's scheme from late 1964 onwards differed considerably from the plans of early 1963, partly as a result of the drastic cutting down in overall size.

'Not a college, not a campus, but an Italian hill town, that was Lasdun's brief. Lasdun had no brief'. By 1963, 'Italian' had become somewhat of an euphemism for a dense development with perhaps some towering structures. But in order to understand the essence of Lasdun's plan one has to begin with the site. It was a longstanding tradition in British architecture for a London architect to come to the provinces, to praise the beauties of a site, to make an effort to determine the *genius loci*, to place massive structures on it and in the end praise the unity of these buildings with the site. If the locals were startled by the size of the buildings the *genius loci* notion would be used as the main defence. It does seem to have worked for many in Norwich, as visitors kept praising the magnificent site, which in reality was, and is, nothing out of the ordinary in a county that never had a reputation for hillyness or variety. Lasdun took as much note of it as any designer of the Picturesque would have done, but his response was different in many ways. One of the chief reproaches made to classic Modernist town planning was that it had remained static, 'two-dimensional' and 'diagrammatic', spreading out in the same way whatever the nature of the site. Lasdun followed, first of all, the contour of the ground. His buildings literally 'step' down, they 'rise and fall' – in places they are even dug in to make them look lower. 'Anti-diagrammatic' meant an avoidance of right angles and rectangular repetition. There was furthermore a reciprocity, or a dialectic between the concept landscape and the concept urban. The idea was to concentrate the buildings to a high degree of density and leave as much as possible of the landscape open, accessible, viewable – although this concept was much less apparent at the very first stage of the plans than in the final, reduced outcome. When Lasdun left at the end of 1968 he took great care to stress that the remainder of the site, next to his structures, should not be built on and if the university was to grow substantially it should seek new land.

The idea of following the site contour led to a sense of the continuity of line, which in turn was linked with the general desire to produce as continuous a design as possible. This, and the principle of 'extendibility' led to the long, single teaching block, or 'Teaching Wall': one continuous block, 460 metres (1510 feet) long serves virtually all teaching and research functions. One of the most tricky questions in the relation between academic and architectural setup in the New Universities was how to express the new unit of the 'school' as a building. All the four designs discussed so far, however novel in some of their features, adopted the conventional method, namely individual buildings for individual subjects. York and Kent, of course, accommodated some of the teaching and research – chiefly the non science subjects – within the residential unity of the college. Lasdun and Thistlethwaite, having decided against the college pattern, did not want the older campus fashion of individual units peppering their site either. Lasdun's Teaching Wall is unified to the extent that all ceiling heights are the same 3.25 metres (or 11 feet) for science as well as for arts. We might thus comment that, as at Sussex, there is no real correspondence between the novel academic concept of the 'school' and its architecture. The only feature which marks out each school is its main entrance off the walkway (figs 2.68–2.73).

It is the 'walkways' that provide a strong directionality. They form the second major feature of UEA's design. A single system is meant to connect all buildings. Like the teaching block, they are responding in a subtle, and yet very real way to the contour of the site. The entrance to the walkway system is at the top, at the highest point of the site. One then goes down, with the site, a short, steep slope. From a certain point onwards, however, the walkways lift off the ground; now there are two levels, one for vehicles on the ground, and one for pedestrians above. Henceforth the grounds go down only very gently and the walkways remain on the same level to the far end of the campus. It is one's elevated position that makes the landscape appear pleasant and even dramatic. As has been said, the main entrances to all the teaching buildings, as well as to the library which forms a large separate block, are all from the walkway system. Although he has denied this, Lasdun's idea is perhaps derived to some extent from the Smithson's 'Berlin Hauptstadt' project of 1958, but he modifies this by concentrating his communications system in a narrow band. The only problem, in east Norfolk, might be the weather; however, Lasdun's meteorologists (UEA did not, as yet, have such a department), maintained that rainfall was only 26 inches (79 centimetres) per annum and that the prevailing winds were southwest!

143

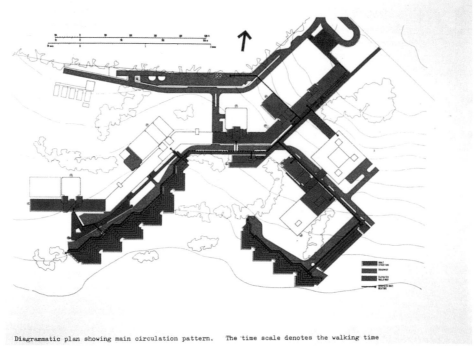

Diagrammatic plan showing main circulation pattern.   The time scale denotes the walking time

2.68   The University of East Anglia, circulation plan. Blue: vehicular access and parking. Red: pedestrian access. (D. Lasdun and Partners, *University of East Anglia Development Plan*, 1969)

Using a term which had recently become fashionable for large estates of public housing, Lasdun's UEA forms a 'spine'. Lasdun's other preferred form is the 'deck', the elevated platform which serves both for groups to gather and to look out – he was to develop this considerably at his London National Theatre shortly afterwards. These walkway platforms, finally, also connect with the third major element of the whole, the residences. The greater part of Lasdun's residences snuggle closely to the teaching spine, separated and connected by the walkway, distinct parts of one large whole. These 'Terraces ' or 'Ziggurats' are extraordinary buildings by any standards. The main idea is for groups of twelve rooms served by a small breakfast-kitchen/common room. Frank Thistlethwaite and Lasdun prided themselves in having found a solution to a pressing problem, namely how to build masses of rooms cheaply

2.69   The University of East Anglia, walkway section (D. Lasdun and Partners, drawing 1967).

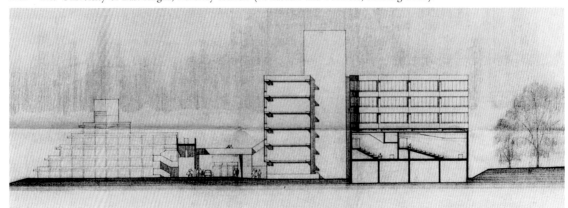

2.70   The University of East Anglia, academic procession 1977: the Chancellor, Lord Franks, followed by the Vice Chancellor Frank Thistlethwaite and the Chairman of the Council Sir Timothy Colman. All the Seven continued the old custom of academic dress. At East Anglia it was designed by Cecil Beaton.

and yet create some groupings which help to identify small 'communities'. This was achieved with 'an architectural device', the Oxbridge staircase. Each staircase is surrounded by the corridors and the bedrooms, which, on each floor, are centred around a communal kitchen. This forms a kind of apex – again conducive to enjoying the panoramic view. Lasdun then bent the stairtowers backwards, that is, the whole block actually steps back. He finally contrasts the all-window side of the complex with a no-window side over the entrances, which appear incredibly dark and messy, but this was the way Lasdun intended them, an astonishing example of 'urban' manipulation on a green field site. Peter and Alison Smithson, not normally showing much

2.71 The University of East
Anglia, walkway encounter
1968. (*TES* 6-12-1968)

2.72 The University of East
Anglia, walkway from below

2.73   The University of East Anglia, air photo of part of Teaching Wall and residences (to the left, 'Norfolk Terrace'), photo
c. 1974. Cf. Cover illustration. (Courtesy Feilden and Mawson)

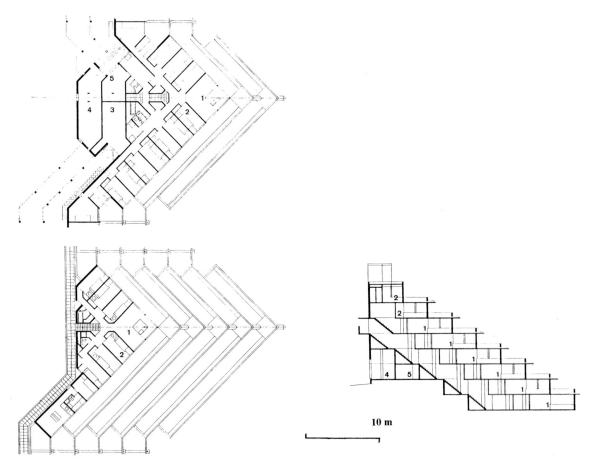

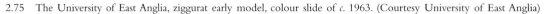

10 m

2.74   The University of East Anglia, plan of the ziggurat student residences (cf. cover illustration). (*Lotus* 7 1970, pp. 208–35)

2.75   The University of East Anglia, ziggurat early model, colour slide of *c.* 1963. (Courtesy University of East Anglia)

interest in the work of their contemporaries, remarked: 'could it be that we like Lasdun's East Anglia student clusters because they are connective, they have a front and a back and counterpart space'. Like Spence at Sussex, Lasdun was one of those accused of overspending the UGC's money; like most of his university the 'Ziggurats' were built with his own system of site-cast, re-inforced concrete panels, and stayed, at just over £1,000 (construction costs) per bedroom, roughly within the early 1960s UGC's stipulations (figs 2.74–2.75 and jacket illustration).

During 1968 the clash between what the architect wanted to see and what the client experienced broke out again. One could now begin to get an idea of the designer's grand and intricate concept. The architects soon declared East Anglia reasonably complete and in 1969 Richard Einzig's and I. A. Niamath's photographs, carefully hiding the gaps, were seen in multi-page displays in many of the major architectural journals around the world. In Norwich, clients and first users complained about incompleteness, leaks, financial problems – the government was now much stricter, too – and Lasdun left at the end of the 1968, peacefully, as neither party could afford to lose face. Trusted Norwich practitioner Bernard Feilden (who was, by then, also England's premier conservation architect) took over. The way he and his partners, especially David Luckhurst, were considered as competent (especially in those cost-cutting times) but unadventurous, reinforced the myth of the reverse qualities in Lasdun's work. Feilden faithfully completed Lasdun's teaching wall and library and set about creating that part which Lasdun never got round to, the social centre. Here, the two differed strongly: Lasdun had not planned a really large open meeting space; he saw the users essentially on the move, 'walking briskly'. Feilden, however, returned to the earlier English urban concepts of Townscape and precinct and provided an arena-shaped main square, partly surrounded by the major communal buildings. By 1974 UEA had completed its campus in a manner which, all in all, was not too distant from Lasdun's original intentions of 1963–4.

Essex

By the autumn of 1963 the New University movement appeared to reach its peak. If the word 'high profile' was ever an understatement, the University of Essex would be near the top of the list. None of Britain's postwar universities was launched with such enthusiasm. But it was to be a double-edged experience: no other British university was ever criticised so vehemently and intricately. The way Essex's hopes turned into despair within the span of a few years, is one of the most extraordinary stories of the decade. It must be stressed that this was not an issue of academic ranking, but an architectural story, or rather, a tale of the fate of a utopianist creation. John Maule McKean's 'Case Study' in the *Architects' Journal* of 1972 presented a most penetrating analysis of the campus, by an architect who had turned theorist and critic, while, in fact, doing his postgraduate work at that university. Faced with what appeared to be the profound failure of a whole institution, the critic's saw it as his task to enquire into the very origins of the design, to go back to the beginning, in order to link inception and realisation with the eventual dissatisfactions. A quarter of a century later, the historian ought to adopt a different approach. The critic insists that his or her actors should have possessed a better foresight. The historian tries to circumvent precisely this position and insists that his or her 'actors' were not in a position to possess the relevant foresight. Therefore, in this account, we propose resolutely to separate the two phases. First come the intentions, the foundation and the realisation of Essex University. The criticism will be dealt with in a separate chapter, in the general context of the late 1960s collapse of New University and Welfare State architectural enthusiasm.

More than any other New University, Essex depended upon the drive of two individuals, its academic leader and its architectural designer. In contrast to the first three New Universities – Sussex, York and Norwich – the 'local effort' was of lesser importance, though no doubt Sir John Ruggles-Brise, Lord Lieutenant of Essex and Chairman of the University Promotion Committee did his job effectively. To begin with, there were arguments about the location: Chelmsford staked its claims first, but Colchester fulfilled the UGC's demands for a self-contained, historic town at a plausible distance from London much better. Local opinion seemed chiefly concerned with the economic impact: 'take hairdressing, another thousand or so girls wanting a hair-do regularly will keep several saloons fully occupied'. While not neglecting local links, the university remained conscious of the fact that a close match could never be expected. What the university really did cherish was the actual site, 'its personality . . . the magic and charm of Wivenhoe Park', an eighteenth-century landscape garden of some repute, which, even more importantly, had been immortalised by John Constable in a painting that had the added distinction of hanging in the National Gallery in Washington.

It was Sir Noël Annan, chairman of the Academic Planning Board in 1961–2, who first insisted that Essex be 'distinct from other universities'. By mid-1962 Annan had appointed Albert Edward Sloman as the vice chancellor. Sloman was Oxford-educated, had taught in California and was professor of Hispanics at Liverpool. During the war he had served as a fighter pilot. At 41, he was the youngest vice chancellor anyone could remember. During late 1963 Sloman gave the BBC Reith Lectures ('the youngest ever Reith Lecturer') which were published in the *Listener* and as a book in early 1964; it became the most widely read text – apart from the Robbins Report – on its subject. Cleverly entitled *A University in the Making*, that university was, in fact, his own. Finally, there came the appointment of Lord ('Rab') Butler as chancellor, securing for Essex the support of one of the most popular politicians of the period, and, what was more, one whose liberal and populist conservatism matched closely the early image of the university.

Superlatives became the hallmark of the now ensuing campaign to launch Essex University. First, size. Until the early 1960s the New Universities were conceived as relatively small institutions, 3,000 students after ten years appeared an ample target. When, in late 1961, Annan asked the UGC what they thought of going to 6,000, Sir Keith Murray hesitated and advised waiting for Robbins. But Sloman, upon his appointment as vice chancellor, immediately emphasised 'more than 6,000'. Whether through intention or luck, he timed the presentation of his university (in the Grocers' Hall in London) and its giant plan and model to coincide exactly with the publication of the Robbins Report, in late October 1963. The report's most important demand was for a vast increase in student population. Now Sloman's plan was for 10,000 students at Essex, with the possibility of going up to 20,000.

Sloman then presented what appeared to be a very substantial rethink of academic education and organisation, perhaps a more striking example of Briggs's dictum, 'redrawing the map of learning' than Sussex itself. Sloman's book, and even more so the press reports, abounded in hopes of the 'exhilaration to be in something genuinely new', for 'one of the most progressive seats of learning in the world'. Essex followed Brighton's model of interdisciplinarity and its 'schools'. But it was more up-front with novel combinations, such as Mathematics with Statistics, to train social administrators, or Science with Communication Studies, or Comparative Studies for languages. Sloman, however, kept something of the older departmental structure in order to attract high-profile heads of departments, some of them being lured away even from the sister universities Sussex and Warwick. Research and teaching should go together as closely as possible. This all necessitated the very closest proximity, the togetherness of all subjects, academically and educationally.

Sloman's greatest 'coup' however, seemed to be his concept of the modern 'independent' student. His discourse began with many of the values of the late 1950s UGC line on student care. Above all, Sloman subscribed to the notion of the residential university. Like Niblett, he stressed the unsatisfactory nature of both lodging in private houses and of living at home. 'A university, should, I believe, provide an experience of living as well as an opportunity for learning' and he wanted students to experience 'the full community life, traditionally associated with universities'. Annan initially recommended a number of halls of residence as a series of 'social centres' or 'nuclei', rather than 'one vast emporium'. Sloman's stated concept was to be virtually the opposite: 'Essex will have no colleges or halls of residence'. Shortly before, Frank Thistlethwaite at Norwich had pointed to a change in student mentality and a new trend towards independence which he sought to combine with greater economy in the construction of the study bedroom blocks. Sloman now went into an all-out recommendation of a new 'non-parental attitude'. In the late 1950s the UGC had still been talking about 'boys and girls' entering university; now Sloman wanted to pioneer a 'new way of life', the total abolition of regulations for the student body. He spoke of 'Students' legitimate desire for independence . . . students do not want to be reminded of school' and went on: 'give them responsibility if you want them to act responsibly'. He wanted to provide enlightenment not paternalism. In stark contrast to Kent and even York, Sloman thought he would hit the crux of desirable modern university life when he stressed that students were adults. There should be no rules, no proctors. If there was severe misbehaviour, then that would be a matter for the police. As regards the older type of residence, he declared that 'halls sometimes perpetuate adolescence . . . in women's halls linger the ghosts of Victorian chaperons'.

So what type of dwelling did Sloman propose for his students? 'Like many Londoners and New Yorkers . . . our students will live in flats and apartments.' Sloman then went on immediately to the central feature of the 'flats': 'groups of a dozen or so [study bed]rooms' with the 'social centre of each group [being] the living room and a small kitchen'. Further on, he explicitly stated the sources of this arrangement and the social policy behind it. He demanded that the 'the social unit' in Essex would be small – here, too, we are reverting to the principle of the Oxford and Cambridge staircase. To underline the new value of independence, it was stressed, as at Norwich, that each Essex flat would have its own 'lockable front door' and that the students 'will each have their own key' – a notion inconceivable in the old hall of residence setup. A further topical issue was coeducation, the question of abandoning the strict separation of the sexes. Essex embraced it wholeheartedly, at least to the extent of putting men and women on alternate floors. Lastly, much was made of the fact that those students who did not live in the residences, but in lodgings outside, often a long way away, had the use of day rooms in the tower blocks. Overall, the social life within the residences assumed very considerable importance because there was to be no other social locus specifically designed for students, no student union – a hotly contested issue throughout the planning of most of the New Universities as we have mentioned. Nor was there to be a senior common room in the university. Sloman wanted social spaces close to the academic departments and eating places distributed throughout the campus. Everything was to be shared by staff and students. Everybody should live and learn close to everybody else. Sloman's map of academic life was thus one which rejected a tight paternalistic framework for student life, but at the same time postulated a strong sense of voluntary cohesion for all members of the institution.

One must not forget that all this was based on an undertone of providing a university for the masses. With all its stress on academic selectiveness, excellence and special conditions, Sloman's project was one of unprecedented size: 10,000, let alone 20,000 were numbers which far exceeded any university in Britain, except London. Essex's primary justification was Robbins, it claimed to serve the 'national need'. Occasionally, Sloman hinted at his profound satisfaction with what the Welfare State provided, what he saw as the 'exceptionally favourable conditions of development' and he felt – in 1963 – 'assured of money . . . not as much as the university would like, of course, but substantial sums both for capital and recurrent expenses'. He had to make his proposals sound cost-conscious throughout. Compactness and judicious distribution of social facilities, would, Sloman was convinced, fulfil their social-political aims economically. In this respect his thinking was close to that of his colleague Eric James at York, though the latter was much more openly Welfare State orientated. Sloman occasionally conjured up the picture of a frugal, but happy student population, 'on the whole students live on tight budgets and [want] simple, inexpensive pleasures . . . happy to sit down with just a cup of coffee talking with a congenial crowd' – a slightly romantic heroism of the parsimonious carried over from an earlier phase of the Welfare State. On the other hand, there were frequent insistences on the university being the 'independent and self-governing master of its own fate'. Sloman, in tune with the whole of New University movement, represents neatly the ambiguous position of the Welfare State professional of that time, that is, 'serving' the community, the nation, but doing so in an acutely self-assured manner. Occasionally, Sloman steps beyond both those values and reveals how he saw the task of the university founder and leader in terms of a publicity seeker, as when he would describe the ethos of Essex by using the term 'brand image'.

But words were only one aspect of Sloman's grand intentions. When he presented Essex to the world, he brought with him a model, which was immediately reproduced in innumerable newspapers and journals. The 'plan . . . which gives physical and visual expression to the academic ideas I have been discussing . . . reflects absolutely what we are trying to do'. As McKean wrote later, Essex authorities had an 'almost reverential attitude towards these buildings'. Sloman and his architect formed one of the most formidable client/designer relationships of the period, an example of architectural patronage of the first order.

2.76 The University of Essex. The Vice Chancellor Albert Sloman and the architect Kenneth Capon (of The Architects' Co-Partnership) in front of Wivenhoe Hall 1962. (*Colchester Express* 6-12-1962)

Kenneth Capon was the architect chosen by Annan and Sloman in September 1962. He was a member of the Architects' Co-Partnership, who became first known for their advanced reinforced concrete construction of the Bryn Mawr Rubber Factory, and then had much to do with schools. Their 1958 study bedroom block for St John's College ('The Beehives') was considered instrumental in introducing Modernist design to Oxford University and it had already taken an anti-diagrammatic form. The firm's ethos was 'not monuments but humane and efficient shelter for social activities . . . not avant-garde, no fashionable gimmicks'. The firm's competition entry for Churchill College Cambridge of 1959 appeared in some ways as a blueprint for Essex, a system of low enclosed courts combined with high-rise residential units (figs 2.10 and 2.76).

After his appointment, Capon immediately set to work and treated Essex as a full-time job. Yet, contrary to what one might have been led to believe, at the beginning one finds very much of the 'no brief' situation similar to that at Norwich. Sloman wrote: 'We spent several months tramping the site and arguing together. I could not give him a precise brief.' They issued a few pages of typescript, entitled 'Development Plan', but, as at East Anglia, this in no way represented a factual or quantitative analysis of the way the complex was to be structured. Later Capon himself stated: 'In contrast to York's diagrammatic plan . . . at Essex the model was the plan.' Like Lasdun's first model, Essex's plan appeared baffling when looked at for the first time; yet

153

2.77 The University of Essex, model, Kenneth Capon, October 1963. The towers left and right contain the student residences, the central complex research/ teaching/administrative/ social facilities interspersed with octagonal restaurants. (A. Sloman, *A University in The Making*, 1964)

2.78 The University of Essex, circulation plan 1966–70. Blue: cars. Red: pedestrian, indicating the platforms or squares, above the roadway. (*AR* 12-1966, p. 405; AJ 14-12-1966; computer adaptation: Tracy Fussell)

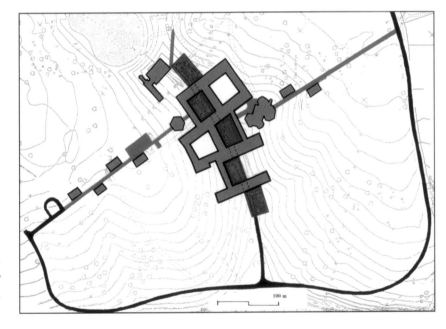

100 m

2.79　The University of Essex, air view, also showing the university library at the upper end of the central complex, as well as the vice chancellor's house near the lake (1964–5) and Wivenhoe Hall. (Courtesy University of Essex)

Sloman's explanations of it were as clear and convincing as any of his pronouncements. Indeed, Sloman acted as Capon's main spokesperson.

How close is the much emphasised relationship between the academic-social ideas or ideals and the layouts and shapes of the buildings at Essex University? We know that Sloman's lectures were written while he walked the site with his architect. Ideas appeared thus to combine from the start – quite unlike the situation at East Anglia, where no clear, or detailed, correspondence between the client's and the architect's ideas could be detected in the early years (except for the residences). At Essex the explanation of the design can follow the same sequence as that of the academic plan. Firstly, size. A university of 10,000 students in Britain would mean an agglomeration of at least 15,000 people overall. Housing them all in one complex of buildings would require a very large structure indeed. Secondly, the demand for close contacts – distances of 'no more than five minutes' (it was common to speak of ten minutes on large new campuses) – would lead to a very high degree of overall density. Thirdly, there was, as at East Anglia, a strong demand for keeping as much as possible of the landscape intact. Student residences in dense blocks of flats would help considerably to achieve this overall density. Moreover, the 'blocks of flats' were said to be placed in such a way at the edge of the teaching blocks that they would not essentially hinder any future extension of the latter (fig. 2.77).

However, 'teaching block', at Essex, is a misnomer. There are no individual 'blocks',

2.80 The University of Essex, Vice Chancellor Albert Sloman 'with some of his students'. (*The Guardian* 17-10-1966, p. 5)

2.81 The University of Essex, student residences, 1965–7. (*AR* 4-1970, p. 268)

2.82 The University of Essex, student residences illustration of 1964. (*Essex County Standard* University Supplement October 1964)

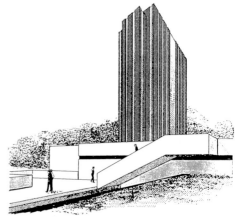

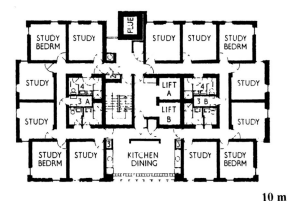

2.85 The University of Essex, student residences, ground floor entrance.

2.83 The University of Essex, student residences: typical floor plan. (*AJ* 14-12-1968, p. 1490)

2.84 The University of Essex, student residences, kitchen in 1966. (*AJ* 21-12-1966, p. 1565)

nor do they contain just teaching or research facilities. In fact, they encompass a very large number of uses which are not accommodated in separate units but all fused into one continuous mesh of four- to six-storey buildings. Unlike East Anglia and a further five of the Seven, in fact unlike almost all kinds of higher education buildings up to that date, Essex incorporates teaching/research of both sciences and humanities, with administration, and most social buildings, into one single multi-winged and intertwined complex. Capon expressed this aim even more forcefully than Sloman: 'It will be impossible to see where one teaching building or social amenity building ends and others begin'. Capon thus took a current design model, the 'mesh' or 'web', practised in some advanced housing complexes, and provided the most literal manifestation of Sloman's idea of the 'togetherness' of all functions of the university. Only a few 'services', those which could not easily be integrated into the low-ceilinged 'teaching

157

blocks', stand out and are easily recognised in their separate function: the lecture theatre group, the library and the main restaurant (figs 2.78–2.81).

What really do stand out from the central complex are the residences. Sloman and Capon's residences and teaching blocks were strongly distinguishable from each other, the buildings contrast rather than merge, as at East Anglia. The rationale of the residential blocks at Essex was twofold. The unit of twelve or so study bedrooms demanded by Sloman, with their associated bathrooms and their communal kitchen are conveniently allocated on one floor. The second step was to stack lots of them on top of each other; in other words, Capon resorted to a formula that was all too familiar in public housing in those decades: tower blocks. In that sense, the Essex blocks of student residences are, indeed, 'blocks of flats'. Moreover, they partake in two particular fashions of late 1950s and early 1960s tower blocks. Firstly, they stand close together to form an impressive, dense massing. Secondly they reflect a conviction that high-rise dwellings are not only suitable for dense inner urban situations, but can also be applied to out-of-town sites, where they can save landscaped grounds and provide powerful visual accents (figs 2.82–2.87).

All these characterisations, do not, however, catch the essence of what is Essex's combined sociological and architectural plan. The rejection of campus and college resulted in the idea of the 'compact small town', which had already been agreed for Essex by the end of 1962. The new kind of 'urban' concept was, for Capon, opposed to that of 'institution'. The post-Smithson designers were no longer interested in social policies which were to be instituted through the provision of facilities and buildings, but in social behaviour which was to be encouraged through new modes in the detailed layout of everyday spaces. This is the ultimate reason for not planning halls of residence, for not wanting a specific students union building, locations where people were led to meet in rooms specially created for the purpose of meeting. Instead, it was assumed, or hoped, that socialisation would happen spontaneously everywhere, within the designer's approximation of an ordinary urban fabric.

High density meant that functions were layered on top of each other, rather than placed side by side. Only now do we come to what, for Capon, was the single most important design element of Essex University: the platforms. Capon adhered to a most radical scheme of traffic segregation, more radical even than Lasdun's at East Anglia. Vehicles were only permitted on the ground, all pedestrian movement was to be exclusively on the roof, so to speak, 20 feet (6 metres) above, over the vehicle area. These 'roofs', or platforms, constitute the very centre of the university, as a series of five descending squares, or piazzas. It is here that the public life of the university is meant to unfold, the life of 'a compact . . . central community . . . a small university town, full of life, with light even at midnight dreaming across squares and pedestrian bridges from the windows of the teaching buildings, study rooms and coffee houses'. It was to provide the guarantee that 'living and learning are one'; or, as Capon evoked even more proudly: 'The Student Union in Paris is the Boulevard St Michel'.

Finally, we must search for a correspondence between Capon's architecture and what Sloman generally saw as the university's situation within the possibilities of the Welfare State. Such a correspondence must, necessarily, be a vague one. We cited the way Sloman conjured up the average student's heroism of parsimony. Capon went for a 'strong image', 'a strong scale' which, according to him was lacking in English architecture: 'the English love . . . softening everything up . . . We decided to do something

2.86 The University of Essex, the Squares (or 'Platforms') 1964–9; late summer evening view.

2.87 The University of Essex, undercroft.

fierce to let them work within . . .'. Whether every aspect of the design can be called 'fierce' must be questioned, there is considerable subtlety in the anti-diagrammatic spacing and shaping of the squares and in the vistas through them. One is aware, furthermore, that this is an architecture without symmetry, without front vs. back; in fact, the 'back' of the building, the 'service side' is underneath. There is, as in Lasdun's East Anglia, no obvious entrance side of the complex; in fact, when Princess Margaret came to visit a ceremonial entrance could only be made by helicopter. Another similarity frequently conjured-up was the 'Italian Hill Town' and there was one in particular, San Gimignano in Tuscany, which, like Essex, was graced with a series of threatening towers. Already in their Churchill College entry in Cambridge, Architects' Co-Partnership proposed towers, chiefly because they wanted to counter any possible suburban sprawl (fig. 2.10). At Essex there was a belief and a fear in the early years that the town of Colchester would soon grow around the university in the form of ordinary low-density suburbia. Unordered, ordinary 'Subtopia' was what the Welfare State planners of around 1960 were most contemptuous of. Against that, Essex 'need[s] a gesture, tense and impervious'.

After the short planning design session phase Sloman and Capon were soon joined by the contractors. Essex was not all words, or models, or pictures, as appeared to be the situation at East Anglia for so long, but action followed immediately. In fact, having started the whole process a year later than East Anglia, Essex, overtook it when it moved into its first permanent buildings (Physics, Sloman's splendid residence) in 1965. Sloman made sure that his relations with the UGC were trouble free, again in marked contrast to Norwich. He explained carefully that a period of three years, no longer or shorter, was needed, from the date of his and Capon's appointment to the opening of the first set of buildings. By the time the model was presented, Capon had already begun to work out a detailed building programme which also included devising a structural frame system; actual building started in June 1964 on a shoe-string budget of about £1 m per year. Capon rejected Clasp because he felt 'the loading and the spans made it unsuitable'. Arguably, the appearance of the structural framework at Essex is more unified than that of the celebrated Clasp system at York. By late 1966 the platforms for all five 'podia' or squares were there and by 1970 it could be claimed that the university had completed '1/3 . . . of the site plan'.

An uncompromising, almost defiant tone comes through in a long architect-inspired analysis of late 1966: 'a considerable architectural and social achievement . . . and it is clear that the highest priority decisions have not been compromised'. 'User requirements are subject to strategic constraints of the development plan and the tactical constraints of indeterminacy . . . If sacrifices in user efficiency had to be made, it was because the overall concept, the overall image of the university as a tightly knit, cohesive organisation . . . was regarded of overriding importance'. Even the constant building noise could be justified: 'Provided that you can hear yourself speak in the Lecture Theatre . . . surely there is some value in being a part of something that is evolving all the time'. However, in terms of the English professional architectural press, interest in new universities was already waning by 1967. Moreover, Capon and his Architects' Co-Partnership did not count among the front runners in British architecture. The Essex model was frequently reproduced, even abroad, Essex's buildings very rarely. And this meant that Essex did not enter the subsequent international architectural books in which Spence figured sometimes and Lasdun regularly (Capon did not even make it into *Megastructures*, cf. below page 272. Did Banham just forget?). Only a few analysts of the New Universities kept up their interest in Sloman's ideas: 'The most imaginative and futuristic version of the integrated pedestrian campus' wrote social historian Harold Perkin. Perhaps the comparisons with Oxbridge were the most revealing: 'Staff have willingly turned their back on the architecture and ethos and glories of Oxford and Cambridge', and yet it could also be observed: 'the university library ['s] position is as significant as that of the Magadelen Tower in the curving High Street of Oxford'.

Lancaster

All the three great 'urban' schemes, East Anglia, Essex, Lancaster, were essentially designed during 1963. Ling's 'urban' plan, Warwick, came a few months later, but was soon to be abandoned on grounds of unrealistic vastness. Lancaster was the last of the three and was intended as the opposite to the grandiosity of Essex and East Anglia. Moreover, it appeared to achieve the greatest degree of consistency in its realisation. A seemingly simple, yet powerful statement by Vice Chancellor Charles Carter in 1971 perhaps best conveys the proud spirit of this university: 'we have got the balance between freedom and order about right'.

As regards its foundation, Lancaster was the last of the Seven and its history is the shortest and least complicated. The first attempts to found a university in north Lancashire go back to 1947 and beyond, but gathered momentum really only during 1961. To begin with, it was Blackpool that was keen to acquire a university, but that idea was soon dropped when it turned out that the plot adjacent to the proposed campus had been earmarked for a large pleasure park. No doubt, the small City of Lancaster, the ancient capital of County Palatine was thought a more suitable location by the UGC – with whom relationships remained excellent throughout. Building at the Bailrigg site, given by the city, began in 1964.

As at Essex, we must begin with the intentions of a team of two, the vice chancellor and the architect. The Academic Planning Board's choice was a Cambridge-trained economist and fellow of St John's, Charles Frederick Carter, then professor at Manchester. Although considerably less flamboyant than his colleagues James at York, or Sloman at Essex, Carter's imprint on the plan of his university was probably even stronger than their's. In the interviews of all the seven vice chancellors in the *Times Educational Supplement* in 1966 Carter came across as the most provocative: he was 'not keen on big ideas or on big speeches', and declared 'I don't have the advantage of being an Oxford philosopher' (a dig at Fulton). One of his tongue-in-cheek beliefs was that it was not only students who should be numerate, but vice chancellors, too. His line was the 'relation of science to industry' yet, the humanities should not be 'trampled on in the rush towards technology'; thus Lancaster went in for both marketing (a first) and Classics, and religious studies. As a Quaker, Carter had 'a religious zeal for the economic use of resources, human and material'. Like Eric James, Carter never thought – at least during the pressing early days – that there was time for the 'gentler processes of democratic consultation'. Order and speed were of prime importance. Moreover, Carter and the Academic Planning Board took a long time to appoint further academics and thus Carter – as the university's meticulous historian Marion McClintock put it – 'enjoyed 10 months of decisionmaking' until late into 1963.

From mid-1963, however, the vice chancellor was sharing his intentions with his architect, Gabriel Epstein. A partner of Bridgwater, Shepheard and Epstein of London, he was the least well known of the architects of the Seven – and, for reasons to be cited in due course, he remained so. Although trained partly in the 1930s Germanic-influenced architecture of Israel, Epstein's architectural and intellectual home appears to be the English municipal work of the early 1950s, with a dose of Townscape; in any case, Epstein stayed pre-New-Brutalist. Lancaster became, and remained, far and away Epstein's most important work. Carter did not go on record with elaborate statements about architecture. But he was very clear, at least in his reminiscences, about what he wanted to avoid: 'eminent' designers intent on building 'a monument to their prowess as architects'; he wanted no 'great towers', nor 'brutal concrete'. Instead, he was looking for designers who could do the job without 'overruns of either cost or time'. Shepheard and Epstein, he mused later, 'seemed to be – I hope Gabi will forgive me – nice ordinary people' and to guarantee 'an agreeable place . . . a place of human scale'. The intense cooperation which followed was based on their first encounter where trust was built in an instant, spontaneous agreement. It came after the first interview, when Carter asked the firm for its general ideas for developing the university: 'Mr. Shepheard was about to give a polite demural . . . "we are honest architects, we do not approach such a project with preconceived ideas". But Epstein interjected: "If you really want to know what we want to do, please give me a sheet of paper".' Thus, almost on the proverbial 'back of an envelope', Epstein sketched out the long pedestrian spine with buildings on either side and the perimeter roads and explained especially how the university could be extended. After the architects had left the room 'Carter put his hand on the table and said "That's it".' The sketch on a single piece of paper 'saved months of discussion afterwards which might have been spent on debating and discarding various alternatives'. Later on, Epstein emphasised again that the master plan was drawn up 'free-hand to prevent precise intepretation'. Epstein made it clear that his 'attitude to work is both modest and assertive'. Para-doxically perhaps – given Carter's emphasis on scientific precision – yet, not surpris-ingly, remembering Essex and East Anglia – we hear in Lancaster, too, that 'we never had a development plan'. It also seemed to follow that Epstein had nothing against other architects joining him, as long as they fitted in with his overall scheme, with the result that only about 50 per cent of Lancaster was designed by his firm.

Did Epstein's attitudes mean a turn away from the trend of 'the architect as brief-maker', which had reached its high point at Essex, or did he confirm it, once again? We might be inclined to think the former, simply because of the absence of the kind of overall socio-academic-architectural rhetoric. In reality, no decisive answer to that question can be given at this point. As with most of the Seven, there is at Lancaster a strong overall correspondence between the architectural and the academic pro-grammes and aspirations: they definitely share a general sense of complexity. The teaching structure at Lancaster still harks back to Sussex, with interdisciplinarity being the fundamental aim. Lancaster, however did not create a number of clearly defined 'schools', and it was 'not particularly worked up about new academic schemes' (Maclure); moreover, teaching patterns remained a subject of constant discussion. Somewhat like Warwick, Lancaster kept the traditional pattern of departments, with comparatively 'strong heads', but created a superimposed structure of 'Boards of Studies' whose concern was the coordination of syllabi, especially for the first year, such as the 'distant minor' which all students had to take. Like East Anglia, Lancaster adopted continuous assessment. Like Sloman, Carter put emphasis on new subjects,

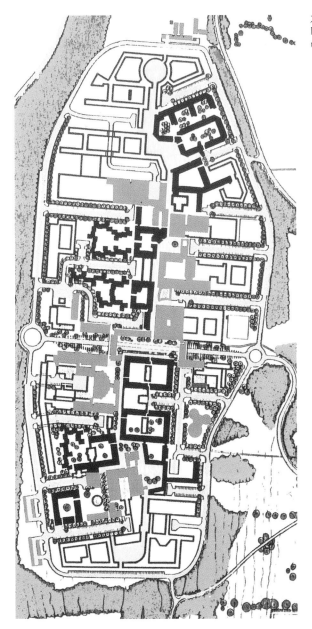

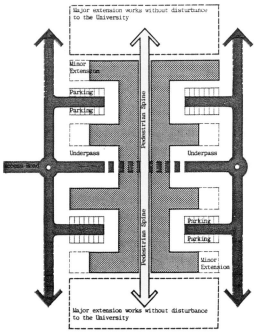

2.88 University of Lancaster, plan early 1970s: colleges in blue, pedestrian area in yellow, car access in pink. (Courtesy Gabriel Epstein)

2.89 University of Lancaster, schematic extension plan, by Bridgwater, Shepheard and Epstein (Gabriel Epstein), designed from 1963. (Courtesy Gabriel Epstein)

such as operational research, which, in turn, were said to reflect the ethos of the institution as a whole, namely that a plan no longer meant adhering to some fixed principles but something that appeared flexible and to be continually evolving.

Trying to comprehend the Epstein/Carter architectural plan one oscillates between stating the plausibility, even the simplicity of it all, and, on the other hand, getting enmeshed in its mind-boggling complexity. Not surprisingly, a look at the layout as a whole leaves one perplexed, and a great number of simplified diagrams were pro-

2.90 University of Lancaster, air view early 1970s. In the centre-foreground the Chaplaincy Centre (Anglican, Roman Catholic and Jewish) by Cassidy and Ashton. (Courtesy University of Lancaster)

duced for guidance. It is worth casting one's mind back to the most straightforward of the Seven, in terms of the overall designation of functions, East Anglia: research and teaching on this side, residences on that side, plus a concentration of social and administrative buildings in a third location. This is precisely what did not happen at Lancaster. It is here extremely hard to identify any of the four functions via 'their' buildings. We already followed the argument at Essex, namely the mixing of teaching, research and social activities in one continuous building. (However, science-laboratory teaching at Lancaster does take place in separate buildings, as at York and most other places, and not in the same overall complex, as at Essex and East Anglia.) Lancaster goes beyond Essex in that the student residences, too, are integrated; as will be explained later, the major components of Lancaster are called colleges. What is crucial to understand is that 'to combine' really meant what it says; innumerable steps were taken to consider everything in close relation to everything else (figs 2.88–2.92).

Thus the majority of the buildings each contain a multitude of functions. In the planning process, nothing was taken for granted. There seemed to be no fixed-purpose institutions. Flexibility of use was the highest aim. In some of the colleges, Epstein devised groups of rooms which could be used for small group teaching, for academic-administrative offices, or for student residences. 'The architect has been careful to plan the buildings so that the decisions remain open.' Epstein here acted in special unison with Carter and his desire to economise. Teaching rooms for arts subject, Carter argued, should not be placed in a separate building because it would remain empty in the evenings, whereas teaching rooms within a college complex might be used for social purposes as well. In the process of consultation between architect and client, Epstein at one point warned Carter that this kind of dispersive

164

planning might disrupt functions which normally belong together. Did Carter really want a 'fruit salad of functions'?

Carter's reply lead straight to the other planning feature which really forms the logical corollary to dispersion, namely communication. As Epstein reports, Carter positively welcomed the 'fruit salad', the mixing of diverse functions. What if, Epstein asked, taking an extreme example, the physicist found himself a long way away from the biologist? Carter replied that there could no be better way of encouraging rapprochement and communication 'than those frequent meetings on the way, sitting down, chatting and having a cup of coffee'. A university is 'held together by an unconscious pattern of cooperation between departments and between students and teachers'. Even more than Essex, Lancaster adhered to what has been termed here the post-institutional, spontaneous idea of achieving a community.

In the jargon of town planning and large public housing estate planning the term was 'spine'; in ordinary language the analogy is the 'high street' of a town, or even a 'village street' which, half a mile long, ties the whole of Lancaster University together: 'The village street is the place where everyone will fall over everybody else.' Epstein points to the older, smaller kinds of towns, where everyone still lives in close proximity to that main street. In the centre there is a large free space, Alexandra Square. Like Essex and East Anglia, Epstein adopts a radical separation of movement. His town street is entirely pedestrianised. And yet, he does not resort to the Futurist kinds of separation of traffic, to the acrobatics in re-inforced concrete of East Anglia and Essex. Only at one point are there two levels of movement, under the square, where a bus underpass drops the visitor a few flights of steps away from the centre. Otherwise Epstein handles access and car parking in a way which town planners call Radburn (after a 1920s housing estate in New Jersey): a group of houses is reached from the back while their front side remains vehicle-free. In the case of houses this means that the gardens are undisturbed; at Lancaster it means that the pedestrian communication areas remain free of cars, which can be left very close by at the back of each building. This had the added advantage (in the early days) of avoiding massed car parks.

All this, in turn, reinforces the desired inward-looking character of the campus. It results in another major feature of Lancaster, or rather lack of feature: there is no real 'outside' of the conglomerate. Lancaster seriously departs from the essential New University concept of the 'landscaped' campus. Although situated on a high plateau, the campus hardly presents a coherent whole from the outside, certainly not from the main approach road. There is only the roofline, enlivened with innumerable vents, penthouses and other excrescences. One further result – a characteristic shared with Essex – is the lack of a plausible 'main' entrance, something the architect later regretted. (The recent library extension and art gallery are meant to remedy this). What could perhaps also not quite have been envisaged was the growth of the private vehicle; today, the complex is surrounded basically by a belt of cars – from that point of view Essex clearly scores in the way it accommodated virtually all cars underneath and kept the access to the surrounding park free.

But by no means everything has been said about the 'streets'. What makes for a 'lively' town is the way the streets are flanked by buildings of diverse purposes and especially those which are used by the whole community. Hence, at Lancaster, Epstein mixes the teaching buildings, administrative and social functions all along the 'spine'. As in a ordinary old town, buildings are hardly differentiated from each other. The

2.91   University of Lancaster, Alexandra Square, mainly by Gabriel Epstein, *c.* 1965–8. (*AR* 4-1970, p. 276)

large central library on the square, for instance, can be recognised as such only when one looks very carefully and discovers its small windows. What identifies it, and the same applies to all other facilities on campus, is a simple sign: 'Library'. It does not need to be large because the regular users know anyway. To forego the architectural impact of major institutions within the university is perhaps the most radical consequence of Epstein's insistence on the cohesive town. All the other Six, and the vast majority of universities all over the world, even Essex, insist on a dominant library building. Epstein even dispensed with the traditional kind of main reading room as 'vast, echoing, intimidating'. All things considered, it was this way of abandoning the traditional (and Classic Modernist) custom of the distinguished individual central building, or set of central buildings, which constituted Lancaster's (and Essex's) most radical innovation.

We must finally come to those units which actually make up much of the campus, the colleges. Lancaster's are more massive than those of York, more of the Kent size with 500 plus students each. True to the Lancaster spirit, 'colleges should be encouraged to experiment'. As at York, the principal discussion was about the relationship between the college and the university as a whole. Lancaster's colleges form part of the university's special definition of unity, the small-town atmosphere. 'At Cambridge [colleges are] too powerful, and the university [is] too weak . . . we have to strike a balance . . . between the community life of the college and the wider world outside . . . we can get the best of both worlds'. Epstein's coup, however, was again in the exact way he ties in the colleges with the 'town': the communal facilities of the colleges, especially their eating and communal drinking facilities ('one always has to pass the bars') are placed alongside the spine. They give out to the pedestrian street. As at Essex, the principle was to line the public centres of the campus with a mixture of functions; simply formulated, turn a '9 to 5' university into a '9 to 9' university. Epstein

166

2.92   University of Lancaster, pedestrian street. Bowland College is on the left.

championed the idea that 'the university is lit up until midnight'. But while at Essex this ideal somehow remained unfulfilled at Lancaster it was taken at its most literal. The diverging ambitions of Essex and Lancaster are further mirrored in the metaphors they conjure up for their eating places: Capon dreamt of the cafés on the Boul' Mich', Epstein wanted users to look for the Fish and Chip shop. Finally, as at Essex, there was to be strictly no students union, that is, no major separate facility for student entertainment (fig. 2.93).

Whereas it appears difficult to differentiate buildings on the plan, there is a very clear vertical division. All the ground floors of the colleges are taken up with quasi public rooms. At the back they give out to quiet courts or to vehicular access facilities. On the floor above we find principally the teaching rooms (a minimum of five teaching departments were housed in each college), whereas the second floor is taken up mainly by the students' study bedrooms and on the roof we find the teachers' penthouse flats, loosely strewn over the roofs. Lancaster does not believe in the virtues of high buildings, largely for reasons of economy (far fewer lifts are needed). The exception to this is Bowland tower, which owes its existence to the need to disguise the boilerhouse chimney.

Whereas in the other universities, colleges and halls of residences were seen as fixed kinds of institutions, Lancaster kept up the experiment in a number of ways. Carter took on Essex's idea of providing day rooms for those living in distant lodgings. In fact, initially, the campus provided no bedspaces for students. Carter took great care to call his colleges 'study, social, teaching and administrative complexes'. The day rooms were to house desks for three or four students each. Sixteen of them were grouped around shower etc. facilities, although it was always stressed that they could easily be turned into student study bedrooms. The issue was, as elsewhere, that the government had a policy not to pay for the construction of student bedrooms. The new univer-

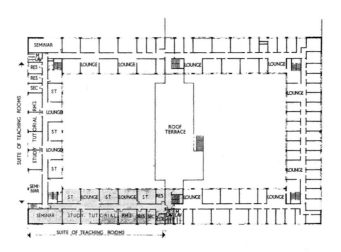

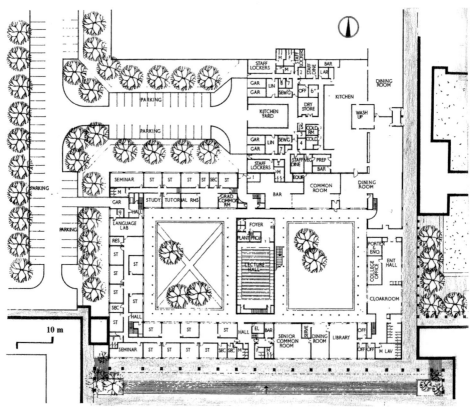

2.93 University of Lancaster, plan of Bowland College ground floor and first floor, *c.* 1965–6, by Gabriel Epstein. At the bottom end are the arcades along Alexandra Square (cf. Fig. 2.91). (*AJ* 12-2-1969, pp. 432–3)

sities would use their own appeal funds for that. In 1964 the UGC went on record as actually helping to pay for the 'non-residential student accommodation' at Lancaster and thus Lancaster could keep its own funds largely for other purposes. A further element of variety was the more lavish County College, actually just a hall of residence, paid for by the County of Lancashire. Finally, in early 1967, Carter introduced the (American) idea that student residences could be self-supporting and loan-

2.94   University of Lancaster, Cartmel College loan-financed, cheap student residences, by Taylor Young and Partners 1967–8. (*AJ* 21-5-1969, p. 1375)

financed. Lancaster, with the annexes to Cartmel, Furness and Fylde Colleges, thus introduced into England the cheapest kinds of student residences, costing little more than £700 per head and built to Parker Morris standards, i.e. to the 1960s standards in public housing (fig. 2.94).

As individual buildings, structures at Lancaster University do not fall into the category of spectacular architecture, even less so than those by RMJM or Capon. The striking Chaplaincy (by Cassidy and Ashton) is a one-off structure which cannot even be seen from the inside of the campus. What is spectacular at Lancaster is conviction and perseverance, demonstrated in the pursuit of the socio-educational aims in the plan. For Carter, this procedure seemed self-evident because he wanted to achieve speed at low cost. Clearly, Lancaster had caught, or rather, foreseen, the flavour of the architectural debate of around 1970, when a critic's praise for Epstein's Furness College reads as follows: 'There are no special structural or service problems and none has been generated by searching for an exciting design solution. . . . In short it is an ordinary building.' The construction of Lancaster, whether in reinforced concrete framework, or simply in brick was also ordinary. Epstein and Carter flew in the face of contemporary advanced opinion in firmly rejecting all kinds of prefabricated 'systems construction'. Instead, Epstein exercised his sober approach by stressing that it was by way of standardising room sizes, windows and other elements that he could gain some of the advantages of 'industrialised building'. In the mid-1960s Epstein's statements must have sounded arrogant to, say, the client and designer at York, with their absolute belief in the efficiency of Clasp. But it appears that Epstein was simply ahead of his time, as by the late 1960s virtually all 'systems' proved to be expensive rather than cheap, or good value, even at York. The comment of 1971 stresses further that Furness College 'does not demonstrate any new constructional system, new materials or dimensional co-ordination techniques'. As regards flexibility inside the building, the 'solid partitions', Epstein disarmingly claimed, 'can be knocked out if the need arises'. What was expensive, however, was the facing brick itself, a creamy yellow 'Stamford Stone' from Lincolnshire, which had also been used in Cambridge for Harvey Court and, in a different colour, for Churchill College. A stated aim was to avoid the dark-brick look of a 'nineteenth-century penitentiary'.

Finally, Lancaster's greatest merit in those years appeared to be in the way it provided for growth. The plan distinguished between two kinds of extensions. The principle was clear from the start, in 1963, when it was formulated as follows: 'From the spine buildings will stretch back in courts and blocks and the expansion needs of any one building will be provided for by further development at the back. Extra buildings (as distinct from additions to existing buildings) will be added as they are needed so as to extend the spine'. In all this 'neither the speed nor the nature of growth can be foreseen', and yet, at every stage, Epstein implies, the institution must have a centre, which, in turn, has to be extendable, too. The complex logic of extendibility will be discussed again later in this book. Lancaster, however, has remained the most unified of all the major campuses, in spite of, or perhaps even because of, this idea of easy extendibility.

Epstein's championship of the 'ordinary' (although not his word – Epstein was not given to much rhetoric) logically precluded fame. Of course, very strong praise and respect were voiced, but this came from those who had studied closely the problems and workings of new university design, such as Perkin, Wilby or Birks. They were convinced that Lancaster was 'the most humane, the most balanced' of the New Universities that it was 'seemingly effortless . . . [the] buildings do not intimidate'. They declared it 'the most successful of the integrated pedestrian campuses' and they thought it offered a solution to the problems of 'pedestrian liveliness'. This must be understood partly as a reaction to the perceived failures of the 'architects' universities' of East Anglia and Essex. Lancaster's unspectacular buildings were now preferred to those that 'have been designed to excite or with an eye to striking camera angles'. Epstein's firm did savour success when they were appointed as planners to sort out the 'mess' at Warwick. However, some criticism of Lancaster did emerge in those years: the 'spine' was not as lively as it had been hoped, chiefly because it was conceived for an institution of 6,000 students, not 3,000 – the usual problem. Epstein's idea of sprinkling shops all over the spine did not work, they had to be concentrated around Alexandra Square. Students were changing their eating habits, old-style dining halls were no longer popular but self-catering 'was the order of the day'. But these were minor criticisms compared with the avalanche of problems experienced by many of the other institutions. The crucial question at the end of our account of the Seven, however, is, did Lancaster became a model? A later chapter will address some elements of the complex story of the new trends in the later 1960s. More topical at this point is to remember the highest praise given to each of the Seven and to consider that, in this regard, Lancaster appeared 'connected . . . like a slice of Oxbridge'. But in the end it is the characteristic Lancaster dialectic of the 'ordinary' which predominates in the appraisals of its buildings; it is that very ordinariness which seemed to ensure the greatest approximation to the utopian aims.

The large new university complexes started on fresh sites during this period in Great Britain number about a dozen. Many of them stem from a movement that originated slightly later than the New Universities with the upgrading of the Colleges of Advanced Technology into Universities of Technology. After a long period of discussion, this was finally decided upon in 1963. The earliest development of these new foundations runs parallel with the peak years of the New Universities and the formulation of their ethos often sounds similar, certainly in the case of Bath (the relocated Bristol College of Technology). Its aim was also to create a 'new' kind of institution, departing both from old Oxbridge and unplanned Redbrick. Admittedly, the practical-professional-vocational teaching ethic was paramount, but this was to be heightened by studying the fundamental aspects of science as well as of the human and social environments. According to Bath's vice chancellor George H. Moore, the university's primary objective sounded familiar: to 'produce well educated men and women', as well as to provide a 'maximum of freedom' in which to conduct 'experiments.'

The first design ideas of 1963–4 were contemporary with Lancaster, but the final detailed *Development Plan* was only formulated in late 1965. 'The architectural plan is intended to express the underlying unity of the university', said Moore, and also: 'we have been fortunate in having a team of architects willing to spend time in acquiring detailed knowledge . . . adding their professional skill to the many discussions'. Their name is, perhaps, not hard to guess: RMJM, Robert Matthew Stirrat Johnson-Marshall of York fame. Hence the decision to use Clasp, although in a specially developed, heavier version with greater spans, called JDP, with a 'Bath Stone coloured concrete cover'. RMJM's Bath can be seen as number four of the 'urban' group of the New Universities. It resembles Lancaster with its 'linear spine', or 'linear centre'. Everything is closely grouped around, and attached to, that centre. There is also the Lancaster idea of the two kinds of extendability, both at the ends of the spine and at the backs of the buildings along the spine. On the other hand, the college mode is not adopted here – it was felt that for science and technology the chief social foci are the groups of the teachers and the students. Each 'school', is however, carefully divided into social, general teaching and laboratory areas. The latter are on the outer fringe, while the social areas give out to the spine, akin to Epstein's mode of thinking. As regards the centre itself, here called 'The Parade', evoking of course the *genius loci* of Georgian Bath, this is shaped somewhat after Essex: a complete pedestrian platform with cars underneath. Another model cited in this respect was the abandoned London County Council overspill town Hook, of 1961/2. In fact, Bath had taken over one of its planners, Hugh Morris. Finally, there are the student dwellings. Some of them are in a position not yet encountered so far: a daring use is made of the third dimension, above the spine, rooms are placed in two large blocks which run at right angles to the spine. Another more purely vertical feature, the 'administration and hotel tower' was never built. To return to the issue of extendibility: 'The plan is thus most determined at the centre, using the most fixed parts of the University, residential space and the communal and general teaching space; the less fixed spaces go out at either side of the parade'. Bath thus seemed plausibly to combine flexibility with the highest degree of density (figs 2.95–2.97).

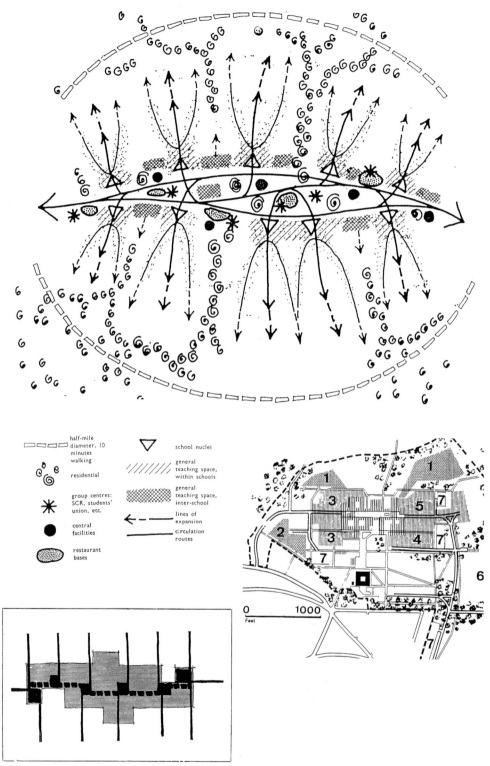

half-mile diameter, 10 minutes walking

residential

group centres: SCR, students' union, etc.

central facilities

restaurant bases

school nuclei

general teaching space, within schools

general teaching space, inter-school

lines of expansion

circulation routes

0   1000
Feet

2.95   University of Bath, schematic plan, begun in 1965, by Robert Matthew and Johnson-Marshall and Partners (RMJM). (*AR* 1-1966, p. 14). Zoning Plan: 1   student residences, 2   staff residences, 3   sciences, 4   engineering, 5   other disciplines, 6   games, 7   parking. (*Ad'A* no. 137 4/5-1968, p. 82)

Bottom left: schematic plan of the Hook New Town Project (1961, for *London County Council*). (*AJ* 20-9-1972, p. 642)

Dr George Moore, Vice-Chancellor, on the roof of Building 2 East, which houses the
School of Electrical Engineering, at the 'topping out' ceremony on 18th December 1968.
It was the first University building erected by the new industrialised system CLASP/JDP.

2.96   University of Bath, 1972.

2.97   University of Bath, central concourse.

Next in line was the University of Surrey, the old Battersea College of Technology, transplanted between 1964 and 1970 to a site on the slope underneath the Cathedral at Guildford. We note some rousing words by George Grenfell Baines of Building Design Partnership: 'Designers . . . have been listened to with respect . . . have been accepted as partners . . . as influencing forces on the nature of the physical environment'. What follows, however, is essentially an older type of zoning, residential on the upper parts, very large teaching blocks on the lower part, with some communal buildings squeezed in between. On the whole, everything is very closely packed. Indeed, there is hardly anything of a larger public space or forum (fig. 2.98).

Finally, RMJM were to have yet another opportunity to try the New University formula, at Stirling, which some say, was an English university transplanted into the Scottish system. Stirling provides a fitting summary for this chapter. Everything seemed to work as planned: Keith Murray, freshly retired from his UGC chairmanship, directed the academic planning efforts himself and they sound radical throughout with the sweeping away of both faculties and departments, no senior common room, and no junior common room. Stirling decided against the college system but built a great number of residences, both of the hall type and the study bedroom type. Building went exactly according to plan: from 1967 onwards for a period of six years, £1m was spent per annum for 3,000 students. The closeness of a small historic town and the site, with its mountain slope, lake, park and country house make Stirling 'the most beautiful of the campus universities' (Tony Aldous). The Principal Tom Cottrell was credited with much understanding of Modernist architecture and acted in complete unison with the project architect, John Richards (fig. 2.99).

And yet, with Stirling we also step beyond the phase of New University planning represented by the Seven. In 1968 we read: 'The university authorities feel that no single pattern of experience is best for all: a student should therefore be given wide opportunities for association with staff and fellow students in the way most satisfying to him as an individual'. Secondly, we experience a return to the older kind of zoning: residential, teaching and even the central social facilities are firmly separated again. 'This is a realistic approach: for mixing teaching and living accommodation poses as many problems as it solves'. The questions of educational-institutional planning were all open again; the continuation of the story of English New University design has to be resumed in the context of international university planning.

1968: INSTITUTIONAL AND ARCHITECTURAL DISILLUSIONMENT

'Dream exposed as sham' . . . 'beyond redemption' . . . 'shut Essex'. In 1977 there were rumours of a sizeable, unofficial list of candidates for closure: Aston, Lancaster, East Anglia, Essex and Warwick. What had gone wrong? Who, or what was to be blamed? It seemed, moreover, that the 'troubles' involved chiefly the most modern institutions, especially the New Universities, with the case of Essex being the most severe, and, true to its past, the most publicised. Only the London School of Economics suffered more. Next in severity came Warwick and East Anglia, at least for short periods, while Sussex experienced fewer problems and the others remained relatively quiet.

What was behind this extraordinary episode? From hindsight, decades later, one is

2.98   University of Surrey, planned from 1964, built mainly 1967–9 by Building Design Partnership (George Grenfell Baines). (Dober (1965))

2.99   University of Stirling, 1967, onwards, by Robert Matthew and Johnson-Marshall and Partners (J.D. Richards). From front to back: teaching, social facilities and student residences. (*AR* 6-1973, p. 354)

Building the New Universities

Tony Birks

photographs by **Michael Holford**

Introduction by Peter Cowan
Professor of Planning Studies, University College, London

DAVID & CHARLES
Newton Abbot

2.100 A view of East Anglia, main entrance to the campus, *c.* 1971. (Birks)

inclined to ask: why should anything have gone so drastically wrong? The stated aim of this book has been, so far, to deal with the bona-fide intentions and resulting buildings first, and to leave the critical reactions for a later discourse. A cynic may begin by saying that after all the hype, some kind of fall was inevitable. More to the point, the New Universities had courted publicity to an unprecedented degree and Briggs and Sloman had had immense success in publicising their superlative programmes. The fact was that the spokespersons of the New Universities had taken public opinion and the press by surprise; in 1960, or even by 1963 journalists had simply not developed any kind of critical discourse to deal with new academic institutions. The media, therefore, just repeated the university press releases. During the next few years, journalists rapidly found their own language. Now it was simply not on merely to repeat what the vice chancellors were saying. The press now had to be critical, or at least mix the positive with the negative. For a number of reasons that lay outside the immediate sphere of the universities, and because of factors which could not have been forseen, high-profile condemnation became rampant by 1970 – although it varied greatly in style, ranging from the reports in the popular press, like the *Daily Mail* and the *Daily Express*, to the more lengthy contributions by specialised journalist-investigators and professional critics, such as Stuart Maclure and Michael Beloff and, a little later Tony Birks, John Maule McKean and Peter Wilby. Their insights were, in themselves, admirable pieces of analysis – not surprisingly, one might be tempted to say in the case of McKean and Wilby, being graduates of Essex and Sussex respectively. The late 1960s also produced a number of dispassionate studies by academics for academics, but for the context of this chapter it is crucial to be aware that the vital discussions took place outside adcademe. Indeed, while we read complaints about pretty much every facet of New University life, one aspect of their work, academic quality, the ranking of research and of the actual procedures of teaching were hardly ever mentioned. From the perspective of the 1990s, high academic reputation was curiously taken for granted, it certainly could not, in the case of Essex especially,

2.101   Oxford, city and university: by the late 1960s the most admired architectural element of Oxford was not the college as such but the way in which the university buildings and the town appear interwoven. (Aerofilms Limited)

prevent any demands for closure. There was more uncertainty about 'new subjects', about interdisciplinarity, and their implications for teaching. By the early 1970s it was noticed that some of the complex plans for new kinds of subject combinations had already been abandoned, or that they did not work as envisaged, and that the old kind of departmental 'straightjacket' was reasserting itself. By the mid-1970s, Wilby declared that Asa Briggs's famous project of 'redrawing the map of learning' had 'without doubt failed'. There had been experiments but no innovation. By 1968, the New Universities' founding (and funding) body, the UGC, had long gone off experiments: 'it might be supposed that the recent wave of new institutions had probably exhausted the stock of new ideas for the time being'. The government was by now concerned plainly with numbers and aimed at providing places for students more cheaply in the older institutions or in new technological colleges.

Finance was, of course, a major issue. There was, firstly, a strong notion that the Seven were cheese-paring structures; for instance the major criticism of the residences at Essex was excessive proximity and noise. Capon and Sloman, understandably, were glad to blame government-stipulated cheapness as the main reason. There was, secondly, the impact of the financial prevarications and of the cuts in government spending from the mid-1960s onwards. It meant that the early megalomaniac dreams of Warwick and Essex, with their 15,000 or even 20,000 places had no chance whatsoever of coming to pass and even the initial New University target of 3,000 was not reached by some after 10 years. Essex was particularly hit by stagnation, by 1973 it had still less than 2,000 students. Others did carry on building and at least completed their initial programme, but in a fashion that was judged, by professional architectural opinion, as mean and cramped. In effect, an unfortunate atmosphere arose in which the New Universities were accused of both profligacy and meanness (figs 2.100 and 2.101).

177

However, financial problems, though contributory, were not at the core of the disillusionment. What was totally new at the end of the decade was a general perception of trouble, or problems, in the universities. '1968' itself, of course, says much. The student protest had taken British universities and the public unawares. It was powerful because it was directed not only against the university authorities but seemingly against the whole of the capitalist world, yet it manifested itself within the confined environment of the universities. It was seen as paradoxical that students made use of Welfare State, and/or bourgeois privileges, while, at the same time, rejecting them in principle. The story of the many ugly scenes needs no retelling here, the maltreatment of a prominent speaker or visitor, or world-events provided the platform for political protest. This usually entailed subsequent troubles, sit-ins and the calling of the police (Essex 1974: 'perhaps the worst ever police confrontation at a British university'). Because the New Universities, in particular, had been conceived as nation-wide institutions, trouble in any of them was felt by parents nationwide, exacerbated by the shrill tones of the more conservative sections of the press. Students were presented as having 'little else to do apart from "sitting round, playing records, drinking coffee and smoking pot" . . . free to smoke pot so far as the University is concerned'. (*The Daily Telegraph* about Essex 1970). The effect was also felt strongly at the local level: there was now a new town/gown issue with special regard to students. Earlier on student pranks could be an occasional nuisance to landladies, now the students' arrogant contempt for their host towns (Colchester was seen as a 'dead', even a 'horrible' town) left local promoters reeling. Students seemed not to value at all the original government intention to place the new institutions close to old and picturesque provincial centres.

The intense questioning went in diverse directions. Was it the fault of a minority of demagogic left-wingers? Or of the university's administration not being strict enough, or efficient enough, or, on the other hand, lacking in democracy? Was there something inherently wrong with university life? And why were the New Universities so much involved in these troubles? For conservative opinion there seemed no real problem in answering the latter question: naturally, it was their new liberal regime that attracted subversive elements; the assumption that students are by definition adults had turned out to be a fallacy. Sloman, on the other hand, did not see any need to change his attitude, which he was on record as formulating long before the troubles: being adults, students' misbehaviour is a matter for the police and not the university. To most parents the chief issues, and fears, were simply promiscuity and drugs. Those of a neutral stance tried a more pragmatic reasoning: the communal educational life in the New Universities had simply not been allowed to develop as originally envisaged, for instance the idea of staff being present on campus for as long as possible during the day. There was perennial criticism of the teachers of the universities in the metropolitan orbit, and their rushed departure after 5 pm: 'I have to catch my train to London'. Other minds were fixed on the afternoon exodus to the distant country cottage or manor house.

An academic/professional discourse arose which delved sociologically into the 'student movement' and its relationship with the structures of the university. The New Universities had suddenly found themselves hosting a new kind of person: the 'New Student'. He or she most likely belonged to one of the student societies which now formed within the institution, flexing their political and demagogic muscle, as 'Student

Power'. Ironically, these new student communities showed a considerable degree of cohesion (Beloff: 'There could be a kibbutz atmosphere in the student-unrest universities'). They usurped the local student unions and were interlinked through international bodies under charismatic leaders, 'kinds of student Lord Franks', as Beloff aptly put it.

We have earlier characterised the way in which the New Universities started off in a spirit of paternalist education and gradually developed a new educational stance of 'responsibility combined with freedom', at Sussex, at UEA and especially at Essex. From the old idea of a community of paternalistic benevolent dependence and benign rule we moved to a community in which there was more of a feeling of equality, especially with the emphasis on small-group teaching. From the beginning, there were attempts to draw students into the decisionmaking process. 'New Universities are a laboratory in staff student relations.' In Sussex students had sat on the university's committees since its inception; Essex began with students running the residences and by 1969 their say had been greatly extended, so that, for instance, they made up half of the membership of the Disciplinary and Appeals Committee. The newest anti-paternalist student movement thus followed in a line of development that had already begun before international Student Power arrived. By 1968 this development was propelled forward to a point at which not only the older paternalistic model but also the newer liberal model was rejected or declared as non-functioning. 'We are fed up being treated as children, . . . [with] paternalism . . . we want the rights of a normal community . . .' declared the student leader David Triesman in early 1968 at Essex. The public's perception of students was traditionally that of earnest young men and women, at least as far as provincial universities were concerned. One of the problems with the public's perception around 1968 was that the new liberal phase, as formulated by Norwich and Essex from 1963, had not had time to gain wider recognition. When the new radical assertiveness arrived, it, and the previous liberal demeanour, were simply seen as one and the same evil.

Whatever went wrong, any trouble, any inconsistency, was blamed on the university as a whole, as an institution; even bad weather, such as the winds at Essex or the purported 200 annual days of rain at Norwich. Indeed, the earlier constant emphasis on the whole of the university was now used in the arguments against them. The 'total university community', as formulated by at least six of the Seven, seemed elusive. 'That nirvana of staff student integration . . . the idea of a single institution was a myth that existed only in Asa Briggs's mind' (Wilby). We even read that 'the word "community", applied to the university, is ostensibly repudiated these days by students and left-wing staff'. Sloman and Capon continued to use the term, and their chief defence, when told about the lack of 'community' at their university, was that their institution had simply not been allowed to grow. None of this helped to counter the most frequent criticisms of the atmosphere, as either 'isolated' or 'claustrophobic'; the two terms could even occur together.

Paradoxically, it seemed that the emphasis on 'the whole' had somehow led to a neglect of individual loci, places to meet, especially club rooms. The greatest single complaint at Essex was the lack of a separate students' facility, a students union. In Norwich the delay in the provision of student facilities in Lasdun's campus was, likewise, a very serious factor. At Warwick the situation was much the same. The argument that the lack of facilities was due to shortage of funds was not listened to. At

Essex the thinking behind not building a students union was economic, in part, but it was the way Sloman and Capon explained its omission on quasi ideological grounds that the critics could not stomach. Nor did the argument that there was no senior common room either cut any ice. It was only after the mid-1970s that Essex arranged some rooms within the existing buildings for the exclusive use of students. The new kinds of student 'flats' also suffered severe criticism: 'Without halls of residence there is no immediate community between flats and the university at large and this has caused a feeling of isolation and bewilderment . . .'. Furthermore, the curriculum itself, especially in the very broadly based multi-departmental first year could mean that the fresher lacked a proper academic home.

We remember Capon's statement from early on that Essex was 'not institutional', but a 'town'. His aim was to allocate all social functions and venues in as dispersed a fashion as would be expected in a town, and not in the way they were usually located within university-specific institutions, whether campus or college. Already by late 1966 a young Essex sociology lecturer, Paul Thompson, stated that Capon's squares were not a success, 'a perpetual valley wind blows through . . . no real physical enclosure'. He questions, or does not want to recognise, Capon's idea that spontaneous contacts in an environment called urban are preferable to those within an institutionally-conceived environment. According to Thompson, the contact zones in the students' flats, 'the arguably more institutional kinds of kitchen/common rooms seem to be working well'. McKean's chief and fundamental point in his penetrating analysis of 1972 is centred around a complex dialectic of the two concepts of institution and town. In the idea and plan of Essex he detects an unsolved dilemma. On the one hand, the basic idea of all the Seven was to see the university as a distinct entity, as a self-contained community, in the campus and the college tradition. But Essex, McKean continues, then tries to recreate a 'society in model', a utopia; and that means that the university wants to become something that is not a university, not an institution, but a town, like a normal town. In the end the campus achieves neither: 'Essex University is not consistently based on either one concept or the other, nor does it explicitly accept, and come to terms with, the paradox of accepting both'. We have cited the architect's concern over not allowing Essex university to become submerged into any future suburban growth of Colchester, which to McKean underlines, once again, the uncertainty of Capon's concept of a town. Many other voices joined the debate. For instance, Mary Douglas, the anthropologist, who threw in another popular socio-psychological and architectural term: Essex departments 'lack territorial identity'. Tony Birks spoke more simply, and yet also in a more sinister way, about '. . . no nooks, no corners, and students have a sense of being under observation by their fellows whenever they are around the campus'.

All this is leading towards the one principal question: was it all architecture's fault? The usual course of a historical investigation of the architecture of an institution begins with the underlying ethos or ideal, leads to the way the institutions were devised, moves on to the details of architectural planning and design, and finally its use. Can we now go backwards, from unhappy users to bad design, to misconceived institutions and to flaws in the ethos? Many commentators of this period of disillusionment would have no problems with this reasoning. In 1970, the *Daily Telegraph* wrote of '. . . the "concrete jungle" of Essex University, towering residential housing, hippies, "pot" smokers and vandals . . . claustrophobic atmosphere makes pot smoking acceptable' or 'Campus claustrophobia and neurosis produced a near-hysteria among students, with Dr. Sloman in their eyes becoming a fascist ogre'; and 'the aesthetic poverty of the very buildings of Essex's isolated campus must contribute to developing delinquent behaviour '. The link between 'bad' buildings and student unrest was obvious to them. The architectural argument appeared strongest at the time of Essex's greatest troubles, in 1974. Lord Annan who was called in to investigate what, to all intents and purposes, was a university he himself had founded, concluded: 'Numbers of staff and students wrote to me to condemn the architecture of the University and to lay at its door the blame for the unhappy life and hence for the disturbances'. One might suspect, though, that Annan felt he had to blame something, rather than somebody, for instance his friend Sloman, and that he wanted to avoid putting too much blame on the students. But Briggs, in retrospect, confirms: 'The trouble in Essex was at least partly attributable to the architecture'. An ironic twist in the argument was, finally, the ways in which some of the planning of the New Universities appeared to provide the perfect frame for the rebellious students. Totally unexpected to the planners of the early 1960s, it became clear that the more residential and dense the campus, the easier it was for the militants to organise themselves (figs 2.102 and 2.103). 'The police, brought on to the campus, immediately encounter concentrated resistance. The students are running down within minutes of the police arriving.'

As regards persistent and comprehensive architectural-institutional criticism, Essex's most radical sister university, East Anglia, must be considered next. The years of its nadir, 1970/1, were slower in coming than at Essex and faster in passing. High spirits, partly based on the international acclaim of its architecture, continued longer, until 1969, and helped staff and students to put up with the chaos and inconvenience of the unfinished campus. But soon Norwich, too, experienced political extremism as well as left-wing staff vs. an 'intransigent administration' etc. By late 1969 a number of architecturally minded undergraduates took the designers to task: 'Lasdun's buildings . . . a dream, socially and educationally a nightmare. . . . They contribute all that is negative at the university'. The architects failed to recognise 'that people need and desire to live an integrated life', and, predictably, critics noted 'a failure of community'. There was little criticism of Lasdun's residences, but more of a certain anonymity and 'office block' character found in his 'Teaching Wall'. A long analysis in the *Architects' Journal* in 1972 took a somewhat more practical line, criticising circulation, in particular car parking (never, of course, a problem at Essex with its vast undercroft). Most pervasive was the dislike of grey concrete – at Essex the mixture was lighter. Critics and lay visitors would agree: the university 'Looks miserable when wet . . .'. 'Expiring dinosaur' was Birks's charming conclusion (figs 2.104 and 2.105).

Warwick must come next in importance in our hierarchy of criticism of the Seven. In a way, Warwick's architectural problems were more severe than those even at Essex, and yet, they were more the ordinary problems resulting from a lack of continuity in planning. This, and the early architectural criticism of the old-fashioned Modernism of YRM's blocks may even have precluded an outburst of the newer kind of architectural criticism around 1970. Some general criticisms were those voiced of many Modernist complexes: 'so big that it is dehumanised' . . . 'cold, impersonal' while complaints about a lack of student-run communal facilities were almost to be expected. Later on Warwick's original main buildings became dogged by the problem of falling

181

2.102 University of Essex. *Square*, drawing (Kenneth Capon), *c.* 1964. (Dober (1965))

tiles. Warwick's serious outburst of trouble came in the spring of 1970, the left-wing students taking on the university's narrow links with industry and an apparent resulting lack of democracy in its running. The unrest was cogently analysed by the university's renowned social and economic historian, E. P. Thompson. By the early 1970s the university tried its utmost to remedy the situation, especially through a series of lavish communal facilities and a new style for student residences (see page 280).

Of the remaining four of the Seven, two do not really figure in our context. The paucity of Kent's student troubles was said, by some, to be a result of its early

2.103 University of Essex: Square, from *The Times* 1968. (*T* 16-5-1968)

182

2.104 University of East Anglia, residences just after opening, photo 1966. (Courtesy University of East Anglia)

decision to chose a paternalistic college system; on the other hand, the severity of their restrictions had already been loosened by the late 1960s. At Sussex the architecture played no problematic role. The dip in the university's reputation was simply a dip in the rate of student applications. Student troubles were frequent, but remained mild. Criticism of the overall planning concept – or lack of it – remained, so to speak, within the profession. The opposite story, in many ways, was provided by York. In fact, it was the only New University which continued to receive much positive publicity, still largely produced by its own spokespersons. Lord James of Rusholme was

Home news

This is the first of a series of occasional photographs of life at universities in Britain. The four casually dressed students above are relaxing on the terrace of one of the blocks of study-bedrooms at East Anglia University. Opened in October, 1963, it was one of the seven new universities built during the expansion programme of the sixties.

2.105 University of East Anglia residences, from *The Times* 1971. (T 29-4-1971)

renowned for both his approachability and his authority – caring but firm. The college system was not much commented upon any more, but continued to be praised for the way it created 'communities'. There was never a strong demand to institute a proper, central student union. Above all, York never suffered from incompleteness. It may, however, be argued that all this was bought at some price, too: a perceived lack of architectural distinctiveness. 'There is a casualness in the way the buildings relate to each other . . . to a visitor it has the slightly unsatisfactory feeling of never having arrived . . .'. We might thus interpret York in 1970 as the opposite of Norwich, where we met architectural satisfaction combined with social/institutional dissatisfaction. At Lancaster the situation was diametrically opposed to that of Essex. Although there were some critical analyses of the college structure. Lancaster, it seemed, during the early 1970s, was all that Essex had aimed for originally, but seemed unable to achieve. And yet, because Lancaster was not that kind of high-profile institution, and had never set out to be one, the positive publicity it received did not remotely match the amount of negative opinion lavished on Essex. Thus we are faced with the irony that the campus which could be called, by certain standards, the institutionally-architecturally most successful one, missed out most on architectural and institutional fame.

In an earlier section we dealt systematically with the correspondences between utopian hopes in housing and town planning and utopianism in university planning. The same parallels apply to the negative story. The adverse reception of the Essex residential blocks comes, in this context, as no surprise at all. At the time of their conception, in 1962–3, they were still in architectural fashion, if only just; but long before the last ones were completed, by 1970, the type was resoundly condemned, for any kind of dwelling. As regards the concepts of the 'town', the one element that all the New Universities shared was their distance from their host towns. While not always as explicitly as in the 'urban' solutions of East Anglia, Essex and Lancaster, all of them had set out to create a town of their own, at least they all agreed on avoiding any kind of '9 to 5' institution. By 1970 none of universities (not even Lancaster) escaped the criticism that this 'urban' promise had not been fulfilled. By the late 1960s the professionals' definition of 'urban' had changed radically. It now stood for variety and comprehensiveness of life and that meant the whole spectrum of life, youth, age, all kinds of jobs etc. An out-of-town university could never, by that definition, become, or function, like a proper town. At this point there was a link with student radicalism, in that it, too, tried to connect the university with the wider world in new ways. A nasty remark, reported by Beloff and too good not to be taken up by Wilby, was aimed at finally demolishing any socio-urban claim of the New Universities: 'Only cemeteries are sited as far out of towns as the universities'. Universities should simply be situated inside the town. The demand, made by a faction of local founders in Norwich in 1960, to place the university in the city centre was now dug up again; it was now held that the actual space occupied by Lasdun's buildings at East Anglia, namely 75 acres (30 hectares), corresponded exactly to one of the proposed central sites. The result of these voltes-face in definitions was that some types of buildings which had been condemned were liable to return to fashion. Dense kinds of terraced housing had been the horror of the planners and designers of 1940 or 1950; by 1975 the type had been fully rehabilitated. In the early 1960s university patrons like Frank Thistlethwaite would look down upon the dull 'municipal' character of the Civics and Redbricks; in 1972 we are told, that, after all, 'working inside a community' was precisely what the older municipal universities were achieving. Finally, it comes as no surprise that the role played by architects was now, in 1970, considered 'excessive', as well as expensive – it came as another volte-face of the *Architectural Review* where seven years earlier critics could not rhapsodise enough about the contribution architects were going to make to the great task. At East Anglia, the low cost of the newest residences were said to be partly the result of the way in which there was 'freedom for the contractor . . . with a minimum of design limitations imposed by the architect'. A conclusion, drawn by the critic, Conrad Jameson, stated that 'the failings represented by the design of the University of Essex represents not too little thought and imagination, it represents too much'.

But the major reasons for the malaise go deeper than the discourses among architectural and planning specialists. We are witnessing, by 1970, the beginnings of a general rejection of Welfare State ideals and a deep criticism of its 'provisions'. At the very least, a rupture had occurred in the way these provisions were received or appreciated. Earlier on there was a prevalent attitude of gratefulness, which would include an understanding of those aspects of the provisions that appeared somewhat parsimonious. This old basis of understanding of the Welfare State included an acceptance of at least a certain amount of paternalism from the agents of the state; it also entailed a recognition of the expert regimes of those professions who served the Welfare State. In any case, there was a widely shared contentment and a sense that the postwar Welfare effort was 'succeeding'. The new attitude of a new generation, by contrast, was to expect what was provided by the Welfare State as of right and to complain if it did not come up to expectations – expectations which had been nourished by the increasing overall standard of life. Paradigm changes in sociology and planning and a new populism, a stress on 'grass-roots power' led to the beginning of a distrust of the expert regimes. It was coupled with a rejection of what was considered the false rhetoric used by the agents of the Welfare State. Those of a more left-wing persuasion held that the original aims of social equality were far from being fulfilled; in fact deprivation appeared on the increase again. As regards the New Universities there was the frequent realisation that, far from fulfilling a broad 'national need', as originally defined, they were, or behaved like, thoroughly upper middle-class institutions. Occasionally we meet with a panoply of outright condemnations, as those by Bernard Crick, Professor of Politics at Birkbeck College: '. . . the New Universities, isolated from the towns . . . elites acted selfishly . . . Oxbridge bias against cities and industrial England . . . civil servants with the mentality of commuterbelt pseudo-gentry'.

It was argued at the beginning of this section that the story told here has, in the end, no real bearing on what universities are ostensibly there for, namely academic research and teaching. Utopia or dystopia, a New University would not share the fate of an abandoned, soon-to-be-demolished 1960s large housing estate. Although some threat of closure hung over a number of the New Universities for a time, it was quite unlikely that this would ever have happened. Already in 1971, Beloff sounded conciliatory: 'Stocktaking of Plate glass' . . . 'student participation, flexible interdisciplinarity . . . Oxford imitated . . . courses'; even a new 'serious student' had appeared. The end of our English story is thus a rather simple one: the most favourable conclusion which the New Universities could hope for in the early to mid-1970s was that there was not that much difference between them and 'the rest'. 'Some assume that in New Universities everything may be made anew each year' Thistlethwaite wrote as early as 1968. Even Essex, according to Annan – in the year of its deepest disillusion, 1974 – 'turned out to be the same as other institutions'. In the early 1960s it would have been hard to think of a more hurtful remark. Altogether, this chapter has attempted a rational analysis of the 'troubles' and its discourses. What it cannot convey is the actual mental pain that the critics' remarks inflicted at the time.

There is, finally, the international dimension. After all, the student troubles happened worldwide. Seen from outside, the English chapter was not rated as a major one. As regards the condemnation of New University architecture, we shall encounter a few similar cases, such as Bochum and Chicago Circle. In France, it was the new campus at Nanterre, as such, which helped to spark the revolt of 1968 (see fig. 5.25). Here the dislike was concentrated on the way the planners had so far omitted to provide anything much beyond the academic/teaching facilities, the 'functional' minimum. This puts an ironical light on the concept of Essex, where dissatisfaction occurred in spite of, or perhaps because of, the planner's conscious, even maximum thought on the facilities for communal living. 'Too much design' (Jameson) or too little design? – The dilemma of the late 1960s. For the context of this book, two factors seem to be confirmed: it is in England where we find both the most intensive manifestations of the utopianist institution, as well as their most nervous rejection.

THE NEW 'URBAN' CAMPUS
IN NORTH AMERICA

Urban . . . like Paris, Bologna or Berlin.
(Richard Dober)

This chapter is, first of all, a straight continuation of the story of the English Seven. While our earlier section on the USA attempted to deal with the intricate web of campus and college design as a whole, the topic here is much more restricted. A highly select number of campuses by 'architects' architects' and architect-planners will be discussed within a further elaboration of the 'urban' version of the university community ethos.

CANADA: THE 'SINGLE STRUCTURE CAMPUS': SCARBOROUGH, SIMON FRASER

It is a commonplace to say that Canada's universities present a mixture of American and English trends. It is important to stress here the Canadian differences with the USA. General growth in the provision of education was almost as strong as it was across the border, but the Canadian 'system' as a whole was much simpler. There were hardly any venerable high-prestige universities, or strong divisions between 'higher' and 'lower' institutions. There was no tradition of notable residential colleges. All major institutions came under the 'provincial' governments (by 1974 the state and federal contributions stood at 70 per cent) which also indicates the localised clientele of each institution. There was, of course, always the proximity of the USA for those preferring something different. As in England and Germany, by 1960, it was felt necessary to set up models for new universities for the whole country. In 1961 *The New University* by the University of Toronto's vice president, Murray G. Ross presented one of the first fully ambitious pleas to combine expansion of numbers, Modernity and all the European and American pedigrees of academic and teaching excellence.

As in so many tracts of its kind, Ross's ideal new university was actually the one he had just helped to found, and begun to serve as a president, York University, Ontario. There was due mention of the American 'liberal' ideal and a boundless admiration for Oxbridge, however, according to Ross the latter's 'social quiet . . . has disappeared'. Ross's solution for his 15,000–strong campus, built from 1964, was to accommodate a good proportion of students in colleges, that is, clusters of four small colleges each, with ample campus central facilities. Ross condemned – without mentioning a country of origin – any style that adopted 'hideous and inefficient skyscrapers of learning'. Another major Ontario foundation was Trent University near Peterborough which adopted the college principle more fully and thus remained unusual in Canada; 'there was to be no single centre of university life' except for the

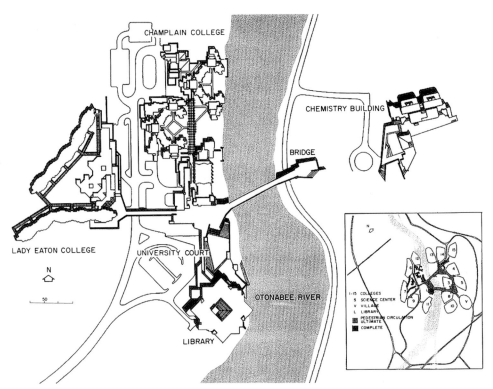

3.1   Trent University (Ontario), from 1964 by Ron Thom. (M. Schmertz, *Campus Planning & Design*, New York, 1972)

lavish library. The plan envisaged twelve smallish colleges of 180 to 220 students each (smaller ones for women); the planned total of 3,000 students was never much exceeded. Colleges were to be relatively independent administratively and academically. There was also a greater than usual mix of tutors' rooms with students' rooms. Dubbed 'Balliol on Trent', there was probably much influence from the University of York (England) – some of Trent's officials and the architect, Ron Thom from Vancouver, had travelled to see English New Universities, including Oxbridge, Sussex and York, in 1963. On the other hand, Trent's 'staircase plan' as well as its architectural elaboration is generally more influenced by some of the new East Coast buildings, which Thom also went to see. With its extremely complex plan and vertical excrescences, Champlain College looks somewhat like Eero Saarinen's Morse and Stiles Colleges at Yale, from where Trent also took the experimental rubble–aggregate method of building (fig. 3.1).

The major Canadian architectural innovations were of a different kind. They were those which precisely did not follow new American, or the old English pattern, but ran parallel to England's newest New Universities. One preliminary explanation for the impact of Simon Fraser University and Scarborough College on the international architectural scene was that they were planned and built with extreme rapidity, within a mere two years, from 1963 to 1965. Secondly, there was the outright enthusiasm of the two young Canadian designers, Arthur Erickson and John Andrews (actually the latter was Australian). Most importantly, their architects' and their buildings' fame was 'institutionalised' by a new faction among Canadian and American architects. At the 1964 Banff Session on university architecture it was stated that 'almost overnight the Canadian university has become a major patron of the architectural profession . . .'. The architects now rallied and proffered their collective expertise, in a way that sounded much like the *Architectural Review/Architects' Journal* campaign of 1957/8 – one of the noted speeches at the session was by Percy Johnson-Marshall of RMJM, the architects of York, England. The Canadian architects' proud summary ran as follows: 'There are . . . many factors at work . . . the academic ping-pong ball bounced back and forth between academics, administrators, provincial purse strings. . . . Finally, the ball often comes to rest in the collective lap of the planner-architect . . . the real problem of university design and growth begins right here . . . we must explore totally new educational and architectural concepts'. The always eloquent Erickson prided himself on the fact that at Simon Fraser 'there was no academic program and we had to make assumptions upon which we based our design'. Later, the official nature of these moves was underlined again, when they declared that 'major university projects manifested the government's embrace of Modernism' and that this meant 'an architecture that is beautiful, happy, healthy, rational and, above all, moral'. One may use comparisons with other state-entrepreneurial entities in this field: with Clark Kerr's elaborate educational planning concepts at Santa Cruz combined with architectural restraint, or with Nelson Rockefeller's drive towards architectural splendour in New York State; Canada went the English way of the 'architect as briefmaker'.

Scarborough College, designed during 1963, is, in fact, not a full university but one of a number of subsidiaries of the University of Toronto for undergraduate study only. Scarborough is essentially non-residential which simplified the programme. Moreover, it has remained somewhat incomplete, as the theatre and sports facilities and the original design for the library were never built. This meant that attention has concentrated even more on the main building. Everything is, indeed, accommodated in one structure, 'a single building for 6,000 people'. Stretched out, it would be about 1300 feet (400 metres) long, that is, nearly the length of East Anglia's 'teaching wall'. There are other similarities with UEA, the 'Ziggurats' in particular – designed slightly before but completed several years later. Situated on a slope, Scarborough has a 'back', much of it windowless, and a 'front', letting in the light and overlooking the landscape. Above all, the complex is 'cranked', forming 'knuckles', the whole presenting the kind of non-rectilinear, non-diagrammatic form beloved to Lasdun and the Smithsons. As at East Anglia, it is the air photograph that is invariably shown. Lastly, what fascinated the planning-minded among architects was, as with Lasdun's first plans, the apparent easy extendibility (figs 3.2 and 3.3).

As with the Smithsons, the zigzagging, or gently angled figuration is suggestive of communication lines. In John Andrew's complex at Scarborough these 'lines' are inside the building, whereas, as we realised at East Anglia, Lasdun operates preferably with external 'spaces'. There was one major practical rationale: five or six months of inclement weather during the academic year suggested the creation of an environment which nobody had to leave during the day. It was in those years that Canada built a number of what were soon to be called 'megastructures' (cf. page 272), huge complexes of indoor urban spaces, especially in Montreal. An internal 'street' links it all, running right through the longer science wing and the shorter humanities wing,

189

3.2 Scarborough College (University of Toronto), 1963–5. (Courtesy John Andrews Associates)

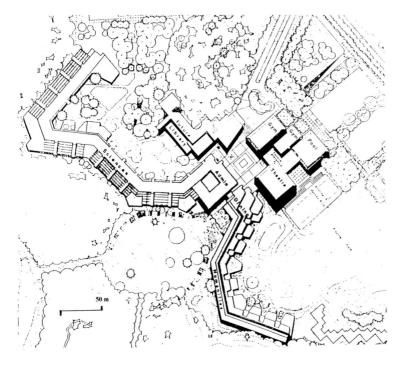

50 m

3.3 Scarborough College, plan.
(*Country Life Annual* 1969, p. 62)

3.4   Scarborough College, interior. (*Canadian Architect* 1-1969, p. 39)

linking up at a large open, i.e. glass-roofed, 'meeting place'. Studying the lines of the plan of Scarborough is one thing. When close by one is overwhelmed by another element, the physicality of the in–situ reinforced concrete. Andrews makes use of an element popular at that time: cantilevering or oversailing. Practically no part of the building goes straight up, floors either project or recede, they are 'splayed or staggered'. All this makes for immense heaviness, as well as for the utmost spatial complexity (fig. 3.4). The international critics' praise was boundless: 'The significance of Scarborough is its totality' writes Oscar Newman and he makes the building the centrepiece of his account of the new 'urban' kind of university. 'Of all completed university complexes in recent years this is by far the most daring, comprehensive and

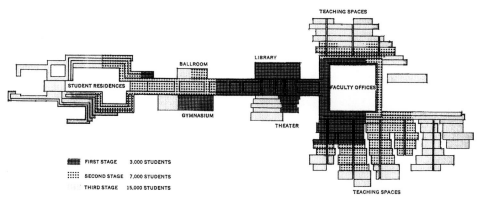

3.5   Simon Fraser University, Burnaby/Vancouver (B.C.), plan by Arthur Erickson (Erickson and Massey); quadrangle (Faculty Offices) by Zoltan Kiss. (*AFor* 12-1965, p. 13)

radical' (Kenneth Frampton in *Architectural Design*) and later it was claimed that 'Scarborough College constitutes Canada's initial claim to the first rank of Modern architecture'.

The praise for Simon Fraser was less complete, but then this new university is very much more complex than Scarborough's teaching block. As everywhere else, the starting point was numbers. More student places were needed in the Vancouver area. Again, the speed was breathtaking. In mid-1962 there were warnings of the need to create extra student places for the year 1965. In early 1963 the decision was taken to found a new institution, Simon Fraser (the eighteenth-century explorer is a house-hold name in the region); a competition for it was held in mid-1963, open only to local designers – an ideas contest, rather in the European way. A 1,200 acre (or 480 hectare), site was given by the local town, Burnaby. Building started a few months later and by autumn 1965 – and after spending about $16,000,000 (£5,700,000) – the first 2,500 students began at Simon Fraser, with an eventual 15,000–17,000 planned.

Efficiency was a shared aim of the architects and the chancellor, Dr Gordon Shrum, a physicist as well as 'a highly experienced university administrator, well-connected politically, eloquently bulldozing when geared to a cause'. In many ways, he provided the motive force – not always popular – for the success at Simon Fraser. 'At no point did the project bog down in red tape or deferred decision' and an English critic duly recommended that 'this policy of defined individual responsibility could well be adopted for Britain'. Shrum had, in fact, stipulated some of the basics of the design concept, such as compactness and the possibility of expansion. While Erickson/Massey had provided the striking overall concept, in order to save time, some parts of the designs by the runner-ups were used for individual buildings, most notably those for the Academic Quadrangle by Zoltan Kiss. It has to be admitted that, as with most of the English New Universities, 'SFU' did not quite fulfil the dreams of the first plan, not all the buildings stood up to Erickson's vision, and more-over, the residential element was, initially, only small (10 per cent of the students). What was impressive about Erickson's original plan was a long series of large squares with repetitive detail, not too unlike Stone's grandiose Albany (see p. 43). But the dif-ferences between Stone and Erickson are crucial: Stone's designs sit geometrically flat

3.6   Simon Fraser University, air view. (*AFor* 12-1965, p. 12)

on a plane, Simon Fraser responds to a 800 feet (260 metre) high hilltop situation with a set of varying levels ('terraces'), gently ascending and descending between two points of the ridge – 'an Acropolis for our time' (Erickson) (figs 3.5 and 3.6).

The success of the building itself lies in the straightforwardness of the 'linear' succession of the two main parts of the campus, the mall and the square, and the way this plan appeared to respond to the basic academic aims of the institution. We have already quoted the architect, boasting the primacy of his plan over the academic concept. The basic aim of the latter was subsequently formulated in a by now familiar form of words: the unity of academic subjects, the 'total body of knowledge'. 'One world, one university, one building'. Erickson untiringly condemns the typical 'North American campus' as 'random separate buildings for separate studies, fragmented . . . little to do with the ideals of education but . . . [rather] with the process of departmental indoctrination'. 'Erickson/Massey have succeeded in expressing both the symbolic unity and the vast heterogeneity of the modern university in their integrated plan for SFU' said the sociologist, Lionel Tiger. Virtually all teaching facilities and offices surround the huge Academic Quadrangle. This then leads, via a grandiose set of steps, to the mall which gives access to most of the social facilities and leads on to the access road. The mall is, on the one hand, open, but also, in view of the inclemency of the weather, covered with a vast, but light 'space frame' roof. In 1969 Canada's senior academic, Claude Bissell, President of the University of Toronto (the 'patron' of Scarborough College) offered his praise: while noting 'tensions' academically, 'in its inception and physical embodiment Simon Fraser was the wonder of the university world' (fig. 3.7).

At Lethbridge University, Alberta, Erickson finally accommodated virtually every-

3.7   Simon Fraser University, view of mall with teaching quadrangle in the background. (*A'dA* no. 137, 4/5-1968, p. 88)

thing into one building. Designed in 1967/9, 'University Hall', about 1,000 feet (300 metres) long and up to nine stories high, contains residences in the lower storey and social offices and teaching spaces above, accessible at different levels from the very uneven grounds. As at Scarborough, reinforced concrete allows for an unusual top heavy shape. As a whole, Lethbridge seemed 'the achitectural statement of an often expressed but seldom implemented educational idea – learning and living are integral parts of the process . . . students meet with unexpected ease and ideas can be exchanged freely' (fig. 3.8).

USA: CHICAGO CIRCLE: THE 'URBAN' CHALLENGE TO CAMPUS AND COLLEGE

By 1965 the Canadian story can be taken across the southern border. Among Erickson's proudest notions was the backwardness of American campus architecture. He even believed that he had overcome the problems of 'multiversity' dispersal, as formulated by Kerr. Indeed, it could be said that American campus planners, like Richard Dober, thought in terms of individual buildings for individual functions, whereas the new kind of planning began with the way buildings are linked. It was the American critics who jumped to an interpretation of Scarborough and Simon Fraser as 'urban' solutions; Thomas H. Creighton, a partner of a Californian firm heavily involved in college design there, Carl Warnecke and Associates, first put it cautiously, at the Banff Conference in 1964: 'Architecture is less and less a series of separate building designs: it is more and more a new discipline called urban design'.

We must interject here an element of surprise, namely, that of Americans taking

194

3.8   University of Lethbridge (Alberta), by Erickson/Murray, planned from 1967/9. The lower floors contain student residences, the fifth floor the main communal facilities and the upper floors teaching and research. 'Plant' is placed on the top.
The block is 912 feet (278 metres) long. (Courtesy Erickson Architectural Corporation)

note of English New University design. Was there anything to be learned from
England apart from Oxbridge? In 1964 it was none other than Richard Dober, who,
having been invited to the Brighton conference on New Universities, came to find
out for himself. His *The New Campus in Britain: Ideas of Consequence for the United
States*, brought out by Educational Facilities Laboratories of New York in 1965 is
rather a short book, yet surprisingly comprehensive. After a few remarks about
financing and commissioning he comes straight to his point: 'The most striking synthesis is the continuous teaching environment, a physical form that preserves communication and contact between all parts of the institution while allowing external
accretion and internal change.' There now appears to be an 'American dilemma' in
that 'too often the rigid distinctions between instructional, communal, and residential
buildings reduce the opportunity for casual and indirect attachment . . . a sense of
belonging is lost'. Much attention is given to student residences: 'The conscious formulation of connections between educational philosophy and housing goals is the
idea of consequence', and he concludes with the question: York or Essex? It is,
however, hard to gauge the exact response to Dober's tract at home, even though it
was printed three times. On the whole there was little mention of English New Universities; and the occasional visits to them by sociologists, such as Riesman or Trow,
resulted in not much more than polite remarks. Journals such as the *Architectural Record*
kept up international reporting without any stress on particular national achievements.

    An important lesson some Americans took from England and Canada in connec-
tion with university design was the plea for architecture's autonomy: 'Many of us

today resent being "handed" a program that was devised by a client who did not know anything about architecture, but knew damn well what he wanted'. 'The New Campus' was the title of a blast by Oscar Newman, Professor of Urban Design in St Louis and editor of *Architectural Forum* in 1966: 'With the suddenness of a coup d'etat, the new campus has come to occupy the dominant position in current architecture'; again, this is coupled with the assertion: 'The profession . . . has been seeking a more relevant role in society . . . as planners we are hamstrung . . . at best we are involved with the design of the ideal while the refuse of the real accumulates around us.' Newman even claims that 'artistic taste is a ladder, paralleling class, the architect, as a professional taste maker, automatically occupies the highest rung. Campus clients . . . are a rung below'. Without mentioning Britain at all, Newman dwells on concepts that were, by 1966, more than familiar to the 'new' English architects, such as generous social-communal facilities, flexibility and growth, traffic separation, hierarchies of circulation frequency, places for spontaneous meetings etc. Immense praise is given to Scarborough, and other examples are made of Berlin and Marburg (see page 270) and the local St Louis, while the hitherto most frequently cited new American campus, at Santa Cruz, is condemned as 'suburban'.

Oscar Newman's proud essay showed only one really convincing American example: Chicago (Congress) Circle. Significantly, here, too, a pronouncedly 'urban' design went with a case of the architect as briefmaker. The same journal, *Architectural Forum* had given it the 'biggest editorial comment ever'. The huge State University of Illinois had decided after World War II to create an additional campus inside the inner city. Mayor Richard J. Daley helped them to acquire a site close to the city centre, the Loop. The story of the acquisition of the site – a *cause célèbre* for many years, suspended between issues of perceived high commercial value and the quite different values of the mixed-race resident population – served to demonstrate the difficulty of escaping the out-of-town campus pattern. The move was aimed at 'solving problems of an urban society', and accommodating students from 'lower income' families. Yet, some of the rhetoric was then aimed at redressing that impression of low class: 'liberal education as a framework for technical and/or specialised training . . . the state university . . . reflecting the spirit of a city, a state and a nation'. Planning and building proceeded quickly after 1961 and the university opened in 1965 for 9,000 students and was meant to grow to 25,000 by 1969; it actually took several decades to reach that target. The campus was to be thoroughly 'Modern' and aimed to break 'with many traditions of college architecture'. Skidmore, Owings and Merrill were the USA's largest architectural office; the job architect was the highly individualistic Walter Netsch, whose previous experience included the Air Force Academy at Colorado Springs.

Netsch's early plans, showing a series of rectangular blocks, did not really differ much from the standard Modernist American campus plan. Indeed, there is still much planting even now between the grand buildings. But the grouping is denser than usual, all is pressed into 106 acres (43 hectares), including surface parking for 6,000 cars. There were to be no student residences. The main buildings are the enormous students union and the library in the centre, the giant science laboratories and 'University Hall', a twenty-eight storey tower. The self-contained nature of the campus was strengthened in the way low buildings dominated its centre with high buildings pushed to the periphery. It is the way the main uses are allocated within this group

3.9 University of Illinois at Chicago Circle, by Walter Netsch of Skidmore, Owings and Merill, begun 1962. (UC University Archives Aerial Photograph by Orlando R. Cabanban).

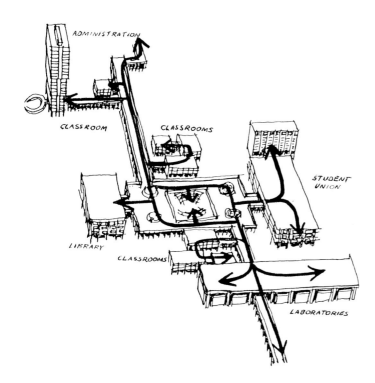

3.10 Chicago Circle, main functions and circulation. (*AFor* 5-1966, p. 50)

3.11   Chicago Circle, central plaza; lecture theatres below. (Courtesy University of Illinois at Chicago)

that is highly unusual. The campus is not divided according to faculties or departments (except for the science building), but according to basic function: all departmental offices and small classrooms are in the tower. The only parallels, vaguely, are
the one-building teaching blocks at UEA or Simon Fraser. All larger classrooms are
housed in separate, smaller buildings. The larger lecture theatres, twenty-one on the
plan, ranging from 75 to 500 seaters, are placed into one central block. It is this central
block which appears to be a building totally without precedent. The theatres are coordinated in geometrical fashion – in that aspect a residue of American Beaux Arts can
still be felt – on the ground floor, between a forest of short columns. These columns
support a platform, a raised plaza, forming a rectangle, measuring 100 by 150 metres.

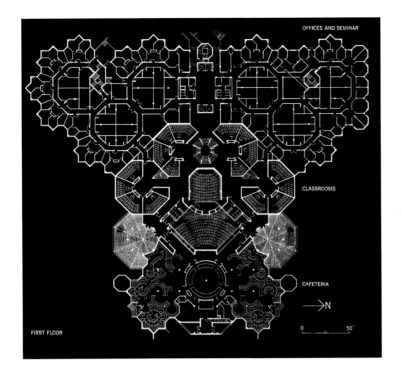

3.12   Chicago Circle,
Behavioural Sciences Center,
'cluster plan', by Walter Netsch.
(*AFor* 11-1970, p. 24)

Part of this plaza is taken up by four circular mini plazas, while the very centre is further sunk in, forming a double amphitheatre, with seating for 10,000. In the end, the idea does not seem that complicated: lecture theatres are usually placed in the centre of the campus, and likewise one expects a large central open plaza. It is the way the two are combined that baffles. It more than baffled the actual users, the climate often being hostile, not only in Canada, but in Chicago, too. Finally, the elevated plaza also served as the centre of an elevated walkway system which, not unlike East Anglia, runs across the entire campus and was meant to double up on the main paths at ground level (figs 3.9–3.11).

All stress was on communication: 'Everybody will be constantly rubbing shoulders' (Norman A. Parker). Netsch's plan meant that teachers had to travel a long way from their offices to the teaching rooms, while for the students the closeness of so many lecture theatres meant a constant mingling. 'What happens between classes came to be regarded as being as important as what happens in classes.' By the mid-1960s this kind of statement was nothing unusual. What was singular at Chicago Circle was the proliferation of the architect's own language and design confidence, backed by his client, University of Illinois President David D. Henry and the Chancellor of Circle, Norman A. Parker, himself a mechanical engineer. The main idea of the 'functional division' was Netsch's and it occurred to him after the start, 'it came . . . with classic suddenness'. Throughout, Netsch found his own words: he claimed 'everything falls into place', and the elevated walkways he called 'pedestrian "expressways"'. The journal probably directly echoed the architect's convictions when it summarised: 'The strength of Chicago Circle is in part the strength of rough-cut granite and coarse textured concrete, of big spaces and of massive forms . . . the strength of consistency achieved without conformity. . . . The strength is in freedom.' Lastly, Netsch was not at all afraid to admit violent changes of mind. From 1965, his major additions to the campus took leave from rectangularity in favour of multi-angled conglomerates of forms of the most complicated kinds of interlocking spaces. Netsch called them, 'galaxies', 'clusters', or 'new geometries' based grandeloquently on his 'field theory' (fig. 3.12). Altogether, Netsch said, he would by that time have adopted 'more of a . . . single system, not a group of objects', which might have led to another one of the gigantic all-in-one building solutions.

Netsch's campus might thus be compared to Capon's Essex; they both stand at the intersection of two modes of thinking. On the one hand there is a new emphasis on informal use, the attempt to encourage spontaneous contacts; on the other hand a preference for large, dominant buildings. We noted the way the new 'urban' campus seemed to mean, on the part of the designer, a sense of doing something daring, unusual. All the more heavy could be the criticism of the designer's work and ideas. Netsch experienced a heavier dose than probably anybody else in the story of our universities. Whereas at Essex it was the whole concept of the institution, conceived by the university authorities as much as by the designer which was criticised, at Chicago Circle it was Netsch alone who had to take the blame, not so much for the character of Chicago Circle as a whole but for more specific malfunctionings, especially of the central piazza. However, such criticism can oscillate: *Time Magazine's* verdict in 1970 was; 'such failures are magnificent ones, architectural experiments that excite bold clients'. And yet, in the early 1990s, after much argument, the platform over the lecture theatres, Netsch's main plaza, was finally taken away.

There appears to have been no real parallel to, or follower of Chicago Circle (but cf. Tolbiac, Paris, page 267 below). While plenty of major individual functions of multiversity complexes were built in dense towns, hardly any major universities were ever planned as a whole in inner urban locations. The famous Canadian 'urban' models, after all, constituted pure American campus tradition in respect of their location, Simon Fraser proudly on the hills, seven miles out of Vancouver, and Scarborough a lonely twenty miles away from Toronto (roughly 10 and 30 kilometres respectively). Nevertheless, 'urban' now became one of the most heavily used terms when discussing, not just issues of town planning, but any groups of buildings. Formulations, like Netsch's 'micro environment of a twentieth century city' does not really point to anything more than what Oscar Newman was trying to drive home, namely an analogy: any new campus in some ways should look and feel like an old-style city. In practice, there could be many variants. Firstly, any larger group with a pedestrianised centre could be called 'urban', especially when it also contained a number of major 'public' buildings for the arts, as at the State University of New York at Purchase, planned from 1967 (fig. 1.21). The centre could also become an elongated covered zone, a kind of shopping mall, such as at Stockton State College, Pomona, New Jersey. Then there is the massed, quasi single building which could take the dramatically dynamic shapes of Paul Rudolph's North Dartmouth Technology Institute, begun in 1963, or an Italian Hill town image, as with the Engineering Department of the University of Colorado at Boulder. Perhaps a fair conclusion is that voiced by *Time Magazine* in 1970: the overall trend was for 'denser and more crowded campuses . . . to make the most of an ever-decreasing amount of open space'.

Architects, no doubt, did share the general sense that American inner cities were experiencing problems. 'Although many notable individual buildings have been constructed, the positive impact of American architects on urban America seems inconsequential' (Paul Heyer 1967). In the first chapter on American university planning and architecture we kept switching discourses. At this point of our account we also have to turn away from the architectural faction and use arguments of practical and economic planning. As emphasised before, 'community' had two meanings, an inward one and an outward one. The new inner 'urban' campus made sense in the efforts to spread higher education to the urban masses, young and not so young, to those who had to stay close to their jobs or families; for these groups an out of town campus was simply too expensive. Locations had to be accessible by public transport (multi-storey car parks would be too expensive to build and run for that sort of student, while surface car parks would take too much land). By now, another interest group had emerged, those who discussed 'urban land' problems. While the earlier definition of campus or college entailed a detachment of the institution from its surroundings, discussion now centered around their interaction. With regard to Chicago Circle, there was disappointment that it appeared to contribute so little to the 'urban renewal' of its area.

Although the oil shock of the 1970s slowed the movement down somewhat, new colleges and campuses continued to be built throughout America. And yet, there were clear signs of some decline in the strict definition of these two institutions. We noted in the first chapter the great diversification of student residences by the late 1960s. The new urban campuses and the community colleges usually built only a small number of student rooms. 'College education' no longer seemed a universal value, and neither was the idea of the educationally self-contained campus. The student movement which, famously, took its origins from the American campuses in the mid-1960s before it reached Europe by early 1968, is of less relevance here than in our account of England because less of a link was constructed between the unrest and the nature of the campus plan or architecture – although some of the severest critics of the unrest maintained that the isolated large campus had lent itself particularly well to rebellious student organisation. Moreover, the unrest in the USA was essentially more concerned with matters external to the university. There was, principally, a different phasing of new university building and student unrest: in England, the unrest came after the buildings and it could thus, as at Essex, be blamed directly on the buildings. In the USA the two ran concurrently and college organisations like Kresge, with its intensely personalised approach and its high degree of student participation, notably in the design process, was in part a response to the revolt. The way Kresge was then not taken seriously, in turn, ran parallel with the dying down of the student movement ideals in the later 1970s. On the whole both the student movement with its ethics of personal altruistic commitment, and its opposite, the aim of just getting good marks so as proceed to a good job, in other words, both the anti-authoritarian and the instrumentalised view of the university contributed to a lessening of the institution's moral and educational authority altogether. To cite once more David Riesman, who after his intensive researches concluded very simply that it was '. . . characteristically American . . . to overestimate what education itself can do'.

'The notion of a campus may be disappearing', said Richard Dober in 1967 – a remarkable turn of mind. 'The quarters of the College for Human Services are properly unprepossessing. As benefits reformers, the place is frugal, a bit drab and hand-me-down. Most of its two hundred students are mothers on welfare . . .'; and yet, to David Riesman, this college on the Lower West Side, New York City, founded in

1965, counts among the major American reformist and experimental institutions. Another new idea was to let higher education come directly into peoples homes. In 1969 the sociologist, Martin Trow, asked the searching question: why do older buildings lend themselves better to spontaneous academic contacts than newly and purposely designed ones? One might even find attractions with the multiversity, precisely because it is 'undesigned'. The main campus in Los Angeles, UCLA, was dubbed 'urban . . . like Paris, Bologna or Berlin', as forming part of a large urban agglomeration and thus the opposite to the American campus tradition, as well as Oxbridge. Berkeley, too, comes close to a common urban mixture. Quoting from Ian Brown, one of the English authors on planning indeterminism of those years, American campus historian Paul Venable Turner would have none of all this: 'This call for impermanence and obsolescence struck at the heart of the American tradition of the campus as a physcical place that is meaningful precisely because of its enduring embodiment of values. Not suprisingly, it [indeterminism] had little effect on American college planning'. One might be inclined to agree, bearing in mind that Turner takes a broad view, being concerned with the whole of American college architecture. In the context of the present book, however, it is tempting to highlight once more the complexity of the situation at the end of the 1960s by giving the last word to some of those who were in charge of Berkeley during that time. DeMars, Alan Temko and Donald Reay were first of all 'steeped in the townscape spirit that pervaded English architecture'. Many of the 'urban' qualities of Berkeley, we read at the time, were directly owed to these architects, for instance the campus entrance: 'This was intended as a Hyde Park corner by the designers and so it has become'; or Upper Sproul Plaza, as the architects shaped it: '. . . its influence instantly locates speakers and organises activities in space. . . . they make it function as an outdoor area . . . a scene of tremendous power when 6,000 to 8,000 people assembled here in the rain to hear Herbert Marcuse'. The Anglo-American campus creators' beliefs were, and remained, boundless. But whereas the designer of Essex University was chided as being directly responsible for the troubles on his campus, at Berkeley the architects were seemingly not concerned with such critiques and carried on extolling the quality and the performance of their architecture. This applied even to occasions when their architecture functioned as a frame for protest, a protest against the very campus creators themselves.

IV   WEST GERMANY: CAMPUS AND COLLEGE
AS 'REFORM'

> *. . . der Sozialbereich der Hochschule als der eigentlich gestaltbare . . .*
> *[. . . the social areas of the university as the part that is really subjected to designing . . .]*
> (Horst Linde, 1970)

THE POST WORLD WAR II REINSTATEMENT OF TRADITION

While England gave us the 'college' and America the 'college campus', Germany was the land of the 'university', no more, no less. And this was by no means just a prevailing pride in German-speaking countries, but something voiced by many American and English academics, too. In a speech, given at the Freie Universität Berlin in 1967, Cambridge University's vice chancellor, Sir Eric Ashby, one of the international experts on matters of university policy, spoke of the 9,000 Americans who studied in Germany between the 1860s and 1914 and of the same number coming from England. Many Americans, almost as devotedly as the Germans, paid homage to that early nineteenth-century intellectual and government adviser, Wilhelm von Humboldt and his role in the foundation of the new university in Berlin in the great Prussian Reforms after 1806. According to Humboldt, a university is first and foremost about *Wissenschaft* – a word that has to be rendered in English with a number of terms, such as scientific precision (which is applied to the humanities as much as to the natural and social sciences) and 'academic' in the sense of the level achieved by research and postgraduate studies. The crucial factor is that the perception of the student is fixed at that 'high' level too. The 'typical' German university student is one who learns through being introduced to research, virtually from the start. They should never have to engage in mere rote-learning. From this derives the most famous of all the Humboldtian maxims, and one from which to this day many academics, anywhere, would hesitate to dissociate themselves: the 'Einheit von Lehre und Forschung', the 'unity of teaching and research'. In order to thrive, what both *Wissenschaft* and university studies need is, above all, freedom, which should apply, in like measure, both to the teacher and the student: *Lehrfreiheit* and *Lernfreiheit*, the completely free choice of what to teach and what to learn. The term 'Einheit' (unity) is used in further permutations, such as the 'Einheit' of the learners and the teachers as well as in the older sense of the unity and purity of all *Wissenschaften* in the face of any instrumentalisation. Humboldt thereby somewhat demoted those subjects which had traditionally provided the mainstay of university teaching, theology, law and medicine, and foregrounded the humanities and above all philosophy, as the chief subject of pure inquiry.

Much less straightforward would be a definition of the German University as an institution. Coming from the traditional Anglo-American position we might find a certain lack of institutional identity. Humboldt himself stated very simply that the university is 'neither a Gymnasium [a high school or grammar school], nor a Specialschule'. The teaching of technology was, indeed, almost entirely undertaken by the polytechnics, the *technische Hochschulen*, traditionally of a slightly lower academic rank. There is, in Germany, no ambiguity in the terms used for our institution: university is the only official word. There is no 'college' and no direct equivalent for the term campus ('Universitatsgelände' is weak, an arbitrary composite word). A major institutional factor on the other hand is the very high social reputation enjoyed by the professoriate, comprising all universities. A crucial difference between Germany and most other countries is the lack of traditional ranking. Each of the two dozen or so pre-World War II German universities enjoyed the same level of reputation. This was, and in many ways still is, linked to the old strong geographical divisions of Germany, the states of the federation or the old principalities, who all created their own university as one of the ways of striving for prestige. A scale of ranking applies, however, to the professoriate; it is the rank of the individual professor which helps the student to make the academic choice of the institution (fig. 4.1). It goes without saying in continental Europe that virtually all institutions are state-owned and state-led and subject to state law. Humboldt's purist conception notwithstanding, the vast majority of students, still study for a profession, law, medicine etc. and not for research, and take examinations which are regulated directly by the state. This state control, in turn, produced, from Humboldt onwards, a constant assertion of 'academic autonomy', but there could never be an independent German university on the model of old Oxbridge or the 'private' American university.

But institutional definition does not necessarily have anything to do with institutional presence. The German university carries a number of unofficial ornamental names, universities literarum, 'Hohe Schule', or confusingly – 'Hochschule' – as a generic term. As in many other Western countries, there is (or was, until recently) the periodic display of medievalist pageantry. In many older towns the institution vies with theatres and museums; in the famous smaller university towns, like Tübingen or Jena, everything turns around the *Alma Mater*. There are always large dignified buildings, usually in the centre of the town, with splendid halls and staircases, with lectures reverberating, the most prestigious ones held in the giant *auditorium maximum* ('Audimax'). In more recent complexes the most prominent building is usually the *Studenten Haus*, the student day centre with its gigantic *Mensa*, feeding lunch to thousands at a time. Thus, the old institutions show a concentrated presence, and largely an urban one. Above all they appear public and open. In the analysis of the Anglo-American campus and college there seemed no special need to differentiate between institution, institutional image and 'institutional presence' because they all appeared congruent. But Germany and most other continental European countries lack the 'campus' or the 'college' and a stranger to the town or the country might mistake the university buildings for another kind of institution. A specific 'institutional presence' concerns the people, the users, rather than the buildings. The correspondence between the aims of the institution and its built manifestations was not something that really mattered for the strict Humboldtians.

All the greater seemed the fall of the German university during the years 1933 to 1945. To the Nazis, freedom or autonomy were useless or dirty words. Not only was there massive repression, with vast numbers of teachers dismissed, on racial as well as

4.1   Universität Göttingen. Eighteenth/nineteenth century dwelling house with plaques of professors and other eminent persons who lived here. Far left: Benjamin Franklin (1766)

intellectual grounds, but the size of the institution as a whole was practically halved by 1939 and of the remaining teachers many completely forgot their allegiance to academic freedom, independence of judgment or institutional autonomy and colluded with the regime. Above all, the regime laid a fierce organisational structure upon the universities' 'liberal' practices.

To most, 1945 meant a reinstitution of freedom. And yet, it has to be asked: perhaps the Nazi phase of the German university was not a complete aberration? Perhaps it had something to do with the fundamental problems of its institutional definition, or the lack of it, the way in which, intrinsically, not much of an institution was needed ·when the stated central purpose was the free pursuit of pure research, ideally undertaken by each individual himself or herself. To quote another crucial Humboldtian term, research ought to be conducted in 'Einsamkeit' (meaning both seclusion/solitude and loneliness). 'Freiheit und Einsamkeit: from these two points flows the whole external [äusserliche] organisation of the university'. The issue that was least determined in German universities was that of the actual education of, or care for, the students. Arguably, in Humboldt's system there was no place for those terms at all. As has already been stated, the student is defined as a researcher, who, to quote another popular formula, proceeds by – 'learning while researching' – 'forschend lernen'. While in the USA students normally begin aged 17 and in Britain at 18, around 70 per cent of West German students in 1961 were aged 21 or over. And yet, the Germans, too, asked the question: should students be considered adults? By a stretch of the imagination, the Humboldtian kind of relationship between teacher and taught, could, and was, also described by a much older definition of the university as the 'community of magistrorum et scholarum'. In practice, one might see the German universities as no different from those anywhere else, presenting several levels of student involvement, from the predominantly professional studies, involving much rote-learning, like law or medicine, 'upwards' to theoretical sciences and humanities. In practice, the Humboldtian ideal of complete freedom could only be applied to a small proportion of university studies – which was also the sector which the Anglo-Saxon visiting students came to know best. It is all these apparent dilemmas which will concern us in what follows below. We shall note how, with increasing diversity overall, steeply rising student numbers, and a growing realisation that the Anglo-American type of university appeared to be 'better organised', a more complex institution overall and a greater degree of institutionality had at least to be considered.

That period, however, was preceded by a relatively uncomplicated decade. The years of the late 1940s until the early to mid-1960s in the Federal German Republic entailed a rapid rebuilding followed by a surge of happy wealth creating, the *Wirtschaftswunder*, in step with the extension of Welfare State provisions. By the mid-1950s student numbers – 128,000 – had reached the pre-Hitler level in the whole of the German Reich and by 1960/1 they had more than doubled. By the later 1950s a system of state support for poorer students ('Honneff') had been instituted. It appeared rather modest in comparison with the British system of students' grants and it did not help to broaden access to higher education in social terms as fully as the American system. On the other hand, Germany was virtually abolishing teaching fees and there was, as always, equal access to any of the universities. As regards research excellence, it was felt that all effort was being made to compensate for the self-inflicted losses during 1933 to 1945. On the whole, it appeared that the old ideals, especially the Humboldtian kind of freedom, could be upheld: 'Without being conscious of it, the learned men and the students of those years [the 1950s] lived through the sunset of the German university.'

THE NEW CONCERN FOR STUDENTS: *WOHNHEIME,*

GEMEINSCHAFTSHÄUSER AND THE *KOLLEGIENHAUS*-PROJECT

Alongside this Humboldtian kind of academic antonomy, however, a new concern for the students' 'education' had arisen which resulted in attempts to create new institutional structures based largely on Anglo-American models. These structures were not applied to the main parts of the institution, but for the subsidiary ones of the student sphere. Initially all this formed part of the measures, instituted by the occupying powers, to rid Germany of the Nazi spirit, 're-education', as it was called. Numerous bodies subordinated to the American and British military authorities dealt with all aspects of university life. A short report by a British University Commission, in 1949, was directed by a group of German public figures who were joined by Lord Lindsay of Birker, Master of Balliol College Oxford, who was, as we saw, the founder of Keele University during the same year. He was, more importantly in this particular context, also an adherent to German (philosophical) idealism. The overwhelming message of the report, surprisingly or unsurprisingly, was: no change as far as the Humboldtian ideals were concerned. Moreover, 'freedom' in the German university acquired a new urgency in the Cold War. It manifested itself directly in the name of the new Freie Universität in West Berlin in 1948, virtually founded and financed by the Americans.

To the West it appeared ironic, or worse, that the original Berlin University, now in East Berlin was renamed Humboldt Universität, when higher education in East Germany was becoming an instrument in the teaching of primarily that which the new state held to be necessary. A closer study of the DDR's system would, however, reveal some similarities with the West, at least during the 1950s and particularly in the strong concern for student welfare.

'Re-education' in the university was an apt term, when, in the years immediately after 1945, the majority of students were returning soldiers. But it also marked the beginning of a long debate on all aspects of 'education' in and around the German university, or, to put it more precisely, a special concern for what the students did and thought outside their special field of study, outside their 'research apprenticeship'. The cited British Report of 1949 was adamant that 'the student should be led not merely to scientific abstraction, but to the creative and formative absolute . . . from conscientious learning . . . into the whole cultural field: in the first place of the civilisation of the West and finally of humanity as a whole'. No doubt we hear the voice of Lord Lindsay. The first academic measure to bring students together beyond their individual specialisations was the 'Studium Generale' which was instituted in most universities and entailed a series of lectures on all subjects, sometimes followed by organised discussion sessions.

However, what really mattered now was a new concern for the whole of the student's life. Traditionally this was of no interest to the university authorities, nor to the teachers. The new axiom here was a Western European fomula, the combination of freedom with responsibility. The first term does not require definition yet again but the second meant a new stress on the way in which the new 'having a say' entailed a sense of facing the consequences of the decisions. A combination of care and strictness was considered the crux of the 're-education' policy. 'Self-administration was the decisive experience for the post-war generation.'

The older American praise of the German ideal of the research university was often followed by stating that it did not work so well for the beginners and that it was 'impersonal'. Yet, again, it would be a mistake to conclude that the German university tradition had no equivalent to Anglo-American undergraduate life. Indeed, it was perhaps more varied than anywhere else, for the very reason that the German student in his or her extracurricular activities was less tied to the institution. There is, or was, a strong perception of 'student life' as something apart from the rest of society. Probably more than in most countries, German students studied away from home. In Göttigen, in 1968, 80 per cent came from outside the town. One of the best-known peculiarities of German student life is (or was) the move from university to university and this could offer such advantages as alternating between skiing in the Alps (the Winter Semester in Munich) and sailing in the Baltic Sea (the Summer Semester in Kiel) – to many a welcome by-product of Humboldt's *Lernfreiheit*.

But there were, of course, not only the individualistic traits of student life, but the corporate ones, too. They predated Humboldt by many centuries. Alongside the university proper there had always been houses to cater for impecunious students, the 'Bursen' or the 'Kollegs' for those coming from a distant region, or those simply seeking a semblance of home, socialisation and contacts for future careers. It was *de rigueur* for those engaged in religious education. By the early nineteenth century all this had faded. Instead, there was a strong development of what amounted to a close equivalent of the

American fraternities, and in some ways English club life, the male *Studentenverbin-dungen* (there was no equivalent to the American sororities). From the late nineteenth century onwards their main activities have been the provocative wearing of uniforms, very serious drinking, mock-dueling, congregating, often with the alumni, in the lavish 'houses', the grand villas owned by the fraternity. All this provided, in fact, a counter image to that of the serious *universitas* itself. In spite of their often rampant nationalism, even militarism, Hitler had these groups phased out. After the war they were by no means liked either, yet, by 1963 they constituted, with 30,000 members and over 100,000 alumni, a sizable minority. Clearly, the strong institutional definition of these groups was, as such, an important model. As in the USA, post World War II German university authorities tried to institute elements of these kinds of 'home' within the university. Now the highest priority was given to building up the organisations purely devoted to student welfare, the *Studentenwerk*, whose origins go back no further than the early 1920s. Their constitutions are similar to, but their briefs are much wider, than that of the British students union, as the German students unions also provide food and some shelter on campus (in the 'Studentenhäuser'). It was in this area, too, that the new postwar democratic principles were meant to be applied; students' organisations are seen to be run by the students themselves.

Our principal concern is, however, with where students lived. To organise student residences under the auspices of the university was something virtually unknown in Germany. Apart from the rather small number of rooms available to members of the 'Verbindungen', the fraternities, German students simply used private rented accommodation, usually a room in somebody's flat. 'Die Bude', digs, can signify the temporary, even the makeshift nature of the shelter, and thus again it fosters the old notion of the student as somebody slightly laughable and immature. It was, as elsewhere, a thoroughly male stereotype, and besides, 'he' would quite possibly end up marrying the landlady's daughter.

The major starting point for organised student residences, to be sure, was a purely charitable one, the general unavailability of digs altogether in the postwar misère. But the beneficiary of a place in a post World War II students' home was to be a different kind of student. He or she was to become a member of an organised community. One has to remember, first of all, that by no means the whole of this seriousness was an import. There had been a strand of German educational thinking, concerned with adolescence and high school age, which stressed independence and self-reliance, to be exercised in small educational communities. The *Jugendbewegung*, the youth movement, from before World War I, as well as the *Landschulheim* movement and its complex German-American affiliations were briefly discussed above (see page 33). Some of these ideas had also found their way into Nazi organisations, where the key word was 'Kameradschaft', comradeship. Hitler, too, had wanted to eradicate the old kind of student, hence he introduced the para-military drill of his 'Kameradschaftshäuser'. Upon a visit to Oxford in the 1930s, Dr Robert Ley in his capacity as Hitler's organiser for work and recreation, boasted that his Ordensburgen 'had just the same ideals of community' as the colleges, but, of course, 'their facilities . . . were far superior'. In general, the postwar German professors did not mind participating in something that appeared good for democracy, which at the same time did not curtail their essential powers in all matters to do with the content of research and teaching. Moreover, it was possible to find German traditionalist formulations such as 'to study in the real sense of the word, conversing with Wissenschaften . . . may shape the psychic and mental constitution of the individual' which could easily run alongside the Anglo-American ideal of liberal education. At the beginning, however, the input of the occupying powers was clearly crucial in the new movement for student residences: '. . . to correct the excessive individualism of the students, the HICOG [(American) High Commission of Occupied Germany] university advisers have tried to encourage activities which would improve student living . . . it was felt that . . . there would be a better chance of producing democratic leaders.' An English voice of 1946 is a little milder: 'From an English standpoint, German students would seem likely to benefit a great deal from living (really living) together.' A glowing report about Oxford in 1950 stressed the 'geistige Zucht', that is, the 'strong mental discipline', or 'drill' ['Zucht', a word, that was dear to the Nazis, too] 'and the control and precision of weekly progress'. The crucial word community – Gemeinschaft – can be heightened in German by prefixing it with 'Leben', 'Lebensgemeinschaft', literally, and somewhat tautologically, the community of those living together, culminating in the 'Akademische Lebensgemeinschhaft'.

The 'Göttinger Definition' for student residences of 1953 described them thus: 'a dwelling installed for spiritual [geistige] support by the university as a social help, a place for communal life and work'. There was an emphasis on limited size, 120–200 for the home as a whole, five to eight for a group using a *Teeküche*, as the small breakfast room was usually called. 'Small groups . . . should behave democratically . . . a self-administrating and self-educating Gemeinschaft, as well as being tolerant to others', – this last to try to help with the integration of the many foreign students in Germany. Coed homes were frequent, usually with men and women on alternate floors. There were even cases of no restrictions to visiting hours. Even more novel was the instalment of 'Tutoren' – a term current from about 1947. In some early student residences, tutors acted in a supervisory and educational function of varying intensity; they were either professors or lecturers who supervised part-time, or advanced students who lived in. Again, this move was organised countrywide and the main support was federal money.

As early as 1951 the Heidelberg historian Walther Peter Fuchs gave a detailed report on the whole of the West German postwar efforts of student housing. His main concern is a further distinction between the *Studenten(wohn)heime* which he sees, somewhat reluctantly, as the normal solution. There is usually no involvement of the university and the inhabitants may even feel like hotel guests. What really mattered for Fuchs were the *Gemeinschaftshäuser* type which had developed the most elaborate communal life. Their very diversity demonstrated the experimental spirit. Fuchs was at that time in charge of the Collegium Academicum at Heidelberg where 150 students lived comfortably, ate together and took part ('were expected' to take part) in an elaborate programme of academic and social activities. Most elaborate was also their participation in the Collegium's government ('Konvent'), according to its own 'constitution'. By contrast, in the Akademische Burse in Göttingen there was no planning, the academic and social events occurred 'completely freely'. There was no constitution, a 'minimum of organisation, rules and duties and external suggestions, . . . in order to achieve a maximum of inner intensity' (fig. 4.2). A measure of elitism (only older students with good marks were admitted) and a certain monasticism were not denied. The extreme opposite was provided by the Wohnheimsiedlung Massmannplatz in Munich. Here students from various higher education establishments were mixed with workers and apprentices: 'The daily life together is conducive to remove social prejudices and to make visible a shared humanity [die menschliche Gemeinsamkeit], beyond all differences of origin, education and employment.' The Leibniz Kolleg der Universität Tübingen, founded under the auspices of 're-education' programme in the French-occupied sector, differed from all other *Gemein-schaftshäuser* in that it actually conducted a full-time preliminary ('propaedeutisches') year of university studies for all its (initially sixty) inmates, provided by teachers from the university in a mix of subjects. The Leibniz Kolleg thus came closest to the Anglo-American pattern, and yet, with its demonstrative individuality, the high conscious-ness of its communal life under a charismatic teacher and leader, Paul Ohlmeyer, a chemist as well as a lettrist, there were limits to its comparability with the 'normal' college.

The building of *Studentenheime*, to return to the main generic term, went apace in lean times. By 1951 eighty-four homes had already been adapted or newly built, with an average of sixty beds each. Much of this was due to the way in which Americans followed words with money: by 1955, they had given a total of DM10.2m, 'a gift of the American people', for student residences and other university buildings – matched by a German contribution of DM8.8m (at the time, $2.5 and $2.2m respectively), mostly federal moneys from the general youth support fund (*Bundesjugendplan*), usually not distributed through the universities themselves, but via the *Studentenwerk*. Most significantly, the growth of residences outstripped, proportionally the growth in student numbers, so that by 1965 12 per cent of all students lived in such homes; thereafter the proportion was to go slightly down. It was a very high figure, if one considers that this was virtually a new institution, but a modest figure compared with the English and the American proportion of one third and more, which was also the stated aspiration of many German policymakers, although a more modest target of 20 per cent was mentioned in the late 1960s. The height of the *Studentenheim* movement came in the late 1950s. In a much quoted statistic 50 per cent, and more among younger students, were said to prefer university residences. There was, we must remember, a strict process of selection and the rooms were usually cheaper than the 'Bude'. The arguments, however, had, by then begun to change. The democratic-educational ideal was stressed less while the homes were now to function principally as a 'haven' from the ever more crowded campus, at least that was what the students' welfare representatives maintained (in the 'Düsseldorfer Wohnheimplan' of 1958).

More fundamental questions also began to be asked, forming part of the nascent *Universitätsreform* debate. Should student residences be drawn more fully into the orbit of the university proper, in order to use them not only for general educational pur-poses, but within a more efficient teaching process? By 1960 there was a pressing sense that something was needed to cope with the mass of new students. There were proposals to combine the last years at school with the first years at university. In 1962 the Wissenschaftsrat, the central university advisory body (see page 217), came with a proposal of *Kollegienhäuser*, one of the most radical ideas ever, certainly within the slow-moving German university world. The main instigator was most likely the chair-man, the professor of jurisprudence, Ludwig Raiser, whose early interest in the subject went back to the postwar Burse in Göttingen. The *Kollegienhaus* project was, as such, unrelated to the *Studentenheime*, the numbers of which also had to be increased. Hence another name was chosen, one that had medieval connotations, but was still in use, in expressions such as 'Kolleg halten', giving a lecture. All students up to the third semester were to be cared for (and most of them housed) in special institutions adjacent to the main campus. Again, the term community was heavily used: 'geistige Gemeinschaften', or 'akademische Lebensgemeinschaften' or 'überschaubare Gruppen', groups which could be easily managed. There was to be an elaborate system of administration, a warden for every twenty students alongside the academic tutors. The head of the *Kolleg* should be a full professor. Much teaching should take place in the *Kolleg*, though this should be dovetailed with the lectures going on in the main part of the university. Many of the earlier arguments for the residences were rehearsed, but there was now a greater emphasis on 'geistige Zucht [mental discipline] und Konzentration', strong words for the 1960s. Humboldt still occasionally comes through: there should be no rote-learning. On the whole, though, the educational functions are stressed more than usual. Education through *Wissenschaft* approaches the American liberal ideal of *Wissenschaft* in the service of education. There is only the occasional reference to recent English thinking here, which to the commission would have been well known, while closer parallels could perhaps be found in the new American Living and Learning Centres (cf. page 23).

The Wissenschaftsrat's idea was, of course, also based on the *Kollegien*, the *Gemeinschaftshäuser* of the early postwar years, but these, as we saw, had remained very exceptional institutions and functioned rather independently of the university. The project of 1962 was gigantic: a university of 8,000 students would have to provide thirty *Kollegienhäuser* for 3,000 new students. And yet, in spite of the attention given to the issue, not a single proper example was ever built and very few appear to have even been planned (fig. 4.16). There was only one well-known institution which took up part of the idea, that created by the educationalist Hartmut von Hentig who had received a strong impression of American higher education when an undergraduate at a small East Coast college. At Bielefeld he opened in 1974 an experimental institution adjacent to, and in many ways linked with the new University, called Oberstufenkolleg. This spanned the last two years of the upper school and the first two years of the university and its ideal was an 'open, questioning and philosophical form of life'. However, looking at its buildings, which consist of a large open plan room for teaching and a *Studentenheim* a short distance away, and with the whole overshadowed by the gigantic building of the university proper, the Oberstufenkolleg hardly qualifies as a college institutionally or image wise (4.23). Already in 1951 we can deduct from Fuchs's deliberations that there was no real chance for the introduction of the English college as a norm in Germany. Indeed, it was in the very nature of his *Gemeinschaftshäuser* to be selective, to counter the 'ungegliederte [amorphous] Masse'.

As in Anglo-Saxon universities, the German debate about student residences from 1960 began to develop a mighty complexity. With more money available generally, and a growing welfare state mentality demanding better care for students in every respect, more homes were built than ever before, or afterwards. Yet, social-academic-educational arguments diverged widely. Some repeated the older reasons of sociability and democracy. But the student body had begun to resent strongly what they called an intrusive system, the university following them to their private sphere, even as far 'as the bedrug' ('bis zum Bettvorleger'). After all, it was pointed out, the tutor

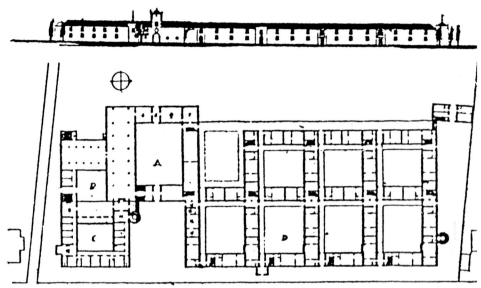

4.2 Universität Göttingen, Akademische Burse Gosslarerstrasse, student residences, early plan 1945 by Dietz Brandi. (*Göttinger Universitätszeitung* 20-1-1946, p. 12)

also wanted to get back home in the evenings. The students, in fact, turned the authorities' argument for new university-controlled residences on its head: because of the nature of new mass university students needed more privacy, not less. At the same time, some students adopted a stronger ideological stance, rejecting any attempts, any measure by the universities to speed up, or regulate the course of study. From the university's side there were new doubts regarding the educational task as a whole. In 1963 Helmut Schelsky (see below page 218) reasserted the pure task of *Wissenschaft*, whereby a 'paedagogische Anleitung', a paedagogical induction, was not necessary. If anywhere, the educational element, the 'heart' of the university would be found in the departments. Statements about the students being adults reasserted themselves. Hence there was no need any more to differentiate between students and the rest of the adult population. Ironically, after all these debates, we read in the late 1960s, as in England, that the whole issue of students residences was lacking in research; what was meant, of course, was empirical, user-oriented research. A rational conclusion at that stage was to advocate a diversity of residences for a diversity of users, from benign care in the *Studentenheim* to the anonymous living in a *Studenten-Appartement*, i.e. completely self-contained dwelling units – which had earlier been called Studenten-hotel and, as such, rejected. A new popular form was the *Wohngemeinschaft*, the self-contained rented student flat. In the end, it is crucial to note again that the universities themselves hardly ever did feel fully responsible for student residences. Money for buildings and for running them usually came from different sources than those used for the university proper. Only in a very few cases are residences placed close to the main university buildings. The notion that the university and the student's residence are part of the same institution was rarely entertained.

To the architects, finally, little of the kinds of disputes cited was of relevance. For the designer, a block of student residences amounted to no more than a special version of an ordinary block of dwellings. The single room which was increasingly requested

4.3 Universität München, Studentenheim Biederstein, by Harald Roth and Otto Roth 1953–4. (Baumeister 4-1954, p. 354)

measured 10–12 square metres (108–30 square feet). As regards the communal rooms, it appears that no home wanted to be without them, but their arrangement, of course, varied greatly. Most designers would have believed in a straightforward relationship of design and community. To cite only one typical comment: 'Through shared living on one floor, the group comes about, friendships and comradeships . . .'.

Change and diversity came with changes in architectural style. Initially there was no model at all. There was virtually nothing in Germany to parallel the traditional college architecture of England or America. Moreover, it must be emphasised that it was only in the early 1950s that West German architects relinquished the pitched-roof *Heimatstil* forms which had prevailed before and under Hitler for educational and minor public buildings. It is thus hard to trace a postwar German affiliation of the Gropius-International Modern collegiate, in spite of its having most of its roots in Germany. In any case, the two most prestigious *Kollegs*, in Heidelberg and Tübingen, made good use of older buildings, whereas the first parts of the Akademische Burse in Göttingen, begun in 1946, adopted a vaguely English fashion of two-storey wings around small courts (fig. 4.2). Most studenten *Wohnheime* looked relaxed, in plenty of greenery, akin to other buildings for young people, such as the youth hostels (which were also built in great numbers during that time). An early example is the Studenten Wohnsiedlung München-Biederstein, built 'in entirely parklike surroundings' . . . 'after a completely unsuitable plot in the inner town was avoided by a hair's breadth' (fig. 4.3). More stylistically advanced houses were to be found in Berlin, as with the small Internationales Studentenheim Eichkamp, built from 1947. The Siegmundshof for the Technische Hochschule, begun in 1957, was for about 700 students, a kind of mixed development including tower blocks. It was adjacent to the Hansa Viertel in the centre of West Berlin and adjoining the International Architectural Exhibition 'Interbau' of 1957 where Germans were seen to rejoin the Modernist Style.

The most elaborate undertaking was probably the Studentendorf (village) Berlin in outer suburban Schlachtensee/Zehlendorf for the Freie Universität of 1959, a late case of American government munificence (providing a total of DM8.8m, then approx. $2.2m). Its foundation sounded like a small re-enactment of the story of the univer-

4.4 Freie Universität Berlin: Studentendorf Zehlendorf, by Fehling/Gogel, begun 1957. View towards central building, residential block on the left. (Courtesy Archiv Freie Universität Berlin. Photo E. von Endt and S.O. Hakanson, HSA FUB. Repro. Sammlung, ehemals Colloqium Verlag Berlin)

sity itself: an 'American Professor', George N. Shuster, had came to Berlin under the auspices of the Ford Foundation and was taken by the idea of building something that 'combats dialectical materialism . . . and shines like a light into the Eastern Sektor'. The renowned literary historian and critic, Professor Walter Killy, in charge of student residence affairs, formulated the brief in 1956 with great care. He was concerned with factors that went 'beyond just accommodation'. Emphasis was very much on 'political education' (students had to elect councillors and a burgomaster) and the 'genuine student community life'. The 'Tutorensystem' was to be particularly strongly developed. One-third of the students were to be female. In short, it was a 'task in which wissenschaftliche, human, social and political aspects are united', serving as a remedy for the 'cultural homelessness of the modern student'. Cooperation with the architects Fehling/Gogel was close. In terms of layout, we meet the familiar Modernist collegiate demand: 'the 630 students constitute a mass which needs to be subdivided (gegliedert)', at the same time the layout must 'show the architectural togetherness of the whole'. There is thus a carefully layered system of sizes: six to eight students around a 'fully equipped' *Teeküche*, with the next unit comprising thirty students with further communal rooms, i.e. the actual residential block. Finally, there is the 'public square', with its building for the burgomaster, the Gemeinschaftshaus, library and shops. The architects adhered to all this with a relaxed low-to-medium-density sprinkling of blocks (figs 4.4 and 4.5).

The expansion of the late 1950s demanded more of these 'villages', even 'Studen-

214

4.6 Cologne/Köln Studentenappartements Luxemburger Strasse 130, by Werner Ingendaay, early 1970s. (A. Paschold (Introd.), *Studenten Wohnen*, Stuttgart, 1971)

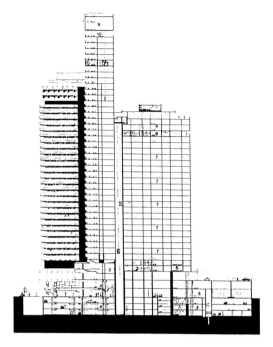

4.5 Universität Hamburg: Studentenwohnheim Karl Andreas Voss, common room, *c.* 1960. (*DUZ* 9-1963, p. 10)

tenstädte' for totals of 500 to 1,500 students. For the largest universities there seemed to be no alternative but to go to the edge of the town; an 'attractive task' for the designer, 'on an empty plot; to begin with [he/she] has a free hand'. By 1961, fifteen such estates were being planned. One of the largest is Munich's Studentenstadt Freimann. However, a major criticism soon arose – that of 'ghettoisation'. In the 1970s diversity increased markedly, with the thirty-five-storey Studentenappartements in Cologne, this time relatively central and closer to the university (fig. 4.6), the colossal Olympic Village in Munich serving the 1972 Olympics and since then providing residence for over 2,000 students, and the Studentenwohnheim Im Pfaffenwald, a notable example of 'low-rise high density' of 1973–4, by a firm which had specialised in this mode in housing since the early 1960s, the Swiss Atelier 5. Here, at last, we find that the homes are located close to the new out-of-town campus of the Technische Universität Stuttgart.

In 1961, a year or so before the *Kollegienhäuser* project of the Wissenschaftsrat, the educationalist Hans Werner Rothe laid down his ideas for a much more rigorous establishment, in his report for a new university at Bremen, the very first postwar German proposal of its kind. Here, at last, the university residences – for a third of all students – were to be an integral part of the plans, taking up major areas of the campus and situated directly adjacent to the teaching buildings. Rothe proposed 'open' residences, as well as *Kollegienhäuser*. He assumes 'a hidden desire' on the part of the students for 'Gemeinschaftsleben'. In fact, he postulates nothing less than an amendment to the philosophy of the German university, in the form of a third element to be added to the existing teaching and research. This was to be the 'Erziehungsauftrag', the 'task to educate', akin to the 'higher education system in the Anglo-American countries'. Rothe demanded 'Gemeinsinn', the civic spirit, 'praised, but never attained by us'; the way he intended to apply this philosophy to the whole campus will be dealt with below. Together with his campus concept, Rothe's

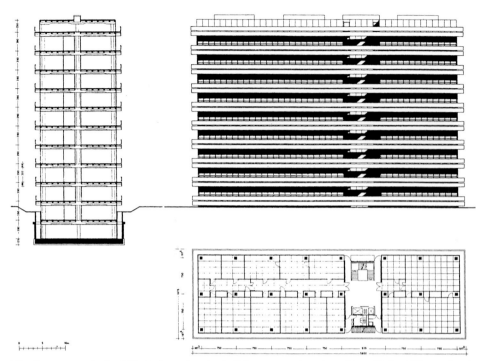

4.7 German standardised block for university buildings: research and teaching (Baden-Württemberg). (*AD* 11-1974, p. 710)

plans for residences fell on deaf ears; the students dubbed the Bremen plan a 'Heimuniversität', 'Heim', or 'home', in the sense of a rigid institution, as in children's homes (fig. 4.8).

What, then, was to be the proper institutional nature of the German university from the 1960s? Should it include frameworks for students' lives while not engaged in the act of studying or researching? We noted that to some extent these questions kept being asked in England and America, too, and increasingly so during the 1960s. Before we carry on with these issues we need to discuss the way in which the trad-itional German university as a whole was put into question.

UNIVERSITÄTSREFORM: ACADEMIC AND/OR INSTITUTIONAL?

The project of Bremen, too, must be seen as one of the countless proposals to 'reform' the German university at large – and the immediate side-lining of the project seemed typical of much of that process, too. An avalanche of pronouncements began in the late 1950s and continued into the early 1970s. 'A strange division of labour has devel-oped: the indefatigable rhetoric of university reform protects the high rank/claims of the system, while administrative emergency measures ensure a superficial fitting in with practical necessities' (Jürgen Habermas, 1965).

To begin with the 'superficial' side of things. What exactly was going wrong? Uni-versities had doubled their intake in the later 1950s; during the 1960s numbers went up again from 320,000 to 520,000 and by 1980 they had reached 1,000,000 (in the whole of the higher education sector). State expenditure on higher education doubled between 1961 and 1964 alone. But by international comparison this was not enough. Still only 5 per cent of the relevant age group went to university in 1965. But worse than the bad figures was the impression that there was no proper plan for expansion. Commenting on the Robbins Report, Ludwig Raiser declared that 'We in Germany have already expanded, while England now has the great advantage of being able to guide its expansion in an orderly manner'. One salient fact about the traditional German university system was that everyone with a high school certificate ('Abitur') could enter any university of their choice, where he or she could stay as long as they liked. Thus while in the USA applicants found access to a great diversity of institutions or sub-institutions and thus brought about the 'multiversity', German students simply filled, and, it seemed, overfilled, an outwardly unified institution and thus created the 'Massenuniversität'. In practice, complaints were much the same as everywhere else: lack of teacher-student contact, anonymity, rigidity of examinations, authoritarianism. As regards new measures in Germany, many were taken from the USA or England; contacts were close, at least between rectors and vice chancellors: 'England, Du hast es besser' remarked Gerhard Hess of Konstanz, gently modifying a word of Goethe's: 'Amerika, Du hast es besser' – you are better off. From the 1960s, the Germans introduced a firmer rule from the top to replace the old revolving government, while lower down the collegial American 'department' replaced the authoritarian 'Institut'. Democratisation was then to extend downwards, through enlarging the 'Mittelbau', the body of young lecturers, and the students' say was increased and institutionalised, something that had been on the agenda since 1945. Restricted entry to oversubscribed subjects was gradually introduced from the 1960s, too, but this 'numerus clausus' was felt to be a most painful reduction of the principle of freedom of choice, as was a new culture of stricter syllabi. The problems of the inordinate length of the period of study were never properly resolved, nor the divisions in the degree structure: talk of introducing a 'BA' (Germans tend even to use the English term) has lasted now (in 1999) for over forty years. The standard German reproach to all these measures is that the institution is being 'verschult', made school-like.

The standard English answer to a perceived general problem is to institute a royal commission which, in typically centralised fashion, is in charge of asking all concerned parties for their views. In the German discourses, contrary to the frequent use of the word 'umfassend', all comprehending, each group pronounced on the proposed reform for itself; and each group asserted its 'Verantwortung', its obligation/responsibility, to study the problem in more fundamental terms than the previous one. Although the chief divisions of the actors were similar to those in England, their number was considerably greater in Germany. There were the rectors and the professors, the junior teachers (Assistenten), the agents of student welfare, the students' own associations, as well as student groups of various political affiliations. Then there were the governments: the *Länder*, West Germany's eleven provinces plus West Berlin, their cultural, finance and other ministries; the federal government and some of its ministries; finally, various bodies composed of delegates from both federal and regional authorities. The latter, in turn instituted new central bodies, such as the Wissenschaftsrat in 1957, which was regarded with the highest degree of trust – although in the end few of its detailed proposals – *vide* the *Kollegienhäuser* – were followed. This, all came under the even more comprehensive umbrella of the new Bildungsrat in 1966. Then, there were the political parties and the representatives of industry who gave money for research. Finally, there were the new research institutes for university planning (see page 222). Of course, all bodies overlapped and the chief players, such as Ludwig Raiser from Heidelberg, sat on several of them. It was a culture of professional associations and interest groups which went back to the nineteenth century and which had been cruelly interrupted by Hitler's unifying measures. One may, of course, draw some parallels here with the multiplicity of agents in American universities, in contrast to the more unified administrations of Britain or France. In the USA we followed the way in which each group pursued its own agenda, according to its own professional interests. But each single institution, each university or college had to function as a unity. Germany was characterised by the way the various groups of agents pursued similar-sounding aims, but each university itself was liable to be divided into various interest groups; the 'university of groups', the 'Gruppenuniversität', was a familiar term of the period.

What unified the discourse was the sense of immense urgency; a typical tract ran *Die deutsche Bildungskatatrophe*, the German educational catastrophe. The newspapers were more and more inclined to chide the gurus. 'The substituting of the university reform through ever new plans of reform has become unbearable' (1968). 'Enough is enough.' It was, of course, divergences in basic beliefs which kept the discussions going. One of the most revered of the commentators was the philosopher Karl Jaspers, respected particularly because of having been silenced during the Nazi period. His solemn tract held that no reform could proceed without the 'precondition to serve truth in its entirety'. Until about 1963 the platform of most university reformers could be summed up in one word: Humboldt. After all, Wilhelm von Humboldt was precisely what everybody was aspiring to, an effective reformer. How could *Wissenschaft* be upheld while numbers increased so drastically? The Germans appeared lumbered with the notion that 'Humboldt' had to comprise the university system of the whole country in equal measure, while in the USA the dilemma of mass vs. excellence was continuously circumvented by simply instituting new graduate schools wherever this made academic and practical sense. But, as we saw, the institutional, the organisational element had been left vague by Humboldt and his definition of the university was, on the whole, an idealistic one. While the latter word was not frequently used by the German reformers around 1960, its opposite, positivist, did still carry a bad odour.

Yet it could not prevent the emergence, around 1963, of a new school of empirical sociology, which, in turn let the older kinds of thinking appear as idealistic and peculiarly German, in contrast to the modern 'American' (and occasionally also 'Soviet') developments. Like most other reformers, the sociologist Helmut Schelsky joined the alarmist school: 'Everybody has failed' (1969). Not only had no reform taken place, German Wissenschaft as a whole was sinking into provinciality. Schelsky demanded that specialisation should not be feared, nor the instrumentalisation of research in the process of professionalisation and practical applicability. In short, the old contemplative values of individual research must be phased out. He claims that the idea of university itself needs to be investigated through empirical sociology, just as any other group or organisation. For Schelsky the overarching occupation of a university is no longer Humboldtian humanist philosophy, but 'theory', of the individual disciplines or of groups of disciplines. He thus pleads for a 'theoretische Universität'. Teaching, too, has to be rationally organised, as everything else, and should itself be the subject of scientific inquiry, the 'Wissenschaftsdidaktik', the research into learning processes and creativity. However, Schelsky also seems to be returning to Humboldt's disregard of institutionalisation, to the latter's simple definition of the teaching process as the contact between the researching teacher and the research apprentice. The solution lies in the assumption of different levels; all proper students should simply arrive ready for the scientific discourse. The whole idea of 'education' at the university, and the paraphernalia prescribed by Rothe for Bremen, as well as the idea of the *Kollegienhäuser*, all are redundant. Schelsky sides with those who simply declare students adults. We shall see how Schelsky's ideas fared at 'his' new 'research' university at Bielefeld.

The third major party in the debate were the students. In Germany the 'student troubles' – which, of course, dominated all university discussions in the late 1960s – were preceded, during the late 1950s and early 1960s, by thorough analyses of the university system, undertaken by student sociologists, largely from the Frankfurt School of 'critical philosophy', guided, to some extent, by its chief younger member, Jürgen Habermas. By no means did the students want to depart from the ideals of *Wissenschaft*, as such, but like Schelsky, and others before him, the students used new kinds of sociological analysis and proclaimed the end of the idealist unity of the institution in the face of modern scientific and industrial society. The old ideals had become a farce. What was left was the 'faschistoid autoritäre Professor'. But unlike Schelsky, the students evaluated the effects of these new scientific developments largely negatively. They considered that within the capitalist system they were bound to lead to a new instrumentalisation and to social and ideological repression – an example of which appeared in the new applied psychology of the student personnel services which was beginning to come over from the USA. The students' demands thus concentrated on the open participation and cooperation of all members of the institution, as well as cooperation with most spheres of the society outside. Their keyword was 'Demokratisierung der Universität'. Predictably, the students' fear of instrumentalisation led to accusations – for instance, by Schelsky – that they, too, ultimately stuck to the old ideals of freedom and thus to the Humboldtian backwardness of the idealists. On the other hand, as we saw, Schelsky was also in their camp; they were all implicit Humboldtians with regard to the educational process, or, rather, their belief in the non-existence of that process.

Occasionally there were attempts to draw attention to the institutional nature of the university, as such. The Wissenschaftsrat demanded, in 1962, the 'fully self-contained institution'. A key term used in many discussions was 'korporativ', 'the 'Korporierung' of the University, as a 'unity of ethos, of place and time, the common activities on the grounds of the university'. The sociological analyses, however, again lead to scepticism. The student congress in 1958 maintained: 'The university cannot actually comprehend the whole human being . . . *Gemeinschaft* through organisation is utopian'. The English college system was deemed not suitable in as much as it did not appear to leave enough room for the student's own initiative. A plea by the educationalist Eduard Baumgarten to conceive of the university environment as an academic club, conducive to informal exchanges, went unheeded. By the late 1960s we meet the demand for the integration of the university with its town, which, as everywhere else, meant a blow to the notion of a self-contained institution. A common denominator suddenly emerged in the late 1960s, in analogy to the 'integrierte Gesamtschule' (comprehensive school), the *Gesamthochschule*. It meant the coordination of the full range of academic and professional schools in a given town within which each level of ability would find the right academic environment – in other words, an organised multiversity. Social justice and equality were now increasingly foregrounded. In our context these *Gesamthochschulen* are not of interest because they usually do not need a unified built structure. In any case, very few of them actually came about.

In the end it will be difficult to answer questions such as: what was the German *Universitätsreform* actually aiming for, and did it succeed? The areas of actual academic research is not our concern here. The issue of this book has been the optimisation of academic learning and education, especially for beginners, through devising the right kind of institution. We noted that in Germany there was a widespread reluctance to consider the individual university as something with a strong institutional character. The German warning not to transform the universities into 'schools' must be understood in this context. Humboldtians, Schelsky and the Frankfurt School student theorists appear united in their disinterest in these matters. The 'unity' of the university was upheld by the academic nature of their discourses, but it was rather an abstract kind of unity. It was perhaps significant that in contemporary English discussions the term 'reform' was not one that was frequently used. It turns out to be a tricky term – in comparison to the much more straightforward Anglo-American terms 'experiment' or 'innovation'. The chief problem in England seemed a straightforward one, how to let more students into university. Until the early 1960s at least, some would object on grounds that the quality of the academic content would suffer. Formulated in that way, this was a problem that concerned all countries. After Robbins, in 1963, such objections could not be voiced any more in England, for socio-political reasons. In England and the USA the perceived problems of the quantitative enlargement were met by what were thought to be qualitative changes and institutional innovations. In Germany the ideal of lonely Wissenschaftlichkeit/scientificness, the ideal of the individualist pursuit of academic studies, proved to be a hindrance for such thinking and procedure. From an Anglo-American point of view at least, German university reform did not seem to believe in an institutional solution of the problems. The new German foundations of the 1960s, to which we shall now turn, pursued their new institutional and architectural ideals in spite of the main German trends and we may thus call them in most respects thoroughly international.

CAMPUS DESIGN AT BOCHUM, REGENSBURG, KONSTANZ AND BIELEFELD

At the beginning of this chapter there was talk about institutional presence and institutional image. The academic university reform pronouncements of the 1960s contain virtually nothing about either of them. The Humboldtians, as we saw, were not interested in this issue; they took for granted the way in which the institution was customarily housed in practical as well as reasonably stately buildings. There simply was no tradition of a special institutional presence, of identifying one's *Alma Mater* with a distinctive type of building, such as the heavy symbolical language of a college chapel. Nevertheless, we can make out three major trends in which reformist statements and the resulting institutions did have an influence on the architectural presence or image of the university. Firstly, the older idealist school would result in large representational buildings and from about 1950–5 onwards these had to be, as everything else in Western Germany, Modernist in style. Secondly, the rationalist theory would result in new and more complex notions of practical planning and perhaps in a denial of other values, such as honorific ones. Thirdly, there were those, like the student reformers, who wanted to minimise the institutional aspect and who might wish to deny architecture's role altogether (cf. page 219).

Of the three new universities founded immediately after the war, Mainz, Saarbrücken and West Berlin, only the latter gained a major reputation for innovation. None of those foundations constituted a completely new campus with entirely fresh buildings. The Freie Universität of West Berlin serves as an example of the continuing lack of concern for a coherent institutional-architectural presence of the German university, at any rate, as it appeared in its newly expanded form. Implanted into the smart suburb of Dahlem, a low density layout was given from the start. University buildings are interspersed with villa homes in leafy surroundings. Basically each subject, each *Institut*, has its own complete setup, even, in many cases, its own lecture theatre. The massive new central buildings, the Henry Ford Bau and the main library, form just one group of buildings among many. It is impossible to locate a real social centre. Stretching for more than two kilometres (1.2 miles), the area is simply too large.

Contrary to expectations, the foundation of the large number of new universities in the 1960s and early 1970s did not, as such, produce nearly the amount of publicity as the general reform debate had done. One reason was that they were not founded by one central agency like the UGC in Britain. The starting sign was said to have been the cautious recommendations of the Wissenschaftsrat in 1960, although individual foundations claimed that they had had the idea before that. The sociologist Ralf Dahrendorf, who was to be involved with Konstanz, echoed English debates when he stated in 1962 that the new universities should not propose a 'constitutionally rigid utopia in the place of an ossified reality', but grasp the chance for reform through experiment. As in England, each university prided itself of a special feature which would provide an example on a national level, such as Konstanz's planning to be a 'research university', while Bochum promised a solution for the mass-university. As regards finance, a crucial agreement had been arrived at between the federal state and the *Länder*, to share the costs in a very complex deal, which was simplified in a new agreement in 1969 when *Land* and *Bund* shared the capital costs equally. The number of planned new establishments grew slowly, only three full new universities were envisaged in 1960, four by 1963, while in 1969 seven were planned or being built; and yet, by 1970 the Wissenschaftsrat demanded 'at least 30 new Hochschulen'. About fifteen were actually founded or built by the early 1980s.

University architecture, whether in old or new institutions, was top of the professional agenda in England for a number of years and aroused considerable interest from the general public. In America its impact was a little slower but some celebrated buildings were created within a rich tradition of campus architecture. In German-speaking lands there was less interest in this type as architecture, partly because of the specific institutional-architectural reasons already explained and partly because German reconstruction after World War II appeared to go primarily for quantity, at least during the first decade or so. By 1955–60 the most important quality of any new public buildings was its Modernism. This International Modern of the Mies or Gropius kind manifested itself mostly in slim slab, or 'Zeilenbau' structures, as in the work of Ferdinand Kramer, university architect in Frankfurt, a survivor of the heady Modernism of the interwar years. An early small residential college, essentially of the new international/American collegiate type, was the Hochschule für Gestaltung, the avant-garde School of Industrial Design at Ulm, built 1953–5 by the Swiss Max Bill. By the late 1950s university extensions on a large scale were planned in most places. Many smaller university towns, such as Heidelberg and Tübingen, built a new campus, usually for the sciences, outside the old town. They offered their users an environment of much increased comfort, but, as almost everywhere else, these were not the sort of buildings to enter the chronicles of Modern architecture or instutional planning. With the increased pressure on space, greater speed and cost-consciousness seemed required and the Wissenschaftsrat in 1963 remarked that 'buildings for research and teaching are utilitarian buildings [Zweckbauten] which do not need to serve for representation; Wissenschaft represents itself through its achievements'.

A complex situation arose with regard to obtaining the services of the architect. In stark contrast to England and the USA, none of the major German new university campuses was straightforwardly the work of one notable designer, as defined in the normal historiography of architecture. In Germany the chief say in the layout was had by the architectural office of the *Land*, or rather its delegation, the special building office for each university. The occasionally mild protest by the 'free architects' – the 'architects in private practice', was of no avail. On the other hand, the German state authorities did tap independent architectural talent by holding competitions, 'of ideas' (whereby there was usually no real commitment for the client to build the winning design), something the English and the Americans usually held to be too cumbersome. The rich international contributions for those at Bochum and Berlin will be discussed in the next chapter. In the State of Baden-Württemberg not even that possibility was open to the free practitioner. Its vast programme of university building was entirely directed by the Staatliche Bauverwaltung in Stuttgart. From 1957 till 1972 its leader was the indomitable Horst Linde. From 1961 he massively increased his influence by concurrently occupying the chair of town planning in the Technische Hochschule Stuttgart, which he changed into a chair for Design for Higher Education. Here Linde developed a research institute and generated a school of designers. In addition he edited the massive four-volume work on all aspects of university design, *Hochschulplanung*, of 1970, as well as setting up an archive, which was recognised by other German states and even internationally. Many German architects felt they could contribute to university design by pooling research, in a way some English designers, such as RMJM, had desired during the mid-1960s (cf. page 106) but were hardly able to institute. In the late 1960s governments began to press particularly for rigorous rationalisation. Planning and construction experiences were, to some extent, pooled and a standard type evolved, dubbed 'elephant', 'jumbo' or 'silo': a 'stacked building' about 120 metres (400 feet) long and a dozen or so storeys high. Ninety-one were built during 1970–1 alone [4.7]. Some architectural critics immediately spoke of a 'frightening monotony'. At the same time the Stuttgart architectural researchers, espe-

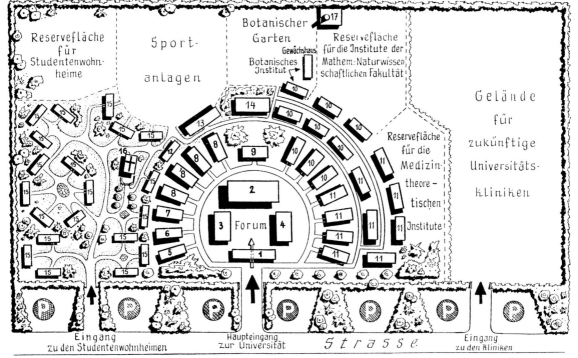

4.8 Bremen, plan for a university 1961 (by Hans Werner Rothe): 1 administration, 2 library, 3 *Auditorium Maximum*, 4 students union and canteen, 5–8 faculties (economic and social, law, protestant theology, humanities), 9 institute for musical and art and crafts education, 10 mathematics and natural sciences, 11 pre-clinical medicine, 12 modern language training, 13 physical education, 14 teachers training college, 15 student residences, 16 church, 17 boilerhouse and workshops, on the right room for extending the clinics. Note also the central entrance from the street. (*Hochschuldienst* 14-5-1961, p. 2)

cially Peter Jokusch, stressed 'the Hochschule als sozialer Ort', the 'university as a place of social interaction'. Linde at one point remarked that the 'social sphere of the university is the one that is really subject to architectural design (eigentlich gestaltbar)'. It was pointed out that in English New Universities one third of the costs went to the 'social' buildings on campus. German university planners could never dream of such a proportion for communal facilities and residences as support was lukewarm on the part of most reformers. In the end, all the new universities did put great stress on the social sphere, and they all did it differently.

The first New University design was conceived not by an architect but by an educationalist, Hans Werner Rothe. We have already dealt with Bremen, in the way it stressed education alongside teaching and research, and that meant, for the first time, perhaps, in the whole of continental Europe the full campus version of a complete university, integral with residences, not only for students, but for teachers, too. It was recognised that land for such a campus could only be found outside the town. The campus was to be compact, no building to be further away than 300 metres from the central library. Cars were to be banned from the centre. Rothe goes Anglo-American the whole way. '"Campus": I could not find a more apt term.' A related term is 'forum', for the centre. The central Studentenhaus he sees as a 'kind of college of the student community.' The 'shared life', the 'harmony of the whole man' entailed, in addition to the actual academic work and a strong *Studium Generale*, a number of other activities, such as fine art, crafts, and music (each with its own building in the centre of the campus), as well as sports, something that had not been given much emphasis by German universities after Hitler. Rothe finds it necessary to underline that the 'functional and architectonic design for the campus is of the greatest importance for the new university', he had clearly taken an interest in those matters himself, citing a number of international examples (fig. 4.8). As already mentioned, Rothe's University plan was not only laid aside for many years – largely because of questions of finance, but doubts increased about his very ideas. When in the early 1970s, the university of Bremen was finally built hardly anything was left of the original proposal.

Rothe's plan, although it stressed that it was only schematic, betrays a crushing directness: all major social buildings are in the centre, from which the other buildings radiate outwards in the form of a half-circle. Rothe does not seem to care about Modernist orientation towards wide open spaces, his plan reminds one more of the dense layouts of the 'social' institutions, the 'panopticon principle' of the prisons and workhouses of the nineteenth century. To the professional architect of 1960 such a layout would have seemed thoroughly old-fashioned. Indeed, the proposal offered to Bremen by Linde's Stuttgart Seminar of 1962/3 shows a pronouncedly asymmetrical and rather loose sprinkling of high and low blocks. Broadly speaking, however, Bremen did set the ball rolling for campus planning in Germany. The Wissenschaftsrat in 1962, in typical cautious parlance, demanded 'a more intensive university-life and a structure which is directed to greater coherence'. A survey on American University planning issued by the Stuttgart Institute, of 1965, defined the campus as being like a 'town, for the people who live here or in the immediate neighborhood'. 'Above all', says the same book, 'students and teachers must be given the possibility to study undisturbed . . .'; this, the simplest possible definition, only goes to show how unfamiliar Germans were at that time with the whole concept of the campus university.

During 1963–4, partly under the impact of the Bochum competition, German architectural commentators had begun to consolidate their concept of the campus. There simply was not enough room inside the towns for new and more expansive users like some sciences and a distance of 2 to 2.5 kilometres (1.2 to 1.5 miles) was recommended. There might be arguments for keeping links with the town, but the space requirements of the individual subjects must be given priority. 150 hectares (370 acres) were considered a minimum. Everything should be placed in close proximity, 10 minutes walking distance to the centre should be the maximum. Design ideas were changing fast. By 1965 Lancaster's architect, Gabriel Epstein, struck up a friendship with the Stuttgart crowd – later he even followed Linde in the chair there. England remained the most admired country for its novel kinds of plans, especially for the concept of 'low-rise high density' as well as, more generally, for the freedom that architects seemed to enjoy there. 'Here we thought only about technical planning' (H.-J. Aminde).

Bochum

The 'Paradestück', the fanfare: this was the real undertaking, to dispel the endless reform discussion on paper. To begin with, all notions of 'problems' should be cast aside. The initiative must, first of all, be called a political one. The Ruhr Universität

Bochum is the creation of its *Land*, Nordrhein-Westfalen. The regionalist process was always similar: the province initiated, but then claimed to provide a model and a service for the nation as a whole. There seemed many natural reasons why North-Rhine Westfalia should take the lead. It was the most populous province, containing the federal capital, Bonn (itself the seat of the most established university of the region), its outlook was Western, with long traditions of both Socialism and Christian Democracy always competing with each other; in short, 'NRW' prided itself as the cradle of the new West German Republic. The story of Bochum's inception and foundation begins with the debates about overcrowded universities in the federal parliament from 1959. Then came the motion of the *Land*'s parliament – under CDU Ministerpräsident Franz Meyers and his Kulturminister Werner Schütz – before the first general pronouncements of the federal Wissenschaftsrat in 1960. Long strategic debates preceded the choice of location. 'The Ruhr' was literally the centre of the province. Here was a population counting many millions, the largest agglomeration of its kind in Europe, without any major institution of higher education. The Ruhr Universität at Bochum was duly placed in the centre of the Ruhr, easily reached, via urban motorways, from all parts of the region. To be precise, it was placed at the southern edge of the area, where the industrial land gives way to the picturesque valley of the river Ruhr itself. While on the one hand explicitly catering for a working-class area, Bochum's beautiful site would also help to alleviate the severe image of a sooty region, badly needed at a time when the erosion of the traditional economic base, coal and steel, had already begun.

It took another year before things could really start; the 'foundation commission' (Gründungsausschuss) under its principal spokesperson and future first rector, Hans Wenke, professor of pedagogy at Hamburg, called in eminent professors from all over Germany, including, in matters of location, Linde. What about 'reform'? Here comments were ambiguous, in spite of the high academic calibre of the foundation commission. While the Konstanz project began to become known as a 'reform university' and Bremen was proposing many novelties, there was a sense that Bochum should, first of all, address the problem of numbers. There was a general assurance that Humboldt's values should be kept, but that the old systems of the powerful institutes and the umbrellas of large faculties should be phased out and replaced by a greater number of smaller institutes (under the neutral term Abteilung, literally department) who would be more ready for interdisciplinary cooperation. Perhaps the most important ambition was the inclusion of engineering, firstly in order to serve the *genius loci*, and also to help it to come closer to other academic discourses, the sciences and the social sciences; medicine was to be treated in that way, too, but the hospital was then built further away. On balance, however, Bochum was not considered a *Reformuniversität*.

Quantity was the major watchword and in those terms Bochum was very largely successful. The speed of its building was breathtaking: the campus was ready for the first 2,000 students in mid-1965, after only two years of building. By 1970 there were already 10,000 students. The campus was essentially completed by the mid-1970s and by 1980 it accommodated 25,000 students. Equally important was the way Bochum managed, straightaway, to raise its proportion of students from working-class backgrounds from the German average of 5 per cent to 9 per cent, and later to even 13 per cent.

By mid-1962 a vast administrative machinery was cranking into gear, as a special branch of the *Staatshochbauamt*, the *Land*'s own design and building authority, under the leadership of Fridolin Hallauer, handling the job 'most unbureaucratically' (Linde). Although there were voices against holding a competition because of the delay it might cause, it was the principle of the state to stage such events in the case of a large building project. While it was running, the university planners got on with measuring the grounds. In any case, it was a competition of ideas for the general layout only, yet it was most carefully formulated and cost DM127,000 in prize money alone. No wonder eighty-five plans were sent in. The competition was open nationally and in addition, a number of very big names were invited from abroad, amongst whom Mies van der Rohe and Aalto, as well as Sir Basil Spence declined. The extremely well publicised and widely diverging entries will be discussed in the next chapter. In any case, the planners knew very much what they wanted. In a most curious process, the state-appointed university planners allowed themselves to take part in the competition (anonymously). The winner was West-Germany's most respected large firm, Hentrich, Petschnigg and Partner (HPP) of Düsseldorf, known above all for their sleek steel and glass skyscrapers – a kind of German SOM. But their design was also that which came closest to that of the university planners and henceforth the teams became jointly responsible. During 1963 the plans were fully worked out, and building started on 2 January 1964.

Bochum was a tour de force. It was also a model of cooperation. Promoted within the state's socio-educational aims, the academics eagerly took the opportunity to provide reformed plans; the architects, the planners and the building industry jumped on the bandwagon. First the state bought the extremely valuable site – extremely generous, too, at 540 hectares (over 1,330 acres). However, the main buildings only occupy a small proportion of it. On it, we are told, we find the 'novelty' of a campus university, yet, to others, Bochum was precisely not to be comfortably spread-out 'within greenery'. They wanted it to be more like a compact town – we shall come back to those arguments. The built complex nevertheless measures an immense 1 kilometre by 400 metres, over half a mile by 1,300 feet. The eighteen departments are accommodated in thirteen virtually identical twelve-storey blocks, arranged almost symmetrically in two parallel rows with the shared facilities in the centre. In ever varied formulations we are told about the 'self-enclosed building form which is a manifestation of the unity of teaching, research and the unity of all the Wissenschaften'. In fact the plan is very much more complicated: the thirteen individual teaching blocks are sitting on a gigantic substructure, a podium, or 'wide foot', which responds to the steep slope and which accommodates stores, workshops, and parking. Thus Bochum, too, can claim to be a 'one building' university (figs 4.9–4.11).

The speed of construction on Europe's biggest building site (campus historian Alexandra von Cube) was down to the rigorous planning procedure and to the repetitiveness of its construction. According to job architect Maximilian Thurn, planners did not bother to devise stages, or phases, there was to be 'no process of cobbling together'. This, again, was in line with the general academic aims: 'the basic aim of the university . . . each house looks almost the same . . . it expresses the required togetherness [*Gemeinsamkeit*]'. There is, indeed, a spirit, or at least a nomenclature of sameness. The thirteen blocks are placed in four groups and each given a letter. Thus one speaks of 'Block GA', or just 'GA', 'GB' etc. 'Serialised thinking' reigned even more in the construction process. In actual fact, though, the earliest blocks largely used a steel construction, while the later ones rely almost exclusively on reinforced concrete, much of it site-cast, including the giant 7.5 × 7.5 metre (67 square feet) floor slabs. As countless other structures of its date, the blocks are clad with prefabricated elements, which also form the obligatory external escape balconies. As the constructors proudly claimed, their methods could be used as generally 'valid results' and were electronically stored.

Just as well, as the costs of this undertaking were immense. Figures vary, giving DM150–200m per annum, for ten years, that is DM2 billion, or even 2.5 billion in total (in 1966/7 this meant £180–220m or $500–60m). It was calculated that a cubic metre of this university cost four times that of a primary school. By the mid-1960s it was pointed out that other countries built their universities very much more cheaply, for half the amount or less. In Bochum the client, that is the state, did not seem to mind. The planners indicated the generous size of the buildings was due to 'the lack of our [planning] experience'. In fact, in 1990 they commented, with some pride, that they had, in effect, built twice as much space as was needed for the student load originally envisaged. As regards construction as such, prefabrication was still at a stage where one hoped that it would lead to an eventual reduction of costs.

The sense of giant size is countered by the planners' assertion that it only takes a maximum of seven minutes to reach the centre. Similarly, the quasi endless regularity of the blocks are meant to be matched by the distinctiveness of the forum. This central area projects over the steep slope on several levels, which contain up to three floors of 'underground' parking. From virtually all parts, the platforms and the forum and more particularly from the large *mensa* and club building at the southern end, one can enjoy panoramic views of the valley. The actual centre is taken up by the library; there is also an arts centre ('musisches Zentrum'), the administration building, as well as the *Auditorium Maximum* which also serves as the main hall, with a capacity of 2,400, it, too, an apotheosis of reinforced concrete construction. There was even an idea of involving the Italian engineer Pier Luigi Nervi, but this would have proved too expensive. The spaces within and around the major buildings, especially the central forum, measuring 120 by 400 metres, that is, about four football pitches, are, according to Hallauer, 'in the truest sense of the word the agora, the market place where the meeting of magistrorum et scolarum can take place' (figs 4.12 and 4.13).

Bochum thus seemed an ideal campus, with a strong sense of unity, a seamless following-through of the academic concept down to the details of construction. This unity of purpose, however, ends, and the arguments begin, at the point where we enter the extracurricular life of the students. We return, once again, to the issues of student residence and its relationship with the university. It began with the argument about whether the university campus should be closely related to the existing town, or whether it should form a unit of its own, detached from the town centre. The combination of both issues led to the simple question: did the members of the university form a community inside, or related to the town, or a special community outside. We have cited the strong voices of 1961–5 which maintained that a large new campus can, almost by definition, only be created outside the town. At Bochum the issue, once the out of town location (or 'edge of town' location) was decided upon, became a narrower one, namely the question of where to place the students' facilities for living. Initially there was to be at Bochum a residential pro-

RUHR·UNIVERSITÄT BOCHUM
Grundstücke · Gebäude · Räume

4.9   Ruhr Universität Bochum, by Hentrich and Petschnigg and Universitätsbauamt, begun 1963, air view of the late 1970s. (Courtesy Ruhr-Universitat Bochum)

4.10   Bochum, sections (early plan): top: through the *Auditorium Maximum*. Bottom: lengthwise, showing the main library. (*Deutsche Bauzeitung* 6-1966, p. 462)

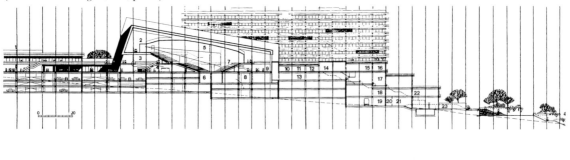

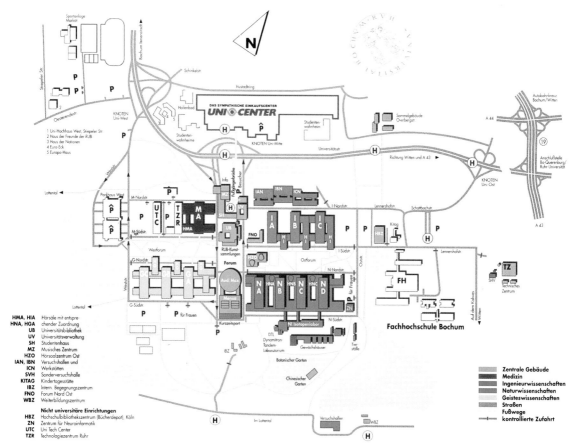

4.11   Bochum, plan/guide: G   humanities, H   lecture theatres, UV   administration, SH   student centre, MZ   fine arts and music, I   workshops. Footpaths in light grey, roads in dark grey (1996). (Courtesy Ruhr Universität Bochum)

4.12   Bochum, view of the side of the *Auditorium Maximum* towards the south

4.13 Bochum, interior *Auditorium Maximum*. (Courtesy Manfred Vollmer, Essen)

portion of 30 per cent, including some *Kollegienhäuser*, yet that whole idea very quickly fell foul of student opinion. All the same, by 1969, 2,000 student residences had been completed. They sport club rooms, but no facilities for university education. But students not only need residences, they need shops and many other facilities. Altogether, the rapidly built complex in Bochum constituted an agglomeration of 20,000 or so people, placed five kilometres (about 3 miles) away from the centre of the city. The university authorities and planners, quite early on, took the decision to exclude the living and many of the social/recreational facilities from the campus proper – a momentous decision for the character of the whole. Instead, a special township was created, immediately north of the university, today called 'Unicenter'. It contains all thinkable facilities, shops, market, cafes; it is, in fact, a most lively mix, a compact town in itself.

However, what this meant, in turn, was that the great forum within the campus receives very much less use than was initially expected. The buildings immediately surrounding the centre are exclusively for academic and honorific use. The main canteen is located at the far end of the forum and is not directly linked to the main open area. The *Auditorium Maximum* was conceived chiefly for special occasions and 'not for the normal, day to day activities'. There remained, at Bochum, a strong element of the old German honorific centre of the institution – but this is no longer, as it always used to be, situated within a town. Bochum might be taken as a 'campus' in the orthodox, in the Dober, sense and it clearly did not yet participate in the newest 'urban' tendency, which called for concentration and a mixing of all functions. In addition, by the late 1960s, the new student movement had already begun to sneer at the old type of university ceremonies: 'Unter den Talaren steckt der Muff von tausend Jahren' the German students chanted, 'under their gowns hides the stale smell of a thousand years'. It shook the foundations of the Bochum concept.

This was, however, not the principal evaluation of Bochum after it had barely opened (indeed, the buildings of the forum were only completed in the early 1970s). In 1967 Germany's most lively architectural journal, the *Bauwelt* in Berlin launched a vitriolic campaign which is reminiscent of the *Architectural Review*'s condemnation of the New Towns in the 1950s and contemporary with the incipient campaigns against tower blocks. The basis of the argument was simple: 'too big' and 'too regular' is detrimental to psychic and physical well-being. 'Monotony', 'mere utility', the rationality of the building method had become something supra-rational, a 'mere aestheticism', the functionality had turned into a 'cliché'. The political aspect of 'bigger, larger', the 'representation-hungry image' are also ridiculed. As von Cube points out, all this amounted to a simple change in architectural fashion, indeed, the years between 1963 and 1965 had seen the publication of the newest English plans and the Berlin design whose forms were diametrically opposed to Bochum. The Ruhr Universität presents an example of the by then largely 'traditional' International Modernism: the early 1960s ideal of rationalisation and industrialisation, loaded with socio-political implications, is combined with a kind of monumentalism that goes a long way back in history – one may think of the city of Brasilia as a parallel. Like Essex and Chicago Circle, Bochum received mainly criticism and was subsequently left out from architectural histories, let alone glossy architectural books. But unlike Essex, Bochum's architecture was only rarely blamed directly for any socio-academic malfunctioning and unlike Chicago Circle, there does not seem to have been much suffering from the climate. Within the history of new university building Bochum can be taken as a Modernist pièce de resistance, somewhat like Warwick; for the next group of German new universities it can be seen as a point of reaction.

Regensburg

Because of the immense time it took most of the founders of the subsequent new universities to establish and plan their institutions it is difficult to devise a precise chronological sequence. Konstanz was founded first; after Bochum, the next major one was Regensburg (a town known outside Germany also under its French name Ratisbon). Decided upon by the Bavarian parliament in 1962 and opened in 1967 with a modest number of 670 students, it was planned that it should eventually cater for 8,000 students. Regensburg, we may say, was everything that Bochum was not. Altogether, for better or worse, Regensburg's rhetoric was rather less well developed than that at Bochum or Konstanz. This resulted in initial statements such as 'consciously [founded] as a normal university' – a pronouncement inconceivable in the context of Anglo-American institutions, but understandable with the background of the old German way of thinking that any example of the institution called 'university' carries conviction. Secondly, such a statement, made at the end of the 1960s, probably addressed the general weariness about the seemingly unfulfilled high hopes of 'university reform'. Thirdly, Regensburg is to all intents and purposes a provincial town of Bavaria, in itself a much more centralised state than any of the others in Germany. Its main university would remain Munich. Regensburg's task was, explicitly, to alleviate the situation in the capital and secondly to help with the development of underprivileged eastern Bavaria.

All discussions about Regensburg's purpose were sealed with the rector's statement of 'a guaranteed unbreakable soldering (Legierung) of old and new'. Regensburg's major single innovation was the public advertisement of all teaching posts – a small, but important step towards a more democratic regime. Like the other reformers, Regensburg, too, pleaded for more cooperation between disciplines. Old plus new meant, of course, something different in each of the foundations. Regensburg was one of the most venerable German towns, seat of the old Reichstag, the diet of the German Empire – long before it became part of Bavaria. Even more importantly, its impressive medieval centre had survived the war unscathed. Attempts to found a university went back to the fifteenth century. A strong initial question was whether there was a chance here to integrate a new university into the old town. But once again, planning and cost considerations necessitated a suburban location. However, planners and commentators missed no opportunity to demonstrate the university's proximity to the old centre, at a 1.5 kilometre (1 mile) distance, and subsequently further supported their case by building expensive student residences in town, using old buildings. The architects even found an effective way of framing the view of the famed Gothic cathedral with their buildings (figs 4.14 and 4.15).

After Bochum's display of power, restraint is the watchword at Regensburg. The site is a 'mere' 100 hectares (250 acres) but appears generous; costs were kept in check (by 1969 DM120m, c. £11m or $28m had been spent). A specially cheap preliminary block for the initial accommodation was built and later successfully integrated into the whole design. Like Bochum, Regensburg prided itself on a seamless cooperation between academic matters, planning and design. The basic formal concept of the plan was similar, too; around a communications centre, with ample parking underneath, the four wings of the major subject areas are spread out, within a ten minutes maximum walking distance from end to end, i.e. about half the size of Bochum overall. But the Regensburg concept had something new, something that had begun to develop during 1962–5, something that Bochum had just missed, or chosen to ignore, a much greater degree of overall flexibility. At Regensburg, there was to be no homogeneous descent from the grand whole to the constructional detail, but a staging of phases and a division between a 'long term planning framework' which was kept as open as possible, and the detailed planning phases of the individual buildings. In line with this logic was the way in which at Regensburg the overall planning was firmly in the hands of the Universitätsbauamt, and its leader, Helmut Gebhard, whereas for individual groups of buildings competitions were held. Much credit was given to the results which avoided the uniformity which the critics now hated, and for which they would have blamed the state building offices. Regensburg at that point also decided against high buildings, in marked contrast to the continuing use of high blocks in the universities of north and west Germany. Perhaps there was here an element of traditional Bavarian 'restraint' and also a deference to the old town, but there was also more than a hint of England's 'low-rise high density', and the Lancaster campus in particular (fig. 2.91).

Finally, the utmost care was spent in the designs of the central spaces. As at Bochum, the gently sloping site is used to create a pedestrian space above a parking undercroft. The main access is from below, leading upwards via somewhat ceremonial sets of open stairs to the campus centre, which is bordered by the usual main buildings. The contrast with Bochum could not be more striking. There we find an overpoweringly vast plaza surface, symmetrical, lined with monolithic buildings within a wide,

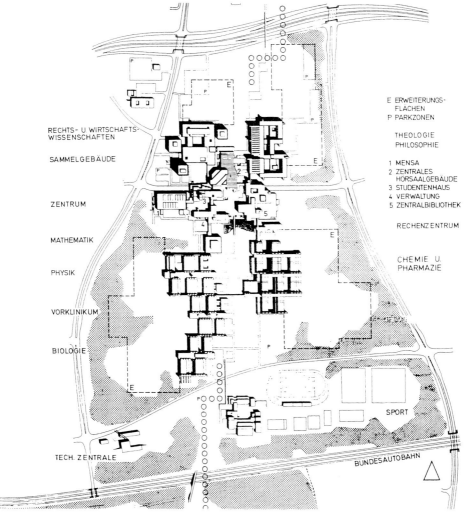

Within the plan, the following labels appear:

RECHTS- U. WIRTSCHAFTS-WISSENSCHAFTEN

SAMMELGEBÄUDE

ZENTRUM

MATHEMATIK

PHYSIK

VORKLINIKUM

BIOLOGIE

TECH. ZENTRALE

E ERWEITERUNGS-FLÄCHEN
P PARKZONEN

THEOLOGIE
PHILOSOPHIE

1 MENSA
2 ZENTRALES HORSAALGEBÄUDE
3 STUDENTENHAUS
4 VERWALTUNG
5 ZENTRALBIBLIOTHEK

RECHENZENTRUM

CHEMIE U. PHARMAZIE

SPORT

BUNDESAUTOBAHN

4.14 Universität Regensburg, plan mid-1970s, chiefly by Universitätsbauamt. Upper left: law and economics; 1 refectory, 2 central lecture theatres, 3 student centre, 4 administration, 5 central library. (*Geplant Gebaut Universität Regensburg* 1977, publ. Universitätsbauamt Regensburg, 1977)

4.15 Regensburg, view of central area, the spires of the cathedral are just visible centre-left

panoramic landscape: here, the impression is one of intimacy, buildings are asymmetrical, interlinked, gently changing their height, framing views into the surrounding green areas. The interiors of the main building carefully communicate with the outer space, especially the library, whose wall facing the square is mostly glass. The choice of designer, Alexander von Branca, Bavaria's most celebrated architect of the older generation, is again typical for Regensburg as a whole, reflecting a certain conservatism but linked with late 1960s socio-spatial convictions. Finally, as at Bochum, student residences are off-campus. The fact that a planned university shopping centre nearby, à la Bochum, was never built, doubtless contributes to the lively use of the central area.

Konstanz

More than any other German new university it was Konstanz that unequivocally stuck its neck out as a 'Reformuniversität'. The claim did not always serve it well: 'a "luxury" project', a 'sweet anachronism' (Dahrendorf), or a 'Harvard am Bodensee', on Lake Constance. How could a German university dare to overlook the burning problem of numbers? Konstanz's argument, and claim, was simply that it could and would serve as a model. Moreover, it claimed to be the earliest of all the new foundations, though it proceeded with majestic slowness. The origin lies again with the region, the *Land* Baden-Württemberg, a part of Germany which contained several of the most venerable European universities, such as Heidelberg and Tübingen. It was Prime Minister Kurt Georg Kiesinger (later for a short time federal chancellor) who himself first mooted the idea in 1959 – virtually a 'princely fiat'. Successive ministers of culture and education of the *Land*, Gerhard Storz and Wilhelm Hahn, who were themselves professors and who were also closely interacting with the Wissenschaftsrat, strongly supported the project. In 1964 the Gründungsauschuss, the foundation commission, began its long discussions. In total contrast to Bochum, a barely medium-sized town was chosen, in an area with little economic but rather more tourist significance. Like

4.16 Universität Konstanz: early model 1964–5 designed by the Institut für Hochschulbau Universität Stuttgart (H. Hofler, L. Kandel). Foreground left: Kollegienhäuser. (Institut für Hochschulbau Universität Stuttgart, S. Heeg (ed.), *Horst Linde Architekt und Hochschullehrer* (publ. Stuttgart) n.d. [*c.* 1980])

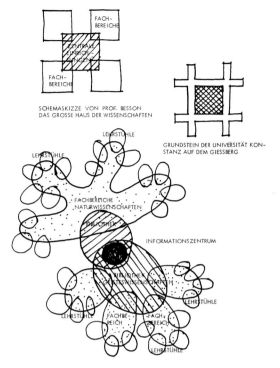

SCHEMASKIZZE VON PROF. BESSON
DAS GROSSE HAUS DER WISSENSCHAFTEN

GRUNDSTEIN DER UNIVERSITÄT KON-
STANZ AUF DEM GIESSBERG

ZUORDNUNGSSCHEMA DER ZENTRALBIBLIOTHEK

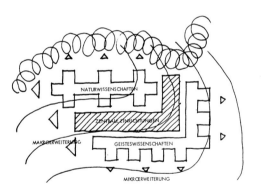

4.17 Konstanz: diagrams, top left and centre: individual disciplines and central facilities; the small circles on the outside represent chairs/departments. Top right: the university's foundation stone. Bottom: diagram of micro and macro-extensions. (*Konstanzer Blätter für Hochschulfragen* no. 29, vol. 8 (no.4) 11-1970, p. 24)

Regensburg, Konstanz had a considerable, and notorious, historic pedigree, the place where, in 1415, the Papal Council condemned to death the Czech religious reformer Jan Hus. In 1966 the university opened in an old monastery in the town; this was followed by a set of quickly built structures which were subsequently turned into student residences (Sonnenbühl). The new main building was only begun in the late 1960s and not opened until 1972, with only 1,479 students; the future total was at that time limited to 3,000. Soon, however, it doubled to 6,000.

A number of lengthy fundamental pronouncements were issued in the preliminary process, notably the memorandum of the *Land* government and the report of the Foundation Commission of 1965, under the founding rector, the linguist Gerhard Hess. The emphasis was on 'pure research', on theory in the humanities and experiment in the sciences, aided by a new emphasis on the social sciences. Early luminaries included Ralf Dahrendorf, the sociologist, later director of the London School of Economics, or Robert Jauss, for literary theory. Important traditional subjects were wholly, or largely excluded, such as medicine, theology and jurisprudence. Technology was not mentioned at all. That was, of course, just the way Humboldt had proceeded with his new university of Berlin. There was to be less emphasis on lectures and more on small group teaching. The natural sciences were open only to those who had studied four semesters elsewhere, a restriction unheard of in a German university. Syllabi were to be more carefully divised than customary. It was to be a place 'in which it is a pleasure to learn and teach' (Dahrendorf). Konstanz, too, preached the principle of cooperation between subjects. Its organisation, however, proceeded in the opposite way to Bochum: it was not divided into many smaller departments, but grouped together in only three faculties, sciences, humanities and social sciences.

About the buildings of Konstanz there is, first of all, a curious kind of anonymity. It is virtually impossible to identify the overall designer. Some credit must go to the Stuttgart Institute and its supremo, Horst Linde (fig. 4.16). The building office in Konstanz was led by Wenzelslaus (Ritter) von Mann and Wilhelm von Wolff. In a very unusual move, in early 1968, Linde called in a high-powered international team to give their opinions, including Gabriel Epstein, Jacob Bakema and Ferdinand Kramer from Frankfurt. The campus then hardly figured in architectural publications, certainly not outside Germany. In stark contrast to Bochum, few passed architectural judgments on Konstanz whether progressive, or old fashioned. Konstanz is a building in which any kind of purely architectural ambition appears to retreat behind the task of responding to the requirements of an exceptionally elaborate institution (figs 4.17–4.19).

The university, first of all, stands by itself, about 3 kilometres (nearly 2 miles) from the town centre. In 1970 the university stipulated that any development of dwellings close to the 'campus' would need to be 'controlled', in other words, the message was: leave us alone. On a slope, Konstanz overlooks the Lake of Constance towards the north east and on the other side it nestles into the edge of a large forest. Konstanz, much more so than either Bochum or Regensburg, is a one-building institution. It is not a long-drawn out solution either, like Scarborough or Simon Fraser, but forms virtually one squarish block of 350 by 350 metres (1,200 × 1,200 feet) Konstanz occupies only 10 per cent of its lavish 220 hectares (540 acres) site. Its general contour follows the site formation, multistorey at the top and low towards the lake. Its construction is standardised over a of grid of 7.2 metre (23 feet) intervals. Total cost: DM525m (c. £50m, or $130m), thus a quarter of Bochum, yet, considering the much smaller number of students, it was an expensive campus as well. The constructional regularity is counteracted by elements which are clearly added-on. Firstly, the intensive colour, secondly a very lavish programme of works of fine art, initiated by a competition, with contributions from eminent German practitioners, such as op artist Otto Piene. Modernism does not allow the use of the word decoration, but the procedure at Konstanz (and, very similarly at Regensburg, whereas Bochum tried and did not succeed and ultra-rationalist Bielefeld hardly tried at all) clearly shows an understanding of the building as utilitarian, which needs to be cheered up – all of it, needless to say, anathema to the contemporary English New-Brutalist conception of architecture.

4.18   Konstanz, air view. (K. Oettinger and H. Weidhase, *Eine Feste Burg der Wissenschaft . . . Universität Konstanz*, Konstanz, 1985)

However, all these considerations appear commonplace when we turn to the seriousness of the principles of the layout. Already at Bochum we saw a strong concern to relate the plan and contents, to 'express in the building the united pursuit of academic research and teaching'. Overall compactness and density, were, of course, major means to that end. The 1965 Report stipulated, even demanded, the working out of the relationships between teaching and research as 'eindeutig', unequivocal. The 'spatial ordering' of the university was to be the exact 'equivalent' of the way the disciplines were grouped. Planning for the 'Raumprogramm' started in 1967, helped by innumerable diagrammatic presentations. It took three 'intensive' years to finalise it. Now it was over to detailed planning. Again, designers began by asserting: 'The relationship between knowledge and how it is housed is neither accidental nor irrelevant'; 'the "quadrangles" of Oxford' could profitably be studied creating, as they do, the necessary quiet for study while, at the same time, 'provoking' intensive contacts between the college's members'. Thus von Mann introduces his own lengthy explanations.

An analysis of Konstanz must begin by moving from the outside inwards. The periphery of most parts of the building serves the individual requirements of the

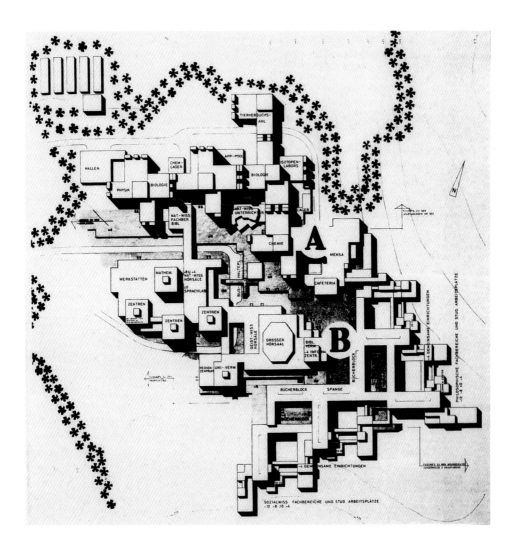

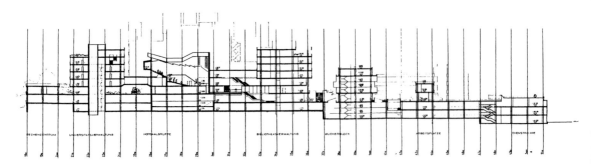

4.19   Konstanz, block plan, by Universitätsbauamt Wencelslaus von Mann, Wilhelm von Wolff and others) 1968 onwards. A sciences, B humanities. Section from left to right: computer centre, administration, lecture theatres, library, administration, library building ('book-block'), workplaces, offices. (*Konstanzer Blätter für Hochschulfragen* no. 29, vol. 8 (no. 4) 11-1970, pp. 34, 51)

teachers. The same principle holds when one moves from the top downwards. The further inwards, and the lower downwards, the more communal the use of the rooms. Beneath the offices of the science blocks are the individual or shared laboratories. Konstanz here combines a kind of planning that was first formulated in Bath and Lancaster. This, however, does not mean that Konstanz looks like Bath or Lancaster (figs 2.89 and 2.95), and even less, of course, like von Mann's cherished Oxbridge. The planning specialists used the term 'spine' for Konstanz, albeit is a 'cranked spine'; this parlance refers to a principle of bundling the lines of communication inside the complex. It is the complex as a whole, the amalgamation of all the communal facilities and the main lines of communication which decides the overall form, while the location of the individual facilities is of secondary importance.

While all this might still sound comprehensible as a general idea, a look at the plan reveals its bafflingly complexity. There is actually not much point in looking at the plan of any one floor, as the contours and the divisions of the building keep changing from level to level. If we think of the new kind of communitarian university as one with a clear central space, a 'forum', as it was intended at Bochum, Konstanz leaves such a notion behind as simplistic. There is here in fact only a relatively small outdoor space called a forum, and even that is difficult to experience as a visual whole. One of its main features is the way it looks out over the lake. Somewhat reminiscent of Lasdun's original concept of East Anglia, users are seen on the move, rather than stationary, inside this 'big house of the Wissenschaften with short distances to go'. The principle mentioned earlier of 'from outside inwards' can also be understood as the transition from a zone where one remains largely stationary to one of intensive movement (cf. Bath page 172). For von Mann, the forum is a wholly exceptional space, one where one might 'loose oneself', because the space is 'funktionslos', without function (fig. 4.20).

The real intricacy of the Konstanz plan, however, lies in the way areas of work and the lines of communication are punctuated with points of rest. In this lavish Reformuniversität, each student had his or her own desk, chair and bookshelf. It is assumed that most users spend the best part of the day within the complex, distant from the town – in this respect the word campus certainly is apposite. The architects thus felt obliged to cater for the precise needs of the various phases of rest. Apart from the central eating rooms and other student facilities, von Mann and his team devised a quite unparalleled system of smaller resting places, or small havens, for short breaks. The architects were adamant that these breaks should not happen at the place of work, no tea-making in people's own offices. In the humanities, the special rest areas are called 'Common Center' ('after the model of English common rooms'), in the science parts they are labelled 'Rekreationsraum', while the larger facilities closer to the centre carry yet another name: 'Erfrischungräume', refreshment rooms (figs 4.21 and 4.22).

It hardly needs stressing that these spaces were designed to encourage students to meet one another and that meant 'spontaneous' and 'less intensive [beiläufige]' kinds of meetings. Yet the intensity and complexity of planning at Konstanz is singular. Along with Lancaster, York and Kresge College at Santa Cruz, Konstanz belongs to a phase in which the strictness of institutional planning meets, and overlaps, with a relaxed type of planning. On the one hand, there was direct instrumentalisation: 'The aim of the new university is to increase the efficiency of research and teaching; the

4.20   Konstanz, 'Forum' Decor by Otto Piene 1972. (K. Oettinger and H. Weidhase, *Eine Feste Burg der Wissenschaft . . . Universität Konstanz*, Konstanz, 1985)

university is a 'severe/strict [streng] environment'. On the other hand, we are told that the student should not be perceived as the user of an institution (here phrased as: 'Anstalt' – the German term for severe kinds of institution, such as the asylum), but as a member of a 'community'. As such, he or she is entitled to rest and to enter associations unrelated to teaching or research, and there should be ample opportunities for that. That said, the designer is then hell-bent on relating these spaces to the working spaces and to the whole. Returning, once more, to the issue of institutional presence, Konstanz must surely count as a high point in the development of an academic-institutional-architectural whole; however, at that time, in the development of institutional architecture, this whole consisted not so much of a tangible form, but of an immaterial presence, by channelling movements, by the dispersal of meeting places. As Peter Jokusch of the Stuttgart Institute remarked: 'a campus must be concentrated as a whole, while social spaces should be decentralised'.

Finally, the library at Konstanz is also subject to this kind of planning. As explained by founding-librarian Joachim Stoltzenburg, it first of all adheres to the Anglo-Saxon manner of having all books concentrated in one place, rather than having most of them disperserd with the faculties or departments, in the traditional German manner. And yet, a little like Lancaster, Konstanz breaks with the tradition of having an entirely separate, prominent-looking building. In addition, the Konstanz library is open-access, something that was only just being introduced to Germany. Konstanz then devises a uniquely complicated division of its library into those parts which are for the more general user and those which are for the specialist user. This translated spatially into

4.21 Konstanz: common centre. (Courtesy Dr Maria Schorpp, Universität Konstanz)

4.22 Konstanz, plan of part of library, with common centres, seminar rooms and professors' offices. (*Baumeister* 9-1975, p. 771)

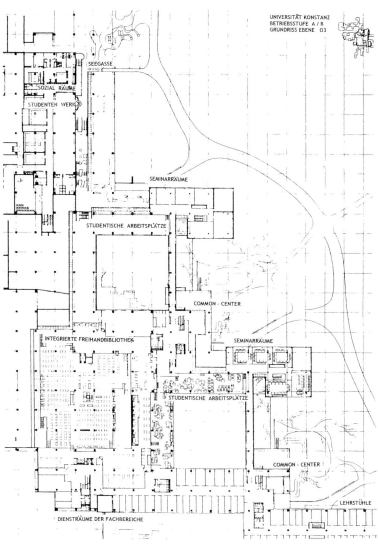

major central parts and smaller parts which reach out towards the relevant departments – at least that was the general idea; in detail the complexity of the arrangement defies description. Lastly, with regard to residences, Konstanz made sure that
there was a provision of 30 per cent, well above the German average, but by occupying the first, quick-built university accommodation (Sonnenbühl) they are about a
kilometre away from the main building. Konstanz early on stated that the students'
'private' living sphere was essentially their own affair. Just as well, some may say.

Bielefeld

At least one thing has become clear: the governments of the German states were
proud of supplying what the academic reform discussion appeared unable to deliver:
new and reformed universities. Work at Bochum had hardly begun when in 1964
North-Rhine-Westfalia dreamt up another major undertaking, a university for the
eastern parts of the state, at Bielefeld. Now the emphasis was to be not, as at Bochum,
on providing places of study for the masses, but on 'reform'. The state got hold of
one of its professors of sociology, Helmut Schelsky, who had just published a book
which, as we saw, advocated a new, somehow more scientific line in university reform.
Schelsky delivered a proposal, entitled 'Structural characteristics . . .'. In it he reasserted
his main theme that a university is there primarily to serve scholarship. The units of
its organisation are the 'institutes', headed by the chairholder though there should be
greater flexibility in the appointments and cooperation should be encouraged. Teaching is closely related to research and tightly organised. Schelsky thus intended to limit
the number of students to 3,600. The university had to ask the state for permission
to limit intake. As at Konstanz, some major vocational subjects, such as medicine and
engineering are excluded. Characteristic of the whole process at Bielefeld, in contrast
to Bochum, was that very much more time was spent on deliberations; every step of
the process was documented and publicised. Large quick-built structures were erected
during 1967–8, to be cast off later to 'lesser' institutes of higher education, and in
1969 the university started to function.

At the same time, during 1968–9, an ideas-competition was held. It was not nearly
as lavish as at Bochum, and thus there are virtually no well-known names. A long
drawn-out dispute arose, when the city of Bielefeld preferred an entry that seemed
more pleasant to look at, while the university and the state, and especially its building supremo, Fridolin Hallauer, insisted on a design (by H. Herzog, K. Köpke and W.
Siepman from Berlin) which, they maintained, fulfilled all the academic and practical
requirements. Hallauer was supported by another professor of Sociology, Dietrich
Storbeck, who was in charge of 'planning of buildings and questions of [university]
structure'. Storbeck maintained that, so far, nobody had paid much notice to the
proper, 'rational' planning of a university. Hallauer insisted that the city was going to
get the 'most progressive educational establishment of the Federal Republic'. There
was a reluctant consensus that a design had to be accepted in which, as it was said,
practicality was given preference to beauty. Clearly, Hallauer did not want to take the
early criticism of Bochum on board. It then took the university planners four years
to organise the details.

The overall ideal and principle was 'Verdichtung', densification, in order to facilitate contacts of all kinds. The reality was that for economic reasons the by then

4.23   Universität Bielefeld, by H. Herzog, Klaus Köpke, Peter Kulka, Wolf Siepmann and others 1970–5.
Centre right: Versuchsschule and Oberstufenkolleg, by Geist, Maier and others. (Photo M. Fricke
Bielefeld)

common German 'jumbo', the high slab block, had to be used. Bielefeld is simply a
group of interlinked jumbos, two rows of them, as at Bochum, but much closer
together. In between there is a space which is covered by a glass roof and which provides the 'forum', over 300 metres (710 feet) in length. What is most elaborate is the
way in which the vertical and horizontal accessways for the high blocks are interlinked
with the forum and the way in which the forum gives direct access to all communal
uses. There was a belief in the utmost rationality of the undertaking. The most elaborate and unusual feature is the library. As at Konstanz the idea was to centralise it, as
well as to 'reach it' into the various departments. This is done at Bielefeld by allocating one whole floor of the building almost entirely to the library; it is here, of course,
that the wholeness of the building is most strongly felt. Altogether, there is 'maximal
use', in this 'purely utilitarian building (reiner Zweckbau)', it is proudly stated; there is
'no hierarchy, no added aesthetic'. 'Nowhere are the contacts between the various parts
of the university closer and is what happens more transparent'. There is the simplest
restatement of the belief that proximity encourages contacts: 'The closer the neighbour
. . . the greater are the chances of informal communication'. Two factors have further
encouraged communication. The number of students had to be doubled from the 3,600
envisaged, and the presence of shops and cafes in the forum make it that much livelier
than the one at Bochum. As regards student residences, far fewer were built than originally envisaged and even those that were built not far from the main complex show
no design relationship with the latter, or with the adjacent 'Oberstufenkolleg', the
buildings of the experimental college (see page 211) (figs 4.23–4.25).

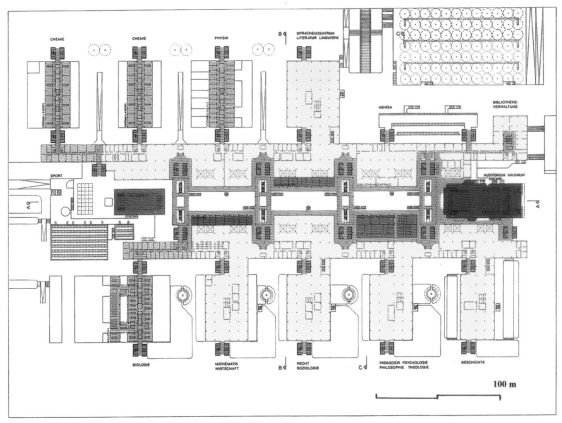

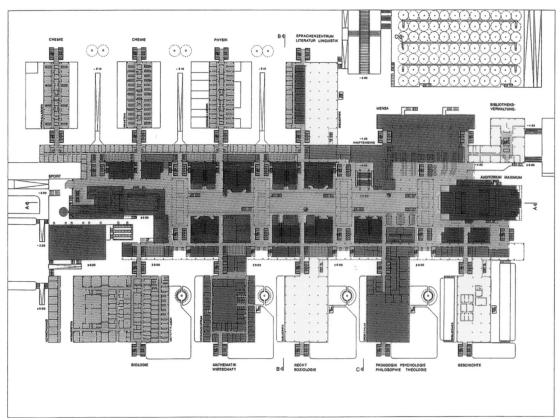

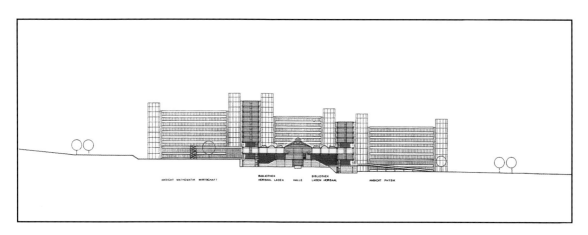

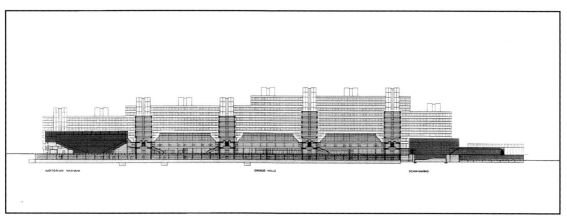

4.24 Universität Bielefeld, plans: ground floor with communal facilities (*Auditorim Maximum* right, swimming pool left); first floor with the library extending though most parts of the complex. Green: teaching rooms and laboratories; blue: offices; yellow: library; purple: lecture theatres; red: restaurants and other communal facilities; brown: 'special areas'; dark blue: seminar rooms; grey: service areas. Sections: cross section; longitudinal section from left, *Auditorium Maximum*, Great Hall, swimming pool. (Courtesy Universität Bielefeld)

4.25   Universität Bielefeld, interior. (Courtesy Universität Bielefeld)

By 1977, the date of the completion of Bielefeld, there was little public interest left (positive or negative) as regards grand new universities. As architecture, Bielefeld received very few professional comments indeed. The numerous new foundations in Germany of the 1970s were usually more modest in scale, and did not, at first, reach the academic level of those of the 1960s. Some of the other more significant projects of the 1960s, for parts of universities, such as those for Berlin, will be discussed in the next chapter. In any case, most architects and especially the town-planning minded architects and their strong critical lobby now demanded a greater integration of the university with the town. In Bremen, where building finally began after 1970, there was even a proposal by the town planning sociologists H. P. Barth, to mix university buildings with ordinary dwellings and other kinds of public buildings, in open disregard of the earlier campus concept. As elsewhere, advanced architectural opinion had begun to doubt the straight causal relationship between building layout and community formation. We may conclude with Helmut Schelsky, who declared in 1965 that what *Universitätsreform* had to bring about was a 'differentiated system of higher education' and that no single new institution could take the claim to be a model for all. And yet plenty of statements could be cited in which each of the new universities claimed 'reform' for themselves, including Schelsky's Bielefeld. In the context of this book it may be concluded that the new German universities did fuse a strong and, to an extent, newly created institutional identity with architectural presence and architectural image. Nobody would, however, dare to proclaim this as a lasting image for the German university – but then nobody could make this claim for the New English and American Universities either.

. . . the desire to have students live among other citizens has turned out to be largely utopian.

[The 'campus à la française'] . . . does not correspond at all to the very complete conception of the American campus.

. . . the only proper university is that which inserts itself profoundly into the town.

(Pierre Merlin, 1995)

Primitive functionalism, which had been the militant force of the pre-war years and had carried architecture through the postwar reconstruction, proved to be illusory by the late fifties.

(Michael Brawne, 1964)

Campus and College have been tackled in this book as two complex and pervasive issues in university planning, especially in Anglo-Saxon countries. There are, however, more straightforward ways of dealing with the university as a building type. One can disregard to a large extent national factors, as well as the issue of global versus regional. Thus, in the context of this chapter it is of lesser importance that the term campus, adopted worldwide from the 1950s, was of North American, as well as Latin, origin. The issue of the 'college' hardly arises any more. The fact that more student residences were built than ever before, may be, but need not be, taken as an element of Anglo-American influence; in many cases it was first and foremost a practical necessity. Likewise, there is much less concern, in this chapter, for any educational or institutional analysis and any utopianism remains implicit. We are dealing in a much narrower sense with the contribution of the architectural profession (figs 5.1–5.4).

   The book began with the proposition that only the USA had a really strong, live tradition of specific, yet varied types of university building. The strength, or impact of Modernism within, or as a development of, that tradition inside the USA was open to question. For the world outside the USA and England, we might state the opposite: there was no tradition to speak of as regards a specific university type of building – it simply looked like any other major public building – and it was Modernist architecture which helped to create a specific university type of building. Campus planning in the American and then in the Modernist, utopianist sense coincided largely with the advent of Modernist town planning. One of the very last examples of the single, dignified, largely symmetrical 'public' building must have been the Université Miséricorde in Fribourg, Switzerland, begun in 1937. Very probably the most exciting complex of university-related buildings of the interwar years is the Cité Universitaire de Paris, a group of halls of residences for foreign students, planned from 1922. The first European 'campus'? Maybe, as it was intended as a 'cité-jardin urbanisée'. Many of its interwar buildings, though, adhere to the old public-building kind

5.1 'Universities': title page in *L'Architecture d'aujourd'hui*, 1968. (*Ad'A* 137, 4/5-1968)

of dignity and symmetry, while the tremendous variety of styles, though exciting for the observer now, is not in line with a Classical, nor a Modernist sense of unity. It is precisely this feeling of unity which is given by the large University of Aarhus, planned from 1927. This now also indubitably forms a campus: buildings are spread out in a landscaped park and have largely abandoned the traditional dignified-public-building look by adopting a homely Danish plain brick. In any case, it has an overall relaxed feel to it.

Not a lot would be gained by attempting a comprehensive, a once-and-for-all definition of the terms Modern or Modernist. The changes within this mode from the 1950s to the early 1970s – that is before the onset of Post-Modernism – are too great. For instance, 'Modern', to most, entailed a thoroughly 'practical' and stringently

5.3 Otto Freese, 'Gedanken zur Universitätsbauplanung'. Cf. ills. 5.17 and frontispiece. (In Günther Feuerstein, *Hochschulen Planen Bauen* (Bundesministerium für Bauten und Technik/Österreichische Bauzentren/G. Feuerstein (eds.), [Documentation of the Exhibition Hochschulen Planen Bauen] Vienna 1969/70)

5.2 A choice of models for planning a university: the size of the plot and the usable surface area inside the buildings remain the same (Hans-Joachim Aminde, 1970). (Linde (1970) vol. 4, pp. 100–1)

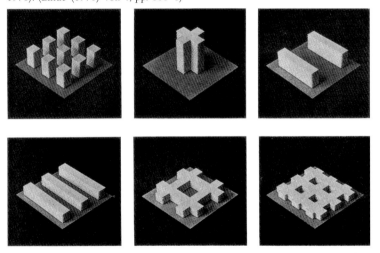

economical approach to planning. But we must begin our post World War II story with another version of the 'Modern', a type of university foundation which we have not encountered so far: the university as the pride, in fact, as the chief new building of a whole state or country. Perhaps following somewhat the model of Mussolini's University of Rome in the 1930s, some Latin American states gave their main universities priority as 'national cultural institutions' and poured scarce money into their buildings, on a scale without parallel. During World War II, South America had become something of a torchbearer of Modernist architecture, which thus found itself considered as an official style rather than a reviled avant-garde (we have noted its meagre progress in the USA before the 1950s). The University of Caracas was planned from 1943 onwards by Carlos Raul Villanueva, 'in the best Bauhaus tradition'. It

5.4 Universidad Nacional Autonoma de Mexico, 1950 onwards by Carlos Lazo and others. Foreground right: teaching, administration and library, the student residences are to the left; in the background the national stadium. (*AR* 11-1953, p. 811)

5.6 (*right*)   Moscow, Lumumba 'University Town', from 1960. 1   student residences, 2   university center, 3   humanities, 4   canteen and assembly Hall, 5   lecture rooms, 6   sciences, 7   engineering, 8   medicine, 9   agriculture, 11–13   other functions, 14   area for extension. (*BW* no. 9, 5-3-1973, p. 284)

5.5 (*below*)   Hyderabad, Pakistan, 'Sind' University, plan by Richard Doecker 1955 onwards. 'The university town': far left the student residences; right, the town itself. (*Baukunst und Werkfrom* 1960, p. 373)

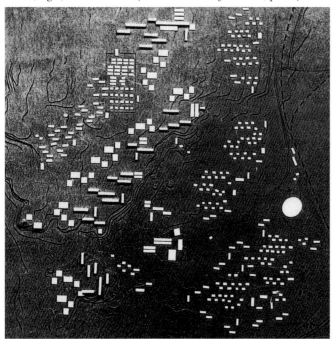

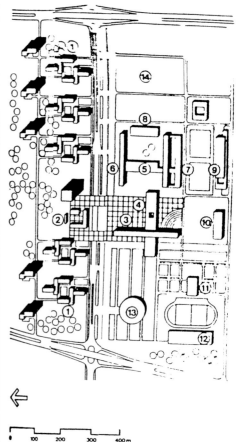

became, moreover, a locus of an exuberant display of Western Modern art. The most lavish campus undertaking of all was Mexico City, built with astonishing rapidity by a great number of architects in 1950–3 for 30,000 students as a 'complete' campus just outside the city. Both Caracas and Mexico made use of the signal of Modernism, the multistorey block. In Mexico, in particular, the Modernist campus now departs decisively from the traditional one-major-building plan and dissolves into a large number of loosely, but still orderly, placed blocks, each housing one of the sub-functions. The architectural order is derived precisely from the careful placing of the blocks and the large spaces between them (fig. 5.5). Another major example, but with far less overall coordination is the Hebrew University on Mount Scopus in Jerusalem, built from 1948. A rather late spate of national prestige building occurred in the 1970s in newly independent Algeria with a grand gesture of calling in non-European master designers, Oscar Niemeyer at Constantine and Kenzo Tange at Oran.

Modernist architecture not only popularised the high point block but also the long thin block. Only 12 to 15 metres (40 to 50 feet) deep, its advantage is the maximisation of daylight, as well as the use of a rationalised, repetitive method of construction when great height as well as length is required. The greater the height, the further the blocks have to be apart for reasons of light. During the 1930s, German designers – especially Gropius – and then English housing architects began to demand high 'slab' blocks, in a parallel, or 'Zeilenbau' formation, as the norm for cheaper kinds of dwellings. It is, of course, easiest to built such groups of buildings on fresh land outside towns. Moreover, ample parks were considered the most desirable kinds of surroundings. Beginning perhaps with Mexico City, campuses around the world adopted this method, including, from the later 1950s onwards, those in Communist countries (fig. 5.6). In the tropics the wide spacing of blocks was considered particularly suitable in order to guarantee a flow of air.

By the mid-1960s new university buildings became the chief focus of architectural effort. *L'Architecture d'aujourd'hui* quoted Lord Robbins: 'if he had to choose between education and prosperity of a nation, he would not consider that the latter was the most desirable' and one of the world's most glossy and high-brow Modernist architectural journals, *Zodiac* proclaimed: 'the universities as institutional archetypes of our age' (Joseph Rykwert). For the architects this meant, above all, the constant working out of new schemes, which entailed, in turn, the constant rejection of earlier solutions. The chief values of the years 1930 to 1960, sunlight and greenery, no longer appeared essential. Preferences were now turning from the rectilinear to the multi-angled, and from the large single shape to the assemblage of smaller units. In the Tropics the prevailing view that buildings should be widely spaced and open in order to make the most of the fresh winds, changed so that now the emphasis was on turning inwards, to the construction of impenetrable walls, most notably in the work of Louis Kahn in South Asia. To what extent English Townscape critics of the 1950s influenced international trends still needs be assessed. American campus models with their emphasis on a lavish central area may have served as much as English ones, for instance in the Rissho Campus near Tokyo, first planned in 1961 by Fumihiko Maki, and in the Universidad del Valle in Cali, Columbia. Gropius's plan for Baghdad [1.10, 1.11], devised from 1957/8 onwards and widely publicised, had become a model for a greater overall density and a non-rectilinear layout. From about 1962–3 we note the influence of Team X, of what the English-international

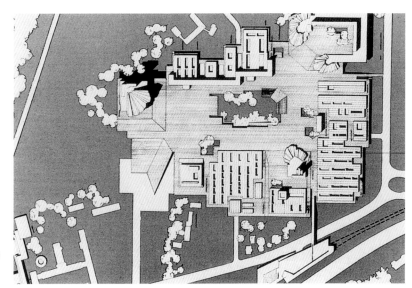

5.7 Stockholms Universitet: competition design by Henning Larsen 1961. (T. Hall (ed.), Frescati. *Huvudstadsuniversitet och arkitekturpark*, Stockholm, 1999)

architectural historian Reyner Banham called New Brutalism. Derived from the work of late Le Corbusier and his international followers as well as on the ideas and drawings of Alison and Peter Smithson, this movement preferred long multi-angled, interconnecting blocks. The straight Zeilenbau block was now virtually phased out. Frequently the new formal preferences were somehow linked with arguments about 'human scale'. The demand for limiting campus size to a maximum of 10 minutes walking distance was now universally repeated. Lastly, the new Townscape preferences were combined with a St Elia – Le Corbusieran desire to keep cars separate. The Danish architect Henning Larsen, in an unbuilt design of 1961 for Stockholm University, proposed a vast podium, only 3–4 metres (10–12 feet) above the ground, which comprised practically the whole campus (fig. 5.7).

Not only England, but also much of continental Europe, North America and Japan now presented designs of breathtaking complexity, as well as diversity. They were first seen in the widely publicised designs for the Bochum competition in 1962. The novelty of the undertaking, the lavish prizes offered by the state of North-Rhine Westfalia, as well as the beautiful, yet difficult site, all provided a huge challenge. If we take only the three best-known names – Gropius, Jacobsen and Broek & Bakema – we meet three solutions that could not possibly be more different from each other. Jacobson's appears the most formalistic, or pure, in a Classic Modern sense. He has several absolutely regular Zeilenbau formations, but, most unusually, the blocks diminish in length in response to the contours and the descent down the valleys. In his proposal Gropius takes elements from Baghdad (figs 1.10 and 1.11) but makes the units smaller and puts them even closer together – in Iraq, we remember, the justification for this was to keep out the burning sun, but in Germany this could hardly be adduced as a plausible reason. Easily the most complex, or at least the most difficult to 'read', was Bakema's scheme. What appears at first sight to be a series of straight lines which run across the hilly site, turns out to consist of stretches of thin slab blocks which contain walkways inside. At many points, especially at the crossings, these vertebrae thicken and we find major

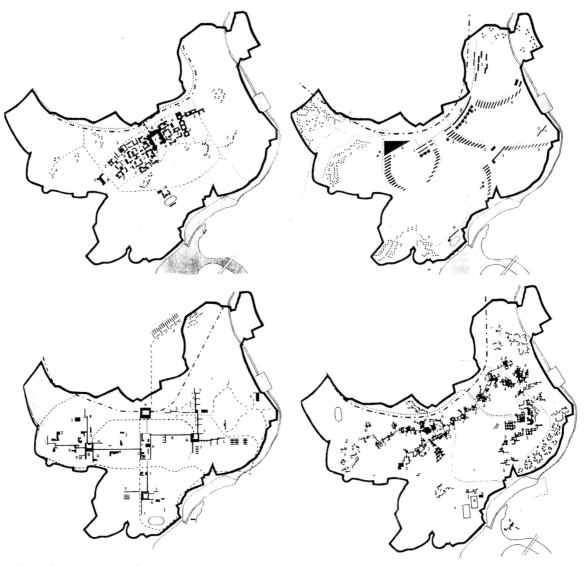

5.8   Ruhr Universität Bochum, competition designs 1962. Top left: W. Gropius; top right: Arne Jacobsen; bottom left: Jacob Bakema; bottom right: Walter Schwagenscheidt, Tassilo Sittmann and others. 1   humanities, 2   technology, 3   sciences, 4 medicine (pre-clinical), 5   medicine (clinical), 6   central facilities, 7   student residences. (*BW* 19/20, 20-5-1963, p. 535 ff.)

5.9   Bochum competition: Jacob Bakema. (*Ad'A* 107, 3/4-1963, p. 10)

5.10   Bochum competition: Candilis, Josic and Woods. Red: communal buildings, yellow: pedestrian routes and student residences. A low rise-high density design, most buildings are only 1–3 stories high, except for the 'A frame' constructions of the meandering residence blocks which are interspersed with the whole. (J. Joedicke (ed.), Candilis, Josic, Woods, *Documents of Modern Architecture* (6), 1968)

5.11   Bochum competition: Eckard Schulze-Fielitz ('Raumgitter'/Spaceframe). (G. Feuerstein, *New Directions in German Architecture*, London, 1968)

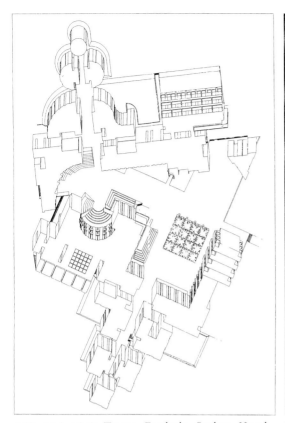

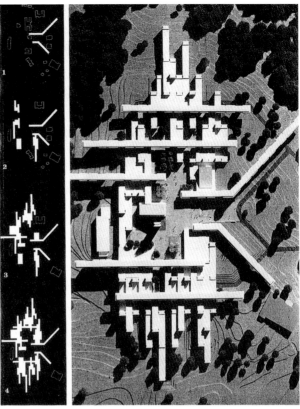

5.12 Universiteit Twente Enschede, Student Hostel project, by Oswald Ungers 1964. (O.M. Ungers, *Architektur 1961–1990*, London, 1991)

5.13 Tougaloo College, Tougaloo Mississippi and by Gunnar Birkerts and Associates, 1965 onwards; the wings accommodate mainly the student residences. (*AFor* 4-1966, p. 57)

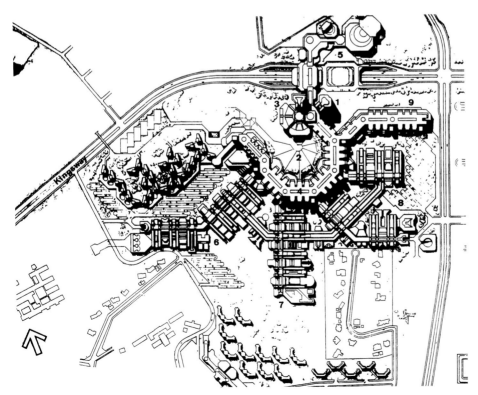

5.14 Johannesburg Rand Universiteit, by Wilhelm O. Meyer and Jan van Wijk, begun 1966. 1 main entrance, 2 University Square, 3 main building, 4 teaching buildings, 5 town square with cultural centre, 6 medicine, 7 sciences, 8 engineering, 9 humanities. (Linde (1970) vol. 4, p. 171)

5.15   Art University Osaka, project by Noriaki Kurokawa 1964; a series of parallel blocks containing the teaching facilities, arranged as bridges over a central roadway. (*AD* 12-1964, p. 606)

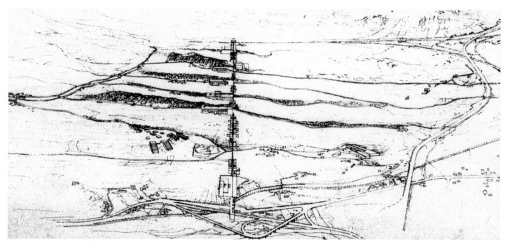

5.16   Università di Calabria, Cosenza, competition design 1973, by Vittorio Gregotti Associati. (*Architetura Chronache i Storia* no.227, 9-1974, p. 298).

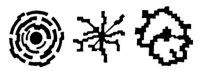

facilities, such as the library. A crucial question, generally, even a dilemma, was whether to cover the very large site with structures or whether to leave large parts untouched (figs 5.8, 5.9 and 5.11). Some competitors opted for an extreme concentration of buildings; the most spread-out design was that by the Paris-international firm Candilis, Josic and Woods, a low-rise high density model along a major pedestrian 'spine' (fig. 5.10). Among its late followers was Griffith University near Brisbane, part of a wave of new campuses in Australia.

Campus designs can further be classed into those which present an agglomeration of separate parts, such as Oswald Matthias Ungers' competition design for student residences for Technisch Universiteit at Twente, consisting of a great number of diversely geometrical blocks around dense 'urban' spaces (fig. 5.12), and those which appear unified, like Giancarlo de Carlo's Student Residences at Urbino, continuously and gently slung around a hill. A similar pair of opposites would be concentration and reaching outwards, such as the various narrow wings branching out, while also being placed on stilts, in Gunnar Birkert's Tougaloo College, Mississippi (fig. 5.13), whereas much of the accommodation of the Rand Afrikaans University at Johannesburg is surrounding, almost concentrically, the open forum (fig. 5.14). As we saw with the English 'urban' designs of 1962–4, the concern for the centre and for the organisation of traffic could turn from a static kind of understanding of the campus into a more dynamic one in which the lines of communication dominate, for instance in elevated walkways. Extreme examples were the projects for Osaka Art University (fig. 5.15) and the University of Calabria at Cosenza by Vittorio Gregotti, where some parts of the teaching blocks are placed as bridges high above roadways; the latter university, in fact, stretches for 3 kilometres (2 miles) through the landscape (fig. 5.16). The Cosenza competition of 1973 may perhaps be taken as an end-point of a decade of international grandiose schemes (fig. 5.17).

5.17   Günther Feuerstein, Hochschulen Planen Bauen: 'A by no means exhaustive diagram of the essential basic types'. Cf. above ills. 5.2 and 5.3. (Günther Feuerstein, *Hochschulen Planen Bauen* (Bundesministerium für Bauten und Technik/Österreichische Bauzentren/G. Feuerstein (eds.), [Documentation of the Exhibition Hochschulen Planen Bauen] Vienna, 1969/70)

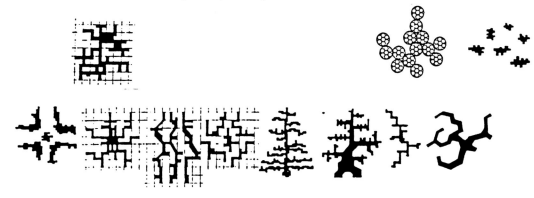

University growth in France from the later 1950s was perhaps more vigorous than anywhere else. Student numbers rose from 150,000 in 1954 to over 600,000 in 1969 and to well over 800,000 in 1977. By the 1970s practically all university buildings were new. But France's planning and institutional story differs considerably from those elsewhere. In France, the 'university', generically and individually, is only one element, albeit by far the largest, within a vast and immensely complex panoply of institutions of tertiary education, comprising 'académies', 'collèges', 'instituts', 'écoles' and, most famously, the Grandes Écoles. Their relationship could not sufficiently be explained by arraying them in the usual simple hierarchies, high to low or vocational to academic. It must also be noted that any particular university in France does not necessarily form a tight unit in itself. Few can memorise the names of the dozen or so universities into which the Université de Paris was dissolved after 1968, let alone distinguish between each sub-university's diverse separate campuses for arts, sciences, for beginners' and for advanced teaching. France's vastly complex multilevel system of degrees, contrasting sharply with the simple Anglo-Saxon custom of the BA, resulted in a much more diffuse notion of 'the student'. The building complexes which are discussed here may house only part of a university, or may even combine parts of several universities; complete new foundations were not as numerous as one might expect.

By the same token, a building for a French university traditionally very rarely provided the same kind of institutional-architectural presence as in Anglo-Saxon countries. There never had been even the notion of a campus (ironically, as one might view it from an American perspective, as French 'academic' planning and drawing styles had contributed so much to the evolution of the impressive American campus ensemble). Moreover, colleges of the old type were virtually extinct and only rarely could one meet with a specially prominent 'public' university building, so familiar in the German system. Neither could one speak of 'university towns', there are no Oxfords, or Heidelbergs, or New Havens. It is often hard to distinguish buildings for higher education from those for secondary education, particularly those for a prestigious lycée. Significantly, this relative lack of identity and esteem continued throughout the postwar expansion and it was reinforced by a perceived low merit of French twentieth-century architecture generally. '1968' of course meant that a new attention was given to all facets of higher education, including planning. In effect, the new turn away from the enclosed, authoritarian institution also brought a turn against the self-contained plan and any kind of imposing architecture, and, instead, a renewed plea to integrate the institution into its immediate urban surroundings. Almost of necessity, the view in this chapter is one from the outside. A summary here could distinguish three phases in France: the adoption of a vaguely American campus model with Zeilenbau formation, followed by a closer attention to a new English kind of integrated campus design, ending with France becoming a member of the consolidated group adhering to international trends of university planning, with a special emphasis on urban integration.

Complete state domination has always been seen as a principal characteristic of French universities – although this may lead to the disregard of cases of specific local or personal initiative. There was always strict control of types, sizes and finance by the

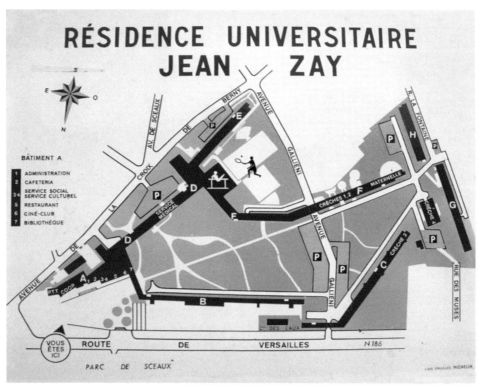

RÉSIDENCE UNIVERSITAIRE
JEAN ZAY

BÂTIMENT A

1 ADMINISTRATION
2 CAFETERIA
3,4 SERVICE SOCIAL
SERVICE CULTUREL
5 RESTAURANT
6 CINÉ-CLUB
7 BIBLIOTHÈQUE

VOUS ÉTES ICI

ROUTE   DE   VERSAILLES   N 186

PARC   DE   SCEAUX

5.18   Antony (Paris) student residences, plan, by Eugène Beaudoin 1954–6.

Ministry of National Education and other state agencies. Nobody could deny that this resulted in complexes that were erected swiftly and cheaply, with buildings that were all eminently practical. By 1965 we count already fourteen major edge-of-town extensions, even excluding those of the Ile de France. The new sites meant above all an escape from the 'asphyxiating' situation in the old town centres. New Bordeaux-Talence, for instance, comprised 260 hectares or 640 acres. The accommodation for each subject was complete and there was adjacent room for expansion. The prevailing type of building was the Zeilenbau. Initially at least, nobody seemed to mind that these universities and the process of their development very much resembled the large public housing estates (the 'HLM', or the 'Grands Ensembles') of the time.

As in Germany, the French system did not concern itself with looking after the student outside teaching hours. Moreover, French universities, at least the provincial ones, usually catered for students who lived at home. And yet the new expansion did embrace student residences and other social and recreational facilities. The thinking behind it was strongly charitable, and it was also to serve the large numbers of foreign students. The first attempts to create 'oeuvres sociales' – corresponding to the German 'Studentenwerke' – barely date back to the interwar years. By 1960, 20,000 bed places had been built, for about 10 per cent of the student population. By 1969, the proportion had been raised somewhat, with a total of 90,000 places. Thereafter growth was small. Conditions were generally rather spartan, with a norm of 9 square metres (97 square feet) or a little more, per room. There were usually thirty to forty rooms

5.19 Paris Université de Nanterre, by J.P. and J. Chauliat and others, from 1962. The long range on the left: faculty of letters; bottom: law and economics; far right: university library; top right: Cité Universitaire (student residences); centre: swimming pool; the square buildings top left and bottom right are restaurants. (J.-P. Duteuil, *Nanterre 1965-66-67-68*, Paris 1988)

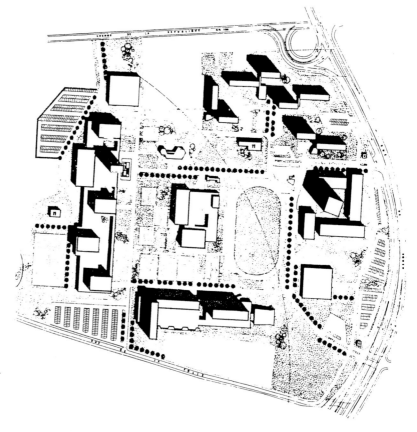

5.20 (*far right*) Université d'Orléans (La Source), by Olivier Cacoub, 1965 view of project for central forum. (*L'Architecture Française* nos. 275–6 1965, p. 68)

along a corridor. Rules were strict until 1968, blocks for 'garçons' and 'filles' were usually rigidly separated. In provincial towns many of the campuses contained student residences. Paris, however, had to build separate colonies of them, of which Antony, deep in the southern suburbs, was by far the largest: about 3,000 students lived there. Over an uneven terrain the massive four- to six- (and up to ten-) storey blocks are spread out irregularly and the way they are linked to each other usually creates quite a sense of spatial coherence (fig. 5.18). Such a scheme was soon considered excessive and 600 students was then cited as an optimal number. Architecturally speaking, there was, of course, no thought of ever taking up the model of the celebrated Cité Universitaire in Paris; as with most other university buildings, Zeilenbau reigned supreme in the new residences, too. Student hostels were an even closer relation of public housing.

The first time the term 'campus' was used was at Caen, from about the mid-1950s onwards, although this group of new buildings represented one of the last – and rare examples – of the compact monumentalised inner urban complex. The first of the outer suburban developments was Dijon, from the early 1950s, with several open Zeilenbau formations, especially for the residences. The last campus of a similar kind was probably the much publicised plan for Grenoble, built from 1962. In 1962–4 the first sets of buildings arose at Nanterre, a new non-science university for Paris, placed in the suburbs just outside the Defense. Spaces are similarly left wide open, although with the main buildings, the faculty of letters, there is an attempt at a careful group-

ing and linking of the blocks (fig. 5.19). Soon, this campus became the cradle of student riots and even before that time, while building was in full swing, criticism of the planning methods had set in.

What was called originally the 'campus à l'américaine' began to be dubbed 'campus à la française', a somewhat negative term from the start. A critique arose which has continued to this day: France supplied quantity but not quality (Pierre Merlin). Already by 1963 we read that architectural concepts are 'static and rigid'. Even the ministry's spokesman admitted that something was lacking and one of France's most eminent representatives of 'hard' Modernism, Bernard H. Zehrfuss, mused that the plans tended towards the orthogonal and unoriginal, but nevertheless were of a 'solid harmony which befits the French tradition'. More annoying was the lack of any kind of social facilities, especially shops and, naturally, there were complaints about insufficient links with the town centres. Fundamental was the perceived absence of a 'milieu de vie'. Later analyses point to the persistence of an inflexible International Style zoning and even of the older formalist French custom of axial layouts. One of the critics' principal conclusions was that the 'campus à la française' was a 'pale imitation' of the Anglo-Saxon campus. This coincided with a greater interest in the English New Universities, where everything appeared to be as carefully thought out as in a 'laboratory'. Moreover, English New Universities appeared to be conceived as urban entities – and that included Essex (sic). It would be difficult, however, actually to find direct acknowledgments of English influence.

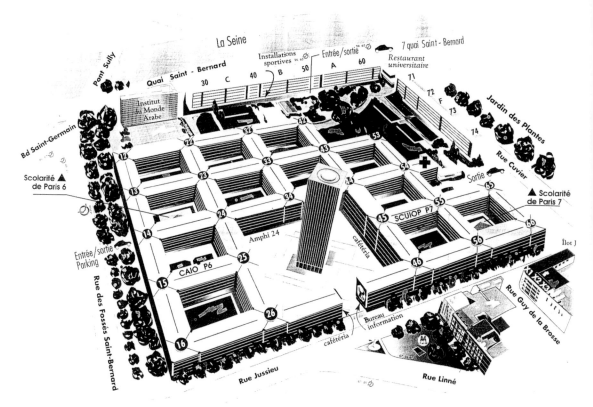

5.21 Université de Paris, Jussieu Science Complex (now the Universités de Paris VI and VII), by Edouard Albert 1963–72 (the long buildings along the river and along the rue Cuvier are part of an earlier project). (Courtesy Université de Paris VII 1996)

As elsewhere, the demand for the 'urban' increased, from about 1963, although it only really came to the fore after 1968. A big impression was made by the project for a new, this time complete, university for Orléans and especially by the lively drawing of its 'forum', perhaps somewhat American in style, complete with a lake, a park, and the distant view of the old cathedral. It also puts much accent on the one prominent building within a French university which carries symbolic weight, the Grand Amphithéatre, the equivalent of the German *auditorium maximum* (fig. 5.20). In contrast to the German tradition the main lecture theatre, or several major ones, are not placed within the great hold-all building of the university but form single exposed structures. Orléans was very much a local initiative, its promoters dubbed it an 'Oxford français', not on account of projected colleges, but because they attempted to create a major university town for the Paris orbit and thereby hoped to transplant some of the Sorbonne's reputation, too. Furthermore, there was the idea of the close link between university and town; yet, Orléans lies four miles outside the old centre, and its close links are with a large new township (la Source). Building progress, however, was far slower than usual.

The one major realisation of a mid-1960s comprehensive architectural project was the Jussieu Science Complex in Paris itself. It is right in the fifth, the university, arrondissement. Its beginnings were highly individual, if not to say irregular. In 1962, the Minister of Culture, André Malraux, no less, and the architect of his choice,

5.22   Paris, Jussieu Complex, view of courts.

Edouard Albert, who, before, had 'seduced the Dean, Marc Zamansky, with his ideas', clubbed together to oust the group of architects who had constructed some buildings on the site earlier on. Jussieu is one of those Modernist buildings which combine apparent ultimate rationality with heavy symbolism. Clearly, its principal value lies in its complete unity and consistency. Malraux and Albert's plan, intended for 40,000 students on just 15 hectares, or 37 acres, consists of a (never quite completed) grid enclosing 4 × 5 rectangular courts (hence also the nickname 'modern Escorial', the 'timeless' epitome of the idea of a large unified complex). There was a new stress on integrating teaching and research and this was to manifest itself in the way in which each of the longer wings of the rectangles was devoted to research and the shorter wings to teaching. Four of the rectangles are thrown into one major court with a tower block in its centre, which is mainly used for administration. Circular staircases and lift towers are placed into all the intersections. All this means that many of the major university facilities, even the 'amphis', are hidden in the basement. According to Dean Zamansky the Campus Jussieu was to 'symbolise the materialisation of scientific thought in the heart of Paris'. Albert had specialised in light-weight steel constructions and he created a highly unified system of thin, concrete-filled steel tubes. The crucial element, however, which was to lead to the 'increasing interaction of the various departments' was 'the assembly of inner connecting cloisters'. Furthermore, the whole of this cloistered groundfloor is open which brings about another astonishing effect: even in the innermost courtyards the ordinary buildings of surrounding streets shine through. We feel embedded in historic Paris, 'close to the precincts of Phillipe Auguste' (Marc Zamansky). To crown this immense effort, Malraux and Albert devised an extremely ambitious collaboration with the artists of the École de Paris,

La cité universitaire

5.23   Paris Université de Nanterre, 'La cité universitaire' student residences, 1966. (J.-P. Duteuil, *Nanterre 1965-66-67-68*, Paris 1988, courtesy J.-P. Duteuil)

including the dying Georges Braque, to decorate the staircases, floors and even the roofs. And yet, independent critics found, at best, lukewarm words for the Jussieu complex. The time for such a grandiose and rigid exercise, whose style, in essence, predated the English and the American campus influence as well as the Zeilenbau phase, seemed past. However, within the context of the major institutional-architectural issue of this book – the comprehensive institutional presence of a university – we can see Jussieu as a major example of the total, 'one-building' concept. The fact that it preceded the 'neutral' grid plan that was to galvanise the attention of young architects soon afterwards, seemed to escape everyone's notice (figs 5.28–5.32). It was Jussieu's extreme formality and the regularity of its detail that was contrary to the taste of the younger designers of the later 1960s (figs 5.21 and 5.22).

The plan for the new university at Amiens of 1967, like Orléans, was for a complete campus. It strenuously avoided rectangularity; multi-angled links reach out from a strong centre to a variety of buildings and sub-centres, a plan that has elements of East Anglia, but would also not be a stranger in a German competition of its date. Candilis and Josic's Faculty of Humanities for Toulouse in the suburb of Le Mirail, from 1966/8, adheres to their entirely novel plan for the Freie Universität Berlin, to be discussed shortly. It goes much further than Amiens in eschewing any grand forms. Ironically, it comes back to the square grid, but not, of course, to a sequence of large rectangles as at Jussieu. It consists rather of an assemblage of diverse small square units. A crucial difference with Berlin consists in the way many of the public areas are not just straight internal corridors but wide open-air platforms or gardens. Both Amiens and Toulouse put high stress on their relationship with the town. Yet their situation hardly differs from that of any large institution which has been located in the suburbs – even though at Le Mirail these contain massive and distinctive public housing blocks by the same architects.

The events of May 1968 were perceived to have turned the French university system inside-out. Because of the concentration of militancy in central Paris, France experienced the university troubles more strongly than any other country. The state responded relatively quickly with reforms which provided, basically, what international student discourse had been demanding for some years: 'participation', the reduction of hierarchies and smaller units of teaching. As regards physical campus planning and architecture, however, 1968 does not mark a very major break. We may see '1968' as merely reinforcing convictions which had been growing at least since 1963. It certainly contributed to the notion that the 'campus à la française' was a failure. It was now held that the incomplete, windswept and somewhat isolated campus at Nanterre had induced close groupings of protest-minded students. As usual in these postulations of causality, there was never ultimate clarity as to whether the environ-ment acted as a principal cause, or as a mere trigger, or catalyst, to bring out funda-mental, socio-political resentments. Or should we believe Alain Touraine that the campus, as such, marked the beginning of protest: 'In its brutality and in the fact that it was so distant from the Quartier Latin, Nanterre was a sign of rupture from the university world of Paris.' (fig. 5.23)

In any case, the 'events' increased the demand for the 'urban'. 'Le modèle français: l'université dans la ville' was the phrase everybody now agreed upon. The architects tried their hardest to apply urbanity in their new creations for a dissolved Sorbonne, partitioned, as it was, into numerous new suburban campuses. Ironically, what had been ridiculed as the 'ordinary' (or worse) suburban surroundings of Nanterre, the architects now had to try and make a virtue of. In the competition for Villetaneuse, in a relatively poor, as well as low-density, area to the north, the team Fainsilber/ Siggurdardottir-Anspach presented the most spectacular plans. They talked fervently about the integration of the campus both with landscaped nature and with an as yet unbuilt 'sufficiently dynamic town', as well as providing a new rapid public transport link to central Paris (fig. 5.24). Very little of this idea was eventually realised. A tour de force of the highest conceivable density was Tolbiac of 1972 (figs 5.26a and b). One half of a hectare ($1\frac{1}{4}$ acres), accommodates a towering structure with several large lecture theatres beneath, with study space and some communal space for 6,700 stu-dents, as well as 400 places for cars. The tops of the souterrainean 'amphis' are covered by open-air theatre-like steps, for the use of the students – probably a hint from Chicago Circle (figs 3.9 and 3.11). None of the massive developments in the capital caught as much international attention as the more gentle forms of another subur-ban 'université pilote', Lyon-Bron (fig. 5.25b), planned from 1969. A multi-angled covered street, constantly narrowing and widening, gives access to all communal facil-ities. The plan is reminiscent simultaneously of East Anglia and Lancaster (figs 2.68, 2.89), though the complete covering of the large central area with a metal and glass roof became much more common in France than in Britain.

All this, however, represented only one half of the new thinking in the wake of later 1960s upheavals. A more profound change was slowly gaining ground, a set of beliefs which doubted the capacity of the planner and designer to influence behav-iour and to determine, or serve, particular functions of a building, beliefs to which we shall come shortly. For many French critics and planners this simply resulted in going back, in fact, in a complete U-turn, to where the French university had come from, to the 'collectivité entière' of the town (Jaqueline Canipel), to the 'tissue de la ville' or more plainly expressed, to a kind of university building which '[is] not treated

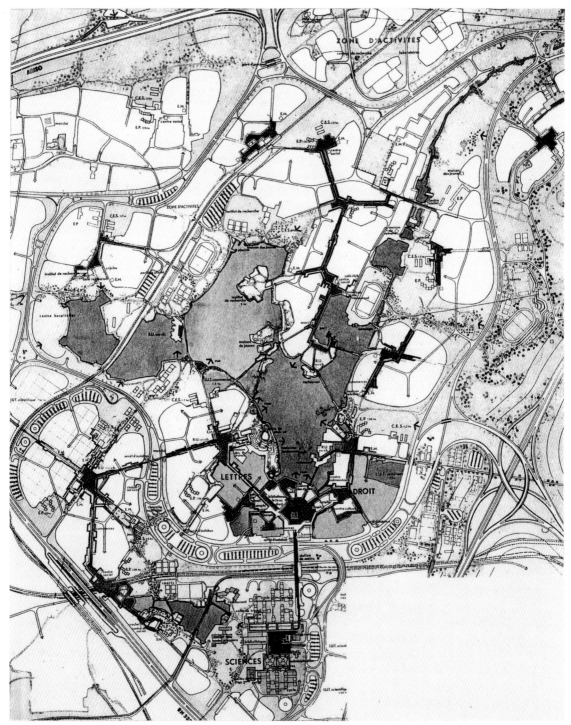

5.24 Université de Paris XIII, Campus de Villetaneuse; competiton design by Adrien Fainsilber and Hogna Siggurdardottir-Anspach, 1967/8. (*Ad'A* no. 137 4/5-1968, pp. 97–101)

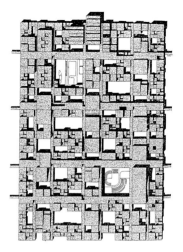

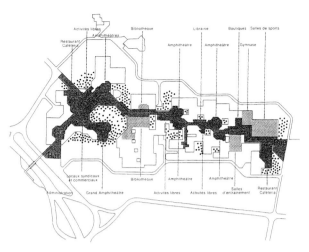

5.25 (a and b) (*above left*) a Université Toulouse Le Mirail, by Georges Candilis and Alexis Josic, from 1966/8, 'plan de masse'. (*Ad'A* no. 137 4/5-1968, p. 58). (*above right*)b. Lyon Bron (Lyon II, Parilly), by Rene Dottelonde and others, from 1969, plan, emphasising 'the street'. (*Arkitekten* 1972, p. 362)

5.26 (a and b) (*left*) a Université de Paris I Panthéon-Sorbonne, 'Tolbiac', 90 rue de Tolbiac, Paris 13e, by Michel Andrault, Pierre Parat, 1972–3. Showing especially the roofs of lecture theatres treated as spaces for open air assembly. The section below, b, shows the underground car parks and other facilities, topped by the lecture theatres, as well as the three towers containing the teaching accommodation. (*Architettura Chronache i Storia*, No. 240 10-1975, pp. 342 and 346)

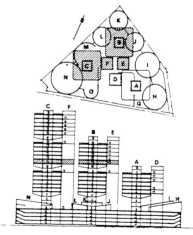

differently from other buildings of the town'. The left-wing philosopher and writer on urban questions and one-time teacher at Nanterre, Henri Lefebvre, wrote of the 'profound spontaneity of the streets, in places which are not occupied by institutions'. The simplest example of the new preferences was of course the Quartier Latin. It was seen as 'un modèle né spontanément', the fruit of 'a mysterious alchemy'. Finally, we might point to one immediate outcome of the 1968 events in Paris, the foundation of two highly experimental institutions, Dauphine and Vincennes – yet neither of them provided new permanent campus buildings, the first being housed in existing buildings, the second in temporary structures.

Returning once more to one of the new suburban universities of Paris, to Créteil, we find the planners at their most serious in their efforts to connect their campus with the surrounding HLMs, even linking across to them via a prominent footbridge. So successful is the intergration that the relatively small campus is far outdone by the spectacular HLMs, the densely grouped, high blocks of dwellings, and, indeed, for any newcomer, it is difficult even to identify. While it is troublesome to define exactly what would be meant by 'urban', the district, with its overall high density, has most decidedly left behind the outer suburban character (fig. 5.27). What should be stressed most in a summing up of the French efforts from the 1950s to the 1970s is probably the seriousenss of, and the continuity in, the Modernist-egalitarian effort. At first, the new university buildings look like blocks of edge-of-town public housing, while later on their planning is integrated with public housing. Thus, it is a kind of utopianism that seems to differ strongly from the Anglo-American one which continued to stress the institutional and architectural distinctiveness and separateness of each university. If, on the other hand, one takes a more purely architectural angle, the French produced, by around 1970, a group of individualised solutions which are hardly inferior to those across the Channel or the Atlantic. However, on the international, especially in the European, scene it was the new urban planning issues which were to gain an ever greater importance. If anywhere, it is here that we find a French contribution to University utopianism.

MEGASTRUCTURAL AND OTHER INDETERMINISMS

By the mid to later 1960s we meet, in the advanced design and critical circles, a vast conglomerate of problematisations. Virtually everything that has been discussed so far was put into question. There was to be the end of the grand gesture, the end of any certainty in planning, and even, for some, the end of the university as a self-contained institution.

The formal and spacial gymnastics in grandiose reinforced concrete were decisively shown the door by a design which was immensely publicised from early 1964 onwards, that of the extension for the Freie Universtät Berlin, by Candilis, Josic and Woods, of Bochum competition fame, with the American Shadrach Woods at the helm. Virtually all the forms described so far have disappeared. Being extremely low rise, basically two storey plus basement, the complex makes absolutely no impact on its indifferent suburban surroundings. There is no major entrance, let alone an entrance front, or any differentiation between a major or a minor side. There is no centre, or central focus. The complex, as originally planned, forms a single rectangle of 14

5.27   Université de Paris XII Val de Marne, Créteil Campus, by D. Sloan, 1972. Part of central elevated area with public housing tower blocks looking in.

hectares, or 34 acres. This is very large if one considers it as one building (it houses parts of the humanities), but not if one thinks of it as a complete and variously subdivided campus. The inside of the Berlin project is, in fact divided up into many small compartments. So far, so simple. But the actual plan is most unusual. We are shown a number of different kinds of plans, not according to floor level, but according to singled-out specific functions: pedestrian circulation, internal courts/green spaces and the rooms as such. When they are superimposed we look at a baffling, and apparently shapeless maze of rectangular elements (fig. 5.28).

With Candilis, Josic and Woods's Berlin plan we enter the sphere of a new kind of abstract planning thinking. When the Berlin building was (partially) completed almost ten years after it had first been published it was only moderately noticed and liked – we shall return to some essential criticisms made by Reyner Banham (see page 286). In the wake of its plans much attention was turned to two other projects devised in the years 1963–6, Marburg an der Lahn and Loughborough. Both showed striking promise but in the end the reality was less inspiring. Like so many others, Marburg felt it had to relocate sciences and medicine entirely outside the town. The building office of the university and the *Land*, Hesse, began by devising a prefabricated building system which promised great flexibility. The way the Marburg designers, in their layout plans, managed to get across the idea that the very large complex of buildings was somehow generated from the small-scale elements of the building system, was impressive (fig. 5.29). The same was true for Loughborough University of Technology which became England's most admired plan after the Seven. It was devised by one of England's most experienced architectural and engineering

DISSOCIATION

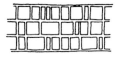

ASSOCIATION

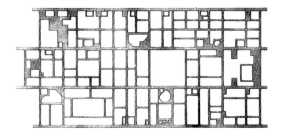

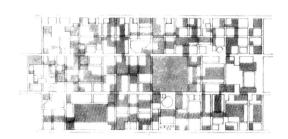

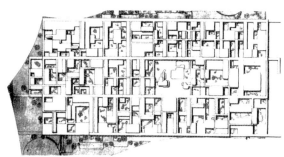

5.28 (West)-Berlin Freie Universität Humanities building, by Candilis, Josic and Woods and Schiedhelm, competiton design 1963. Top: Shadrach Woods: diagram of university socio-dynamics. Plans: top left: pedestrian network; top right: open spaces; bottom left: open spaces and pedestrian network superimposed; bottom right: 'Aerial view of built form'; longitudinal section. (*Architectural Association Journal* vol. 80 no. 883 1-1965, pp. 14–17; *AA* 1967)

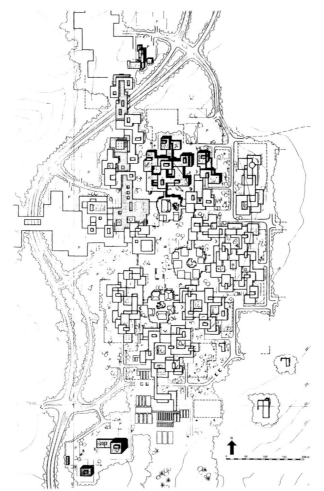

5.29   Phillips Universität Marburg an der Lahn, Lahnberge extensions, design from 1964, by Universitätsbauamt. (*Ad'A* no. 137, 4/5-1968, p. 47, p. 137)

firms, Ove Arup Associates (figs 5.30 and 5.31). Here we find a 15 metre square (50 by 50 feet) constructional net, or grid, into which any conceivable use was to be fitted. Odense University followed with a 'Bandraster', a grid arranged in bands. This, too, appeared very much open-ended; this time it was largely built as intended (fig. 5.32). At Ulm University there is a series of square courts and a complete indoor network of communication while the 1967 competition for Bremen University was virtually dominated by 'net' patterns.

The 'net' or 'mat' principle was fed from three sources. Firstly, the way in which, from about the mid-1950s, the grand regular form was eschewed in favour of a concern for small-scale situations, the places where small groups meet (e.g. by the Smithsons). A 'whole' must now be thought of as an agglomeration, a cluster, of an infinite number of those small places and spaces. The Smithsons took some cues from a number of lesser-known designs by Le Corbusier of the 'mat type,' such as the Roc et Rob project. Candilis, Josic and Woods, disciples of Le Corbusier's, took all this on board at the same time as the Smithsons. The second ideal, emerging in the late 1950s, mainly in Japan

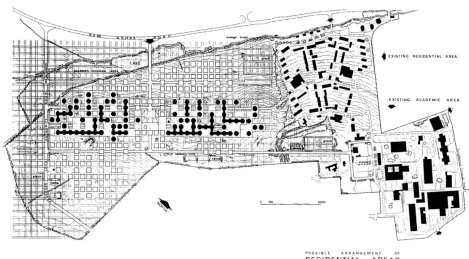

POSSIBLE ARRANGEMENT OF
RESIDENTIAL AREAS
WITHIN THE MASTER GRID

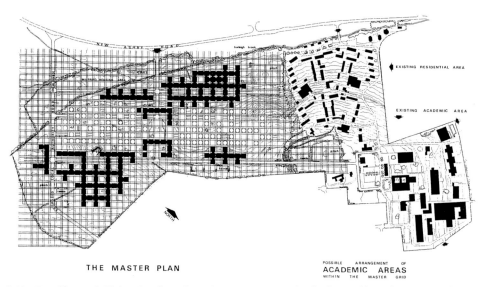

THE MASTER PLAN

POSSIBLE ARRANGEMENT OF
ACADEMIC AREAS
WITHIN THE MASTER GRID

5.30 Loughborough University, plans. (Arup Associates, *Master Plan for the Loughborough University of Technology*, 1966)

and England, was the concept of the megastructure. It was basically meant for whole new towns, but could be applied to all large types of building requiring a complex amount of organisation. There is often a grandiosity about the structures and an avant-garde science-fiction look and there has been much debate about the degree of seriousness, or otherwise, of the drawings of the Archigram or Metabolist groups. Large educational institutions have what the megastructurists loved: a multiplicity of functions. Rather than squeezing these diverse functions into a close and neatly outlined whole, 'megastructures' emphasise the amalgam of the most diverse shapes. In a general sense, many of the new universities of the 1960s, such as Essex or East Anglia, Scarborough and Simon Fraser, or many of the entries for the Bochum competition could already be called megastructures. In a narrower sense, the megastructure dreams of the

272

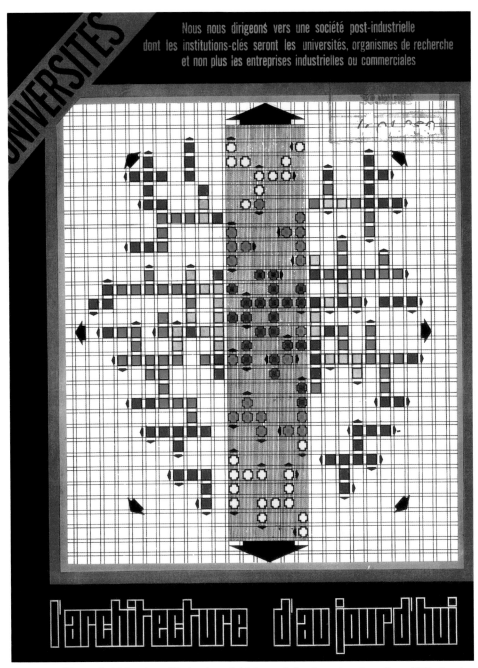

5.31   Loughborough University of Technology (additions to), by Arup Associates from 1966, showing micro and macro extensions. (*Ad'A* no. 137, 4/5-1968, cover)

1960s evolved around the notion of giant permanent infrastructures with interchangeable temporary excrescences, something which then moved on to the High-Tech movement of the 1970s, of the Paris Pompidou Centre kind.

One may thus be surprised to be told that Candilis, Josic and Woods's Berlin university was the 'nearest thing' thus far to a built megastructure. It does not look 'mega',

273

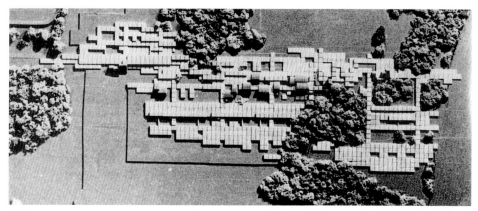

5.32   Odense Universitet, by Knud Holscher (Bureau Krohn and Hartvig, Rasmussen), from 1966. (*Ad'A* no. 137, 4/5-1968, p. 67)

nor does it show very diverse features, and yet Banham tries to justify the label by pointing out its qualities of extendibility, the way it seemingly incorporates parts which are more and parts which are less permanent, and, finally, its 'modularity'. The latter term brings us to the third source of indeterminism: a new concept of planning altogether. The Berlin building was not, in fact, meant as a work of 'architecture', but as a 'framework', as an 'Ordnungsprinzip', a 'method into which the university can develop'. From the megastructure movement we now move on to a core issue with the architectural and planning profession, or rather with a new theoretical faction of that movement.

A combination of factors had led to the new trend. In postwar Europe the planners of towns and large housing estates had acquired an unprecedented professional power. It was linked to a conviction of the scientific solvability of society's problems. We noted in the USA the ever-growing expertise of student personnel services and their scientific backers. We saw the way in which in England the Robbins Report of 1963 demanded and undertook an investigation of a hitherto unknown systematicity. In Germany policy makers like Schelsky demanded a new 'theoretische Universität' as well as the coordination of all higher education into the 'Gesamtuniversität'. There was a requirement for greater cooperation all-round. At the same time, each group involved claimed its territory, its own scientific specialism. In 1974 Peter Jokusch, in the forefront of Germany's university planning science, maintained that there was a great need for more full-time planners. All major countries maintained central planning and architectural research organisations, such as the New York based Educational Facilities Laboratories. In England RMJM, backed by one of their clients, Eric James, tried to make a start by demanding the pooling of research during 1964, without much direct success, but soon afterwards the architectural schools of Cambridge and London University began to conduct much sustained research. Probably Germany's research institutions (see page 222) were the most powerful because of the close state involvement with the whole building process.

On the face of it, the 'planning' of university buildings should be something quite straightforward. True, there are a vast number of details, but once they are put into the right order, so to speak, a complete and well-functioning whole should emerge.

The 'whole' would mean precisely that: 'completeness', maximal and optimal use, and 'not bits and pieces', to quote again the defenders of the vast and complex Bochum plan. The architect's or planner's main task was to translate the requirements as stated by the academics and administrators into 'space requirements'. The Americans had progressed considerably in this field, by considering the diversity of students' activities, and devising 'optimal space use studies'. There was early talk of simulating planning processes on the computer. The conviction that solutions come about logically was crucial: 'The Campus grows by logical building increments' (Dober). At Bochum, the director of planning, Fridolin Hallauer, maintained: 'The analysis of the programme gave us 472,000 square metre requirements. The design of the university is a logical result from this.' It is, further, based on the 'Strukturprogramm [i.e. the plan of the academic divisions], traffic movements, topography and the building components'. Now there appeared essentially only two types of buildings, stackable ones and non-stackable ones. In Cambridge Bullock, Dickens and Steadman arrived, by 1968, at even more precise calculations as to what students did where and when. The Germans tried to refine the various stages of the planning process by devising further terms such as 'Leitplanung' (directional (overall) planning) and 'Bedarfsplanung' (planning for use). A further shift in procedure was the demand for what the Germans coined 'Musterprogramme' or 'Richtwerte', model programmes and guiding figures. Architects maintained that the planning of a university building should no longer be a matter of listening to the individual client, because what physics professor Y wants tomorrow might be totally different from what physics professor X wants today. Instead, demanded Ferdinand Kramer at Frankfurt, when devising buildings for science, one ought to develop generally valid criteria.

A crucial new shift, however, was the increased stress on the links between functions, a new interest in circulation and its differentiation, in 'connectivity'. This meant a reduction in the attention given to all that was merely stationary, to the individual functions themselves. The greater togetherness demanded by the educationalists and academics in England led the architects to study much more intensively the nature of interaction between departments. The Leeds plan of 1960 was the first to investigate quantitatively all contacts, all movements, between all parts of the campus and the architects' extraordinarily complex diagram was often reproduced (fig. 2.31). Candilis, Josic and Woods's Bochum design of late 1962 [5.10] and the English 'urban' plans of 1963 led the way to a kind of 'plan' in which one can discern the lines of communication, but in which it is hard to make out individual zones or functions as they all appear completely interwoven. Megastructural planners followed in this line.

All this turned out to be a prelude to more fundamental shifts of opinion. On the one hand, the complexity of methods grew apace, on the other hand, doubts arose as to the aims and the capacities of planning as a whole. The planners thus found themselves in a paradoxical situation where they wanted to appear to know both more, and less. A number of new outside pressures bore on the planners, too. After the mid-1960s the British government had to hold back on finance and a new climate of uncertainty arose. There was no longer, in Britain, a prospect of many more new campuses. Further expansion had to be piecemeal. In Germany and many other countries there was the continuous demand to step up, and to cheapen output.

Two new and related ways of thinking emerged: 'change' and 'indeterminism'. To put it at its bluntest, a building cannot really be planned at all: 'the built forms do not, in fact, control the activities within them' (Michael Brawne). The hospital planner John Weeks had postulated his idea of 'indeterminacy' as early as 1960. By 1968 several theorists turned against what appeared the earlier 'commitment or "fix" of the building, [that] was the fabric itself, inert . . .' (Michael Cassidy). It was 'change' which preoccupied the planners' minds. While in the period of early and Classic Modernism 'change' was chiefly a utopian or reformist platform, something that seemed urgently needed, now change was felt more as something that happened anyway, and happened ever more rapidly. The German architect whom we cited earlier on university planning, Peter Jokusch, put it most clearly: 'Functional obsolescence usually predates physical obsolescence', and: 'this conflict is getting more and more serious'. All the factors which were earlier listed as relevant for the planner to analyse and find forms for, such as the structure of teaching, technical equipment, density, town–gown relations, to name only a few, all these were now considered factors of uncertainty. Other typical formulations of the direction planning theory was taking were from 'static master plan' to 'evolutionary plan', or perhaps, most drastically, Linde's: from 'recipe' to 'problem'. Planners and architects wanted to hive themselves up to a higher plane of scientificness, using terminology from social sciences and management sciences, they aspired to a practice of 'systemreine Planung', that is, planning purified of the accidental and the pragmatic. Terms such as 'systems analysis' or 'operational research and design' came into currency, i.e. the use of 'mathematical and computable models' which can, firstly, predict, and then accommodate projected changes into their calculations. The new kind of planning, finally, greatly increased the flood of diagrammatic drawings, of schemata of the decision-making processes as well as drawings showing categories of linking and growing. The visual presentation of planning had moved a long way beyond the traditional 'plan of a building'.

Even 'social space' became a problematic issue. We noted a fundamental change in the understanding of the institution from one that was expected to induce certain predetermined kinds of social modes to one which should principally encourage spontaneous social behaviour. We noted further the way in which sociologists, when asked for advice in these matters by architects, now maintained that they had not, as yet, done enough research. Planners adopted an attitude of indeterminism here, too: proximity, we hear, does not necessarily lead to intensified socialisation. Hence, interest for a central gathering space, for the forum or agora, waned. Candilis' Berlin most decidedly did not show such a centre and Konstanz put much stress on its small, dispersed rest areas. 'No part of the university is devoted exclusively to social purposes; on the other hand, there is no area in the university which could not be considered as a social space'.

It was part of the comprehensiveness of the new planning movement to take in construction as well. The old view was to first devise a plan of a building and then to devise the construction accordingly. Now the two were seen as interdependent from the very start. This notion had a good pedigree in British Welfare State school architecture and the use of Clasp at York had been a major talking point. Subsequently German universities erected many large teaching blocks out of prefabricated elements. The new concept of construction at the end of the 1960s was not one of the complete determination of all the elements of a building, but the creation of a flexible framework of 'modules' or 'grids', with room for the desired variety and flexibility of infilling. Frameworks could be in metal, such as the 'Raumgitter'/space-frame proposal for Bochum by Eckhard Schultze-Fielitz (fig. 5.11), or, more universally, in pre-cast re-inforced concrete, of which Loughborough was the most often cited example. Now construction, that is the framework, is basic; 'planning' concerns the detailed and varied infilling. Soon, planners would add to this a generalised notion of the services as equally, if not more important than the construction, in the 'performance' of a building.

The greatest problem for this new thinking was to combine the idea of unplannability with the notion of 'planning for growth'. The old way in campus planning, was simply to leave space around each building in its 'zoned' area. Altogether, international Modernist low density layouts now appeared simplistic. Considerations of growth must begin with a careful analysis of the existing whole and the formulation of the general principles of change. According to Weeks, it was the communication pattern of an institution that directed the possibilities of growth. An intense concern set in for the classification of all plans, with a strong trend towards abstraction, accompanied by ever varied kinds of schematic drawings. The most influential model on the whole was probably the Lancaster/Bath model, which allowed two kinds of extension, major ones lengthwise, at the 'ends', and minor ones on the sides. The major alternative was the Loughborough kind of grid which could be extended equally in all directions. There were many metaphors used, the most common being 'spine'; it could be straight as Bath, or 'cranked', even to a painful 90 per cent, as at Konstanz. At Essex the method of extendibility was likened to pushing along the 'meat inside a sausage' (John Jordan). (Frontispiece)

As far as the majority of campuses were concerned, their planning for expansion was not so clearly conceptualised. Sometimes their clients and designers took advantage of the new indeterminism, when they met criticism of their early lack of planning methods, by declaring either that there cannot be a plan (Lasdun at East Anglia), or that planning is pointless (Kent). Thus the new systematic concern for growth frequently led architects' interests back to the brave plans of the Seven; and yet, the new mistrust of any concept of completeness made the Seven appear old-fashioned, even while they were still being built. We noted the way in which much blame was laid on Essex and other new campuses when they turned out to function well for the student troublemakers in a way that was completely unforeseen.

The new frame of mind finally stretched to a denial of 'architecture' overall. Propositions voiced from time to time under Modernist 'Functionalism', for instance under Hannes Meyer at the Bauhaus in 1928–30 began to be repeated, with phrases such as, 'architecture free from the constraints of aesthetics . . .'. (John Weeks 1969) and 'The quality of buildings is no longer only judged through architectural criteria but more and more according to those of utility.' Others claimed that the concern with the plan, as such, has nothing to do with 'form', or with architecture as an 'artistic element'. But there were yet more extreme positions vis-à-vis not only 'architecture', but the whole university institution. The university was now seen not as a building but as a 'teaching and learning system' (Günther Feuerstein). There was much fascination with 'learning machines', tv and others; 'the "university" in those terms could exist without a clearly defined physical structure; its campus would be invisible within a community'. Here, indeed, we must add our last 'campus', Cedric Price's Potteries Thinkbelt. It was entirely the product of an architect's imagination (Price was close

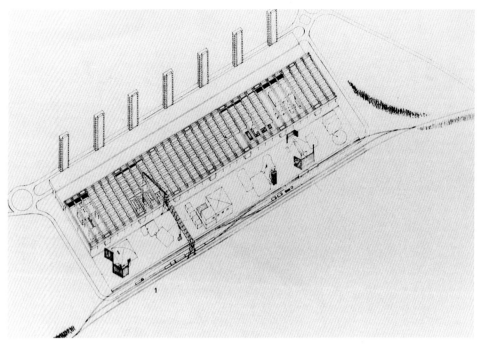

5.33 Potteries Thinkbelt project: by Cedric Price. 'A plan for an advanced educational industry' in North Staffordshire. Parts of the educational facilities travel to students' homes, instead of students coming to the institution. (*AD* 10-1966, p. 488)

to the Archigram circle): 'a plan for an advanced educational industry in North Staffordshire'. The New Universities so far were merely 'a service run by gentlemen for the few'; what was needed was something that really served a whole region, by actually bringing teaching facilities to its users, that is, by moving around mobile teaching facilities by rail or road through a large urbanised area (fig. 5.33). A somewhat similar proposal for a mobile university was found in a Bremen competition entry of 1967, by Rathke, Szabo and Behrendt. Finally, one might state that perhaps the only really new university was the Open University, founded in 1970, and its German descendant, the Fernuniversität, of 1980.

Sometimes the designers paraded complete scepticism about the whole process. 'There is no body of tested or expert knowledge on university planning', one of the main theorists admitted in 1974. It was a statement that logically followed from indeterminism, but it somehow sounded strange after so much research had just been done. Challenged by the sociologist Martin Trow, who asked why old buildings are best in creating spontaneous academic meeting spaces, Robert Anderson of John Andrews Architects (of Scarborough fame) admitted meekly: 'we really don't know what we are doing about the design of space at all'. On the other hand, all this was part of a much more pervasive weariness, part of a growing condemnation of Modernism and a turning away from what now appeared as its technologist/constructional determinism. Like most architectural movements, even the seemingly most profoundly committed and the most theoretically based, 'indeterminism' came to an end, too; but this lies beyond the scope if this book.

There was, finally, yet another version of the non-institution, non-plan university: the university embedded into the town. This was an almost entirely new issue of the

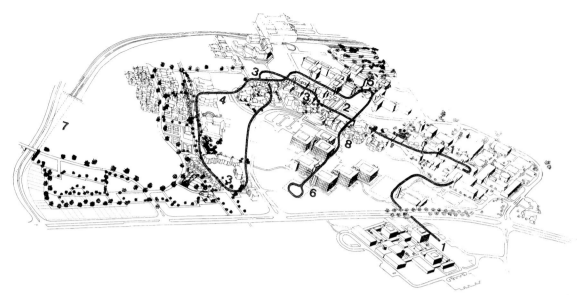

5.34   Université Louvain la Neuve at Woluwe-St Lambert (Brussels), by Groupe Urbanisme et Architecture: 'Perspective with promenade through the pedestrianised streets'. 1   applied sciences, 2   place des sciences, library, science administration, 'le "pub"', and university restaurants, 3   dwellings and commerce, 4   Ecole de Bierau, 5   chemistry, geology, geography, 6   biology, 7   railway tunnel, 8   computer centre. (*Techniques et Architecture* 11-1973 pp. 56–7)

1960s. Everybody was aware of traditional Oxbridge and its 'town-gown' relationship – largely an euphemism for a non-relationship. By the late 1960s universities could see themselves literally as an urban 'Experimentierfeld' (H. J. Aminde). We have followed in great detail the way in which a number of campuses professed to take up 'urban' elements, or argued that they actually had created 'towns', such as Essex, Chicago Circle or even Bochum. Planners of some of the new out-of-town campuses, such as Regensburg, tried desperately to prove that they were close to the old town centre and somehow integrated with it. But there were early demands, for instance at the general German Students' Meeting of 1962, that the university should not be at all a closed complex, but entirely open to the institutions of the town. By the late 1960s, many planners and policy makers valued town-integrated universities higher than out of town campuses. There was clearly a unison between the notion of the unplannability of the university and the new oppositional town planning, of the Jane Jacobs type, which also maintained the unplannability of a good town. Many analysts of student residence patterns now saw 'digs' or the 'Bude' as socially the most desirable solution. Among the many urban campuses where planners took special care to re-integrate them with the town centres one could cite, again Leeds, the Scottish urban universities, such as Strathclyde University in Glasgow, RMJM's Edinburgh University reorganisation, the 'Manchester Education Precinct' plan, and, by the late 1960s, most of the newly constituted English Polytechnics. There were, furthermore, many entirely new town centre projects, such as the proposal for a new university at Hamburg-Harburg, planned to be built across the S-Bahn station. The strong French manifestations of this trend have already been cited. One of its best-known examples Louvain la Neuve near Brussels was built as, or like, actual pieces of infill in a town (fig. 5.34). We might, finally, cite, once again, the way in which the very highest praise for some of the English New Universities was to be reminded, not of the Oxbridge College, but of Oxford as an integrated 'university town'.

5.35   University of Warwick: Whitefields student residences, by Goodman and Short 1972–3. Each house contains twelve single study bedrooms and a communal kitchen and bathroom.

As the very last consideration we must introduce yet another style of building, restricted, it appears, to England – though one might cite Santa Cruz Colleges 1–4 (figs. 1.26 and 1.27): the design of student residences like small houses. It was probably Surrey University which made a start with the steeply-roofed blocks by Maguire and Murray: 'a most original alternative to Oxbridge'. Warwick then provided several versions of the type, including the tiny 'Whitefields' houses (fig. 5.35). Even Essex considered a 'village style low-level plan' of residences – but this piece of news only reached the local newspaper. These houses, of course, follow trends in town planning, too, but this time it was hardly 'town' planning, but suburban planning. The final consideration is that one could hardly think of a more decisive break with the architectural, and by implication, institutional unity of the campus, not only of the new 'urban' campus of the 1960s, but the traditional campus and college as a whole.

UTOPIAN RHETORIC AND ITS RECIPIENTS

We may take rhetoric as a condition of man's survival in society.
(J. Kopperschmidt 2000)

LANGUAGES OF IMPORTANCE

At the end of the introduction there was a preliminary attempt to tackle the issue of value, as such, to take stock of values and to address the epistemological issue of the standpoint of the author vis-à-vis the values held by the protagonists of this story. The proper historical procedure seemed to be to keep a distance by bringing in value judgments only as quotes; in other words, there was an attempt to adhere to the principles of authenticity and objectivity. However, the chief characterisation of the historical episode described in this book, as an example of utopianism, was the very way it appeared so heavily value-laden overall, and the way it constantly enunciated totality. At the end of the story, the historian has to acknowledge that it was this preconception which guided the selection of quotes. The whole story was grouped around the evidence of high aspirations, whether in words or in the special efforts taken to devise an institution or a design. As well as the actual contents of the aspirations, it was the high pitch of their formulation to which the book wanted to draw attention. All this can, of course, be summed up very bluntly: what this story amounted to was just so much rhetoric.

The term rhetoric, however, lands us with a further epistemological problem. It was emphatically not used by our main protagonists. During most of the nineteenth and twentieth centuries rhetoric had largely negative connotations; at best it was held to be something superfluous. Our protagonists thought of themselves as dealing with secure facts and honest, strong and necessary convictions and did not therefore feel that this would come under the heading 'rhetoric'. The term rhetoric was, however, used by the detractors of our protagonists, cautiously in the early 1960s and more forcefully later on. To sociologists or philosophers like Habermas or Touraine, and later on to the student protest leaders, the pronouncements of virtually all the educationalists, university founders and reformers were classified as rhetoric, and that decidedly in the pejorative sense of the word. This may seem to put severely into doubt the whole of the motivation behind the efforts reported here. Where does the historian stand at that point? Does one have to admit, that after the strenuous effort to present things dispassionately, one ends up with a negative assessment overall? In the section on the English '1968' such a position was circumvented by analysing the actual course of the debates presented by the detractors, by the critics. In the end, it was found that the detractors' days came, and went, too. Even their language was subject to change. This final chapter presents a further attempt at this procedure which aims to relativise the languages of importance, this time using the term rhetoric openly. Post-Modern considerations have largely reinstituted traditional 'rhetoric', or at least they have eliminated the Romanticist and Modernist negative assessment of it. Moreover, Post-Modern analysis has established that in spite of the adversity to rhetoric, many of the twentieth-century Modernist pronouncements on architecture and institutions did form part of the rhetorical tradition. Ostensibly, rhetoric is concerned with the out-of-the-ordinary, yet, at the same time rhetoric is something quite normal. The difference in the old days, in the period pre-1965–70, was that rhetoric, almost by definition, remained the preserve of the privileged, and it was this status which ultimately gave it absolute authority. The rest, and that included the students in a university, were there just as its recipients.

Another term which has been loosely employed so far was 'discourse'. In this context rhetoric and discourse can be seen as closely related. Discourse deals with the way any kind of statement, rhetoric included, is related to the professional aspirations, or the position in the wider networks of society, of those who pronounce it. A pervasive issue in university planning was the construction of the contrast mundane-honorific. 'Rhetoric' deals specifically with the latter, with the value-laden aspects of pronouncements. It can be taken simply as the language of praise. Discourse includes considerations about the mundane as well. A consideration of discourse as the totality of pronouncements will reflect on the changes in the relationship of honorific and mundane commentaries. Rhetoric and discourse are thus taken as subjects in themselves, as well as aides in the explanation of values, especially of the ways in which values are liable to change. Although rhetoric is commonly characterised as a kind of speech that keeps repeating old tropes, it also entails a constant repositioning of those tropes.

Naturally, those most interested in keeping up the praise were the founders of the new institutions, the vice chancellors and their circle of senior academics and educationalists, invariably Oxbridge or public-school oriented. Many of the postwar protagonists, such as Lindsay, Moberly and Niblett had a strong Christian background. Their extensive deliberations, within, for instance the University Teacher's Group, were devoted, not to any specific academic content, nor to any technicalities of the running, or the founding, of universities, nor even much to actual teaching methods, but were kept on a generalised level throughout. As the Oxford historian Marjorie Reeves once concluded: 'One of the assertions made in various ways in this book is that "meaning" in academic studies cannot be separated from the meaning of life as a whole and that academic vitality stems . . . from the total human experience'. Or: 'What is higher education for? My own tentative answer would be that its purpose is to understand the needs of the community today and help to meet them.' Such convictions may seem at first – especially in the way they use one of the oldest rhetorical tricks, that of understatement – a far cry from the German way of citing nothing but the very highest values, such as Karl Jaspers and his 'truth', or Clark Kerr's frequent evocation of the American nation, but some of the terms, such as 'total', indicate much the same essentialism.

Soon, another group of discussants, another discourse, emerged, in the reporting about universities in the press. In the chapter on 1968 we noted that until about 1963–4 newspapers did not possess their own critical mode of writing about the New Universities and gullibly took on what the university spokespersons held forth. But by 1965–6 journalists, such as Stuart Maclure, had developed their own expertise and, as was to be expected, because of the nature and the tone of their publications generally, be it *The Observer*, or *The Listener*, the journalists' language was not nearly as praiseful as that of the university founders and the professional academics. During the subsequent years of trouble most newspapers were no longer on the side of the New Universities. During the same years, 1963–4, a third faction arose in Britain, that of the academic researcher of all issues of higher education, in particular sociological ones. Their cool, detached language differed strongly from the polemics of the newspapers, as well as from the statements of faith by the founders. In Germany, academic sociologists, like Schelsky, tried hard to render all discourses more 'scientific', those in, as well as on, the universities. Welcomed at first, in fact, initiated by the academic world, the new research also soon began to cast doubt on the older kind of academic rhetoric. By 1964 the sociologist Peter Marris commented: 'Outside senior common rooms . . . the institutions are . . . incoherent, the sociologist who studies them is forced to devise his own conception of their purpose'. Marris's concept of the university is then formulated very much more modestly as 'the growth of understanding', and his book is entitled *The Experience of Higher Education* by which he largely means that of the recipients, the students, an issue to which we shall come shortly.

All this had the effect that, by 1963–5, the unity of university values appeared split and some vice chancellors, although not necessarily abandoning the old methods of rhetoric, tried to maximise emphasis on the 'new'. While Templeman at Kent was still insisting on 'elite' training, Sloman at Essex kept on about large size and outright Modernity. Carter at Lancaster did, too, but here we note a further change in the style of the pronouncements – we remember his quip 'I don't have the advantage of being an Oxford philosopher'. Although a closer analysis of the actual content of Carter's pronouncements reveals that his basic values, such as 'community', remained close to the Oxbridge ethos, it was the tone of his press releases that seemed new and entirely un-pompous. It was thus the development of the style of the pronouncements which drove forward the development of the notion of the university and which could help to strengthen, individually, a new institution and determine its image for a long time.

The chief difference between England and the USA was the way in which in the latter country a great diversity of disourses existed side by side, whereas in the former they appeared in succession, a situation which called for a more diachronic treatment in England and a more synchronic treatment in the USA. The much-vaunted unity of discourse in England arose from the way in which it had become embedded into the pronouncements of the Welfare State. That discourse, in turn, was institution-creating par excellence. It entailed, furthermore, a firm hierarchy amongst the pronouncements, between those of the specialist 'technicians' and their quasi-neutral specialist languages and the heightened tone of a moralist and even emotional language. When, however, the main beliefs in England were shattered, this affected most protagonists, while in the USA the situation remained more diffuse, and also more open throughout. In Germany discourse and rhetoric were highly unified throughout by one word, *Reform*. It appeared at times that the rhetorical power of that word, or rather, the power the protagonists tried to endow it with, helped to prevent actual change taking place.

The architectural profession's verbal rhetoric cannot match the academics' rhetoric in profundity; on the other hand, architects have a very long tradition of 'art' discourse behind them, and that means they know how to formulate, and how to vary the formulation of praise. The issue of verbal rhetoric in architecture is, of course, a tricky one. First of all, we meet again the Modernists' dilemma, the way in which some architectural elements of Modernism have been called rhetoric by their detractors, while the Modernists themselves did not apply the term to their own pronouncements. We must return, in this context, to the way in which so many architects in England and elsewhere had associated themselves with the power of Welfare State discourses. We cited in detail the English profession's social-architectural 'onslaught' of 1957/8, the clever rhetoric in the launch of their professional platform in the planning of new campuses. In this process architects also adopted a strong division between the mundane technical discourses, pronounced, typically, by the *Architects' Journal* – and the sociological-aesthetic discourses, taken care of by its sister journal, the *Architectural Review*. Town planners, too, divided their attention between 'technical objectives' and 'social goals'. In that context we cited the *Canadian Architect* of 1962, drawing a strong contrast between 'the stylistic gymnastics of artist-architects South of the border' and the way the British evolved 'prototypes of social forms' – remarks made at a time when Canada had begun designing its spectacular new universities. The journal concludes with a demand for a synthesis of 'these basically opposing philosophies'. The pages in the journal which follow are, in fact, mainly devoted to Lasdun, as somebody who did appear to combine social concern with an insistence on artistic individuality. To accompany one's work with statements on generalised social values, often in the style of a 'manifesto' (as opposed to simply praising the overall qualities of a particular building) had become virtually a must for the architect in twentieth-century Modernism – quite in contrast to the way most of the masters of the late nineteenth century completely eschewed public pronouncements. The importance of adopting a high degree of rhetoric was driven home by the fact that those of the Seven – Warwick and Kent – which, for a number of reasons, largely avoided an institutional-architectural rhetoric, appeared, in the end, least successful with their architecture overall.

Our very brief outline of the definition of rhetoric in 'social architecture' thus largely runs parallel with the old Vitruvian definition of architecture, as 'practical and . . .', as function plus aesthetics, whereby the actual 'position' of the aesthetic value varied strongly. Sometimes it was purposely underemphasised, sometimes it went without saying, sometimes beauty was emphasised as one of the factors that could contribute to the fulfilment of the social aims. York's and Sussex's pronouncements provided, at first sight, a strong contrast. 'Beauty . . . the level of aesthetic appreciation usually marks the standard of achievement of a civilisation': with this kind of statement Spence represented an older tradition of architectural aesthetics, that of added ornament, which is then declared to stand for the honorific side of the institution. We remember, too, in this context, the ways in which at Konstanz the plan and structure of the buildings were considered something purely utilitarian, to which fine art had to be added. At York words like beauty are hardly found in the otherwise exceptionally lengthy pronouncements. Emphasis was on a thorough dovetailing of plan and educational purpose, and the retreat of the traditional architectural 'ego' behind the requirements of the institution, although a purely aesthetic issue, the colour of the concrete, did remain.

Quite in contrast, the architect at East Anglia, Denys Lasdun, ceaselessly promoted himself as designer, and even, during the early years, as the chief spokesperson for the whole undertaking. The 'architect as briefmaker's' most often repeated statement was that about the client not knowing what s/he wanted, but in the end accepting the architect's solution as the one s/he 'had always wanted'. Like Le Corbusier, Lasdun was a compulsory rhetorician; as his vice chancellor reminds us, he 'was marvellous at exposition'. Lasdun 'talks with great conviction and passion of the things he really believes in' (*The Times*), although other judgments were not quite so favourable: 'Patrons and committees manage to swallow the polemical idealism whole, only to find the concrete artifact somewhat indigestive.' Some of Lasdun's expressions were of a novel kind, where he was indebted to the Smithsons and to the American town planning writer Kevin Lynch (fig. 2.29). Buildings and their functions are not considered in a contemplative mood (as in the case of Spence), but actively and dynamically. Metaphors abound, taken from physics and biology, such as 'nucleus', 'spine', or 'circuit', others are topological-geographical, or geological, such as 'concentration', 'linkage', 'strata', 'cascading', 'landlocked harbour'. On occasions Lasdun simply tries to heighten the mundane with statements such as: on the walkways 'every moment of walking is a moment of thinking'. What his pronouncements do not contain is older terms, such as 'beauty' or 'monumental'. It was Lasdun who had no time for 'art', in the sense of beautifying the architecture and landscape, say, with sculptures. Lasdun did not worry unduly about the colour of his concrete either. It is uniformly grey and bleak when it rains. The way in which Lasdun managed to square the apparent priority given to the users and the new notion of spontaneous behaviour with the prioritising of himself, as the designer, must be called a major feat of rhetoric (of course, Lasdun did not use that word itself). Finally, more than any of the other architects, Lasdun made use of the visual rhetoric of photography and models, and, indeed, of carefully staged photographs of the models, publicising the latter even at a time when much of the structure had been built! In fact, the critics' most enthusiastic judgments of East Anglia occurred at the stage of the early models.

The situation at Essex, with regard to verbal architectural rhetoric, was far less impressive. Usually placing himself behind Sloman, Capon spoke little in public; when he did, he sounded much more uncompromising than Lasdun, which did not go down well in the surge of anti-Modernism in the late 1960s (of course, Lasdun suffered from that trend, too). At Lancaster, Carter and Epstein decided to forego the architectural rhetoric of Lasdun, and even that of York's designers, which was noted most positively by some critics of around 1970 but, again, one might claim, that this procedure was responsible also for a lack of architectural recognition later on.

We have so far treated the pronouncements of architects about their own designs and the texts of architectural critics as one and the same discourse. Indeed, in many cases the critics simply repeated what the designers had put out for them. In the context of Welfare State public building campaigns there seemed to be no real reason for the critic not to adopt the architect's stance of enthusiasm, at least in general terms. The journals, especially the *Architectural Review*, saw themselves as launchpads for new phases of architectural activity, as with university design in 1957/8. In 1963 Lionel Brett had a profound admiration for Lasdun's models and used some of

Lasdun's metaphors. And yet, criticism, by its very definition, could not leave it at that, it could not stand still. Brett duly goes on in his short piece on East Anglia by stating: '. . . a great cathedral. But will the monument then be what people want? This is the question that hangs over this deeply felt and imaginative concept.' The journal, which a few years before had admonished architects to intensify their design efforts and begged clients to become, or remain sympathetic, now indicates that a lack of design might, in the end be an advantage. Brett concludes on East Anglia: 'It would be ironical if the vaguely disposed campus universities were found, because of their very imprecision, to have a higher survival value.' Critics were, of course, deemed to have a particular sensitivity for the course of time and were almost compelled to a kind of short-termism which could articulate a strong distance from events that occurred barely ten years previously. 'The boom years of the sixites', or 'the atmosphere of the mid-sixties . . . [is] almost impossible to recapture', we read in the mid-1970s. It could thus occur that the 'turning time' for criticism arrived when the campus was not even completed. What lay at the heart of the problem was one of Modernism's most basic dilemmas, the clash between its universalist claims and its sense of up-to-dateness.

Continuous change and indeterminsm were, as we saw, the watchwords of some planners and commentators from the mid-1960s. They purged the critics' language, say that of Reyner Banham, of most essentialisms. In this context, 'rhetoric' re-entered the vocabulary and was used to criticise pronouncements as well as buildings. In 1968 RMJM defended the 'lack of focus' of their preliminary structures at Stirling by referring to the 'surfeit of rhetorical gestures' of some of the new universities' – there was then no need to give any names. The Essex concept as a whole was chided by Conrad Jameson in 1972 as 'dressed in the rhetoric of libertarian values', while remaining 'authoritarian'. Among the plans of the years 1964–6 which excited the profession most was Candilis, Josic and Woods's Freie Universität Berlin, which was understood as 'making places for people, not . . . rhetorical gestures'. In particular, the 'rhetorical gesture' of height was to be completely avoided. However, in one of his more acidic reviews, of the partially completed building, Banham condemned Berlin's attempts to avoid rhetoric as failed and claimed that the building does not 'say anything at all', and yet he concluded that, in the end, the building's social ambitions were still rhetorical, as was, for Banham, the new general 'Big Metaphor, The City', i.e. the much-vaunted value of the 'urban'.

It was the general Welfare State consensus, combined with a long, unbroken tradition of elaborate professional architectural-cultural discourses which had helped to bring about the 1950s and 1960s English architectural-institutional rhetoric and provided it with an audience. The participants within this discourse were relatively free to voice strong opinions and provoke clashes of judgment. A somewhat comparable situation arose in Canada, but it was much less the case in the USA. Here there was less of a homogeneous socio-architecturally-minded audience, and architectural criticism on the whole appeared more cautious. Provocative rhetorical voices, such as Walter Netsch's or Oscar Newman's, remained relatively isolated. In Germany architectural discussion remained, by and large, more technical and homogenous – although the case of Bochum, its praise and its early rejection, did provide parallels with England.

The reduction of paternalism in educational discourses, the descent from the old high rhetoric of 'beauty' of the Spence kind (as well as the newer one of the Lasdun kind), the new apparent designer modesty as well as the new planning 'indeterminacy' and even the new 'urbanism'; all this may be bundled together and taken as a new movement which focused on the users of the building. We may begin by referring to the way in which Michel Foucault changed his views during those decades, from a belief in the strong impact of clients' and architect's concepts on the users to a belief in more arbitrary kinds of effects, with much more 'credit' given to the users' own intentions. In the early to mid-1960s we witness many architects and critics and especially the new kind of academic socio-architectural researcher devising a new terminology of the user, emphasising a notion of user-freedom; primarily this applied to housing and town planning. Since then, the issue of designer domination vs. user freedom has been frequently addressed. Strictly speaking, however, the concept of a separate architectural 'user discourse' is a tautology because to design and build architecture without users in mind is hard to imagine; such a discourse arises chiefly in those cases in which the users appear to have changed their mind after they first accepted the designated use (as in the case of public housing tower blocks). The new user discourse was, in fact, conducted very largely by the design professionals themselves and soon also by 'investigative' journalism. The chief aim of the new discourse was to attack the primacy of the authorial intention of the designer and to favour a more democratic regime. However, there always remained an unclear definition, especially with regard to the borderline between patron/client and user. University architecture was 'imposed' on its users not only by designers but by a growing diversity of agents, in the USA chiefly by those who organised the money, in Germany by government officials, in 1960s England by the UGC and the vice chancellors. It was the designers who now laid much more stress on their consultation with the users. But there were, again, problems about actually pinpointing the 'real' users. Some advocated that there was not much point in asking individual prospective users, say a science professor, as his or her successor was likely to want something rather different, but that more general research into a building's use should be undertaken – naturally under the auspices of the designer. We must refer back to the new trends in planning thinking: a major difference was now perceived between the generic user, and the users as individuals, whose habits might vary considerably.

It can, however, be maintained that in a school or a university the most numerous group of users, the students, had no input at all into the design process. All the more apposite would seem an examination of their reactions to the buildings. A brief survey of opinions of a small number of the first users of the English New Universities, randomly chosen and restricted to the question of the overall impression of the campus, reveals a thoroughly mixed picture. There were those who disliked Modernist architecture; one frequent complaint was that it was difficult to find one's way around the unusual plans. Many others had only a vague notion of the newness of the architecture and stressed that the excitement of their new free student life left little time for reflecting on the buildings as such. Others again did choose the campus and the institution for its novelty or modernity. An English investigation of 1969 gave the latter proportion as 19.7 per cent. This was a high percentage, considering, firstly, that students' preferences were spread quite evenly over a wide range, such as academic reputation, presence of friends etc. and secondly, 1969 was already a low point in the New Universities' reputation and we can therefore assume that in the years before student applicants were even more enthusiastic about the new campuses. On the whole, though, little can be said about students' appreciation of the more narrowly architectural aspects of the institution.

Recently, a book by Harold and Pamela Silver, simply entitled *Students*, made a late claim that there has never been a proper account of what students' life in the university was really like, that is, their lives outside formal teaching. This would appear to take no account of the myriads of postwar investigations on all aspects of student affairs, but the Silvers emphasise that these were always undertaken merely instrumentally, to improve the students' academic results and to keep them out of trouble. In practice, though, the book's themes are virtually all to do with the students' position in relation to the institution, including the issue of hostility towards the institution. One must try and trace here, parallel to the changes in the providers' and the architect's rhetoric, the development of the discourse of the students' existence, as such. Before about 1960 the notion of the student as an independent 'agent' hardly existed. 'The values of American students are remarkably homogenous', we still read in 1962 (J. D. Millett). At Vassar, 'the typical freshman begins her college life with eagerness and confidence. She is orientated primarily to the social group. . . .' But a contemplative mood was also assumed: the student 'expects an elevated intellectual atmosphere and looks forward to a mysterious experience which will result in intellectual transformation . . .'. A survey of the mood of students in Oxford and Manchester in 1962 concluded firmly: that they were 'honest and sincere young men'. In Germany such characterisations are more rarely found, but Professor Fuchs of the Collegium Academicum in Heidelberg contended in 1960 that 'the normal student believes far too much in authority'.

The early 1960s, again, marked a period of conflicting opinions. The rapidly increasing number of students from poorer backgrounds were deemed to require, by some, even more rules or care. Eric James's enormous institutional complexity at York must be seen as a result of this kind of thinking. On the other hand, there had for a long time also been a liberal inflection of compulsion, i.e. it is entered voluntarily. In England, in the years of transition of 1962–7 a similar solution was formulated, that of freedom combined with responsibility, notably at Essex, though it was cautiously formulated in order not to upset anxious middle-class parents. Investigations of the relationship between student and institution could lead, as we saw in the USA, to a logical impasse, to a dilemma. Under the definition of 'college fit' two worst-scenario situations could be constructed in both of which the educational effect would be nil: one in which the fit between the student's mentality and the college outlook are too close, and one in which they are too divergent.

The new liberal outlook did, however, mark the beginning of a definite answer to an old question, the age of maturity: students are not adolescents, they cannot be called boys and girls, they are adults. The legal lowering of the age of maturity from 21 to 18 finally came in England in 1969, in the USA in 1971 and in Germany in 1975. There were other factors, too. When we followed the development of university residences in England, we noted that the early 1960s saw the beginning of the breakdown of the old social and class concepts. To institute and to enforce discipline and conformity simply became too expensive. Gradually, older colleges abolished most of their elaborate rules. Paradoxically, the new emphasis on the spontaneous was matched by a new emphasis on detailed user research. Following only to a limited extent the American lead of instrumentalised research, England developed a body of primarily sociological investigations on student life and student needs. Accounts of the 'student experience' usually began by saying that one knew nothing about what students were up to, an astonishing statement after so many centuries in college education. But the English caution vis-à-vis instrumentalised research meant that the results of the large body of empirical work remained equally inconclusive, for instance as regards residential preferences (see page 83). In any case, researchers in most countries had begun to undermine the notion of the eager student waiting to receive his or her liberal education. According to Marris (in 1964), there were essentially two kinds of students: those whose fathers had a degree, and who were firmly aiming for a specific job qualification, and the lower-class student who had been sent by their teachers; very few students actually fitted neatly the liberal education-community ideal. Most students seemed to have only minimal awareness of the university as a whole and social life was student-rather than institution-generated.

In the context of demands for a general democratisation, student participation in university decisionmakeing was gradually introduced. But by the time participation was really getting into gear, by the late 1960s, many student activists were, so to speak, taking matters into their own hands entirely, and the 'autonomous student movement' emerged. It led to the troubles, but, on the other hand, it also reinforced the notion that students were normal members of the population – at least in their own perception (J. M. McKean: 'there is no student housing, only housing'). The peak of that movement was probably reached when Ivan Illich preached the complete dissolution of institutionalised education and hinted at the 'learning for a lifetime' principle, which was to diversify the student body considerably. What needs to be further investigated are the ways in which the student revolutionaries did make good use of the new campus and college planning. We noted some Americans stating that the out-of-town-situation and the spaciouness of the Modernist campus lent itself well to the gathering large protest forces, while at Essex it was the very proximity of the residences to the centre which was said to enable the students to get organised so rapidly. In the discussion of Nanterre we noted a number of contradictory causalities. However, within the more general terms of the new user definitions, all this only served to confirm that institutional planning was bound to fail.

During the 1970s the categorisations of users diversified further. Co-existent with left-radicals was a new group, the new specimen of cost-conscious student who demanded more instrumentalised kinds of education and training. In the USA the call for more student places of the 1950s and 60s turned into a dearth of students for many universities in the 1970s. Students were now treated as consumers or customers, that is, formulated for our context of investigating discourses about users, they were deemed to define themselves as consumers or customers. To them, neither the old idealists, nor the new protesters were of much concern. Whatever the theorists' categorisation of the user, in the end one can also adopt a simple view: life at the university carried on as it had always done, especially on the best campuses and that usually meant the oldest ones. Whether or not the users appreciated the special con-figuration of the new totality of campuses or 'colleges' in the 1960s, and whether or not they entertained the further new modes of user-consciousness of the institution, the institution's components, the residences, lecture halls, or canteens functioned in virtually the same way in which they had always functioned. While one may always find a few spectacular cases of mis-planned buildings, by the same token a situation of an average satisfactory use also applies. The adage about perpetual change ('when it works, it's obsolete') which was paraded by some advanced designers in the 1960s turned out to be vastly exaggerated. In the end, some of the user discourses may be subsumed under rhetoric, too.

UTOPIA OR INSTRUMENTALISM?

At the beginning we insisted that 'utopianist', and not utopian, was the word which, at least in the most general terms, characterised what was held to be the specific idealist-cum-practical frame of mind of our protagonists. However, utopian and utopi-anist are mostly used interchangeably and 'utopia' did play an important, even a con-stitutive role in many pronouncements, explicitly in the USA and rather more implicitly elsewhere. Now after the foregoing, the proclaimed end of architectural determinism and rhetoric, and after what appeared to be the new manifestations of the users as agents, utopianism appeared gravely undermined. It was now increasingly claimed that some forms of utopia could have a bad influence. This was certainly what happened in housing, when a declaration of indeterminacy, of the impossibility of planning, coincided with the new conviction that high blocks had, per se, a bad effect. The issue now became a fundamental one: any utopia, soon after its formula-tion, or after its partial realisation, was liable to turn into its opposite, a dystopia. A whole type of building could be rejected. With universities there was never such a strong counter-reaction as in housing, but the rejection of the university-organised student residence – not to mention the college as a whole – and the proposals to 'dissolve' the university campus into the ordinary fabric of the town (cf. Bremen in the 1970s, page 246) were radical enough. An opinion that was rarely publicised, but very frequently voiced privately by the users, was that the *ésprit de corps* of the New Universities was strongest in its very early days, in its temporary accommodation, before members moved into the first parts of the massive new structures (as at Essex and East Anglia).

Utopia's opposite was instrumentalism. By that was meant the pursuit of particu-larised, often material or materialist aims as well as overly bureaucratic methods. But now, spurred by the denial of utopia, one may follow the analysis of instrumentalisa-tion right through and conclude that there never was, that there never could have been a utopia because any utopian claim in universities was always informed by par-ticular agendas, which would include even the founders' old-fashioned elitism as well as the architects' seemingly selfless pursuit of 'social architecture'. In our analysis of the American scene it appeared that even 'traditional' architectural decor and its rhetoric were not what they pretended to be – that is serving, the institution as a whole – but that they were detached from a 'whole' which had never quite existed in any case, and that they were instrumentalised for ulterior ends, to maximise the fame of the designers or the alumni-donors. Utopia was nothing but disguised instrumentalism; the contrast between the mundane and a sphere of heightened aspirations which underpinned our whole story was a construct, too. Utopia was nothing but a figure of rhetoric a set of ideologies, however high the pitch of praise and however strong the sense of unity or totality of purpose.

Earlier in this chapter, a parallel was drawn between traditional architectural decoration and the traditional rhetoric of education in academe, on the one hand, and Modernist architecture and new 'liberal' approaches in education, on the other. To some, the greatest disappointment was the way in which the project of Modernity seemed to have foundered, too. In the early 1970s the theoretician and critic of architecture Manfredo Tafuri regretted the way the Modernist architectural and town planning utopias were turning into capitalist-technoid instrumentalism, but he also saw this change as the inevitable outcome of the very procedures of Modernism itself. Part of his argument is familiar from our discussion of the 'campus' and of the oscillation in the meanings of community and urban. For Tafuri the chief problem lay with the way in which the utopianist Modernist housing estate turned in on itself, while it ought to have remained open to the great diversity of urbanity.

Today, however, at the turn of the twenty-first century, the issue of utopia or instrumentality, or of the clash between them, does not seem to bother members of the university any more. The major argument of the 1960s, that student places must be increased, is still upheld. But the coherence of each institution generally no longer seems such a vital issue, except perhaps to the professional administrators within each institution. Architects would not be asked to prepare idealistic schemes for large and complex, all-comprehensive institutions. The definition of architecture appears to have returned to a pre-war and older Vitruvian one, in any case, to a stronger separation of the issues of economic construction, user-friendliness and beauty or special visual impact. The simple issue facing each individual university today is the rating of 'quality', with the quality of teaching, of research and of the buildings all assessed separately; in addition, the university has to get across the right kind of a very generalised 'image'.

How, then, do the utopianist efforts of the 1960s look today? One thing we can say is that they did not turn into dystopia. That was probably because the founders and designers did not want actual utopias; in their view, they combined as much utopianism as possible with as much instrumentalism as necessary. To 'combine idealism with realism' is of course one of oldest rhetoric tropes. Today, probably the whole of the founders' verbal rhetoric belongs, as they say, to history and languishes on the shelves of their university libraries. What about their built rhetoric? Between the seemingly unproblematic charm of the old and the always neatly contextualised attractiveness of the Post-Modern, we may search out for that specific combination of starkness and complexity of the 1960s New Universities.

ABBREVIATIONS

AA 1967	M. Brawne (ed.), *University Planning and Design. A Symposium, Architectural Association [London] Paper No. 3*, 1967 (mainly papers of a conference at Sussex University, 1964).
AD	*Architectural Design*
Ad'A	*L'Architecture d'aujourd'hui*
AFor	*Architectural Forum*
AJ	*Architects' Journal*
AR	*Architectural Review*
ARec	*Architectural Record*
B	*The Builder*
BW	*Bauwelt*
Beloff	M. Beloff, *The Plateglass Universities*, London, 1968
Birks	T. Birks, *Building the New Universities*, Newton Abbot, 1972
Brubacher	J. S. Brubacher and W. Rudy, *Higher Education in Transition* (3rd ed.) New York, 1976
Dober (1963)	R. Dober, *Campus Planning*, New York, 1963
Dober (1965)	R. Dober, *The New Campus in Britain. Ideas and Consequences for the United States* (publ. Educational Facilities Laboratories), New York, 1965
DUZ	*Deutsche Universitätszeitung*
Linde (1970)	H. Linde (ed.), *Hochschulplanung* vols 1–4, Düsseldorf, 1970
OECD	Organisation for Economic Co-operation and Development (Paris)
Perkin	H. Perkin, *New Universities in the United Kingdom.* (Case Studies on Innovation in Higher Education), OECD Paris, 1969
PRO	Public Record Office (London)
RIBA	Royal Institute of British Architects
Ross	Murray G. Ross, *New Universities in the Modern World*, London, 1966
ST	*The Sunday Times*
T	*The Times*
TES	*The Times Educational Supplement* (London)
THES	*The Times Higher Education Supplement* (London)
Turner	P. V. Turner, *Campus. An American Planning Tradition*, Cambridge MA and London, 1984
UGC	University Grants Committee (London)
UQ	*University Quarterly*

INTRODUCTION

For Utopia and Community see: L. Hölscher, 'Utopie', *Utopian Studies* vol. 7 no. 2 1996, pp. 1–65 (first publ. in O. Brunner & oth. (eds.), *Geschichtliche Grundbegriffe*, vol. 6, Stuttgart, 1990); E. J. Green, 'The Social Functions of Utopian Architecture', *Utopian Studies* vol. 4 no. 1 1993, pp. 1–13; K. Kumar (ed.), *Utopianism*, Milton Keynes, 1991; K. Kumar (ed.), *Utopias*, Melbourne, 1987; R. Moos & R. Brownstein, *Environment and Utopia* New York, 1977; K. Mannheim, *Ideology and Utopia* (1936, New York, 1955); P. Selznick, *The Moral Commonwealth. Social Theory and Promise of Community*, Berkeley, 1992; D. Lyon, 'Community as ideology and utopia', *UQ Culture, Education and Society* vol. 38 no. 3 Summer 1984, pp. 243–69; Centre for Educational Research and Innovation, *The University and the Community*, OECD Paris, 1984.

C. Rowe, 'The Architecture of Utopia', pp. 206–16 in: C. Rowe, *The Mathematics of the Ideal Villa and other Essays*, Cambridge MA and London, 1976; I. Todd & M. Wheeler, *Utopia*, London, 1978; H. Rosenau, *The Social Purpose in Architecture*, London, 1970; R. Fishman, *Urban Utopias in the Twentieth Century*. Cambridge MA and London, 1982. E. Howard, *F. L. Wright and LeCorbusier*, London, 1977; V. Margolin, *The Struggle for Utopia*, Chicago, 1997; F. Borsi, *Architecture et Utopie*, Paris, 1997.

F. Toennies, *Community and Society*, East Lansing, 1957 (*Gemeinschaft und Gesellschaft. Abhandlung des Communismus und des Sozialsmus als empirischer Culturform*, Leipzig, 1887); N. Goodman & P. Goodman, *Communitas*, New York, 1947; G. Hillery, Jr., *Communal Organisations. A Study of Local Societies*, Chicago, 1968; R. Plant, *Community and Ideology*, London, 1974; C. Bell & H. Newby, *Community Studies*, London, 1971; for the English post World War II surge of the term cf. M. Glendinning & S. Muthesius, *Tower Block. Modernist Public Housing in England, Scotland, Wales and Northern Ireland*. New Haven and London, 1994, pp. 94ff.

For a recent multifaceted investigation of an institution which shows some similarities with universities cf. J. F. A. Hughes, *The Brutal Hospital. Efficiency, Form and Identity in the National Health Service*, PhD London University, 1996.

P. Ricoeur, *Lectures on Ideology and Utopia* (ed. G. H. Taylor), New York, 1986.

'Utopian moment': K. Kumar, *Utopia and Anti-Utopia*, Oxford, 1987, p. 400.

On architectural theory see notes for pages 297, 304, 326, 330.

'Architecture are the . . . vehicles . . .': Ross, p. 184.

Architects' universities: cf. M. Brawne, 'An Appraisal', *AR* 4-1970, pp. 250–4.

Did the new educational planning of the 1960s succeed? Cf. the elaborate inconclusiveness regarding 1960s open-plan schools: T. Husen & T. N. Postlethwaite (eds.), *The International Encyclopedia of Education*, Oxford, 1985, pp. 2582–8.

I   USA: CAMPUS VS. COLLEGE

The post World War II multiveristy

'Although knowledge . . .': from Clark Kerr's lectures, quoted in V. A. Stadtman, *The University of California 1868–1968*, New York, 1970, p. 423.

'Relation of the university . . .': C. Kerr, *The Uses of the University*, 3rd ed. Cambridge MA, 1982 (1st ed. 1963), p. 150; cf. R. M. Hutchins, *The University of Utopia*, Chicago, 1953; cf. recently: M. Sellers, *An Ethical Education*, Oxford, 1994.

'Shaped by the desire . . .': Turner, p. 305; cf. R. Dober, *Campus Architecture. Building in the Groves of Academe*, New York, 1996; cf. C. Summerfield & M. E. Devine, *International Dictionary of University Histories*, Chicago, 1998; J. C. Smart (ed.) *Higher Education. Handbook of Theory and Research*, New York, vol. I 1985 – vol. XIV 1999; J. S. Brubacher & W. Rudy, *Higher Education in Transition* (4th ed.) New Brunswick, 1997.

'Justice, compassion . . .': *The Report of the President's Commission on Campus Unrest*, Washington, 1970, p. 75.

Schools: W. W. Cutler III, 'Cathedral of Culture: The Schoolhouse in American Educational Thought and Practice since 1820', *History of Education Quarterly* vol. 29 no. 1 Spring 1989, pp. 1–40.

'Everyone's right': D. Riesman, 'The urban university', *Massachusetts Review* 8-1967, pp. 476–86 (p. 486).

'No student who wants . . .': quoted in: L. Hall & Associates, *New Colleges for New Students*, San Francisco, 1974, p. viii.

Having entered the system: J. Ben-David, *American Higher Education*, New York, 1972, p. 3.

'To the English concept . . .': Brubacher, p. 404.

'Oxbridge an expression . . .': W. R. Harper, *The Prospects of the Small College*, Chicago, 1900, pp. 17–18, 45–6, quoted in Brubacher, p. 406; cf. A. Flexner, *Universities: American, English and German*, New York, 1930 (new edition 1968); H. Röhrs, 'The Influence of Humboldt's Concepts on the Universities in the USA', in: H. Röhrs (ed.), *Tradition and Reform of the Universities under International Perspective*, Frankfurt am Main, 1987; A. Touraine, *The Academic System in American Society*, New York, 1973; A. Duke, *Importing Oxbridge. English Residential Colleges and American Universities*, New Haven and London, 1996.

'Non-profit-making . . .': R. Dober, 'Form and Style in Campus Design', *Progressive Architecture* 9-1960, pp. 122–30 (p. 122).

English universities run by faculty . . . : Brubacher, p. 409.

Trustees, president . . . : C. Kerr, *The Uses of the University*, 3rd ed. Cambridge MA, 1982 (as in 1st ed. 1963), pp. 29–30.

Image: J. D. Millett, *The Academic Community*, New York, 1962, pp. 220ff.; O. Handlin & M. F. Handlin, *The American College and American Culture*, New York, 1970, p. 77; J. Ben-David, *American Higher Education*, New York, 1972, p. 36.

'The true American University . . .': C. Kerr, *The Uses of the University*, 3rd ed. Cambridge MA, 1982 (as in 1st ed. 1963), p. 85.

A. Touraine, *The Academic System in American Society*, New York, 1973, p. 1.

'The foundations . . .': Brubacher, p. 354.

Johns Hopkins: R. Hofstadter & C. DeWitt Hardy, *The Development and Scope of Higher Education in the United States*, New York, 1952, p. 61.

Polarity state vs private: T. Parsons & G. M. Platt, *The American University*, Cambridge MA, 1973, pp. 331–2; cf. R. Hofstadter & C. DeWitt Hardy, *The Development and Scope of Higher Education in the United States*, New York, 1952, p. 61.

'First comprehensive rationale . . .': D. D. Henry, *Challenges Past, Challenges Present. An Analysis of American Higher Education since 1930*, San Francisco, 1975, pp. 71–3. U.S. President's Commission, Higher Education for Democracy: *A Report*, vols 1–6, New York, 1947–8.

71% state aid . . . : Cost of producing . . . 5% . . . : E. Ashby, *Any Person, Any Study. An Essay on Higher Education in the United States*, New York, 1971, p. 3.

Proportion of women, blacks . . . : C. Kerr, *The Uses of the University*, 3rd. ed., Cambridge MA, 1982, p. 171.

Drop-out rate . . . : E. Ashby, *Any Person, Any Study. An Essay on Higher Education in the United States*, New York, 1971, p. 18; N. Sanford (ed.), *The American College*, New York, 1962, p. 117.

'Americans' higher expectations . . . : *The Report of the President's Commission on Campus Unrest*, Washington, 1970, p. 74.

'Higher education . . . research complex . . .': T. Parsons & G. M. Platt, *The American University*, Cambridge MA, 1973, p. vi.

J. Ben-David, *American Higher Education*, New York, 1972.

'The multiversity is a confusing place . . .': C. Kerr, *The Uses of the University*, 3rd ed. Cambridge MA, 1982 (1st ed. 1963), p. 42.

Multiversity . . . suffered from: *ARec* 1-1955, p. 124.

Liberal College to student personnel service

Community: cf. P. Goodman, *The Community of Scholars*, New York, 1962.

'Lernfreiheit': C. Kerr, *The Uses of the University*, 3rd ed. Cambridge MA, 1982 (1st ed. 1963), p. 42.

'Liberal studies . . . charm . . .': A. Bush-Brown, 'Cram and Gropius: Traditionalism and Progressivism', *The New England Quarterly* vol. 25 3-1952, pp. 3–22 (p. 8).

H. Lefkowitz Horowitz, *Alma Mater. Design and Experience in the Women's Colleges from their 19th Century Beginnings to the 1930s*, New York, 1984, pp. xvi–xviii.

Small institutions . . . numbers: Brubacher, p. 69.

John Dewey, *Democracy and Education*, New York, 1916.

'Support . . . from disinterested respect . . .': R. Hofstadter & C. DeWitt Hardy, *The Development and Scope of Higher Education in the United States*, New York, 1952, pp. 133–4.

A. Meiklejohn, *The Experimental College*, 1932 (new ed. New York, 1971) and as he established it at the University of Wisconsin.

Reform Colleges: G. Grant & D. Riesman, *Reform and Experiment in the American College*, Chicago, 1978; A. Heiss, *An Inventory of Academic Innovation and Reform*, San Francisco, 1973.

'The academic community . . .': N. Sanford (ed.), *The American College*, New York, 1962, p. 962.

On Theodore Newcomb: D. F. Alwin, R. L. Cohen, T. M. Newcomb, *Political Attitudes over the Life Span. The Bennington Women after Fifty Years*, Madison Wis., 1991.

'College students adolescents': D.S. Arbuckle, *Student Personel Services in Higher Education*, New York, 1953, p. 1.

'Mental hygiene': Arbuckle, *op. cit.*, p. 33.

Student psychology: See *Journal of Educational Psychology* from 1958; N. Sanford (ed.), *The American College*, New York, 1962, p. 962; S. Leibfried, *Die angepasste Universität. Zur Situation der Hochschulen in der Bundesrepublik und in den USA*, Frankfurt am Main, 1968; J. Scherer, *Students in Residence. A Survey of American Studies* (publ. Dept of Higher Education, Univ. of London Institute of Education), 1969; K. A. Feldman & T. M. Newcomb, *The Impact of College on Students*, San Francisco, 1969 (1973); K. A. Feldman (ed.), *College & Student, Selected Readings in the Social Psychology of Higher Education*, New York, 1972; A. W. Chickering & Associates, *The Modern American College*, San Francisco, 1981; E. T. Pascarella & P. Terenzini, *How College affects Students*, San Francisco, 1991; R. Barnett & A. Griffin, *End of Knowledge in Higher Education*, London, 1977.

All students need help: D. S. Arbuckle, *Student Personel Services in Higher Education*, New York, 1953, pp. 1, 22.

'College psychologist helps . . .': G. B. Blaine, Jr. & C. L. McArthur, *Emotional Problems of the Student*, New York, 1961 (1971) pp. x–xi.

'"College Press" and productivity': A. W. Astin, A Re-Examination of College Productivity', *Journal of Educational Psychology* vol. 52 no. 3, 1961, pp. 173–8 (p. 173).

'Freshmen-to-senior changes . . .': K. A. Feldman, College & Student, *Selected Readings in the Social Psychology of Higher Education*, New York, 1972, p. 326; cf. K. A. Feldman & T. M. Newcomb, *The Impact of College on Students*, San Francisco, 1973 (1969), pp. 332, 341.

'Typical college graduate rubber . . .': J. Floud & J. Rosselli, 'Studying Higher Education in Britain and America', *UQ* vol. 17 no. 2, 3-1963, pp. 128–45 (p. 137).

'We house and feed them . . . : E. Raushenbush, 'A larger Role for the Small College', *Atlantic Monthly* 8-1968, pp. 67–73 (p. 67).

Student Unions: Brubacher, p. 337; Association of College Unions – International, *Planning College Union Facilties for Multiple-Use* (publ. Educational Facilities Laboratories, New York), 1966.

College Housing Loan: H. Hewes, 'The College Housing Program', *American Association of Architects Journal* 9-1973, pp. 73–8.

Facilites Act, 'cheap shelter': Dober (1963), pp. 135–7, 142–3.

Residential proportions: J. Scherer, *Students in Residence. A Survey of American Studies* (publ. Dept of Higher Education, Univ. of London Institute of Education), 1969, p. 28; J. Ben-David, *American Higher Education*, New York, 1972, pp. 80–1; O. Handlin & M. F. Handlin, *The American College and American Culture*, New York, 1970, pp. 80–1.

Dormitories: Turner, pp. 244–5; G. S. Blimling, 'The Influence of College Residence Halls on Students', in: J. Smart, (ed.), *Higher Education Handbook, Theory and Research*, vol. 9, pp. 248–307, New York, 1993; J. Scherer, *Students in Residence. A Survey of American Studies* (publ. Dept of Higher Education, Univ. of London Institute of Education), 1969.

Sororities / Fraternities: R. C. Angell, *The Campus. A Study of Contemporary Undergraduate Life in an American University*, New York, 1928; R. Hofstadter & C. DeWitt Hardy, *The Development and Scope of Higher Education in the United States*, New York, 1952, pp. 112–13; Brubacher, pp. 126–31; O. Handlin & M. F. Handlin, *The American College and American Culture*, New York, 1970, p. 57.

'Reintegration of curriculum . . .': Brubacher, pp. 330ff.

'Half college and half monastery . . .': R. A. Cram, *The Gothic Quest*, New York, 1918, p. 342, quoted in Turner, p. 217; R. A. Cram, 'Recent University Architecture in the United States', *RIBA Journal*, 1912, pp. 497–519.

'Sways men's minds . . .': R. A. Cram, *The Gothic Quest*, New York, 1907, p. 94, quoted in A. Bush-Brown, 'Cram and Gropius: Traditionalism and Progres-sivism', *New England Quarterly* vol. 25 3-1952, pp. 3–22 (p. 4); P. Horsbrugh, 'Environmental Crisis and the University', in: S. D. Kertesz (ed.), *The Task of University in a Changing World*, Notre Dame, 1971, pp. 131–52 (pp. 142–3).

Neo-Gothic Colleges: Turner, p. 227 etc; cf. also J. F. Block, *The Uses of Gothic, Planning and Building the Campus of the University of Chicago*, Chicago, 1983.

Harvard Houses: Turner, pp. 244–5; C. S. Jencks & D. Riesman, 'Patterns of Residential Accommodation: A Case Study of Harvard', pp. 731–75 in: M. Sanford, *The American College*, New York, 1962; R. Vreeland & C. Bidwell, 'Organisational Effects on Student Attitudes: A Story of Harvard Houses', pp. 301–18 in: K. A. Feldman (ed.), *College & Student, Selected Readings in the Social Psychology of Higher Education*, New York, 1972.

'Residence adds about 12 per cent . . .': G. S. Blimling, 'The Influence of College Residence Halls on Students', pp. 248–307 (p. 259) in: J. Smart, (ed.), *Higher Education Handbook, Theory and Research* vol. 9, New York, 1993; cf. M. S. Gerst & R. H. Moos, 'Social Ecology of University Student Residences', *Journal of Educational Psychology* vol. 63 no. 6 1972, pp. 513–25; R. Moos & oth., 'A Typology of University Student Living Groups', *Journal of Educational Psychology* vol. 67 no. 3 1975, pp. 359–65.

English ideal expensive: Brubacher, p. 339.

'Education . . . coffee and doughnuts . . .': N. Sanford, *The American College*, New York, 1962, p. 960.

'Still debated': Dober (1963), p. 119, cf. pp. 122, 137, 140.

'Way to integrate more closely . . .': Brubacher, pp. 337–8.

Student independence: Brubacher, pp. 347–8.

Pluralistic residential solution: E. Raushenbush, 'A larger Role for the Small College', *Atlantic Monthly* 8-1968 pp. 67–73 (p. 71).

Coed issue: there appears relatively little on this before the 1970s: see N. Sanford (ed.), *The American College*, New York, 1962, pp. 95–6; Brubacher, pp. 66–9; as regards mixed residences Britain may possibly have been ahead of the USA in the 1960s. For instance in the 1960s colleges in Santa Cruz (see below) men's and women's blocks were well separated. Cf. A. Touraine, *The Academic System in American Society*, New York, 1974, pp. 98–9.

Michigan: D. Riesman, *On Higher Education*, San Francisco, 1980, p. 208; cf. A. W. Chickering & Associates, *The Modern American College*, San Francisco, 1981, pp. 672–88; G. S. Blimling, 'The Influence of College Residence Halls on Students', pp. 248–307 (p. 288), in: J. Smart (ed.), *Higher Education Handbook, Theory and Research*, vol. 9, New York, 1993; cf. M. S. Gerst & R. H. Moos, 'Social Ecology of University Student Residences', *Journal of Educational Psychology* vol. 63 no. 6 1972, pp. 513–25; H. C. Rioker and F. G. Moore, *College Students live here. A Study of College Housing*, New York, 1961; H. Linde (ed.), *Universitätsbau in den USA (Schriften des Zentralarchivs für Hochschulbau Stuttgart, 3)*, Düsseldorf, 1965, p. 12.

1973–1980 student numbers: *ARec* 7-1974, p. 119; R. Field, *The Community College Movement*, New York, 1962.

'More than a high school': P. Heyer, *Architects on Architecture*, 1967, p. 119.

'Social life of the living . . .': *AFor* 11-1959, pp. 132–3.

Claremont, W. W. Clary, *The Claremont Colleges*, Claremont CL 1970; K. A. Feldman (ed.), *College & Student, Selected Readings in the Social Psychology of Higher Education*, New York, 1972, pp. 438–9; 'Conference on Cluster College concept [at Claremont]', *Journal of Higher Education* 10-1967; Cf. J. G. Gaff & Associates, *The Cluster College*, San Francisco, 1970.

'Concern for the "whole student" . . .': Brubacher, p. 331.

'American student most guided . . .': Brubacher, p. 348.

'Optimal community size': N. Sanford (ed.), *The American College*, New York, 1962, pp. 762, 765; cf. A. W. Chickering, *Education and Idenity*, San Francisco, 1969, pp. 185–95; cf. G. Sutherland, 'Is there an optimum size for a university', *Minerva* 1-1973, pp. 48ff.; Ross, pp. 170–89; H. E. Rich & P. M. Jolicour, *Student Attitudes and Academic Environments*, New York, 1978.

Campus planning

Campus – field: Turner, pp. 4, 47.

Yale etc.: *ARec* 4-1962, pp. 125–38; *Progressive Architecture* 9-1960, pp. 124–5.

Univ. South Florida, Tampa Fl, 1957 onwards, Dober (1963), p. 306; Ross, pp. 134–69.

On Campus planning: cf. J. Hudnut, 'On Form in Univeristies', *ARec* 12-1947, pp. 88–96; W. T. Middlebrook, *How to Estimate the Building Needs of College and Universities* (publ. University of Minneapolis), 1958; G. Fesel, 'Universitätsplanung in den USA', *DUZ* 12-1964, pp. 3–10; H. D. Bareither & J. L. Schillinger, *University Space Planning*, Urbana Ill., 1968; T. Mason, 'La Dynamique de la planification dans l'enseignement supérieur', *Ad'A* 137 4/5-1968, p. xxxvii; Doxiadis Associates, Inc., *Campus Planning in an Urban Area. Master Plan for Rensslaer Polytechnic Institute*, New York, 1971; H. O. Krasnoff (President, Association of University Architects), *Campus Buildings that Work*, Philadelphia PA, 1972; S. F. Brewster, *Campus Planning and Construction* (publ. Administration of Physical Plant Administration of Universties and Colleges; Washington D.C.), 1976; M. W. Peterson, 'Continuity, Challenge and Change: 'An Organisational Perspective on Planning Past and Future', *Planning for Higher Education* vol. 14 no. 3 1986, pp. 6–15.

Audio-visual etc.: Architectural Association Journal, vol. 80 no. 883 6-1965, pp. 18–19; cf. 'Higher Education Teaching Support Services . . .', pp. 2253–7 in: T. Husen & T. N. Postlethwaite (eds.), *The International Encyclopaedia of Education*, Oxford, 1985.

'Master plans': Dober (1963), p. 37.

'Hit an run techniques': R. Dober, 'Form and Style in Campus Design', *Progressive Architecture* 10-1960, pp.

122–33 (p. 124); J. D. Millett, *The Academic Community*, New York, 1962, pp. 10, 221; G. Fesel, 'Universitäts-Planung in den USA', *DUZ* 12-1964, pp. 3–10; 'Institutional Planning', in: *International Encyclopaedia of Higher Education*, vol. 7, San Francisco, 1977.

'Educated guesses . . .': Dober (1963), p. 72; Academic . . . Nobel Prize . . . : *ibid.*, p. 177; 'Harvard . . . heating plant': *ibid.*, p. 250.

'Programme analysts, space experts': R. E. Alexander, 'Comprehensive Architectural Practice. College and Universities', *American Institute of Architects Journal* 4-1963 pp. 103–11.

'Campuses grow by logical . . .': Dober (1963), p. 73; 'Planning modules': *ibid.*, p. 57; 'Relatively flat' . . . several sites . . . : *ibid.*, p. 289.

'UCLA is a four-year . . .': quoted in Turner, p. 267.

'Physical elements' . . . 'the circulation systems . . .': Dober (1963), p. 61; 'pedestrian precinct': *ibid.*, p. 261; 'Gradual pedestrian-scale transition . . .': *ibid.*, p. 288.

'Need physical and psychical . . .', 'rarely do people . . .': R. Dober, 'Form and Style in Campus Design', *Progressive Architecture* 10-1960, pp. 122–33 (p. 133).

'Social and living patterns . . .': Dober (1963), p. 137; 'to bring all things . . .': *ibid.*, p. 58; 'chessboard . . .': *ibid.*, p. 61; 'not necessary to establish illustrative . . .': *ibid.*, p. 53; 'planning module may imply . . .': *ibid.*, p. 61; 'residences . . . express . . . density . . .': *ibid.*, p. 53.

'Family resemblance . . .': R. Dober, 'Form and Style in Campus Design', *Progressive Architecture* 10-1960, pp. 122–33 (p. 127); cf. Dober (1963), p. 219.

'The recognition . . .': Dober (1963), p. 61; 'social phenomena', educational programmes: *ibid.*, pp. 200–3; 'I write as a general practitioner . . .': *ibid.*, Preface.

Assigning architecture's role

G. Grant & D. Riesman, *The Perpetual Dream. Reform and Experiment in the American College*, Chicago, 1978.

Cf. S. E. Harris, *Higher Education in the United States*, Cambridge MA, 1960; M. S. Gerst & R. H. Moos, 'Social Ecology of University Student Residences', *Journal of Educational Psychology* vol. 63 no. 6 1972, pp. 513–25; F. Sturner, 'The College Environment', pp. 71–86 in: D. W. Vermilye (ed.), *The Future in the Making*, San Francisco, 1973; F. D. Case, 'Dormitory Architecture Influences', *Environment and Behaviour* vol. 13 no. 1 1-1981, pp. 23–41; H. L. Cohen, 'Behavioural Architecture', *Architectural Association Journal* vol. 80 no. 883 6-1965, pp. 7–11 (also: H. L. Cohen, 'Ecology of Educuation', *Inland Architect* 11-1961); 'The Psychological Dimension of Architectural Space', *Progressive Architecture* 4-1965, pp. 159–67.

'Aesthetic experience': N. Sanford (ed.) *The American College*, New York, 1962, pp. 966–8.

'Expensive': *op. cit.*, p. 764.

'Energy should be directed not to plant': Arthur W. Chickering, 'Undergraduate Academic Experience', *Journal of Educational Psychology* vol. 63 no. 2 1972, pp. 134–43.

'Aesthetic and social purpose . . .': O. Handlin & M. F. Handlin, *The American College and American Culture*, New York, 1970, pp. 57–8; cf. R. W. Talley, 'Trends in College Buildings', *American Institute of Architects Journal* 11-1953, pp. 212ff.; Howard Dwight Smith, 'The architectural integrity of the College Campus', *American Institute of Architects Journal*, 7/9-1955, pp. 118–20, 123ff.; cf. S. E. Harris, *Higher Education in the United States*, Cambridge MA, 1960, p. 120.

'My . . . imagination . . .': H. S. Canby, *Alma Mater*, New York, 1939, p. 23.

'Tasteless and imitative': D. Riesman in N. Sanford (ed.), *The English College*, New York, 1962, pp. 91–9, 732.

'Alumni concerned about . . . style': J. D. Millett, *The Academic Community*, New York, 1962, p. 195.

'Total environment', 'the state's art and architectural bodies . . .': J. R. Thelin & J. Yankovich, 'Bricks and Mortar: Architecture and the Study of Higher Education', pp. 57–83 in: J. Smart, (ed.), *Higher Education Handbook. Theory and Research*, vol. 3, New York, 1987.

'Full attention to aesthetics . . .': *The University of Illinois at Congress Circle. Antecedent Event Architectural Design Educational Programme* (publ. by Univ. of Illinois at Chicago), ea. 1960s (Courtesy UiC Archives).

Yale: Turner, pp. 262 etc.; cf. J. Barnett, 'New College Architecture at Yale', *ARec* 4-1962, pp. 125–38; T. Howarth, 'Architect on the Campus', *Listener* [London] 2-1-1958, pp. 14–16.

J. K. Shear, 'Design is Desired under the Elms', *ARec* 8-1957, p. 136; cf. George Cline Smith, 'One Billion a Year on the 1965 Campus', *ARec* 8-1957, p. 137.

'Beauty': 'Campus Architecture The Architect's View The President's View', *American Association of Architects Journal* 4-1964, pp. 68–76.

'Rational, justifiable . . .': R. E. Alexander, 'Comprehensive Architectural Practice. Colleges and Universities', *American Association of Architects Journal* 4-1963, pp. 103–6; cf. further articles in that issue.

'Exclusively utilitarian standpoint . . .': 'College and University Business selects 16 outstanding Examples of Campus Design for the '70s', *College and University Business* 1-1970, pp. 39–62 (p. 39).

All quotes up to: 'who produce high quality': *AFor* 7/8-1968, pp. 75–84.

S. E. Bleeker, *The Politics of Architecture. A Perpsective on Nelson A. Rockefeller*, New York, 1981, pp. 135–77 (pp. 142, 150).

Four major American architectural periodicals: M. Filler, 'American Architecture and Its Criticism: Reflections of the State of the Arts', pp. 27–32 in: *The Critical Edge. Controversy in Recent American Architecture* (Exh. J. V. Zimmerli Art Museum Rutgers Univ. etc., curated by T. A. Marder, 1985).

'Desire to make a modern building . . .'; 'design a pleasing facade . . .': 'Matching Modern Campuses to People', *American School and University* vol. 39 6-1967, pp. 38–41.

'Age of beauty . . .': *American Association of Architects Journal* 8-1965, p. 3.

American and English architectural trends and definitions of the profession: cf. A. Saint, *The Image of the Architect*, 1983, pp. 155–60; cf. R. A. M. Stern, *Pride of Place. Building the American Dream*, Boston, 1986; G. Stevens, *The Favored Circle. The Social Foundations of Architectural Distinction*, Cambridge MA and London, 1998.

International Modern Collegiate

Modernist architecture: Cf. recently: J. C. Loeffler, *The Architecture of Diplomacy. Building America's Embassies*, Princeton, 1998; D. Upton, *Architecture in the United States*, Oxford, 1998; K. Harries, *The Ethical Function of Architecture*, Cambridge MA and London, 1997.

'Aesthetic victory . . .': J. Burchard & A. Bush Brown, *The Architecture of America*, London, 1961 (1967), p. 321.

Advanced / cautious: Turner, p. 249; see Turner for details about most buildings mentioned here; most architects are dealt with in P. Heyer, *Architects on Architecture*, London, 1967.

Cf. R. Dober, *Campus Architecture*, New York, 1996, p. 146; a very brief work is: T. A. Gaines, *The Campus as a Work of Art*, New York, 1991.

'The Bauhaus, Hitler . . .': G. Grant & D. Riesman, *The Perpetual Dream. Reform and Experiment in the American College*, Chicago, 1978, p. 23. On Gropius: 'Walter Gropius et son Ecole', *Ad'A*, no. 28, 2-1950; 'Genetrix', *AR* 5-1957; cf. K. Herdeg, *The Decorated Diagram, Harvard Architecture and the Failure of the Bauhaus Legacy*, 1983; L. H. Cormier, *Gropius in Exile*, Providence R.I., 1986; cf. on the Bauhaus ethos in J. Ockman, 'Towards a theory of normative architecture', pp. 122–52 in: S. Harris & D. Berke (eds.), *Architecture of the Everyday*, Princeton, 1997.

Foreign trends: T. Howarth, 'Architect on the Campus', *Listener* [London], 2-1-1958, pp. 14–16.

'Both Cram and Gropius . . .': A. Bush-Brown, 'Cram and Gropius: Traditionalism and Progressivism', *New England Quarterly* vol. 25 3-1952, pp. 3–22 (p. 4); 'their mission . . .': *ibid.*, p. 18; cf. W. Creese, 'Architecture and Learning. A Collegiate Quandry', *Magazine of Art* 4 1950, pp. 136–41.

Gropius chiding Gothic: W. Gropius, 'Not Gothic but Modern for Our Colleges', *New York Times Magazine*, 23-10-1949, reprinted as: 'Archeology or Architecture for Contemporary Buildings?', pp. 70–5, in: W. Gropius, *The Scope of Total Architecture*, New York, 1943.

'Americans visited . . .': A Bush-Brown, 'College Architecture: An Expression of Educational Philosophy', *ARec* 8-1957, pp. 154–7; cf. J. S. Coleman (foreword by), *Between Elite and Mass Education. Education in the Federal Republic of Germany*, Albany, 1983, pp. 11–15 (publ. Max Planck Institut für Bildungsforschung, Berlin 1979; publ. also as: *Das Bildungswesen in der Bundesrepublik Deutschland*, Hamburg, 1979); K. Hahn, *Reform mit Augenmass. Ausgewählte Schriften eines Politikers und Pädagogen*, Stuttgart, 1998 (the founder of Salem and Gordonstoun Reform Boarding Schools);

H. Röhrs (ed.), *Die Schulen der Reformpädagogik heute*, Düsseldorf, 1986.

'Relating their educational undertaking . . .': J. B. Conant, *Education in a Divided World*, Cambridge MA, 1948, p. 83, quoted in A. Bush-Brown, 'Cram and Gropius: Traditionalism and Progressivism', *New England Quarterly* vol. 25 3-1952, pp. 3–22 (p. 16).

'Create the conditions . . .'; Erlangen: H. Probst & C. Schädlich, *Walter Gropius*, vol. 2, Berlin, 1986, pp. 70–1; R. R. Isaacs, *Walter Gropius. Der Mensch und sein Werk*, vol. 1, Berlin, 1984, pp. 332–3.

Impington: H. Probst & C. Schädlich, *Walter Gropius*, vol. 2, Berlin, 1986, pp. 98–100; A. Saint, *Towards a Social Architecture. The Role of Schoolbuilding in Post-War England*, New Haven & London, 1987, pp. 42–4.

Possibly the next major example after Impington of the informal, splayed layout of interlinked buildings is Graham Dawbarn's University College of the West Indies near Kingston, Jamaica, begun in 1949. However, Dawbarn, like Fry involved at that time in pioneering solutions of council housing in London, still provides a 'formal element', a circular road surrounding the universitiy's centre, and a long staight avenue leading off it (*AR* 10-1953, pp. 221–30).

Wheaton, Williamsburg, Goucher: J. D. Kornwolf (ed.), *Modernism in America 1937–1941, A Catalogue . . .* Wheaton College, Goucher College, College of William and Mary, Smithsonian Institution, Williamsburg Va., 1985; Turner.

Black Mountain College, Lake Eden, North Carolina: H. Probst & C. Schädlich, *Walter Gropius*, vol. 2, Berlin, 1986, Turner, pp. 258–9; M. Duberman, *Black Mountain . . .* , New York, 1972.

Harvard Yard: *AFor* 12-1950, pp. 62–9; *American Institute of Architects Journal* 9-1963, pp. 79–84; W. Gropius & oth. (eds.), *The Architects Collaborative*, London, 1966; pp. 63–9; Turner, pp. 267–8.

'Philosophical concept . . .': *AFor* 12-1950, p. 70.

Baghdad: W. Gropius & oth. (eds.), *The Architects Collaborative*, London, 1966; pp. 119–220; *ARec* 4-1959, pp. 147–51; *Bauen und Wohnen* 1959, pp. 391–2; *Ad'A* no. 91–2, 9/10/11-1960, pp. 94ff.; G. C. Argan, 'La Citta-scuola', *Casabella* no. 242 1960; *ARec* 2-1961, pp. 107–21; *Baukunst und Werkform* 1-1961, pp. 31–2.

'As a whole the university . . .': R. R. Isaacs, *Walter Gropius. Der Mensch und sein Werk*, vol. 2, Berlin, 1984, p. 1046.

Early attempts at campus unity: Frank Lloyd Wright's Florida Southern College at Lakeland, begun 1938; *Listener* [London] 2-1-1958, p. 14; I. M. Pei & Partners at Frededonia State University College, New York, 1964: Turner, pp. 254–5, 274.

L. Kahn: H. Ronner & oth., L. I. Kahn. *The Complete Works 1935–74*, Basel etc., 1977.

Eero Saarinen: R. M. Stern, Pride of Place. *The Building of the American Dream*, Boston, 1986, pp. 78–80.

Michigan State University: R. M. Crane, 'Coed and Co-Academic Residence Halls', *American Institute of Architects Journal* 9-1963, pp. 79–90; P. L. Dressel,

College to University. The Hannah Years at Michigan State 1935–1969, East Lansing, 1987.

Community Colleges: Eberle M. Smith, 'Project Analysis Services for Community Colleges', *American Association of Architects Journal* 4-1963, pp. 107–11; 'The Community College achieves a Complete Unity of Form', *American School and University* vol. 41 9-1968, pp. 55–7.

'Many campuses handsome . . .': *ARec* 7-1974, p. 119.

'Thoroughly planned college . . .': *American Institute of Architects Journal* 3-1970, pp. 36ff.

E. Kump, 'Architecture for the College Campus', *American Institute of Architects Journal* 3-1963, pp. 75–8; Dober (1963), pp. 96, 203.

Quotes Foothill: *AFor* 11-1959, pp. 134–9; (by Alan Temko): *AFor* 2-1962, pp. 54–7; P. Heyer, *Architects on Architecture*, 1967, p. 444.

Campus: Modern and Big. Albany

Cf 'Building Campuses from the Ground up', *Fortune*, 11-1964.

Hawai: Dober (1963), p. 296.

IIT: D. Spaeth, *Mies van der Rohe*, New York, 1985, pp. 117ff.; there is much by Mies on the issue of academic teaching of architecture. Cf. H. Linde and Zentralarchiv für Hochschulbau, Stuttgart (eds.), *Planung Wissenschaftlicher Hochschulen*, Stuttgart, 1965, pp. 50–3; U. Kultermann, 'Internationale Hochschulreform', in *Baukunst und Werkform* 2-1958, p. 66.

Air Force Academy: R. Bruegmann (ed.), *Modernism at Mid-Century; the Architecture of the US Air Force Academy*, Chicago, 1995; cf. J. Sanders (ed.), *Stud: Architectures of Masculinity*, Princeton, 1996.

Albany: Turner, p. 297; cf. 'Expansion de l'université de l'état de New York', *A d'A* no. 123, 12-1965/1-1966, pp. 56ff.; *ARec* 6-1967, pp. 50–5; *ARec* 5-1966, pp. 165–8; G. A. Dudley, 'Billion Dollar Client', *AFor* 8-1968, pp. 75–87; S. E. Bleeker, *The Politics of Architetcure. A Perspective on Nelson A. Rockefeller*, New York, 1981, pp. 135–76; E. A. Dunham, *Colleges of the Forgotten Americans. A Profile of State Colleges and Regional Universities*, New York, 1969, pp. xiii, 96ff.; T. A. Gaines, *The Campus as a Work of Art*, New York, 1991, pp. 145–7.

W. P. Vogt, *The State University of New York at Albany, 1844–1984 A Short Story* (mimeographed, 1984); K. A. Birr, *A Tradition of Excellence. The Sesquicentennial History of the University of Albany . . .* , Virginia Beach, 1994 (Courtesy SUNYA Archives, G. P. Williams University Archivist).

'Pioneer . . .': *Albany Knickerbocker News* 6-11-1962.

'Free from limitations'; 'a great formal . . .', 'Venice': E. D. Stone, *The Evolution of an Architect*, New York, 1962, pp. 154, 147; cf. E. D. Stone, *Recent and Future Architecture*, New York, n.d. [1967], pp. 48–53. Cf. Stone's design for the International College, Beirut: a series of round pavillions, E. D. Stone, *Evolution . . .* , pp. 152–3.

Size: State University of New York at Albany, *Comprehensive Campus Plan Report Action Plan* 1-5-1965, p. 8.

Old College idea . . . : 'Stone on Stone', *University Review* (publ. by . . . State University of New York, Albany) Fall 1966, pp. 7–11.

'White' concrete: *Knickerbocker News* 11-6-1962; E. Galanty, 'Architecture', *The Nation* 23-5-1966, pp. 629–30.

Free to plan: K. A. Birr, *A Tradition of Excellence. The Sesquicentennial History of the University of Albany . . . ,* Virginia Beach, 1994, p. 126.

Extensions: see State University of New York at Albany, *Comprehensive Campus Plan Report Action Plan* 1-5-1965; residences; *ibid.*, p. 10.

'Decorated box': R. Stern, *New Directions in American Architecture*, 1969, p. 31.

'Needless to say . . .'; 'Authoritarianism': E. Galanty, 'Architecture', *The Nation* 23-5-1966, pp. 629–30.

Stone and his critics: P. Goldberger 'E. D. Stone . . .' *The New York Times* 8-8-1978 C10.

San Matteo: *Progressive Architecture* 4-1965, pp. 190–5.

Other main new university developments: campuses of State University of New York (SUNY): Stony Brook, Binghampton, Buffalo: see [Booklet] *State Universities of New York*, 1965 (in SUNY Albany Archives, G. P. Williams University Archivist); cf. also Old Westbury, Long Island and Fredonia: Turner, pp. 267, 274; S. E. Bleeker, *The Politics of Architetcure. A Perspective on Nelson A. Rockefeller*, New York, 1981, pp. 135–76.

Purchase: Social Sciences Building by Venturi & Rauch, Dance Building by Gunnar Birkerts & Associates, Art Museum by Philip Johnson & John Burgee: Museum of Modern Art New York (eds.), *Architecture for the Arts. State University of New York at Purchase*, 1971; *AFor* 11-1970, pp. 34ff.; S. Stevens, 'Such Good Intentions . . . Purchase', *Art Forum* 1-1976 pp. 26–31. K. Herdeg, *The Decorated Diagram. Harvard Architecture and the Failure of the Bauhaus Legacy*, Cambridge MA and London, 1983, pp. 74–7.

'Uniformity': E. Galanty, 'Architecture', *The Nation* 23-5-1966, pp. 629–30.

A new comprehensiveness in California

'Make university seem smaller . . .': C. Kerr, in *University of California Sta Cruz Undergraduate Bulletin* 1965, quoted V. Stadtman, *The University of California*, New York, 1970, p. 416; on Kerr see *ibid.*, pp. 377 etc.

C. Kerr, *The Uses of the University*, Cambridge MA, 1963, 2nd ed. 1972, 3rd ed. 1982.

'Great universities . . .': C. Kerr, *The Uses of the University*, Cambridge MA, 1963, pp. 87; 'maintain and even increase . . .': *ibid.*, p. 84; on UGC, *ibid.*, p. 72 Cf. A. Nevins, *The State University and Democracy*, Urbana, 1962; *DUZ* 12-1964, p. 3.

'President of a multiversity . . .': C. Kerr, *The Uses of the University*, Cambridge MA, 1963, p. 36; 'Multiversity is inherently . . .': *ibid.*, p. 37; 'mechanism . . .': *ibid.*, p. 20.

'Campus Planning. California's New Campuses, *ARec* 11-1964, pp. 175–85; *A Masterplan for Higher Education in California* 1960–75, Sacramento CA., State Department of Education 1960; S. M. Lipset & S. S. Wolin (eds.), *The Berkeley Student Revolt*, Garden City NY, 1965; H. Rich & P. M. Lolicour, *Student Attitudes and Academic Environments. A Study of California Higher Education*, New York, 1978.

State 'appropriations': V. Stadtman, *The University of California*, New York, 1970, p. 415; C. Kerr, *The Uses of the University*, Cambridge MA, 1963, p. 7.

'Public system of higher education': 'Campus Planning. California's New Campuses, *ARec* 11-1964, p. 175; 'California's New State Colleges', *ARec* 11-1964, pp. 200–4; 'College Buildings', *ARec* 9-1959, p. 159.

'The top 12.5% . . .': V. Stadtman, *The University of California*, New York, 1970, pp. 395–6.

'The determination . . .' etc.: *ARec* 11-1974, p. 200.

Wurster's & Kerr's efforts: V. Stadtman, *The University of California*, New York, 1970, p. 414.

'Pulled together into close groups': 'commercial lift slab blocks', 'youth vehement': W. W. Wurster, 'Campus Planning', *ARec* 9-1959, pp. 161–7; M. Treib (ed.), *Everyday Modernism. Houses of W. Wurster*, London, 1996.

'Kerr . . . worked hard . . .': V. Stadtman, *The University of California*, New York, 1970, p. 430.

'The big campus lacks . . .': 'Campus Planning. California's New Campuses', *ARec* 11-1964, p. 175.

Irvine: V. Stadtman, *The University of California*, New York, 1970, p. 416ff.; *ARec* 11-1964, pp. 186–91.

San Diego: Quotes from: *ARec* 11-1964 192–9; V. Stadtman, *The University of California*, New York, 1970, pp. 410–12; *The UCSD Master Plan Study and its Antecedents. A History of Physical Planning at the University of California, San Diego*, publ. University of California, 1995 (Courtesy UCSD); *Bauen & Wohnen* 11-1969, pp. 390–3.

Santa Cruz: V. Stadtman, *The University of California*, New York, 1970, pp. 412ff.; J. Warnecke & Assoc, *Long Range Development Plan University of California Sta Cruz*, Berkeley, 1963; *ARec* 11-1964, pp. 176–85; *Ad'A* no. 137, 4/5-1968, pp. 97–8; *ARec* 5-1969, pp. 146–56; *AD* 11-1969, p. 618; *Architecture Canada* 7/8-1969, pp. 50–1; P. Berdge, *Solomon's House. A Self-conscious History of Cowell College*, Felton CA., 1970; R. A. M. Stern, *Pride of Place. Building the American Dream*, Boston, 1986 p. 79ff.; *Architecture at UCSC: The First 20 Years . . .* (Exhibition 1986), n.d. publ. by UCSC (Courtesy UCSC); A. Duke, *Importing Oxbridge. English Residential Colleges and American Universities*, New Haven and London, 1996.

'Climate of curricular innovation'; 'distinctive collegiate environment'; 'renewed emphasis on teaching', 'work towards an enriched student-faculty interaction': G. Grant & D. Riesman, *The Perpetual Dream. Reform and Experiment in the American College*, Chicago, 1978, p. 287; Teachers from Oxbridge . . . : *ibid.*, pp. 261–2.

'Medieval Colleges Britain': *Architecture at UCSC: The First 20 Years . . .* (Exh. 1986), n.d. publ. by UCSC, p. 3.

The English influence: R. Montgomery, 'Center for Action', *AFor* 4-1970, pp. 65–70.

East Coast reformers: G. Grant & D. Riesman, *The Perpetual Dream. Reform and Experiment in the American College*, Chicago, 1978, pp. 77–81; 'humanistic psychology', 'a living-learning community . . .': *ibid.*, pp. 27–8; 'encounter and sensitivity training techniques': *ibid.*, pp. 80, 82; 'encourage students to let go': *ibid.*, p. 277; 'participation . . .': *ibid.*, p. 104; not taken seriously: *ibid.*, p. 77; cf. comments about Santa Cruz's difficulties: R. Niblett, 'Colleges under attack at Santa Cruz', *THES* 23-6-1972, p. 15.

Kresge: *Progressive Architecture* 5-1974, pp. 76–83; *AR* 7-1974, pp. 28–30; *Baumeister* 9-1975, pp. 797–9; *Ad'A* no. 184, 3/4-1976 p. 60. On holiday villages: M. Goldfinger, *Villages in the Sun*, New York, 1969, cf. review in *AFor* 6-1970, p. 76.

Hierarchy: H. Klotz, *The History of Post-Modern Architecture*, Cambridge MA and London, 1984, pp. 186–9.

Hierarchy . . . institutions: *Progressive Architecture* 5-1974, pp. 76–83.

'Joyous academic . . .': *The Work of Charles Moore, A + U (A Monthly Journal of World Architecture and Urbanism) Extra Issue*, 1978, p. 276.

An integral approach?

'Multiversity has no bard . . .': C. Kerr, *The Uses of the University*, Cambridge MA, 1963, p. 6.

Aesthetic and socio-political outlook: e.g P. Heyer, *Architects on Architecture*, London, 1967.

'College and University Business selects 16 outstanding Examples of Campus Design for the '70s', *College and University Business* 1-1970, pp. 39–62.

Riesman, Octets: G. Grant & D. Riesman, *The Pepetual Dream. Reform and Experiment in the American College*, Chicago, 1978, pp. 92–3.

Riesman on Santa Cruz: D. Riesman, *On Higher Education*, San Francisco, 1980, pp. 208–9.

'Major groups work alone': G. R. Larke, 'Building Systems . . . Higher Education Construction,' *College and University Business* 1-1970, p. 63.

Selectivity: G. Grant & D. Riesman, *The Pepetual Dream. Reform and Experiment in the American College*, Chicago 1978, p. 2.

While French and German architects studied American university design eagerly, there is very little evidence that English architects did: cf. Bartlett School of Architectural Studies (University College London) Institute for Architectural Studies: *Paper 4: North American Visit, February 1971*; the *AR* illustrated only a small number of new American campuses.

E. McHenry, 'The problem of impersonality and size', Speech given at Utah Conference on Higher Education Salt Lake City (February 1966), quoted in J. Scherer, *Students in Residence. A Survey of American*

Studies (publ. Dept of Higher Education, Univ. of London Institute of Education 1969), p. 19.

II ENGLISH NEW UNIVERSITY DESIGN

COLLEGE AND CAMPUS

N. B. Unless otherwise mentioned the place of publication in this chapter is London

'You do what you like . . .': *AA* 1967, pp. 25–6.

D. Chablo, *University Architecture in Britain*, DPhil. Wolfson College Oxford University, 1987; S. C. Roberts, *British Universities*, 1947; J. Mountford, *British Universities*, 1966. Bibliographies: H. Silver & S. J. Teague, *History of British Universities, 1800–1969, A Bibliography* (Society for Research into Higher Education), 1970; *History of Universities* (Oxford), vol. 1 1981–.

Campus: Civics, Redbricks and Overseas

Downing College: C. M. Sicca, *Committed to Classicism. The Building of Downing College Cambridge*, Cambridge, 1987.

Nuffield College, completed in 1960, by Harrison Barnes & Hubbard; cf. their University of Ghana, A. M. Carr-Saunders, *New Universities Overseas*, 1961, pp. 82–3.

'The college theme . . .': *AR* 10-1957, [p. 225] table of contents.

'In any newly planned "campus"': *UQ* vol. 7 no. 2 2-1953, p. 188.

Manchester University: *AJ* 9-1-1957, pp. 58–61.

See Univerity of East Anglia, *Vice-Chancellor's Report for 1961–2*: 2 April 1962: British Vice Chancellors meet with the Association of American University Presidents to see 14 American Universities (no details given).

'New Dehli Style . . .': M. Girouard, 'The English University of the Future', *Country Life Annual* 1961, pp. 22–4.

'University in a garden': L. Brett, 'Universities 2: Today', *AR* 19-1957, pp. 240–51 (p. 240).

A. P. Fawcett & Neil Jackson, *Campus Critique The Architetcure of the University of Nottingham*, Nottingham, 1998; *AJ* 9-1-1958, p. 61.

Reading: *AJ* 9-1-1958, pp. 64–5; Exeter: B. W. Clapp, *The University of Exeter*, Exeter 1982.

Birmingham University: ; *AJ* 31-10-1957, pp. 646–9; *AR* 10-1957, p. 250; *AJ* 9-1-1958, p. 39; Dober (1965), p. 36; *Town Planning Review* 4-1958, pp. 7–26.

Sheffield University: *AJ* 9-1-1958, pp. 66–7; *AR* 9-1966, pp. 172–3; *Country Life Annual* 1961, pp. 22–4. Library and Arts (and Architecture) Tower built 1958–9, by Gollins, Melvin, Ward.

Southampton: *AJ* 9-1-1958, pp. 69–70.

Africa: Linde (1970), vol. 1, pp. 90–4; A. M. Carr-Saunders, *New Universities Overseas*, 1961.

Ibadan: 'much more concentrated . . .': *AD* 5-1955, pp. 154–61; External Degree System: *8th Congress of the Universities of the Commonwealth, Montreal, 1958* (Proceedings publ. by Association of British Commonwealth Universities, London 1959); K. Mellanby, *The Birth of Nigeria's University*, 1958; K. Mellanby, 'Establishing a new University in Africa', *Minerva* vol. 1 no. 2 Winter 1963, pp. 149–58; A. I. Richards, 'Adaptation of Universities to the African Situation', *Miverva* vol. 3 no. 3 Spring 1965, pp. 336–42; 'University Development in Nigeria, *Minerva* vol. 3 no. 2 Winter 1995. Cf. Graham Dawbarn's University College of the West Indies near Kingston, Jamaica, begun in 1949, *AR* 10-1953, pp. 221–30.

University of Nigeria, Nsukka: *AR* 2-1959, pp. 133–6; pp. 86–104 in: Ross; N. Okafor, *The Development of Universities in Nigeria*, 1971.

University of the Panjab: *AR* 11-1959, pp. 275ff. (N. B. Panjab University is in Chandigarh, India); for Asia: Linde (1970) vol. 1, pp. 85–9.

A. G. Ling and R. S Johnston, 'Proposed University College in Coventry', August 1958; *ABN* 10-12-1958, pp. 770–1.

The new Cambridge contribution

Oxbridge patrons: D. Croghan, 'The Cambridge Scene', *B* 20-1-1961, pp. 122–7 (p. 116); D. Booth, 'Recent Buildings in Oxford', *B* 31-3-1961, pp. 593–8; G. Shankland, 'What is happening in Oxford & Cambridge?', *AD* 3-1960, pp. 85–90.

Gropius: P. Booth & N. Taylor, *Cambridge New Architecture*, 1964, 2nd ed. 1965, here 3rd ed. 1970, p. 14; see for all buildings mentioned here.

Sidgwick Avenue Art Faculties: *AJ* 29-10-1953, pp. 529–35; *AJ* 2-1-1958, p. 42.

For an example of high-profile design cf. Stirling & Gowan's History Faculty: 1964–8: *AR* 11-1968, pp. 328–44; *AD* 10-1968, pp. 456–74; *AFor* 11-1968, pp. 36–47.

P. Carolin & T. Dannatt (eds.), *Architecture Education Research. The Work of Sir Leslie Martin. Papers and Selected Articles*, 1996.

Planning: *UQ* vol. 4 no. 4 8-1950, pp. 41ff.; *AR* 7-1966, pp. 17–18.

Churchill College: PRO UGC 2 42, 27-3-1958; *T* 15-5-1978, p. 16; *Nature* 7-2-1959, pp. 349–50; *B* 14-8-1959, p. 4; *AJ* 13-8-1959, pp. 3–4; *AJ* 3-9-1959, pp. 118–19; Competition Entries: (first four): *AJ* 13-8-1959, pp. 7–31; (remainder): *AJ* 3-9-1959, pp. 120–42; *AD* 3-1960, pp. 85–90; *AJ* 6-12-1961, p. 1102; *T* 5-6-1964; (R. Banham) *AR* 12-1964, pp. 174–9; M. Webb, 'Massive simplicity beside the Cam', *Country Life* 25-11-1965, pp. 1394–7; C. Rowe, 'The Blenheim of the Welfare State', *The Cambridge Review*, 31-10-1959 (reprinted in: C. Rowe, *As I was saying, Recollections . . .*, vol. 1, 1996, pp. 143–51); interview Lord Annan, 1998.

'Clearly identifiable group . . .': *B* 14-8-1959, p. 4.

'Bulldogishly English': *Country Life* 25-11-1965, p. 1394. Look of 'quality': Lord Annan Interview 1998.

Banham: *AR* 12-1964, pp. 175–178; cf. R. Banham, 'Cambridge Mark II', *New Society* 26-9-1968, pp. 454–5; R. Banham, 'Ravished Groves of Academe', *New Statesman*, 3-3-1961, p. 356.

New Hall: *AR* 7-1966, pp. 16–19. For Lasdun's college buildings and projects see also R. F. Jordan, 'Lasdun', *Canadian Architect* 9-1952, pp. 55–66.

Harvey Court: all quotes from P. Booth & N. Taylor, *Cambridge New Architecture*, 1964, 2nd ed. 1965, here 3rd ed. 1970, pp. 155–60; cf. *AR* 7-1959, pp. 42–8; *Bauen und Wohnen* 11-1964, pp. 428–9.

'The Collegiate Plan', *AR* 7-1959, pp. 42–9; 'Cambridge Courts', *AJ* 11-4-1984, pp. 55ff.; cf. College Hall, Leicester University Student Residences by Sir Leslie Martin with Trevor Dannatt, *AR* 6-1961, pp. 378–83; *TES* 21-6-1963, p. 1354; *Casabella*, no. 268 1962, pp. 25–32.

Robinson College: Competition: *AJ* 20-11-1974, pp. 1195–1257; built by Gillespie, Kidd & Coia: *AJ* 5-8-1981, pp. 242–57.

Oxford: *AJ* 9-1-1958, pp. 63–4; *B* 26-9-1958, pp. 526–8; D. Booth, 'Recent Buildings in Oxford', *B* 31-3-1961, pp. 593–8; G. Shankland, 'What is happening in Oxford & Cambridge?', *AD* 3-1960, pp. 85–90; D. Reed & P. Opher, *New Architecture in Oxford* (Oxford Polytechnic), 1977.

Oxford Library Group: *AR* 10-1963, pp. 280ff.

St Catherine's College: *AR* 10-1963, pp. 279–80; (R. Banham) *AR* 12-1964, 175–9; *AD* 12-1966, pp. 595–6; *AJ* 17-11-1971, pp. 1105–18; cf. M. Brawne (on Wolfson College) *AR* 10-1974, pp. 219–20.

'We nearly unpacked it . . .'; 'ordinary standard modern . . .': *AJ* 17-11-1971, pp. 1108, 1118.

College, hall of residence, study bedroom block

J. Brothers & S. Hatch, *Residence and Student Life*, 1971; M. Brawne, 'Student Living', *AR* 10-1963, pp. 289–98; 'University Residence', *TES* 21-6-1963, pp. 1349–54; P. Marris, 'Halls or Digs for Students', *New Society* 16-5-1963, pp. 8–10; J. Donat, 'Living in Universities', *AD* 12-1966, pp. 589–632; E. Shove (University of York, Social Policy Research Unit), *Student Accommodation: Social Issues* (publ University of York), 1986; H. & P. Silver, *Students*, Buckingham, 1997. For a good early summary: S. Hatch, *Student Residence: A Discussion of the Literature* (publ. Society for Research into Higher Education Ltd.), 1968.

Statistics: *AJ* 21-50-1969, pp. 1381–2 (on Lancaster); D. Morgan & L McDowell, *Patterns of Residence. Costs and Options in Student Housing* (Society for Research in Higher Education, London), 1979.

1998: 55% in private rented accommodation, 45% in university residences: *The Guardian* 14-10-1998, p. 11.

'Digs': J. W. L Adams, 'Halls of Residence', *UQ* vol. 2 no. 3 5-1948, pp. 239–46; A. Eden, 'Social Life in a provincial University', *British Journal of Sociology* vol. 10 no. 4 1960, pp. 291–310.

'University residence desirable . . .': *UGC University Development 1957–62 (Parliamentary Papers*, Cmnd. 2267) 1964, p. 97; cf. E. Ashby, 'A Note on an Alternative to Halls of Residence', *UQ* vol. 5 no. 2 2-1951, pp. 150–4.

'Robbins Report': Committee on Higher Education, *Higher Education* (under chairmanship of Lord Robbins, *Parliamentary Papers*, Cmnd 2154), 1963, pp. 194–7; cf. Sir W. Moberly, *The Crisis in the University*, 1949, pp. 214–24.

Oxbridge college: E. Warren, Collegiate Architecture', *RIBA Journal* 1912, pp. 265–96; 'Halls of Residence' (review of Niblett, see below), *UQ* vol. 13 no. 1 11-1958, pp. 94–7. For a polemic on Oxbridge recently see: W. Ellis, *The Oxbridge Conspiracy*, 1994; cf. A. H. Halsey, *Decline of Donnish Dominion. The British Academic Profession in the 20th century*, Oxford, 1992.

Teaching function of college: Sir W. Moberley, *The Crisis in the University*, 1949, p. 218.

On residences in civics: D. Thoday, 'Halls of Residence', *UQ* vol. 12 no. 1 11-1957, pp. 45–56; D. Thoday, 'Residence and Education in Civic Universities', *International Journal of Social Psychiatry* vol. 4 no. 3 1958.

Teacher Training Colleges: 'Robbins Report': Committee on Higher Education, *Higher Education (Parliamentary Papers*, Cmnd 2154), 1963, pp. 27–30; J. Brothers & S. Hatch, *Residence and Student Life*, 1971.

J. Murray, 'Halls of Residence in Universities', *UQ* vol. 3 no. 2 2-1948, pp. 563–70; J. W. L. Adams, 'John Murray on Halls – a Comment,' *UQ* vol. 3 no. 4 8-1949, pp. 814–16; J. Murray, 'Universities and Residence', *Contemporary Review* 6-1962, pp. 289–92; for Boarding Schools: R. Lambert, *The Chance of a Lifetime. A Study of Boys' and co-educational Boarding Schools in England and Wales*, 1975.

'[Keith] Murray Report': *The Planning of University Halls of Residence. A Report . . .* Committee of Vice-Chancellors Great Britain & Ireland, publ. Oxford, 1948: 'make for quicker . . .': *ibid.*, p. 5; 'to relax . . .': *ibid.*, p. 15; 'atmosphere of academic calm': *ibid.*, p. 38.; 'member of staff . . .': *ibid.*, p. 43; selection: *ibid.*, p. 72; 'laundry and sewing rooms . . .': *ibid.*, p. 18; 'healthy competition': *ibid.*, p. 57.

50% total cost: W. Taylor, 'Student Culture amd Residence', *UQ* vol. 19 no. 4 9-1965, pp. 331–45 (p. 335).

'Niblett Report': UGC, *Report of the Subcommittee on Halls of Residence* July 1957 (Chairman W. R. Niblett; members: A. L. C. Bullock, D. G. Christopherson, Dorothy Dymond, Eric James, N. F. Mott, Mary Ogilvie, L. H. A. Pilkington, Mary Stocks).

'Requires a revolution . . .': *ibid.*, p. 9; 'much of the liberalising . . .': *ibid.*, p. 2; 'two atmospheres . . .': [Keith] Murray Report, op. cit. note above, p. 5; all further quotes from Niblett Report: 'blend of dignity . . .:, *ibid.*, p. 15; 'pass easily ceremonies . . .': *ibid.* p. 16; 'every evening . . .': *ibid.* p. 15. low background: *ibid.*, pp. 8–9; 'life in hall . . .'; 'shy and awkward . . .':

ibid., p. 16; 'staircase plan': *ibid.*, p. 12; cf. also R. Niblett, 'Halls of Residence. Students in Isolation', *TES* 12-12-1958, p. 1777.

Lionel Brett: 'most important . . .': *AR* 10-1957, p. 240.

Increase of residence: 'Robbins Report': Committee on Higher Education, *Higher Education* (Parliamentary Papers, Cmnd 2154), 1963, pp. 194–7; Sir W. Moberly, *The Crisis in the University*, 1949, pp. 154, 193–5.

'University life a bus ride': M. Girouard, 'The English University of the Future', *Country Life Annual* 1961, pp. 22–4; cf. 'Halls of Residence' (review of Niblett Report), *UQ* vol. 13 no. 1 11-1958, pp. 94–7.

£1,500 to £840: PRO UGC 2 46, paper 74/58; PRO UGC 2 50, 19-2-1959.

Own cooking: *AJ* 11-8-1971, p. 304 (on Lancaster).

Oxbridge changes: J. Brothers & S. Hatch, *Residence and Student Life*, 1971, pp. 56–8, 222; A. Peake & T. Phipps, 'New Student Accommodation', *Isis* [Cambridge], 20-11-1963, pp. 13–15.

'Superfluidity of common rooms . . .': *AR* 10-1957, p. 242.

'We do not know': D. Thoday, 'University Expansion and Student Life', *UQ* vol. 14 no. 3 6-1960, pp. 272–7; 'A Policy for Higher Education', *Socialist Commentary* 9-1959, pp. 17–30; cf. A. Giddens, 'Aspects of Social Structure of a University Hall of Residence', *Sociological Review* no. 8 1960, pp. 97–108.

'Residence does not influence . . .': P. Marris, 'Halls or Digs for Students', *New Society* 16-5-1963, pp. 8–10.

'Impose arbitrary segregation': P. Marris, *The Experience of Higher Education*, 1964, p. 182.

'Retard the process of reaching maturity': *TES* 21-6-1963, p. 1349.

Reject excessive discipline: M. Brawne, 'Student Living', *AR* 10-1963, pp. 289–98.

Scandinavia: *UQ* vol. 2 no. 3 5-1948, p. 239; *AR* 10-1963, pp. 289–98; *TES* 21-6-1963, p. 1352; *AD* 12-1966, p. 591; University of Leeds, *Confidential Report of the House and Estates Committee by the Delegates sent studying Housing in Continental Countries* (publ. by Univ of Leeds, 1962); J. Hands & R. Bingham, *Housing Students in Scandinavia*, SCD (Student Co-operative Dwellings Ltd, London) *Research Paper*, c. 1972 (copy in Library of Bartlett School University College London).

'"Study bedroom"': *AR* 1-1961, p. 10; *AR* 10-1963, p. 292.

Against just sleeping accommodation: 'Niblett Report': UGC, *Report of the Subcommittee on Halls of Residence* July 1957, pp. 16–17.

Coed: '[Keith] Murray Report': *The Planning of University Halls of Residence. A Report . . .* Committee of Vice-Chancellors Great Britain & Ireland (publ. Oxford 1948), p. 57; A. P. Fawcett & N. Jackson, *Campus Critique, The Architecture of the University of Nottingham*, Nottingham, 1998, p. 61; for Halls at Nottingham: *Association Internationale des Universités, Bulletin*, VIII 1960 1, pp. 52–3; *UQ* vol. 15 no. 1 12-1960, p. 61; *TES* 21-6-1963, p. 1349; *Lancaster*

Guardian, 10-5-1963; *Essex Country Standard University Supplement*, 14-10-1964; J. Brothers & S. Hatch, *Residence and Student Life*, 1971, pp. 330ff.; F. Gibb, 'Out of the Commune and into the Community' *THES* 14-2-1975, p. 7; H. & P. Silver, *Students Changing Roles, Changing Lives*, Buckingham, 1997, pp. 25, 43–9; cf. M. Birney Vickery, *Buildings for Bluestockings. The Architecture and Social History of Women's Colleges in late Victorian England* (Univ. Delaware Press) London, 2000.

'Living together . . .': *THES* 14-2-1975, p. 7.

Statistics: H. & P. Silver, *Students. Changing Roles, Changing Lives*, Buckingham, 1997, pp. 25–6, 45–9.

Government Guidelines for planning and building of student residences: Department of Education and Science, Building Bulletin No 37: Student Residences, 1967; on student residences: *AJ* 7-4-1965, pp. 851ff.; *AJ* 14-4-1965, pp. 903ff.; *AJ* 21-4-1965, pp. 971ff., *AJ* 28-4-1965, pp. 1025ff.; 'Some new university and college buildings' [on interiors], *Interior Design* 11/12-1960, pp. 90–105; 'The student in Residence', *AR* 4-1970, pp. 287–91.

Weeks Hall: *AJ* 5-12-1957, p. 837; *Architect and Building News* 20-4-1960, pp. 501–10; *AD* 3-1960, pp. 94–7; *TES* 21-6-1963, p. 1354; *AR* 10-1963, pp. 244–9, 294; *AJ* 28-4-1965, pp. 1027–39; Dober (1965), pp. 13–16; H. Schmalscheidt, *Studentenheime*, München, 1973, pp. 54–8.

Leeds, Bodington Hall [also spelt Boddington], Otley Road, by Jones & Stocks, 1959–63: N. Pevsner (revised by E. Radcliffe), *Buildings of England Series, Yorkshire West Riding*, Harmondsworth, 1967; illustration in UGC, *University Development 1957–62 (Parliamentary Paper* Cmnd. 2267), 1964.

University of Leeds Report of a Committe on Student Accommodation (Grebenik Report) Leeds 1962 (see P. H. J. H. Gosden & oth. (eds.) *Studies in the History of a University 1874–1974*, Leeds, 1975, pp. 62ff.); *TES* 21-6-1963, p. 1352; *AD* 12-1960, p. 603; *AR* 4-1970, pp. 287–71.

Reading: *AJ* 3-3-1965, pp. 527–35.

Owen's Village, by Building Design Partnership: *TES* 21-6-1963, p. 1349; *AD* 12-1966, pp. 609–10; 'An experiment in living', *Twentieth Century* vol. 174 Summer 1965, pp. 60–1; Perkin, pp. 29, 87; *Architecture and Building News* 16-3-1966, pp. 477–83.

Tower blocks: *AJ* 9-1-1958, p. 44; *TES* 21-6-1963, p. 1350; *AD* 12-1966, p. 612; cf. M. Glendinning and S. Muthesius, *Tower Block. Modern Public Housing in England, Wales, Scotland and Northern Ireland*, 1994.

Liverpool, Carnatic Scheme, Mossley Hill by Manning and Clamp: *AJ* 3-10-1962, pp. 805–16; *TES* 21-6-1963, p. 1353.

The Lawns Cottingham, Hull: *AR* 1-1963, pp. 24–5; *AR* 10-1968, pp. 261–7, Linde (1970) vol. 4, pp. 157–9.

Student Health Services: N. Malleson [Director Research Unit for Student Problems, University of London Institute of Education], 'University Students, 1953. IV Different Sorts of Students', *UQ* vol. 15 no. 1 12-1960, pp. 54–63; P. Halmos (ed.), *Sociological Studies in British University Education*, Keele (Univ. of Keele), 1963 (*Sociological Review Monograph*, No. 7); N. Malleson, *A Handbook on British Student Health Services*, 1965; A. Mair, *Student Health Services*, Oxford, 1967; J. Payne, *Research in Student Mental Health* (Society Research into Higher Education) 1969; H. & P. Silver, *Students*, Buckingham, 1997, pp. 3, 36ff.

'We cannot say . . .': J. Brothers & S. Hatch, *Residence and Student Life*, 1971, p. 353.

Why student residence . . . : J. Donat, 'Living in Universities', *AD* 12-1966, pp. 589–632.

'Luxurious accommodation': W. Mullins & P. Allen, *Student Housing*, 1971, p. 22.

Only housing: 'John McKean asks: do university students need special housing?', *RIBA Journal* 10-1975, pp. 9–20.

Rooms in older houses: *TES* 21-6-1963, p. 1354; *AD* 12-1966, p. 631; J. Brothers & S. Hatch, *Residence and Student Life*, 1971, pp. 237ff.

College into campus: institutional to spontaneous

Gowns: F. W. Haycroft (revised by C. A. H. Franklin), *The Degrees and Hoods of the World's Universties and Colleges*, 5th ed. Lewes (Sussex) 1972.

'Loyalty': 'Niblett Report': UGC, *Report of the Subcommittee on Halls of Residence*, July 1957, p. 15.

3,000: S. Maclure, 'Whither Britain's New Universities?', *Listener* 26-1-1967, pp. 121–2; G. Sutherland, 'Is there an Optimum Size for a University?', Minerva 1-1973, pp. 57–63.

Students' Unions: see H. & P. Silver, *Students*, Buckingham 1997.

Union too big: J. W. L. Adams, 'Halls of Residence', *UQ* vol. 2 no. 3 5-1948, pp. 239–46 (p. 244).

'Some students would prefer . . .': 'Niblett Report': UGC, *Report of the Subcommittee on Halls of Residence*, July 1957, pp. 17, 33, 40.

'Membership' of the hall: 'Niblett Report': UGC, *Report of the Subcommittee on Halls of Residence*, July 1957, pp. 36, 40.

Durham: D. Parsons, 'A Hall for Non-Residents', *British Universities Annual* 1964, pp. 96–101.

E. Ashby, 'A Note on an Alternative to Halls of Residence'. *UQ* vol. 5 no. 2 2-1951, pp. 150–4.

'Student houses': 'Niblett Report': UGC, *Report of the Subcommittee on Halls of Residence*, July 1957, p. 43.

Norwich: no shops on edge of campus: *T* 19-3-1963; *Eastern Daily Press* 15-6-1963.

Meet in Department: P. Marris, 'Halls of Digs for Students?' *New Society* 16-5-1963, pp. 8–10; W. Taylor, 'Student Culture and Residence', *UQ* vol. 19 no. 4 9-1965, pp. 331–44.

'Non-artificial': P. Marris, 'Halls of Digs for Students?' *New Society* 16-5-1963, pp. 8–10.

'Meet casually . . .': *AA* 1967, p. 10;

'Chance contiguity . . .': Dr N. Malleson, 'Other Ways of Living, *TES* 21-6-1963, p. 1354.

'Do not . . . impose community structure . . .': *AR* 10-1963, p. 292.

'Unforced associations . . .': PRO UGC 7 503 1-1964 (Halls at Warwick).

'Free group discussion', M. Cassidy, 'Architecture and the Sociology of University Life', *UQ* vol. 18 no. 4 9-1964, pp. 353–65.

'Unplanned and spontaneous . . .': *AD* 12-1966, p. 589.

'We need wardens . . .': D. Parsons, 'A Hall for Non-Residents', *British Universities Annual* 1964 pp. 96–101 (p. 99).

'Idealism, spontaneity . . .': John Davis, *Youth and the Condition of Britain*, 1990, p. 63; cf. K. Kumar, *Utopia and Anti-Utopia*, Oxford, 1987, pp. 394ff.; cf. D. Chapman, 'The Autonomous Generation', *Listener* 17-1-1963, pp. 107–8; Bryan Wilson, *The Youth Culture and the Universities*, 1970; P. Jackson and P. Young, 'Death of the Student,' Twentieth Century vol. 174 1965 pp. 61–2.

Dober (1965), pp. 35ff.

Cf. *AD* 12-1966, p. 632; S. Van der Ryn (Univ. of California, cf. page XX), 'The University Environment', *AD* 11-1969, pp. 618–20.

Academic supervision . . . : R. Niblett, 'Halls of Residence', *TES* 12-12-1968, p. 1777.

A. H. Halsey, 'University Expansion and the College Ideal' *UQ* vol. 16 no. 1 12-1961, pp. 55–8 (p. 58).

Thistlethwaite: 'college . . .': F. Thistlethwaite, *The Founding of UEA. A Reminiscent Chronicle*, November 1963, mimeographed Univ. of East Anglia Archives.

Town planning and public housing paradigms: precinct, townscape, urban cluster and the elevated pedestrian

'No difficulty . . . universities . . .': L. Brett, 'Universities Today', *AR* 10-1957, pp. 240–52 (p. 242).

'Freedom from traffic . . .': M. Girouard, 'The English University of the Future', *Country Life Annual*, 1961, pp. 22–4.

W. Curtis, 'L'université la ville et l'habitat collectif', *Archithese* 14 1975, pp. 29–36. Le Corbusier quote from *Quand les cathédrales étaient blanches*, Paris 1937, pp. 200–1.

'Scatter . . .': L. Brett, 'Universities Today', *AR* 10-1957, pp. 240–52 (p. 242).

'Finite areas . . .': M. Cassidy, 'Architecture and the Sociology of University Life', *UQ* vol. 18 no. 4 9-1964, pp. 353–65 (p. 357).

Housing and Townscape: M. Bottero, 'Urban and public housing paradigms', *Zodiac* 18 [1968] pp. 256ff. f M. Glendinning & S. Muthesius, *Tower Block. Modern Public Housing in England, Wales, Scotland and Northern Ireland*, 1994; L. Esher, *A Broken Wave*, Harmondsworth, 1981; D. Gosling, G. Cullen. *Vision of Urban Design*, 1996.

Imperial College: *AR* 7-1955, pp. 30–5.

'Living stream of university life . . .': *AJ* 29-10-1953, p. 529.

Leeds: P. H. J. H. Gosden & A. T. Taylor, *Studies in the History of a University 1874–1974 . . . Leeds*, Leeds, 1975; *University of Leeds Development Plan*, Chamberlin, Powell & Bon (Architects) (publ. Univ. of Leeds) April 1960; *AJ* 19-5-1960, p. 749, *AJ* 26-5-1960, pp. 786–8; *AR* 1-1965, p. 23; Dober (1965), pp. 37–41; *Deutsche Bauzeitung* 2-1969, pp. 90–4, *AR* 4-1970, pp. 251ff.; *AR* 1-1974, pp. 4–21.

A. & P. Smithson: R. Banham, *The New Brutalism, Ethic or Aesthetic*, 1966; A. & P. Smithson, *Ordinariness and Light, Urban Themes 1952–1960*, 1970; M. Glendinning & S. Muthesius, *Tower Block. Modern Public Housing in England, Wales, Scotland and Northern Ireland*, 1994; pp. 121ff.

Sheffield University etc.: *AR* 10-1963, pp. 289–98; *AJ* 22-7-1964, p. 201.

Hook: 'Two High Density Redevelopment Schemes . . .', *RIBA Journal* 2-1964, pp. 51–9; *Stadtbauwelt*, 1 1964, pp. 25–40.

R. Banham, *Megastructures. Urban Futures of the Past*, 1976; cf. S. Adler, *The Situationist City*, 1998.

THE 1960S NEW UNIVERSITIES

'The alliance . . .': A. H. Halsey, 'The Universities and the State', *UQ* vol. 23 no. 2 Spring 1969, pp. 128–48 (p. 143).

On Newspapers: Beloff, pp. 15, 56, 151; cf. Beloff in: *Encounter*, 5-1968, pp. 14–23; *Daily Telegraph* 18-11-1968; *Sunday Telegraph* 3-11-1968; *Sunday Telegraph* 17-11-1968.

On the New Universities in general: PRO UGC 2 60, Paper 48/60: 'New University Institutions. Memorandum by the UGC; K. Murray, 'The Development of the Universities in Great Britain', *Journal of The Royal Statistical Society*', vol. 121 no. 4 1958, pp. 931–419; K. Murray, 'England's new Universities', *Commonwealth Journal (Journal of the Royal Commonwealth Society)* vol. 5 no. 2, 3/4-1962, pp. 91–3; *Economist* 26-11-1960, pp. 852–3; B. B. Raboni, 'L'università in Inghliterra. Un problema aperto', *Zodiac* 18 (1968) pp. 212–20 (Universities in England: Still an Open Question', pp. 278–82); *Listener 1965, 1966, 1967*. UGC, *University Development 1962–1967 (Parliamentary Papers* Cmnd. 3820), 1968. Other general works: Perkin; H. E. Smith Rhett, *Creating University Communities: Four New Universities in England*, Ph.D, Graduate School Cornell University, 1968. J. Lawlor (ed.), *The New Universities*, 1968; H. J. Perkin, 'Was ist neu an Englands neuen Universitaten', *Unesco Dienst*, Köln no. 11 1971, pp. 8–12; Perkin; 'The new Universities' (articles by H. Perkin, A. Briggs, G. Darley & oth.) *Higher Education Quarterly*, vol. 45 no. 4 Autumn 1991, pp. 285–367.

Hess: 'England . . .': Foreword to J. F. Embling, *Die neuen Britischen Universitäten als Instrumente der Reform*, Konstanz (publ. by Universität) 1969.

The UGC and the local founders

State proportion: A. H. Halsey, 'The Universities and the State', *UQ* vol. 23 no. 3 Spring 1969, pp. 128–48 (p. 138).

'National need': UGC, *University Development 1957–62 (Parliamentary Papers* Cmnd. 2267), 1964, p. 153; cf. 'Robbins Report' : Committee on Higher Education, *Higher Education (Parliamentary Papers,* Cmnd 2154), 1964; *The Years of Crisis, Report of Labour Party's Study Group on Higher Education* (1962); Peter Scott, *The Crisis of the University,* 1984; on the *Crowther Report on Education* of 1959: see John Davis, *Youth and the Condition of Britain,* 1990, p. 95.

4,500: 'Bursting which Seams?': *The Economist* 9-7-1960, pp. 120–3.

On UGC; K. Murray, *Recollections* (privately printed, 1992, courtesy Michael Murray), pp. 49–53; Obituary, *T* 12-10-1993; cf.; M. Shattock, *The UGC and the Management of British Universities,* Buckingham, 1994; J. (Lord) Wolfenden, 'The UGC: A personal view', *THES* 2-4-1976, p. 13; G. H. Dodd, 'The UGC' [Lecture Cologne], in: *Informationen 34* (ed. by Zentralarchiv für Hochschulbau Stuttgart), Stuttgart, 1976; R. O. Berdahl, *The British Universities and the State,* Cambridge 1959; G. C. Moodie & R. Eustace, *Power and Authority in British Universities,* 1974.

'Possess full range . . .': Obituary, *T* 12-10-1993.

Redbricks and Civics; B. Truscot: *Redbrick and these vital days,* 1945; W. H. G. Armytage, *Civic Universities,* 1955; *The Twentieth Century,* 2-1956; J. Mountford, 'University Expansion', *Manchester Guardian* 16-5-1957, 17-5-1957, 18-5-1957; E. J. Morse, 'English Civic Universities and the Myth of Decline', *History of Universities* 11 1992, pp. 177–204; S. V. Barnes, England's Civic Universities and the Triumph of the Oxbridge Ideal', *History of Education Quarterly,* vol. 36 no. 3 Fall 1996, pp. 271–305.

30 applications: Perkin, p. 70; UGC, *University Development 1957–62 (Parliamentary Papers* Cmnd. 2267), 1964, pp. 63–93.

'Dismal and unattractive . . . : G. Tilsley, UEA. A Personal Reminiscence (MS 1988 in University of East Anglia Library Archives), p. 83.

W. G. V. Balchin, 'University Expansion in Great Britain', *New Scientist* 12-3-1959; M. Wright, 'The Design of Universities', *Town Planning Review* 7-1974, pp. 233–5.

Norwich early plan: R. G. Jobling, 'The Location and Siting of a new University', *UQ* vol. 24 no. 2 Spring 1970, pp. 123–36.

'De facto control . . .': A. H. Halsey, 'The Universities and the State', *UQ* vol. 23 no. 2 Spring 1969, pp. 128–47 (p. 137); cf. A. H. Halsey, *Decline of Donnish Dominion. The British Academic Professions in the 20th century,* Oxford, 1992.

'Hands-on, highly personal . . .': M. Shattock, *The UGC and the Management of British Universities,* Buckingham, 1994, p. 148.

'"Clubbale", enjoyable . . .': K. Murray, *Recollections* (privately printed, 1992, courtesy Michael Murray), p. 44; cf. K. Kerr, *The Uses of the University,* Cambridge MA, 1963, p. 72; *DUZ* 19/20 1955 [no date], pp. 10–11; Linde (1970) 1, pp. 56–7.

'Good' academic staff: 'Sites chosen to attract dons?', *Observer* 21-5-1961.

'Born Free': quoted in: Beloff, p. 26.

The Balliol/'Liberal' Ethos.
The 'schools' setup

'1/3 numbers, 2/3 ideas': P. Wilby, 'Interesting Experiments but no radical change', *THES* 18-6-1976, p. 6; 'experiments' see Beloff, H. Perkin; 'The University Explosion. New Life on the Campus', *Observer Magazine* 8-5-1966.

'Patchwork'; haphazard growth': B. Ford, 'Creating the New Universities', *ST* 17-6-1962 (Magazine), pp. 28–9.

'Elitist, hierarchical': Perkin, p. 45; cf. B. Ford, 'Creating the New Universities', *ST* 17-6-1962 (Magazine Section) pp. 28–9; B. Ford, 'What kind of education?', *ST* 24-6-1962 (Magazine Section) p. 24.

'University graduates . . .': K. Amis, 'Lone voices. View of the 1950s', *Encounter* 15-7-1960, pp. 6–11; cf. Debate in the House of Lords on 11-5-1960: *T* 12-5-1960, pp. 4–5; A. Briggs, 'A New Approach to University Degrees', *Listener* 24-5-1962, pp. 899–900; N. Annan,

TABLE OF TIMING OF 'SEVEN'

	Govt. Announcement	APB established	VC appointed	Main Buildgs begun	Student numbers 1961–2	1963–4	1966–7
Sussex	Feb. 1958	April 1958	Feb. 1959	Jan. 1960	52	885	2763
York	April 1960	April 1960	Jan. 1962	Dec. 1963	–	225	1070
East Anglia	April 1960	May 1960	Aug. 1961	Nov. 1964	–	112	1225
Essex	May 1961	Sept. 1961	July 1962	Nov. 1964	–		600
Kent	May 1961	Sept. 1961	Aug. 1962	Jan. 1964	–		700
Warwick	May 1961	Sept. 1961	Nov. 1962	Nov. 1964	–		670
Lancaster	Nov. 1961	Feb. 1962	Dec. 1962	Nov. 1964	–	–	600

'The Universities', *Encounter* 4-1963, pp. 3–14; on Robbins Report, *Listener* 14-11-1963, p. 780; S. Black and M. Sykes, 'More means worse revisited', *UQ* vol. 25 no. 3 Summer 1971, pp. 289–325. Oxbridge full: *T* 2-10-1959, p. 13 (leader).

Briggs: 'qualitative / quantitative': *AA* 1967, p. 12.

'Not mere specialists . . .': 'Robbins Report': Committee on Higher Education, Higher Education (*Parliamentary Papers*, Cmnd. 2154), 1964, pp. 6–7.

'Men are men . . .': J. St Mill, Inaugural Lecture, St Andrews, in F. A. Cavenagh (ed.), *James & John St Mill on Education*, 1931, pp. 133–4, quoted in W. R. Niblett (ed.), *Higher Education*, 1969, p. 112.

Sir. W. Moberly, *The Crisis in the University*, 1949; cf. A. Löwe, *The University in Transformation*, 1940.

F. R. Leavis, *Education and the University*, 1943.

'Liberal Arts College planned at Nottingham University', *Bulletin Association Internationale des Universités*, vol. 9 no. 1 1961, B. Pattison, 'Liberal Education', *Contemporary Review* 12-1962, pp. 283–7; J. Floud, J. Rosselli, 'Studying Higher Education in Britain and America', *UQ* vol. 17 no. 2 3-1963, pp. 126–48; A. D. C. Peterson, 'The Relevance of Liberal Arts Colleges', *UQ* vol. 17 no. 4 9-1963, pp. 346–52; cf. G. Grant & D. Riesman, *The Perpetual Dream, Reform and Experiment in the American College*, Chicago, 1978, pp. 43, 48–9; F. Thistlethwaite of East Anglia liberally uses 'liberal' in 1963: F. Thistlethwaite, *The Founding of UEA. A Reminiscent Chronicle*, November 1963 (mimeographed Univ. of East Anglia Archives).

New Universities not Liberal Arts . . . : S. Maclure, 'Whither Britain's New Universities?', *Listener* 26-1-1967, pp. 121–2, second article, *Listener* 2-2-1967, p. 1578.

Balliol; 'a close-knit community . . .': R. H. C. Davis & R. Hunt, *A History of Balliol College*, Oxford, 1963, p. 263; C. Driver, *The Exploding University*, 1971, pp. 132–53.

Keele: W. B. Gallie, *A New University. A. D. Lindsay and the Keele Experiment*, 1960; J. Mountford, *Keele. A Historical Critique*, 1972; *Listener* 28-1-1965, pp. 137–8; *AJ* 6-3-1968, pp. 545–58; Obituary Lindsay, *T* 29-3-1952, p. 9.

'Remarkable proportion . . .': W. R. Niblett, 'Halls of Residence', *TES* 12-12-1958, p. 1777.

'Leaders': cf. H. Huseman, 'Anglo-German Relations in Higher Education' in: A. Hearnden (ed.), *The British in Germany*, 1978, pp. 158–73.

'Governing class . . .': W. R. Niblett (ed.), *The Expanding University*, 1962, p. 123.

'Buccaneers . . .': *TES* 'Seven Builders': A. E. Sloman [Essex], 9-12-1966, p. 1416; the others: Fulton [Sussex], 4-11-1966, p. 1078; James [York], 11-11-1966, p. 1152; Thistlethwaite [East Anglia], 18-11-1966, p. 1218, Carter [Lancaster], 25-11-1966, Butterworth [Warwick], 2-12-1966, p. 1354, Templeman [Kent], 16-12-1966, p. 1471; cf. *AR* 10-1963, p. 231; Beloff, p. 106; Perkin, p. 149.

'Balliol Society . . .': Perkin, p. 230.

'Balliol-by-the-Sea': *T* 16-8-1961, p. 9.

'Allegiance': Perkin, p. 84.

'Insider': W. R. Niblett, (ed.) *The Expanding University*, 1962, p. 124.

James: 'Students . . . directionless': W. R. Niblett (ed.), *The Expanding University*, 1962, p. 135.

'Fundamental . . . community': A. Briggs, 'A University for Today', *Listener* 7-9-1961, p. 346; cf. P. H. Man, 'University Community', *British University Annual* 1963, pp. 104–15; H. E. Smith Rhett, *Creating University Communities: Four New Universities in England*, Ph.D. Graduate School Cornell University, 1968; R. Startup, 'Is the University a Community', *Higher Education Review* 5 1 1972, pp. 6–20; D. Christopherson, *The University at Work*, 1973; Centre for Educational Research and Innovation, *The University and the Community*, OECD Paris 1982; see M. Glendinning and S. Muthesius, *Tower Block. Public Housing in England, Wales, Scotland and Norther Ireland*, pp. 104ff.; N. Blake, 'Truth, Identity, Community in the University', *Curriculum Studies* 3 3 1995; R. Barnett & A. Griffin, *The End of Knowledge in Higher Education*, 1997.

Reeves: 'the academic community . . .': Quoted in B. Ford, 'What is a university?', *New Statesman* 24-10-1969, p. 561.

C. P. Snow, *The Two Cultures and the Scientific Revolution* [The Rede Lecture 1959], 1960; 'almost all high tables . . .': C. P. Snow, *The Two Cultures. A Second Look*, 1964, p. 102.

Oxbridge influence extending: R. Niblett, 'Oxbridge and Redbrick: The Debt and the Interest', pp. 161–70, in: P. Halmos (ed.), *The Sociologcal Review Monograph*, No 7: *Sociological Studies in British University Education*, Keele, 1963.

Oxbridge graduate figures: 'Robbins Report': Committee on Higher Education, *Higher Education* (*Parliamentary Papers*, Cmnd. 2154), 1963, p. 99.

'Highly articulate, Oxbridge type . . .': F. Thistlethwaite, *Doing Different in a Cold Climate, The St John's Lecture, 25-10-1988* (publ. St John's College Cambridge), p. 7.

F. Thistlethwaite: 'Norwich should become an outstanding teaching university', quoting, as he writes, the Norwich Academic Planning Board in 1962–3, in: Ross, p. 62. Eric James: much was made of the fact that James had been previously a headmaster at a prestigious grammer school: 'All I wanted to be was a schoolmaster': *THES* 17-8-1973, p. 7.

'Redrawing the map . . .': A. Briggs, 'Universities for Tomorrow. Maps of Learning', *New Statesman* 3-3-1961, pp. 338, 340; A. Briggs, 'A University for Today', *Listener* 7-9-1961, pp. 345–6.

'School': one may note that in the US 'School' usually denotes the opposite of Brighton's ideal: e.g. the 'Law School' etc., cf. J. D. Millett, *The Academic Community*, New York, 1962.

'Everyone is guarding . . .': A. Briggs, 'A New Approach to University Degrees', *Listener* 24-5-1962, pp. 899–900; cf. Perkin, p. 31; Beloff, p. 42; M. B. Campbell, *Non-specialist Study in the Undergraduate Curricula of the New Universities and Colleges of Advanced Technology in*

England (publ. University of Michigan School of Education), AnnArbor 1966.

DEGREE COMBINATIONS:

The following ostensibly simplified survey was given to applicants for 1969/70:

Sussex: Students major in one of about 45 subjects, many of which can be studied in several schools. Within each school students take 'contextual studies' linking the subject of their major to the interests of their schools.

York: There are no schools or faculties: supervision of studies is by boards, and teaching is organised by departments, but teaching in non-science subjects takes place in colleges.

East Anglia: . . . now eight schools. Each school has a broadly based two-term introductory course followed by a choice of integrated options.

Essex: Students are based on one of the four schools of study: comparative, mathematical, physical and social. Each school has a broadly-based first year scheme combining three or four subjects . . . most subjects . . . can be studied in more than one school . . . each school with its own distinctive emphasis.

Kent: The degree structure and range of subjects is traditional; there are no highly experimental courses and only the broad four term Part I within each of the three faculties. . . .

Warwick: allows disciplines to develop freely but with a marked emphasis on combined degrees and broad first year with a chance to sample the unfamiliar.

Lancaster: A large range of degree subjects. . . . Students are expected to study at least one course unrelated to that in which they are 'majoring' and this may be a science course for arts students and vice-versa. Quoted from *ST* 9-11-1969 (Magazine) pp. 84–5.

Varied views of Oxbridge: 'Advice from Lord James', *TES* 4-5-1962, p. 888; 'Universities', *Observer* 4-11-1962; 'Elite system of education sustained by a democracy', P. Marris, *The Experience of Higher Education*, 1964, p. 180; B. Wilson, 'In Defence of Oxbridge', *Spectator* 15-4-1966, p. 458; A. H. Halsey, 'Ancient Grip on new Universities', *THES* 5-7-1974, p. 5; T. Tapper & B. Salter, *Oxford and Cambridge and the Changing Idea of University*, Buckingham, 1992.

Nicknames: (Verse: *Observer* 14-6-1964, p. 12). 'The Shakesesperan Seven': *AR* 4-1970, p. 241, Sir Edward Boyle is credited with that term. Other nicknames: Greenfield, Whitbrick, White Stone, Pinktile, Newbridge; Plateglass appears to have been Beloffs invention: Beloff, p. 11. 'Hardboard': *Arkitekten*, 1966, p. 257; 'Beadecker Universities' (Harold Wilson 1967): M. Shattock, *The UGC and the Management of the British Universties*, Buckingham, 1994, p. 73; 'Mushroom universities': M. Thompson, 'Natural Sciences in the New Universities', in: 'The New Universities', *Higher Education Quarterly* vol. 45 no. 4 Autumn 1991, p. 346.

Welfare State 'Social Form' The Architects Devise Cost-Cuting Briefs

'What is the Modern equivalent . . .': 'The Design of New Universities', *RIBA Journal* 7-1964, pp. 301–9 (p. 308).

'New University Movement . . .': *AA* 1967, p. 7.

'Neither the mind nor the face . . .'; 'Pent-up flood . . .': 'The Universities Build', *AR* 10-1963, pp. 231–2.

'British architects as briefmakers . . .': *AD* 12-1966, p. 592.

'Architects' universities . . .': B. Ford, 'New University in Essex', *New Statesman* 11-12-1964, pp. 919–21.

'Odd way architects . . .': B. Ford, 'University Planning', *Architectural Association Journal* vol. 80 no. 888 6-1965, pp. 159–63; cf. *AA* 1967, p. 20; *AR* 4-1970, p. 251.

Word of mouth / letter . . .: H. Rees, *A University is Born*, Coventry 1989, p. 70; G. Martin, *From Vision to Reality the Making of the University of Kent*, Canterbury 1990.

Situation of postwar architects: cf. J. Summerson, Introduction to Arts Council of GB Exhibition, *Ten Years of British Architecture 1945–55* (exh. cat.) 1955.

UGC, *University Development 1957–62 (Parliamentary Paper* Cmnd. 2267), 1964, pp. 115ff. (a series of illustrations of new university buildings which are hardly illustrated elsewhere).

'British Universities': 'New university buildings', *T* 8-3-1957, p. 5; *AJ* 2-1-1958, pp. 1–3 (Introduction), pp. 4–33; 'British Universities 2', *AJ* 9-1-1958, pp. 37–70; cf. D. Chablo, *University Architecture in Britain*, DPhil. Wolfson College Oxford University, 1987.

On 'routine functional' see J. M. Richards, 'The next Step', *AR* 3-1950, pp. 170–8; cf. M. Glendinning & S. Muthesius, *Tower Block, Public Housing in England, Wales, Scotland and Northern Ireland*, 1994, pp. 104–9.

'Primitve functionalism . . .': *AA* 1967, p. 7.

Stirling and Gowan at Cambridge (History Library), Oxford (Florey Building) and Leicester (Engineering Faculty).

'Building Allocations': UGC, *University Development 1962–1967*, (Parliamentary Paper Cmnd. 3820), 1968, p. 152.

L. Brett, 'Universities Today, *AR* 10-1957, pp. 225, 240–51; preceded by a potted history of university buildings by Nikolaus Pevsner, 'Universities Yesterday', pp. 235–9; cf. on the *AR*: M. Spens (ed.), *AR* 100. *The Recovery of the Modern 1980–1995*, 1999.

'More humane and adaptable . . .'; 'administrative buildings . . .': *AR* 10-1957, pp. 243, 242.

'Restore to the designer . . .': *AR* 10-1957, p. 251.

'Supreme social importance . . .': G. Shankland, 'What is happening in Oxford and Cambridge?', *AD* 3-1960, pp. 85–90.

Criticism of the architecture of Keele: *AR* 10-1957, pp. 246, 251; *AJ* 9-1-1958, pp. 51–2; *UQ* vol. 19 no. 4 9-1965, pp. 331–45; *AJ* 6-3-1968, pp. 545–52; *AJ* 30-10-1968, pp. 1003–16; Perkin, pp. 28, 60.

'While we are dazzled . . .': R. Furneaux Jordan, 'Lasdun', *Canadian Architect* 9-1952, pp. 55–66.

'Social Architecture', see A. Saint, *Towards a Social Architecture. The Role of School Building in Post-War England*, 1987; cf. R. Llewellyn-Davies, 'The Science Side: Human Sciences', *AR* 3-1960, pp. 185–90.

William Stone Building for Peterhouse, by L. Martin and C. St J. Wilson: P. Booth & N. Taylor, *Cambridge New Architecture*, 1970, pp. 39–41.

A. Briggs, Interview 1999: 'St Catherine's College Oxford cost about 3 times per square foot as Sussex'.

Bochum: see below.

'Gater Report', UGC, *Methods used by Universities of Contracting and of Recording and Controlling Expenditure (Parliamentary Paper* Cmnd. 9) 1956; 'Rucker Report', UGC, *Methods used by the Universities of Contracting and of Recording and Controlling Expenditure (Parliamentary Paper* Cmnd. 1235) 1960; UGC, *Non-Recurrent Grants. Notes on Procedure*, 1963.

Appeal sums: M. Shattock, *Making a University* (publ. Univ of Warwick), 1991, p. 124.

Question of development architect: PRO UGC 2 73, 21-9-1961.

Thistlethwaite and UGC: PRO UGC 7 213, K. Murray internal note.

Unpublished reports by A. E. Parnis filed with individual universities, PRO UGC 7; cf. below on York, p. 311.

'Designing New Universities' (Meeting at RIBA, 3 March 1964: Robert Matthew, Stirrat Johnson-Marshall, Lord James, Lord Esher, Henry Swain, Sir William Holford, Peter Shepheard, Sir Gordon Russell, David Medd, Peter Newnham, John Stillman & others): *Architect and Building News* 11-3-1964, p. 438; *AJ* 11-3-1964, pp. 568–9; *B* 20-3-1964, pp. 627–9; *RIBA Journal* 7-1964, pp. 301–10; S. Johnson-Marshall, 'Architectural Dilemma', *Guardian* 26-11-1964, p. 10. cf. M. Fry, 'The Aesthetics of New University Building', *UQ* vol. 18 no. 4 9-1964, pp. 341–51; J. Fielden & G. Lockwood, *Planning and Management in Universities*, 1973; P. Jokusch & F. J. Mertens, *Gesamtplanungen britischer Hochschulen. Bericht . . . Studienreise in GB* (*Schriften Zentralarchiv für Hochschulbau*, Stuttgart, 5), Düsseldorf, 1967; 'University Buildings, Notes by a Building Officer', *British Universities Annual* 1963, pp. 129–39.

'UGC policy, as distinct . . .': PRO UGC 7 216, Letter to B. D. Fraser 16-12-1958.

Exclusivity of English universities: cf. R. Löwe, *The Welfare State in Britain, Manchester*, 1993, pp. 224–7.

Sussex

Briggs: *AR* 10-1963, pp. 233–4.

'Liberal education': PRO UGC 7 215, 5-6-1956; *UQ* vol. 12 no. 3 5-1958, pp. 223–7.

'Trade may follow . . .': PRO UGC 7 215, Memo Feb. 1956, pp. 24–30; cf. *T* 15-2-1956.

General: D. Daiches (ed.) *The Idea of a New University. An Experiment in Sussex*, 1964; J. Fulton, *Experiment in Higher Education*, 1964; Birks; H. E. Smith Rhett, *Creating University Communities in England,* PhD. Cornell University 1968; R. R. Blyn-Stoyle (ed.), *The Sussex Opportunity*, Brighton 1986.

'Eight persons . . .': Daiches, *op. cit.*, p. 186.

J. Mountford, *Keele*, 1972, pp. 55–9.

'Incredibly varied public life': *TES* 4-11-1966, p. 1078; Fulton at University College of Wales Swansea: D. Dykes, *University College Swansea*, Gloucester, 1992; P. Morgan, *The University of Wales 1939–1993*, Cardiff, 1997.

Norwich dropped 'college': PRO UGC 7 212, Letter C. Wilson 18-5-1960; Memo 27-5-1960.

Size: *T* 21-2-1959, p. 4; *T* 25-3-1960; cf. *T* 21-2-1958, p. 10; PRO UGC 218 7, 24-6-1959; *UQ* vol. 15 no. 2 3-1961, pp. 139–51; cf. 'Dreams of Regency Red Brick', *Manchester Guardian* 20-2-1959, p. 8.

'Freedom . . .': PRO UGC 7 215, 29-11-1959.

'Completely free . . .': A. Briggs in R. R. Blyn-Stoyle (ed.), *The Sussex Opportunity*, Brighton 1986, p. 3.

'Merely to turn out . . .': A. Briggs, 'A University for Today', *Listener* 7-9-1961, pp. 345–6.

See Daiches, *op. cit.*; J. Fulton, 'Sussex' pp. 32–52, in Ross; S. Maclure, 'The "with-it" University', *Listener* 25-2-1965, pp. 290–2; A. Briggs, 'University Social Studies: The Sussex Idea', *New Society* 18-10-1962, pp. 20–2; see also the *University of Sussex Handbook and Guide for Applicants* series; H. C. Jones, G. Lockwood, N. Mackenzie, 'The University of Sussex', in: V. Gonushkin (ed.), *Planning the Development of Universities* vol. 1 (I I E P Seminar Paris 7-11-7-1969; Paris UNESCO, International Institute for Educational Planning), 1969.

'Throughout the world . . .': 'Balliol by the Sea faces its Future', *T* 16-8-1961, p. 9.

3,100 applicants: *T* 12-10-1962, p. 6.

'Oxford, Cambridge . . .': *T* 12-11-1964.

'PR and Colour Supplement . . .': *New Statesman* 11-12-1964, pp. 932–4.

'Unlike London . . .': *T* 12-11-1964.

Borough Surveyor: PRO UGC 7 215 n.d (c. early 1957); PRO UGC 7 215, 19-8-1957.

Stone interviews: Daiches, *op. cit.*, p. 192; PRO UGC 7 216, 5-8-1958.

On Spence: L. Campbell, *Coventry Cathedral*, Oxford, 1996; Cambridge: P. Booth & N. Taylor, *Cambridge New Architecture*, 1970, pp. 41 ff.; Southampton, Liverpool etc. see *AJ* 2-1-1957.

Architectural Sources: *AJ* 31-3-1960, pp. 511–3; *B* 1-4-1960, pp. 643–6; *Ad'A* no. 91-2 9/10/11-1960, pp. 134–5; *AR* 1-1962, pp. 40–1; *AJ* 4-4-1962, p. 712; *Architecture and Building News* 19-12-1962, pp. 917–23; 'Precast Structure at Sussex', *Architecture and Building News* 19-12-1962, pp. 924–6; *Yorkshire Post*, 18-12-1962; *AR* 10-1963, pp. 264–274; *AR* 12-1964, pp. 403–9; *Ad'A* no. 1123 12-1965/1-1966, pp. 80–1; Dober (1965), pp. 67–9; *DUZ* 3-1966, pp. 14–15; *AR* 10-1970, pp. 255–8; on Stanmer House: C. Musgrove, 'New Life for Great Sussex House', *T* 8-6-1963, p. 11.

'One of the most interesting . . .': B. Spence, 'Building a new University', in Daiches, *op. cit.*, p. 208.

Stone's determination: PRO UGC 7 217, 1-12-1959.

Fulton and residences: PRO UGC 7 217, 1-12-1959; yet the Appeal (n.d., c. end 1959/beginning 1960) asked for £1m for residences.

'Father and mother . . .'; 'completeness': Spence in Daiches, *op. cit.*, pp. 202, 208–12.

'Our alternative to a college system': *AA* 1967, p. 15; interview Lord Briggs 1999.

'Care was taken . . .': Daiches, *op. cit.*, p. 49.

'Staff and Students mix . . .': *Yorkshire Post* 18-12-1962. On one occasion Briggs found himself with Spence in the lunch queue and asked him 'how long will this take?' Spence: 'not as long as in the queue for mass in Coventry Cathedral' (interview Lord Briggs 1999).

'Chest of drawers . . .'; 'to stand up to hard wear': Spence in Daiches, *op. cit.*, pp. 202–12.

'Axis of our main entrance archway . . .': Spence in Daiches, *op. cit.*, p. 207.

Meeting House: *T* 9-6-1965, p. 12; *T* 15-6-1965, p. 13; *T* 23-6-1965, p. 8. Here an important role was played by the Chairman of the University Council, Alderman Sydney Caffyn of Eastbourne.

'I am against the rigid formal plan': Spence in *AA* 1967, p. 27.

Materials: Daiches, *op. cit.*, p. 205; *T* 25-3-1960; *Guardian* 25-5-1965, p. 14.

'Peaceful pastoral scene': Spence in Daiches, *op. cit.*, p. 205.

Sylvia Crowe: *Guardian* 25-5-1965, p. 14. Cars: Birks, pp. 58–9.

'Careful interrelationship . . .': Birks, p. 51; cf. Brawne in *AA* 1967, p. 10.

'Avoid an institutional type . . .': *Architect and Building News* 19-12-1962, pp. 917–23.

'Should help sixth-formers . . .': Spence in Daiches, *op. cit.*, p. 203.

'The undergraduate is still . . .': 'University should get protection', *TES* 11-11-1966, p. 1153.

'Series of interlocking . . .': Spence in Daiches, *op. cit.*, p. 203.

'Established a university presence . . .' *Listener* 25-2-1965, p. 291.

'Beauty' . . . "aesthetics" . . .'; 'committees do not know . . .'; 'Sussex esprit'; Spence in Daiches, *op. cit.*, pp. 203, 215, 202–3.

Fulton's ideas about College House: Daiches, *op. cit.*, pp. 202–3.

Briggs: 'the academics . . .': Lord A. Briggs, 'A Founding Father reflects', pp. 311–33 (p. 323) in: 'The New Universities', *Higher Education Quarterly* vol. 45 no. 4 Autumn 1991.

UGC . . . more economic: PRO UGC 7 485, 28-4-1961.

Guy Oddie Interview 1997.

'It might be reasonable to allow . . .': PRO UGC 7 217, 1-12-1959 (Internal Memo by Copleston).

Not out of line . . . : Parnis in PRO UGC 7 486, 13-2-1967.

Later architecture: see *AR* 4-1970, p. 255; Birks, p. 54; cf. Brett in *AR* 10-1963, p. 259.

Unpredictability: Fulton in Ross, p. 23; cf. G. Lockwood, 'Das Planungsverfahren an der Universität Sussex,' *Konstanzer Blätter für Hochschulfragen*, no. 30, vol. 9 (no. 1) 2-1971, pp. 63–78; Univ. of Sussex, Site Development Projects, Discussion Paper, January 1973.

First Hall for Men by Ronald Sims, for Women by H. Hubbard Ford: *TES* 21-6-1963, p. 1353; for the village-like Brighthelm Residences by Phippen, Randall & Parkes see *AJ* 9-5-1979, pp. 948–50.

Later Assessements: A. Briggs, 'The "Distinction" of Sussex', *THES* 31-12-1971, p. 10; 'The State of English – II: The University of Sussex', *TLS* 11-2-1972, p. 147; 'Staff claim Sussex Ideas eroded', *THES* 2-2-1973, p. 1; P. Wilby, 'Sussex', *THES* 30-4-1976, pp. 6–7; 'Bold Idea that kept its Promise', *T* 7-2-1986, p. 25.

Warwick

General: H. Rees, *A University is Born, The Story of the Foundation of the University of Warwick*, Coventry, 1989; PRO UGC 7 224, 503–5; M. Shattock, *Making A University, A Celebration of Warwick's First 25 Years*, publ. University of Warwick, 1991; M. Shattock, *The UGC and the Management of British Universities*, Buckingham, 1994; H. E. Smith Rhett, *Creating University Communities in England*, PhD. Cornell University 1968; Birks.

Search for a vice chancellor, M. Shattock, *op. cit.*, p. 20; cf. *TES* 2-12-1966, p. 1354.

Determining the architect(s) PRO UGC 7 224, December 1962–January 1963; 'cost conscious': Rees, *op. cit.*, pp. 55–6; PRO UGC 7 503, January 1963 onwards; Rees, *op. cit.*, pp. 70–2. 'The architects are anxious . . .': PRO UGC 7, 503 6-8-1963. YRM discussed: PRO UGC 7 503, 28-10-1963.

Development Plan: PRO UGC 7 503; '2nd Draft' 31-12-1963.

Appeal: Shattock, *Making A University* (publ. University of Warwick) 1991, p. 124.

'Co-operation . . . industrial side . . .': Rees, *op. cit.*, pp. 89–90.

'"Real world"': Beloff, p. 143.

Oxbridge professors: Rees, *op. cit.*, p. 79; *Guardian* 9-12-1965, p. 10.

'Best to let professors . . .': Lord A. Briggs, 'A Founding Father reflects', pp. 311–33 (p. 324) in: 'The New Universities', *Higher Education Quarterly* vol. 45 no. 4 Autumn 1991.

'No straightjacket', 'no "complex whole"', A. P. Griffiths, 'The New Universities: The New Humanities', pp. 333–45 in: 'The New Universities', *Higher Education Quarterly* vol. 45 no. 4 Autumn 1991.

'It is regarded as essential . . .': *University of Warwick Development Plan* (A. Ling) (publ. Univ. of Warwick) April 1964, p. 3; cf. *AA* 1967, p. 61.

University of Warwick Development Plan (A. Ling) (publ. Univ. of Warwick) April 1964.

'10 minutes walk': Rees, *op. cit.*, p. 90.

'Final answer to student living': PRO UGC 7 503, 31-12-1963; cf. Ling a little earlier PRO UGC 7 224, 4-4-1963 (Univ. War. Report, no. 1, p. 2 UGC Paper 56/63); cf *AJ* 27-5-1964, pp. 1201–6; Dober (1965), pp. 58–61; *T* 10-4-1964.

'58 millions'. . . : *Coventry Evening Telegraph* 9-4-1964.

Architectural sources: *AJ* 27-5-1964, pp. 1201–6; *AR* 7-1964, p. 5; *AD* 5-1964, p. 206; *AR* 1-1965, p. 18; *AR* 1-1966, p. 16; *AJ* 5-10-1966, p. 833; *AD* 6-1966, pp. 301–4; *AJ* 23-11-1966, pp. 1271–84; *AR* 4-1970, pp. 273–4; *Baumeister* 1-1972, p. 52–3; *AJ* 13-9-1972, p. 577; *AJ* 24-3-1976, pp. 583–93; *AR* 5-1975, pp. 266–8; *Baumeister* 9-1975, p. 781.

'Faster . . . , a big office', on YRM (Yorke, Rosenberg and Mardell): PRO UGC 7 503, 28-10-1963; on YRM: *AD* 6-1966, p. 277ff; *University of Warwick Development Plan* (YRM; Univ. of Warwick) 1966; R. Banham (introd.), *YRM 1944–1972*, 1972.

YRM on Churchill College: 'Avoid . . . the conscious protective sense . . .': *AJ* 3-9-1959, p. 135.

Eugene Rosenberg himself : *Guardian* 28-9-1966, p. 13.

'It will not be possible . . .': PRO UGC 7 503, 31-12-1963.

'University has deliberately chosen . . .': *AJ* 23-11-1966, pp. 1271–84.

'Solid' . . . 'cool' . . .': *Guardian* 28-9-1966, p. 13.

'Classic simplicity . . . austerity . . .': G. Lewison & R. Billingham, *Coventry New Architecture*, Warwick, 1969, p. 88.

'Which we call Halls'. *University of Warwick Development Plan* (A. Ling) (publ. Univ. of Warwick) April 1964, p. 17.

'Nothing will stop a student . . .': *AJ* 27-5-1964, p. 1206.

Halls for 1000–1500: G. Lewison & R. Billingham, *Coventry New Architecture*, Warwick, 1969, p. 82:

No high blocks: PRO UGC 7 505, memo, n.d. c. end of 1966.

University of Warwick Development Plan (YRM, Univ. of Warwick) 1966; cf. *AA* 1967, pp. 62–3; PRO UGC 7 504, 12-8-1965 and 3-11-1965.

'A system of internal roads'; 'hoped for'; 'be put in hand . . .': *AA* 1967, pp. 62–3; *AJ* 23-11-1966, p. 1293; *AR* 4-1970, p. 274.

'Town sized machine'; 'needlessly regimented': *Guardian* 28-9-1966, p. 13.

'Dehumanised . . .': Birks, p. 107.

'Yesterdays' planning philosophy': *AJ* 13-9-1972, p. 577. P. Wilby, 'The fragmented Dream of Warwick', *THES* 26-3-1976, pp. 6–7; E. P. Thompson, *Warwick University Limited*, Harmondsworth, 1970; Falling tiles: see below.

For the later type of student residences at Warwick see below, page 291.

Kent

General: G. Martin, *From Vision to Reality. The Making of the University of Kent at Canterbury* (publ. Univ. Kent),

1990; E. Fox & T. Barker, 'Canterbury Campus', *New Education* vol. 1 no. 3 1-1965.

Templeman: H. Rees, *A University is Born, The Story of the Foundation of the University of Warwick*, Coventry, 1989, p. 70.

'Personifying the older academic style': *T* 31-3-1986, pp. 22–4.

'Paternalistic' Beloff, p. 136.

'Not about gimmicks': *TES* 16-12-1966, p. 1471. cf. PRO UGC 7 449, 11-12-1962; *Times* 4-4-1963.

Tutorials: M. Maclure, *Listener* 17-2-1966, pp. 235–7; Beloff, p. 137.

'Merging of learning and living': PRO UGC 7 449, 10-1962; *T* 27-4-1964.

Choosing the architect: PRO UGC 7 449, 8-10-1962.

'Among the top few in the world league': Martin, *op. cit.*, p. 74.

Holford: G. E. Cherry & L. Penny, *Holford: A Study in Architecture, Planning and Civic Design*, 1986.

'Single whole . . .': . . .': PRO UGC 2 92, Paper 50/63; cf. G. Templeman, 'Research and Education in a New University', *Nature* 16-5-1964, pp. 636–9; G. Templeman, 'The Responsibility of Institutions of Higher Education', pp. 30–5 in: M. Reeves (ed.), *Eighteen Plus. Unity and Diversity in Higher Education*, 1965.

Plenty of room between them: PRO UGC 7 449, 11-12-1962 ('Kent Development Plan').

'Finest site . . .': *TES* 16-12-1966, p. 1471.

Holford's early sketch: Martin, *op. cit.*, pp. 84–5; Holford Papers Liverpool University Archives D. 147/C75/19.

Architectural Sources: *Architecture and Building News* 2-1-1963, p. 5 (on Holford); *Architecture and Building News* 6-11-1963, p. 717; *AR* 1-1965, p. 19; *AJ* 17-11-1965, pp. 1141–52; *AR* 4–197, pp. 271–2; Birks.

Templeman's recipe of dispersal: PRO UGC 7 450, Paper 15/64 16-1-1964.

'At least 10 self-contained colleges': *Architecture and Building News* 6-11-1963, p. 717; cf. *T* 27-4-1964, p. 22; *Illustrated London News* 23-10-1965, pp. 26–29; *Guardian* 11-10-1965, p. 6.

'"Grand manner" . . . a bleakness . . .': *AJ* 17-11-1965, p. 1147.

R. Banham, 'The Outhouses of Academe', *New Society* 6-10-1966, pp. 546–7.

UGC costs limits . . . : PRO UGC 7 449, 21-1-1963, 22-1-1963; PRO UGC 7 504, 16-4-1964.

'A clash of personalities': Martin, *op. cit.*, pp. 76–80.

'The thing that really fascinates . . .': *TES* 16-12-1966, p. 1471.

'Each college is as compact . . .': *AA* 1967, p. 57.

Master's House: *T* 27-4-1964; Martin, *op. cit.*, Chapter 4.

First coed university college . . . : Martin, *op. cit.*, pp. 115; *T* 19-2-1964, p. 6.

'Community of masters and scholars': Martin, *op. cit.*, pp. 109, 115.

Old college ritual: Beloff, pp. 131–3.

'No rules': *Wyvern* (Essex University student newspaper) 5 2-11-1965, quoted in *AJ* 20-9-1972, p. 645.

Offspring looked after: Martin, *op. cit.*, pp. 113–15.

'Holford's buildings incorporate': *Listener* 17-2-1966, pp.

235–6; cf. 'Ancient and Modern touch but they do not embrace', *THES* 18-4-1975, p. 9; S. Berlyn, 'Kent's Stunted Growth', *New Statesman*, 21-1-1977, p. 85; P. Wilby, 'The Time for Adventure has now passed', *TES* 4-6-1976, pp. 6–7; 'dream works come true': *T* 31-3-1986, pp. 22–4; 'Town and Gown make it a chaste Affair', *T* 31-3-1986, p. 24; 'Hints of the Old in Modern Halls', *T* 31-3-1986, pp. 22–4.

York

Memorandum: PRO UGC 7 218, February 1947.

'One of the most beautiful towns . . .': PRO UGC 7 218, 24-6-1959.

'York's ultimate aim': PRO UGC 7 218, memo 3-1959.

'Whole English speaking world': PRO UGC 7 218, 24-6-1959.

E. James: 'An Apostle of the Intellectual Elite', *T* 20-2-1961, p. 2; *TES* 4-5-1962, p. 888; *Yorkshire Evening Press*, 10-2-1962.

Three further New Universities by RMJM: see below: Bath, Ulster and Stirling.

B. Wood, 'Old Buildings for a new University', *Country Life* 3-10-1963, pp. 822–7.

'Of all the [early] decisions taken . . .': E. James, 'The Start of a New University', *Transactions of the Manchester Statistical Society* 1965–6, pp. 1–26 (p. 6).

A. Saint, pp. 214–23 in: *Towards a Social Architecture, The Role of School Building in Post-war England*, 1987.

Architectural Sources: *AJ* 13-6-1962, pp. 1323–36; *AJ* 6-3-1963, p. 486; *AJ* 15-12-1965, pp. 1435–48; *AR* 12-1965, pp. 409–11; *AR* 1-1966, p. 22; *AR* 4-1970, pp. 259–62; *T* 15-1-1971, Supplement; *AJ* 23-2-1972, pp. 415–26; Birks; *Werk* vol. 53 no.1 1966, pp. 6ff.

'It is doubtful . . .': E. James, 'The Start of a New University', *Transactions of the Manchester Statistical Society* 1965–6, pp. 1–26 (p. 6).

James – Derbyshire relationship: *TES* 21-6-1963, p. 1351.

'Cost limits': 'Design of New Universities': *AJ* 11-3-1964, p. 568.

University of York Development Plan 1962–1972 publ. University of York (May) 1962.

'Sociometric diagrams': Joan Abbott, 'The University Environment . . .', *Twentieth Century* no. 175 Summer 1966, pp. 45–8.

James's motto 'the identity . . .': *AJ* 13-6-1962, p. 1328. Cf. on Sussex and York, *ST* 24-6-1962.

University of York Development Plan 1962–1972, York, 1972. Foreword: p. 3.

'Propositions': *Development Plan, op. cit.*, p. 13.

'Distaste for pomp and circumstance': *THES* 17-8-1973, p. 7

'Schoolmaster': title of article *THES* 17-8-1973, p. 7.

'The academic community, the clerisy . . .': E. James, 'The Start of a New University', *Transactions of the Manchester Statistical Society* 1965–6, pp. 1–26 (p. 25).

'His sort of university . . .': Parnis in PRO UGC 7 502, 23-2-1967.

York least eager: E. James, 'The Start of a New University', *Transactions of the Manchester Statistical Society* 1965–6, pp. 1–26 (p. 14).

Choice whether single or combined . . .': *Guardian* 22-10-1965, pp. 18–19.

'Breadth is more likely . . .': E. James, 'The Start of a New University', *Transactions of the Manchester Statistical Society* 1965–6, pp. 1–26 (p. 14).

Colleges: 'personality', 'endowments': PRO UGC 7 218, memo 12-1959, cf. *Yorkshire Evening Press* 23-11-1960; *T* 15-5-1962.

Colleges 'build up a body . . .': PRO UGC 7 219, Interim Report APB [Academic Planning Board] 3-1961.

'Encourage isolation . . .': and a parochial attitude': *University of York Development Plan 1962–1972*, York, 1962, p. 11.

English Department . . . colleges: P. Wilby in *THES* 27-2-1976, pp. 8–9.

Each college originally three departments: *TES* 21-6-1973, p. 1351.

'Mixing of different interests . . .': *University of York Development Plan 1962–1972*, York, 1962, p. 10, pp. 9–13; cf. S. Maclure, *Listener* 6-5-1965, pp. 633–5.

'Opportunities for meeting . . .': *Development Plan, op. cit.*, p. 11.

'Excessive concentration . . .': *AJ* 13-6-1962, p. 1330.

Centrally . . . teaching timetable: *Development Plan, op. cit.*, pp. 31, 35.

'Membership is distributed . . .': *Prospectus 1969–70*, p. 26.

'Non-resident members . . .': *Prospectus 1969–70*, pp. 69–70.

Nothing should substitute: E. James, 'The Start of a New University', *Transactions of the Manchester Statistical Society* 1965–6, p. 10; cf. *Yorkshire Post* 7-2-1966; *Nouse* (York Student Newspaper) 16 5-5-1966; see also: *University of York Development Plan Review* (publ. University of York), 1995.

Honorary memberships . . . : *Prospectus 1970–1*, p. 21.

'Comparatively few . . . student politicians': James in Ross, p. 40.

Size: *AJ* 23-2-1972, p. 416; *ST* 9-11-1969 (Magazine), p. 84.

Maximum number could get to know . . . : *AA* 1967, p. 33.

Each staircase a tutorial room: *TES* 21-6-1963, p. 1351.

'Students, staff, porters . . .': *Prospectus 1970–1*, p. 26.

'Here students sit and talk': (article on E. James): *TES* 11-11-1966, p. 1152.

'Libertarianism': E. James, 'The Start of a New University', *Transactions of the Manchester Statistical Society* 1965–6, pp. 19–20; J. Brothers & S. Hatch, *Residence and Student Life*, 1971, pp. 330–1.

CLASP: see A. Saint, *Towards a Social Architecture. The Role of School Building in Post-war England*, 1987.

'Minimum study bedroom . . .': *TES* 21-6-1963, p. 1351.

System was somewhat modified: UGC 7 502, 2-3-1965; *AJ* 15-12-1965, p. 1448; cf. *Spectator* 24-4-1964; PRO UGC 7-501, 13-2-1963; PRO UGC 7 502, 2-3-1965.

Later buildings were constructed conventionally, but covered with Clasp-like panels: *AJ* 23-2-1972, p. 421.

Science buildings: Dober (1965), pp. 30–3.

Frank Clark, Landscape Consultant (of Edinburgh University) *Guardian* 2-10-1965, p. 18; PRO UGC 2-3-1965, p. 502; D. O. Manning, 'Landscapes Revisited. Campus of York', *Landscape Research*, 20-2-1995, pp. 68–76.

'Casualness in moving around': *AJ* 23-2-1972, p. 422.

'Community', ... [rather than] ... : *University of York Development Plan 1962–1972*, York, 1972, p. 47.

Andrew Saint: A. Saint, *Towards a Social Architecture. The Role of School Building in Post-war England*, 1987, p. 214.

J. M. Richards: 'The only master plan ...': *THES* 3-10-1975, p. 6.

'The collegiate system ... expensive': *T* 15-5-1962.

Above UGC norms by 10 %: *University of York Development Plan 1962–1972*, York, 1972, p. 71.

Site works ... cost: PRO UGC 7 502, 2-3-1965.

More expensive than piecemeal: PRO UGC 7 502 1-8-1966.

'A monument to ... any abstract aesthetics ...': *University of York Development Plan 1962–1972*, York, 1972, p. 13.

'I want beautiful places ...': *AJ* 11-3-1964, p. 568.

'Quality of memorableness': *University of York Development Plan 1962–1972*, York, 1972, p. 14.

'In the style of the Cambridge ...': quoted in A. Saint, *Towards a Social Architecture. The Role of School Building in Post-war England*, 1987, p. 217.

Lacking aesthetic qualities: C. Feinstein (ed.), *York 1831–1981. 150 Years of Scientific Endeavour and Social Change*, York, 1981, p. 306; Parnis at York: PRO UGC 7 502, memo February 1965.

'York is a disarming place: *AD* 12 1966, p. 605.

'Strongly built form' *AR* 12-1965, pp. 409–10.

'Scattered', or 'confused' PRO UGC 7 502, 23-2-1967.

'Amorphous': PRO UGC 7219, York Academic Planning Board 26-1-1961.

Integrated 'Urban'

'University ... social place': P. Jokusch in Linde (1970), 2, p. 84.

East Anglia

General: P. Dormer and S. Muthesius, *Concrete and Open Skies. Architecture at the University of East Anglia 1962–2000*, 2000; M. Sanderson, *A History of UEA* (forthcoming).

Kate Wharton ('Family Forum'), *Daily Telegraph* 29-11-1963.

UGC discussions about vice chancellors' residences: PRO UGC 7 440, Paper 143/63 17-10-1963, memo on UEA 17-7-1963 ('notional cost of new house £20,000').

University Village: Medway System, chiefly timber panels; finally demolished in the late 1980s. *Architecture and Building News* 27-11-1963, pp. 887–980; P. Thompson, 'The Architecture of the New Universities', *Country Life* 28-10-1965, pp. 1116–19; *Illustrated London News* 23-7-1966, p. 15.

W. Curtis, *Denys Lasdun* 1984; R. Furneaux-Jordan on Lasdun, *Canadian Architect* 9-1962, pp. 55–65 (especially for Cambridge).

Note by G. Tilsley 10-11-1961 (UEA Docs. Est FN/213).

Mackintosh: 'one mind ...': Report of meeting 8-7-1961 (UEA Docs. Est. FN/213 10-7-1961).

R. Banham, *The New Brutalism, Ethic or Aesthetic?* 1966.

On Lasdun's 'Draft I plans and model: *TES* 26-4-1963; *T* 26-4-1963; *B* 21-4-1963, pp. 875–7; *AJ* 8-5-1963, p. 976; *AR* 10-1963 261–2; UEA in *AA* 1967, pp. 36–45.

L. Brett in *AR* 10-1963, pp. 261–2.

'Cathedral-coloured': Executive Committee Extraordinary Meeting 30-9-1963 (UEA Doc. Est FN/213).

Troubles: see especially PRO UGC 7 440.

'Not a College ... no brief': Interview Frank Thistlethwaite 1996.

Residences: UEA Academic Planning Board, Student Residences as a Factor in the Development Plan, Paper I 10 Januray 1962; quote from Paper II 15 February 1962 (filed with Residences Sub-Committee Minutes 13-1-1964–21-9-1964). Chief designer in Lasdun's office for the UEA residences was Edward Cullinan; Michael Brawne worked on the other buidings.

'Smithsons: 'Could it be ...': A. & P. Smithson, *Without Rhetoric*, 1973, p. 34; W. Curtis, *Denys Lasdun*, London, 1994, p. 99.

Later Architectural Sources: *AD* 6-1965, pp. 288–91; *AJ* 5-1969, pp. 245–68; *Official Architecture and Planning* 4-1968, pp. 513–15; *Arup Journal* 3-1968, pp. 36–41; *Concrete Quarterly* 10/12-1969, pp. 18–25; F. Hawes, 'UEA Revisit', *Concrete Quarterly* Spring 1990, pp. 8–11; S. Upjohn and A. F. Crawshaw, 'Case Study UEA', *AJ* 14-6-1972, pp. 1331–8; T. Aldous, 'Adventures in Architecture. The New Universities', *Country Life* 29-1-1976, pp. 222–4; A. H. Th. Vercruysse, 'Plan voor een nieuwe universitet in Engeland', *Tijdschrift voor architectuur en beeldende kunsten* 10-1965, pp. 461–7; *L'architettura Chronache i Storia* no. 123 1-1966, pp. 662–3; *Arkitekten* (Stockholm) 1966, pp. 256–60; *Zodiac* 18 (1968), no p. nos.; *Deutsche Bauzeitung* 6-1969, pp. 470–5. *ARec* 7-1969, pp. 99–110; C. Dardi, 'Lettura di D. L.', *Lotus* vol. 7 1970, pp. 208–35; W. Curtis (& oth.), *A Language and a Theme. The Architecture of D. Lasdun & Ptrs.*, RIBA 1976; W. Curtis, 'D. Lasdun and his place in the Modern Tradition', *World Architecture* vol. 14 1991, pp. 34–53.

'Walking briskly': S. Upjohn & A. F. Crawshaw, 'Case Study: University of East Anglia', *AJ* 14-6-1972, pp. 1321–38.

Essex

John Maule McKean, 'University of Essex. Case Study', *AJ* 20-9-1972, pp. 637–78; 'Essex Comeback', *AJ* 6-12-1972, pp. 1292–4; 'Essex Comeback', *AJ* 13-12-1972, pp. 1348–50; cf. J. Langfield 'Not-so-Ivory Towers overshadow Essex piazzas' (summary of AJ articles), *THES* 20-10-1972, p. 7.

Other major sources: A. E. Sloman, *A University in the Making* (The Reith Lectures 1963), publ. BBC London 1964; also as: 'A University in the Making', *Listener* 14-11-1963, pp. 777–9, 810; 21-11-1963, pp. 823–6; 28-11-1963, pp. 875–8; 5-12-1963, pp. 924–8; 5-12-1963, pp. 980–3; 19-12-1963, pp. 1026–7, 1030–1; H. E. Smith Rhett, *Creating University Communities in England*, PhD. Cornell University 1968.

'Take hairdressing . . .': *Essex County Standard* 26-5-1961; cf. *T* 13-10-1959, p. 8.

'Its personality, magic . . .': *Listener* 12-12-1963, p. 983.

Annan: 'Distinct . . .': *ST* 17-6-1962.

6000?: PRO UGC 7 233, letters 21-11 1961, 22-11-1961.

'More than 6000': *T* 5-7-1962.

'Exhilaration . . .': *Listener* 14-11-1963, p. 840.

'Most progressive seats of learning . . .': *Eastern Daily Times* 1966, quoted in McKean *AJ* 20-9-1972, p. 653; cf. *T* 5-7-1962.

'A University should . . .'; 'full community life . . .': *Listener* 5-12-1963, p. 924.

'Social centres' or 'nuclei': PRO UGC 2 81, Report of Essex Academic Planning Board Feb. 1962.

'No colleges or halls of residence'; 'students do not want to be reminded . . .': *Listener* 5-12-1963, p. 924.

'Provide enlightenment, not paternalism'; responsibility: *Guardian* 17-10-1966, p. 5.

'Halls sometimes perpetuate . . .': *Listener* 5-12-1963, p. 925.

'Like many Londoners . . .': *Listener* 5-12-1963, p. 924.

'Groups of a dozen . . .': *Listener* 5-12-1963, p. 927.

'Each have their own key': *Essex County Standard, University Supplement* October 1964, p. VI. Cf.: *AJ* 21-12-1966, pp. 1559–1573; *RIBA Journal* 7-1964, p. 305; Beloff p. 112; M. Crossick (Society for Research into Higher Education Ltd. London), *Student Residence: A New Approach at the University of Essex: A Study of Rayleigh Tower 1965–6*, 1967.

Criticisms: see McKean in *AJ* 20-9-1972, pp. 667ff.; 'Life in the Tower Blocks', *Essex County Standard* 8-2-1980 (views divided).

Live and learn close to everybody: *Listener* 5-12-1963, p. 928.

'National need', Sloman, *Listener* 21-11-1963, p. 824.

'Assured of money . . .': *Listener* 14-11-1963, p. 810.

'On the whole students live on tight budgets': *Essex County Standard* 20-12-1963.

'Independent . . .'; 'serving' the community: *Listener* 14-11-1964, p. 810.

'Brand image', *Listener* 14-11-1963, p. 779.

Architectural sources: *Architect and Building News* 23-10-1963, p. 637; *AR* 11-1963, p. 609; *B* 1-11-1963, p. 899; *AJ* 6-11-1963, pp. 640–1; cf. *T* 23-1-1963, p. 6; *Colchester Express*, 24-10-1963; *Essex County Standard*, 25-10-1963; *AR* 1-1964, p. 5; *AR* 1-1965, p. 20; *AJ* 14-12-1966, pp. 1489–1508; *AJ* 21-12-1966, pp. 1559–73; *AR* 12-1966, pp. 402–12; 'The Landscape of the new Universities', *Journal of Landscape Architects*, no. 78 1967, pp. 6–7, *AR* 5-1968, pp. 343–51; *AR* 4-1970, pp. 267–70; P. Thompson, 'Essex . . . What it is like to live there', *AJ* 4-1-1967, pp. 4–6; McKean see above; S. Lyall, 'Citadels of Faded Dreams', *New Society* 16-9-1982, pp. 467–9; Birks.

'Plan . . . which gives physical . . .': *Listener* 12-12-1963, p. 980.

'It reflects absolutely . . .': *Guardian* 17-10-1966, p. 5.

'Reverential attitude . . .': quoted in *THES* 20-10-1972, p. 7.

'Not monuments . . .': M. Emanuel (ed.), *Contemporary Architects*, 1980, p. 41.

'Not avant-garde . . .': *Essex County Standard* 19-10-1962.

No clear plans: *AA* 1967, p. 47.

Development Plan, PRO UGC 2 100, Paper 191/63 of 21-11-1963.

'In contrast to York . . .': quoted in *AJ* 20-9-1972, pp. 649–65.

'It will be impossible to see . . .': C. K. Capon, 'Bright Lights at Midnight', *Essex County Standard University Supplement* October 1964.

'Small town': *Colchester Express* 7-12-1962.

'Urban' . . . ; 'institution': *AR* 10-1963, p. 309.

'Central community'; 'small university town': C. K. Capon, 'Bright Lights at Midnight', *Essex County Standard University Supplement* October 1964.

'Living and learning are one': *Guardian* 17-10-1966, p. 5.

'The Student Union in Paris . . .': *Listener* 2-2-1967, p. 158.

'English love softening . . .': Capon, quoted in McKean, *AJ* 12-9-1972, p. 656.

Princess Margaret: McKean in *AJ* 20-9-1972, p. 661.

San Gimignano: illustration in McKean in *AJ* 20-9-1972, p. 648.

Churchill College . . . suburban sprawl: *AJ* 3-9-1959, pp. 119–21.

'Need a gesture . . .': *New Statesman* 11-12-1964, p. 920.

Contractors: Holloway Bros. (London) Ltd.

3 years: *Listener* 14-11-1963, p. 810.

Costs: cf. PRO UGC 2/94, Paper 81/63.

No Clasp: 'the loading . . .': PRO UGC 2 100, paper 191/63 Development Plan, 21-11-1963.

'Considerable architectural and social . . .'; 'if sacrifices in user efficiency . . .': *AJ* 14-12-1966, p. 1492.

'Provided that you can hear . . .': *Architectural Association Journal* vol. 80 no. 888 1-1965, p. 167.

'The most imaginative . . .': Perkin, p. 96.

'Staff have willingly turned . . .': N. Annan, *Report of the Disturbances in the University of Essex* (publ. Univ. of Essex), 1974, p. 31.

'The university Library . . . : Statement by Registrar A.

Rowland-Jones on the Development Plan, quoted in McKean, *AJ* 20-9-1972, p. 653.

Lancaster

'We have got the balance . . .': G. Brosan, C. Carter & oth., *Patterns and Policies in Higher Education*, Harmondsworth, 1971, p. 113.

General: M. E. McClintock, *University of Lancaster: Quest for Innovation* (Univ. of Lancaster) 1972; cf. later briefly M. McClintock, *The First Thirty Years, A Lecture . . .* (publ. Univ of Lancaster) 1994.

City of Lancaster: see submission of 1961, quoted in C. Driver, Lancaster in: *The Exploding University*, 1971, pp. 172–85 (p. 172).

'Not keen on big ideas . . .': *TES* 25-11-1966, p. 1292.

'Not only students should . . .': C. Driver, Lancaster in: *The Exploding University*, 1971, pp. 178–9.

'Relation of science to industry . . .'; 'the humanities not trampled on': *TES* 25-11-1966, p. 1292; cf. C. Carter, Measuring Productivity of Universities, *T* 17-5-1966, p. 13.

'Relgious zeal . . .': C. Driver, Lancaster in: *The Exploding University*, 1971, pp. 178–9.

'Gentler processes of democratic . . .': McClintock, *op. cit.*, pp. 59–60.

'Enjoyed 10 months of decisionmaking': McClintock, *op. cit.*, pp. 242–3.

'Seemed to be – I hope Gabi . . .': H.-D. Laubinger (ed.), *Hommage à Epstein* (publ. Institut für öffentliches Bauen und Hochschulplanung, Universität Stuttgart) 1987, p. 13.

'Mr. Shepheard was about to . . .': McClintock, *op. cit.*, pp. 48–9; H.-D. Laubinger (ed.), *op. cit.* pp. 13, 95.

'Free-hand to prevent . . .': *AJ* 11-8-1971, p. 297.

'Attitude to work is both modest . . .': H.-D. Laubinger (ed.), *op. cit.* p. 62.

'Never had a development plan': PRO UGC 7 456, 2-8-1967; Lancaster and brief: *Architectural Association Journal* vol. 80 no. 888 1-1965, p. 167.

'Not particularly worked up . . .': *Listener* 5-5-1966, pp. 645–6.

Groups of rooms which . . .': PRO UGC 7 455, 6-11-1963.

'The architect has been careful . . .': McClintock, *op. cit.*, pp. 332–8.

Architectural Sources: *AD* 4-1964, p. 206; *B* 24-4-1964, pp. 862–3; *AJ* 27-5-1964, pp. 1206–8; *AR* 1-1965, p. 21; *AJ* 26-7-1967, p. 208; *AJ* 12-2-1969, pp. 429–40; *AJ* 21-5-1969, pp. 1379–85; *AR* 4-1970, pp. 275–6; *AJ* 11-8-1971, pp. 295–308; *Baumeister* 7-1972, pp. 73–5; cf. *T* 14-4-1964; *T* 24-11-1964, p. 6; *Lancaster Guardian and Observer* 18-12-1964 (Supplement), *Lancaster Guardian and Observer* 22-1-1965, 25-6-1965 (Supplement); Birks.

Teaching rooms . . . separate . . . : PRO UGC 7 455, 6-11-1963; 28-1-1964; H.-D. Laubinger (ed.), *op cit.*, p. 13; McClintock, *op. cit.*, p. 334.

'Fruitsalad of functions': G. Epstein, 'Die Universität Lan-

caster . . .', pp. 39–47 in: *Information 34* (publ. by Zentralarchiv für Hochschulbau Stuttgart) (year 9), 1976; McClintock, *op. cit.*, p. 51.

'Held together by an unconscious . . .': *TES* 25-11-1966, p. 1292.

'The village street . . .': *B* 24-4-1964, pp. 862–3.

Reading room: 'vast, echoing . . .': UGC 7 455 5-11-1963: Building Programme 1964–5 Explanatory Memorandum.

'Cambridge [colleges are] too powerful': (Professor M. M. Willcock 1964) McClintock, *op. cit.*, p. 338, cf. p. 331ff.

'Meets at the bars . . .': G. Epstein, 'Die Universität Lancaster . . .', pp. 39–47 in: *Information 34* (publ. by Zentralarchiv für Hochschulbau Stuttgart) (year 9), 1976, PRO UGC 7-455, 6-11-1963 28-1-1964.

'University is lit up until midnight': Epstein in: 'Gemeinsames Gutachten fur die Universität Konstanz' [Protokoll], Konstanz 13-2-1968 (Archives Universität Konstanz, see below), p. 18.

No student union: McClintock, *op. cit.*, p. 358.

No bedspaces for students: *T* 15-7-1968, p. 10; on the issue generally: PRO UGC 2 109, Paper 169/64; PRO UGC 2 103, paper 33/64.

'Study, social, teaching . . .': PRO UGC 7 455, 28-1-1964.

'Non-residential student accommodation': quoted in McClintock, *op. cit.*, p. 332.

McClintock, *op. cit.*, pp. 72–5; 342; *AJ* 21-5-1969, pp. 1379–86; *AJ* 11-8-1971, pp. 304–5; *T* 28-11-1967, p. 11; *The University of Lancaster Loan Financed Student Residences* (publ. Lancaster University), 1969.

Early Buildings on Lancaster Campus: By Epstein: University House August 1966; Bowland College 1966/8; Lonsdale College 1967/68; Great Hall Complex (Nuffield Theatre etc.) 1968/69; Furness College 1970; Grizedale and Pendle Colleges 1974. By T. Mellor & Partners Library 1966/69/71; Physics and Chemistry 1967/68. By Haydn Smith: Cartmel College 1968; Furness College residences 1969, Fylde College 1971. By Cassidy and Ashton: Chaplaincy Centre 1970; by Lancashire County Council (Roger Booth): County College 1969.

'There are no special structural . . .': *AJ* 11-8-1971, p. 301.

'Industrialised building': UGC 7 455, 6-11-1963.

'Does not demonstrate any . . .': *AJ* 11-8-1971, p. 301.

'Solid partitions . . .': *AJ* 27-5-1964, p. 1208.

'19th century penitentiary' (Sir Noel Hall, of the Academic Planning Board), quoted in McClintock, *op. cit.*, p. 56.

Extra buildings will be addded: PRO UGC 7 455, 5-11-1963 Memorandum.

'Neither the speed . . .': *AJ* 12-2-1969, p. 434.

Institution must have a centre: G. Epstein, 'Die Universität Lancaster . . .', pp. 39–47 in: *Information 34* (publ. by Zentralarchiv für Hochschulbau Stuttgart) (year 9), 1976, p. 39.

'Most humane . . .': P. Wilby in *THES* 13-2-1976, p. 8.

'Buildings do not intimidate . . .': *AJ* 11-8-1971, p. 301.

'Most successful of . . .': Perkin, p. 99.

'Have been designed to excite . . .': *AJ* 12-2-1969, p. 434.

6000/3000 students . . . : *AJ* 12-2-1969, p. 437.

Self-catering: *AJ* 11-8-1971, p. 305; cf. McClintock, *op. cit.*, pp. 272–91.

'Model for university plans . . .': Birks, p. 127.

'Connected like a slice of Oxbridge': *AR* 4-1970, p. 276.

Cf. C. H. Church, 'The collegiate experiment at Lancaster: a case study in the problems of innovation in the new universities', *Higher Education Review* (publ. Lancaster), vol. 6 no. 3 Summer 1974, pp. 3–23.

Bath and others

G. Walters, *A Technological University: an Experiment in Bath*, Bath, 1966; G. H. Moore, *The University of Bath. The Formative Years*, Bath, 1972.

'Produce well educated men . . .': *AA* 1967, p. 73.

Development Plan Report No 1 (Robert Matthew Johnson-Marshall & Partner) (publ. Bath University) 1965; *AJ* 17-11-1965, pp. 1120–4.

'The architectural plan is intended to express . . .'; 'We have been fortunate . . .': *AA* 1967, p. 73.

In charge: Peter Newnham and Hugh Morris; *AR* 1-1966, pp. 14–15; Linde (1970) vol. 4, pp. 183–4.

Joint Development Project UGC and Department of Education and Science (DES), *AR* 4-1970, p. 281; *AJ* 8-1-1969, pp. 79–80; cf. P. Jokusch, 'Bauliche Hochschulplanung in GB', pp. 17–29 (p. 22) in: *Information 34* (publ. by Zentralarchiv für Hochschulbau Stuttgart) (year 9), 1976.

'Bath Stone coloured . . .': G. H. Moore, *The University of Bath. The Formative Years*, Bath, 1972, p. 52.

Resembles Lancaster with its 'linear spine': *AA* 1967, pp. 74–9.

Science buildings generally: cf. L. Martin, 'Science Buildings . . .', *AD* 12-1964, pp. 595–600.

Surrey: G. G. Baines: 'Designers . . .': *AA* 1967, pp. 86–94 (p. 88). Cf. *AR* 2-1965, p. 97; *AR* 1-1967, p. 44; *AR* 4-1970, pp. 282–5; *AJ* 16-12-1970, pp. 1409–10; *AJ* 17-3-1971, pp. 585–600; *Baumeister* 10-1972, pp. 1126–7; Dober (1965), pp. 63–6; cf. *T* 4-5-1971.

Other new, or re-founded universities in Britain or by British architects:

Bradford University of Technology, also mostly newly designed by Building Design Partnership from the mid-1960s onwards. Although situated much further into the town, it loosened the urban density by meandering its buildings, mixing teaching and residential, along a communal spine (*AA* 1967, pp. 104–12).

The central buildings on the Brunel University Campus at Uxbridge by Richard H. Sheppard received much attention (*AR* 1-1965, p. 22; *AA* 1967, pp. 80–5; Dober (1965), pp. 6–9).

The last major relocation was Heriott Watt University at Riccarton, Edinburgh (*AJ* 18-2-1970, pp. 394–5; *AJ* 27-12-1976, pp. 783–92), by A. Reiach, E. Hall & Pts.

The New University of Ulster in Coleraine has been little publicised, although it constituted as complete a project as any of the Seven (although there were no early plans for student residences). First mooted in 1963, by 1968 it already taught 4,500 students. Its 'school' structure à la Sussex is accommodated in a dense conglomerate of buildings, again designed by RMJM. Ulster did not come under the UGC; it is now merged with Belfast Polytechnic to form the University of Ulster. (Information from *RMJM*; *ST* 9-11-1969 (Magazine), p. 84; *AR* 4-1970, p. 285; *AJ* 9-11-1977, p. 905; J. Brothers & S. Hatch, *Residence and Student Life*, 1971, p. 335; Perkin, pp. 73–4; *THES* 19-5-1972, p. 8; *THES* 26-5-1972, p. 8; *THES* 26-6-1972, p. 2).

Finally, one of the most elaborate plans of the spine type is Zambia Cross (Lusaka) designed by Anthony Chitty, partly built as planned. (*AR* 1-1968, pp. 1–2; Linde (1970) vol. 1 pp. 94–5; (I. O. Horvitch FRIBA, MZIA, Resident Architect), *The University of Zambia*. Report on Physical Development (publ. Univ. of Zambia), 1971.)

For Giancarlo de Carlo's 'linear' proposal for University College Dublin of 1963 see *Ad'A* no. 137, 4/5-1968, pp. 12, 15; *Bauen & Wohnen* 11-1969, pp. 397–9.

Loughborough: see below page 329.

Stirling: 'Sweeping away both faculties . . .': P. Wilby in *THES* 21-5-1976, p. 6; *Report on the Policies and Running of Stirling University from 1966–1973, made to the University Court, 22-10-1973* (The Roger Young Enquiry) (publ. Univ. of Stirling, 1973) p. 3; *University of Stirling Development plan Report* (RMJM) (publ. Univ. of Stirling) 1968; *AJ* 5-6-1968, pp. 1283–95; *AJ* 29-5-1968, pp. 1231–6; *AR* 6-1973, pp. 349–62; *Baumeister* 10-1973, pp. 1270–7; Information RMJM; Interview with John Richards 1997; R. G. Bomont, *The University of Stirling* (publ. Univ. of Stirling), 1995.

'The university authorities feel . . .': *AJ* 29-5-1968, p. 1233.

'Most beautiful . . .': T. Aldous, 'Higher Education at Lower Cost. The New Universities III', *Country Life* 12-2-1976, p. 56.

1968: INSTITUTIONAL AND ARCHITECTURAL DISILLUSIONMENT

'Dream exposed as sham': *Observer* 19-5-1968; 'beyond redemption': *Colchester Express* 23-5-1974; close Essex: *Wivenhoe The Newspaper of the University of Essex* vol. 2 no. 16 17-2-1977, referring to editorial: 'Shut down Essex', *ST* 13-2-1977, p. 16. Further: 'Essex heads university closure list – claim'. 'A national newspaper report two weeks ago named Kent, Aston, Lancaster and East Anglia as those included in the alleged list. But privately, students, officials and lecturers at other universities add the names Essex and Warwick.': [Colchester] *Evening Gazette* 7-2-1977.

Beloff; cf. earlier: S. Maclure 'Whither Britain's New Universities', *Listener* 26-1-1967, pp. 121–2; *Listener* 2-2-1967, pp. 157–8; even earlier A. Tropp & A. Little, 'Blueprint for a University', *New Society* 6-6-1963, pp.

10–11; M. Irwin, 'A Framework for Contraction', *New Statesman* 15-12-1972, pp. 892–4.

'Without doubt failed': P. Wilby in *THES* 18-6-1976, p. 6; 'Sussex Ideals eroded', *THES* 2-21973, p. 1.

'It might be supposed the recent wave . . .': UGC, *University Development 1962–1967* (*Parliamentary Paper* Cmnd. 3820), 1968, 69; cf. Lord Wolfenden, 'The UGC a Personal View', *THES* 2-4-1976.

Cheapness as the chief reason: J. M. McKean, 'Essex . . .', *AJ* 20-9-1972, p. 670; cf. Beloff, pp. 18–19.

Some figures: 1967–8 envisaged capital grants: £35.1m, actual: £31.9m. 1969–70 envisaged: £31m, actual 18.7: UGC, *University Development 1967–1972* (*Parliamentary Paper* Cmnd. 5728), 1974, p. 40.

Cf. C. J. Crouch, *Student Revolt in Britain*, 1970; M. A. Rooke, *Anarchy and Apathy. Student Unrest 1968–70*, 1971.

Essex 1974: 'perhaps the worst ever . . .': *New Statesman* 29-3-1974, p. 435.

'Little else to do . . .': *Daily Telegraph* 26-11-1970, p. 9.

Colchester: 'a dead . . .': *Essex County Standard* 14-10-1966. cf. *THES* 7-6-1974, pp. 8–9, 21.

'Liberal regime – subversive': R. Boston, 'The Essex Affair', *New Society* 23-5-68, pp. 745–6.

'Students . . . adults . . .': *Daily Telegraph* 26-11-1970, p. 9.

'New Student': Beloff, p. 20; 'Kibbutz': *ibid.*, p. 56; 'student Lord Franks': *ibid.*, p. 58.

'Laboratory in staff student relations': Perkin, pp. 33, 193, 246; cf. a good brief survey: 'The New Universities *ST* 9-11-1969 (Magazine), pp. 84–5; H. & P. Silver, *Students*, Buckingham, 1997, Chapter 5.

'We are fed up being treated . . .': *Daily Express* 13-3-1968, quoted in *AJ* 20-9-1972, p. 672; cf. *T* 17-5-1968, p. 13.

'Everything is blamed on the institution': *Report on the Policies and Running of Stirling University from 1966–1973, made to the University Court, 22-10-1973* (The Roger Young Enquiry) (publ. Univ. of Stirling) 1973, p. 113; cf. also Cf. C. H. Church, 'The collegiate experiment at Lancaster: a case study in the problems of innovation in the new universities', *Higher Education Review* (publ. Lancaster), vol. 6 no. 3 Summer 1974, pp. 3–23.

'That nirvana of staff student . . .': D. Wilby in *THES* 13-2-1976, p. 9.

'The word "community", applied to . . .': V. Brittain, 'The Aging of the New Universities', *Illustrated London News* 2-1975, pp. 40–2.

Not been allowed to grow: McKean in *AJ* 20-9-1972, p. 655.

'Isolated', 'claustrophobic': *T* 23-3-1974, p. 2.

'Without halls of residence . . .': *THES* 7-6-1974, pp. 8–9, 21.

Freshers lacked a proper institutional home: Lord Annan, *Report of the Disturbances in the University of Essex* (publ. University of Essex), 1974, p. 29.

'Perpetual valley wind . . .': *AJ* 4-1-1967, pp. 4–6.

'Essex is not consistently based . . .': *AJ* 20-9-1972, pp. 675, 638.

'Lack territorial identiy': letter to the Times, *T* 3-8-1974, p. 13.

'No nooks, no corners . . .': Birks, p. 96.

'The "concrete jungle"': *Daily Telegraph* 26-11-1970, p. 9.

'Campus claustrophobia and neurosis': *New Statesman* 29-3-1974, p. 435.

'The aesthetic poverty': *New Society* 28-3-1974, pp. 757–8.

'Numbers of staff and students condemn': Lord Annan, *Report of the Disturbances in the University of Essex*, (publ. University of Essex) 1974, p. 32.

Interview Lord Briggs 1999.

'The police, brought on . . .': *THES* 7-6-1974, p. 9.

Sheila Upjohn and A. F. Crawshaw, 'Case Study: University of East Anglia', *AJ* 14-6-1972, pp. 1321–38.

'Lasdun's buildings . . . a dream': R. Hutchinson & R. Osborne, 'The Failure of UEA', *Mandate* (University of East Anglia Student Newspaper), January 1970; R. Haynes, in *Mandate*, November 1969.

'Looks miserable when wet . . .': Birks, p. 82.

'Dinosaur': Birks, p. 75.

'So big that it is dehumanised'; 'cold . . .': Birks, pp. 107, 109.

Cladding tiles: *Building Design*, 17-7-1970, pp. 1–2; *ST* 27-3 1988, p. A 11; *AJ* 9-3-1988, p. 14; *Building* 4-3-1988, p. 7; *Building Design* 10-6-1988, p. 1.

E. P. Thompson, 'The Business University', *New Society*, 19-2-1970, pp. 301–4; E. P. Thompson, *Warwick University Limited*, Harmondsworth 1970.

Lord James: *T* 15-1-1971, Part IV, Universities and Polytechnics Supplement.

York Colleges: *T* 3-9-1985 Special Report.

'There is a casualness . . .': *AJ* 23-2 1972, p. 422.

'On a wet Sunday': *T* 3-9-1985 Special Report.

'Only cemeteries . . .': P. Wilby, 'Interesting experiments but no radical change', *THES* 18-6-1976, p. 6.

Thistlethwaite on 'municipal': Interview 1996.

'Excessive': *AR* 4-1970, p. 251; cf. *AR* 10-1973.

University of East Anglia: 'Freedom from contractor': *Vice Chancellor's Report 1967–8*.

'Not too little thought . . .': *AJ* 13-12-1972, p. 1349.

Late Welfare State: cf. I. Culpitt, *Welfare and Citizenship. Beyond the Crisis of the Welfare State*, 1992.

B. Crick, '"Garden suburb" university lambasted', *THES* 28-1-1977, p. 2.

'Stocktaking . . .': *Daily Telegraph* 16-10-1971, p. 16.

'Serious student': *T* 26-7-1975, p. 13.

'Some assume everything new . . .': Univ. of East Anglia: *Vice Chancellor's Report 1967–8*.

'Turned out to be the same . . .': Lord Annan, *Report of the Disturbances in the University of Essex* (publ. University of Essex) 1974, p. 35.

Cf. G. Statera, Death of Utopia, *The Development and Decline of the Student Movements in Europe*, New York, 1975, p. 142ff.

Nanterre: M. Crozier, 'French Students: a letter from Nanterre la folie', *The Public Interest* 13 1968, p. 153, quoted in N. Abercrombie, *The University in an Urban Environment*, 1974.

III THE NEW 'URBAN' CAMPUS IN NORTH AMERICA

Canada: The 'Single Structure Campus': Scarborough, Simon Fraser

'Urban . . .' Dober (1963) p. 201.

J. Porter, 'The Democratisation of the Canadian Universities and the Need for a National System', *Minerva* 7-1970, pp. 325–36; D. V. Verney, 'Government . . . University – A Canadian Experience', pp. 277–86, in: S. D. Kertesz, *The Task of Universities in a Changing World*, Notre Dame/London 1971; J. Katz, *Education in Canada*, Newton Abbot 1974, pp. 76–7; M. Skolnik, 'Higher Education Systems in Canada', pp. 15–34, in: A. D. Gregor & oth., *Higher Education in Canada* (publ. Secretary of State of Canada, Ottawa), 1992.

'Social quiet has disappeared': M. G. Ross, *The New University*, Toronto, 1961, p. 78.

York University Toronto: M. G. Ross, *York University*, pp. 69–86, in: Ross; *Canadian Architect*, 8-1968, p. 31ff.

'Hideous and inefficient skyscrapers . . .': M. G. Ross, *The New University*, Toronto, 1961, p. 14.

A. O. C. Cole, Trent, *The Making of a University* (publ. Trent University), 1992.

Canadian Architect 12-1967, pp. 29–37; *Baumeister* 4-1970, pp. 377–85; M. F. Schmertz (of Architectural Record), *Campus Planning and Design*, New York, 1972, pp. 209–13.

'Balliol on Trent', D. V. Verney, 'Government . . . University – A Canadian Experience', pp. 277–86 (p. 265) in: S. D. Kertesz, *The Task of Universities in a Changing World*, Notre Dame/London, 1971.

Banff Fine Art School, Alberta.

'Almost overnight the Canadian university . . .': 'Banff Session 1964', *Journal Royal Architectural Institute Canada* (RAIC) 7-1964, pp. 48–66 (p. 48); cf. 'Campus Planning and Architets', *Architecture Canada* 7/8-1969, p. 35ff.

'There are . . . many factors . . .': 'Banff 64', *Canadian Architect* 5-1964, pp. 39–54.

'We must explore totally new . . .': *Journal Royal Architectural Institute Canada* (RAIC) 7-1964, p. 50.

'There was no academic program . . .': *Canadian Architect* 5-1964, p. 54.

'Architecture that is beautiful . . .': L. Whiteson, *Modern Canadian Architecture*, Edmonton, 1983, p. 13.

Scarborough: J. L. Ball, *The First Twenty-Five Years. Scarborough College University of Toronto* (publ. Scarborough (?)), 1989; J. Taylor, John Andrews. *Architecture a Performing Art*, New York, 1982, p. 31ff; *Journal Royal Architectural Institute Canada* (RAIC) 7-1964, pp. 61–6; *Canadian Architect* 5-1966, pp. 39–62; Oscar Newman, 'The New Campus', *AFor* 5-1955, pp. 30–40, 53–4; *Ad'A* no. 129, 12-1966/1-1967, pp. 85–90; (Kenneth Frampton) *AD* 4-1967, pp. 178–87; *ARec* 9-1966, pp. 161–7; (J. Rykwert) *Zodiac* 18 (1968) pp. 61–3; A. Erickson, *The University and the New Intellectual Environment*, Toronto, 1968; M. Webb, 'Linear Planning in New Universities', *Country Life Annual* 1969, pp. 62–5; R. Banham, *Megastructure*, 1976, pp. 130–63.

'Canada's claim . . .': L. Whiteson, *Modern Canadian Architecture*, Edmonton, 1983, p. 125.

On G. Shrum: 'Canada. Sermon on Mount', *Interbuild* 2-1966, pp. 12–17; D. V. Verney, 'Government . . . University – A Canadian Experience', pp. 277–86 (pp. 266–7), in S. D. Kertesz, *The Task of Universities in a Changing World*, Notre Dame/London 1971; cf. *Journal Royal Architectural Institute Canada* (RAIC) 7-1964, pp. 51–4.

'Acropolis': Erickson, quoted in L. Whiteson, *Modern Canadian Architecture*, Edmonton, 1983, p. 24; cf. *AR* 4-1968, pp. 263–75; *Ad'A* no. 137, 4/5-1968, p. 85; 'In Canada, the Continent's first single structure Campus', *AFor* 12-1965, pp. 11–18.

'Total body of knowledge': *Canadian Architect* 2-1966, p. 39ff.; cf. *AD* 8-1966, pp. 403–5.

'One world'; 'North American campus . . .': A. Erickson, The University: A New Visual Environment', *Canadian Architect* 1-1968, pp. 25–37.

'Erickson/Massey have succeeded . . .': Lionel Tiger, *Canadian Architect* 2-1966, p. 42.

C. Bissell: 'Institutes of Higher Education in Canada . . .', p. 145 in: W. R. Niblett (ed.), *Higher Education. Demand and Response*, London, 1969.

Lethbridge: by Erickson & Massey; first planned 1967, *Architecture Canada* 7/8-1969, pp. 48–9; *ARec* 5-1973, pp. 114–23 ('architectural statement': p. 114); *Ad'A* no. 183 1/2-1976, pp. 46–50; cf. a similar plan: Le Corbusier's Maison des Jeunes et de la Culture at Firminy, begun 1961: W. Boesiger (ed.), *L'oeuvre complète de Le Corbusier*, vol. 7, London, 1965.

USA: Chicago Circle: The 'Urban' Challenge to College and Campus?

T. H. Creighton, *Canadian Architect* 5-1964, p. 43.

'The most striking . . .'; 'American dilemma': Dober (1965), p. 9.

'The conscious formulation . . .': Dober (1965), p. 9. Earlier evidence of new European ideas in American campus design: University. *Four Universities in the State of New York designed by Students of the School of Architecture under Direction of Michale Mosteller with Patrick de Saulles . . .* , Student Publication of the School of Architecture Van Rensselaer Polytechnic, Troy, N.Y. vol. 3 Fall 1965.

M. Trow, 'The Idea of a New University', *UQ* vol. 19 no. 2 3-1965, pp. 162–72; D. Riesman, 'Notes on New Universities: British and American', *UQ* vol. 20 no. 2 3-1966, pp. 128–46.

See *ARec*; M. F. Schmertz, *Campus Planning and Design*, New York, 1972.

'Many of today resent . . .': T. H. Creighton, *Canadian Architect* 5-1974, p. 42.

O. Newman, 'The New Campus', *AFor* 5-1966, pp. 30–54. St Louis: Forest Park Community Centre by Harry Weese & Associates (p. 46).

Santa Cruz 'suburban': *AFor* 5-1966, p. 43.

G. Rosen, *Decision-Making Chicago-Style. The Genesis of a University of Illinois Campus*, Urbana/Chicago/London 1980; *A For* 9-1965, pp. 21–45; A. S. Weller, *University of Illinois. 100 Years of Campus Architecture . . .* (publ. University of Illnois), 1968; Information Dr F. Beuttler, UIC.

'Solving problems urban society'; liberal education . . .': handout ('Portfolio'), signed Norman A Parker, n.d. [*c.* 1965]; *The University of Illinois at Congress Circle* [information booklet], c. late 1961 (Courtesy UIC).

Dober (1963), p. 298; Turner, pp. 271–6.

'Everybody will be constantly . . .': *AFor* 9-1965, p. 44.

'What happens between classes . . .'; 'it came with classic suddenness . . .'; 'everything falls into place': *AFor* 9-1965, p. 27.

'The strength of Chicago Circle . . .': *AFor* 9-1965, p. 44.

'Galaxies', 'clusters', 'Field Theory': *AFor* 12-1968, pp. 25ff.; *AFor* 11-1970, pp. 24–33; 'Field Theory': *Progressive Architecture* 3-1969, pp. 96–7.

'More a single system': *AFor* 9-1964, p. 44.

'Such failures are magnificent . . .': 'The Campus: Architecture's Show Place', *Time Magazine* (US ed.) 21-9-1970, p. 82.

Netsch's main plaza taken away: *Inland Architect* 3/4-1993, pp. 52–5.

'Micro environment . . .': *AFor* 9-1965, pp. 23–45.

Stockton State: by Geddes Brecher Qualls Cunningham, *c.* 1970: Turner, pp. 278–80.

North Dartmouth Technology Institute / South Eastern Massachusetts University: Turner, pp. 301–2; *Ad'A*, no. 122, 10-1966, pp. 2–3; S. Moholy Nagy (Introd.), *The Architecture of Paul Rudolph*, London, 1970; M. F. Schmertz, *Campus Planning and Design*, New York, 1972, pp. 161–76.

Boulder: Engineering Science Center by Sasaki Walker & Associates with P. Belluschi, *Ad'A* no. 137, 4/5-1968, p. ix.

'Denser and more crowded': 'The Campus: Architecture's Show Place', *Time* (US ed.) 21-19-1970 pp. 76–82.

Cf. R. A. M. Stern, *Pride of Place. Building the American Dream*, Boston, 1986, p. 74.

'Although many notable . . .': Paul Heyer, *Architects on Architecture*, London, 1967, p. 10.

Inner urban locations: J. O. Merill (of Skidmore, Owings & Merrill), 'The Urban Campus', *Urban Land* [Washington] 12-1966, pp. 3–4; cf. K. R. Petshek, 'A new role for City Universities. Urban extension programmes', *Journal of the American Institute of Planners*, 11-1964, pp. 304–16.

Cf. K. R. Petshek, 'A new Role for City Universities. Urban Extension Programs', *Journal American Institute of Planners*, 11-1964, pp. 304–16.; M. Klotsche, *The Urban University and the Future of our Cities*, New York, 1966; A. Schlesinger, 'The University in an Urban Society', *Massachusetts Review* 8-1967, pp. 470–6; D. Riesman, 'The Urban University', *Massachusetts Review* 8-1967, pp. 476–85; W. Rovetch, 'Architecture for the Urban Campus', pp. 78–81 in: G. K. Smith (ed.), *Agony and Promise. Current issues in Higher Education*, San Francisco, 1969; M. R. Berube, *The Urban University in America*, Westport Con., 1978.

Unrest on large campuses: *The Report of the President's Commission on Campus Unrest*, (publ. Washington), 1970, pp. 79–80.

Dying down of the student movement: G. Grant & D. Riesman, *The Perpetual Dream. Reform and Experiment in the Architectural College*, Chicago, 1978, p. 280; R. A. M. Stern, *Pride of Place. Building the American Dream*, Boston, 1986; cf. S. M. Lipset & S. S. Wolin, *The Berkeley Student Revolt*, Garden City N.Y., 1965.

Just getting good marks: J. Floud & J. Rosselli, 'Studying Higher Education in Britain and America', *UQ* vol. 17 no. 2 3-1963, pp. 126–48 (p. 137).

'Overestimate what education itself can do'. G. Grant & D. Riesman, *The Perpetual Dream. Reform and Experiment in the Architectural College*, Chicago, 1978, p. 7.

'The notion of a campus . . . : *AA* 1967, pp. 120–1; cf. E. K. Thompson, 'College Building and Planning', *ARec* 5-1969, p. 145.

College for Human Services, New York: G. Grant & D. Riesman, *The Perpetual Dream. Reform and Experiment in the Architectural College*, Chicago, 1978, pp. 135ff.

Higher education into peoples homes: S. van der Ryn, 'The University Environment', *AD* 11-1969, pp. 618–19, from *The Daily Californian* [weekly magazine], 18-2-1969.

UCLA: Dober (1963), p. 201.

Berkeley: cf. W. W. Wurster, 'Campus Planning', *ARec* 9-1959, pp. 161–7.

Turner, p. 276; I. Brown, 'Irrelevance of University Architecture', *ARec* 11-1975, pp. 105–16 (publ also: *Higher Education Review* [London] vol. 2 no. 1 Autumn 1969, pp. 31–54; and in T. Burgess (ed), *The Shape of Higher Education*, London, 1972).

'Steeped in townscape . . .'; 'this was intended as a Hyde Park . . .': R. Montgomery, 'Center of Action', *AFor* 4-1970, pp. 65–70.

IV WEST GERMANY: CAMPUS AND COLLEGE AS 'REFORM'

The post World War II reinstatement of tradition

'Sozialbereich': Linde (1970) vol. 1, p. 12.

A. Flexner, *Universities American English German*, New York, 1930 (new ed. 1968).

E. Ashby, 'Die Zukunft der Universitätsidee des 19. Jahrhunderts in Grossbritannien und Deutschland', *DUZ* 6-1967, pp. 14–20; (same in English): *Minerva* vol. 6 no. 1 Autumn 1967, pp. 3–17; cf. C. Kerr, *The Uses of the University*, Cambridge MA, 1963, p. 11; C. Diehl, 'Innocents abroad: American Students in German Universities', *History of Education Quarterly* Fall 1976, pp. 257–300.

W. Nitsch, U. Gerhardt, C. Offe, *Hochschule in der Demokratie*, Neuwied 1965; cf. G. Kloss, 'University Reform in West Germany', *Minerva* vol. 6 no. 3 Spring 1968, pp. 323–53. C. Bode, W. Becker, R. Klofat, *Universitäten in Deutschland / Universities in Germany*,

Munich, 1995; L. Boehm & R. A. Müller, *Universitäten und Hochschulen in Deutschland, Oesterreich und der Schweiz* (Hermes Handlexikon), Düsseldorf, 1983; T. Ellwein, *Die deutsche Universität*, Königstein im Taunus, 1985; M. B. Baumgarten & oth., *Die deutsche Universität im 20 Jahrhundert*, Köln 1994; H. Brockmann, *Wissen und Widerstand. Geschichte der deutschen Universität*, Berlin 1999.

W. von Humboldt, *Über die innere und äussere Organisation der höheren wissenschaftlichen Anstalten in Berlin* (1810), in: Gesammelte Schriften, ed. by Preussische Akademie der Wissenschaften, vol. 10, Berlin, 1902, pp. 250–60; also in W. v. Humboldt, *Die Idee der deutschen Universität*, Darmstadt, 1956.

On institutionality: W. Nitsch, U. Gerhardt, C. Offe, *Hochschule in der Demokratie*, Neuwied, 1965, pp. 18ff.

Linde (1970) vol. 1, pp. 25ff.; K. Rückbrod, *Universität und Kollegium. Baugeschichte und Bautyp*, Darmstadt, 1977; cf. on the earlier architecture of university buildings for the sciences: H. Kristenson, *Vetenskapsbyggnader under 1800. Lund och Europa* (publ. Stockholm Arkitektur Museet), 1990; L. Ziegert-Hackbarth, *Die Entwicklung des Typus des deutschen Universitätsgebäudes*, Dissertation University of Königsberg 1942.

H. Kuhn et al., *Die deutsche Universität im Dritten Reich. Acht Beiträge*, Munich, 1966; R. G. S. Weber, *The German Studentenkorps in the Third Reich*, London, 1986.

'From these two points . . .': W. V. Humboldt, *Litauischer Schulplan* (1809), quoted in E. Hinterman, 'Das Studentenwohnheim . . .', *DUZ* 9-1963, p. 27.

Age of students: S. Uhlig, 'Gedanken über studentisches Wohnen', *DUZ* 2-1964, p. 22. Here a wrong figure of 95% is given for 1964.

'A system of state support': T. Ellwein, *Die deutsche Universität*, Königstein im Taunus, 1985, pp. 296–8.

'Without being conscious . . .': H. P. Schwarz, *Die Ära Adenauer, 1949–1957*, Stuttgart, 1981, pp. 417–420.

The concern for students as students: Wohnheime and *Kollegienhaus*-Project

D. Phillips (ed.), *German Universities after the Surrender. British Occupation and the Control of Higher Education* (Univ. of Oxford Dept. of Educational Studies), 1983; A. Hearnden, *The British in Germany, Educational Reconstruction*, London, 1978. J. Mountford, *Keele*, London, 1972, pp. 135ff.; Lindsay Papers at the University of Keele; Lord Birkner, 'The Commission on German Universities', *UQ* vol. 4 no. 1 11-1949, pp. 82–90; Special Issue: Educational Policy and Reform in Modern Germany, *History of Education Quarterly* Fall 1982.

J. F. Tent, *The Free University of Berlin*, Bloomington Indiana, 1988.

DDR/GDR: Cf. M. Gibas & P. Pasternack, *Sozialistisch behaust & bekunst. Hochschulen und ihre Bauten in der DDR*, Leipzig, 1999.

'The student should be led . . .': [United Kingdom]

Foreign Office, University Reform in Germany. Report by a German Commission (publ. His Majesty's Stationary Office London), 1949, p. 43; cf. Lidell (ed.), *Education in Occupied Germany / L'Education de l'Allemagne occupée*, Paris, 1949; H. P. Pilgert, *The West German Educational System* (publ. by Historical Division of the Office of Executive Secretary of the U.S. High Commissioner for Germany [Bad-Godesberg-Mehlem]), 1953.

'Studium Generale': 1949 Report (*op. cit.*, previous note), pp. 46–9; W. Killy, *Studium Generale und studentisches Gemeinschaftsleben*, Berlin, 1952; *DUZ* 8-1962, pp. 25ff.; *DUZ* 9-1962, pp. 6ff.

'Self-administration': [various articles on Studentenwohnheime], 'Eine pädagogische Chance' (Prof. W. Fuchs), *Baukunst und Werkform* 1960, pp. 297–313 (p. 297).

'Impersonal': Brubacher, p. 331.

80% Göttingen: K. Weber, *Wunsch und Wirklichkeit des studentischen Wohnens in Göttingen*, Hannover, 1968, p. 85.

Studentenverbindung(en) is the generic term; Corps is used for upper-class associations, Burschenschaft for the middle-classe ones. A Latin name mostly refers to a region, such as Corps Saxonia or Corps Borussia; 'Alte Herren': 'old boys' i.e. the alumni. Cf. L. Koslowski, 'Burschenschaft und Hochschule', *DUZ* 9-1962, pp. 3–7; *Hochschuldienst* 23-11-1963; P. Krause, *O Alte Burschenherrlichkeit*, Graz, 1979.

Studentenwerk: *Göttinger Universitäts Zeitung* (the forerunner of *DUZ*), 11-12-1945, p. 1; ['Blaues'] *Gutachten zur Hochschulreform* (publ. Studienausschuss für Hochschulreform) Hamburg; 1948, see R. Neuhaus (ed.), *Dokumente zur Hochschulreform 1945–1959*, Wiesbaden, 1961, pp. 289–297; D. von Beulwitz & oth., *Kantine und Mensa*, Stuttgart,1973; cf. W. P. Fuchs, *Studentische Wohnheime und Gemeinschaftshäuser in Westdeutschland* [no place of publication (Heidelberg/Frankfurt a. M.)], 1951, pp. 37–9.

R. Ley in Oxford: S. D. Stirk, *German Universities through English Eyes*, London, 1946, p. 64; Fuchs hints at some continuities between the Nazi period and the post war periods: W. P. Fuchs, *Studentische Wohnheime und Gemeinschaftshäuser in Westdeutschland* [no place of publication (Heidelberg/Frankfurt a. M.)], 1951, pp. 17–8, 52, 89.

'To study in the real sense . . .': W. P. Fuchs in *DUZ* 12-9-1955, p. 4.

'To correct the excessive individualism . . .': H. P. Pilgert, *The West German Educational System* (publ. by Historical Division of the Office of Executive Secretary of the U.S. High Commissioner for Germany [Bad-Godesberg-Mehlem]), 1953, p. 86.

'From an English standpoint . . .': S. D. Stirk, *German Universities through English Eyes*, London, 1946, p. 64.

'Geistige Zucht': E. Blochmann, 'Lebensgemeinschaft College', *DUZ* 15-12-1950, pp. 17–18; cf. H. Schneider, 'Zwischen Konservatismus und Modernität. Oxford . . .', *DUZ* 120-1960, pp. 22–5; cf. *DUZ* 12-9-1955, p. 4.

'Göttinger Definition' of 1953; 'a dwelling installed for

spiritual . . .': see *Architekturwettbewerbe, Sonderheft* May 1960, pp. 2–3; *Architekturwettbewerbe* 81 1975 p. vi.

'Self-administrating . . .': *DUZ* 9-1963, pp. 20, 22.

'Tutoren': *DUZ* 10-1961, pp. 18–21.

W. P. Fuchs, *Studentische Wohnheime und Gemeinschaftshäuser in Westdeutschland* [no place of publication (Heidelberg/Frankfurt a. M.)], 1951.

'Hotel . . .': Fuchs, *op. cit.*, p. 25.

Gemeinschaftshäuser: Fuchs, *op. cit.*, pp. 26–34. Fuchs presents the following tentative list of 'Gemeinschaftshäuser' or 'Kollegs' in the narrow sense of that term: Göttingen: Akademische Burse, Fridtjof Nansen-Haus; Heidelberg: Collegium Academicum; Köln: Burg Wahn; Marburg: Bettina-Haus, Collegium Gentium; München: Wohnheim Siedlung Massmannplatz; Münster: Aasee-Haus; Tübingen: Leibniz-Kolleg; Villigst (Schwerte an der Ruhr): Evangelisches Studienwerk. One might add: Studentendorf Rüstersiel (near Wilhelmshaven) of the Hochschule für Arbeit, Politik und Wirtschaft (pp. 131–4).

Heidelberg Collegium Academicum: Fuchs, *op. cit.*, pp. 80–4; founded in 1946, housed in an 18th-century university building (Seminarium Carolinum) in the undestroyed old town, largely upon America initiative. H. P. Pilgert, *The West German Educational System* (publ. by Historical Division of the Office of Executive Secretary of the U.S. High Commissioner for Germany [Bad-Godesberg-Mehlem]), 1953, p. 79; *Frankfurter Allgemeine Zeitung* 4-7-1998; P. A. Riedl (ed.), *Gebäude der Universität Heidelberg*, Berlin, 1987, pp. 167–75.

Göttingen Akademische Burse: Fuchs, *op. cit.*, pp. 66–70; *Göttinger Universitats Zeitung* (precursor to *DUZ*) 20-1-1946, pp. 12–3; *DUZ* 26-5-1950, p. 14; *DUZ* 5-12-1951, p. 15; A. Hearnden (ed.) *The British in Germany, Educational Reconstuction after 1945*, 1978, p. 152.

'Minimum, maximum . . .': Fuchs, *op. cit.*, p. 69.

München Wohnheimsiedlung Massmannplatz, Hessstrasse 77: Fuchs, *op. cit.*, pp. 113–17; built from 1947 by the Bayerische Jugendsiedlungswerk; initiated by Hermann Mau; the initial architect was Werner Wirsing ('then a student of architecture'); second phase 1951; the building is flat-roofed and grouped around courtyards. Bayerischer Architekten- und Ingenieur-Verband e.V. (ed.), *München und seine Bauten nach 1912*, München, 1984, pp. 341–2 (I owe thanks to N. Huse); *DUZ* 26-5-1950, p. 11; *DUZ* 23/24-1955, p. 23; R. Neuhaus, *Dokumente zur Hochschulreform 1945–59*, Wiesbaden, 1961, p. 373.

Tübingen Leibniz Kolleg: Fuchs, *op. cit.*, pp. 124–7; M. Behal & F. Schmoll, *Studium Generale, Studium sociale. Das Leibniz Kolleg 1948–1998* publ. Leibniz Kolleg Tübingen 1998; *DUZ* 26-5-1950, p. 11; *DUZ* 10-3-1950, pp. 14–15; *DUZ* 5-12-1951, p. 15; R. Neuhaus, *Dokumente zur Hochschulreform 1945–59*, Wiesbaden,1961, pp. 371–2. I have to thank the Director, Michael Behal for his help (the Kolleg is now independent of the university).

Cf. H. Ohl, *Hochschule und Studentenwohnheim* (*Schriften des Hochschulverbandes* 11), Göttingen, 1962, p. 133: 'since 1955 no Kolleg has been founded'.

Early Studentenheime: E. Kimmerle, 'Das deutsche Studentenwohnheim 1913–1963', *DUZ* 9-1963, pp. 18–27; 'Ansätze neuer studentischer Gemeinschaftsformen', *DUZ* 26-5-1950, pp. 10ff.; 'Lohnen sich Studentenheime?', *DUZ* 5-12-1951, pp. 14–15; W. P. Fuchs, 'Studentenwohnheime', *DUZ* 12-9-1955, pp. 3–7; 'Studentische Wohnheimtagung München', *DUZ* 7/8 1956, pp. 30–2; F. W. Kraemer, 'Das Studentenwohnheim als architektonische Aufgabe', *Umschau in der Arbeit der deutschen Studentenwerke* no. 27 1959, p. 19ff.; 'Anmerkungen . . . ', *Baukunst und Werkform* 1960, pp 295–312; H. Kimmerle, 'Studentenheime ante portas', *DUZ* 2-1961, pp. 16–20; H. Bachmann, 'Zur Frage: Studentenwohnheim', *DUZ* 1-1961, pp. 6–9; Dr R. Nunn, 'Die Bildungsaufgabe des Studentenwohnheims', *DUZ* 10-1961, pp. 18–21; H. Kimmerle, Der Studentenwohnheimbau in Deutschland', *DUZ* 10-1961, pp. 12–17; J. Fischer, 'Das Studentenwohnheim und seine Hochschule', *DUZ* 6-1962, pp. 7ff.; H. Kimmerle, Cités Universitaires – Studentenwohnheime', *DUZ* 2-1963, pp. 26–30; S. Uhlig, Gedanken uber studentisches Wohnen und akademische Freiheit', *DUZ* 2-1964, pp. 20–3; Deutsches Studentenwerk (ed.), *Studentenwohnheime 1960/63*, Bonn 1963; cf. below, Note Berlin Zehlendorf-Schlachtensee; E. Hintermann, 'Das Studentenwohnheim – zeitgemässe Losung des studentischen Wohnens oder Instrument der Hochschulreform?', *DUZ* 9-1963, pp. 6–17; Numerous articles by W. Nahrstedt in *DUZ* 1970, 1971; Kramer, Pfennig, Sieverts, *Neue Studentenwohnheime*, Braunschweig, 1968.

By 1951 already 84 homes: *DUZ* 10-1961, p. 12.

DUZ 12-9-1955, p. 3; H. P. Pilgert, *The West German Educational System* (publ. by Historical Division of the Office of Executive Secretary of the U.S. High Commissioner for Germany) [Bad-Godesberg-Mehlem], 1953, pp. 82–5; *DUZ* 2-1961, p. 18; *DUZ* 9-1963, p. 25; *Hochschuldienst* 8-2-1961, p. 4.

H. Linde (*Schriften des Zentralarchivs für Hochschulbau*, Stuttgart) (eds.), *Planung wissenschaftlicher Hochschulen* . . . , Stutgart, 1965, p. 38; cf. *Hochschuldienst* 8-4-1966; '20 Jahre Hochschulbau', *Konstanzer Blätter für Hochschulfragen* no. 73, vol. 19 (no. 4) 1-1982, pp. 6–7.

50% students were said to prefer . . . : *Architekturwettbewerbe, Sonderheft* May 1960, pp. 2–3; *Hochschuldienst* 8-2-1959, pp. 1–4.

'Düsseldorfer Wohnheimplan'. *Memorandum des Kuratoriums des Deutschen Stundentenwerks e.V.* . . . , November 1958; cited in R. Neuhaus, *Dokumente zur Hochschulreform 1945–59*, Wiesbaden, 1961, pp. 256ff.

For general educational purposes: *DUZ* 9-1963, pp. 10–11.

Wissenschaftsrat, *Anregungen des Wissenschaftsrates zur Gestalt neuer Hochschulen*, Tübingen,1962, pp. 73–87.

Project gigantic: *DUZ* 11-1962, p. 10; *DUZ* 2-1963, p. 29; Linde (1970) vol. 1, p. 85. Cf. Konstanz, early design, fig. 4.16. Cf. H. Ohl, *Hochschule und Studentenwohnheim* (*Schriften des Hochschulverbandes* 11), Göttingen, 1962, p. 133: 'since 1955 no Kolleg has been founded'.

'Oberstufenkolleg des Landes Nordrhein-Westfalen', Information Leaflet supplied by Universität Bielefeld (n.d.); H. von Hentig, 'Do we need a college in the German educational System?', pp. 245–66 in: H. Röhrs (ed.), *Tradition and Reform under International Perspective* (*Studien zur Erziehungswissenschaft*, vol. 21, Frankfurt, 1987.

'Mass . . .': W. P. Fuchs, *Studentische Wohnheime und Gemeinschaftshäuser in Westdeutschland* [no place of publication (Heidelberg/Frankfurt a. M.)], 1951, p. 114.

More homes were built: *DUZ* 12-1966, p. 23.

Sociability and democracy: Dr W. Nahrstedt in *DUZ* 1970, many articles.

'Bis zum Bettvorleger': *DUZ* 9-1963, p. 26.

Tutor also wanted to get back home: *DUZ* 11 1962, pp. 8–11.

Students needed more privacy: not less: 'Ein Wohnhaus für Studenten', *Konstanzer Blätter für Hochschulfragen* no. 12, vol. 4 (no. 3) 8-1966, pp. 58–63.

Rejecting attempts by the universities: H. Baier, *Studenten in Opposition*, Bielefeld, 1968, pp. 134–49.

H. Schelsky, *Einsamkeit und Freiheit, Idee und Gestalt der deutschen Universität und ihrer Reformen*, Hamburg, 1963 (ed. of 1970), pp. 193–4.

Students are adults: Schelsky cites H. Heimpel, *Schuld und Aufgabe der Universität*, Frankfurt, 1954: 'We treat the student as an adult on principle – this is a fiction which we want to uphold, because it leads to freedom and responsibility' (Heimpel p. 12).

Residences not really needed: H. Ohl, 'Hochschulen und Studentenwohnheime', pp. 133–46 in: *Schriften des Hochschulverbandes* 11, Göttingen, 1962.

Empirical research: K. Weber, *Wunsch und Wirklichkeit des Studentischen Wohnens in Göttingen*, Hannover, 1968.

Studentenappartments: Cf. *Architekturwettbewerbe* 81 1975, p. iv; cf. *DUZ* 10-1961, p. 14; *DUZ* 1-1961, pp. 6–7; against 'Studentenhotel': *DUZ* 5-12-1951, p. 14.

'Through shared living . . .': *DUZ* 10-1961, p. 14.

Generally on the architecture of the immediate postwar years: See W. Durth, *Deutsche Architekten, Biographische Verflechtungen 1900–1970*, München, 1992.

München-Biederstein: *Baumeister*: 4-1954, p. 354.

Eichkamp Berlin: by H. Chr. Müller, W. Rausch, S. Wewerka; H. Hoffmann und K. Kaspar, *Neue Deutsche Architektur*, Stuttgart, 1956, pp. 60–3; W. Killy, *Studium Generale und studentisches Gemeinschaftsleben*, Berlin, 1952, pp. 47–8.

Siegmundshof Berlin: by Peter Poelzig and K. H. Ernst, *DUZ* 10-1971, p. 15; *Ad'A* no. 104 10/11-1962, pp. 78–9.

Berlin Zehlendorf-Schlachtensee: 'Combats dialectical materialism . . .': H. Engel & oth. (eds.), *Geschichtslandschaft Berlin. Orte und Ereignisse*, vol. 4: Zehlendorf, Berlin, 1992, pp. 362–77 (p. 366); cf also R. Zunder, *Studentendorf Schlachtensee 1959 bis 1989. Eine Dokumentation* (*Schriften zur Hochschulsozialpolitik*, 1), Berlin, 1989. The money came from the US State Department. Cf. also the Evangelisches Studentenheim der TU Berlin at Eichkamp Dauerwaldweg, by Peter Lehrecke, of 1960 (*AR* 10-1963, p. 298) and the way it groups the small pavilions along a communal space.

'Political education . . .'; 'genuine student . . .'; 'beyond just accommodation'; 'Tutorensystem' 'task in which wissenschaftlich . . .'; 'cultural homelessness . . .': Der Rektor der Freein Universität Berlin, Exposé . . . Errichtung eines Studentenwohnheimes . . .', 2-3-1956, University Archive (HSA FUB: Kuratorium, Hg. d. Sitzgs.-Prot. nebst Vorlage (Vorlage A 091/56 zur 71. Kur. Sitzg.), courtesy Universitätsarchiv, Dr A. Spiller.

'Fully equipped'; 'intimate courts'; 'public square': *BW* 51/52 21-12-1959, pp. 1488–9, 1494–7, cf. *DUZ* 10-1961, p. 16.

'On an unbuilt-on plot': *DUZ* 9-1963, pp. 7–8, 14.

Munich Studentenstadt Freimann: by E. M. Lang & S. Pogadl: *DUZ* 9-1963, pp. 7ff.; A. Paschold & P. Jesberg (ed. by Deutsches Studentenwerk, Bonn), *Studenten wohnen . . .*, Stuttgart/Bern, 1971, pp. 34–7: 'Isolation in der Studentenstadt'.

Cologne (Köln) Luxemburgerstrasse: 1971–3, built by DEBA; see: A. Paschold & P. Jesberg (ed. by Deutsches Studentenwerk, Bonn), *Studenten wohnen . . .*, Stuttgart/Bern, 1971, pp. 12–15; pp. 34–7.

Stuttgart Pfaffenwald: A. Paschold & P. Jesberg (ed. by Deutsches Studentenwerk, Bonn), *Studenten wohnen . . .*, Stuttgart/Bern, 1971, pp. 42–4; *Ad'A* no. 170 11/12-1973, pp. 18–19.

H. W. Rothe, *Über die Gründung einer Universität in Bremen*, Bremen, 1961, pp. 61, 94, 98, 86; also in pp. 265–482 in: R. Neuhaus (ed.), *Dokumente zur Gründung neuer Hochschulen*, Wiesbaden, 1968.

Task to educate' . . . 'Anglo-American countries . . .': H. W. Rothe, 'Bremen . . .': pp. 103–32 (p. 111) in: *Schriften des Hochschulverbandes* 11, Göttingen 1962.

'Heimuniversität', W. Nitsch, U. Gerhardt, C. Offe, *Hochschule in der Demokratie*, Neuwied, 1965, pp. 203, 329; cf. H. Schelsky, 'Wie gründet man Universitäten', in *Frankfurter Allgemeine Zeitung* no. 239 14-10-1961 (Section: 'Bilder und Zeiten'); H. T. Jüchter, *Bremer Studentenhausplan. Studentische Vorstellungen zum Universitätsleben zwischen Arbeit und Geselligkeit* (publ. Verband deutscher Studenten VDS), Bonn, 1965.

Universitätsreform: academic and/or institutional?

'A strange division . . .': in Preface to W. Nitsch, U. Gerhardt, C. Offe, *Hochschule in der Demokratie*, Neuwied, 1965, p. v.

On Universitätsreform: R. Neuhaus (ed.), *Dokumente zur Hochschulreform 1945–1959*, Wiesbaden, 1961; R. Neuhaus (ed.), *Dokumente zur Grundung neuer Hochschulen*, Wiesbaden, 1968; *UQ* vol. 21 no. 4 9-

1967, pp. 453–61; G. Kloss, 'University Reform in West Germany', *Minerva* vol. 6 no. 3 Spring 1968, pp. 324–53; E. Böning & K. Roeloffs, *Case Studies on Innovation in Higher Education: The German Universities Aachen, Bochum, Konstanz*, OECD Paris, 1970; Publications of The Wissenschaftsrat (Tübingen / Bonn), 1960–70. Cf. for GDR / DDR: W. Flaschenträger & oth., *Magister und Scholaren / Professoren und Studenten, Deutsche Universitäten und Hochschulen im Überblick*, Leipzig 1981; cf. also note page 319.

Raiser on Robbins: L. Raiser, 'A German View . . . , *Minerva* vol. 2 no. 3 Spring 1964, pp. 336–42.

Hess: 'England . . .': J. F. Embling, *Die neuen britischen Universitäten als Instrumente der Reform* (publ. by the University) Konstanz, 1969, p. 7.

G. Picht, *Die deutsche Bildungskatastrophe*, Olten/Freiburg, 1964.

H. Schlager, 'Jetzt ist's genug', *Die Zeit* 19-4-1968.

K. Jaspers & K. Rossmann, *Die Idee der Universität*, Berlin, 1961; K. Jaspers, *The Idea of the University*, (Beacon Press USA 1959) 1960; cf. R. Schwarz (ed.), *Universität und moderne Welt*, vols 1, 2, Berlin, 1962.

Failure: H. Schelsky, *Abschied von der Hochschulpolitik*, Bielefeld, 1969, p. 133.

H. Schelsky, *Einsamkeit und Freiheit. Idee und Gestalt der deutschen Universität und ihrer Reformen*, Hamburg, 1963 (here the 1970 ed. (Bielefeld) was used, including the 'Nachtrag 1970', pp. 242ff.). On Kollegienhäuser: pp. 190ff.; 'theoretische Universität': p. 205.

'Faschistoid Professor': H.-A. Jacobsen & H. Dollinger (eds.), *Die Deutschen Studeten* [reprints of statements], Munich, 1968, p. 255. Cf. (Verband deutscher Studentenschaften (ed.), *Gutachten einer Kommission des V.D.S. zur Neugründung wissenschaftlicher Hochschulen, Studenten und die neue Universität* (publ. Bonn), 1962 (2nd. ed. 1968); W. Nitsch, U. Gerhardt, C. Offe, *Hochschule in der Demokratie*, Neuwied, 1965; H. Baier (ed.) *Studenten in Opposition*, Bielefeld, 1968; J. Habermas, *Protesbewegung und Hochschulreform*, Frankfurt, 1969.

On student personnel services: S. Leibfried, *Die Angepasste Universität. Zur Situation der Hochschulen in der Bundesrepublik und in den USA*, Frankfurt, 1968; cf. S. Liebfried (ed.), *Wider die Untertanenfabrik, Handbuch der Demokratisierung der Hochschule*, Köln, 1967.

H. Schelsky, *Einsamkeit und Freiheit. Idee und Gestalt der deutschen Universität und ihrer Reformen*, (Hamburg 1963) here 1970 ed. (Bielefeld), 'Nachtrag 1970': p. 255.

Self-contained institution: Wissenschaftsrat, *Anregungen des Wissenschaftsrates zur Gestaltung neuer Hochschulen*, Tübingen, 1962.

'Restaurieren, reparieren, reformieren', 5. Deutscher Studententag, Karlsruhe 1958: in R. Neuhaus (ed.), *Dokumente zur Hochschulreform 1945–1959*, Wiesbaden, 1961, pp. 222–9.

E. Baumgarten, *Zustand und Zukunft der deutschen Universität*, Tübingen, 1963, pp. 104ff.; cf. W. Killy, *Studium Generale und studentisches Gemeinschaftsleben*, Berlin, 1952, pp. 61–3.

Institutional and/or architectural innovations: Campus design at Bochum, Regensburg, Konstanz and Bielefeld

Berlin Freie Universität (FU): On the American-inspired central buildings at the Berlin Freie Universität (FU): 'Bücherturm', Lecture Theatres ('Henry Ford Bau'), and Mensa, by. F. H. Sobotka and G. Müller: *Neue Bauwelt* [precursor of Bauwelt (*BW*)] no. 46, 11-12-1951, pp. 750–1; *BW* no. 5, 30-1-1956, pp. 97–106.

Wissenschaftsrat, *Empfehlungen des Wissenschaftsrats zum Ausbau der wissenschaftlichen Hochschulen*, Tubingen, 1960; *Hochschuldienst* 8-8-1963, p. 1.

R. Dahrendorf, 'Starre und Offenheir der deutschen Universität: die Chancen der Reform', *Archives Européennes de Sociologie* vol. 3 no. 1 1962, pp. 263–93 (p. 293).

Finance: B. B. Burn & oth., *Higher Education in Nine Countries*, New York, 1971, p. 181.

Land and Bund shared: *DUZ* 8/9-1969, pp. 19–23.

Ulm: H. Lindinger (ed.), *Hochschule für Gestaltung Ulm*, Berlin, 1987.

1960: Bremen, Konstanz, Bochum. By 1963: plus Regensburg. Cf. *Hochschuldienst* 23-2-1963, p. 2. 1969: plus Ulm, Bielefeld and Dortmund: *Deutsche Bauzeitung* 7-1971, p. 737, see Linde (1970); *Baumeister* 6-1971; *Baumeister* 9-1975.

F. Kramer, 'Hochschulplanung Gestern und Heute', *Bauen und Wohnen* 1962, pp. 315ff.; *DUZ* 6-1960, pp. 20–1; cf. A. Hansen, 'Insel der Moderne. Die Frankfurter Universitätsbebauung der 50iger Jahre', pp. 68–79 in: D. Bartetzko (ed.), *Sprung in die Moderne. Frankfurt am Main, Die Statdt der 50er Jahre*, Frankfurt, 1994.

'Buildings for research . . .': Wissenschaftsrat, *Empfehlungen des Wissenschaftsrates zur Aufstellung von Raumprogrammen für Bauvorhaben der wissenschaftlichen Hochschulen*, 23-11-1963, p. 8.

Protests by the 'freie Architekten': *DBZ* 7-1971, p. 740.

On competitions: cf *Architekturwettbewerbe, Sonderheft Bremen* 1967; J. Jordan, 'University Planning in Western Germany', *AJ* 15-4-1970, pp. 941–58.

H. Linde: Institut für Hochschulbau Universität Stuttgart, S. Heeg (eds.), *Horst Linde Architekt und Hochschullehrer* (publ. Stuttgart), n.d. [*c.* 1980]; Linde (1970) vols. 1–4.

Wissenschaftsrat, *Empfehlungen des Wissenschaftsrates zur Struktur und zum Ausbau des Bildungswesens im Hochschulbereich nach 1970* (publ. Bonn, 1970), pp. 178–81; *AD* 11-1974, p. 711; *DUZ* 12-1969, p. 1; H. U. Schmidt, Institutsbauten – *Hochschulgebäude in der Bundesrepublik Deutschland* (*Planen und Bauen*, 20; publ. Zentralarchiv für Hochschulbauten Stuttgart), Munich, 1980; (Wissenschaftsrat), *Vergleich von Kosten deutscher und ausländischer Hochschulbauten: Bericht einer vom Wissenschaftsrat beauftragten Arbeitsgruppe über eine Untersuchung ausgewählter in- und ausländischer Beispiele*, Wiesbaden, 1968.

91 built: *DUZ* 2-12-1971, p. 821.

'Frightening monotony': *Deutsche Bauzeitung* 7-1971, pp. 740–1.

P. Jokusch, 'Die Hochschule als sozialer Ort', pp. 82–6 in: Linde (1970), vol. 2; also in *Konstanzer Blätter für Hochschulfragen* no. 40, vol. 11 (no. 3) 9-1973, pp. 45–56.

'Social sphere . . . .': Linde (1970), vol. 1, p. 12.

'"Campus" I find': H. W. Rothe, 'Bremen . . .': pp. 103–32 (p. 114) in: *Schriften des Hochschulverbandes* 11, Göttingen, 1962.

'College of the Student Community', H.W. Rothe, *Über die Gründung einer Universität in Bremen*, Bremen, 1961, p. 87; cf. *Hochschuldienst* 14-5-1961, pp. 2–3.

'Harmony of the whole man'; 'functional and architectonic': H. W. Rothe, 'Bremen . . .': pp. 103–32 (pp. 119, 114 in: *Schriften des Hochschulverbandes* 11, Göttingen, 1962).

Bremen: *BW* no. 1, 1-1-1962, p. 5; W. M. Luther, 'Die Stellung der Universitätsbibliothek nach den Vorschlägen des Bremer Gutachtens', *DUZ* 4-1962, pp. 15–17; *BW* nos. 42/43, 23-10-1967; *Architekturwettbewerbe Sonderheft Bremen* 1967; *BW* no. 30, 28-7-1969, pp. 1006ff.; Controversy about architectural quality: *BW* no. 47, 24-11-1969, pp. 1665, 1694, 1696; *BW* no. 1, 2-1-1970, pp. 2, 4; *BW* no. 24, 25-6-1976, pp. 736–8; *Baumeister* 9-1977, pp. 832–3; 'Humboldtscher Geist oder linke Modell-Universität', *DUZ* issue 1 + 2 of August 1969, pp. 16ff. The university planners provided the 'Grossraster', the main layout pattern, various architects designed the buildings.

M. Foucault, *Surveiller et punir: naissance de la prison*, Paris 1975 (*Discipline and Punish*, New York, 1977); cf. H. Rosenau, *Social Purpose in Architecture*, London, 1970.

Bremen plan in Linde's Seminar: H. Linde: Institut für Hochschulbau Universität Stuttgart, S. Heeg (eds.), *Horst Linde Architekt und Hochschullehrer* (publ. Stuttgart), n.d. [*c*. 1980], p. 67.

'More intensive university-life . . .': Wissenschaftsrat, *Anregungen des Wissenschaftsrats zur Gestalt neuer Hochschulen*, Tübingen, 1962, p. 82.

'Town for people . . .': H. Linde (ed.), *Universitätsbau in den USA, Schriften des Zentralarchivs für Hochschulbau* 3, Düsseldorf, 1965, p. 10.

P. Conradi, 'Probleme bei der Planung von Hochschulen', *Bauen und Wohnen* 1964, pp. 295–9; also as: P. Conradi & H. Reichenecker, 'Gedanken zur Gesamtplanung von Hochschulen', *Konstanzer Blätter für Hochschulfragen*, no. 5, vol. 2 (no. 3) 11-1964, pp. 44–52; cf. 'Zur Situation unserer Hochschulen', *BW* no. 48, 1-12-1958, pp. 1163ff.; 'Hochschulen bauen', *Baumeister* 12-1265, p. 1369; *BW* no. 10, 9-3-1964, pp. 295–9; *BW* nos. 19/20, 20-5-1963, pp. 536, 563; 'Bauwelt Gespräch: Universitätsbau': *BW* nos. 42/43, 23-1967, pp. 1054 ff.; 'Hochschulentwicklung and Planungsmethodik', *Deutsche Bauzeitung* 7-1967, p. 582; 'Studienreform = Hochschulreform', *Deutsche Bauzeitung* 3-1968, pp. 151ff.

Institut für öffentliche Bauten und Hochschulplanung, Stuttgart, H. D. Laubinger (eds.), *Hommage à Gabriel Epstein* (publ. Stuttgart), 1987.

'Here we thought only about technical . . .': H.-J. Aminde, interview 1999.

Anglo-German contacts: Cf. 'Umbau der deutschbritischen Hochschulbeziehungen', *Hochschuldienst* 13 8 23-4-1960; 'Lord Hailsham gegen Trennung von Forschung und Lehre', *Hochschuldienst* 14 19 8-10-1961, pp. 2–3; 'Der Versuch von Brighton', *Hochschuldienst* 14 10 23-5-1961, p. 9; 'British Council Kurs über Universitätsverwaltung', *Hochschuldienst* 16 17/18 23-9-1963, pp. 2–3; A. Nathan, 'Sensationelle Hochschulpläne [Robbins Report]', *DUZ* 11-1963, pp. 4–5; 'Universitätsbau in GB', *BW* no. 5, 4-2-1963, pp. 137–43; 'England's neue Universitaten . . .', *DUZ* 6-1966, pp. 29–31; 'Das englische Hochschulwesen' *DUZ* 3-1966, pp. 9–17; K. Steiner (ed.), *Probleme der Hochschulerweiterung*, Teufen 1966, pp. 221–33; W. Lantz, *New University Building England Reisebericht 1966*, Wiesbaden, 1966; A. Sloman, *Eine Universität im Aufbau*, Düsseldorf, 1967 [cf. above: Essex University]; P. Jokusch, *Gesamtplanung Britischer Hochschulen*, (*Schriften Zentralarchiv für Hochschulbau Stuttgart* 5), Düsseldorf, 1967; C. Schneider, 'Hochschulplanung in England', *Konstanzer Blätter für Hochschulfragen* no. 24, vol. 7 (no. 3) 9-1969, pp. 75–84; 'Bauliche Hochschulplanung in GB', *Information 34* (Zentralarchiv für Hochschulbau Stuttgart 1976 (ed.), pp. 17–24; cf. 'Reform and Tradition in German Universities Today', *UQ* vol. 21 no. 4 9-1967, 45–61; G. Epstein, 'Building universties in Germany' *Listener* 3-11-1966, pp. 647–9; J. Jordan, 'University Planning in Germany', *AJ* 15-4-1970, pp. 941–58; P. Jokusch, 'University Campus Design', *AD* 11-1974, pp. 702–17.

Bochum

General: A. von Cube, *Die Ruhruniversität Bochum, Bauaufgabe-Baugeschichte-Baugedanke. Eine kunsthistorische Untersuchung*, Bochum, 1982; Gesellschaft der Freunde der Ruhruniversität (eds.), *Materialien zur Geschichte der Ruhruniversität Bochum*, 1, 1971; 2, 1972 (publ. Bochum); R. Knümann, *Die Universität Bochum*, Stuttgart, 1965; H. Linde (ed.), *Planung Wissenschaftlicher Hochschulen* (*Schriften des Zentralarchivs für Hochschulbau 1*), Stuttgart, 1965, pp. 81ff.; Linde (1970), vol. 3, pp. 185ff.; E. Böning & K. Roeloffs, *Case Studies in Innovation in Higher Education. Three German Universities. Aachen, Bochum, Konstanz*, OECD Paris, 1970; I have to thank Archivar Joerg Lorenz.

'Paradestück', *DUZ* 8-8-1963, p. 1.

Problem of numbers: P. Mikat, 1965, quoted in A. von Cube, *op. cit.*, p. 23.

Academic System: Ruhr Universität Bochum, *Denkschrift des Gründungsausschusses, Empfehlungen zum Aufbau der Universität Bochum*, Dezember 1962; *Hochschuldienst* 8-6-1962, p. 9; *DUZ* 4-1963, pp. 13–16.

5%, 9%: E. Böning & K. Roeloffs, *Case Studies in Innovation in Higher Education. Three German Universities.*

323

Aachen, Bochum, Konstanz, OECD Paris, 1970, p. 58; Hochschuldienst 23-6-1966.

'Most unburaucratically': Linde (1970) vol. 1 p. 113.

'Novelty' campus university: E. Böning & K. Roeloffs, op. cit., p. 22.

'Manifestation of unity . . .': F. Hallauer, 'Werden und Gestalt der Ruhruniversität. Eine bautechnische Anthologie', in: Gesellschaft Freunde der Ruhruniversität Bochum (eds.), Die Ruhruniversität, Stuktur – Planung – Bauen (publ. Bochum) 1966, pp. 22–5.

'Europe's biggest building site': von Cube, op. cit., p. 57.

'No process of cobbling together': BW no. 49, 4-12-1967, pp. 1298–9. cf. AD 11-1974, p. 711.

'Basic aim of the university . . .': Michael Zotter, project architect, quoted by von Cube, op. cit., p. 117.

'Valid results' electronically stored:, H. Linde (ed.), Planung Wissenschaftlicher Hochschulen (Schriften des Zentralarchivs für Hochschulbau 1) Stuttgart, 1965, p. 84. Costs: Hochschuldienst 8-12-1964, pp. 3–5; BW no. 19, 8-5-1967, pp. 461ff.; E. Böning & K. Roeloffs, op. cit., p. 128.

Much more cheaply: Hochschuldienst 8-12-1964, pp. 3–5; cf. K. Herzog, 'Kostenvergleich von Hochschulbauten', Der Ruhrstudent no. 13–14 1968, pp. 12–14.

'The lack of our experience'(Rüdiger Thoma): von Cube, op. cit., p. 120.

'In the truest sense agora': F. Hallauer, 'Werden und Gestalt der Ruhruniversität. Eine bautechnische Anthologie', in: Gesellschaft Freunde der Ruhruniversität Bochum (eds.), Die Ruhruniversität, Stuktur – Planung – Bauen (publ. Bochum), 1966, p. 30.

Kollegienhäuser: Hochschuldienst 23-2-1963, pp. 2–3; Hochschuldienst 23-5-1965, p. 4; fallen foul of student opinion: Linde (1970) vol. 2, p. 85; BW no. 19/20, 20-5-1963, pp. 533–4.

Residences: BW no. 19/20, 20-5-1963, p. 534; 'Bochum. Die Wohnstadt Zentren', Die Bauverwaltung, 12-1966, pp. 726–51; 1-1967.

1969: 2,000 student residences: E. Böning & K. Roeloffs, op. cit., p. 116.

Momentous decision: Ad'A no. 107, 4/5-1963, p. 10; cf. R. Knümann, Die Universität Bochum, Stuttgart, 1965 and von Cube, op. cit., about the town/campus arguments.

On 'unicenter' plans: 'Die Universitätswohnstadt', Die Bauverwaltung 12-1966 / 1-1967; Die Ruhruniversität (a Journal publ. by Gesellschaft der Freunde der Ruhruniversität), 9-5-1966, p. 38; Linde (1970) vol. 4, p. 78.

'Not for the normal . . .': Interview project architect Rüdiger Thoma, von Cube, op. cit., pp. 118–21.

Against Bochum: 'monstrous', 'bigger, larger', rationality . . . aestheticism . . .: 'Der Irrationalismus mit der "Rationalität" in Bochum', BW no. 19, 8-5-1967, pp. 461–5; 'monotony', 'mere utility', functionality a cliche: BW no. 23, 5-6-1967, pp. 581–4; cf. BW no. 41, 9-10-1967, pp. 1012–13; BW no. 42/3, 23-10-1967, p. 1048; BW no. 49, 4-12-1967, pp. 1298–1301; DUZ 2 February issue 1971, pp. 114–15; Baumeister

8-1971, pp. 936–8; cf. K. Bonacker, Beton. Ein Baustoff wird Schlagwort, Marburg, 1996.

Von Cube, op. cit. about criticism: pp. 91ff.

Regensburg

I am grateful to Dr R. F. Dietze for help.

Geplant Gebaut Universität Regensburg 1977 Pläne Daten Photos Texte des Universitätsbauamtes (publ. University Regensburg), 1977; Gruppe "Arttraktion" (eds.), Rund um die Kugel. Ein Wegweiser zu den Kunstwerken an der Universität Regensburg, Regensburg, 1992; Konstanzer Blätter für Hochschulfragen no. 11, vol. 4 (no. 2) 5-1965, pp. 67–9; Hochschuldienst 5-6-1966, pp. 5–6; 'Bildungszentrum in der weissblauen Provinz', DUZ 1st December issue 1969, pp. 22–3.

'Consciously a normal university': Linde (1970) vol. 1, p. 116.

'A guaranteed unbreakable . . .': Regensburger Universitätszeitung vol. 4 no. 4 4-1968, pp. 2–7.

Public advertisement: UQ vol. 23 no. 4 Summer 1969, pp. 408–19; cf. E. Böning & K. Roeloffs, Case Studies in Innovation in Higher Education. Three German Universities. Aachen, Bochum, Konstanz, OECD Paris, 1970, pp. 135–7.

Residences in town: Linde (1970) vol. 4, pp. 153–5; Deutsches Studentenwerk (ed.), Studenten wohnen . . . , Stuttgart/Bern, 1971, pp. 60–2.

View of Cathedral: Linde (1970) vol. 4, p. 179.

Preliminary tower: DUZ 10-1966, p. 9.

Planning: H. Gebhard, 'Bauplanung . . .': Regensburger Universitätszeitung vol. 3 10-1966, pp. 2ff.; H. Gebhard, 'Planung . . .', Regensburger Universitätszeitung vol. 3 10/11-1967, pp. 38–54; Linde (1970) vol. 4, pp. 179–81; H. Gebhard, 'Bauleitplanung . . . Regensburg', Bauen und Wohnen no. 24 11-1969, pp. 392–4; Der Architekt, 3-1975, pp. 140–2;

Konstanz

K. Oettinger & H. Weidhase, Eine Feste Burg der Wissenschaft, Konstanz 1985; Konstanzer Blätter für Hochschulfragen (hereafter in this section KoBL) nos. 50/1, vol. 14 (no. 1/2) 6-1976. I have to thank Frau Dr Maria Schorpp.

'A "luxury" project': E. Böning & K. Roeloffs, Case Studies in Innovation in Higher Education. Three German Universities. Aachen, Bochum, Konstanz, OECD Paris, 1970, p. 46.

'Sweet anachronism': R. Dahrendorf, 'Konstanz, "der süsse Anachronismus". Eine persönliche Notiz zum 10. Geburtstag . . .', KoBL nos. 50/1, vol. 14 (no. 1/2) 6-1976, pp. 14–23.

'Harvard am Bodensee', KoBL nos. 82/83/83, vol. 22 (nos. 1–3) 4-1984, p. 108.

Foundation: Bericht des Gründungsausschusses, KoBL no. 8, vol. 3 (no. 3) 8-1965, pp. 5ff.; cf. Denkschrift über die Errichtung von Wissenschaftlichen Hochschulen in

Baden-Württemberg, 1963, printed also in *KoBL* no. 2, 12-1963 and no. 3, 5-1964.

Virtually a 'princely fiat': *KoBL* nos. 50/1, vol. 14 (nos. 1/2) 6-1976, pp. 14–23.

Student residences (at the Sonnenbühl): J. Jordan, 'University Planning in Germany', *AJ* 15-4-1970, pp. 941–58 (pp. 956–7).

Pure research: *KoBL* no. 8, vol. 3 (no. 3) 8-1965, pp. 9–11.

'Pleasure to learn and teach': *Hochschuldienst* 8-7-1966, pp. 4–5.

Architectural Sources: *BW* no. 31/32, 5-8-1968, pp. 989ff.; *BW* no. 10, 11-3-1974, pp. 403ff. (Library); 'Umfrage' [user survey], *BW* (no.) 31, 19-8-1974, pp. 1057–63; *Baumeister* 9-1975, pp. 769–75; *Baumeister* 9-1977, pp. 829–31; *Architekt* 1-1975, p. 138.

Linde: Institut für Hochschulbau Universität Stuttgart, S. Heeg (eds.), *Horst Linde Architekt und Hochschullehrer* (publ. Stuttgart), n.d. [*c.* 1980], pp. 70, 133.

Gemeinsames Gutachten für die Univesität Konstanz [Protokoll], Konstanz 13-2-1968, mimeogaphed in University Archive (Courtesy E. Pook). This was instigated by Linde (Interview Linde 1998).

Development 'controlled': *KoBL* no. 29, vol. 8 (no. 4) 11-1970, p. 18; E. Böning & K. Roeloffs, *Case Studies in Innovation in Higher Education. Three German Universities. Aachen, Bochum, Konstanz*, OECD Paris, 1970, p. 127.

Art by Otto Piene and others, *KoBL* no. 29, vol. 8 (no. 4) 11-1970, pp. 60–2; K. Oettinger & H. Weidhase, *Eine Feste Burg der Wissenschaft*, Konstanz, 1985; pp. 50ff.

Bochum: 'Manifestation of unity . . .': F. Hallauer, 'Werden und Gestalt der Ruhruniversität. Eine bautechnische Anthologie', in: Gesellschaft Freunde der Ruhruniversität Bochum (eds.), *Die Ruhruniversität, struktur – Planung – Bauen* (publ. Bochum) 1966, p. 22–5.

'Eindeutig', definitively, 'spatial ordering': *KoBL* no. 8, vol. 3 (no. 3) 8-1965, p. 34.

'Relationship . . .'; *KoBL* no. 29, vol. 8 (no. 4) 11-1970, p. 9. 'Big house of the Wissenschaften . . .': *ibid.*, p. 27; Stationary to movement: *ibid.*, pp. 10–11.

'Loose oneself', Gemeinsames Gutachten für die Universität Konstanz [Protokoll], Konstanz 13-2-1968, mimeogaphed in University Archive, p. 12.

Own desk, chair: K. Oettinger & H. Weidhase, *Eine Feste Burg der Wissenschaft*, Konstanz, 1985; p. 42.

'Commoncenter' etc.: *KoBL* no. 29, vol. 8 (no. 4) 11-1970, pp. 53, 111; 'spontaneous': *ibid.*, p. 56; 'The aim of the new university . . .': *ibid.* p. 24; users of an 'Anstalt': *ibid.* p. 111; 'severe environment': *ibid.*, p. 64. Cf. Peter Marris: 'It matters less where people meet to dine than where they drink coffee together. If each department were equipped with a coffe lounge, and informal study room. . . . [this] would break down reserve'. P. Marris, *The Experience of Higher Education*, London, 1964, p. 181.

'University . . . social place': P. Jokusch in Linde (1970), vol. 2, p. 84; P. Jokusch, 'Die Hochschule als sozialer Ort', *KoBL* no. 40, vol. 11 (no. 3) 9-1973, pp. 45–56.

Library: *KoBL* no. 29, vol. 8 (no. 4) 11-1970, pp. 74–93; also in *BW* no. 10, 11-3-1974, pp. 403ff.

30% residences at Sonnenbühl: K. Oettinger & H. Weidhase, *Eine Feste Burg der Wissenschaft*, Konstanz, 1985, p. 90.

'Wohnheime . . . here the students' private realm should purposely be kept, thus there should be no obligation to take part in social functions': *KoBL* no. 8, vol. 3 (no. 3) 8-1965, p. 90.

Bielefeld

H. Schelsky, *Einsamkeit und Freiheit. Idee und Gestalt der deutschen Universität und ihrer Reformen*, Hamburg, 1963 (2nd ed. Bielefeld, 1970).

'Structural characteristics . . .': 'Strukuturmerkmale der neuen Universität in Ostwestfalen', *DUZ* 9-1969, pp. 31–2; cf. *Hochschuldienst* 23-11-1965, pp. 6–7; *Zwischenstation. Universität Bielefeld 1979* (publ. Univ. Bielefeld), 1979, p. 23ff. K. Köpke, P. Kulka & oth., *Universität Bielefeld, Bauen in der industriellen Welt*, Kunsthalle, Bielefeld, 1975.

Competition: *BW* no. 49, 8-12-1969, pp. 1759–65; cf. *BW* no. 10, 12-3-1976, pp. 284–5; *Ad'A* no. 183, 1/2-1976, pp. 42–5.

Press Reports, including Hallauer's comments, in: Universitat Bielefeld, *Bauplanung der Universität Bielefeld*, (publ. Univ. Bielefeld), 1974, p. 141ff.

'Rational' planning: *DUZ* 10-1970, p. 3.

'A purely utiltitarian . . .'; 'no hierachy'; 'maximal use': D. Storbeck, *Neue Universität. Standort und Baustruktur. Erfahrungen aus dem Aufbau der Universität Bielefeld* (publ. Univ. Bielefeld), 1985, pp. 21–3; 'nowhere contacts . . .': *ibid.*, p. 30.

'The closer the neighbour . . .': Universität Bielefeld, *Bauplanung der Universitat Bielefeld* (publ. Univ. Bielefeld), 1974, p. 52.

Bremen: H. P. Barth, *DUZ* 8-1969, pp. 16–7; cf. notes above page XX.

P. Mikat & H. Schelsky, *Grundzüge einer neuen Universitat. Zur Planung einer Hochschulgründung in Ostwestfalen*, Bielefeld, 1966, p. 37.

H.-A. Jacobson & H. Dollinger (eds.), *Die deutschen Studenten 1968*, Munich, 1968, p. 13.

V   CAMPUS PLANNING WORLDWIDE

P. Merlin, *L'urbanisme universitaire à l'étranger et en France*, Paris, 1995, pp. 246, 387, 264.

'Primitive functionalism': *AA* 1967, p. 7.

General: for international universities see *Bulletin Association Internationale des Universités International Association of Universities*, (Paris), 1955;

A. M. Carr-Saunders, *New Universities Overseas*, London, 1961–; R. Schwarz, *Universität und moderne Welt*, vols 1 and 2, Berlin 1962; Various contributors, 'Universität im Umbau', Archives Européennes de Sociologie vol. 3 no. 1 1962, vol. 3 no. 2 1962; 'Robbins Report': United Kingdom, Committee on Higher Education, *Higher Education (Parliamentary Papers* Cmnd. 2154, publ. London), 1963, see especially Appendix vol. five; Ross; *Minerva* 1963–; J. Dreze & J. Debelle, *Conceptions de l'université*, Paris, 1968; 'Common Outline for the Preparation of Case Studies': Preface to the publications on universities by OECD Paris (printed e.g. in: C. Grignon & J. C. Passeron, *French Experience Before 1968*, OECD Paris, 1970); B. B. Burn (ed.), *Higher Education in Nine Countries*, New York, 1970; S. D. Kertesz, *The Task of Universities in a Changing World*, Notre Dame/London, 1971; M. S Archer (ed.), *Students, University and Society*, London, 1972; V. G. Onushkin – International Institute for Educational Planning (eds.), *Planning the Development of Universities* (series) (publ. Unesco Press Paris), 1975; G. Statera, *Death of Utopia. The Development and Decline of the Student Movement in Europe*, New York, 1975; J. Ben-David, *Centers of Learning: Britain, France, Germany, United States*, New York, 1977; A. S. Knowles (ed.) *The International Encyclopaedia of Higher Education*, New York, 1977; B. R. Clark (ed.) *Perspectives on Higher Education*, Berkeley, 1984; H. Röhrs (ed.), *Tradition and Reform of the University under an International Perspective* (*Studien zur Erziehungswissenschaft* 21), Frankfurt, 1987; S. Vassal, *L'Europe des universités. France, RFA, RU*, Thèse (Géographie), Caen 1988; B. R. Clark, *The Encyclopedia of Higher Education*, Oxford, 1992.

For international buildings see U. Kultermann, 'Internationale Hochschularchitektur', Baukunst und Werkform 2–1958, pp. 65–7; 'Internationale Wohnheimkonferenz in Dijon und Paris', Hochschuldienst 23-10-1963; H. Linde (ed.), *Planung Wissenschaftlicher Hochschulen* (*Schriften des Zentralarchivs fur Hochschulbau* 1), Stuttgart, 1965; K. Steiner (ed.), *Probleme der Hochschulerweiterung*, Teufen, 1966; O. Newman, 'The New Campus, *AFor* 5-1966, pp. 30–54; C. Pellicia & P. Sartogo, 'Campus Design', *Casabella*: in issues 322, 323, 326, 332, 333, January 1968–February 1969; W. D. Schrader, 'Planungen moderner Hochschulen im In- und Ausland', *Regensburger Universitätszeitung*' vol. 4 no. 3 3-1968, pp. 2–13; J. Rykwert, 'Universities as Institutional Archetypes of our Age', *Zodiac* no. 18 (1968), pp. 61–3; *Ad'A* no. 137, 4/5-1968; G. Feuerstein, *Hochschulen Planen Bauen* (Cat Exh. Bundesministerium für Bauten und Technik / Österreichische Bauzentren 1969/70, publ. Vienna); *Deutsche Bauzeitung* 2-1969; *Bauen und Wohnen* 11-1969; *AR* 4-1970, Bibliography on p. 312; Linde

(1970) vols. 1-4; Unesco, *Planning Buildings and Facilities for Higher Education*, Unesco Paris/ London, 1975; W. Curtis, 'L'Université, la ville at "habitat collectif"', *Archithese* 14, 1975, pp. 29–37; *Ad'A* no. 183, 1/2-1976; P. Merlin, *L'Urbanisme universitaire à l'étranger et en France*, Paris, 1995; P. C. Pignatelli & D. Mandolesi, *L'Architettura delle Università. Campus Architecture*, Roma, 1997.

Modern campus in USA: Turner, pp. 249ff.

Fribourg, Switzerland, by Denis Honegger: *Werk* 1942, pp. 33–59. Andrew Saint drew my attention to this building.

Cité Universitaire, Paris: B. Lemoine, *La Cité Internationale Universitaire de Paris*, Paris 1990, 'cité jardin', p. 27.

Aarhus: by K. Fisker, P. Stegmann and C. F. Möller; *Bygninger en arkitektonisk helhed*, Steno Museet, 1994; C. F. Möller, *Aarhus Universitets Bygninger*, Aarhus, 1978.

Caracas: 1, H. Linde (ed.), *Planung Wissenschaftlicher Hochschulen* (*Schriften des Zentralarchivs fur Hochschulbau* 1), Stuttgart 1965, pp. 45–6. S. Moholy-Nagy, *Carlos Raul Villanueva*, Caracas, 1964, pp. 72ff.

Mexico City: *AR* 11-1953, pp. 307–18; *American Institute of Architects Journal* 1-1953, pp. 6ff.; J. R. Alvarez Noguera, *La arquitectura de la Ciudad Universitaria* (publ. Universidad Nacional Autónoma de México), 1994.

Jerusalem: Master Plan by Kaufman, Klarwein and Rau, from 1948: *AD* 5-1961, pp. 201; *Ad'A* no. 77, 4-1958, pp. 69–80.

Constantine, 1971: *Ad'A* no. 183, 1/2/1976, pp. 19–23. Oran, 1971, *Ad'A* no. 183, 1/2-1976, pp. 24–9. Cf. University of Brasilia, by Oscar Niemeyer, Linde (1970), vol. 1, pp. 82–3.

'Zeilenbau' in housing: W. Gropius, *The New Architecture and the Bauhaus*, London, 1935; cf. M. Glendinning & S. Muthesius, *Tower Block Modern Public Housing in England, Wales, Scotland and Northern Ireland*, New Haven & London, 1994, pp. 39ff.

USSR: Linde (1970) vol. 1, pp. 65–9; A. J. Aminde, 'Neue Wissenschaftsstädte und Hochschulplanung UdSSR', *BW* no. 9, 5-3-1973, pp. 382–90; *Deutsche Architektur* [Berlin-DDR], 20 4-1971, pp. 200–49.

Another notable example of an essentially Zeilenbau plan is A. Aalto's Helsinki Technical University at Otaniemi (from 1949): P. D. Pearson, *A. Aalto*, New York, 1978, p. 216.

R. Banham has to be corrected with regard to Tucuman University in Argentine, which he claims to be the first major example of a one-building university, by Horacio Caminos, 1951-2 (R. Banham, *Megastructure*, 1976, pp. 10, 36 etc.). The plans (*AR* 11-1952, pp.

322–30) in fact consist of the usual Zeilenbau formation, only the large community centre shows an early
example of an all-covering space-frame roof.

Widely spaced out: e.g. Campus for 'Sind' university,
Hyderabad in Pakistan, begun 1955 by Richard
Döcker (of Stuttgart): *Baukunst and Werkform* 1960, pp.
361–73; University Karachi, planned from 1954-6 by
M. Ecochard, P. Riboulet, G. Thurnauer: *Bauen und
Wohnen* 1959, pp. 393–4.

'If he had to choose . . .': *Ad'A* no. 137, 4/5-1968,
p. cxxv.

'Archetypes', J. Rykwert, 'Universities as Institutional
Archetypes of our Age', *Zodiac* no. 18 (1968), pp.
61–3.

L. Kahn, e.g.: Institute of Management, Ahmedabad India
1962-74: H. Ronner & oth., L. I. Kahn, *The Complete
Works 1935–74*, Basel etc., 1977.

Rissho University: *AFor* 5-1970, pp. 34–5.

Universidad del Valle, Cali: Linde (1970) vol. 1, pp. 84–5.

Stockholm 1961: T. Hall (ed.) *Frescati. Huvudstadsuniversitet och arkitekturpark* (publ. Stockholms Universitet),
1998, pp. 62ff.

Bochum competition: A. von Cube, *Die Ruhruniversität
Bochum, Bauaufgabe-Baugeschichte-Baugedanke. Eine kunsthistorische Untersuchung*, Bochum, 1982, pp. 28–51;
R. Knümann, *Die Universität Bochum*, Stuttgart,
1965; 'Zum Ideenwettbewerb . . .': *Die Bauverwaltung*
6-1963, pp. 271–96; *BW* no. 19/20, 20-5-1963,
pp. 533–48; *Ad'A* no. 107, 4/5-1963, pp. 10–11; *AD*
8-1964, pp. 376ff.

Griffith, begun 1971: R. Johnson, *Griffith University Site
planning Report* (publ. Griffith University Brisbane)
1973, *Town Planning Review* 7-1964, pp. 246–7; 'New
Universities' in Australia included Monash 1958 (pp.
1–15 in: Ross), Macquarie 1964, LaTrobe 1964 ('coll-
giate': *Interbuild* 7-1967, pp. 20–4), Flinders 1966. D.
S. Macmillan, *Australian Universities A Descriptive Sketch*,
Sydney, 1968.

O. M. Ungers Studenthostel 1964 (not built), for Universiteit Twente (Enschede): O. Ungers, *Architecture
1951–1990*, Stuttgart, 1991; cf. P. Huygen, *Vormgeven
aan de Campus / Designing the Campus*, (publ. Univ.
Twente / Enschede), n.d. [c. 1990].

Urbino: 1962: Zucchi, *Giancarlo de Carlo*, Oxford, 1992;
cf. Aldo van Eyck on Urbino: *Zodiac* no. 16 [1966],
pp. 180–7; G. DeCarlo, 'Why/How to Build School
Buildings', *Harvard Educational Review* (spec. no. *Architecture and Education*) 39 1969.

Tougaloo College, from c. 1965: Turner, pp. 267, 271;
M. Schmertz, *Campus Planning and Design*, New York,
1972, pp. 193ff.; *AFor* 4-1966, pp. 56ff.; *ARec* 11-1973,
pp. 110–16.

Rand: by W. O. Meyer and Jan van de Wijk, founded
1966, Linde (1970) vol. 4, p. 171; *Bauen und Wohnen*
11-1969, pp. 379–89.

Osaka Art University: plans by Noriaki Kurokawa 1964:
AD 12-1964, pp. 606–7; built by Dai-ichi-Kobo; *Japan*

Architect 8-1966, pp. 57–64; *Japan Architect* 12-1968,
pp. 45–52; *Japan Architect* 3-1972, pp. 21–36; *Baumeister*
2-1975, pp. 95–101.

Cosenza (University of Calabria) founded, 1972; by
Gregotti Associati: competition 1973: *Architettura
Chronache e Storia* No. 227, 9-1974, pp. 296–324;
R. Banham, *Megastructure*, 1976, pp. 147–8; *Lotus*
no. 11 1976, pp. 146–53; *Ad'A* no. 183 1/2-1976, pp.
30–50.

France

General: *La Réforme de l'université*, (contrib. by G.
Antoine, J. C. Passeron), Paris, 1966; J. Dreze & J.
Debelle, *Conceptions d'université*, Paris, 1968; C.
Grignon & J. C. Passeron, *French Experience before
1968*, OECD Paris, 1970; F. Bourricaud, *Universités à
la dérive. France, États Unis, Amérique du sud*, Paris, 1971;
Linde (1970) vol. 1 pp. 40–7; J. Abram, *L'Architecture
moderne en France*, Tom. 2 1940–66, Paris, 1999; G.
Monnier, *L'Architecture moderne en France* Tom. 3
1967–99, Paris, 2000.

Student numbers: (151,000; 619,000; 838,000): *Les
Cahiers de l'IAURP* (Institut d'Aménagement et
Urbanisme de la Région Parisienne), vol. 23, 5-1971,
p. 10; J. Verger, *Histoire des Universités en France*,
Toulouse, 1986.

'1970 over 80 per cent of all university buildings were
less than ten years old'. *Les Cahiers, op. cit.*, p. 10.

Cf. D. Alexandre-Bidon, M. M. Compère & oth., *Le Pat-
rimoine de l'éducation nationale* (Collection Le Patri-
moine des Institutions Politiques et Culturelles,
Flohic Editions) Charenton le Pont, 1999; P. Merlin,
L'Urbanisme universitaire à l'étranger et en France, Paris
1995; *Ville Architecture Université. Réalisations du Schéma
Université 2000* (Ministère de l'éducation nationale
. . .), Paris, 1998.

14 campuses: F. Gaussen, 'L'université hors les murs' (II),
Le Monde 29-4-1966, p. 10.

'HLM': Habitations à Loyer moderé, cf. J. Lemoine,
'De l'habitation à l'urbanisme', *Techniques et Architecture*
7-1959.

Up to early 1960s: cf. P. Donzelot, 'Les constructions
universitaires, de 1947–1957', *Revue de l'enseignement
supérieur* 1958 no. 1, pp. 67–78; *Esprit* (Novelle Serie)
no. 327, 32 4-1964, *Esprit* (Nouvelle Serie) no. 328,
32 5/6-1964; *Ad'A* no. 107, 4/5-1963, pp. 2–32; *Architecture Française* nos. 275–6, 1965, pp. 1–116; *Ad'A* no.
123, 12-1965/1-1966. *Urbanisme Revue française* no. 32
(79) 1963; H. Linde (ed.), *Planung Wissenschaftlicher
Hochschulen*, (*Schriften des Zentralarchivs für Hochschulbau* 1) Stuttgart, 1965; Linde (1970), vol. 1, pp. 40–6.

Early student residences: *Urbanisme Revue française*, vol. 32
(79) 1963, p. 19. In 1936 the minister of Education,

the left-winger Jean Zay, laid the foundations of
CNOUS. (Centre National des Oeuvres Universitaires
et Scolaires).

Student residences: P. Merlin, *L'Urbanisme universitaire à
l'étranger et en France*, Paris, 1995, p. 362; D. Alexandre-
Bidon, M. M. Compere & oth., *Le Patrimoine de
l'éducation nationale* (Collection Le Patrimoine des
Institutions Politiques et Culturelles, Flohic Editions)
Charenton le Pont, 1999; *DUZ* 2-1963, pp. 26–9;
DUZ 9-1963, p. 19.

Antony, Residence Universitaire Jean Zay, Avenue
Général de Gaulle, by Eugène Baudouin, one of the
most respected early Modernists, 1954–6; *L'Architecture
Française* nos. 171–2, 1956, pp. 76–7; *DUZ* 8-1960,
pp. 20–2; *DUZ* 2-1963, pp. 26–9.

Size of residences: *Les Cahiers de l'IAURP* (Institut
d'Aménagement et Urbanisme de la Région Parisienne), vol. 23, 5-1971, p. 13.

Caen: by Henri Bernard, completed 1957. *Les Cahiers de
l'IAURP, op. cit.*, pp. 4, 10; *Revue de l'enseignement
supérieur* 1966 no. 4.

Dijon-Montmuzard, *c.* 1953–65, by Roger Barade. *Centre
Universitaire de Dijon. La Faculté des sciences de Dijon*
(Extrait de la *Revue d'hygienie et confort des collecitivités*
no. 13) [n.d.]; H. Linde (ed.), *Planung Wissenschaftlicher
Hochschulen* (*Schriften des Zentralarchivs für Hochschulbau*
1) Stuttgart, 1965, p. 39; *Les Cahiers de l'IAURP, op.
cit.*, p. 16.

Grenoble, Saint Martin d'Hères by G. Bovet and J.
Royer. H. Linde (ed.), *Planung Wissenschaftlicher
Hochschulen* (*Schriften des Zentralarchivs für Hochschulbau*
1) Stuttgart, 1965), pp. 39–40; *Ad'A* no. 123,
12-1965/1-1966, p. 69.

Nanterre: *Techniques et Architecture* 12-1964, pp. 100–1;
L'Architecture Française nos. 275–6, 1965, pp. 74–5; *Techniques et Architecture* 2-1968, pp. 130–1; see also note
below.

'Campus à l'Américaine': *Urbanisme Revue Française* vol.
32 (79) 1963, p. 22.

'Campus à la française': *Les Cahiers de l'IAURP* (Institut
d'Aménagement et Urbanisme de la Région Parisienne), vol. 23 5-1971, p. 5; P. Merlin, *L'Urbanisme universitaire à l'étranger et en France*, Paris, 1995.

'Bilan . . . aussi négatif sur le plan qualitatif qu'il est
positif sur le plan quantitatif', Merlin, *op. cit.*, p. 264.

'Static and rigid': *Ad'A* no. 107, 4/5-1963 [no p. nos.,
beginning of issue].

G. Mesmin, Directeur de l'équipement scolaire universitaire et sportif au ministère de l'éducation nationale,
'Problèmes des constructions scolaires et universitaires', *Ad'A* no. 107, 4/5-1963, pp. [0]-1

'Une solide harmonie qui semble bien s'inscrire dans la
tradition française', B. Zehrfuss, 'Les programmes d'enseignement vont-ils favoriser en France l'évolution de
l'architecture?', *Ad'A* no. 107, 4/5-1963, pp. 3, 9.

'Millieu de vie': *Les Cahiers de l'IAURP* (Institut d'Aménagement et Urbanisme de la Région Parisienne), vol.
23 5-1971, p. 14; C. Grignon & J. C. Passeron, *The
French Experience before 1968*, (*Case Studies on Innovation in Higher Education*) OECD Paris, 1970, pp. 61–3.

Cf. H. van Mang & J. P. Muret, *Essai pour une nouvelle
conception de l'architecture et de l'urbanisme à propos du
thème de l'université*, Paris, 1967: 'La France n'a pour
ainsi dire pas consacré à l'enseignement supérieur
un édifice digne de cet nom', p. 20; *Ville Architecture
Université. Réalisations du Schéma Université 2000*,
(Ministère de l'éducation nationale . . .), Paris, 1998,
pp. 21–2.

'Pale imitation . . .': *Les Cahiers de l'IAURP* (Institut
d'Aménagement et Urbanisme de la Région Parisienne), vol. 23 5-1971, p. 5.

English universities: *Les Cahiers de l'IAURP, op. cit.* p. 7,
pp. 29–39; see also *Ad'A* no. 123, 12-1965/1-1966,
pp. 74–91; *Ad'A* no. 137, 4/5-1968.

English 'urban': *Les Cahiers de l'IAURP, op. cit.*, pp. 33,
49.

'Urban': *Urbanisme Revue Française* vol. 32 (79) 1963,
pp. 22 etc.

Orléans-La Source: Oliver Clément Cacoub (Louis
Arretche was involved at the beginning). *Urbanisme
Revue Française* vol. 32 (79) 1963 (The XIIIe Jour
Mondial de l'Urbanisme was held in Orleans in
1962); R. Secretain, 'Un Oxford Français à Orléans',
Revue des Deux Mondes 15-3-1963, pp. 237–49; *Le
Grand Larousse*, 'Universités', 1964; *L'Architecture
Française* nos. 275–6, 8-1965, pp. 68–71; *Techniques et
Architecture*, 9-1967, pp. 86–7; B. Godet, *Combat* 14-6-
1967, pp. 8–9.

Somewhat similar in their distinctive departure from the
Zeilenabau principle were the campus designs for the
new universities of Nantes and Rennes, of 1963, by
Louis Arretche; *Le Grand Larousse*, 'Universités', 1964;
L'Architecture Française nos. 275–6, 8-1965, pp. 68–71.

'Amphis': cf. those at Reims University; see
D. Alexandre-Bidon, M. M. Compere & oth., *Le
Patrimoine de l'éducation nationale* (Collection Le
Patrimoine des Institutions Politiques et Culturelles,
Flohic Editions) Charenton le Pont, 1999, p. 917;
'Horsäle in Holzbauweise', *BW* no. 20, 27-5-1974,
p. 747.

'Seduced the Dean . . .': B. Marrey, 'La Faculté des
Sciences de Paris', *Revue de l'Art*, 29 1975, pp. 100–6
(p. 101). The plan was devised 1962–3, building began
1964; the tower was built to a simplied formula after
Albert's death in 1968; *L'Architecture Française*, nos.
275–6, p. 73; B. Marrey, *Edouard Albert*, Paris, 1998;
BW no. 8, 24-2-1969, pp. 263–7; D. Oboussier, *Le
Centre Universitaire Jussieu, Thèse du Doctorat Paris I*,
1982; *Campus Universitaire de Jussieu. Naissance d'une
grande Bibliothèque*, Paris, 1993. Today the complex
houses parts of the universities of Paris 6 Pierre et
Marie Curie and Paris 7 Denis Diderot.

'Modern Escorial': *Acier Stahl Steel*, vol. 32, 1967 no. 5,
pp. 210.

'Materialisation of scientific . . .': quoted in: 'Être étudi-
ant à Paris 6' (student guide), 1999, also in 'Modern
Escorial: New Faculty of Sciences . . .', *Acier, op. cit.*,
pp. 209–19.

'Increasing interaction . . . cloisters . . .': *Acier, op. cit.*,
p. 211.

'Close to the precincts Phillipe Auguste . . .': *Acier, op. cit.*, p. 209.

Jussieu criticism: P. Merlin, *L'Urbanisme universitaire à l'étranger et en France*, Paris, 1995, p. 281.

Amiens, Université de Picardie by J. Le Couteur: *Techniques et Architecture* no. 39, 1967, pp. 17–19.

Université Toulouse Le Mirail: *Ad'A* no. 137, 4/5-1968, pp. 57–60; Linde (1970) vol. 1, p. 46.

Reforms: cf. H. S. Cohen, *Elusive Reform: The French Universities, 1968–78*, Boulder, Colorado, 1978; cf. *La Réforme de l'université* (contrib. by G. Antoine, J. C. Passeron), Paris, 1966.

Campus . . . failure ('échec'): D. Alexandre-Bidon, M. M. Compère & oth., *Le Patrimoine de l'éducation nationale*, (Collection Le Patrimoine des Institutions Politiques et Culturelles, Flohic Editions) Charenton le Pont, 1999, p. 914.

Nanterre: see note above; Y. LeVaillant, 'Nanterre-la-Folie', *Nouvel Observateur* no. 171, 21, 27-2-1968, pp. 21–3; H. Lefebvre, *L'Interruption de Nanterre au Sommet*, Paris, 1968 (new ed. 1998); M. Crozier, 'French Students: a letter from Nanterre la folie', *The Public Interest* 13 1968, p. 153, quoted in N. Abercrombie, The *University in an Urban Environment*, 1974; J. P. Duteuil, *Nanterre 1965-66-67-68*, Paris, 1988.

'In its brutality . . .': A. Touraine, *Le Movement du mai ou le communisme utopique*, Paris, 1968, p. 101.

'Le modèle français . . .': *Ville Architecture Université. Réalisations du Schéma Université 2000* (Ministère de l'éducation nationale . . .), Paris, 1998, p. 19.

Villetaneuse (Université de Paris 13, Campus de Villetaneuse; the competiton preceeded '1968'): *Ad'A* no. 137, 4/5-1968, pp. 97–101; Linde (1970) vol. I, p. 46; *Les Cahiers de l'IAURP* (Institut d'Aménagement et Urbanisme de la Région Parisienne), vol. 23 5-1971, p. 55; *Techniques et Architecture* 4-1972, p. 88ff.; P. Merlin, *L'Urbanisme universitaire à l'étranger en France*, Paris, 1995, pp. 263, 283.

'Tolbiac': Centre Pierre Mendès-France, 90 rue de Tolbiac, Paris 13e, part of Université Paris I Panthéon-Sorbonne, a campus for beginners (1er cycle) only, by Michel Andrault and Pierre Parat, 1972–3; *Architettura Chronache i Storia*, no. 240, 10–1975, p. 346.

Lyon II Bron-Parilly: *Les Cahiers de l'IAURP* (Institut d'Aménagement et Urbanisme de la Région Parisienne), vol. 23 5-1971, p. 6; *Architekten* [Stockholm] 18 361 1972, pp. 361–7; *BW* no. 31, 19-8-1974, pp. 1048–51; cf. the similar buildings for the University of Compiègne: *Techniques et Architecture* 11-1973, p. 54ff.

J. Canipel, 'Architecture et Université', *Techniques et Architecture*, 11-1973, pp. 27–8.

'Tissue de la ville': *Ville Architecture Université. Réalisations du Schéma Université 2000* (Ministère de l'éducation nationale . . .), Paris, 1998, p. 22.

'Not treated differently . . .': *Les Cahiers de l'IAURP* (Institut d'Aménagement et Urbanisme de la Région Parisienne), vol. 23 5-1971, p. 6.

H. Lefebvre, *L'Interruption de Nanterre au Sommet*, Paris, 1968 (new ed. 1998), p. 67.

'Model né spontanement . . .': *Les Cahiers de l'IAURP* (Institut d'Aménagement et Urbanisme de la Région Parisienne), vol. 23 5-1971, p. 9.

Créteil, Université de Paris XII Val de Marne: P. Merlin, *L'Urbanisme universitaire en etranger et en France*, Paris, 1995, p. 283; D. Alexandre-Bidon, M. M. Compère & oth., *Le Patrimoine de l'education nationale*, (Collection Le Patrimoine des Institutions Politiques et Culturelles, Flohic Editions) Charenton le Pont, 1999, p. 915.

Dauphine, Vincennes: P. Merlin, *L'Urbanisme universitaire à l'étranger et en France*, Paris, 1995, pp. 291–4.

Megastructural and other indeterminisms

Berlin FU: by Candilis, Josic & Woods, with M. Schiedhelm and J. Greig, building system designed by Jean Prouvé. J. F. Tent, *The Free University of Berlin*, Bloomington Indiana, 1988; Competition announcement: *BW* no. 52, 30-12-1963, p. 1518; *Hochschuldienst* 8-1-1964, p. 9; *BW* no. 6, 10-2-1964, pp. 161–76; *Architectural Association Journal* vol. 80 no. 883, 1-1965, pp. 14–7; *AFor* 5-1966, p. 44; *AA* 1967, pp. 113–19; *Deutsche Bauzeitung* 7-1967, p. 551ff.; S. Woods, 'The Education Bazaar', *Harvard Education Review* 39 4 1969, pp. 116–26; R. Banham, 'Ground Scraping', *New Society* 12-18-1976, pp. 352–3; *Techniques et Architecture* 4-1972, pp. 67–74. Cf. On the earlier work by Candilis, Josic and Woods: *Ad'A* no. 101, 4/4-1962, p. 50ff.; *AD* 1-1965, p. 35ff.; R. Banham, *The New Brutalism*, 1966, pp. 70, 71, 75; *Free University Berlin. Candilis, Josic, Woods Schiedhelm*, (by G. Feld & oth.), publ. by Architectural Association [London] Series *Exemplary Projects*, 1999.

Universität Marburg: Status Report. Ausbauprogramm und Entwicklungslinien der Phillips-Universität Marburg/Lahn, Sonderheft 1966 of *Alma Mat.̈ Phillipina*; *BW* no. 31/32, 10-8-1964, p. 313; *Bauen und Wohnen* 1964, pp. 311–18; *AFor* 5-1966, p. 48; *Ad'A* no. 137, 4/5-1-1968, pp. 45–51; *AD* 11-1974, p. 710; *Techniques et Architecture* 4-1972, pp. 75–85.

Loughborough: Arup Associates *Master Plan for Loughborough University of Technology* (publ. Loughborough), 1966; *AJ* 22-6-1966, pp. 1510–13; *Architect and Building News* 22-6-1966, pp. 1114–16; *Arena/Interbuild* 9-1967, pp. 40–3; *Zodiac* 18 (1968), pp. 78–9; *AR* 1-1968, p. 49; *AJ* 31-1-1968, p. 317; *AR* 4 1970, p. 277; *Ad'A* no. 137, 4/5-1968, pp. 53–6; *AA* 1967, pp. 94–103; *Architecture East Midlands*, 3/4-1979, pp. 7–11.

Odense, by Knud Holscher, Bureau Krohn & Hartvig, Rasmussen: *Ad'A* no. 137, 4/5-1968, pp. 67–9; *BW* no. 42/43, 210-1967, p. 1076; *Deutsche Bauzeitung* 3-1966, pp. 82–7; Linde (1970) vol. 1, p. 51; Linde (1970) vol. 4, pp. 182–3; cf. the competition for Oulu (Finland), *Deutsche Bauzeitung* 2-1969, pp. 86–79.

Universität Ulm, by Hochbauamt Baden Württemberg, begun 1969: Linde (1970) vol. 1, pp. 114–15; Linde (1970) vol. 4, pp. 185–6, *AD* 11-1974, pp. 711–12; cf.

Ecole Polytechnique Fédérale de Lausanne, plans by Zweifel + Strickler and others: *Werk* 5-1971, p. 309ff.

Le Corbusier: Roq et Rob Project (Hotel for Cap Martin), 1949; A.&P. Smithson, Berlin Hauptstadt project 1958 (R. Banham, *The New Brutalism*, 1966. pp. 94, 82); cf. A.&P. Smithson, 'Team X at Royaua-mont', *AD* 11-1975, pp. 664–89.

R. Banham, *Megastructure*, 1976, p. 207 (cf. *AD* 12-1968, p. 565).

'Structuring principles . . .': *AD* 8-1964, p. 380.

Jokusch / planners: P. Jokusch, 'University Campus Design', *AD* 11-1974, pp. 702–16.

RMJM 1964: see above, page ••.

'Bits and pieces' (or: 'a patch-up job'), 'Flickschusterei': *BW* no. 41, 9-10-1967, p. 1013.

Computer: T. Mason, 'La dynamique de la planification dans l'enseignement supérieur', *Ad'A* no. 137, 4/5-1968, pp. xlix–xl (also English version).

'Campus grows by logic . . .': Dober (1963), p. 73; cf. 'Optimal space use studies': W. T. Middlebrook, *How to Estimate the Building Needs of College and Universities* (University of Minneapolis) Minneapolis, 1958.

'The analysis of the programme . . .': F. Hallauer, Bochum, pp. 81–5 in: H. Linde (ed.), *Planung Wissenschaftlicher Hochschulen*, (*Schriften des Zentralarchivs für Hochschulbau* 1), Stuttgart, 1965.

'Stapelbar': Linde (1970) vol. 3, p. 15.

'Bedarfsplanung': Linde (1970) vol. 2;

'Bauleitplanung': *Bauen und Wohnen* 1969, p. 379.

N. Bullock, P. Dickens, P. Steadman, *A Theoretical Basis for University Planning* (publ. Cambridge University School of Architecture) April 1968; N. Bullock, P. Dickens, P. Steadman, 'A theoretical model . . .', *Official Architecture and Planning* 4-1968, pp. 505–11; N. Bullock, P. Dickens, P. Steadman, 'Activities, Space and Location', *AR* 4-1970, pp. 299–306.

'Musterprogramme', 'Richtwerte', P. Conradi, 'Probleme bei der Planung von Hochschulen', *Bauen und Wohnen* 1964, pp. 295–9; also as: P. Conradi & H. Reichenecker, 'Gedanken zur Gesamtplanung von Hochschulen', *Konstanzer Blätter für Hochschulfragen*, no. 5, vol. 2 (no. 3) 11-1964, pp. 44–52; cf. H.-J. Aminde, 'Zeitlich-funktionale Elemente der Bau-Leitplanung für Hochschulgebäude', *Bauen und Wohnen* 11-1969, pp. 379–89.

Generally valid criteria: F. Kramer, 'Hochschulplanung Gestern und Heute', *Bauen und Wohnen* 1962, p. 315ff.; 'Zur Situation unserer Hochschule', *BW* no. 48, 1-12-1958, p. 1163; *DUZ* 6-1960, pp. 20–1.

'Connectivity': R. Banham, *Megastructure*, 1976 p. 119; *Official Architecture and Planning*, 4-1968, pp. 496–504; R. Banham, 'The Outhouses of Academe', *New Society* 6-10-1966, p. 546; traffic separation: Turner, p. 276.

'The built forms do not': *AR* 4-1970, p. 284.

'Commitment or "fix" . . .': M. Cassidy, 'Who was right?', *Official Architecture and Planning*, 4-1968, pp. 469–503.

'Functional obsolescence . . .'; 'more serious': P. Jokusch, *AD* 11-1974, p. 708.

J. Jordan, University Development Plans', *AJ* 31-1-1968, pp. 313–20.

'Static master plan' to 'evolutionary plan': *Canadian Architect* 12-1967, p. 40.

'Recipie' to 'problem': Linde (1970) vol. 1, p. 4.

'Systemreine Planung': H. Linde: Institut für Hochschulbau Universität Stuttgart, S. Heeg (eds.), *Horst Linde Architekt und Hochschullehrer* (publ. Stuttgart), n.d. [c. 1980], p. 76.

Operational research: G. Broadbent, *Design in Architecture. Architecture and the Human Sciences*, London, 1970.

'Mathematical and computable models': *AD* 11-1974, p. 714.

Not enough sociological research: *AJ* 22-7-1964, pp. 201–2; Cf. N. Malleson in *AA* 1967, p. 23.

Proximity: Linde (1970) vol. 1, p. 11.

'No part . . . exclusively to social purposes . . .': Linde (1970) vol. 2, p. 84.

'Modules', 'grids': *AD* 11-1974, p. 709.

Schultze-Fielitz: G. Feuerstein, *New Directions in German Architecture*, London, 1968. cf. B. Russell, *Building Systems*, Chichester, 1981; M. Glendinning & S. Muthesius, *Tower Block Modern Public Housing in England, Wales Scotland and Norther Ireland*, New Haven and London, 1994, p. 308ff.

J. Weeks, 'Planning for Growth and Change', *AJ* 7-7-1960, pp. 20–2; cf. Jonathan Hughes, *The Brutal Hospital. Efficiency, Form and Identity in the National Health Service*, PhD London University, 1996; J. Hughes & S. Sadler (eds.), *No Plan*, Oxford, 2000.

Meat inside a sausage: *AJ* 31-1-1968, p. 317.

Cf. statements by clients and designers in *AA* 1967; cf. J. K. Page, 'Academic Goals and University Buildings', *UQ* vol. 18 no. 3 6-1964, pp. 301–8.

J. Weeks, 'Architecture free from . . .': *Baumeister* 12-1969, pp. 1486–1490.

'The quality of buildings . . .': P. Jokusch, 'Entscheidungsbildung bei der Bedarfsplanung wissenschaftlicher Hochschulen', *Konstanzer Blätter für Hochschulfragen* no. 22, vol. 7 (no. 1) 3-1969, pp. 40–54.

'Form', 'artistic element', *AJ* 31-1-1968, pp. 313–20; (on Bremen) *BW* no. 42/43, 23-10-1967, pp. 1072–5.

'Teaching and learning system': G. Feuerstein, *Hochschulen Planen Bauen* (Cat Exh. Bundesministerium für Bauten und Technik/Österreichische Bauzentren 1969/70, publ. Vienna), p. 81.

Campus invisible: within a community': *AJ* 20-9-1972, p. 676.

Potteries Thinkbelt: *AD* 10-1966, pp. 484–7; R. Banham, P. Barker, P. Hall, C. Price, 'Non-Plan: An Experiment in Freedom,' *New Society* 20-3-1969, pp. 435–3; cf. Megastructural projects *Casabella* no. 323, 2-1968, pp. 10–19; *Casabella* no. 325, 4/5/6-1968, pp. 32–7; *Casabella* no. 326, 7-1968, pp. 26–31.

There is no body of tested . . .': *AD* 11-1974, pp. 70–5.

'We really dont know . . .': *Sarah Lawrence Alumnae Magazine* Fall/Winter 1969, pp. 20–6 (p. 25; courtesy P. F. Owen, Archivist Sarah Lawrence College).

Away from technologist determinism: cf. Linde (1970) vol. 4, p. 163; *AD* 11-1974, pp. 714–15; G. Fesel, 'Planungsirrtümer', *BW* no. 23, 16-6-1978, pp. 867–8.

Urban 'Experimentierfeld': H. J. Aminde, interview 1999.

German Students' Meeting of 1962: (Verband deutscher Studentenschaften), *Gutachten einer Kommission des V.D.S. zur Neugründung wissenschaftlicher Hochschulen, Studenten und die neue Universität* (publ . Bonn), 1962 (2nd. ed. 1968), pp. 90–2.

Strathclyde: Dober (1965), pp. 17–19.

Edinburgh: *AR* 7-1954, pp. 45–51.

Manchester Education Precinct. Final Report of Planning Consultants H. Wilson & L. Womersley (publ. Manchester), 1967. First planned 1963; *AJ* 31-5-1967, pp. 1265–7; Linde (1970) vol. 4, p. 66; H. J. Aminde, in *Bauen und Wohnen*, 11-1969, pp. 386–9.

English Polytechnics: *AR* 1-1971.

Hamburg-Harburg: *Stadtbauwelt* 1964, no. 3, p. 213.

Université Catholique de Louvain, Louvain-la Neuve at Woluwe-St. Lambert (Brussels), 1970 onwards, by groupe Urbanisme et Architecture. *Baumeister* 9-1977, pp. 791–828; *Techniques et Architecture* 11-1973, pp. 54–66.

E. W. Gilbert, *The University Town in England and West Germany* (Univ. of Chicago Dept. of Geography Research Paper 71) Chicago, 1961; 'Urban' universities: cf. A. Tropp & A. Little, 'Blueprint for a University', *New Society* 6-6-1963, pp 10–11; 'Universität und Stadt', *Stadtbauwelt* no. 3 1964; F. Gaussen, 'L'Université hors les murs', *Le Monde* 28/29/30–4 1966; *Casabella* no. 326, 7-1968, pp. 26–31; J. Canipel, 'Architecture et Université', *Techniques et Architecture* 11-1973, pp. 27–8; N. Abercrombie & oth., *The University in an Urban Environment*, London, 1974; C. Alexander, M. Silverstein & oth., *The Oregon Experiment* [Master Plan for the University of Oregon], New York, 1975; P. Merlin, *Urbanisme Universitaire à l'étranger et en France*, Paris, 1995; cf. N. Ellin, *Postmodern Urbanism*, Oxford, 1996; cf. S. Sadler, *The Situationist City*, London, 1998; cf. J. Holston, *The Modernist City . . . Brasilia*, Chicago, 1999. 'A most original alternative . . .': *AJ* 16-12-1970, pp. 1409–22; *AJ* 17-3-1971, pp. 585–600; *Country Life* 12-12-1976, pp. 5–6.

Essex: *Colchester Evening Gazette* 14-5-1974.

VI   UTOPIAN RHETORIC AND ITS RECIPIENTS

Languages of Importance

J. Kopperschmidt (ed.), *Rhetorische Anthropologie*, Munich 2000 (quoted after Frankfurter Allgemeine Zeitung 10-5-2000)

Habermas, see above page 216; A. Touraine, *The Academic System in American Society*, New York, 1973, p. 4: '. . . the tiresome rhetoric and . . . preoccupation with noble sentiments, high-sounding principles, and self satisfaction . . .'.

Welfare State language: cf. I. Culpitt, *Welfare and Citizenship*, London, 1992, pp. 5–9.

W. Nash, *Rhetoric*, Oxford, 1998; G. Ueding (d.), *Historisches Wörterbuch der Rhetorik*, Tübingen, vol. 1-1992.

'One of the assertions . . .'; 'what is higher education for' (the latter quote from Mary R. Glover, Director of Social Service Training at Keele University): M. Reeves (ed.), *Eighteen Plus. Unity and Diversity in Higher Education*, London, 1965, pp. 215, 119; cf. W. R. Niblett (ed.), *The Expanding University*, 1962; D. Christopherson, *The University at Work, London*, 1973 (under the auspices of the Student Christian Movement, see Preface to that book).

For this kind of discourse cf. further: J. Wyatt, *Committment to Higher Education, Seven West European Thinkers on the Essence of the University*, Buckingham, 1990.

'Outside senior common rooms . . .': P. Marris, *The Experience of Higher Education*, London, 1964, pp. 172–3.

'Elite': G. Templeman, 'The Responsibility of Institutions of Higher Education', pp. 30–5 in: M. Reeves, (ed.), *Eighteen Plus. Unity and Diversity in Higher Education*, London, 1965.

'I don't have the advantage . . .': *TES* 25-11-1966, p. 1292.

'Technical objectives' . . . : *Tomorrow's London, A Background to the the Greater London Development Plan*, (publ. Greater London Council (GLC) n.d. [c. 1971], p. 44.

'The stylistic gymnastics . . .': *Canadian Architect* 9-1962, p. 55.

C. Braegger, *Architektur als Sprache*, Munich, 1982; B. Colomina (ed.) *Architecturereproduction*, Princeton, 1988; R. Williams, 'Representing Architecture: The British Architectural Press in the 1960s', *Journal of Design History* no. 4 1996, pp. 285–96. T. Benton, 'The Myth of Function', pp. 412–52 in: P. Greenhalgh (ed.), *Modernism in Design*, London, 1990.

Sussex: D. Daiches (ed.) *The Idea of a New University. An Experiment in Sussex*, London, 1964, p. 202.

D. Lasdun, 'An Architect's Approach to Architecture', *RIBA Journal* 4-1965, p. 185; the lecture is also reproduced in W. Curtis, *Denys Lasdun*, Oxford, 1994.

Frank Thistlethwaite: 'Lasdun at exposition': Interview 1996.

'Talks with great conviction . . .': *T* 2-3-1975.

'Patrons and committees swallow . . .': H. Smith, 'The Concrete Reality', *Spectator* 14-8-1976, p. 19.

The Smithsons: see above page 92; K. Lynch, *The Image of the City*, Cambridge MA, 1960.

'Nucleus', 'spine', 'circuit' were used by the Smithsons and Lasdun.

'Linkeage', 'strata': *RIBA Journal* 4-1965, p. 184ff.

'Landlocked harbour': *ST* 1-10-1967.

'Every moment of walking': *Zodiac* vol. 18 [1968], pp. 7–17; cf. P. Dormer and S. Muthesius, *Concrete and Open Skies. Architecture at the University of East Anglia 1862–2000*, 2000.

Brett: *AR* 10-1963, p. 263.

'The sixties', 'boom years': K. Smith, 'Appraisal [of Warwick]', *AJ* 24-3-1976, p. 586.

'Lack of focus': *AJ* 5-6-1968, p. 1290.

'Dressed in the rhetoric . . .': *AJ* 11-12-1972, p. 1349.

R. Banham, 'Ground Scraping', *New Society* 19-8-1976, pp. 352–3; cf. A.&P. Smithson, *Without Rhetoric An*

Architectural Aesthetic, 1973; B. Colomina, *Privacy and Publicity. Modern Architecure as Mass Media*, 1994.

Changing User Discourses

Michel Foucault: *Discipline and Punish. The Birth of the Prison*, New York, 1975 and 'Space, Knowledge and Power (Interview with Paul Rabinow)', in *Skyline 3-1982* (extracts from both in N. Leach (ed.), *Rethinking Architecture, a Reader in Cultural Theory*, London, 1997, pp. 350–80; cf. S. J. Ball, *Foucault and Education. Disciplines and Knowledge*, London, 1990.

Users: cf. J. Hill (ed.), *Occupying Architecture. Between the Architects and the User*, London, 1998.

Cf. user voices in R. Blyn-Stoyle (ed.), *The Sussex Opportunity*, Brighton, 1986, p. 3.

N. Abercrombie & oth., *The University in Urban Environment*, London, 1984, p. 141.

Keep them out of trouble: H. & P. Silver, *Students. Changing Roles, Changing Lives*, Buckingham, 1997, pp. 8, 11; cf. S. Haselgrove (ed.), *The Student Experience*, Buckingham, 1994; cf. H. Lefkowitz Horowitz, *Campus Life. Undergraduate Cultures from the End of the 18th Century to the Present*, New York, 1987.

'The values of American students . . .': J. D. Millett, *The Academic Community*, New York, 1962, p. 142; cf. only eight years later: C. M. Otten, *University Authority and the Student. The Berkeley Experience*, Berkeley, 1970.

'The typical freshman begins . . .': N. Sanford (ed.), *The American College*, New York, 1962, p. 253.

'Expects an elevated . . .': Bryan Wilson in: M. Reeves (ed.), *Eighteen Plus. Unity and Diversity in Higher Education*, London, 1965, p. 53.

F. Zweig, *The Student in the Age of Anxiety*, London, 1963, p. xiii.

'Normal student believes . . .': *Baukunst und Werkform* 12-1960, p. 60.

Rules: cf. M. Reeves (ed.), *Eighteen Plus. Unity and Diversity in Higher Education*, 1965, p. 111.

E. Jones: cf. *TES* 21-6-1963, p. 1351.

Investigations of 'the student': cf. B. Simon, *A Student's View of the University*, London, 1943; D. Thoday, 'How Undergraduates work', *UQ* vol. 11 no. 2 2-1957, pp. 172–81; N. Malleson, 'University Students 1953: IV Different Sorts of Students', *UQ* vol. 15 no. 1, 12-1960, pp. 54–63; and subsequent articles in *UQ*; 'Death of the Student', *Twentieth Century* vol. 174 Summer 1965, pp. 61–3; F. M. Katz, 'The ideal student . . .', *UQ* vol. 25 no. 3 Summer 1971, pp. 277–88; cf. also: *Report on the Policies and Running of Stirling University from 1966–1973, made to the University Court, 22-10-1973* [The Roger Young Enquiry] (publ. Univ., of Stirling), 1973.

Two kinds of students: P. Marris, *The Experience of Higher Education*, London, 1964, p. 31.

Social life: G. Little, *The University Experience. An Australian Study*, Melbourne, 1970, p. 159.

Student participation: E. Ashby & M. Anderson, *The Rise of the Student Estate in Britain*, London, 1970; cf. above:

the development towards 'spontaneity'; cf. H. L. Horowitz, 'The 1960s and the Transformation of Campus Cultures', *History of Education Quarterly*, vol. 26 no. 1 Spring 1986, pp. 1–38.

I. Illich, 'The Deschooled Society', pp. 263–73 in: D. W. Vermilye (ed.), *The Expanded Campus*, San Franciso, 1972.

H. E. Rich & P. M. Jolicoeur, *Student Attitudes and Academic Environment*, New York, 1978; D. Riesman, *On Higher Education. The Academic Enterprise in an Era of Rising Student Consumerim*, San Francisco, 1980; cf. already J. D. Millett, *The Academic Community*, New York, 1962 114ff.; cf. recently: Anthony Smith & F. Webster, *The PostModern University?* Buckingham, 1997; R. Barnett & A. Griffin (ed.), *The End of Knowledge in Higher Education*, London, 1997; W. Shumar, *College for Sale: A Critique of the Commodification of Higher Education*, London/Washington D.C. 1997.

Utopia or instrumentalism?

Cf. Utopia: D. Lyon, 'Community as Ideology and Utopia', *UQ* vol. 38 no. 3 Summer 1984, pp. 253–69; see note to Introduction.

Undermine utopia: E. Kamenka (ed.), *Utopias*, Melbourne, 1987.

'When it works . . .': *RIBA Journal* 7-1964, p. 308.

Nostalgia for first years: 'The University of Essex', *The Cambridge Review* 22-1-1966, pp. 199–209. cf. *AJ* 20-9-1972, p. 643; cf. York, in *Twentieth Century* 175 1966 Summer, p. 47; *Times Literary Supplement* 11-2-1972, p. 147 (Sussex).

Ross, p. 184.

M. Tafuri, *Architecture and Utopia*, Cambridge MA, 1975, pp. 117, 119, 124, 139.

For some of the most recent views cf. P. Mitchell, *Beyond the University in Higher Education*, Aldershot, 1998.

Illustration Sources: Every effort has been made to trace copyright holders. If anybody has been over looked please contact the author via the publisher.

INDEX